MICROECONOMICS
THEORY AND APPLICATIONS

MICROECONOMICS
THEORY AND APPLICATIONS

G.S. Maddala
University of Florida

Ellen Miller
The University of North Carolina at Charlotte

McGraw-Hill
Book Company

New York
St. Louis
San Francisco
Auckland
Bogotá
Caracas
Colorado Springs
Hamburg
Lisbon
London
Madrid
Mexico

Milan
Montreal
New Delhi
Oklahoma City
Panama
Paris
San Juan
São Paulo
Singapore
Sydney
Tokyo
Toronto

MICROECONOMICS: THEORY AND APPLICATIONS
INTERNATIONAL EDITION

1 2 3 4 5 6 7 8 9 0 CMO PMP 8 9 4 3 2 1 0 9

This bookwasset in Meridien by General Graphic Services, Inc.
The editors were Scott D. Stratford and Ira C. Roberts;
the designer was Chuck Carson;
the production supervisor was Friederich W. Schulte.

Library of Congress Cataloging-in-Publication Data

Maddala, G. S.
        Microeconomics: theory and applications.

        Includes index.
        1. Microeconomics.   I. Miller, Ellen M.
II. Title.
HB172.M29   1989   338.5   88-23147
ISBN 0-07-039415-6

When ordering this title use ISBN 0-07-100220-0

ABOUT THE AUTHORS

G.S. Maddala has been Graduate Research Professor of Economics at the University of Florida since 1975. Prior to that he taught at Stanford University and the University of Rochester. Dr. Maddala received his Ph.D. in economics from the University of Chicago and is author of *Econometrics* (McGraw-Hill, 1977, Spanish edition, 1985), *Limited Dependent and Qualitative Variables in Econometrics* (Cambridge University Press, 1983), and *Introduction to Econometrics* (Macmillan, 1988).

Ellen Miller is Assistant Professor of Economics at the University of North Carolina at Charlotte. She received her Ph.D. in economics from the University of Florida, with specialization in microeconomics and industrial organization.

CONTENTS

LIST OF APPLICATIONS AND EXAMPLES

PREFACE

With all the acceptable books on microeconomics available, why have we produced yet another one? The reason is that no one book develops the core topics patiently and clearly, while also giving students a sense of microeconomics as a field of study that is vibrant and always evolving. In addition to an exposition of the core topics that is more painstaking than most, to help the students develop the foundation so critical to economists' thinking, we include in this book references to the specific theorists and developments of the past. We also give, particularly in the later chapters, a sense of the "interesting edge" topics that involve the thinking of today's (and tomorrow's) microeconomists. These topics can be dealt with depending on the available time and needs of the instructors.

SPECIAL FEATURES OF THE BOOK

The following are some of the special features of this book.

1. The book offers exceptionally patient and careful coverage of the core topics in microeconomics. Some examples are Chapters 4 and 5 (Theory and Analysis of Demand), Chapters 10 and 11 (Monopoly) and Chapter 19 (Externalities and Public Goods). In our opinion, this degree of care not only sets this book apart; it also helps students establish the strongest possible foundation in microeconomic analysis.

2. The book also features in-depth coverage of many topics from current microeconomic research. Such topics as the rigidity of prices, advertising and market structure, the economics of uncertainty, the economics of information, and inter-temporal choice and risk provide students with a sense of the dynamic nature of contemporary microeconomics. These topics can, however, be treated as optional and the instructor can pick and choose among them, as time permits, according to his/her and the student's interest.

3. The book presents microeconomics in the context of its historical development, both in giving the development of core topics and explaining modern research. Numerous references to the classic economic literature help students understand the fabric of economic thought. In the discussion of indifference curves in Chapter 4, we point out that Edgeworth, who derived indifference curves, believed in cardinal utility rather than ordinal utility. In Chapter 18, we think students will find it interesting that one of the greatest mathematical economists, Walras, who developed general equilibrium theory, failed twice in a mathematics entrance examination and went to study literature before coming back to economics.

4. The book features many innovative examples and applications of microeconomic theory. The applications in the book are both numerous and detailed.

They are designed to be of interest to both majors and non-majors and serve to demonstrate the relevance of the theory to the analysis of current issues and problems. The applications also cover a wide range of areas: energy economics, environmental economics, health economics, transportation economics, urban economics, and many others.

Some applications worked out in detail include: illegal activities and black markets (Chapter 2), food-stamp programs, gasoline tax (Chapter 4), welfare programs and negative income tax (Chapter 5), transportation improvement and land values (Chapter 9), medical insurance (Chapter 9), rent controls (Chapter 10), minimum wage laws (Chapter 15), the market for nurses (Chapter 16), economics of sports (Chapter 16), excess profits tax (Chapter 17), highway tolls and mass transit (Chapter 19), housing prices and Proposition 13 (Chapter 20), and the market for durable goods (Chapter 20).

5. The book features in-depth coverage of welfare economics for instructors who want to include this material in courses. It also treats the important topics of externalities and public goods with unusual clarity and completeness.

THE IMPORTANCE OF MICROECONOMICS

In microeconomics we study the economic behavior of individuals and firms, the different types of market organization, and how individuals and firms interact with the government. Though generalizations cannot be taken literally, many economists argue that it is in courses in microeconomics that students learn the fundamental principles of economic theory. The principles that are most important to the economists' way of thinking include the fundamentals of supply and demand, the distinction between accounting and opportunity cost, the relationship between the marginal and the average, and so on. In this book we present the basic principles of microeconomics in a thorough manner, and introduce numerous applications and policy problems throughout. Students thus learn both the tools of analysis and how to apply them to practical problems.

WHO CAN USE THE BOOK?

This text is appropriate for undergraduate intermediate level microeconomics courses in economics departments. It is also ideal for undergraduate or MBA courses in the business administration curriculum. The book covers all the basic material required for courses in microeconomics and also includes several supplemental topics so that instructors can choose the ones that they consider most appropriate. Knowledge of calculus is not required of the reader and, hence, this text can be used in more basic courses as well. We have paid careful attention to the figures that illustrate the arguments. The details of the figures are explained in the text so that the arguments flow in a logical way. For instructors who would like to adopt an algebra-based coverage, we have included a mathematical appendix in the *Instructor's Manual*.

Chapters 8, 9, 14, 18, 21, and some sections of the other chapters might be omitted in the more basic courses. Chapters 2 and 3 can be omitted in the more advanced courses. The book permits considerable flexibility in the choice of topics, particularly because the applications are included in each chapter.

PEDAGOGICAL AIDS

The book contains a wide variety of pedagogical learning aids, including:

- Chapter introductions
- Numerous diagrams and illustrations
- In-depth chapter summaries
- Lists of key terms in each chapter
- Questions and problems (solutions are given in the *Instructor's Manual*)
- A full glossary of terms at the end of the book
- Numerous examples of current topical interest

Supplemental readings are provided in the footnotes when the particular topic is discussed in the book. The students can, thus, pick the relevant supplemental readings that are of interest to them.

In addition to the many applications in the text, specially highlighted examples of particular current interest are often used to illustrate theory in a more in-depth manner. They include: the markets for copper, orange juice, and sugar (Chapter 2); the demand for gambling (Chapter 3); Christmas gifts (Chapter 4); doctor-nurse substitution (Chapter 6); pricing admissions to Disney World (Chapter 9); Texaco vs. Pennzoil (Chapter 13); and the costs of the 55 mph speed limit and gasoline mileage standards (Chapter 19).

SUPPLEMENTS

There are two supplements available with the book: an *Instructor's Manual* and a *Study Guide*. The *Instructor's Manual* provides general and specific comments on the development of the topics in each chapter, answers to the end of chapter questions, a test bank, and a mathematical appendix to the book. It also discusses a few additional topics and examples not fully covered in the book.

The *Study Guide,* prepared by professors Wayne Joerding and Rodney Fort of Washington State University, is intended to give the students further practice in the use of microeconomic theory. It provides several comprehensive tests for the students. These tests are in addition to the chapter overviews and self-study questions (multiple choice, true/false, problems). The answers to these tests are included in the *Instructor's Manual* so that professors can decide whether to use this material as additional self-study questions or as examinations.

ACKNOWLEDGMENTS

We would like to thank Parthasaradhi Mallela of Northern Illinois University and Michael Morgan of the College of Charleston for their important contributions in the development stages of this book. We would also like to thank Pat Mitchell, who was then economics editor at McGraw-Hill, for her encouragement in the early stages of the project. However, this book would not have been successfully completed without the constant encouragement, keen interest, and enthusiasm of Scott Stratford, economics editor at McGraw-Hill. We owe him special thanks.

We would also like to thank Ira Roberts, editing supervisor, for his constant effort in the efficient production of this book. Thanks are also due to Liz Lawrence, Judy Motto, and San Rao for their share of the effort. We would also like to thank Adele Koehler, Sandy Ostrofsky, and Betty Sarra for their efficient typing; Teresa Kauf for her careful assistance in preparing the index; and Marcie Guira for her assistance in proofreading. Finally, we would like to thank our colleagues for their many informal comments and suggestions.

We have received many helpful comments from several reviewers, though we could not incorporate all of their valuable suggestions (sometimes because of conflicting opinions). We would like to thank the following for their comments: Jack Adams, University of Arkansas; Kirk Blackerby, San Jose State University; Ken Boyer, Michigan State University; Paul G. Farnham, Georgia State University; R.P.H. Fishe, University of Miami; Charles Geiss, University of Missouri; Herb Kessel, Saint Michael's College, Winooski, Vermont; Pramila Krishnan, San Francisco State University; Craig MacPhee, University of Nebraska; John G. Marcis, University of Toledo; Gerald M. Miller, Miami University; Michael Peddle, Holy Cross College, Worcester, Massachusetts; Janet Rives, University of Northern Iowa; John Schnell, Syracuse University, and Larry Sgontz, University of Iowa.

G. S. Maddala
Ellen Miller

MICROECONOMICS
THEORY AND APPLICATIONS

PART ONE
INTRODUCTION

Part One (Chapters 1 to 3) presents an introduction to microeconomic analysis. Chapter 1 deals with scarcity and choice as the fundamental basis of microeconomic analysis, the different types of microeconomic analysis, goals of microeconomic policy (efficiency and equity), and the nature of microeconomic models (assumptions and reality). It also presents a summary of the book. Chapter 2 presents a review of the general principles of demand and supply analysis, a determination of equilibrium price and quantity, and some exceptions to the conventional models of demand and supply. Chapter 3 deals with the different concepts of elasticity and their applications. Chapters 2 and 3 review basic material that students learn in a beginning course. However, there is some new material in these review chapters that students who already have had a beginning course in economics will find interesting.

In these and the subsequent chapters in the book, the presentation of the theory is reinforced throughout with applications of the theory as well as real world examples.

CHAPTER 1

INTRODUCTION TO MICROECONOMIC ANALYSIS

The basic problems of economics are simple; the hard part is to recognize simplicity when you see it. The next hardest part is to present simplicity as common sense rather than ivory tower insensitivity.

Harry G. Johnson*

Common sense is not so common.

Voltaire

*Harry G. Johnson, "The Study of Theory," *American Economic Review*, Papers and Proceedings, May 1974, p. 324.

1.1 WHAT IS MICROECONOMICS?

In the beginning there was only one "economics." Then after the great depression of the 1930s, there became two: microeconomics and macroeconomics.[1] "Micro" means small. "Macro" means large. We will explain soon what small and large mean in this context. Although the two branches of economics existed side by side for centuries, the division became transparent only during the 1930s. Ragnar Frisch (1895–1973), a Norwegian economist (who along with the Dutch economist Jan Tinbergen won the first Nobel prize in economics), coined the words "micro-dynamics" and "macro-dynamics" in 1933 to denote roughly what we now mean by microeconomics and macroeconomics.[2]

In distinguishing between macroeconomics and microeconomics, one often hears the analogy that microeconomics views the economy through a microscope whereas macroeconomics views the economy through a telescope. This analogy does not give a correct impression of either of these fields, and someone viewing the economy through a microscope or telescope is not likely to get a good picture of the economy at all.

The main differences between the two fields are the following:

1. Microeconomics deals with the choices of individuals—individual households or individual firms. Macroeconomics deals with economic aggregates—total consumption, total production, etc. The distinction, however, is subject to some qualifications. Even in microeconomics we deal with aggregates like total market demand for oranges, market demand for labor, industry supply of automobiles or wheat. However, the important difference is that these aggregates are derived from individual choices. In macroeconomics we do not consider individual choices. Furthermore, in microeconomics we study only *aggregates over homogeneous or like products.* For example, we talk of market demand for apples but do not combine oranges and apples. In macroeconomics we talk of GNP (gross national product) which is an aggregate over many different products.

2. In microeconomics, relative prices play an important role. In macroeconomics, relative prices are of secondary importance. In microeconomics we study the response of consumers and producers to changes in relative prices of domestic versus foreign cars, apples versus oranges, beef versus chicken, etc. In macroeconomics we pay attention only to changes in the price level, interest rates, etc. And if we consider relative prices at all, it is relative prices of broad commodity groups, such as producer prices versus consumer prices or wage rates relative to the price

---

[1] Recent years have seen the addition of the suffix "nomics" or "omics" to politicians' names: Nixonomics, Carteromics, Reaganomics, Volckeromics, Thatcheromics, Gandhinomics, and so on. Alan Abelson, editor of *Barrons,* a weekly magazine, once wrote that one reason why Walter Mondale could not be a viable candidate for the presidency (in 1984) was that the word "Mondalenomics" sounded a bit awkward and difficult to pronounce. So was McGovernomics, which could be mispronounced as "Misgovernomics." A presidential candidate with a short name ending in "n" is better off. Otherwise, you may have to drop the "n" and use words like "Thatcheromics," "Carteromics," and so forth, and then you do not know whether the suffix is coming from "economics" or "comics." At any rate, these individual philosophies do not constitute branches of economics and will not concern us.

[2] The words appeared in R. Frisch, "Propagation Problems and Impulse Problems in Dynamic Economics," in R. Frisch (ed.), *Economic Essays in Honor of Gustav Cassel,* Allen & Unwin, London, 1933. The words "microeconomic" and "macroeconomic" were perhaps first used by the Dutch economist P. DeWolff in his paper, "Income Elasticity of Demand: A Micro-economic and Macro-economic Interpretation," *Economic Journal,* 1941, pp. 140–145.

level. Again, the difference is that in microeconomics we consider relative prices of somewhat homogeneous products such as apples versus oranges, domestic cars versus foreign cars. We do not combine apples and cars and talk of a general price level in microeconomics.

Some economists feel that even when we study total employment, general price level, total gross national product, and other problems from the area of macroeconomics, we should approach these problems from the microeconomic point of view, or from the point of the individual decision-making unit. These economists talk of "microfoundations of macroeconomics." The approach is also called in common language "the bottoms-up approach" as compared with the usual macroeconomic approach of starting with national money income, aggregate employment, total money supply, etc., which is a "tops-down approach."

In summary, the major emphasis in microeconomics is on the decision making of individual consumers and producers (or firms) and on a discussion of relatively homogeneous products.

1.2   SCARCITY AND CHOICE

In the previous section we talked of individuals and firms making decisions. What are these decisions? An individual has many decisions or choices to make:

- Whether to go to college after high school
- Whether to buy a Chevy or a Dodge car
- Whether to marry

In fact, our whole life is a complex multiple-choice problem. Similarly, firms also have many choices to make:

- Whether to expand output
- Whether to close down a plant
- Whether to produce output in the United States or in an overseas plant

Not all choices are economic. For example, whether to marry is not usually considered an economic choice. However, some economists such as Gary Becker from the University of Chicago analyze this as a pure economic problem. Becker talks of couples "who separate when the utility expected from remaining married falls below the utility expected from divorce and possibly remarriage," of people "who marry when the utility expected from the marriage exceeds the utility expected from remaining single," and so on.[3] We will be mostly concerned with more conventional economic choices involving the allocation of scarce resources.

[3]Gary Becker, "A Theory of Marriage," *Journal of Political Economy*, 1973, pp. 813–846 and 1974, pp. S-11 to S-26. Also, Gary Becker, Elizabeth Landes, and Robert Michael, "An Economic Analysis of Marital Instability," *Journal of Political Economy*, 1977, pp. 1141–1187, and Gary Becker, *A Treatise on the Family*, Harvard University Press, Cambridge, Mass., 1981.

Choices are dictated by scarcity—scarcity of the resources at our command. Productive resources are usually classified under the following categories:

1. *Natural resources:* land, water, air, minerals, forests
2. *Human resources:* skilled and unskilled labor
3. *Capital resources:* machines, equipment, buildings
4. *Entrepreneurial resources:* a special category of human resources that consists of people who combine natural, human, and capital resources to produce output, take risks, etc.; entrepreneurs are the ones who make the decisions about the organization of production.

We will be discussing these resources as *factors of production.*

Firms must decide how to combine these scarce productive resources to produce goods and services. These goods and services will also be scarce and must be allocated among society's consumers. Most allocation of goods and services, under capitalism, is through markets. Here, consumers must decide how to allocate their limited (or scarce) purchasing power among the various scarce goods and services.

Economics has sometimes been referred to as the "science of scarcity" because it focuses on the allocation of society's scarce resources. The emphasis of this book will be on the analysis of individual decisions made by consumers, firms, and, to a much lesser extent, by government which affect the ultimate allocation of society's scarce resources.

EXAMPLE 1.1 Butter versus Guns

One example often cited for economic choice on a grand scale is that of choosing between defense expenditures and expenditures on social and environmental programs. Before the Vietnam war many believed that the United States was so rich in resources that it could afford to wage two wars—the Vietnam war abroad and the so-called war on poverty at home. Of course, there is a limit on the amount of resources any country has, and there is a limit on how much of each of guns and butter the country can afford to have. The following list of defense and social programs with comparative cost (as of 1985) is taken from Melman.[4] Of course, each side of the ledger taken by itself can be demonstrated to have a lot of waste. The equality of cost is as estimated by the government, and we all know the definition of an elephant as "a mouse built to government specifications." The interesting things here are the comparative costs of the different programs.

Defense Program	Cost	Social Program
Navy (EA6B) airplane program for surveillance and communication jamming	$2.8 billion	Proposed cut in funds for mass transit systems
1986 budget for the M-1 Abrams heavy tank	$2.3 billion	Proposed 1986 cuts in guaranteed loans and in campus-based financial aid for students

[4]Seymour Melman, "Butter That's Traded Off for Guns," *Gainesville Sun*, April 27, 1985, p. 15A. (Also appeared in the *New York Times* and other papers around that time.) The article lists 24 items of which only 6 are listed here.

The stealth radar-evading bomber program	$40.6 billion	Mayor Koch's 10-year plan for repairing New York City's infrastructure
Navy's Trident II submarine and F-18 jet fighter programs	$100 billion	Estimated cost of cleaning up 10,000 toxic waste dumps that contaminate the nation's soil and water
The Army's Patriot ground-to-air missile system	$12.2 billion	1982–1985 cuts in federal income and nutrition programs for the 35.3 million living in poverty
The Army's single-channel ground and air-borne radio system	$5.3 billion	A one-third increase for the federal school-lunch program, food stamp program, and Women, Infants, and Children (WIC) program

1.3 TYPES OF MICROECONOMIC ANALYSIS

The answers to many problems in microeconomics will depend on the type of analysis we conduct.[5] For convenience it is customary to divide the different types of analysis into the following categories:

1. Positive and normative analysis
2. Statics, comparative statics, and dynamics
3. Short-run and long-run analysis
4. Partial and general equilibrium analysis

An understanding of the distinctions between different analyses will often help to resolve some differences in conclusions that two economists might arrive at for the same problem.

1.3.1 Positive and normative analysis

It is common knowledge that economists often disagree. These disagreements can be reconciled if we know whether they result from different assumptions or working hypotheses or from different views about how things ought to be. The former is a difference of opinion about what is, and the latter is a difference of opinion of what ought to be.[6] It is possible that two economists starting with the same premises would come to different conclusions because of differences in opinion about what ought to be done. This conflict is extremely prominent when it comes to analyzing the different policies of the government.

---

[5]The different approaches to a problem might yield different conclusions. That is why if you ask an economist a question, you get an answer that goes like this: "On the one hand . . ., but on the other hand. . . ." President Harry Truman was reported to have asked his advisors to get an economist with only one hand.

[6]We are assuming that there are no mistakes in logic. Those economists that make mistakes in their arguments are excluded from our discussion.

Positive economics is said to deal with the question of what is, and *normative economics* is said to deal with the question of what ought to be. Normative economics involves prescriptive statements. For example, the statement that the government should guarantee a minimum income for every individual is a prescriptive statement. Another such prescriptive statement would be that the government should stop all aid to farmers or to a particular country. These are statements in normative economics.

What does positive economics consist of? Statements in positive economics are statements that start with assumptions and derive some conclusions (which can be checked with data). For example, "A minimum wage law increases youth unemployment" is a statement in positive economics because it can be verified with actual data. A statement such as "A profit-maximizing firm will set its price equal to its marginal cost" is a statement in positive economics. Positive statements do not involve values or opinions. Note, however, that we have only given a simple description of positive and normative economics. There is, actually, considerable dispute as to what is positive and what is normative. For example, if positive economics is "what is" then we should be talking about how consumers actually *do* behave when they go shopping, or how firms actually *do* price their products and so on. But to study this we have to go and observe the actual behavior of individuals and firms and study their psychology. In this book, we will start with some assumptions such as "consumers maximize utility," "firms maximize profits," and then derive some implications from these assumptions. Some will call this normative economics, arguing that in essence we are assuming that consumers ought to maximize utility, producers ought to maximize profits, and so on.

All these assumptions are considered by economists as *rational*. However, in actual life many consumers are *partly irrational* and so are many firms.[7] There are two reasons for this:

1. The real world problems are much more complicated than those that we study in microeconomics texts, and it is impossible to be as rational as assumed there. In real life you have to make so many approximations, rough-and-ready calculations, etc., and the human mind is capable of assimilating only a limited amount of information.

2. The decisions made by consumers and firms are not all based on pure economic reasoning. There is a lot of psychology involved.

This area of studying individuals and firms at the actual decision-making level comes under what the Harvard economist Harvey Leibenstein called "micro-microeconomics."[8] Since this is a book on microeconomics, not micro-microeconomics nor psychological economics, when we talk of an individual or a firm we will often be talking of a rational individual (maximizing utility) or a rational firm (maximizing profit), except for a digression in Chapter 8.

There are two reasons why we discuss only rational economic behavior.

[7]Herbert Simon calls this "bounded rationality." See Herbert Simon, *Models of Man,* Wiley, New York, 1957.

[8]Harvey Leibenstein, "The Missing Link: Micro-Micro Theory," *Journal of Economic Literature,* June 1979, pp. 477–502.

1. Individuals can be rational in only one way, but they can be irrational in several ways. Furthermore, it is hard to predict the actions of irrational individuals.

2. Many of the important conclusions we derive in microeconomics theory are not substantially altered by irrational behavior.[9]

In summary, this book discusses the behavior of economically rational consumers and firms. Furthermore, we derive conclusions about the behavior of consumers and firms from some simple assumptions, without imposing value judgments.

1.3.2 Statics, comparative statics, and dynamics

It is customary to classify economic analysis into three categories: *statics, comparative statics,* and *dynamics.* In this book we will be concerned with statics and comparative statics only.

Before we define these terms, we have to define another term: equilibrium. *Equilibrium* is defined in economics as a position from which there is no reason to move. If a hot dog stand at a football stadium sells hot dogs at 80 cents each and the entire stock of hot dogs is exactly finished at the end of the day, then we say the hot dog market was in equilibrium. It is not in equilibrium if at the end of the day some hot dogs are left over, or if the hot dogs were sold out halfway through the game, and some people who wanted to buy hot dogs could not get them. In either of these cases the price should have been different from the price of 80 cents. Positions of equilibrium are very rarely attained, but they are considered important because they indicate the direction in which economic variables will tend to move if they are not in equilibrium.

Statics is the branch of economics which studies the properties of positions of equilibrium in the economic system. *Comparative statics* is the branch of economics which compares equilibrium positions when external circumstances change. For example, in the case of the hot dog vendor at the football stadium, suppose the equilibrium position is 5,000 hot dogs with a price of 80 cents per hot dog. If there is a change in the weather so that it is a very hot day, not as many people will want to eat hot dogs, and the vendor might want to bring fewer hot dogs and sell at a lower price. The new equilibrium might be 2,000 hot dogs with a price of 50 cents per hot dog. In comparative statics we compare the new hot weather equilibrium with the old one.

In both statics and comparative statics we concentrate only on equilibrium positions. We are not concerned with how long it takes to achieve the equilibrium position or by what path the equilibrium is attained.

Dynamics is the branch of economics concerned with whether an economic system in disequilibrium reaches an equilibrium position, how long it takes, and the path it follows to do this.

In this book we will not be concerned with dynamics except for the "cobweb model" presented in Chapter 3, because an analysis of dynamic models requires more mathematical background than is assumed in this book. Thus, when we

[9]Gary S. Becker, "Irrational Behavior and Economic Theory," *Journal of Political Economy,* February 1962, pp. 1–13.

analyze the effect of, say, a hard winter freeze on the price and output of oranges, all we ask is what effect this has on the new equilibrium price and output of oranges. We are not concerned with how long consumers and producers take to adjust to the new situation. Nor do we ask whether the increase in price is: (1) gradual as shown by arrow (*a*) in Figure 1.1, (2) overshooting (because of everyone overestimating the damage at first) as shown by arrow (*b*), or (3) oscillatory as shown by arrow (*c*).

Comparative statics looks at points *A* and *B* only but not at the paths of adjustment from *A* to *B*. This does not mean that comparative static analysis is not useful. The analysis does give us a lot of information on where we will be going, and this information is a prelude to a dynamic analysis. Thus, our concentration in this book on statics and comparative statics is not a limitation. Furthermore, we have to study these first before we go to dynamic models.

1.3.3 Short-run and long-run analysis

Although we will not be concerned with full-fledged dynamic analysis in this book, we will be talking about short-run and long-run analysis. A *short run* is a time period during which consumers and producers have not had enough time to make all the adjustments to the new situation. A *long run* is a time period during which consumers and producers have had enough time to make all the adjustments to the new situation. Consider, for instance, a sudden increase in the oil price by OPEC. The immediate impact would be an increase in the prices of oil and other products requiring oil. After some time, consumers would adjust to this situation by using more energy-efficient cars and appliances, building energy efficient homes, and so on. These adjustments would eventually reduce demand and bring the price of oil back down.

How short a short run is and how long a long run is are very difficult questions to answer. For instance, in the case of the oil price increase by OPEC in 1973, the famous economist Milton Friedman was wrong in predicting a decline in oil prices

FIGURE 1.1   Three dynamic paths (*A* is initial position, *B* is final position).

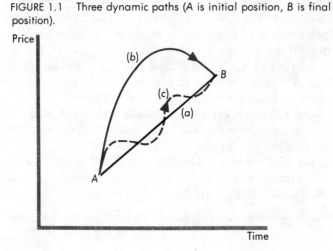

shortly thereafter. Oil prices rose continuously through the 1970s and began to decline only in 1980. The automobile manufacturer, Chrysler Corporation, continued to insist in the mid-1970s that the oil price increase was temporary and refused to switch over and manufacture more energy-efficient cars thus postponing adjustment. Here we see that a long run can be many years. And the adjustment time depends in part on whether a change is perceived as temporary or permanent by individuals and firms who can be wrong in their perceptions.

Though we cannot exactly say how short a short run is, and how long a long run is (this varies from case to case), the short-run and long-run analysis that we study in this book will be helpful in organizing our ideas. Furthermore, an analysis of the long-run effects is helpful in avoiding drastic policies that attack the short-run effects and thereby actually increase the time required to achieve the long-run position. For instance, a policy of domestic price control on oil prices is a policy that attacks the short-run problem created by the OPEC price increase for oil. But such a policy actually delays adjustment to the long-run equilibrium.

1.3.4 Partial and general equilibrium analysis

Partial equilibrium analysis uses the *ceteris paribus* (a Latin phrase which means "other conditions being equal") assumption. Of course, in practice, other things are never "equal," or the same. But if the changes in the "other things" are small, the *ceteris paribus* assumption is a reasonable approximation.

Partial equilibrium analysis is used in two cases:

1. The first case is when we are concerned with an event or occurrence that affects only a given industry. An example would be a strike which occurs only in one industry, with the impact on other industries almost negligible.

2. The second case is when we are concerned with *first-order* effects. For example, we might want to analyze the effect of a quota on automobile imports on automobile output and prices. Of course, the quota will have an impact on the steel industry, on the aluminum industry, on the glass manufacturing industry, and so on, but these are effects of the second and third order that we may not be immediately interested in.

In general, the smaller the sector being considered, the better the possibility that partial equilibrium analysis can predict its behavior.

Partial equilibrium analysis was popularized by the English economist Alfred Marshall (1842–1924). This is the approach we will adopt in this book, partly because the problems we analyze fall in the two types mentioned earlier, and partly because the alternative method of general equilibrium analysis requires more mathematical background than is assumed in this book.

General equilibrium analysis is concerned with the study of the effects of certain changes and policies after all the interactions in the economy have taken place. For example, the import quota on automobiles will have impacts on the gasoline, steel, aluminum, glass, platinum, and other industries, and these in turn will have further effects on the automobile industry.[10] General equilibrium is achieved only

[10]There was a saying that "what is good for General Motors is good for the economy as a whole." The effect of increased employment in the automobile industry can have an impact on the housing industry as well.

when all these industries are in equilibrium *simultaneously*. In economics, everything depends on everything else. Thus, one would think that every problem in economics should be approached from the point of view of general equilibrium. In general, it is often the case that macroeconomic theories tend to be general equilibrium in character and microeconomic theories tend to be partial equilibrium in character.

General equilibrium theory was first systematically studied by the French mathematical economist Leon Walras (1834–1910). This analysis is fairly complex for the purpose of this book. Except for a brief introduction in Chapter 18, we will be concerned throughout with partial equilibrium analysis.

1.4   GOALS OF MICROECONOMIC POLICY: EFFICIENCY AND EQUITY

Broadly speaking, microeconomic policies have two objectives: *efficiency* and *equity*.

One of the primary goals of microeconomic policy is the efficient allocation of resources. One aspect of efficiency requires that it be impossible to increase the output of some goods without reducing the output of others. For example, if we currently produce 100 cars and 1 million loaves of bread, but by reshuffling our resources we could produce 102 cars and 1 million loaves of bread, then we have not currently attained efficiency. Another aspect of efficiency requires that it be impossible to improve one person's well-being without making someone else worse off. We will discuss the different aspects of efficiency in Chapter 9.

Another primary goal of microeconomic policy is equity or fairness in the distribution of goods and services among the people in an economy. There are different ways in which the equity concept has been interpreted. Some interpret it as elimination of income inequality. Suppose that a bus driver, college professor, and a doctor are all paid the same (or almost the same) wage. This would certainly promote income equality. This is roughly the concept of equity in socialist and communist countries. Some people do not feel that this is a proper concept of equity. By equity they mean equality of opportunities, not equality of rewards.

The first goal, efficiency, is achieved through the use of appropriate prices. The second goal can be achieved by changing incomes (taxes and subsidies). Government policies to break up monopolies are designed to promote efficiency. As for promoting equity, government has a host of policies such as personal income tax, public housing policies, unemployment insurance, and several welfare programs. Many policies followed by the government have not served the purpose they were designed for. Two examples follow:

1. The farm price support program was adopted to help some farmers with low incomes, but it has actually increased income inequality within the farm sector and has resulted in an inefficient use of resources.

2. Minimum wage laws are often enacted to protect the incomes of youth. Usually they have a perverse effect on youth unemployment.

Failure of the above mentioned policies resulted from the use of the wrong instruments. In both of the previous examples, a policy of meddling with prices was used in an attempt to achieve the goal of equity. Broadly speaking, prices should be used for resource allocation problems. Problems of income distribution should be solved solely by income taxes and income subsidies, not by tinkering with the price system.

Throughout the different chapters of the book, we will be discussing the consequences of different government policies. The conditions that need to be satisfied for efficient allocation of resources are discussed in Chapter 9. Almost all of microeconomic theory is concerned with the efficiency question, and the equity problem is usually treated only cursorily. Part of the reason that the equity problem receives very little attention is that its analysis is often considered to be outside the realm of microeconomic theory. This is because the definition and evaluation of equity involve value judgments, and this precludes any sort of positive analysis.

It is, however, interesting to note that the way conservatives, liberals, and radicals approach economic problems usually depends on the emphasis given to the efficiency versus equity goals (apart from their attitudes toward the government). Conservatives emphasize the efficiency aspect, almost to the complete neglect of the equity problem. In general, they believe that if a bigger pie is produced then everyone will be better off sharing the bigger pie. The liberals believe that the equity problem is not solved by just producing a bigger pie and that we need some special policies on the part of the government. The radicals believe that because of strong special interest groups, the bigger pie might even result in a less equitable distribution of the pie.

These are, of course, broad characterizations, and the only way to bring forth the true differences in these views is to analyze specific problems from the three different points of view.[11]

1.5 MICROECONOMIC MODELS: ASSUMPTIONS AND REALITY

Economic analysis begins with models. What is a model? It is simply a description of the economist's view of how things work. Economists first construct simple models and then progressively complicate them. Given that the real world is complicated, the economist's task of constructing a simple model is not a simple one. In constructing a simple model, the economist has to make some "simplifying" assumptions such as, there is no uncertainty, all consumers have the same tastes, there is only one homogeneous product. None of these assumptions is, of course, realistic, but there are always some aspects of reality that are irrelevant or of negligible importance for any problem. Thus, some of the "unrealistic" assumptions made by the economist are justified on the ground that they enable us to concentrate on the essential aspects of the problem while ignoring irrelevant detail.

For instance, suppose we want to analyze the demand for automobiles. We would say that the price of automobiles, family income, price of gasoline, and so on, are the important factors to consider. Of course, in a remote sense, the demand

[11]See Robert B. Carson, *Economic Issues Today: Alternative Approaches*, 4th ed., St. Martin's Press, New York, 1987, for such a discussion. About 16 issues (8 in microeconomics and 8 in macroeconomics) are analyzed, presenting the conservative, liberal, and radical approaches to each problem. The first chapter defines these ideologies.

for automobiles will also depend on the price of ice cream, because if the price of ice cream goes up people can substitute cars for ice cream. But no one considers this as a realistic or important factor.[12]

We might, therefore, say that *a model is a simplified representation of the real world.* Many scientists have argued in favor of simplicity, because simple models are easier to understand, communicate, and test with data. For instance, the philosopher Karl Popper says: "Simple statements, if knowledge is our objective, are to be prized more highly than less simple ones because they tell us more; because their empirical content is better, and because they are testable."[13] Milton Friedman also argues: "A hypothesis is important if it 'explains' much by little, that is, if it abstracts the common and crucial elements from the mass of complex and detailed circumstances surrounding the phenomena to be explained and permits valid predictions on the basis of them alone."[14]

The choice of a simple model to explain complex real world phenomena often leads to two criticisms: (1) the model is oversimplified and (2) the assumptions are unrealistic. To the criticism of oversimplification we can argue that it is better to start with a simplified model first and then progressively construct more complicated models. This is the approach we will follow in this book.

To the criticism that the assumptions are unrealistic, it has been argued, most notably by Friedman, that the assumptions of a theory are never descriptively realistic. He says:

> To be important, therefore, a hypothesis must be descriptively false in its assumptions ... the relevant question to ask about the "assumptions" of a theory is not whether they are descriptively "realistic" for they never are, but whether they are sufficiently good approximations for the purpose at hand. And this question can be answered only by seeing whether the theory works, which means whether it yields sufficiently accurate predictions.[15]

The statement that the assumptions *must* be descriptively false is a provocative statement (and it provoked a lot of controversy), but there is a point here. What we should mean by "realistic" assumptions is that they take all the relevant variables into account but are descriptively inaccurate in the sense that they simplify and idealize rather outrageously. If simplicity is a desirable criterion, then the assumptions have to be descriptively inaccurate. But this does not mean that we can make any assumptions that we want. All it means is that we can make assumptions that do not flatly contradict anything observable and then proceed to test the predictions.

For instance, suppose we consider the market for cigarettes, and we are interested in studying the effect of an excise tax on the output and price of cigarettes.

[12]Note, however, the following passage from E. A. G. Robinson, *The Structure of Competitive Industry*, University of Chicago Press, Chicago, 1958, p. 6: "The butchers of a large town complained some years ago that owing to the reduction in the price of motor-cars the demand for sirloins of beef had fallen off. Their customers bought a little meat paste for sandwiches for the Sunday picnic, and no longer the necessary preliminaries to a somnolent Sunday afternoon. The competition of almost identical goods is different in kind, from the competition of more distinct substitutes." (The book was first published in 1931.)

[13]K. Popper, *The Logic of Scientific Discovery*, Hutchison, London, 1959, p. 142.

[14]M. Friedman, "The Methodology of Positive Economics," in *Essays in Positive Economics* (Chicago, University of Chicago Press, 1953), p. 14.

[15]Ibid., pp. 14–15.

Suppose also that we conduct our analysis on the assumption of perfect competition, which implies (as discussed in Chapter 10 later in the book) that the product is homogeneous (all units are identical) and there is virtually an infinite number of sellers. Clearly both the assumptions are descriptively false. The product is not homogeneous. There are a large number of brands and some people prefer Marlboro while others prefer Benson & Hedges. Also, there are only a few cigarette manufacturers, certainly not infinity, not even 100. How do we know whether the assumption of perfect competition is valid or not? Should we reject the whole analysis because the assumptions are unrealistic? We cannot test this assumption by its realism, because we do not know whether the departures from the ideal situation of product homogeneity and a large number of sellers are significant. Thus, we have to resort to the approach of testing the theories on the basis of their predictions. Bear and Orr suggest this approach because assumptions are difficult to test.[16] Therefore, we should, as a second-best solution, test economic theories on the basis of their predictions. The real world situation will always be a departure from the ideal situation postulated by economic theory, but the practical question is whether this departure is significant, given the problem at hand. This issue can be resolved only by checking the predictions of the model against reality.

Not all economists buy this irrelevance-of-assumptions thesis. The major criticism of this argument is that you cannot use accuracy of predictions as the *only* test of economic theories, because there can be many spurious correlations. The fact that a theory A gives better predictions than another theory B does not necessarily imply that theory A is a better theory. As an illustration, David Hendry compared two theories that try to explain movements in the U.K. price level over the period 1964 to 1975.[17] The first theory uses money supply as an explanatory variable, and the other uses a variable C. The latter theory does much better in predicting movements in the price level, except that the variable C is simply the *cumulative rainfall in the United Kingdom*!

Of course, not all competing theories contrast variables such as money supply and rainfall. But if one is arguing that economic theories are to be judged on the basis of predictions alone, there ought to be some stringent definitions laid down concerning what "accuracy of predictions" means.

Many economic theories do not generate any predictions (we will discuss this in Chapter 13 when we discuss monopolistic competition). This does not mean that these theories are useless. These theories suggest new avenues of approach and focus attention on problems that were ignored earlier. Some other economic theories are just exercises in pure deductive logic. If assumptions A, B, C, etc., are made, then conclusions X, Y, Z, etc., follow. There are many examples of these exercises in mathematical economics.

In the following chapters in this book we will be making some assumptions to enable us to start with simple models that are easy to understand. To understand the basic principles of microeconomics, we cannot start with a huge model with all the complications built into it. We have to go step by step starting with the simplest models and many simplifying assumptions.

[16]D. V. T. Bear and D. Orr, "Logic and Expediency in Economic Theorizing," *Journal of Political Economy*, April 1967, pp. 188–196.

[17]David Hendry, "Econometrics—Alchemy or Science?" *Economica*, November 1980, pp. 387–406.

This propensity of economists to always start with some assumptions is the butt of a popular joke narrated by economists themselves at social gatherings. The story is about three men on a deserted island, and all they have is one huge can of tuna. The three men are starving and discussing how to open the can. The first man, a physicist, suggests a way to make a fire hot enough to melt the can. The second, an engineer, suggests a slingshot that will hurl the can against a rock with enough force to puncture it. The third, an economist, suggests that they "assume a can opener" and proceed from there.

1.6   A SUMMARY OF THE BOOK

Before we proceed, it is important to understand the following elements of microeconomic analysis:

1. There are three types of economic agents: consumers, producers, and government.
2. There are two sides to each problem: demand and supply.
3. Prices depend on demand and supply and the way output and input markets are organized.

The interaction between consumers, producers, and government is set out in Figure 1.2. Corresponding to these interrelationships, the book is organized in the following chapters:

Basic elements of demand and supply

Chapters 2 and 3

Output markets

Demand by consumers: Chapters 4 and 5
Supply by producers: Chapters 6, 7, and 8
Market organization and pricing: Chapters 10, 11, 12, 13, and 14

FIGURE 1.2   Interaction between consumers, producers, and the government.

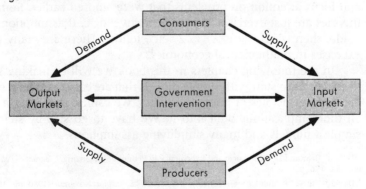

Input markets

Labor: Demand and supply, Chapter 15
Market organization and pricing: Chapters 15 and 16
Other inputs: Chapter 17

Government intervention

This is discussed in all the chapters as the occasion arises, but the rationale for government intervention is discussed in Chapter 19.

Other topics

Efficiency
The formal conditions of economic efficiency are discussed in Chapter 9.

Economic surplus
The concepts of consumers' and producers' surpluses, which form the basis of applied welfare analysis, are discussed in Chapter 9. This chapter follows the theory of the producer but precedes the other chapters because these concepts are used frequently in the later chapters.

Welfare economics and general equilibrium analysis
These are advanced topics and, hence, are dealt with in Chapter 18.

Multiperiod analysis
Most of the book is based on a single-period analysis, although there is a discussion of short run and long run. Chapter 20 presents an introduction to the analysis of multiperiod consumption and production decisions.

Imperfect information and uncertainty in microeconomics
Throughout the book we assume perfect information and lack of any uncertainty. In Chapter 21 we present an introduction to these two problems.

The use of mathematics would have simplified the exposition at several places. However, this might have intimidated many students, and so we have avoided that course. In any case the following quotation from Alfred Marshall might be of interest to some students:

> But I know I had a growing feeling in the later years of my work on the subject that a good mathematical theorem dealing with economic hypotheses was very unlikely to be good economics: and I went more and more on the rules:
> (1) Use mathematics as a shorthand language rather than as an engine of enquiry.
> (2) Keep them till you are done.
> (3) Translate into English.
> (4) Then illustrate by examples that are important in real life.
> (5) Burn the mathematics.
> (6) If you can't succeed in 4, burn 3.
> This last I did often.[18]

---

[18]Letter from Marshall to Bowley, A. C. Pigou, ed., *Memorials of Alfred Marshall*, Macmillan, London, 1925, p. 427.

CHAPTER 2

DEMAND AND SUPPLY

You can make even a parrot into a learned political economist—all he must learn are the two words "Supply" and "Demand."

Anonymous

2.1 INTRODUCTION

Economists, like carpenters, need a good set of tools. One of the strongest tools of microeconomics is demand and supply analysis. In this chapter we will discuss the basics of demand and supply. Some of the material covered should be a review from your introductory course.

For clarity, we will look first at each side of the market separately. We will begin by examining an individual's demand. We will next consider how we can aggregate individuals' demands into a market demand. Some of the factors which result in changes in demand will then be discussed. And we will emphasize the very important distinction between a change in demand and a change in quantity demanded.

Following our examination of demand, attention will turn to the other side of the market—the supply side. Here we will be focusing on the behavior of sellers. Again, we will consider an individual's supply as well as the derivation of a market supply schedule. We will then consider some factors that affect the position of the supply curve.

Having examined each side of the market independently, we will be able to combine the two and study the market equilibrium. What will be the equilibrium price, and what will be the equilibrium quantity bought and sold? The determination of price by the market is extremely important, because under capitalism, the price system ultimately answers the questions of "What will be produced?" "How will it be produced?" and "For whom will it be produced?" We will also look at how changes in demand and supply affect the market's equilibrium position.

Finally, we will be able to apply our basic tools to examine how and why various types of market intervention by the government affect price and quantity. We will look at the effects of different types of taxes and subsidies on output and price. We will consider the impact of meddling in foreign trade through import tariffs and export subsidies. The effects of various types of price and quantity controls, like rent controls and quotas, will be analyzed, and we will look at the markets for illegal goods and at black markets. Clearly the tools of demand and supply analysis can be applied to study many different issues.

2.2 INDIVIDUAL AND MARKET DEMAND

Before considering the interaction of buyers and sellers in the marketplace, it will be useful to examine the two sides of the market independently. We will begin arbitrarily by looking at the behavior of buyers, or the demand side.

When we talk of *demand* for a good (say oranges), to whose demand are we referring—an individual, a household, a group of individuals, or a country as a whole? At this stage it really does not matter, but we will start with the demand by a household. So by an individual, we mean an individual household. Similarly, on the supply side we will mean by individual, a single supplier.

By way of definition, *demand* simply indicates the quantities of a good (or service) which the household would be willing and financially able to purchase at various prices, holding other things constant.

Demand can be illustrated through a demand schedule. For instance, for the Jones family, a hypothetical demand schedule is given in Table 2.1. The schedule is hypothetical because we can get these numbers only by asking the members of the Jones family a hypothetical question of how many oranges they would buy at different prices. One alternative is to watch how many oranges the Jones family actually does buy at different prices. But there is a problem with this. We have to assume that nothing besides the price of oranges has changed during the course of our observation (e.g., Mr. Jones has not lost his job, none of the children has gone away on a camping trip). Of course, in reality, "other things" do not stay the same, but we will first assume that other things stay the same and then examine what happens if other things change. It is always useful to start with some simple models and then introduce real world complications later.

You will notice a pattern in the numbers appearing in the schedule in Table 2.1. Price and quantity demanded vary inversely, or quantity demanded rises as price falls. This is because the demand schedule obeys the law of demand. Simply stated, the *law of demand* says: Other things staying the same, the quantity demanded of a commodity will be smaller at higher market prices and larger at lower market prices.

Let's consider why the law of demand is intuitively reasonable. Remember that as we change the price of oranges, we are holding other things constant. Those other things include consumer incomes and the prices of other goods. If the price of the commodity we are considering rose and consumers did not reduce their consumption of this commodity, then they would have to cut their consumption of other commodities. Usually, the consumer would cut the consumption of this and some other commodities. If there are substitutes, such as grapefruit, available, the consumer would switch, cut the consumption of this commodity, and increase the consumption of the now relatively cheaper substitute. The law of demand will be examined in much greater detail in a later chapter. For now it will suffice to see that it is generally plausible.

As with all laws in social science, there will of course be exceptions to the law of demand, but these exceptions are very few and isolated (see Section 2.8).

TABLE 2.1 A Hypothetical Demand Schedule for Oranges

Price per Orange (cents)	Quantity Demanded (dozens)
12	3
10	6
8	9
6	12
4	15
2	18

It is frequently useful to illustrate demand graphically through a demand curve. Figure 2.1 presents the demand curve which corresponds to the demand schedule from Table 2.1. In this figure we measure quantity on the horizontal axis and price on the vertical axis because this is the common practice. This may seem backward since from the previous discussion quantity is the dependent variable and as such should appear on the vertical axis. Actually, the practice of measuring quantity on the horizontal axis and price on the vertical axis goes back to the English economist Alfred Marshall (1842–1924) who viewed the demand curve from the sellers' point of view. The seller might ask "if I produce 10 units, what is the highest price at which I can sell each unit?" Thus, from the seller's viewpoint, quantity is the choice or independent variable, and price depends upon that quantity.

An important question concerns the slope of the demand curve. Why is it downward sloping (negatively sloped)? The answer is because of the law of demand. If quantity increases as price falls then the curve illustrating this relationship must slope downward from left to right. There is, incidentally, no reason to believe that a typical demand curve will have a constant slope or that the relationship between price and quantity will be a linear relationship. Demand curves are sometimes drawn this way merely for simplicity.

Although for some purposes it is useful to examine an individual consumer's demand, it frequently is necessary to analyze demand for an entire market made up of many consumers. We will now show how we derive the market demand curve from individuals' demand curves. In Figure 2.1 we have shown the demand curve for an individual consumer. We can take curves like this for each consumer, and by adding the quantities demanded by all consumers at each price we get the aggregate demand curve for the market as a whole. Let us, for the sake of exposition, assume that there are only two consumers in the market. Their demands and the market demand are shown in Table 2.2. The individual demand curves and the market demand curve are shown in Figure 2.2. D_1D_1 is the demand curve for consumer 1, D_2D_2 is the demand curve for consumer 2, and DD is the market demand curve. At the price OA (or $10), the quantity demanded by consumer 1 is AB_1 (or 5 units), the quantity demanded by consumer 2 is AB_2 (or 8 units), and,

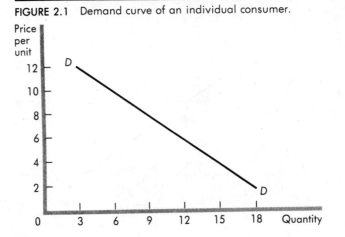

FIGURE 2.1   Demand curve of an individual consumer.

TABLE 2.2   Demand Curves for Two Consumers and the Market Demand Curve

Price	Quantity Demanded		Market Demand
	Consumer 1	Consumer 2	
12	4	6	4 + 6 = 10
10	5	8	5 + 8 = 13
8	6	10	6 + 10 = 16
6	7	12	7 + 12 = 19
4	8	14	8 + 14 = 22

hence, total quantity demanded is $AB = AB_1 + AB_2$ (or 13 units). Note also that $B_1B = AB_2$. We obtain the other points on DD in a similar fashion. This operation is what is often called *horizontal summation*.

2.3   CHANGES IN DEMAND

Before discussing changes in demand, some very important and somewhat confusing terminology must be emphasized. To an economist, *demand* refers to the entire relationship between price and quantity, as long as other things remain the same. This is what is known as the "ceteris paribus" condition. The words "ceteris paribus" are Latin for "other things remaining the same." Demand is thus composed of many price and quantity pairs for a given set of circumstances. So an entire schedule or curve illustrates demand.

Now, for any single price there is a corresponding *quantity demanded*. So the term "quantity demanded" refers to a particular point on a demand curve. As long

FIGURE 2.2   Derivation of the market demand curve.

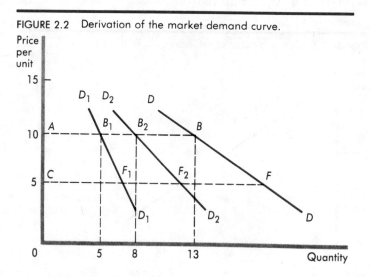

as the ceteris paribus conditions hold we can move along a stationary demand curve. We are merely changing quantity demanded.

If something other than price changes so that the ceteris paribus condition is violated, then an entirely new demand curve results. We say that there is a change in demand, and the demand curve shifts.

We are now ready to examine some changes which would result in a change in demand:

- Changes in tastes
- Changes in weather
- Changes in incomes
- Changes in prices of other commodities
- Changes in expectations

All these factors produce a *shift* in the entire demand curve. If more of the commodity is demanded at every price, then the demand curve shifts to the right as shown in Figure 2.3(a). This is called an *increase* in demand. If less of the commodity is demanded at every price, then the demand curve shifts to the left as shown in Figure 2.3(b). This is called a *decrease* in demand.

The following are some illustrations of changes in demand:

1. *Change in tastes:* Suppose Americans, imitating the British, start drinking tea more often. This will result in an increase in the demand for tea and a decrease in the demand for coffee.

2. *Change in weather:* An unusually dry summer results in a decrease in the demand for umbrellas. The demand curve shifts to the left.

3. *Changes in prices of other goods:* An increase in the price of heating oil results in an increase in the demand for natural gas. The demand curve for natural gas shifts to the right.

FIGURE 2.3 Shifts in the demand curve.

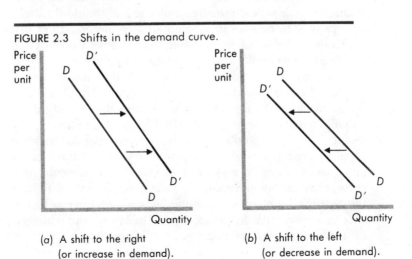

(a) A shift to the right (or increase in demand).

(b) A shift to the left (or decrease in demand).

4. Changes in income: An increase in family income increases the demand for video recorders. The demand curve shifts to the right.

5. Changes in expectations: Rumors that next year's new cars will be considerably more expensive increase the demand for this year's models. The demand for this year's cars shifts to the right.

Economists use special terminology to describe how demand responds to certain changes. For example, if an increase in consumer incomes leads to an increase in demand for a good, then that product is said to be a *normal* good. Most goods are normal. Tennis racquets, beer, pizza, and movie tickets are all examples of normal goods. However, if an increase in consumer incomes leads to a decrease in demand for a good, then that good is said to be an *inferior* good. Canned meat products and used clothing are examples of inferior goods.

Another set of terms deals with how the demand for one good reacts to a change in the price of another good. If an increase in the price of good X leads to an increase in the demand for good Y, then these two goods are said to be *substitutes*. Examples of substitutes are beef and chicken, pizza and hamburgers, or skateboards and roller skates. If instead, an increase in the price of good X leads to a decrease in the demand for good Y, then these two goods are said to be *complements*. Examples of complementary goods are gym shorts and tennis shoes, pizza and beer, cars and gasoline.

We will look at the demand side of the market in more detail later in this chapter as well as in subsequent chapters, but now we turn our attention to the other side of the market. The supply side of the market reflects the behavior of sellers or suppliers.

2.4   INDIVIDUAL AND MARKET SUPPLY

Again we will begin by examining supply for an individual seller or supplier. We will then aggregate to obtain a market supply. The supply side of the market is similar in some ways to the demand side and should thus now be easier to grasp.

By way of definition, *supply* indicates the quantities of a good (or service) which the seller is willing and able to provide at various prices, ceteris paribus.

Supply can be illustrated through a supply schedule or, graphically, through a supply curve. A hypothetical supply schedule for oranges is presented in Table 2.3, and the corresponding supply curve appears in Figure 2.4. In graphing supply we again measure quantity on the horizontal axis and price on the vertical axis. Examining either the supply schedule or the supply curve, a pattern again appears. As the price of the product rises, the quantity supplied increases as well. Thus, the supply curve has a positive slope or slopes upward from left to right. That is, price and quantity supplied vary directly. Our supply schedule, and, hence, our supply curve, obey the law of supply. The *law of supply* says the following: Ceteris paribus, the quantity supplied of a commodity will be larger at higher market prices and smaller at lower market prices. Again, the law of supply will be analyzed in greater detail in future chapters when we look behind the supply curve at the cost structure

TABLE 2.3 A Hypothetical Supply
Schedule for Oranges

Price per Orange (cents)	Quantity Supplied (dozens)
4	3
6	6
8	9
10	12
12	15

of the firm. For now it will suffice to understand intuitively why this law makes sense.

We can explain the upward-sloping supply curve through the *law of diminishing returns*. A simple example will illustrate this concept. Suppose there is a factory which assembles bicycles. If 10 workers are employed, then daily output is typically 100 bicycles. If 20 workers are employed then output increases to 200. But if 30 workers are employed, output increases to only 270. The law of diminishing returns has set in. The successive units of input, or labor in this case, do not produce the same extra output. So assuming that the wage rate is constant, the cost of these extra bicycles is higher than the earlier ones. Hence, they will be produced only at a higher price. This is the basis for the upward-sloping supply curve.

Once again, it is sometimes useful to examine a single seller's supply curve. But many times a market supply curve is needed. We can sometimes derive the market supply curve from individual supply curves in the same manner that we derived a market demand curve, that is, by adding up the quantities supplied by all individuals at each price. But we can do this only if no specialized inputs are involved in the production process. Otherwise, some adjustments must be made.

FIGURE 2.4 Supply curve of an individual producer.

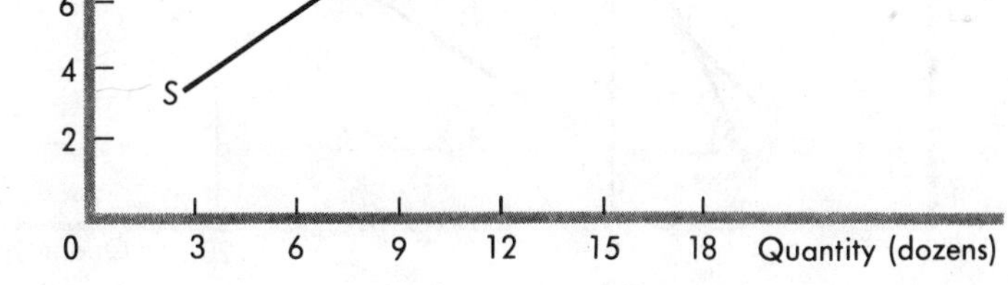

TABLE 2.4 Supply Curves for Two Suppliers and the Market Supply Curve

Price	*Quantity Supplied*		Market Supply
	Supplier 1	Supplier 2	
4	5	6	5 + 6 = 11
6	7	7	7 + 7 = 14
8	9	8	9 + 8 = 17
10	11	9	11 + 9 = 20
12	13	10	13 + 10 = 23

We will discuss this problem further in Chapter 10. For now we will simply assume that no specialized inputs are involved. This means that all firms can move along their individual supply curves without affecting input prices and, hence, production costs.

Again, for ease of exposition, we will make the simplifying assumption that there are only two suppliers in the market. Table 2.4 shows the quantities supplied by the two suppliers and the market supply. Figure 2.5 shows this diagrammatically.

2.5 CHANGES IN SUPPLY

With the supply side of the market, it is again important to clarify some otherwise confusing terminology. Supply refers to the entire relationship between price and

FIGURE 2.5 Derivation of the market supply curve from individual supply curves when input prices are constant.

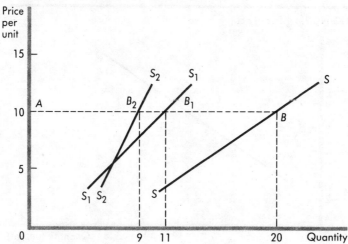

quantity, ceteris paribus. So an entire supply schedule or supply curve illustrates supply. And corresponding to any single price, there is a single *quantity supplied*. So the term "quantity supplied" refers to a particular point on the supply curve. You will see that the distinction between supply and quantity supplied is analogous to the demand side of the market.

As long as the ceteris paribus conditions are satisfied, we can move along a single stationary supply curve, merely changing quantity supplied. But if something other than the price of the product changes, then an entirely new supply curve results. We say that there is a change in supply, and the supply curve shifts.

As with the demand curve, there are several factors that produce shifts in the supply curve. These are new discoveries, availability of a new technology, changes in the prices of alternate outputs, changes in the supply of inputs, changes in weather, and so on. If more of a commodity is supplied at every price, then we say that there is an increase in supply. The supply curve shifts to the right. If less of a commodity is supplied at every price, then we say that there is a decrease in supply. The supply curve shifts to the left. This is shown in Figure 2.6.

The following are some examples of changes in supply.

1. Discoveries: The supply curve of natural gas shifts to the right because of the discovery of a number of new gas fields.

2. New technology: The supply curve for personal computers shifts to the right because of rapid developments in computer technology.

3. Changes in weather: Because of bad weather, the supply curve of wine shifts to the left.

4. Changes in prices of alternative outputs: If the price of soybeans rises, some farmers will plant more soybeans and less wheat. The supply curve of wheat shifts to the left.

5. Changes in input supply: A reduction in the supply of steel will cause the supply curve for cars to shift to the left.

FIGURE 2.6   Shifts in the supply curve.

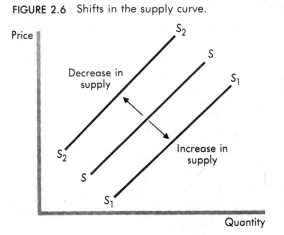

2.6   MARKET EQUILIBRIUM AND THE IMPACT OF CHANGES IN DEMAND AND SUPPLY

We have now examined each side of the market separately. It is now time to put the two together. Alfred Marshall compared demand and supply to the two blades of a pair of scissors. There is no point in arguing which of the two blades is doing the cutting. Similarly, prices are determined by the interaction of demand and supply, and one cannot ignore either element. So now we will examine how market price is determined and how the transaction takes place.

The determination of price depends on what market organization we are considering and whether there is price discrimination (that is, the seller charges different prices to different customers). These are topics we discuss in detail in future chapters (Chapters 10 through 14). For the present we shall assume that the market is *competitive*. This means that there is a large number of buyers and sellers and, hence, no one buyer or seller has control over the market price. In this case the point of intersection of the aggregate or market demand and supply curves gives the price that will prevail in the market. This is shown as the price P^* in Figure 2.7. This is the price that every buyer will pay. The corresponding quantity Q^* is the total quantity transacted by the buyers and sellers.

The price P^* is determined by the intersection of the market demand and supply curves and is called the *equilibrium price*. The quantity transacted Q^* is called the *equilibrium quantity*.

The word "equilibrium" denotes a state of rest from which there is no tendency to change. In Figure 2.7 the point C describes a position of equilibrium because this is the point where all buyers and all sellers are satisfied.

If the price is higher than P^*, say P_1, then the buyers can buy what they want to buy at that price, but the sellers cannot sell all they want to sell. This is a situation of *excess supply* or *surplus* in the market. The suppliers are dissatisfied. This situation cannot be sustained and the market price has to come down.

FIGURE 2.7 Determination of equilibrium price and quantity (competitive markets).

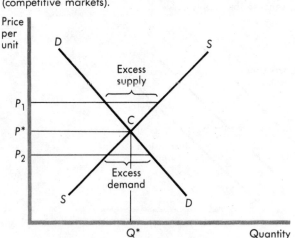

If the price is lower than P^*, say P_2, then the sellers can sell what they want to sell at that price, but buyers cannot buy all they want to buy. This is a situation of *excess demand* or *shortage* in the market. The buyers are dissatisfied. This situation cannot be sustained and the market price has to go up.

When prices are above or below P^* we say the market is in *disequilibrium*. There is, of course, the question of how one gets to the equilibrium point C in actual practice. One story goes like this: There is an auctioneer who calls off prices and asks for bids from buyers and sellers.[1] She then adds up the bids on the demand side and on the supply side. If there is excess supply she lowers the price and calls for bids again. If there is excess demand, she raises the price and calls for bids again. This procedure continues until the equilibrium price is found. *Then and only then does trade take place.* This process of getting to the equilibrium price is called a *tatonnement* process.

There are, of course, several problems with this story. All this auctioning takes time. Furthermore, we have to assume that buyers and sellers tell the truth, that both buyers and sellers keep their commitments, and that the auctioneer is doing a free service in finding the equilibrium price (quite a curious assumption for economists to make).

Very few markets have such auctioneers. However, the argument goes that many markets function *as if* there were an invisible auctioneer.

The simple model of market equilibrium does indeed provide a useful framework for the analysis of many practical problems as we will presently illustrate. We do not have to delve deeply into the question of how the equilibrium point is reached. An equilibrium position need not be realized for equilibrium analysis to be a useful tool. When the external circumstances change, the equilibrium will be disturbed, and in actual practice this happens all the time. However, an analysis of the equilibrium position shows in what direction economic variables are headed.

We can now discuss the effects of changes in demand and supply on the equilibrium price and quantity. What we will be doing falls in the area of *comparative statics*. That is, we study the effect on equilibrium positions if the demand and supply curves shift.

Let us consider an increase in demand. What happens to the equilibrium price and quantity depends on whether (1) the supply curve is unchanged, (2) there is an increase in supply, or (3) there is a decrease in supply. These situations are described in Figure 2.8.

In all three cases D_0D_0 is the initial demand curve and S_0S_0 the initial supply curve. D_1D_1 is the new demand and S_1S_1 is the new supply curve. The initial equilibrium price and quantity are P_0 and Q_0 respectively and the new equilibrium price and quantity are P_1 and Q_1 respectively.

In Figure 2.8(*a*), when supply remains unchanged, the effect of an increase in demand is that both the equilibrium price and quantity increase.

In Figure 2.8(*b*), when there is an increase in supply, equilibrium quantity increases, but we cannot say anything about equilibrium price. This is because the increase in demand puts upward pressure on price while the increase in supply

---

[1] This auctioneer is usually called a "Walrasian" auctioneer after the name of a famous French economist Leon Walras (1834–1910).

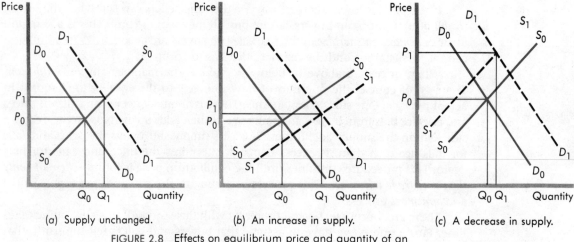

(a) Supply unchanged.   (b) An increase in supply.   (c) A decrease in supply.

FIGURE 2.8   Effects on equilibrium price and quantity of an increase in demand.

puts downward pressure on price. Price can go up, stay the same, or go down. It all depends on the relative magnitudes of the shifts in the demand and supply curves. In Figure 2.8 we see that the equilibrium price goes up, but we can get the other conclusions by changing the magnitudes of the shifts in the demand and supply curves.

In Figure 2.8(c), when there is a decrease in supply, the equilibrium price goes up, but we cannot say anything about the equilibrium quantity. This time, the decrease in supply puts downward pressure on output while the increase in demand puts upward pressure. The net effect can be either an increase or decrease. Again, it all depends on the relative magnitudes of the shifts in the demand and supply curves. Only one of the three possibilities is illustrated in Figure 2.8 but it is easy to show the other cases by just changing the magnitudes of the shifts in the demand and supply curves.

We can analyze the case of a decrease in demand in a similar fashion. All these cases are shown in Table 2.5. For compactness we use the following notation:

$P(+)$ means the equilibrium price goes up

$P(-)$ means the equilibrium price goes down

$P(?)$ means we cannot say whether the equilibrium price goes up, stays the same, or goes down

$Q(+)$, $Q(-)$, and $Q(?)$ are defined similarly and refer to equilibrium quantities

The results can be verified by drawing the demand and supply curves.

EXAMPLE 2.1   Winter Freezes in Florida and the Price of Orange Juice

The orange juice market demonstrates fluctuations in price resulting from shifts in the supply curve (and during recent years shifts in the demand curve as well). During the early 1980s, with demand fairly stable, shifts in supply produced price

TABLE 2.5 Effects of Shifts in the Demand and Supply Curves
on Equilibrium Price and Equilibrium Quantity

Supply	Demand		
	Increase	No Change	Decrease
Increase	P(?) Q(+)	P(−) Q(+)	P(−) Q(?)
No Change	P(+) Q(+)	No change	P(−) Q(−)
Decrease	P(+) Q(?)	P(+) Q(−)	P(?) Q(−)

changes. Prices shot up whenever the Florida orange crop was threatened by winter freezes. In January 1982, the nearby futures price of orange juice went up from $1.15 to $1.65 per pound.[2] In January 1984, it again went up from $1.25 to $1.65 (and rose to $1.90 by April). In January 1985, it rose again from $1.55 to $1.85. Then several changes took place on the supply side: The Florida citrus industry moved further south from Orlando so that winter freezes stopped having as much impact on the supply side, and Brazil emerged as a major producer of oranges and a major exporter of orange juice. With these developments, orange juice prices fell steadily from $1.85 in June 1985 to $0.80 in March 1986. Since then prices crept up so that they stood around $1.70 toward the end of 1987. This latter movement in prices has nothing to do with winter freezes. This has been mainly a consequence of the rise in demand for orange juice. With the growth in health consciousness here and in Europe, people started drinking more orange juice.

A detailed analysis of the orange juice market would involve a discussion of the several factors that contributed to shifts in the demand and supply curves, import restrictions in the United States, growth in the Brazilian orange industry, fluctuations in worldwide demand, and relocation of the Florida citrus industry. This is left as an exercise for interested students.

EXAMPLE 2.2 The Copper Market

The copper market showed wide price swings in the 1980s. These price swings were produced by changes in both the demand and supply conditions. Copper prices were over $1.00 per pound in 1980. They fell to about $0.60 per pound in 1986. The price decline was a result of a decrease in demand (use of fiber optics rather than copper wire in phone cables and other communications, use of plastic pipes in home construction, and so on) and an increase in supply from low-cost producers such as Zaire, Chile, and Zambia. Many U.S. producers whose costs of production were higher than $0.65 per pound had to shut down production. Between 1982 and 1986, nearly half of U.S. copper producers left the market, and others trimmed in size. Copper producers like Phelps Dodge and Magma Copper modernized their plants. The costs of production in the industry were $0.65 per

---

[2]We are talking of nearby futures price because it is readily available. It is the price on a contract for delivery in the near future. The wholesale price would exhibit a similar behavior. For the purpose of our illustration, which price does not matter. Interested students can collect data on wholesale prices and retail prices.

pound in 1987 as compared to $0.90 per pound in 1982 and were expected to go down further. The industry produced 1.3 million tons in 1987 compared with 1.1 million tons in 1981—with a work force one-third of the total 28,000 workers employed in 1980.

In the latter part of 1987, however, copper prices shot up. From about $0.62 per pound in June 1987, prices rose to $1.20 per pound in November 1987. This was the result of a decrease in supply caused by troubles in the African countries, labor unrest and strikes in Chile, and a decline in the domestic productive capacity in the United States. Simultaneously, there was an increase in the industrial demand from South Korea, Japan, and Taiwan. Once the problems in the African countries and Chile were settled, it was expected that the copper price would come down.

There was even some talk of some individual buying up the available stocks and creating a temporary squeeze. However, one needs to be reminded of the attempt by the Hunt brothers from Texas to "corner" the silver market in 1980. They kept on buying silver and pushed the prices from $6 an ounce to $50 an ounce within a few months. But then the roof caved in. At that price, every one wanted to sell the silver in their house. Many antiques were melted. A lot of silver was recovered from scrap. The price of silver came down faster than it had gone up. The Hunt brothers were left holding the bag. From billionaires, they turned into millionaires.

2.7   GENERAL PRINCIPLES OF DEMAND AND SUPPLY ANALYSIS

We turn our attention now to some applications and extensions of basic demand and supply analysis. These applications focus on the impact of various types of government intervention on market equilibrium. The first form of intervention to be examined is the imposition of taxes and subsidies.

2.7.1 Taxes and subsidies

Two important things to remember in demand and supply analysis are:

1. The distinction between shifts in the demand and supply curves and movements along the curves.
2. In the presence of taxes, subsidies, and other distortions, the price buyers pay and the price suppliers keep are different, and the quantity demanded depends on the former price whereas the quantity supplied depends on the latter price.

We will illustrate these principles with a simple example of a per unit or excise tax. Other examples will be given in later sections.

An excise or per unit tax
An excise tax is a tax of a fixed amount T on each unit of commodity. Per unit or excise taxes are currently imposed on goods such as gasoline, liquor, and cigarettes. This is different from a sales tax which is a percentage tax. (The analysis of a sales tax is similar, and we will point out the minor modifications later.)

The effect of a per unit tax of T is illustrated in Figure 2.9. The per-unit tax

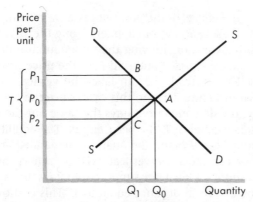

FIGURE 2.9 Effect of a per unit tax.

implies that: the price buyers pay = the price sellers keep + the tax T. In Figure 2.9 DD is the demand curve and SS the supply curve. Without the tax the equilibrium price is P_0. This is the price buyers pay and the price sellers keep. With the excise tax, there is a wedge of height T between the price buyers pay and the price sellers keep. Buyers move up the demand curve, and sellers move down the supply curve until the vertical distance between the two is equal to T. This is shown by the points B and C in Figure 2.9. P_1 is the price buyers pay, and P_2 is the price sellers keep. The difference $P_1 - P_2 = T$ is the tax the government collects. At the price P_1 the quantity demanded is Q_1, and at the price P_2 the quantity supplied is again Q_1, and, thus, there is equilibrium. Since there is equilibrium, there are no forces producing any change.

From the buyers' point of view the price has *risen* from P_0 to P_1, but from the sellers' point of view the price has *fallen* from P_0 to P_2.

Politicians, however, are accustomed to looking at only one side of the story. The following is a common argument: "The effect of a tax on a commodity might seem at first sight to be an advance in price to the consumer. But an advance in price will diminish the demand. And a reduced demand will send the price down again. It is not certain, therefore, after all, that the tax will really raise the price."[3] A similar argument was made by President Carter regarding his tax on gasoline. When asked by reporters whether the tax would raise the price of gasoline, he said that initially the tax would push the price up, but the higher price would discourage demand and bring the price down. All this merely shows the confusion among the press reporters and even high-ranking politicians about a very simple matter.

The rise in the price paid by buyers to P_1, reduces the *quantity demanded* to Q_1, but, since suppliers also get a lower price, the fall in the price to P_2 reduces the *quantity supplied* to Q_1. Thus, quantity demanded is equal to quantity supplied, and there is no more incentive for the buyers or sellers to change anything. Note that there are no shifts in the demand and supply curves that the politicians are talking about when they talk of "decrease" in demand. Further, a rise in the price of a commodity does not produce shifts in demand for that same commodity. All you have is a movement along the demand curve for that commodity.

[3]The quotation is in H. D. Henderson, *Supply and Demand*, Cambridge, London, 1922, p. 27.

We have shown the effects of the per unit tax as a movement of buyers along the demand curve from A to B and of suppliers along the supply curve from A to C. There are alternative ways of showing the new equilibrium. In Figure 2.9 we labelled the vertical axis as "price" and said P_1 is the price paid by buyers and P_2 the price kept by sellers. Instead, we can label the vertical axis as "consumers' price." This is shown in Figure 2.10. In this case, since the vertical axis measures the price buyers pay, the demand curve stays the same but the supply curve shifts up by a vertical distance equal to T, the per-unit tax. The equilibrium market price (price paid by consumers) is P_1, and the quantity demanded and supplied is Q_1.

Alternatively, we can label the vertical axis as "sellers' price." In this case, since this is the price suppliers keep, the supply curve stays the same but the demand curve shifts down by a vertical distance equal to T. This is shown in Figure 2.11. The equilibrium market price (sellers' price) is P_2, and the quantity demanded and supplied is Q_1.

Thus, there are several ways of looking at the same problem. The important things to note are the following:

1. The per unit tax raises price for buyers only. This results in a reduction in the quantity demanded. But the per unit tax lowers the price for the sellers, and this reduces the quantity supplied as well. The result is an equilibrium position with a lower quantity and a *higher price for buyers* and *lower price for sellers*. No further changes will take place. We can show this effect as a movement of buyers along the demand curve and of sellers along the supply curve.

2. By labeling the vertical axis as consumers' price (looking from the demand side) we can show the effect as no change in the demand curve and a decrease in supply. See Table 2.5, which shows the result as $P(+)$, $Q(-)$.

3. By labeling the vertical axis as sellers' price (looking from the supply side) we can show this effect as no change in the supply curve and a decrease in demand. See Table 2.5, which shows the result as $P(-)$, $Q(-)$.

A sales tax (percentage tax)

We can now analyze a sales tax which is a percentage tax. Suppose the tax rate is 8 percent. If we are analyzing it in Figure 2.9 we have to measure the wedge

---

FIGURE 2.10   Effect of a per unit tax shown as a shift in the supply curve.

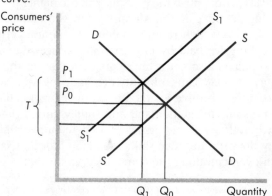

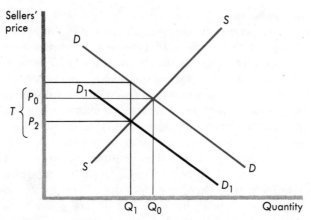

FIGURE 2.11   Effect of a per unit tax shown as a shift in the demand curve.

$(P_2 - P_1)$ as 8 percent of P_2. Thus, we keep on moving a vertical wedge from A to the left till $BC = 8$ percent of the vertical distance CQ_1. Then that will give P_1 as the price paid by the buyer, P_2 as the price the seller gets, and Q_1 as the equilibrium quantity.

If we are analyzing it as in Figure 2.10, the shift in the supply curve will not be a parallel shift as in the case of the per unit tax. At lower prices, the distance between SS and S_1S_1, which measures the per unit amount of the tax, is smaller than at higher prices. In fact, with linear supply curves as we have been drawing, and an 8 percent tax, the slope of S_1S_1 will be 1.08 times the slope of SS. This is shown in Figure 2.12. (The shifts are thus rotations.)

If we are analyzing it as in Figure 2.11, the shift in the demand curve will not be a parallel shift as in the case of the per unit tax. Again at lower prices, the distance between DD and D_1D_1, which measures the per-unit amount of the tax, is smaller than at higher prices. With linear demand curves and an 8 percent tax, the slope of D_1D_1 will be 0.92 times the slope of DD. This is also shown in Figure 2.12.

FIGURE 2.12   Rotation of the supply and demand curves with a sales tax (a percentage tax).

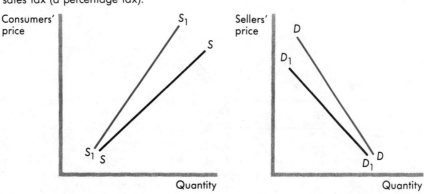

A production subsidy

The case of a production subsidy is similar to that of the per unit tax and sales tax. Suppose it is a per-unit subsidy of an amount Z. Examples of goods thus subsidized are milk and corn. The effect is shown in Figure 2.13, which is similar to Figure 2.9. DD is the demand curve, and SS is the supply curve. The initial equilibrium price is P_0 and equilibrium quantity is Q_0. With the subsidy, the price buyers pay differs from the price sellers get. From the equilibrium point A, we move a wedge to the right until the vertical distance is equal to the subsidy Z. P_2 now gives the price suppliers get, and P_1 gives the price buyers pay. $P_2 - P_1 = Z$, the amount of subsidy. At the price P_2, that sellers get, the quantity supplied is Q_1 and at the price $P_1 = P_2 - Z$ that buyers pay, the quantity demanded is Q_1. Thus, there is equilibrium in the market. Note that from the sellers' point of view the equilibrium price has risen from P_0 to P_2 but from the buyers' point of view the equilibrium price has fallen from P_0 to P_1. (Whether press reporters and politicians would call this an increase in price or decrease in price is a good question.) Note that the equilibrium quantity has increased from Q_0 to Q_1.

Again, we can analyze this in terms of shifts in demand and supply curves as done earlier. If the vertical axis is labeled "price including subsidy" (or price that producers get), then we can depict it as unchanged supply and increase in demand. From Table 2.5 we see the result as $P(+)$, $Q(+)$. If the vertical axis is labeled "price excluding subsidy" (or price paid by consumers), then we can depict it as unchanged demand and an increase in supply. From Table 2.5 we see the result as $P(-)$, $Q(+)$.

A percentage subsidy can be analyzed in a manner similar to the analysis of a sales tax. We will, therefore, not pursue this further.

2.7.2 Import tariffs and export subsidies

We have until now discussed the effects of a per unit tax and a production subsidy. The same techniques of analysis can be used to analyze import tariffs and export subsidies.

Import tariffs are commonplace in virtually all countries. The United States currently imposes an import tax or tariff on items such as clothespins, chickens

FIGURE 2.13   Effect of a production subsidy.

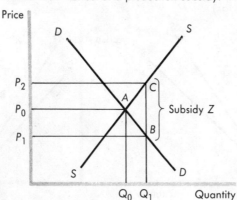

(dead), tomatoes, cork, and champagne. At the same time, many underdeveloped countries subsidize the export of industrialized goods, and our government effectively subsidizes the export of grain to Russia. So what are the results of such import tariffs and export subsidies?

Let's look first at an import tariff. Consider a commodity that is both domestically produced and consumed and also traded in the world market. Let P_f be the foreign price or world price of the commodity and let us assume that domestic buyers can buy any amount they want at this price and domestic sellers can sell any amount they want at this price in the world market. (We are abstracting from all transportation costs and so on.) Then without the tariff, the domestic price is also P_f.

The situation is shown in Figure 2.14. D_dD_d is the domestic demand curve, S_dS_d the domestic supply curve. Without any tariffs the domestic price is the foreign price P_f. At this price DE is the quantity supplied domestically, and DF is the domestic quantity demanded. The difference is made up by imports which are given by EF.

With the imposition of a tariff T, the domestic price P_d is equal to $P_f + T$, domestic quantity supplied rises to AB, and domestic quantity demanded falls to AC. The difference is made up by imports which now fall to BC. The government collects a revenue of T per unit of imports. Thus, the government's revenues are given by the shaded area $BCHG$.

The argument for the import tariff is to protect domestic production and employment. However, instead of a tariff on imports, suppose the government gives a subsidy equal to T to domestic producers. The effect is that producers get a price P_d and, hence, the quantity supplied rises to AB. But consumers still pay P_f, and, thus, domestic quantity demanded does not change. It is still DF. The difference GF is made up by imports.

However, along with a production subsidy of T, if the government imposes a consumption tax of T per unit, the consumers also pay the price P_d, and thus demand is curtailed to AC as before. The government now collects revenues of T per unit on the total consumption, which is AC. This revenue is given by the area $ACHD$. But it pays out $ABGD$ to producers as a subsidy. Thus, its net revenue is as before $BCHG$ (which is the revenue from the import tariff).

FIGURE 2.14 Effect of an import tariff.

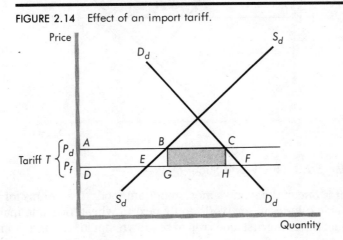

What this shows is that *a tariff of T per unit has exactly the same effects as a production subsidy of T per unit plus a consumption tax of T per unit.* It should now be clear who is paying the costs of import tariffs.

The case of export subsidies is exactly analogous. This is shown in Figure 2.15. D_dD_d is the domestic demand curve, and S_dS_d is the domestic supply curve. Without any tariffs and subsidies, the domestic price is the foreign price P_f. At this price DG is the domestic quantity demanded, and DH is the domestic quantity supplied. The difference GH is exported.

Now, the government wants to stimulate exports and introduces an export subsidy of Z per unit. The domestic price rises to $P_d = P_f + Z$. Domestic quantity demanded falls to AB, and domestic quantity supplied increases to AC. The difference is the exports BC, which are higher than GH. The cost to the government is the subsidy of Z per unit for the exports BC. It is thus the area of the shaded rectangle $BCFE$.

Now exactly the same result is achieved by a production subsidy of Z per unit and a consumption tax of Z per unit. The cost to the government for the production subsidy is $ACFD$. The revenues from the consumption tax are $ABED$. The difference is the net cost to the government, which is $BCFE$.

Thus, *an export subsidy of Z per unit is exactly equivalent to a production subsidy of Z per unit plus a consumption tax of Z per unit. And so it also follows that both import tariffs and export subsidies are equivalent to a production subsidy plus a consumption tax.*

In the above discussion we have, of course, abstracted from the costs of tax collection and disbursal of subsidies which can be substantial. But the analysis shows how we can demonstrate the equivalence of different policies by using a simple demand and supply analysis.

FIGURE 2.15   Effect of an export subsidy.

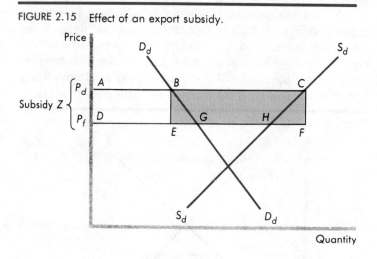

EXAMPLE 2.3   The World Sugar Market

Sugar is one of the world's most important foods. It accounts for 10 percent of the available calories in the world (only next to wheat, rice, and maize). Sugar is also unique: It was the first food crop to be grown, not for eating at home, but for export.

It was brought to Europe from the Middle East by the Arab invaders in the eighth century along with cotton, rice, and oranges. However, it was not until the conquest of Barbados in 1627 and the subsequent development of sugar plantations that it achieved any importance as a food. By 1800 it became a necessity, and by 1900 it was supplying nearly one-fifth of the calories in the British diet. If one looks at per-capita sugar consumption, one finds that it increases steadily with per-capita income until a per-capita income of say $6,000 to $8,000 and then declines because of the increase in health consciousness and calorie counting. (Japan, the United States, Canada, some European countries, and Australia are examples.) Such populous countries like Bangladesh, China, India, and Indonesia are at the low end of per-capita income, and with economic development their demand for sugar is expected to grow.

Sugar is both an agricultural and an industrial business. Refining sugar is more complicated than processing wheat, coffee, and other crops. Since it is advantageous to have refineries where sugar cane is grown, sugar gives many countries their first taste of industrialization. The sugar plantations were perhaps the first examples of industrial capitalism. By the late seventeenth century a typical plantation would have 80 acres and a work force of 100. When farms of over 30 acres were uncommon in Britain, the sugar plantations in the Caribbean were the biggest enterprises in the world, predating by a century the development of industrial capitalism in other areas.

Sugar was also the center of a three-way trade. Britain sent cloth, tools, beads, and weapons to Africa, shipped African slaves to the Caribbean to work on the sugar plantations, and brought Caribbean sugar to Britain.

From 1670 to 1820, when it was overtaken by raw cotton, sugar was Britain's biggest single import. In the nineteenth century, however, Britain levied taxes on the imports of sugar, and sugar became the focus of arguments about free trade. The free traders won, and taxes were removed in 1843. However, after more than almost a century and a half, the free trade issue remains.[4]

The sugar market is an interesting example of a market that is enslaved by government subsidies and import restrictions. The U.S. government has been regulating sugar imports in one way or another almost continuously since 1789, which is some sort of proof that governments do not learn from past mistakes. In 1934 a quota system was set up and has continued ever since with an interruption in the 1970s.

The U.S. government subsidizes the price of domestic sugar (the subsidized price is 20 to 22 cents per pound, whereas the world market price was as low as 3.5 cents per pound in 1985 and was about 6.5 cents per pound in 1987). But the U.S. government is not alone. The European common market (EEC) pays its farmers about 20 cents and Columbia pays its farmers about 21 cents. The resulting surpluses are dumped in the world market. Because of the subsidies, the European farmers increased their annual production between 1977 and 1985 from 10.8 million to 13.3 million tons. During those 8 years, the EEC "sold" 38 million tons of sugar on world markets at world prices. The European taxpayers lost more than $12 billion.

[4]"Return to Where We Left Off in 1843," *The Economist*, August 10, 1985, p. 51; and Sidney W. Mintz, *Sweetness and Power: The Place of Sugar in Modern History*, Viking Press, New York, 1985.

Not all sugar traded on world markets is sold at world market prices. Around one-third of sugar traded internationally is sold under fixed contracts. Russia guarantees a market for Cuban sugar, the United States a market for its third-world friends, and the EEC for former British colonies and others. Since the importers pay the same high price as they pay for the domestic producers, this sounds like a good deal for the exporting countries. However, none of the exporting countries except a few (Cuba and Mauritius, for instance) sell more than half their output at these subsidized prices, and they have to sell the rest at world market prices. Some other countries (Thailand, Australia, and the Philippines, for instance) do not have a "sugar daddy."

As far as the United States is concerned, there is no restriction on domestic production, and the imported sugar is also bought at the high domestic subsidized price, not at the much lower world price. The domestic supply has been rising when demand has been falling because U.S. consumers have become more diet conscious. Between 1983 and 1987 sugar production in the United States increased by 1 million tons whereas quantity consumed decreased by 1 million tons. The high price of sugar has also encouraged the production of cheaper substitutes like high-fructose corn syrup. The price support for sugar has created a lovely market for the corn people, and now the grain growers from the corn belt join the plantation owners in the south in lobbying for price supports for sugar. Pretty soon a time will come when the United States would have to reduce import quotas to zero or drop the price support program, or else dump on the world market the supplies it buys from the domestic sugar producers. In 1986 the Commodity Credit Corporation decided that it was not going to hold sugar any more and sold 150,000 tons of sugar to China. It had paid 18 cents a pound for it and China got it for 4.75 cents a pound. The world price at that time was 6.33 cents, and the U.S. bargain sale brought it down to 4.96 cents in 2 days. The foreign sugar exporters like Fiji, Australia, and Thailand were infuriated.[5]

If cars that cost $8,000 to make had to be sold at $2,000, all the world's automobile manufacturers would go bust, starting with the least efficient ones. However, with the blessings of the different governments around the world, the only growers in the sugar market that will be going out of business are the most efficient ones (in Australia, Brazil, Cuba, Fiji, the Philippines, and so on).

2.7.3 Controls on prices and quantities

There are several governmental policies that are designed to: (1) prevent prices from rising to their market equilibrating level, or (2) prevent prices from falling to their market equilibrating level, or (3) prevent quantities from reaching their market equilibrating level.

Examples of case (1) are interest rate controls, rent controls, controls on natural gas prices, and controls on several consumer prices. Examples of case (2) are the price support programs for different agricultural commodities and minimum wage laws. An example of case (3) is an import quota.

In the case of controls on maximum prices, what the government has in mind

---

[5]Lindley H. Clark, Jr., "How Protectionism Soured the Sugar Market," *The Wall Street Journal,* November 5, 1987, p. 36.

is the idea that low-income consumers are likely to suffer a great hardship if prices are "too high." In the case of agriculture, the argument for the price support programs is that farm incomes suffer if prices are "too low." In the case of minimum wage laws, again the stated purpose is to protect workers from employers' exploitation. In all these cases, one can argue that one should attack the income problem by changing incomes directly (income subsidies) rather than by tinkering with prices.

As can be seen from a simple demand and supply diagram like the one in Figure 2.7, fixing the price below the market equilibrating level creates an excess demand or shortage, and supporting the price above the market equilibrating level creates an excess supply or a glut. What happens to this excess supply or excess demand depends on the specific case we are considering. For instance, in the case of agricultural price support programs the government purchases part of the excess supply and subsidizes the farmers in storing the remainder. In the case of minimum wage laws, the excess supply of labor goes into the pool of unemployed. Among this pool, those who qualify get unemployment insurance, some of the workers get discouraged and drop out of the labor force, and some others find jobs at lower wages among occupations not covered by the minimum wage laws or in an illegal way even among those occupations covered by minimum wage laws.

In the case of consumer goods subject to price controls, a black market will develop as a consequence of excess demand. We will discuss this issue in the next section.

In the case of price controls on natural gas, the excess demand (those customers that cannot get natural gas) spills over into the demand for alternative fuels (for example, heating oil, electricity, and, in the case of industrial customers, into coal).

In the case of rent controls, the excess demand will go into alternative housing arrangements. Furthermore, the actual market price can really be higher than the controlled price, because landlords can make tenants buy furniture from them at exorbitant prices and in some cases demand "key money" (down payment for the privilege of renting the apartments).

Since one of the major objectives of the price controls (controls on natural gas prices, rent controls, and so on) is to prevent large income transfers to the owners of these resources, it might be interesting to see under what conditions this is possible. Consider the case where the quantity supplied is fixed and equal to Q_0. The effects of price controls in this situation are illustrated in Figure 2.16.

The supply curve SS is vertical at the quantity Q_0. DD is the demand curve. The equilibrium price is P_0 and, of course, the quantity supplied and demanded is Q_0.

Suppose the price is controlled at P_c, which is less than P_0. Then the quantity supplied is still Q_0 as before. There is, of course, an excess demand equal to BC, but this will remain unsatisfied. One thing that has happened is that there is an income transfer equal to the shaded area shown in Figure 2.16 from the producers or resource owners to consumers. Earlier consumers spent $P_0 \cdot Q_0$ for the amount Q_0. Now they spend only $P_c \cdot Q_0$ for the same amount Q_0.

In the case of rent controls, assuming the quantity of housing to be fixed, there is an income transfer from landlords to the tenants that are currently occupying the apartments or houses. Of course, the rent control draws new consumers into

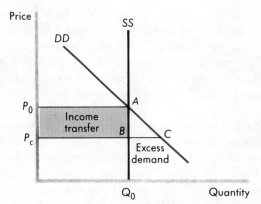

FIGURE 2.16   Effect of price controls under conditions of fixed supply.

the market, and this is what causes the excess demand. But since quantity supplied is fixed, they cannot get any rental housing in this market.

A similar story can be told for price controls on natural gas. The price controls result in an income transfer from natural gas producers or pipeline companies to the consumers. Of course, the low controlled price draws new customers into the market, and this is what produces the excess demand. But since the quantity supplied is fixed, these new customers cannot get natural gas and must find alternative energy sources.

Of course, quantity supplied is not fixed except in the very short run and, thus, the above arguments may not hold good in the long run. But the argument about income transfers is based on an implicit assumption of fixed supply.

EXAMPLE 2.4   Cattle Raisers' Lament

Governments can create shortages by legislating prices below the market equilibrium price and gluts by legislating price supports above the market equilibrium price. The surpluses created by price supports are disposed of in a number of ways, sometimes by selling them even to communist countries at prices below world market prices (by dumping them) and sometimes by novel methods. One particular example is that of the slaughter of milk cows in 1986.

The price support program for milk created an oversupply of milk. In the spring of 1986 the Agriculture Department (USDA) came up with a plan to reduce national milk production through a buy out of surplus milk cows. About 1.6 million milk cows were to be slaughtered or exported over a period of 6 months.

The cattle raisers, however, were not too happy with this plan and protested that this undermines the market for fed cattle. However, this is not true. The cow meat is entirely different from grain-fed steer beef. It cannot be branded as "USDA Choice." It is only useful for the production of hamburgers, hot dogs, bologna, and so on. Thus, the USDA plan would affect only the ranchers who cater to this market. Since the meat industry anyway imported more than 1 billion pounds of boneless beef annually, the cow meat would affect mostly the countries that supply the United States with boneless beef. Australia, New Zealand, and Canada were the major suppliers to this market. Ireland was the only country in Europe from which these supplies came. Thus, the meat from the dairy herd buy out would have exerted pressure on the foreign suppliers and would have even helped the trade balances for the U.S. The cattle raisers would not have been seriously affected.[6]

Finally, we come to the case of quantity controls. As mentioned earlier, an example of quantity control is an import quota. The effect of an import quota is the same as that of an import tariff as shown in Figure 2.14. Going back to that figure, if the government restricts imports to the level BC, the domestic price will rise to P_d. The government can restrict imports by issuing import licenses equal to the amount BC. If these are issued at random (by say a lottery), then the lucky importers who obtain the licenses will reap the benefit which is $BC \cdot T$ or the shaded area $BCHG$ in Figure 2.14. However, if the government auctions the import licenses, then it will get revenues equal to the shaded area $BCHG$, which is what the government gets from an import tariff. *This shows the relationship between a quantity control and a price control.*

Actually, the case of a per unit tax considered earlier in Section 2.7.1 can also be viewed as one of quantity control. Instead of letting the amount produced be Q_0, the government restricts output to Q_1 by issuing production licenses for that amount. This amount will fetch the price P_1 in the market, but the suppliers are willing to supply this quantity at a price P_2. Thus, $(P_2 - P_1)Q_1$ represent the profits that the lucky producers who get the licenses make, if the government gives away licenses in a lottery. However, if the production licenses are auctioned off, the government will get revenues of $(P_2 - P_1)Q_1$, which is exactly the revenue it gets from a per unit tax. The situation is similar to an import quota.

There are several other examples of quantity controls. The government policy of "pollution standards" is a policy of pollution quotas where each firm is given a quota on the amount of pollution it can generate. We will be discussing this problem in Chapter 19. In the field of agriculture, acreage controls control not output but an input in production. We will discuss this as well in Chapter 15.

2.7.4 Illegal activities and black markets

In the previous section, when we discussed price controls, we argued that some of the excess demand generates a "black market." In other words, some transactions will take place at the controlled price and some other transactions will take place above the controlled price in an illegal market often called the "black market." In the case of minimum wage laws, these transactions are below the price supports (employment at wages below the minimum wage). To study the black market let us first consider demand and supply in a completely illegal market.

Suppose buying and selling a good X is illegal. This could be babies, some drugs, human organs, or U.S. jeans in Russia. The demand and supply curves are shown in Figure 2.17. DD and SS show the demand and supply curves if the buying and selling were legal. The equilibrium would be at A.

Now suppose there is a penalty for those caught buying or selling the product. The consequence of this is a decrease in demand and a decrease in supply. The

[6]See Emerson Moran, "Cattlemen's Beef Is Just Baloney," *Wall Street Journal*, May 14, 1986, p. 30.

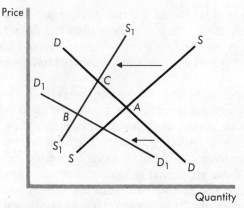

FIGURE 2.17 Demand and supply for illegal goods when penalties are imposed on both buyers and sellers.

equilibrium quantity falls but we can't say anything about the equilibrium price (see Table 2.5, the case of a decrease in both demand and supply).

In actual practice, frequently only the sellers are penalized. In this case, only the supply curve shifts, and equilibrium price clearly rises. However, the reduction in equilibrium quantity will not be as dramatic. This demonstrates that if the objective of outlawing certain goods is to curtail their use, then penalties should be imposed on both buyers and sellers.

Black markets develop when the government attempts to control the price of a product and that price is below the equilibrium price. All trade in this product is not illegal, rather only trade at a price in excess of the controlled price. For example, "scalping" Superbowl tickets is against the law in many places. Selling most items at above an official price is illegal in most communist countries—and, as a result, black markets are prevalent.

The black market situation is shown in Figure 2.18: DD is the demand curve and SS the supply curve.[7] The market equilibrium occurs at A. Suppose the price is controlled at level P_c. This generates an excess demand equal to BC. These unsatisfied buyers enter the black market. If there are no penalties on the buyers, then their demand curve is EC. Suppose there is a penalty on the seller. Then the supply curve shifts leftward to S_1S_1. The equilibrium is now at the point F. The black market price is higher than the market-equilibrating price. Actually, the average market price (the weighted average of the legal price and black market price) could also be higher than the market-equilibrating price (although it is not the way the diagram is drawn).

Now suppose the buyers also pay a penalty. In this case the black market demand curve shifts leftward to D_1D_1. The black market equilibrium is at the point G. In this case the black market price is below the market equilibrium price but one can get other results by changing the magnitudes of the shifts. If no penalties are imposed on sellers and penalties are imposed on buyers only, the black market

[7]The analysis here is based on Kenneth E. Boulding, "A Note on the Theory of the Black Market," *Canadian Journal of Economics and Political Science*, February 1947, pp. 115–118. The exposition and diagrams are, however, different and relate to the preceding discussion of illegal activities.

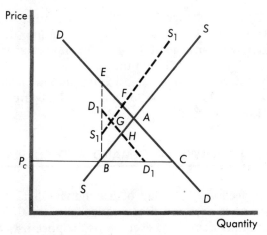

FIGURE 2.18   Price determination in black market.

equilibrium is at H (since the supply curve does not shift). Thus, *if our concern is with the price in the black market, it is better to penalize the buyers rather than the sellers.*

Also, note that if the penalties are sufficiently high, then the black market demand curve D_1D_1 and the black market supply curve may not intersect and, thus, no transactions can take place.[8]

Finally, some supplies currently available in the "free" market might disappear into the black market. Of course, in the extreme case where all supplies disappear we can apply the analysis of the illegal markets we discussed earlier. The case where some of the supplies from the free market disappear into the black market is illustrated in Figure 2.19. All the curves and equilibrium points are defined as

[8]This is not shown in the diagram, but we can just move S_1S_1 upward and D_1D_1 downward. Note that any meaningful intersection has to be to the right of the point B.

FIGURE 2.19   Price determination in black market when part of the legal supply disappears into the black market.

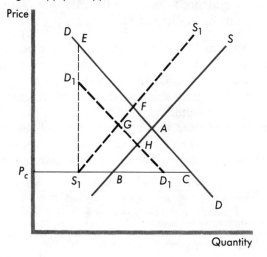

in Figure 2.18. The only change is that the black market supply S_1S_1 starts at a point to the left of B. S_1B is the supply disappearing into the black market. The excess demand is now S_1C instead of BC. One can draw conclusions similar to those drawn with Figure 2.18. We will omit the details here.

Note that the IRS estimated that it lost $90 billion in unpaid taxes due to black market activity and tax cheating in 1981 and that the figure would likely grow to $135 billion by 1985.[9]

2.8 EXCEPTIONS TO THE LAWS OF DEMAND AND SUPPLY

As stated earlier in Section 2.2, the law of demand says that ceteris paribus quantity demanded falls as price rises and rises as price falls. Are there any exceptions to this law? Does quantity demanded ever rise as the price rises and fall as the price falls? The answer is yes, and the following are some examples:

1. Goods with snob appeal: Many items such as jewelry are valued for their "snob appeal." The economist Thornstein Veblen coined the phrase, "conspicuous consumption" to describe the consumption of items that are valued just because of their high price.[10] If prices are reduced, the buyers' satisfaction from possessing them goes down, and the quantity demanded goes down. The same thing happens for fur coats and fancy cars as well. If they are "cheap," then there is nothing great about possessing them.

2. Goods with uncertain product quality: There are many goods for which we do not know the quality, and we sometimes judge the quality by the price. We often say "if it costs so much, it must be really good." In markets where prices act as "signals" of quality, people tend to assume that quality has gone up when prices are raised and hence may demand more of the commodity at a higher price.

3. Giffen goods: For completeness our list should include Giffen goods, named for the nineteenth-century English economist Robert Giffen. He argued that the demand curve for some inferior goods would slope upward for theoretical reasons. There is no empirical evidence to establish the existence of a Giffen good, but we will examine his argument in Chapter 4.

As with the violations of the law of demand, there are cases of violations of the law of supply. That is, there are cases where less will be supplied at a higher price and more at a lower price. One example is based on imperfect information. This is similar to the uncertainty about product quality discussed in the case of the violations of the law of demand.[11]

In summary, the violations of the laws of demand and supply we discussed are to be found in (1) markets for goods with snob appeal, (2) markets with imperfect information and uncertainty, and (3) the case of Giffen goods.

[9]See O. Friedrich, "Tax Cheating—Bad and Getting Worse," *Time*, March 28, 1983, pp. 26–32.

[10]Thornstein Veblen, *The Theory of the Leisure Class*, Macmillan, New York, 1899.

[11]This problem is discussed in Joseph E. Stiglitz and Andrew Weiss, "Credit Rationing in Markets with Imperfect Information," *The American Economic Review*, June 1981, pp. 393–411. Some other examples pertaining to used cars, medical insurance, and so on can be found in G. Akerlof, "The Market for Lemons: Qualitative Uncertainty and the Market Mechanism," *Quarterly Journal of Economics*, August 1970, pp. 488–500.

EXAMPLE 2.5 Supplier-Induced Demand—The Case of Physicians

The conventional demand and supply model we have discussed is based on the assumption that price and output can be explained by the interaction of *independent* supply and demand. This assumption has been called into question in the market for medical services. It has been argued that medical practitioners have the ability to generate demand for their services directly, that they have the ability to shift the position of the consumers' demand curve. This is a case of supplier-induced demand, and the inducement hypothesis in this case states that doctors generate demand for their own services.[12]

The first evidence on the inducement hypothesis was provided by Fuchs and Kramer, who found, using data for different states, that visits per capita are positively associated with the number of physicians per capita when income, price, insurance benefits, and hospital beds per capita are held constant.[13] Thus, more doctors means more doctoring. The findings by Fuchs and Kramer were criticized on empirical and logical grounds by Sloan and Feldman, Yett, and others.[14] A question that was asked by Yett was: "After all, if physicians really do have the power to raise fees and sell more of the same service to a small number of patients in areas where physician density is high, why don't they do this sort of thing in all circumstances? If the answer is that they aim for a target income, what determines the height of the target?" Fuchs and Kramer were also criticized on grounds that they used aggregate data for states.

To respond to these criticisms, Fuchs reexamined the supplier-induced demand hypothesis using in-hospital surgery rates and the supply of surgeons.[15] He again found that more surgeons per capita mean more operations per capita! He found that "other things equal, a 10 percent increase in surgeon/population ratio results in a 3 percent increase in *per capita* utilization. Moreover, differences in supply seem to have a perverse effect on fees, raising them when the surgeon/population ratio increases." As for surgeon supply, Fuchs found that it was determined in part by factors unrelated to demand, especially by the attractiveness of the area as a place to live.

The supplier-induced demand hypothesis has profound implications for public policy. We cannot expect to reduce the price of medical care by increasing the supply of physicians and surgeons. More doctors mean more doctoring and higher fees. More surgeons mean more operations and higher fees. Maybe this is why the medical profession is not too opposed to the expansion of medical schools.

Price controls applied to physicians' fees to restrain total health care spending may be unproductive. They may merely lead to more visits, substitution of costly procedures for simple ones, increased use of hospital care, and so on. There is substantial empirical evidence to show this. The greatest 2-year change in physi-

[12]J. Richardson, "The Inducement Hypothesis: That Doctors Generate Demand for Their Own Services," in J. Van der Gaag and M. Perlman, eds., *Health, Economics and Health Economics*, North Holland, Amsterdam, 1981, pp. 189–214, presents evidence from Australian data.

[13]V. R. Fuchs and M. J. Kramer, "Determinants of Expenditures for Physicians' Services in the U.S. 1948–68," National Bureau of Economic Research, Occasional Paper No. 117, New York, 1972.

[14]See A. C. Enthoven, "The Behavior of Health-Care Agents: Provider Behavior," in Van der Gaag and Perlman, *Health, Economics*, pp. 173–188 for a survey of this literature.

[15]V. R. Fuchs, "The Supply of Surgeons and the Demand for Operations," *Journal of Human Resources*, Supplement, Fall 1978, pp. 35–36.

cians' services occurred during the 2-year period when price controls were in effect (fiscal year 1973 and fiscal year 1974).[16] Physician utilization rates increased 6.3 percent and 5.5 percent, respectively. The increases were 3.9 and 4.3 percent the previous 2 years, and 2.5 and 2.8 percent in the 2 subsequent years. Thus, physicians may have increased billings to compensate for their inability to raise fees.

The theoretical underpinnings of the supply-induced demand hypothesis are weak. But there is considerable empirical evidence to suggest that it might be valid. And the policy implications if it is valid are very important.

2.9   SUMMARY AND CONCLUSIONS

The demand curve relates price to the desired quantities of purchase. Other conditions remaining the same, quantity demanded falls as price increases. The market demand curve is obtained by summing the individual quantities demanded at each price; similarly, the supply curve relates price to the desired quantities of sale. Other things remaining the same, quantity supplied rises as price increases. The market supply curve can be obtained by summing the individual quantities supplied at each price, if no specialized inputs are involved.

It is important to distinguish between the terms "demand" and "quantity demanded." In common conversation they may be used interchangeably, but in economics they mean two different things. Demand refers to the entire relationship between price and quantity. Quantity demanded refers to the quantity which buyers are willing to purchase at a particular price. Thus, when we say there is an increase in demand, we mean that the demand curve shifts to the right so that quantity demanded increases at *every* price. Similarly, a decrease in demand means a shift of the demand curve to the left. The terms "increase in supply" and "decrease in supply" are similarly interpreted as shifts in the supply curve.

Market equilibrium occurs at the point of intersection of the market demand and supply curves. Market equilibrium changes when there is a change in one or more conditions that influence the behavior of either buyers or sellers so that there is a shift in the demand and/or supply curves.

Shifts in the demand curve occur when there is a change in tastes or income or the prices of related goods. Shifts in the supply curve occur with changes in input supply, the state of technology, changes in the prices of alternate outputs, new discoveries, and changes in weather.

Taxes (subsidies) will also cause the demand or supply curves to shift. An excise tax (per-unit tax) can be described as an upward shift in the supply curve by an amount equal to the tax, when the price paid by consumers is plotted on the vertical axis (Figure 2.10). Alternatively, it can be shown as a downward shift in the demand curve when the price kept by sellers is plotted on the vertical axis (Figure 2.11).

The effect of import tariffs and export subsidies can be shown as movements along the given demand and supply curves.

A tariff of T per unit is exactly the same as a production subsidy of T per unit

[16]Z. Y. Dickman, *A Study of Physicians' Fees*, Council on Wage and Price Stability, Washington, D.C., 1978.

plus a consumption tax of T per unit. A similar conclusion applies to export subsidies. Both import tariffs and export subsidies are equivalent to a production subsidy plus a consumption tax.

Controls on prices or quantities produce a situation of excess demand or excess supply. These require measures of "rationing" if there is excess demand or "surplus disposal" if there is excess supply.

In markets for illegal goods, suppliers are usually highly penalized. However, this causes the equilibrium price to rise, but the quantity transacted may not fall much. If the government would like to control both the price and the quantity of a good transacted illegally, then it should penalize not only the sellers but the buyers as well.

Price controls may produce black markets. The analysis of black markets is similar to that of illegal markets.

KEY TERMS

Black Market
Ceteris Paribus
Change in Demand
Change in Quantity
   Demanded
Change in Quantity Supplied
Change in Supply
Complements
Conspicuous Consumption

Demand
Disequilibrium
Equilibrium Price and
   Quantity
Excess Demand or Shortage
Excess Supply or Surplus
Export Subsidy
Import Tariff
Inferior Good

Law of Demand
Law of Supply
Market Demand
Market Supply
Normal Good
Substitutes
Supply
Tatonnement Process

QUESTIONS

1. Listed below are six statements. Indicate which is an increase or decrease in demand, an increase or decrease in quantity demanded, an increase or decrease in supply, or an increase or decrease in quantity supplied.

   a. TWA reduces its average plane fare by 30 percent in order to attract more passengers.

   b. The government grants an export subsidy to the producers of oranges in order to increase the sale of oranges abroad.

   c. Wheat farmers in Nebraska decide to withhold some of their product from the market because prices are too low.

   d. The higher price of imported whiskey causes more people to drink Kentucky bourbon.

   e. The government imposes an excise tax on automobile tires, and sellers cannot pass much of this tax on to consumers. As a result, the number of tires offered on the market for sale drops.

   f. Saudi Arabia opens its "oil spigot" in order to teach those OPEC members who discounted price in the international market a lesson.

2. What does the term "ceteris paribus" mean? How does it relate to the distinction between a change in quantity demanded and a change in demand?

3. Consider the market for video cassette recorders (VCRs). How will each of the following changes affect demand, supply, and equilibrium price and quantity? Discuss why.

   a. Consumer incomes increase dramatically.

   b. Penalties on the recording of copyrighted materials are imposed and enforced.

   c. Movie theaters reduce their prices.

   d. An improvement in technology dramatically reduces production costs.

   e. The price of recording tape increases.

   f. It is rumored that prices of VCRs will rise sharply next year.

4. The table below is a demand and supply schedule for oranges. The quantity is measured in boxes of 48 oranges each.

Price per Box (48 per box)	Quantity Demanded (millions of boxes per year)	Quantity Supplied (millions of boxes per year)
$6	25	125
5	50	100
4	75	75
3	100	50
2	125	25
1	150	0

   a. What are the equilibrium price and quantity in the orange market?

   b. At a price of $6 per box, does a surplus or shortage exist in the market? What is the magnitude of this disequilibrium condition?

   c. If the government controlled the price of oranges at $3 per box, what would happen in the orange market?

   d. Suppose that the world price of oranges is $2 per box. Will there be imports into or exports from the domestic market? Why? By how much?

5. If the equation for a market demand curve is $Q_d = 10 - 4P$, and the equation for the market supply curve is $Q_s = 4P$, find the market equilibrium price and quantity. Verify your answer graphically.

6. The following statement was recently made by one of this nation's top political leaders: "With the price of crude petroleum falling so rapidly, it will be difficult for the oil refineries to keep up with the increase in demand for gasoline."

   a. Criticize the statement. Can you find a flaw in the leader's reasoning? Explain.

   b. What effect will the falling price of petroleum have on the supply of gasoline? Explain.

7. From January of 1979 through January of 1980, the price of gold nearly tripled. Yet as the price of gold rose, sales of gold increased as well. Does this imply that the demand for gold is upward sloping? Why or why not?

8. For each of the following statements, answer "true" or "false," and then provide a reason for your answer.

a. An increase in demand and a decrease in supply will always result in a higher equilibrium price and a lower equilibrium quantity.

b. Ceteris paribus, if the government supports a product's price below its equilibrium price, neither a surplus nor shortage will exist.

c. An increase in the price of mink coats will cause quantity demanded to fall.

d. An increase in demand and an increase in supply have an indeterminate effect on product price, but equilibrium quantity increases.

e. If the government imposes an import tariff on Japanese televisions, the supply of imported televisions decreases.

9. During the summer of 1985, some watermelons were accidentally contaminated with an herbicide. Several consumers became seriously ill. This accident had two immediate results. First, consumers were frightened. Second, the agricultural authorities destroyed a large number of suspect melons. Using demand and supply analysis, explain the impact of this incident on the market for watermelons. Could you have predicted the impact on equilibrium price? On equilibrium quantity consumed? Why or why not?

10. From time to time, the federal government gives away surplus agricultural commodities (cheese, butter, and so on), and retail grocers often complain that the "giveaways" reduce their sales. Is this complaint valid? Is there a change in demand or quantity demanded? Explain your answer.

11. In April of 1981, Japan imposed a "voluntary quota" on the export of cars to the United States. Many people believed that they agreed to voluntarily restrict exports because they feared that the alternative would be the imposition by the United States of an import tariff on Japanese cars. Why would the Japanese prefer the quota to the tariff?

12. Every year there is a shortage of Superbowl tickets at the "official" price. (What does this imply about the official price relative to the equilibrium price?) Generally, a black market (scalping) then develops in which tickets are sold for several hundred dollars or more. If tickets were instead auctioned to ensure that they sold for the equilibrium price, how would the average price paid be affected? If stiff penalties were imposed on scalpers, how would the current black market price be affected? Demonstrate your conclusions using demand and supply analysis.

PRICE ELASTICITY
OF DEMAND AND SUPPLY

*When you can measure what you are speaking about,
and express it in numbers, you know something about
it; but when you cannot measure it, when you cannot
express it in numbers, your knowledge is of a meager
and unsatisfactory kind; it may be the beginning of
knowledge, but you have scarcely, in your thoughts,
advanced to the stage of <u>science</u>.*

Lord Kelvin (1824–1907)
Popular Lectures and Addresses (1891–1894)

3.1 INTRODUCTION

In Chapter 2, we stated the laws of demand and supply and studied the effects of shifts in the demand and supply curves on the equilibrium prices and quantities. We also studied the effects of a per unit tax, import tariff, export subsidy, and so on. In all these cases we made statements concerning the direction of change in price and quantity. In this chapter we examine the magnitudes of these changes. For example, the law of demand states that if the price rises by 10 percent, then quantity demanded will decline. But will it decline by 10 percent? By more? By less? Just how responsive is quantity demanded to a change in price?

The measures of responsiveness we will examine are *elasticities*. The ratio of percentage change in the quantity demanded to percentage change in price is called the *price elasticity of demand*. (This ratio is, however, generally expressed as an absolute value.) Similarly, the ratio of percentage change in quantity supplied to percentage change in price is called the *price elasticity of supply*. Thus what we are asking is whether the elasticity of demand is equal to 1, less than 1, or greater than 1.

We will consider elasticity of demand from the seller's point of view. Several revenue concepts will be introduced, and their relationship to demand elasticities will be explored. What, for example, happens to total expenditure on a product as the price of that product rises or falls? The answer depends on the price elasticity of demand.

We will also quantify many of the applications of demand and supply analysis which we looked at in Chapter 2. For instance, in our discussion of the per unit tax, we said that a tax T results in an increase in the price paid by buyers and a decrease in the price the seller gets. In other words, the tax is "shared" by buyers and sellers. An important question is: Whose share of the burden of the tax is bigger? We will show that the answer depends on the price elasticities of demand and supply.

Finally, we will review some problems with the estimation of demand and supply functions from actual data on prices and quantities. And we will look at a simple dynamic model of price determination.

Chapter 3 is an important chapter. It is one of the "cornerstones" of this text. Although some of it should be review, students should make certain that they fully understand these concepts.

3.2 PRICE ELASTICITY OF DEMAND AND SUPPLY

We define the price elasticity of demand as the absolute value of the ratio of percentage change in the quantity demanded to the percentage change in price, ceteris paribus. Note that this is the same as the ratio of *relative* changes or *proportionate* changes. It is customary to use the Greek symbol η (eta) for price elasticity of demand. Thus, price elasticity can be written as

$$\eta = \left| \frac{\Delta Q/Q}{\Delta P/P} \right| = \left| \frac{\Delta Q}{\Delta P} \cdot \frac{P}{Q} \right|$$

The vertical lines denote that we take the absolute value of the ratio, and ΔQ and ΔP denote the changes in quantity and price.[1]

The price elasticity of supply can be similarly defined as the ratio of percentage change in quantity supplied to the percentage change in price, ceteris paribus. Using ϵ (epsilon) to denote the price elasticity of supply, we can write

$$\epsilon = \frac{\Delta Q/Q}{\Delta P/P} = \frac{\Delta Q}{\Delta P} \cdot \frac{P}{Q}$$

Clearly the definition of ϵ is very similar to that of η. The only difference is that Q now denotes the quantity supplied instead of the quantity demanded. Also, the absolute value signs have been dropped, because the law of supply tells us that ϵ is already positive (why?) and, hence, the absolute value signs are no longer needed.

Now we are ready to consider why we work with proportionate or percentage changes rather than simple magnitudes of changes. Why don't we just calculate $|\Delta Q/\Delta P|$ and use this to measure responsiveness of quantity demanded (or supplied) to a change in price? Graphically this number is the inverse of the slope of the demand curve (or supply curve) expressed in absolute terms.

One reason is because $|\Delta Q/\Delta P|$ depends on the units of measurement for both P and Q and, hence, is somewhat difficult to interpret. Suppose, for instance, that we are told that $|\Delta Q/\Delta P|$ for corn is 7.3. How responsive is the quantity demanded of corn to a change in its price? What if P is measured in cents and Q is in millions of bushels? A 1-cent increase in the price of corn would cause a 7.3 million bushel decrease in the quantity demanded of corn. But suppose instead that P is measured in dollars and Q is in bushels. The picture changes dramatically.

Elasticities, however, are pure numbers and are thus much less cumbersome to interpret. If the price elasticity of demand for corn is 4.1, a 1 percent increase in the price of corn leads to a 4.1 percent reduction in quantity demanded, holding other things constant. The units of measurement for P and Q are immaterial.

EXAMPLE 3.1   Price Elasticity of Demand for Whole Life Insurance

In the insurance literature, life insurance has often been characterized as a "sold good, not a bought good" in the sense that the initiative in a life insurance transaction in the ordinary (individual) life insurance market comes typically from the seller (insurance agent who works on commissions) rather than the buyer. Since the complexity of a whole life insurance contract is not easily amenable to price comparisons, it is inferred that consumers are insensitive to variations in the price of life insurance.

Some other indirect evidence has also been suggested to argue that quantity demanded of life insurance is not especially sensitive to price. Most of the studies conducted into the competitiveness of policy pricing among insurers have found wide ranges in the prices of ostensibly similar policies. It has also been observed that few consumers make the comparisons that characterize consumer shopping behavior for other goods and services of similar price. Some have even argued that the mere existence of whole life contracts is evidence of consumer irrationality (the

---

[1]In terms of derivatives we have $\eta = |dQ/dP \cdot P/Q|$ or $|(d \log Q)/(d \log P)|$.

argument being that a rational person could be economically ahead by purchasing term insurance and investing the difference).

Babble discusses all these arguments and demonstrates why they are not valid.[2] He constructs a real price index for whole life insurance sold in the United States from 1953 to 1979. He finds a price elasticity of 0.71 to 0.92 for nonparticipating and 0.32 to 0.42 for participating individuals. He also finds an income elasticity of 0.62 to 0.98. Thus, new purchases of whole life insurance are responsive to changes in the price index, contrary to what has been accepted in the insurance literature but consistent with economic theory. This, he argues, does not however ensure that the insurance industry manifests a high degree of competition.

3.3 ARC AND POINT ELASTICITIES

We defined the elasticity of demand as

$$\eta = \left| \frac{\Delta Q/Q}{\Delta P/P} \right|$$

The quantities ΔQ and ΔP, which are the changes in Q and P, respectively, are easy to define. But the question arises as to what value of Q and P we use. Are we supposed to take beginning values or final values or some average? For example, suppose the price per unit of a watch went up from \$10 to \$11, and the number of watches demanded went down from 100 to 95. Clearly, $\Delta P = \$1$ and $\Delta Q = -5$. If we take the initial values, then $(\Delta Q)/Q = -5/100 = -1/20$ and $(\Delta P)/P = 1/10$ and $\eta = 0.5$. It seems reasonable to consider the starting values for both P and Q. However, economists more frequently calculate the *arc elasticity*, which uses the average of the initial and final values. Thus, if P_1 and Q_1 are the initial price and quantity respectively, and P_2 and Q_2 are the final price and quantity respectively, then $\Delta Q = Q_2 - Q_1$ and $\Delta P = P_2 - P_1$. For the divisors we use the average quantity and average price, which are $(Q_1 + Q_2)/2$ and $(P_1 + P_2)/2$.

Thus, the arc elasticity is (cancelling the factor 2 in both the denominator and numerator)

$$\eta = \left| \frac{\Delta Q/\Delta P}{(Q_1 + Q_2)/(P_1 + P_2)} \right| = \left| \frac{\Delta Q}{\Delta P} \cdot \frac{P_1 + P_2}{Q_1 + Q_2} \right|$$

And in the example from the preceding paragraph

$$\eta = \left| \frac{-5}{1} \cdot \frac{21}{195} \right| = 0.54$$

Figure 3.1 shows the arc elasticity. As the point B gets closer to the point

[2]David Babble, "Price Elasticity of Demand for Whole Life Insurance," *Journal of Finance*, March 1985, pp. 225–239. The paper contains numerous references to early studies on this topic.

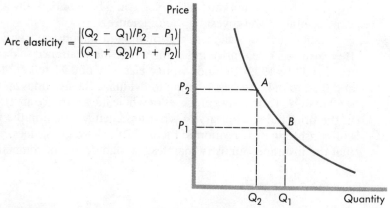

Arc elasticity $= \dfrac{\left|(Q_2 - Q_1)/P_2 - P_1)\right|}{\left|(Q_1 + Q_2)/P_1 + P_2)\right|}$

FIGURE 3.1   Arc elasticity.

A, so that the changes in price and quantity get smaller, we get the *point elasticity* at *A.*[3]

EXAMPLE 3.2   Elasticity of Demand for Gambling

Estimates of elasticity of demand for legalized gambling are important for use by governments in devising the tax rates that maximize the revenue to the government. Suits estimates these elasticities and finds them considerably higher than unity (in absolute value).[4] The estimates he obtains arc in the range of 1.6 to 2.7. This high elasticity of demand, he argues, places severe limits on gambling as a source of tax revenue. An important source of this high price elasticity is the availability of illegal establishments.

Gambling is a recreational activity. For most gamblers the purpose of gambling is not to get rich but to have fun and to experience excitement. Gamblers are perfectly aware that they will lose on the average, but they view this expectation of loss as the price paid to engage in the game.

What is the price and what is the quantity in the case of gambling? Gambling establishments pay out in winnings only a fraction of the total dollars bet. The fraction of the total that the gambling establishment withholds is called the *take-out rate.* This is the price for any game. In the case of casinos the take-out rate is highest for slot machines (usually around 0.90) and lowest for games such as roulette (which is around 0.06). The rate is usually 0.15 to 0.20 at race tracks and 0.50 or more for lotteries. Different games constitute different products and are not even close substitutes in the minds of the players. For any particular game the take-out rate is the price P for playing that game. The quantity Q is the total value of bets placed and is called the *handle.* It is measured in dollars, but it is not revenue. The revenue for the gambling establishment is PQ, that is, take-out rate multiplied by the total value bet.

To derive an elasticity of demand, Suits looked at the experience of Nevada betting parlors when at the end of 1974 the federal excise tax on bookmaking was

[3] As ΔP and $\Delta Q \to 0$ the arc elasticity becomes $\left|(dQ)/(dP)\right| \cdot P/Q$ or $(d \log Q)/(d \log P)$.

[4] D. B. Suits, "The Elasticity of Demand for Gambling," *The Quarterly Journal of Economics,* February 1979, pp. 155–162.

reduced from 10 percent to 2 percent of handle. The per-quarter betting rates preceding the reduction of the tax rate and following it were as follows:

Activity	Year	Federal Tax (%)	Take-Out Rate (P)		Handle (Q) ($ million)
			Operator (%)	Total (%)	
Off-track Horse Betting	1974	9.1	14.5	23.6	5.1
	1975	2.0	14.0	16.0	9.6
Sports Betting Parlors	1974	10.0	8.0	18.0	1.4
	1975	2.0	8.0	10.0	5.0

The arc elasticities are

$$\text{Off-track horse betting} = \left| \frac{4.5}{7.6} \cdot \frac{39.6}{14.7} \right| = 1.6$$

$$\text{Sports betting parlors} = \left| \frac{3.6}{8.0} \cdot \frac{28.0}{6.4} \right| = 2.0$$

Consider the sports betting parlors. The government revenues have declined from $140,000 to $100,000, that is, by $40,000. The gambling establishments' revenues have increased from $112,000 to $400,000 or by $288,000 or seven times the loss in government revenue. The gambling and racing establishments and the gamblers and racing fans all constitute a strong lobby against increased taxes, since the lobby has much to gain and the state has relatively little to lose from low tax rates. More empirical evidence and more detailed calculations can be found in the paper by Suits.

3.4   GEOMETRIC REPRESENTATION OF POINT ELASTICITY

We all know that the slope of a straight line is constant and that the slope between any two points is given by the change in y divided by the change in x. Thus, with a linear demand curve $\Delta Q/\Delta P$ is constant. However, since Q/P is not constant, the demand elasticity will be different at different points on the demand curve. There is, however, a simple rule for finding the demand elasticity at any point. This rule, for a linear demand function, is

$$\text{Point elasticity of demand} = \frac{\text{Distance of the point from the } Q \text{ axis}}{\text{Distance of the point from the } P \text{ axis}}$$

with both distances *measured along a demand curve*. Figure 3.2 illustrates this.

This result can be proven as follows: $\Delta Q/\Delta P = EC/AE$, and at the point C we have $Q/P = OF/OE$. Hence, $\eta = (EC/AE)/(OF/OE) = OE/AE$ since $EC = OF$. Since CF and OA are parallel lines, $\eta = OE/AE = CB/CA$.

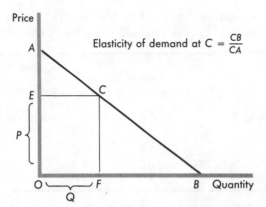

FIGURE 3.2 Geometric representation of elasticity for a linear demand curve.

As a consequence, we get the result that $\eta = 1$ at the midpoint M of AB, $\eta > 1$ for points on the demand curve between A and M and $\eta < 1$ for points on the demand curve between M and B (Why?). This is shown in Figure 3.3.

For a nonlinear demand curve the same rule for calculating elasticity applies except that we have to consider the tangent to the demand curve in place of the linear demand curve we considered earlier. (Note that the slope at a point on a curve is the slope of the tangent to that curve at that point.) This is shown in Figure 3.4. All we have to do is draw a tangent to the demand curve at the point we are considering and then use the rule for the elasticity at a point on a linear demand curve given earlier.

Let's now turn our attention to the elasticity of supply. With a linear demand curve, as we have shown in Figure 3.3, $\eta = 1$ at the midpoint of the demand curve, $\eta < 1$ below the midpoint, and $\eta > 1$ above the midpoint. With a linear supply curve, the elasticity can equal, be less than, or be greater than 1 at *all* points on the supply curve. In Figure 3.5 we show supply curves with elasticity of less than, greater than, and equal to 1 at all points.

FIGURE 3.3 Elasticity of demand at the different points on a linear demand curve.

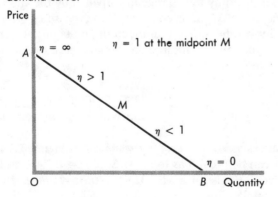

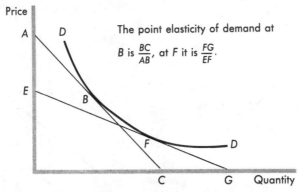

FIGURE 3.4 Price elasticity of a curvilinear demand curve.

The rule for calculating the elasticity of supply at a point can be derived the same way we did for elasticity of demand. Consider, for instance, Figure 3.5(*b*).

$$\text{Elasticity of supply } \epsilon = \frac{\Delta Q/Q}{\Delta P/P} = \frac{\Delta Q}{\Delta P} \cdot \frac{P}{Q}$$

But

$$\frac{\Delta Q}{\Delta P} = \frac{1}{\text{slope}} = \frac{AD}{CD}$$

and

$$\frac{P}{Q} = \frac{CD}{OD}$$

Hence,

$$\epsilon = \frac{AD}{CD} \cdot \frac{CD}{OD} = \frac{AD}{OD}$$

but

$$\frac{AD}{OD} = \frac{AC}{BC} = \frac{\text{Distance of } C \text{ from the } Q \text{ axis}}{\text{Distance of } C \text{ from the } P \text{ axis}}$$

Both distances are measured *along the supply curve.*

Note that the elasticity of supply is less than 1 if the supply curve has a negative intercept as in Figure 3.5(*a*). Take any point *C* on the supply curve. Its distance *along the supply curve* from the quantity axis is *CA*, and its distance from the price axis is *CB*. Since *CA* < *CB*, the elasticity of supply is less than 1. If the supply curve has a positive intercept as in Figure 3.5(*b*), then we have *CA* > *CB*, and the elasticity of supply is greater than 1.

Finally, if the intercept is zero, so that the supply curve passes through the origin, the distance of the point, along a supply curve, is the same from both the quantity and price axes. Hence, elasticity of supply equals 1. Thus, all the supply curves shown in Figure 3.5(*c*) have elasticity of supply equal to 1.

Note that there are no linear demand curves with elasticity equal to 1 at all points, but several linear supply curves have elasticity equal to 1 at all points.

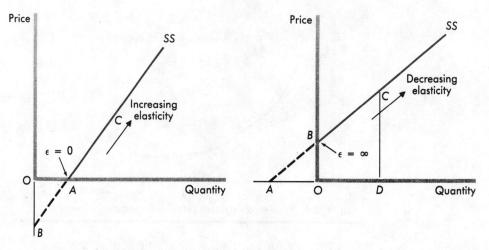

(a) Elasticity of supply less than 1 (CA < CB).   (b) Elasticity of supply greater than 1 (CA > CB).

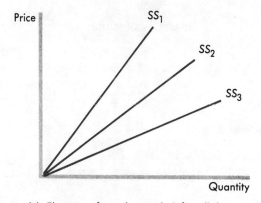

(c) Elasticity of supply equals 1 for all the curves.

FIGURE 3.5   Elasticity of supply for linear supply curves.

Similar is the case with elasticity less than 1 or elasticity greater than 1. There are no linear demand curves with such elasticities at all points, but there are several linear supply curves whose elasticities are either less than 1 or greater than 1 at all points.

Also, for nonlinear supply curves, we just draw a tangent to the supply curve at the point we are considering and then use the same rule as for a linear supply curve. Since the tangent line can have a positive or negative intercept at different points, we will have the elasticity of supply greater than 1 at some and less than 1 at other points. The elasticity of supply declines from ∞ to 0 along the nonlinear supply curve the way it declines for the linear demand curve as shown earlier in Figure 3.3. The decline of elasticity for the supply curve is shown in Figure 3.6.

Finally, we will show what a demand curve with elasticity equal to 1 at all points looks like. This is a curve for which $P \cdot Q$ is constant and is called a rectangular hyperbola. This is shown in Figure 3.7. Note that for a supply curve with elasticity

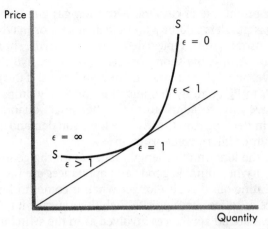

FIGURE 3.6   Changes in the elasticity of supply along a curvilinear supply curve.

equal to 1, P/Q is constant and for a demand curve with elasticity equal to 1, PQ is constant.[5]

3.5   SHORT-RUN AND LONG-RUN PRICE ELASTICITIES

When the price of a product changes, it takes some time for consumers to fully respond. For instance, the effect of a rise in the price of heating oil results in consumers switching to alternative fuels only after some time. Consumers initially will try to economize on the usage with existing appliances, but eventually they also switch to alternative fuels. With a rise in the price of gasoline, consumers will

[5]Mathematically the equation $Q = AP^\alpha$ is a curve with constant elasticity α, since $(d \log Q)/(d \log P) = \alpha$. For demand curves, α is negative. For supply curves, α is positive.

FIGURE 3.7   A demand curve with elasticity equal to 1 at all points: A rectangular hyperbola.

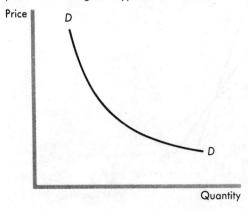

try to economize on the use of gasoline with their gas guzzlers but will eventually get rid of their gas guzzlers and buy fuel-efficient cars or maybe join a car pool.

Figure 3.8 illustrates some typical demand curves in the short run, intermediate run, and long run. A_1B_1 is the short-run demand curve, A_2B_2 is the intermediate-run demand curve, and A_3B_3 is a long-run demand curve. If the price of the product increases from P_1 to P_2, quantity demanded immediately drops from Q_1 to Q_2. But as consumers have time to adjust to the higher price, quantity drops to Q_3 and eventually to Q_4 in the long run. Clearly, the long-run demand curve is more elastic than the short-run or intermediate-run curves.

How long is the long run? Its length depends on the goods being considered. Clearly it is longer when durable goods and appliances are involved as in the case of gasoline or heating oil. It is also longer when it comes to long-standing habits. Suppose the price of coffee goes up. Although theoretically it is easy to switch from coffee to tea (there are no appliances involved as in the switching from natural gas to heating oil), we do not observe many people making such a switch immediately. For many individuals drinking tea is not the same as drinking coffee. It takes time for them to change their drinking habits.

In actual practice there is no such thing as complete adjustment. Suppose the price of gasoline goes up 10 percent and *stays there*. Then, ceteris paribus we can ask by what percentage the quantity demanded of gasoline goes down. Suppose the initial quantity demanded is 100 (million gallons). Then we observe the demand in successive years until the decline peters off. In Table 3.1 we show the decline over the first 10 years.

The figures in Table 3.1 are, of course, hypothetical because, in practice, it is not possible to maintain the ceteris paribus assumption, nor is it possible to maintain the price of gasoline at the 10 percent increased level. To compute the elasticities in practice we have to use multiple-regression analysis to control for the other factors and estimate appropriate dynamic demand functions to disentangle the short-run and long-run effects. We have chosen a hypothetical example to illustrate the difference between short-run and long-run elasticities.

FIGURE 3.8   Short-run and long-run demand curves.

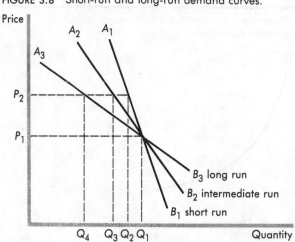

TABLE 3.1 Effect of a Price Increase on the Quantity of Gasoline Demanded
Initial demand = 100 million gallons
Increase in price = 10 percent

Year	Quantity Demanded	Cumulative Decline	Price Elasticity	
1	98.0	2.00	0.200	← Short run
2	97.0	3.00	0.300	
3	96.5	3.50	0.350	
4	96.0	4.00	0.400	
5	95.7	4.30	0.430	← Intermediate run
6	95.4	4.60	0.460	
7	95.2	4.80	0.480	
8	95.05	4.95	0.495	
9	95.01	4.99	0.499	
10	95.00	5.00	0.500	← Long run

Note: Initial quantity was 100 million gallons, and increase in price was 10 percent.

In Table 3.1 we have stopped at 10 years because the decline in quantity demanded seems to have almost petered out in 10 years. If we went another 10 years, we would have observed a little more decline, but for all practical purposes 10 years is enough. If we treat 1 year as short run, 5 years as intermediate run, and 10 years as long run, we have the respective elasticities as 0.2, 0.43, and 0.5.

Note that the definition of what constitutes short run and intermediate run is somewhat arbitrary. For the definition of long run we have used the idea that it is the time taken for the decline in quantity to peter out (almost). In any case, it is important to note that the short-run elasticity is less than the intermediate-run elasticity, which, in turn, is less than the long-run elasticity.

The distinction between short-run and long-run elasticities becomes a bit complicated when we discuss the demand for *durable goods*. Again, if we consider the demand for *services* provided by durable goods, the long-run elasticity would be higher than the short-run elasticity. However, if we look at the *current purchases* of durable goods, the short-run price elasticity may appear higher than the long-run price elasticity. Consider, for instance, the case of automobiles. We buy automobiles for the services they provide. Assume that the *flow of services* is proportional to the *stock* of automobiles. Suppose the current stock of automobiles is 80 million. If the long-run price elasticity of demand for automobiles (services they provide) is 0.5, then a 10 percent decrease in the price of automobiles results in an ultimate increase in the desired stock by 4 million. However, if consumers initially increase their *current purchases* by, say, 3 million, and the normal level of yearly purchases is 10 million, we observe a 30 percent increase in current purchases of automobiles. This would imply a short-run price elasticity of 3.0, and one might be tempted to conclude that the short-run elasticity is higher than the long-run elasticity. However, this is not true. When we computed the long-run elasticity we considered the flows of services or the stock of automobiles. When we computed the short-term elasticity, we considered the *current purchases* of automobiles, not the current stock. If we define the variables consistently, we would find that the short-run increase in purchases is 3 million, whereas the long-run increase in purchases is 4 million, so that the short-run elasticity of purchases is 3, which is less than the long-run elasticity of 4. Similarly, the short-run increase in the stock is 3.75%, whereas the long-run increase is 5 percent, making the long-run elasticity of the stock greater than the corresponding short-run elasticity. In both cases the usual pattern in short-run and long-run elasticities holds.

When we consider the demand for automobiles, we have to make sure what we are talking about. Is it the demand for services of automobiles (which we have assumed to be proportional to the stock of automobiles) or is it the current purchases of automobiles (addition to the stock)? From the consumers' point of view the former is the relevant concept. On the other hand, from the automobile manufacturers' point of view, what counts is the elasticity of current purchases. In both cases, if the elasticities are properly defined, the short-run elasticities will be lower than the long-run elasticities.

Houthakker and Taylor estimated the following short-run and long-run elasticities for three energy uses[6]:

Good	Elasticity	
	Short Run	Long Run
Natural gas	0.15	10.74
Gasoline and oil	0.14	0.48
Electricity (residential)	0.13	1.90

Note that the short-run elasticities are all about the same but the long-run elasticities differ considerably. The results imply that gasoline has very few substitutes, electricity has some substitutes, and natural gas has many substitutes.

Actually, many estimates of the demand elasticity of energy sources derived during the days of the "energy crisis" of the 1970s varied considerably, although one could see that the short-run elasticities were all considerably below 1 and the long-run elasticities generally were above 1.

Suppliers also require time to react to price changes. For example, it might take considerable time to interview the necessary additional labor required to produce a larger output in response to a higher price. Thus, supply curves also tend to be more elastic, the longer the time frame considered. This point will be considered further in future chapters when we look behind a supply curve.

3.6   OTHER ELASTICITY CONCEPTS

Elasticities can be defined with respect to any two variables. Next we will examine the income elasticity of demand and the cross-price elasticity of demand.

[6]H. S. Houthakker and L. D. Taylor, *Consumer Demand in the United States: Analysis and Projections,* 2d ed., Harvard University Press, Cambridge, Mass., 1970.

Income elasticity

The income elasticity of demand, u, is defined as

$$u = \frac{\Delta Q}{\Delta Y} \cdot \frac{Y}{Q}$$

where Y stands for income and Q denotes quantity demanded. Again, the assumption of ceteris paribus applies. But this time we are assuming that everything except consumer incomes remains the same. In particular, the price of the given good and also the prices of all related goods are assumed to remain constant.

Income elasticity tells us how responsive quantity demanded is to a change in income. If income elasticity of demand equals 2.3, then a 1 percent increase in income leads to a 2.3 percent increase in quantity demanded, ceteris paribus.

You will notice that when we defined the income elasticity of demand, we did not take the absolute value. That is because the sign is of interest. For most goods, when income increases, the quantity demanded of the good also increases. In this case, the income elasticity of demand is positive, and the good is a normal good at the level of income considered. However, if the quantity demanded of the good falls when income increases, the good is an inferior good at the income level considered, and, in this case, income elasticity of demand is negative. Remember that no good is inferior at all income levels. Almost all goods are normal at sufficiently low levels of income and are inferior at sufficiently high levels of income. For example, at lower levels of income, the demand for poultry increases as the income level rises, but at sufficiently high levels of income, quality cuts of beef will be substituted for poultry, causing the quantity demanded for poultry to decrease. Thus, poultry is a normal good at lower levels of income and an inferior good at higher levels of income.

Normal goods are further classified as necessities and luxuries. A good is called a *necessity* if its income elasticity of demand is positive and less than 1. Thus when income rises, demand for the product increases, but less than proportionately. Similarly, if income elasticity of demand exceeds 1, the good is called a *luxury*. A good can be a necessity at high levels of income and a luxury at low levels of income. In empirical studies, however, economists generally either assume a constant elasticity or report the elasticity at the mean (or median) level of income. In Table 3.2, we present some estimates of income elasticity computed for the United States on the basis of quarterly data for the years 1967 through 1979.

As with price elasticities, we can talk of short-run and long-run income elasticities. Because consumers can make the necessary adjustments in the long run, we would expect the long-run income elasticities to be higher than short-run income elasticities in absolute value. However, as mentioned earlier in connection with short-run and long-run price elasticities, in the case of durable goods we must be again careful whether we are discussing stocks or flows.

Are there *any* cases where the short-run elasticity is higher than the long-run elasticity? Yes, if there is *over-shooting*.[7] In models of flexible exchange rates, an increase in money supply ceteris paribus would have an impact on domestic price

[7] This terminology is commonly used in models of flexible exchange rates, where the short-run effect is higher than the long-term effect.

TABLE 3.2 Estimates of Income Elasticity of Demand

Commodity Group	Elasticity	Commodity Group	Elasticity
Beef	0.94	Housing	0.41
Pork	0.32	Other services	0.72
Broilers	0.65	Transportation	0.64
Milk	0.24	Household operation	0.03
Eggs	0.52	Electricity and gas	0.56
Clothing and shoes	1.72	Gasoline and oil	0.36
Other nondurables	0.91	Fuel oil and coal	0.27

Source: Dale Heien, ''Seasonality in U.S. Consumer Demand,'' Journal of Business and Economic Statistics, vol. 1, no. 4, October 1983, p. 283.

level and the exchange rate. However, if prices are sticky and exchange rates are not, then initially the brunt of the adjustment falls on the exchange rate and it would have to overadjust or "overshoot." The short-run effect on the exchange rate is consequently higher than the long-run effect. Similarly, a decrease in consumers' income would eventually be felt on *all* commodities. However, in the short run, consumers would overadjust (cut down drastically) the expenditures on commodities whose purchase they can easily postpone. These are usually big-ticket items such as houses, cars, or some appliances. These adjustments would produce an effect that is higher in the short run than the long run. This would be an argument why the demand for automobiles (or other durables or owner-occupied housing) can be more income elastic in the short run than in the long run.

Cross-price elasticities

Another useful concept is the *cross-price elasticity of demand.* (Price elasticity of demand discussed in Section 3.1 is sometimes referred to as *own* price elasticity.) The elasticity of demand for good Y with respect to the price of good X measures responsiveness of demand for Y to a change in the price of X and is defined (with obvious notation) by

$$\eta_{Y, P_x} = \frac{\Delta Q_y}{\Delta P_x} \cdot \frac{P_x}{Q_y}$$

Again, the assumption of ceteris paribus applies, and this time we assume that everything remains the same except the price of X.

A cross-price elasticity of -1.4 means that a 1 percent increase in the price of good X leads to a 1.4 percent reduction in the demand for good Y. Again, the sign of the elasticity is important. A positive cross-price elasticity means that an increase in P_x leads to an increase in Q_y, and the two goods are substitutes. Fuel oil and natural gas are examples of substitutes for heating. However, a negative cross-price elasticity implies that an increase in P_x causes a reduction in Q_y so that products X and Y are complements. Gasoline and motor oil are complements. If the price of gasoline rises, the quantity demanded for gasoline falls but so does the demand for motor oil. If the cross-price elasticity is 0, the goods are independent or unrelated.

With respect to two goods X and Y there are two cross-price elasticities.

$$\eta_{Y.P_x} = \text{elasticity of demand for } Y \text{ with respect to the price of } X$$

and

$$\eta_{X.P_y} = \text{elasticity of demand for } X \text{ with respect to the price of } Y$$

These two elasticities need not be equal.[8]

Note that cross-price elasticities frequently tell us something about the magnitude of the own price elasticity of demand. Why? Because an important determinant of own price elasticity is the availability and closeness of substitutes. Consider the demand for Pepsi. If the price of Pepsi increases, many consumers quickly switch to Coke or similar cola products. What does this tell us about the cross-price elasticity of demand for these products? It should be positive and fairly large, indicating that these two goods are close substitutes. In turn, what does the high cross-price elasticity imply about own price elasticity of demand for Pepsi? Demand should be fairly elastic. So, in general, when close substitutes are available, own price elasticity will be larger.

EXAMPLE 3.3   Use of Cross-Price Elasticity in an Antitrust Case

The Antitrust Division of the U.S. Department of Justice brought suit against the Du Pont Company for monopolizing the sale of cellophane. Du Pont sold 75 percent of the cellophane used in the United States. However, Du Pont argued that the relevant market was that of packaging materials that included aluminum foil, waxed paper, polyethylene, and so on. In fact, cellophane accounted for only 20 percent of this market. To prove its point, Du Pont produced cross-price elasticities between cellophane and the other substitute products. In 1956 the U.S. Supreme Court agreed with Du Pont and dismissed the case.[9]

EXAMPLE 3.4   Demand for Liquor

Estimates of price and income elasticities vary a lot depending on the time periods, type of data, country for which the data apply, and so on. Of particular importance are elasticities of demand for some items whose consumption is considered detrimental to individuals' health or has adverse social consequences (e.g., drunken driving).

Hogarty and Elzinga estimated the price elasticity of demand for beer as 1.13.[10] McGuiness finds with U.K. data that consumption of alcohol is not sensitive to

---

[8]In Chapter 5 we will discuss the income and substitution effects of a price change. At that time we will discuss what is known as an income-compensated demand curve. For such demand curves these two elasticities are equal.

[9]See *U.S. Reports*, vol. 351, U.S. Government Printing Office, Washington, D.C., 1956, p. 400. See also the analysis in G. W. Stocking and W. F. Mueller, "The Cellophane Case and the New Competition," *The American Economic Review*, March 1955, pp. 29–63.

[10]T. F. Hogarty and K. G. Elzinga, "The Demand for Beer," *Review of Economics and Statistics*, May 1972, pp. 195–198.

price changes although it goes up with income.[11] He also finds large elasticity of consumption with respect to number of licensed premises. The two studies give different answers to the question of whether an increase in the taxes on liquor restricts alcohol consumption.

3.7 THE SELLERS' VIEW: TOTAL REVENUES, AVERAGE REVENUES, AND MARGINAL REVENUES

In Chapter 2, when we discussed the concept of the demand curve, we said that the demand curve gives the *hypothetical* quantities that a consumer would buy at different prices. In this view, quantity is the dependent variable, and strictly speaking, we should measure quantity on the vertical axis and price on the horizontal axis. However, we followed the usual convention of measuring price on the vertical axis and quantity on the horizontal axis, a procedure that is justifiable if we view the demand curve from the seller's point of view. We will now discuss this view.

From the seller's point of view, the demand curve tells what price the sale of a number of units will fetch. Note that we are not talking of selling one unit of the commodity at a time. What we are asking is a hypothetical question as to what price sellers would get if they *block-auctioned* different quantities.

If a seller offers 10 units of a commodity for sale and gets $100, then $100 is called the *total revenue. Average revenue* or per-unit revenue is total revenue divided by the number of units sold or $10. This is actually the *bid price* when 10 units are offered for sale.

Table 3.3 shows a demand curve from the buyers' point of view and the sellers' point of view. Note that the average revenue curve is the demand curve. For the data in Table 3.3 we can compute the total and average revenue.

Also listed in Table 3.3 is marginal revenue. *Marginal revenue* of the *n*th unit is the *extra* revenue that the seller gets by offering *n* units instead of $(n - 1)$ units for sale. Since marginal revenue is the increase in total revenue for a one unit increase in the quantity Q offered for sale, we can write

$$MR = \frac{\text{Change in } TR}{\text{Change in } Q} = \frac{\Delta TR}{\Delta Q}$$

where MR denotes marginal revenue and TR denotes total revenue.[12] Graphically, the MR at a point on the TR curve is the slope of the TR curve at that point.

Henceforth, we will use the abbreviations TR, AR, and MR to denote total revenues, average revenue, and marginal revenue, respectively.

Note that like the demand curve (which is also the AR curve from the sellers' point of view), the TR and MR curves are hypothetical. Transactions do not take place at all the points. This does not mean they are not useful. We discussed this point in Chapter 2 in connection with demand curves.

---

[11]T. W. McGuiness, "The Demand for Beer, Spirits and Wine in the U.K. 1956–79," in M. Grant, M. Plant, and A. Williams, eds., *Welfare Economics and Alcohol,* Croom Helm, London, 1983.

[12]For an arbitrarily small change in Q, $MR = d(TR)/dQ$.

TABLE 3.3   A Demand Curve from the Buyers' and Sellers' Points of View

	Buyers' View		Sellers' View			
Price	Quantity Demanded	Total Expenditures	Quantity Offered for Sale	AR (Bid Price)	Total Revenue	Marginal Revenue
12	1	12	1	12	12	12 − 0 = 12
10	2	20	2	10	20	20 − 12 = 8
8	3	24	3	8	24	24 − 20 = 4
6	4	24	4	6	24	24 − 24 = 0
4	5	20	5	4	20	20 − 24 = −4

Examining Table 3.3, we see that the AR declines at a rate of 2 per unit, whereas the MR declines at the rate of 4 per unit, and MR is equal to 0 when TR is maximum.

Figure 3.9 shows typical average and marginal revenue curves when the demand curve is linear. Note that in Figure 3.9, $OC = (1/2)OB$. Since the MR and demand curves have the same vertical intercept, this means that the MR curve is twice as steep as a corresponding linear demand curve. We will prove this result in the next section.[13]

Figure 3.10 shows a typical TR curve for a linear demand curve. With a linear demand curve, MR is strictly diminishing as Q increases. And since MR at any point on the TR curve is the slope of the TR curve at that point, diminishing marginal revenue means that the slope of the TR curve is diminishing. This implies a humped shape for the TR curve. In Figure 3.10, the slope diminishes as we go from A to B to C. At the point C, or at maximum total revenue, the slope is 0. After that, the slope turns negative as it is at the point D and continues to diminish or become increasingly negative.

[13]Mathematically we can derive this as follows: $p = \alpha - \beta q$ is a linear demand curve. $TR = pq = \alpha q - \beta q^2$. Hence, $MR = d(TR)/(dq) = \alpha - 2\beta q$. Thus, the MR curve is linear. The intercept on the quantity axis (obtained by setting $p = 0$) is $-\alpha/\beta$ for the demand curve. For the MR curve (at $MR = 0$) it is $-\alpha/2\beta$. Thus, $OC = (1/2)OB$ in Figure 3.9.

FIGURE 3.9   Linear AR and MR curves.

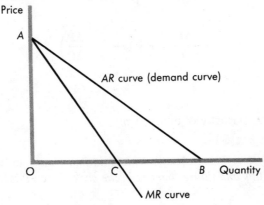

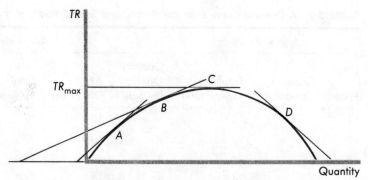

FIGURE 3.10   A typical *TR* curve for a linear demand curve.
Diminishing marginal revenue implies that the slope of the *TR*
curve diminishes as quantity offered for sale increases.

We will now discuss how the shapes of the *TR, AR,* and *MR* curves are related
to the elasticity of the demand curve.

3.8   RELATIONSHIP BETWEEN ELASTICITY OF DEMAND,
PRICE (*AR*), *TR,* AND *MR*

The elasticity of demand plays a crucial role in the relationship between *TR, AR,*
and *MR* and in shaping these curves.

To examine these relationships, let us start with an initial price of *P* and quantity
Q on the demand curve. Then total revenue $TR = P \cdot Q$. Now increase *Q* to *Q* +
ΔQ, where ΔQ is very small. With a downward-sloping demand curve, the price
falls to $P - \Delta P$. (Note that we are taking the absolute values of ΔP.) Since ΔQ is
very small, ΔP will also be. The total revenue now is $(Q + \Delta Q)(P - \Delta P) =$
$PQ + P(\Delta Q) - Q(\Delta P)$. We have omitted the term $\Delta Q \cdot \Delta P$, since if ΔQ and ΔP
are very small, their product will be negligible. Subtracting the initial total revenue
of *PQ* we get:

$$\Delta TR = P(\Delta Q) - Q(\Delta P)$$

hence

$$MR = \frac{\Delta TR}{\Delta Q} = P - Q \cdot \frac{\Delta P}{\Delta Q} = P\left(1 - \frac{Q}{P} \cdot \frac{\Delta P}{\Delta Q}\right)$$

but

$$\frac{\Delta Q}{\Delta P} \cdot \frac{P}{Q} \text{ is the elasticity of demand } \eta$$

So finally, $MR = P(1 - [1/\eta])$. *This is an important relationship which we will
use repeatedly in this and future chapters in the book.* Since *P* is the same as *AR,* we
can also state

$$MR = AR \left[1 - (1/\eta)\right]$$

This establishes the relationship between MR and AR. We can note the following results:

1. Since we have defined elasticity of demand as a positive number, $1 - (1/\eta)$ is less than 1, and, hence, $MR \leq AR$.
2. As η keeps decreasing, $1/\eta$ keeps increasing, and MR keeps falling.
3. If $\eta > 1$, $[1 - (1/\eta)]$ is positive. Hence, $MR > 0$, or TR will be increasing as Q increases.
4. If $\eta < 1$, $[1 - (1/\eta)]$ is negative. Hence, $MR < 0$, or TR will be decreasing as Q increases.
5. If $\eta = 1$, $[1 - (1/\eta)] = 0$ and $MR = 0$. Thus, the TR will be constant.
6. If $\eta = \infty$, $[1 - (1/\eta)] = 1$ and, hence, $MR = AR$.

We can now study these results in relation to the linear demand curve. (Figure 3.3 showed how the elasticity η changes along the demand curve.) We will now superimpose the results for MR. This is shown in Figure 3.11.

FIGURE 3.11 Elasticity of demand, MR, and TR for a linear demand curve.

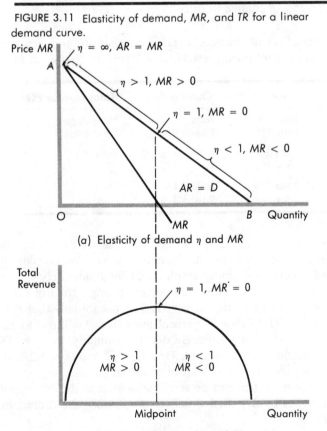

(a) Elasticity of demand η and MR

(b) Elasticity of demand η and TR.

The behavior of *TR* is shown in Figure 3.11(*b*). When $MR > 0$, *TR* will be increasing, and when $MR < 0$, *TR* will be decreasing. At the maximum value for *TR*, $MR = 0$. Why? (Note that for the hyperbolic demand curve shown in Figure 3.7, $\eta = 1$ at all points. Hence, $MR = 0$ and $TR =$ constant. In fact, the demand curve with a constant $P \cdot Q$ means *TR* is constant.)

The hump-shaped *TR* curve shown in Figure 3.11(*b*) is for a linear demand curve. For a curvilinear demand curve with elasticity less than 1 at all points, the total revenue will be falling steadily, and for a curvilinear demand curve with elasticity greater than 1 at all points, *TR* will be rising steadily.

We can get a hump-shaped *TR* curve even for a curvilinear demand curve if η is steadily falling as Q increases. However, the peak of the hump need not be at the midpoint. This is true only for a linear demand curve because $\eta = 1$ at the midpoint of a linear demand curve.

We have until now considered changes in total revenue *TR* when quantity changes. The price elasticity of demand will also tell us whether total revenue will increase or decrease with changes in price. To see what happens to total revenue all we have to do is note that the elasticity of demand is defined as

$$\left| \frac{\text{Percentage change in quantity}}{\text{Percentage change in price}} \right|$$

and see the effect of changes in price on quantity and hence on total revenue. Thus, we get the following results for a 1 percent change in price:

	Price P	Quantity Q	Total Revenue PQ
$\eta = 1$	Rises 1%	Falls 1%	No change
	Falls 1%	Rises 1%	No change
$\eta > 1$	Rises 1%	Falls >1%	Falls
	Falls 1%	Rises >1%	Rises
$\eta < 1$	Rises 1%	Falls <1%	Rises
	Falls 1%	Rises <1%	Falls

Thus if $\eta < 1$, the seller can get more total revenue by raising prices. If $\eta > 1$, the seller can get more total revenue by cutting prices. We consider only a small price change of 1 percent—similar results hold for moderately higher percentages of, say, 5 percent. If we consider a 20 percent change, then of course we cannot say that *TR* will show no change if $\eta = 1$. Suppose initially that $P = 10$ and $Q = 10$ so that $TR = 100$. With a 20 percent price rise, P will rise to 12, Q will fall to 8, and $TR = 96$, which is a 4 percent decline. Similarly, for $\eta = 0.9$, if P rises by 20 percent, Q declines by 18 percent. Thus $P = 12$ and $Q = 8.2$ and $PQ = (12)(8.2) = 98.4$. Thus total revenue, instead of rising, has fallen.

The reason for this can be seen by looking at the expression for the change in *TR*. If P rises by ΔP, then Q falls by ΔQ. Hence the change in total revenue is given by

$$\Delta TR = (P + \Delta P) (Q - \Delta Q) - PQ$$
$$= Q\Delta P - P\Delta Q$$

if we ignore the term $\Delta P \cdot \Delta Q$. Thus

$$\frac{\Delta TR}{\Delta P} = Q - P\frac{\Delta Q}{\Delta P}$$

$$= Q - Q\left(\frac{P}{Q} \cdot \frac{\Delta Q}{\Delta P}\right) = Q(1 - \eta)$$

Hence if $\eta < 1$, this expression is positive and ΔTR is positive, and if $\eta > 1$, this expression is negative and ΔTR is negative, as we obtained earlier. However, all this assumes that ΔP and ΔQ are small and hence their product is much smaller in magnitude and can be ignored. If they are not small, the cross product $\Delta P \cdot \Delta Q$ cannot be ignored.

EXAMPLE 3.5 Demand for Shakespearean Plays

Nonprofit lively arts often lose money and depend on patronage to cover losses.[14] An estimation of price elasticities of demand would help us to see whether prices could have been raised to increase revenues. Gapinski estimated demand functions for performances by Britain's Royal Shakespeare Company (RSC) during the 1965 to 1980 period and for the Aldwych Theater in London and the Shakespeare Memorial Theater in Stratford-upon-Avon.[15] He obtained a price elasticity of 0.657 (implying that the RSC could have raised price and thereby revenue) and an income elasticity of 1.327 (implying that Shakespeare performances were a luxury item). Gapinski estimates that profit maximization would require prices to more than double at Aldwych and exactly double at Stratford. According to his calculations, real profit would rise from −£505,000 to £5,000 at Aldwych and from −£214,000 to £317,000 at Stratford.

3.9   APPLICATIONS OF THE ELASTICITY CONCEPTS

We will now return to the problems of taxes, subsidies, tariffs, and quotas, that we discussed in Chapter 2 and show how the elasticities of demand and supply determine who bears the burden of taxes, who benefits more from subsidies, and so on. First, we will start with the excise tax discussed in Section 2.7.

3.9.1 Who bears the burden of excise taxes?

As we discussed in Section 2.7 we can analyze a sales tax (a percentage tax) the same way as a per unit tax with minor changes. Hence, we will analyze only a per unit tax here.

[14]W. J. Baumol and W. G. Bowen, *Performing Arts—The Economic Dilemma*, Twentieth Century Fund, New York, 1966.

[15]J. H. Gapinski, "The Economics of Performing Shakespeare," *The American Economic Review*, June 1984, pp. 458–466.

In our discussion, we said that the effect of a per unit tax is to raise the prices the buyers pay and reduce the prices sellers get. Thus, the tax is "shared" by buyers and sellers. The question is whose share is larger? The answer depends on the elasticities of demand and supply. The general rule is that if supply is less elastic than demand, then the suppliers pay the greater portion of the tax. If demand is less elastic than supply, then the buyers pay a greater portion of the tax. We illustrate the extreme cases of completely inelastic and perfectly elastic supply curves in Figure 3.12. We follow the same notation as in Section 2.7 of Chapter 2. DD is the demand curve, SS the supply curve, and P_0 the market equilibrium price without the tax. With the tax, P_1 is the price buyers pay, and P_2 is the price sellers get. $P_1 - P_2 = T$, the tax per unit.

As we did in Section 2.7 of Chapter 2, we have to find P_1 and P_2 such that $P_1 - P_2 = T$, the tax, and quantity demanded at the price P_1 is equal to the quantity supplied at the price P_2. In Figure 3.12(a) when supply is completely inelastic, quantity supplied is the same at all prices. Hence, P_1 stays at the price P_0 (the buyers pay the pretax price), and P_2 falls by the *full* amount of the tax (the price suppliers get falls by the full amount of the tax). Thus, suppliers bear the total tax burden.

In Figure 3.12(b) when supply is perfectly elastic, the price suppliers get cannot change and so stays at P_0. Hence, the price buyers pay has to rise by the full amount of the tax. Buyers bear the full burden of the tax. One can illustrate the cases of perfectly elastic and completely inelastic demand curves in a similar fashion. This will be left as an exercise. Now we must consider the case where the demand and supply curves are neither perfectly elastic nor completely inelastic but with elasticities very low or very high. This is shown in Figure 3.13. The figure is self-explanatory, and the conclusions are straightforward.

One additional result concerns the impact of the tax on output. If both the demand and supply curves are inelastic, the effect of the tax on quantity is minimal, but if both the curves are highly elastic, then there will be a drastic reduction in output. This result is obvious, since if the elasticities are high, a given percentage

FIGURE 3.12　Effect of a per unit tax with completely inelastic and completely elastic supply.

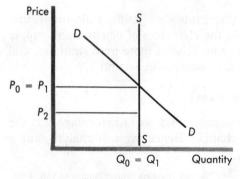

(a) Supply completely inelastic—
tax is completely borne by
the suppliers.

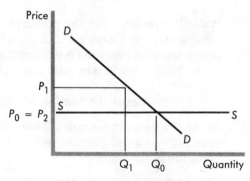

(b) Supply perfectly elastic—
tax is completely borne
by buyers.

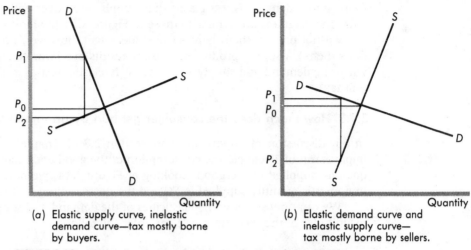

(a) Elastic supply curve, inelastic
    demand curve—tax mostly borne
    by buyers.

(b) Elastic demand curve and
    inelastic supply curve—
    tax mostly borne by sellers.

FIGURE 3.13   Effect of per unit tax with an elastic supply curve
(with an inelastic demand curve) and an inelastic supply curve
(with an elastic demand curve).

increase in price results in a higher percentage reduction in output. We show this
in Figure 3.14.

3.9.2 Who benefits from production subsidies?

A production subsidy is similar to the excise tax. We said in Section 2.7 of Chapter
2 that a production subsidy raises the price for the producer and reduces the price
for the buyer. Thus, both share the benefit. The question is: Who gets the bigger
share?

Again, if supply is less elastic than demand, then the supplier gets the bigger

FIGURE 3.14   Effect of a per unit tax on output.

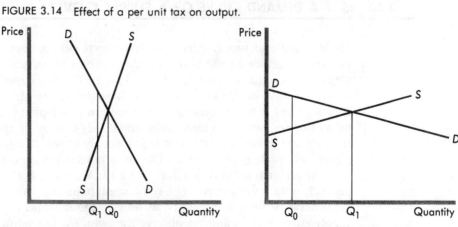

(a) Both demand and supply
    inelastic—output reduction
    is small.

(b) Both demand and supply highly
    elastic—output reduction
    substantial.

share, and if demand is less elastic than supply, the buyer will get a bigger share. Since the diagrams are similar to those in Figure 3.13 (by looking at Figure 2.13), we will not present them here. (The student will, however, find it instructive to draw them.) Also, the production subsidy results in a large change in output only when the demand and supply curves are very elastic (just as in the case of the per unit tax).

3.9.3 How much does the consumer get hurt by an import tariff?

In our discussion of import tariffs in Section 2.7 of Chapter 2, we said that an import tariff of T reduces the consumption of the good and increases the domestic quantity supplied of the good. Looking at Figure 2.14, we note that the increase in domestic quantity supplied is EG and the decrease in consumption is HF.

We can now see how the elasticities of the demand and supply determine the magnitudes of these changes. We can infer the following:

1. If supply is inelastic and demand very elastic, there will be very little increase in domestic quantity supplied (EG will be very small). The reduction in imports will come almost entirely from reduction in consumption (it will come almost entirely from HF). The effect is merely a rise in domestic price to benefit the suppliers.

2. The opposite will be our conclusion if demand is inelastic and supply is very elastic.

3. If both demand and supply are very elastic, we would need only a small tariff to reduce imports.

All these conclusions follow directly from the definitions of elasticity and from Figure 2.14.

3.10 IS IT A DEMAND CURVE OR A SUPPLY CURVE?

The demand and supply curves we have been talking about are hypothetical in the sense that not all the points on these curves are actually observed. Suppose we are given actual data on quantity and price (of, say, a commodity such as wheat or sugar). How do we know whether these points are on a demand curve or a supply curve? If these points give us a downward-sloping curve, we are tempted to say that we have a demand curve, and if they give us an upward-sloping curve, then we are tempted to say that it is a supply curve. But this conclusion is not correct, as Working demonstrated in his famous paper of 1927.[16]

The problem is illustrated in Figure 3.15. At time 1, D_1D_1 is the demand curve, and S_1S_1 is the supply curve. The equilibrium point is C_1, and this is the only point we observe at time 1. Similarly, at time 2, the demand curve is D_2D_2, and the supply curve is S_2S_2, and we observe the point C_2. The points we observe are C_1

[16]E. J. Working, "What Do Statistical Demand Curves Show?" *Quarterly Journal of Economics*, February 1927. Reprinted in American Economic Association, *Readings in Price Theory*, Irwin Publishers, Homeward, Illinois, 1953, pp. 97–118.

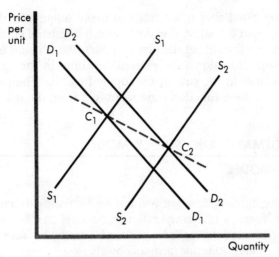

FIGURE 3.15   Observations on quantity and price when both the
demand and supply curves shift over time.

and C_2 alone, and if we join them we get a downward-sloping line. But C_1C_2 is
neither a demand curve nor a supply curve. This is called the *identification problem.*
We cannot *identify* the observed curve as a demand curve or a supply curve. We
can do this only if one of the two curves is stable.

Suppose the demand curve is stable over time but the supply curve shifts as
shown in Figure 3.16(*a*). Then the observations we have will all be on the same
demand curve. Similarly, if the supply curve is stable but the demand curve shifts,
as shown in Figure 3.16(*b*), then the observed points will trace out a supply curve.
Thus, we can identify from the observed data the curve that is stable.

FIGURE 3.16   Identification of the demand or supply curves from
market data on quantity and price.

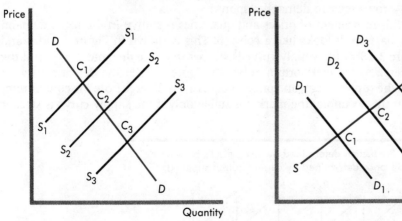

(a) Demand curve stable;
    demand curve identified.

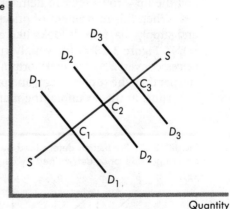

(b) Supply curve stable;
    supply curve identified.

Working suggested that if we want to make inferences about demand and supply functions from actual market data (which consist of equilibrium quantities and prices only), we should get data on variables that account for the shifts in the demand and supply functions, for example, income in the case of the demand function and weather in the case of the supply function. Then we can control for the shifts in one of these functions and identify it from the market data.

3.11 A DYNAMIC DEMAND AND SUPPLY MODEL:

THE COBWEB MODEL

As we said in the introduction, we will not be discussing dynamic models in this book. However, there is one simple dynamic model that is easy to explain: the cobweb model. The model is called a "cobweb" model because the path taken by the observed price and quantity form a cobweb.

In a dynamic model every variable has to be dated. Let P_t, Q_t be the price and quantity transacted at time t. We consider a market where supply decisions have to be made one time period (say a year or 6 months) in advance. This is a reasonable assumption in the case of many agricultural commodities. The suppliers are assumed to be very naive, and they look at last period's price and make their supply decisions (assuming that price to prevail this year as well). Once they produce the output, they have to sell it for whatever price it fetches. Since the quantity is given, the price they get is determined by the demand curve.

Suppose we start with some price P_0. Suppliers look at this and decide how much to produce for the next period. Thus, this determines Q_1, the quantity brought into the market at time 1. The price they get, P_1, is determined by the demand curve. The suppliers go back and change their production based on P_1. Next time period they come to the market with output Q_2. Again, the demand curve determines the price P_2 they get. This process keeps on going. The situation can be depicted by the arrows in Figure 3.17. The down arrows refer to supply response, and the up arrows refer to demand response.

When this movement of prices and quantities is shown in the usual demand and supply diagram, it looks like a cobweb. This is shown in Figure 3.18(a) and (b). In Figure 3.18(a) the supply curve is steeper than the demand curve, and the prices converge to the equilibrium point. In Figure 3.18(b) the demand curve is steeper than the supply curve, and prices progressively diverge from the equilibrium.

Thus, in this example, the market is stable only if the supply curve is steeper

FIGURE 3.17 Production determined by last period's price and current period's price determined by current output supplied.

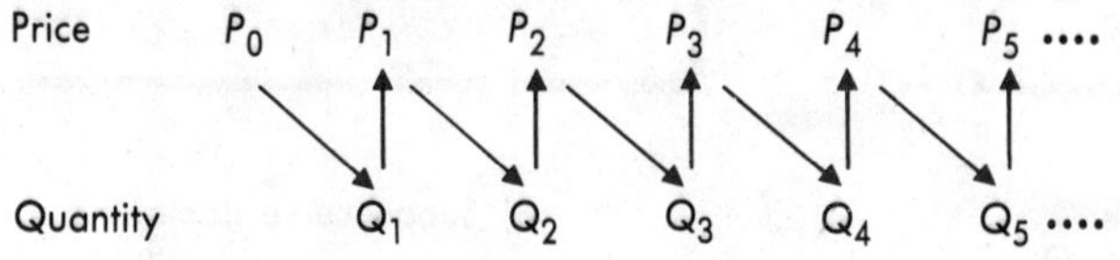

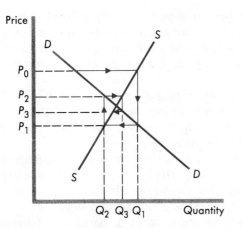

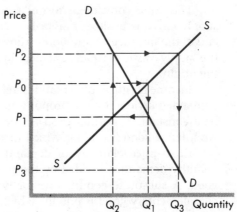

(a) Supply curve steeper than the demand curve: prices converge to an equilibrium.

(b) Demand curve steeper than the supply curve: prices are explosive.

FIGURE 3.18

than the demand curve. If both the demand and supply curves have the same slope, one can easily check that prices continually oscillate between two limits. Prices neither converge to an equilibrium, nor diverge from the equilibrium.

3.12 SUMMARY AND CONCLUSIONS

Elasticity measures the responsiveness of quantity to changes in some other variable. Price elasticity of demand is defined as the ratio of percentage change in quantity demanded to percentage change in price. It is given by

$$\eta = \left| \frac{\Delta Q/Q}{\Delta P/P} \right| = \left| \frac{\Delta Q}{\Delta P} \cdot \frac{P}{Q} \right| = \left| \frac{1}{slope} \cdot \frac{P}{Q} \right|$$

Point elasticity measures the elasticity at a given point on the demand curve, or equivalently, at a given price. Arc elasticity is an approximate average of the elasticities at two points on the demand curve.

For a linear demand curve the slope is constant, and since P/Q falls as we move down the demand curve, price elasticity declines as we move down the demand curve. A convenient formula to use to compute elasticity at a point C is

$$\eta = \frac{\text{Distance of the point } C \text{ from the } Q \text{ axis}}{\text{Distance of the point } C \text{ from the } P \text{ axis}}$$

with both distances being measured along the demand curve in the case of a linear demand curve and along a tangent to the demand curve at the point C, if the demand curve is nonlinear.

The same convenient formula applies for supply elasticity as well. Since a supply curve is positively sloped, it can pass through the origin. For this supply curve, the distance of any point from the Q axis or the P axis is the same. Hence, the supply elasticity equals 1 at all points for any linear supply curve passing through the origin.

Income elasticity of demand is defined as the proportionate change in quantity demanded divided by the proportionate change in income, with prices and tastes held constant. A normal good is one for which the income elasticity is positive. An inferior good is one for which income elasticity is negative.

Cross-price elasticity of demand is defined as the proportionate change in quantity demanded divided by the proportionate change in the price of a related good. A substitute good is one for which the cross-price elasticity is positive. A complementary good is one for which the cross-price elasticity is negative.

Total revenue is the product of the price and quantity demanded of the good at that price. Equivalently, it is the product of the quantity offered for sale and the price the offered quantity fetches in the market place. Average revenue is total revenue divided by the quantity sold. Marginal revenue is the change in the total revenue divided by the change in the quantity sold.

Total revenue (TR), marginal revenue (MR), and average revenue (AR) are related as follows:

1. MR is the slope of the TR curve.

2. TR is increasing if $MR > 0$ and decreasing if $MR < 0$. TR is maximum when $MR = 0$.

3. $MR = AR[1 - (1/\eta)]$ where η is the elasticity of the demand curve at that point.

The effects of excise taxes, subsidies, import tariffs, and so forth on price and output depend on the elasticities of the demand and supply curves. Other things remaining the same, the effect on quantity is greater if the elasticities of the demand and supply curves are high. If the supply curve is perfectly elastic but the demand curve is not, the taxes are entirely borne by the buyers. However, if the demand curve is perfectly elastic but the supply curve is not, the taxes are entirely borne by the suppliers. Thus, the distribution of the burden depends on the elasticities of the two curves.

In practice, from given data on quantities and prices we cannot determine whether we have a demand curve or a supply curve. If the demand curve is stable and the supply curve shifts, then the observed data on quantities and prices will give us a demand curve. If the supply curve is stable and the demand curve shifts, the observed data will give us a supply curve. If both the curves shift, then we do not know what we have. This is called the identification problem.

If quantity demanded depends on current price and quantity supplied depends on last year's price, we have the cobweb model. Prices converge to an equilibrium point if the supply curve is steeper than the demand curve. Prices move away from the equilibrium level if the demand curve is steeper than the supply curve.

KEY TERMS

Arc Elasticity
Cobweb Model
Complementary Goods
Cross-Price Elasticity
   of Demand
Identification Problem
Income Elasticity of Demand
Inferior Goods

Intermediate-run
   Elasticity
Long-run Elasticity
Luxury Goods
Necessities
Normal Goods
Point Elasticity

Price Elasticity of
   Supply
Price (Own) Elasticity
   of Demand
Short-run Elasticity
Substitute Goods
Total Revenue

QUESTIONS

1. In Table 3.2, we presented estimates of the income elasticity of demand for certain commodity groups. Which commodities are necessities? Which are luxuries? Which are inferior? Explain your answer.

2. Market analysts often use cross-price elasticities to determine a measure of the "competitiveness" of a particular good in a market. How might cross-price elasticities be used in this manner? What would you expect the cross-price elasticity coefficient to be if the market for a good was highly competitive? Why?

3. Suppose that the demand curve for product X is

$$Q = 100 - 5P$$

where Q is the number of units of X demanded, and P is the per-unit price of X in dollars. Express the total revenue and marginal revenue functions for product X. Graph both the demand and MR curves and determine over what range of output demand is elastic and inelastic. Calculate elasticity at an output of 50 both algebraically and graphically? What is MR at an output of 50?

4. Suppose that you are the president of a firm that produces and sells four products: apples, oranges, grapefruit, and kiwi fruit. Each product has the following price elasticity of demand:

Product	Price Elasticity
Apples	2.50
Oranges	1.00
Grapefruit	1.75
Kiwi fruit	0.65

Because the company is experiencing serious cash flow problems, your immediate objective is to increase total revenue. What is your pricing strategy for each product? Why? Would it help to know cross-price elasticities? Why?

5. The price elasticity of demand for table salt is very small. Why is this the case? Could this explain why table salt is seldom advertised at a "special price" by grocers?

6. Suppose that when the price of pork chops in a certain town was $2.20 per pound, the quantity of chicken sold was 1,200 pounds per week. But when the price of pork chops rose to $2.75 per pound, the quantity of chicken sold increased to 1,800 pounds per week. Nothing changed over this period except the price of the pork chops. Calculate and interpret the cross-price elasticity of demand. How are these two products related?

7. Underdeveloped countries frequently argue that unless they industrialize, they will remain forever poor relative to the rest of the world. Does this argument make sense in light of the small (but positive) income elasticities for the agricultural commodities typically now produced by many of these countries? Explain.

8. During the summer of 1986, the southeastern United States experienced one of the worst droughts of this century. It was argued that farm relief programs were essential because the reduced agricultural output meant that farmers would not have the revenues needed to meet their mortgage payments. Do you agree with this conclusion? Does the price elasticity of demand enter into your answer?

9. Over the past few years, college and university administrators have been increasing tuition rates (sometimes quite substantially), even though there have been significant declines in student enrollment. Is this a rational decision on the administrators' part? What assumptions do they make about the price elasticity of demand for higher education?

10. Using the appropriate diagrams, graphically show that a linear supply curve intercepting the vertical axis at some point above the origin is elastic at every price and that the elasticity of supply declines as price increases.

11. Would you expect the demand for Skippy Peanut Butter to be more or less elastic than the demand for peanut butter in general? Why? What general conclusion can you draw about the elasticity of a specific product or brand name as opposed to a product class?

12. Suppose that products A and B are produced by different firms and are substitutes. Do you think that a change in the price of product A will affect the marginal revenue of the firm producing B? Explain your answer with diagrams.

13. Using the demand curve in Figure 3.2, show that the price elasticity of demand is also equal to FB/OF.

14. When the federal government increased the excise tax on whiskey and other distilled spirits, many retailers complained that the tax would cause a reduction in their sales. On whom do you think that the burden of the tax fell? Were retailers able to pass the tax on to consumers? Why or why not?

15. A diabetic individual must take a prescribed amount of insulin per time period to avoid severe health risks. Draw the individual's demand curve for insulin. What is the price elasticity of demand? Who would bear the burden of a tax on insulin?

16. Explain, intuitively, why the law of demand implies that $MR \leq P$ for all output levels.

17. Consider the following demand curve for product Y:

$$Q = 100 - 10P$$

where Q is the number of units of Y demanded and P is the per unit price of Y in dollars. Demonstrate graphically and mathematically that the demand for Y is more elastic than the demand for X (from problem 3) at any price.

18. Show that commodities which take up a large percentage of a consumer's budget generally have relatively small income elasticities of demand.

19. The price elasticity of demand for a given commodity is alleged to be greater:

a. The more numerous and closer the substitutes

b. In the long run as opposed to the short run

c. At high prices rather than low prices

Give supporting arguments in each case.

20. An airline is considering introducing an advance purchase fare to supplement its existing economy fare. It conducts a study to assess the patronage of such a fare. The following table summarizes the projected weekly sales for various advance purchase sales. The economy class fare is $200.

Advance Purchase Fare ($)	Number of Advance Purchase Tickets	Number of Economy Tickets
50	2,000	200
100	1,200	400
120	900	500
150	600	600
180	200	1,000

a. What is the own-price elasticity of advance purchase tickets when the fare rises from $100 to $180?

b. What is the cross-price elasticity of economy tickets in response to advance purchase fares when the advance fare increases from $50 to $150?

c. Would you expect the cross-price elasticity of advance purchase tickets to economy fares to be lower or higher than your answer to question b?

PART TWO
CONSUMER AND PRODUCER BEHAVIOR

Part Two (chapters 4 through 9) presents a detailed analysis of the underlying forces behind demand and supply: consumer behavior determining demand (Chapters 4 and 5) and producer behavior determining supply (Chapters 6 and 7). Chapter 4 presents an analysis of consumer behavior based on utility and indifference curves. It then discusses applications of the theory to the study of taxes and subsidies and price and nonprice rationing. Chapter 5 explains how demand curves can be derived from indifference curves and how one can analyze the effects of price changes on the quantity demanded. This chapter also applies the concepts to problems of labor supply (leisure-work choice), consumption over time (borrowing and lending), and cost-of-living indexes. Finally, a new approach to consumer theory in terms of characteristics rather than goods is presented. This completes the analysis of demand, and we move next to the analysis of supply.

Chapter 6 discusses the theory of production or how producers combine resources or inputs to produce final commodities. Chapter 7 looks at the same problem from a different angle—costs. Whereas Chapter 6 deals with maximization of output for given total cost, Chapter 7 deals with cost minimization for given total output. Chapter 7 also contains a discussion of short-run and long-run costs. Chapter 8 presents alternative theories of the firm wherein production is carried out under some constraints. It discusses alternatives to the traditional profit maximization hypothesis. It also presents the linear programming model, which is essentially a problem of output maximization or cost minimization subject to constraints which are linear.

Chapter 9 integrates the theory of demand and supply (or consumption and production) and discusses efficiency in consumption and production as well as consumers' and producers' surpluses. Several applications of these concepts are also discussed.

THEORY OF CONSUMER BEHAVIOR

4.1   INTRODUCTION

In Chapter 2 we examined an individual's demand curve. We plotted various prices and the corresponding quantities demanded. In this chapter, we will look behind the demand curve and examine how the consumer decides what quantities of various commodities to consume.

We will argue that consumers choose the commodity bundle which provides them with the greatest satisfaction. In economics we call this satisfaction utility. Of course, consumers are not free to select any commodity bundle. They must choose from among the bundles which they can afford, and whether they can afford a particular bundle depends on their income as well as the prices of the various commodities.

We begin the chapter by introducing the concept of utility and the notion that consumers attempt to maximize their utility. Many a student has argued that utility functions do not exist and, hence, the consumer cannot possibly seek to maximize utility. The question of the existence of utility functions or the realism of the conscious weighing of utility by the consumer is somewhat immaterial. These theoretical tools provide a useful model which can be employed to explain and accurately predict consumer behavior in a variety of settings. In other words, we can argue that consumers behave as though they were seeking to maximize utility.

After introducing the concept of utility, we will develop a graphical representation—the consumer's indifference curve map. The next step is to graphically depict the consumer's budget limitations. Finally, we combine the indifference curves and the budget line to determine the commodity bundle which is optimal. We then demonstrate how a demand curve can be derived from an indifference curve map and the budget line.

Finally, we demonstrate the applicability of our new tools. We use indifference curve analysis to compare the impact of an income tax versus a selective excise tax on consumer well-being. We extend this example to examine the relative benefit of a cash subsidy as opposed to an in-kind subsidy. We study the issue of whether, and when, quantity allotments are preferable to price rationing. All these issues and many others can be analyzed using our basic theory of consumer behavior.

4.2   THE CONCEPT OF UTILITY AND ITS RELATION
TO THE VALUE OF GOODS AND SERVICES

The satisfaction a consumer derives from the consumption of commodities is termed *utility* by economists. Suppose a consumer eats five oranges. The total satisfaction he gets from this is called *total utility*. Suppose he now consumes an extra orange. The *extra* satisfaction he gets from consuming this orange is called the *marginal utility* of the sixth orange. We assume that the consumer compares the utility of different commodity bundles and chooses the one with the highest utility from among all the bundles he can afford.

The term "utility" is associated with the British philosopher Jeremy Bentham (1748–1832). However, neither he nor the economists of the time understood the relationship between the value of goods and the utility derived from their consumption. Adam Smith (1723–1790) distinguished between *value in use* and *value in exchange* and gave the famous example of diamonds and water.[1] Diamonds have a high price (value in exchange), but they are unnecessary for life (a low value in use). Water has a low price (value in exchange) but is necessary for life (a high value in use).

David Ricardo (1772–1823) and later Karl Marx (1818–1883), the founder of communism, thought of value as congealed labor. According to Marx, if it took 2 units of labor to produce a commodity X and only 1 unit of labor to produce a commodity Y, then the value of X is twice the value of Y. Many economists did not like this explanation at all.

It was the English economist William Stanley Jevons (1835–1882) who pointed out the relationship between utility and price (or value in exchange). In a paper read to the British Association for the Advancement of Science in 1862, he introduced the concept of marginal utility. He argued that it is marginal utility, not total utility, that is related to price.[2] His book, *Theory of Political Economy* (1871), contains a systematic development of the marginal utility concept. Going back to the example of diamonds and water, the result he derived can be written as

$$\frac{\text{Marginal utility of diamonds}}{\text{Price of diamonds}} = \frac{\text{marginal utility of water}}{\text{price of water}}$$

This is the connection between utility and value. The relationship makes intuitive sense; consumers who purchase both commodities will distribute their expenditures so that the last dollar spent on each commodity yields the same extra utility. Otherwise, consumers could increase total utility, without additional expenditure, by consuming more of the good with the higher marginal-utility-to-price ratio and less of the other product. We will return to this point later in this chapter.

There are two questions we need to ask at this stage:

1. How do you measure utility?
2. What is the relationship between prices of goods and their utility?

4.3 CARDINAL AND ORDINAL UTILITY

Is utility measurable? The cardinal utility theory says that it is measurable just as prices and quantities are. That is, we can assign a number of *utils* to each commodity. For example,

An orange = 5 utils
An apple = 6 utils

---

[1]This is commonly known as the "Diamond-Water Paradox," as described in his book, *Wealth of Nations.*

[2]The Austrian economist Karl Menger (1840–1921) and the French economist Leon Walras (1834–1910) are said to have discovered the same independently. Menger is widely known as the founder of the "Austrian School of Economists." Joseph Schumpeter (1883–1950), who wrote the monumental book *History of Economic Analysis,* called Walras the greatest of all economists.

The ordinal utility theory says that utility is not measurable like prices and quantities. But one can *order* the utilities from different goods. That is, we can say whether the utility of an orange is less than, equal to, or greater than the utility of an apple.

In the cardinal utility theory, total utility and marginal utility are both measurable. As we defined earlier, total utility for n units of commodity is the total satisfaction derived from the consumption of n units, and marginal utility of the nth unit is the *additional* utility obtained from consuming the nth unit. Table 4.1 gives a hypothetical example.

One thing we notice in Table 4.1 is that marginal utility decreases as more and more units are consumed. This is the law of *diminishing marginal utility*. The assertion that products are characterized by diminishing marginal utility as consumption rises is an empirical one. This assertion is widely believed despite the absence of a generally accepted measuring device for utilities. It corresponds to our commonsense notion that the first orange or apple gives more satisfaction than the second, that the first million a person makes gives more thrill than say the tenth million, and so on.

Total utility will be increasing as long as marginal utility is greater than 0. At the point of maximum utility, marginal utility is 0.[3] If the consumer whose total utility is as shown in Table 4.1 maximizes her utility, she will be consuming eight oranges. We will see later that she will consume fewer if she has to pay a price.

Note that, although we illustrated the law of diminishing marginal utility with an example that assumes cardinal utility (utility measured in absolute magnitudes), the law does not depend on cardinal utility. Even if utility were to be measurable on an ordinal scale, we could still make statements like "marginal utility of the

[3]In mathematical terms if $U(x)$ is total utility, dU/dx is marginal utility. $U(x)$ is maximum where $dU/dx = 0$ and $U(x)$ is an increasing function of x if $dU/dx > 0$.

TABLE 4.1 Total and Marginal Utility

Number of Oranges	Total Utility	Marginal Utility
0	0	
1	20	20
2	35	15
3	45	10
4	50	5
5	53	3
6	55	2
7	56	1
8	56	0
9	55	−1
10	53	−2

first orange is greater than the marginal utility of the second orange, which is greater than the marginal utility of the third orange," and so on.

Economists who believed in cardinal utility can be divided into two groups. Those who believed in (1) cardinal and additive utility and (2) cardinal but not additive utility.

Nineteenth-century economists such as Jevons, Walras, and Marshall (1842–1924) belonged to the first group. They considered utility to be not only *measurable* but also *additive,* that is, if an orange gives 5 utils of utility and an apple gives 6 utils of utility then the utility of both an orange and an apple is 5 + 6 = 11 utils.

Economists such as Edgeworth (1845–1926) and Irving Fisher (1867–1947) belonged to the second group. They argued that utility is measurable but not additive, that it depends simultaneously on all the amounts of the different goods consumed. In the above example, the utility of both an apple and an orange could be less than 11 utils. This approach assumes some amount of interdependence in the satisfaction derived from each good. The marginal utility a consumer derives from another ounce of butter normally depends on the consumer's current rate of consumption of other commodities such as margarine or bread. With additive utility, the marginal utility of any commodity is independent of the amounts consumed of other commodities. Clearly, the assumption that utility is additive is not a reasonable assumption to make given the interdependencies that exist in the consumption of several goods.

In mathematical terms, we say that utility is a function of the quantity consumed of all the commodities. If there are two commodities, we write this function as

$$U = U(x_1, x_2)$$

where U = utility, and x_1 and x_2 are the quantities consumed of the two goods. With additive utility, we can write

$$U(x_1, x_2) = U_1(x_1) + U_2(x_2)$$

where $U_1(x_1)$ is the utility derived from the consumption of the first good alone, and $U_2(x_2)$ is the utility derived from the consumption of the second good alone.

If the commodities are substitutes in consumption $U(x_1, x_2)$ will be less than $U_1(x_1)$ plus $U_2(x_2)$. Examples are butter and margarine, apples and oranges. If the commodities are complements, so that when used together, the consumer derives more satisfaction than when used separately, then $U(x_1, x_2)$ will be greater than $U_1(x_1)$ plus $U_2(x_2)$. An example is catsup and french fries.

Until now we have discussed cardinal utility. Next, we will consider ordinal utility. As we said earlier, the law of diminishing marginal utility is valid whether utility is measured on a cardinal scale or on an ordinal scale.

The Italian economist, Wilfredo Pareto (1848–1923), laid the foundations for the modern theory of consumer behavior by removing the measurability associated with the cardinal theory of utility. It is assumed that the consumer need not be able to assign numbers that represent utility, but can rank commodities in order of preference. For example, the consumer may prefer an apple to an orange but cannot say that the apple gives 6 units of utility and the orange 5 units of utility. Similarly, with reference to Table 4.1, the consumer can say that the marginal utility of the first orange is greater than the marginal utility of the second but cannot give 20 units to the marginal utility of the first orange and 15 units to the marginal utility of the second orange.

The modern theory of consumer behavior, based on ordinal utility, uses the technique of *indifference* curves. Indifference curves are curves that show combinations of goods that give the same total utility to the consumer. We will now examine these curves.[4]

4.4   INDIFFERENCE CURVES

As defined earlier, an *indifference curve* shows combinations of two commodities that a consumer is indifferent about. It gives the combinations from which the consumer derives the same total utility or level of satisfaction. Thus, it can also be called an *isoutility curve* ("iso" means same).

Figure 4.1 shows an indifference curve. It shows the combinations of oranges and apples from which the consumer derives the same level of satisfaction (i.e., is indifferent about). For example, point E represents a bundle containing 5 apples and 5 oranges. Point F depicts a combination of 3 apples and 8 oranges. Because these two points lie on the same indifference curve, we know that this consumer derives the same satisfaction from either combination of the two goods.

We will consider only two commodities. With more than two commodities we have to talk of *indifference surfaces*. It is hard to show indifference surfaces on paper (which is two-dimensional). Furthermore, almost all the principles of consumer behavior can be discussed in terms of two commodities and illustrated in two-dimensional diagrams.

[4]As a historical note, although it was Pareto who argued in favor of ordinal utility, indifference curves were derived by Edgeworth, who believed in cardinal utility theory. Irving Fisher, too, used indifference curve analysis, although he, too, believed in cardinal utility.

FIGURE 4.1   An indifference curve for two goods.

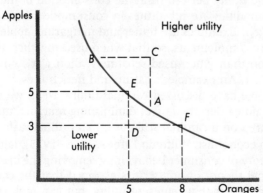

First, why have we drawn the indifference curve as downward sloping? (We will discuss the curvature toward the origin in the next section.) If both apples and oranges give positive satisfaction to the consumer, then increasing the number of apples while holding the number of oranges constant would increase the consumer's total utility. So, if we want to hold utility constant, as the number of apples increases, some oranges will have to be taken away. Thus, as we move along an indifference curve, the quantity of one commodity rises and the other falls. This, of course, implies a negatively sloped indifference curve.

One more thing to note is that every point, and, hence, every commodity bundle, lies on some indifference curve. In Figure 4.1 all points above the indifference curve correspond to combinations where the consumer has more apples and no fewer oranges, or more oranges and no fewer apples, than the points on the indifference curve. So, these points represent higher levels of satisfaction. Thus, they lie on higher indifference curves.

For instance, consider any point C above the indifference curve. Let the vertical line from C intersect the indifference curve at the point A, and let the horizontal line from C intersect the indifference curve at B. Compared with A, at the point C the consumer has the same number of oranges but more apples and, hence, is better off at C than at A. Similarly compared with B, the consumer has the same number of apples but more oranges and, hence, is better off at C than at B. Thus, C is a point on a higher indifference curve.

By similar reasoning, we can show that a point D below the indifference curve has to be a point on a lower indifference curve. Compared with the point E, the consumer has the same number of oranges and fewer apples at D. Or compared with F, the consumer has the same number of apples but fewer oranges. Thus, D has to lie on a lower indifference curve than E and F.

Of course, with some commodities, the individual gets less total utility by having more of the commodity (see the example in Table 4.1). Thus, the "good" becomes a "bad." In this case, the consumer would be better off having less of the commodity than more. Such a commodity might be garbage or pollution.

Indifference curves for goods versus bads are shown in Figure 4.2. The curves

FIGURE 4.2   Indifference curves for goods versus bads.

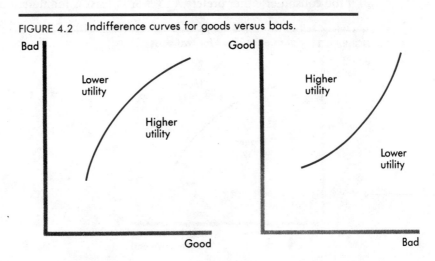

are upward sloping as they should be. If the consumer is given more of a bad then the consumer needs more of the good to keep the consumer on the same indifference curve. As for the curvature of the curves, we will again discuss this problem in the next section, where we discuss the concept of marginal rate of substitution.

We can also consider indifference curves between two bads. For instance, if we assume that unemployment is bad, and inflation is bad, then the indifference curves of consumers will be as shown in Figure 4.3. The indifference curve is downward sloping like the indifference curve for two goods shown in Figure 4.1. It has the opposite curvature, but this will again be discussed in the next section.

In the cases of the indifference curves presented in Figures 4.2 and 4.3, the points of higher and lower utility shown in the figures can be verified as we have done earlier with the points in Figure 4.1.

Finally, two fundamental assumptions are usually made that translate into some properties of indifference curves: (1) *completeness* of the ordering of preferences and (2) *transitivity* (or consistency) in the ordering of preferences. Completeness implies, in our example, that given any two combinations A and B of oranges and apples, the consumer is able to rank them. For instance, let

A = 2 oranges and 3 apples
B = 4 oranges and 2 apples

Then the consumer is able to say whether A is preferable to B, B is preferable to A, or the consumer is indifferent between A and B. This assumption means that there is an indifference curve passing through every point in the positive quadrant of Figure 4.1.

To illustrate transitivity, suppose there are three combinations A, B, C of goods:

A = 4 apples and 3 oranges
B = 5 apples and 1 orange
C = 2 apples and 5 oranges

We will illustrate a little bit of our own notation. If A is preferred to B, we will write A ⊘ B. If the consumer is indifferent between A and B, we will write A ⊖ B. If the consumer either prefers A to B or at least is indifferent between A and B

FIGURE 4.3   Indifference curve for two bads.

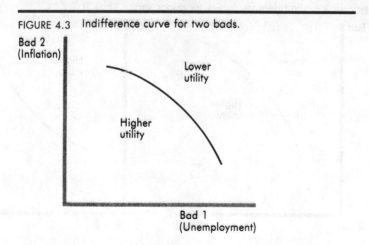

Bad 2
(Inflation)

Lower
utility

Higher
utility

Bad 1
(Unemployment)

(i.e., does not prefer B to A) we will write $A \circleddash B$. We have put circles over the inequality and equality signs because these are preference statements, not simple inequalities and equalities as in algebra. The assumption of transitivity says that if $A \circleddash B$ and $B \circleddash C$ then $A \circleddash C$, and also if $A \circleddash B$ and $B \circleddash C$ then $A \circleddash C$.

The implication of this assumption is that two *indifference curves cannot intersect.* Figure 4.4 shows how we would arrive at inconsistent conclusions if indifference curves did intersect. From the diagram we see that $A \circleddash C$ and $C \circleddash D$, so, by transitivity, $A \circleddash D$. But this cannot be so because A lies on a higher indifference curve indicating $A \circleddash D$. Thus, the preferences are intransitive or inconsistent.

It is not impossible for us to observe such inconsistencies in actual practice. However, such instances are very rare, and we cannot build a theory on such inconsistent behavior. Hence, in our analysis we will assume that indifference curves do not intersect.

4.5 MARGINAL RATE OF SUBSTITUTION AND CONVEXITY OF INDIFFERENCE CURVES

Earlier we talked of marginal utility. Now we need to define another concept, the *marginal rate of substitution,* and examine its relationship to the slope of the indifference curve and to the ratio of marginal utilities.

Consider the hypothetical indifference curve shown in Figure 4.5. It gives the combination of oranges and apples that the individual is indifferent about. The figure corresponds to the following combinations of oranges and apples.

Bundle	Oranges	Apples
A	2	15
B	5	9
C	7	6
D	17	2

FIGURE 4.4 Intersecting indifference curves show preferences are inconsistent.

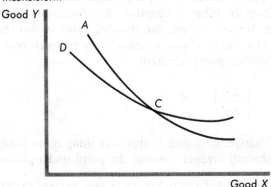

Good Y

Good X

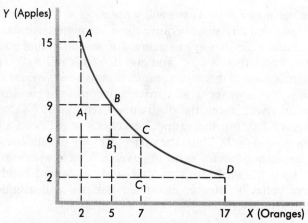

FIGURE 4.5   An indifference curve convex to the origin.

The slope of the indifference curve is negative, since the consumer is willing to give up some oranges to get more apples (and vice-versa) and still have the same total utility or satisfaction.

Let us now consider the movement of the consumer from A to B. Suppose we ask how many apples the consumer is willing to give up to get 3 more oranges. The answer is clearly 6. The ratio of 6 to 3 is called the marginal rate of substitution (MRS) of oranges for apples. (The consumer is substituting oranges for apples.) Of course, if we consider the reverse movement from B to A, the consumer is substituting apples for oranges. So, instead of calling this a substitution of oranges for apples, or apples for oranges, we should just call it marginal rate of substitution in consumption.[5] If we are considering two goods X and Y, we define the marginal rate of substitution of X for Y as the quantity of Y that the consumer is willing to give up to gain a marginal unit of X. (This is also the quantity of Y that the consumer has to be given to compensate for a unit loss of X.) Thus, holding utility constant,

$$MRS_{X \text{ for } Y} = \left| \frac{\text{Change in } Y}{\text{Change in } X} \right|$$

The fact that the indifference curve has a negative slope means that if one of these changes is positive the other is negative. It is customary to define the MRS as a positive number. Hence, we take the absolute value of this ratio. Thus, if ΔY and ΔX denote the changes in Y and X respectively between two points on an indifference curve, holding utility constant,

$$MRS_{X \text{ for } Y} = \left| \frac{\Delta Y}{\Delta X} \right|$$

For very small changes in X and Y, this is nothing more than the absolute value of the slope of the indifference curve at the point under consideration.

[5]This is the definition used by J. R. Hicks in his famous book, *Value and Capital*, Clarendon Press, Oxford, 1939.

In Figure 4.5, denoting oranges by X and apples by Y, we have the following marginal rates of substitution.

$$MRS_{X \text{ for } Y}$$

Between A and B: $\dfrac{AA_1}{A_1B} = \dfrac{6}{3} = 2.0$

Between B and C: $\dfrac{BB_1}{B_1C} = \dfrac{3}{2} = 1.5$

Between C and D: $\dfrac{CC_1}{C_1D} = \dfrac{4}{10} = 0.4$

Thus, $MRS_{X \text{ for } Y}$ diminishes with increasing X. This is the principle of *diminishing marginal rate of substitution*. It makes intuitive sense, since the consumer is willing to give up more apples for another orange when the consumer has more apples (and fewer oranges) as at A, than when the consumer has fewer apples (and more oranges) as at C. Clearly, this intuitive principle explains the fact that the indifference curve is convex to the origin, or bowed in toward the origin.[6] Look at Figure 4.6. The absolute value of the slope of A_2B_2 is lower than the absolute value of the slope A_1B_1. Thus, the absolute value of the slope of the indifference curve diminishes as we increase the consumption of X. This is all that is required for convexity.

If the consumer were instead willing to give up the same number of apples for another orange, no matter how many apples the consumer had, that is, if the MRS were constant, then the indifference curve would be a straight line as shown in Figure 4.7.

[6]Some economists do not like this explanation. We will see in the next section after discussing the budget constraint that there is an alternative explanation that does not rely on this "intuitive" explanation.

FIGURE 4.6 Convexity of the indifference curve implies diminishing marginal rate of substitution.

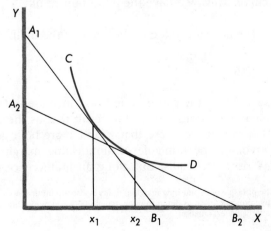

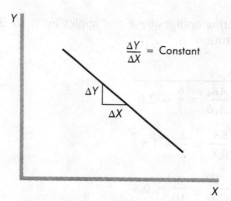

FIGURE 4.7   An indifference curve with a constant marginal rate of substitution.

Relationship to marginal utilities

One important relationship to note is that the absolute value of the slope of the indifference curve is also equal to the ratio of the marginal utility of X to the marginal utility of Y. Consider a small decrease in Y and a corresponding small increase in X that will leave the consumer on the same indifference curve. The decrease in utility due to a decrease in the consumption of Y is $\Delta Y \cdot MU_y$. The increase in utility due to an increase in the consumption of X is $\Delta X \cdot MU_x$. Since the consumer is on the same indifference curve, the net change in utility must be 0. Hence, we have:

$$| \Delta Y \cdot MU_y | = | \Delta X \cdot MU_x |$$

or

$$\left| \frac{\Delta Y}{\Delta X} \right| = \frac{MU_x}{MU_y}$$

But for small values of ΔY and ΔX, $| \Delta Y/\Delta X |$ is the absolute value of the slope of the indifference curve. Thus, we have the important result:

$$MRS_{X \text{ for } Y} = \text{The absolute value of the slope of the indifference curve}$$
$$= \frac{MU_X}{MU_Y}$$

Earlier, we said that as the consumption of X increases, $MRS_{X \text{ for } Y}$ decreases. This is only an alternative statement of the result that as the consumption of X increases, MU_X/MU_Y falls. In the case that X and Y are both goods, it is easy to explain this by invoking the principle of diminishing marginal utility.[7] As the consumption of X rises, MU_X falls. But along an indifference curve, if the con-

_____

[7] As we argued earlier, the principle of diminishing marginal utility is also an intuitive principle. Some economists do not like to invoke intuitive principles such as diminishing marginal utility and diminishing MRS. See footnote 6 and the next section for an alternative explanation.

sumption of X rises, the consumption of Y falls, and, hence, MU_Y goes up. Thus, the ratio MU_X/MU_Y goes down (the numerator goes down, the denominator goes up). As the consumption of X increases, eventually we might come to a point where $MU_X = 0$ but $MU_Y > 0$. At this point the slope of the indifference curve would be 0 and the indifference curve would be parallel to the X axis. Similarly, as the consumption of X falls and that of Y rises, we might come to a point where $MU_Y = 0$ (but $MU_X \neq 0$). At this point, the slope of the indifference curve would be infinity and the indifference curve would be parallel to the Y axis.

Curvature of other types of indifference curves

We have until now discussed the convexity of the indifference curves for two goods. The shape of the indifference curves between a good and a bad or between a bad and a bad that we have shown in Figures 4.2 and 4.3 can also be inferred from the rule that the absolute slope of the indifference curve = MU_X/MU_Y. Again, if we invoke the intuitive principle of diminishing marginal utility for a "good" and increasing marginal "disutility" for a bad (or diminishing marginal utility for a bad) then the slopes implied by the curvatures in Figures 4.2 and 4.3 result.

4.6 THE BUDGET CONSTRAINT AND THE EQUILIBRIUM OF THE CONSUMER

We have discussed the concepts of indifference curves and the diminishing marginal rate of substitution. Now we will discuss the consumer's choice of a bundle of commodities. For this we must describe the *budget line*. The budget line consists of all the possible combinations of the two commodities that the consumer can purchase with a given total expenditure (budget).

Suppose the price of oranges is 20 cents per orange and the price of apples is 25 cents per apple and our consumer can spend $10. Then her budget is said to be $10. She can buy 50 oranges or 40 apples or some combinations of apples and oranges like 25 oranges and 20 apples. The line joining these points is the budget line shown in Figure 4.8. The consumer can buy less and save money (be *within* her budget). But she cannot buy more. Thus, all the feasible purchases are *on* the budget line or lie *under* it, in the triangular area below it. The budget line is negatively sloped, and its absolute slope = 40/50 = price of oranges/price of apples.

More generally, if x and y are the quantities of good X and Y and if the prices are P_X and P_Y respectively, then the equation of the budget line is

$$(x \cdot P_X) + (y \cdot P_Y) = M$$

where M is the total money the consumer has to spend. Note that $x \cdot P_X$ is the amount of money spent on good X, while $y \cdot P_Y$ is the amount of money spent on good Y. They must sum to total expenditure.

Now, if the consumer buys only good X, she can just afford M/P_X with her budget so that M/P_X is our horizontal intercept. Similarly, the vertical intercept is M/P_Y. In going from the vertical intercept to the horizontal intercept, $\Delta Y/\Delta X = (-M/P_Y) \div (M/P_X) = -P_X/P_Y$, which is the slope of the budget line.

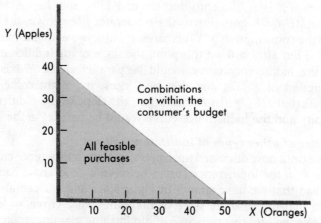

FIGURE 4.8   A budget line (slope of the budget line = $-P_X/P_Y$).

Shifts in the budget line

There are only two things which will cause a budget line to shift:

1. Changes in the budget
2. Changes in the prices of the commodities

With a change in the budget but no change in prices, we will have parallel shifts in the budget line as shown in Figure 4.9. With an increase in the budget, for example, both intercepts increase, but the price ratio (the absolute value of the slope) is unaffected. The budget line will also shift in a parallel manner if both prices are changed proportionately, because the price ratio and, hence, the slope will be unaffected.

If the price of one commodity increases, then that intercept (M/P) decreases. The opposite is true for a price reduction. Figure 4.10(b) shows the effect of an

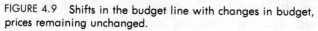

FIGURE 4.9   Shifts in the budget line with changes in budget, prices remaining unchanged.

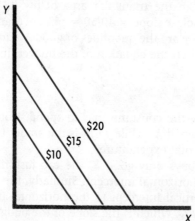

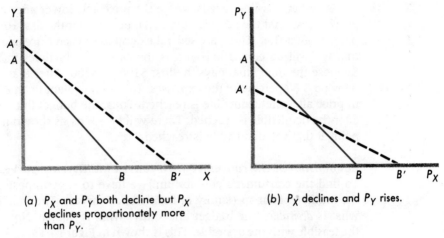

(a) P_X and P_Y both decline but P_X declines proportionately more than P_Y.

(b) P_X declines and P_Y rises.

FIGURE 4.10 Shifts in the budget line with different changes in the prices.

increase in one price with a decrease in the other. Of course, the slope declines in absolute terms. (Why?) If both prices change in the same direction but by different amounts, then again both the intercepts and the slope are altered. This is demonstrated in Figure 4.10(a).

Different shapes of the budget line

Until now we have assumed that the prices P_X and P_Y remain the same regardless of how much is purchased. This need not always be the case. If there are quantity discounts, then the per-unit price goes down as the quantity bought increases. In this case, returning to our example of oranges and apples, the consumer would be able to buy, say, 50 apples or 60 oranges, but if she tried to split her expenditures between apples and oranges, she could not get 25 apples and 30 oranges—she might get just 15 apples and 25 oranges. The budget line in this case will be convex to the origin as shown in Figure 4.11.

FIGURE 4.11 A budget line with discounts based on quantity purchased.

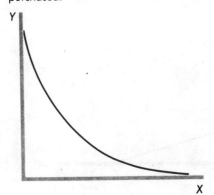

Another possible case is where the price gets lower after an initial volume of purchase, so that the price is, say, $1.00 per unit for the first 100 units but 80 cents per unit after that. There are several examples of such price changes. One example that we will be concerned with is the case of deductibles in medical insurance. Suppose the individual pays the first $100 or $200. After that the insurance company pays 80 percent of the expenses. This is equivalent to an 80 percent reduction in price after the deductible is reached. Thus, the budget line will change its slope after the deductible is reached. There will be a kink as shown in Figure 4.12 at the point B that the deductible is reached.

Equilibrium of the consumer with convex indifference curves

To find the consumer's equilibrium, we have to superimpose the budget line on the indifference map (family of indifference curves). The indifference map shows what is *desirable*. The budget line shows what is *feasible*. Now we have to match the feasible with the desirable. This is shown in Figure 4.13. I_1, I_2, I_3 are indifference curves; I_2 gives a higher utility than I_1; I_3 gives a higher utility than I_2; and so on. AB is the budget line: The consumer's feasible combinations of the goods X and Y are given by the points on the budget line AB or in the triangular area under AB. The consumer would like to get to the highest possible indifference curve representing the highest level of utility. This is shown as I_2 in Figure 4.13. The point of tangency C gives the optimal bundle of X and Y. Points on the curve I_3 are not within the reach of the consumer. As for I_1, the consumer can do better, since all points in the shaded area are still within the consumer's budget and yet yield more satisfaction.

Note that at the point D the slope of the indifference curve is higher than the slope of the budget line (both in absolute values). Thus, $MRS_{X \text{ for } Y} > P_X/P_Y$. Substituting MU_X/MU_Y for the MRS and rearranging, gives us $MU_X/P_X > MU_Y/P_Y$ at point D. Spending one less dollar on Y will reduce total utility by MU_Y/P_Y. But spending that same dollar on X will now increase utility by MU_X/P_X. The consumer

FIGURE 4.12   A kinky budget line with deductibles in medical insurance.

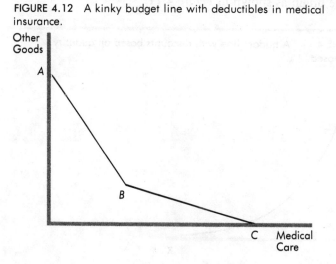

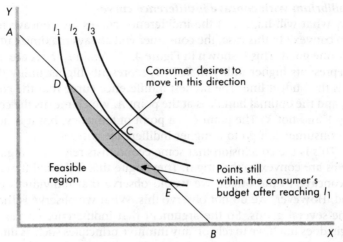

FIGURE 4.13 Equilibrium of the consumer with convex indifference curves.

can increase her total utility, without spending more, simply by purchasing additional units of X and fewer Y, thus, moving toward C. The opposite is true at a point such as E. And at the optimum, MU_X/P_X must be equal to MU_Y/P_Y, which is merely a restatement of the tangency condition. This is also the connection between utility and value presented by William Jevons and discussed in Section 4.2.

Now it is possible that a consumer with convex indifference curves would maximize utility by consuming only one product. This situation is shown in Figure 4.14. Note that there is no tangency between the budget line and an indifference curve. The first unit of product X is simply not worth its cost to the consumer. That is, MU_X/P_X for the first unit of X is less than MU_Y/P_Y for the last unit of Y which the consumer can afford. We will argue shortly that this is not a typical case.

FIGURE 4.14 Specialization in consumption with convex indifference curves.

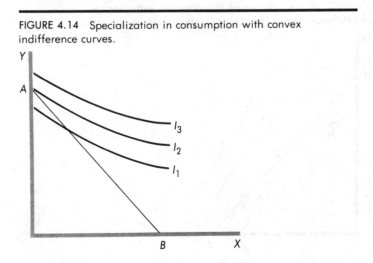

Equilibrium with concave indifference curves

Now what will happen if the indifference curves are concave to the origin rather than convex? In this case, the consumer will always maximize utility by consuming only one good. This is shown in Figure 4.15. Again I_1, I_2, I_3 are indifference curves; I_2 represents higher utility than I_1; I_3 represents higher utility than I_2; and so on. AB is the budget line. The highest indifference curve that the consumer can attain is I_2 and the optimal bundle is at the point A, which means the consumer consumes only Y and not X. The point C is a point of tangency, but it is not optimal because the consumer can go to a higher indifference curve I_2.

This is the conclusion that some economists rely on to argue that indifference curves are convex to the origin. They argue that if the indifference curves were to be concave to the origin, we would observe that individuals consume only one good. However, we do not observe this. What we observe is that individuals consume several goods. So the argument that indifference curves are convex to the origin does not have to rely on any intuitive principles such as diminishing marginal utility or diminishing marginal rate of substitution.[8] All that is needed is the empirical observation that consumers choose to consume several goods.

Equilibrium with convex and concave segments

If the indifference curves were to have both convex and concave segments, sometimes the consumer would choose points on the convex segment. This is shown in Figure 4.16, where the optimum point C lies on the convex portion of the indifference curve. However, in Figure 4.17 the optimum lies on the concave segment. C is a point of tangency on the convex segment, but this is on a lower indifference curve I_1. The consumer can do better by moving to I_2. Thus, B is the optimal point.

---

[8]As one illustration of this assumption see Gary S. Becker, *Economic Theory*, Alfred A. Knopf, New York, 1977, p. 28. Becker goes on to argue (using a specific case) that the indifference curve can have both convex and concave segments, but in this case points on the concave segment would never be optimal. They would never be chosen. That this is not always true is illustrated in Figure 4.17.

FIGURE 4.15 Equilibrium of the consumer with concave indifference curves: The consumer specializes in one good.

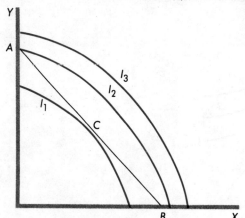

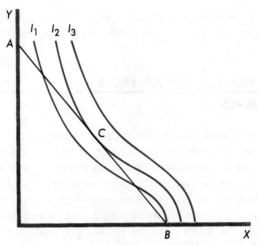

FIGURE 4.16 Indifference curves with convex and concave segments. The consumer's optimum is on the convex segment (at C).

Synopsis

In summary, when working with two goods (not bads) and linear budget lines, we have the following results.

1. If both commodities are consumed, then either the entire indifference curves are convex to the origin or the indifference curves contain some convex portions.

2. Consumption of only one good can occur with either concave or convex indifference curves. Specialization can also occur where indifference curves have both concave and convex segments.

3. Because we do not generally observe specialization in consumption, we assume that indifference curves are convex to the origin. (This is equivalent to

FIGURE 4.17 Indifference curves with convex and concave segments. The consumer's optimum is on the concave segment (at *B*).

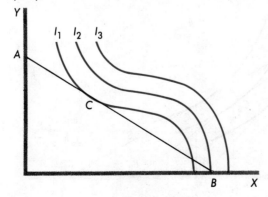

ignoring any concave portions which might exist.) We also assume that a tangency point between the budget line and an indifference curve exists.

4.7 DERIVATION OF DEMAND CURVES FROM INDIFFERENCE CURVES

In the previous two sections we discussed the convexity of indifference curves, the budget line, and the equilibrium of the consumer. We will now show how the law of demand (that quantity demanded of a good ceteris paribus increases when the price declines and decreases when the price increases) can be derived from the theory of indifference curves presented so far.

We will assume that there are two goods X and Y, and that it is only the price P_X of X that changes, the money income (or budget) and the price of Y remaining unchanged. The effect on the quantity demanded of X as P_X changes is shown in Figure 4.18.

Suppose initially the budget line is AB_0. The consumer's equilibrium is at C_0 with the quantity of X demanded being x_0. If the price of X rises, the budget line becomes AB_1, the consumer's equilibrium is at C_1, and the quantity of X demanded falls to x_1. If the price of X falls, the budget line becomes AB_2, the consumer's equilibrium is at C_2, and the quantity of X demanded rises to x_2. So a reduction in the price of X leads to an increase in quantity demanded and vice-versa.

Thus, we have verified the law of demand. However, there can be some exceptions. Suppose the indifference curves have the curious shape as shown in Figure 4.19. Then as the price of X falls, the quantity of X demanded also *falls*. Again, the initial budget line is AB_0, with the consumer's equilibrium at C_0, and quantity of X demanded is x_0. The price of X falls, the budget line shifts to AB_1, the consumer's equilibrium is at C_1, and we see that paradoxically, the quantity of

FIGURE 4.18   Changes in the quantity demanded of X as the price of X changes.

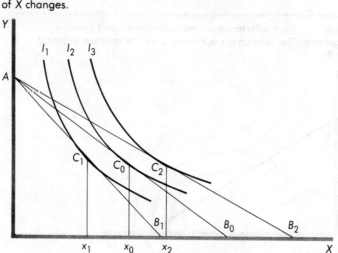

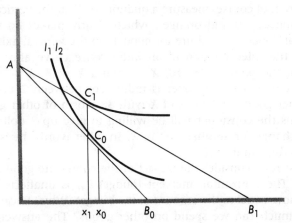

FIGURE 4.19 Giffen's paradox: Quantity of X demanded falls as the price of X falls.

X demanded has fallen to x_1. (Note that the consumer is on a higher indifference curve.) This paradox was supposed to have been pointed out by an economist named Giffen and is called the *Giffen paradox*. As mentioned earlier, a good for which the quantity demanded falls as price falls, is called a Giffen good. Such goods are, however, very rare (for further discussion see the next chapter, Section 5.5).

The derivation of a demand curve from an indifference curve map is very straightforward. In Figure 4.18, only the price of X changes. So all we need to do is plot the various prices of X against the various quantities demanded. For example, the price of X associated with budget line AB_0, and the quantity x_0 is one point on the demand curve. (The price of X associated with AB_0 is equal to income/B_0 or the absolute value of the slope of AB_0 times P_Y.) The lower price associated with budget line AB_2 and the quantity x_2 define another point on the demand curve and so on.

We have now discussed

1. The different types of indifference curves
2. The different types of budget lines
3. The consumer's equilibrium as the point of tangency of the budget line with the indifference curves
4. The derivation of demand curves from indifference curves

We will discuss further properties of the demand curves (as derived from the properties of indifference curves) in the next chapter.

4.8   THE COMPOSITE GOOD CONVENTION

Students frequently argue that the application of indifference curve analysis is extremely limited because we do not live in a two-commodity world. We can frequently, as we will see, extend the application by defining good Y to be all other goods except X.

We cannot, of course, measure a quantity of Y on the vertical axis. This would involve adding apples and oranges, which clearly makes no sense. Instead, we measure total dollar expenditure for good Y on the vertical axis.

How is the interpretation of an indifference curve affected? Only slightly. Suppose that the points $Y = 10$, $X = 2$ and $Y = 8$, $X = 3$ lie on the same indifference curve. The consumer is indifferent between 2 units of X with \$10 worth of other goods or 3 units of X with \$8 worth of other goods. The $MRS = 2$. This means the consumer will be willing to give up 2 dollars worth of other goods in exchange for another unit of X. In other words, he is willing to pay up to \$2 for his third unit of X.

We must now consider the impact of the composite good convention on the budget line. The horizontal intercept (budget/P_X) is unaffected. But the vertical intercept is now equal to the amount of the budget. Why? Because, if we purchase no X, how much can we spend on other goods? The answer, of course, is the budget. The slope of the budget line was previously demonstrated to be $-P_X/P_Y$. But now we are measuring Y in terms of expenditure on other goods. Clearly, one more dollar of other goods costs \$1 so that P_Y is, by design, equal to 1. This means that the slope of the budget constraint becomes $-P_X$.

4.9   APPLICATIONS: TAXES AND SUBSIDIES

Taxes have come to be accepted as a "necessary evil" under capitalism. Many a politician has promised to reduce taxes. In fact, most of us are convinced that lower taxes would improve our well-being. Although this may be true, it is not simply the overall tax bill that affects consumer welfare. Different types of taxes affect us differently even though they yield the same revenue to the government.

In this section we will use indifference curve analysis to compare two different taxes. We will demonstrate that the typical consumer is better off with an income tax than with a comparable excise tax on a single commodity. We will then generalize our analysis to consider the relative benefits of a cash subsidy versus an in-kind subsidy (or a pay raise versus an increase in fringe benefits). Here our conclusion will depend on whether the in-kind subsidies are taxable.

It should be noted that our analysis focuses on a single consumer (or possibly a small group). Some of our conclusions do not hold for society as a whole. We will discuss this problem as we proceed.

4.9.1   Selective excise tax versus income tax

Consider the case of two goods X and Y (Y stands for all goods other than X). The total income or budget of the consumer is M. By a selective excise tax, we mean an excise tax on X only. A proportional tax on both X and Y is the same as an income tax. In Figure 4.20 we compare the two situations. The budget line with no taxes is AB. With an excise tax on X, *assuming that the sellers can pass on the whole tax to the consumers,* the price of X will rise by the amount of the tax. The budget line is now AB_1. The consumer's equilibrium before the tax is at the point

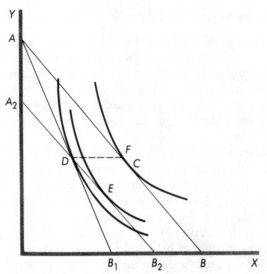

FIGURE 4.20 Selective excise tax versus an income tax: The consumer is better off with an income tax.

C, and after the tax the equilibrium is at the point D. The consumer, thus, moves to a lower indifference curve and is, as is to be expected, worse off.

Now with an income tax, or a proportional tax on both goods, the budget line will shift down and be parallel to AB. This is because both intercepts decline but the price ratio is unchanged. If the income tax gives the same revenue as the excise tax on A, this budget line has to pass through the point D.[9] This is shown as the line A_2B_2. But with this budget line the consumer's equilibrium is at the point E on a higher indifference curve. Thus, the consumer is better off with an income tax than with a selective excise tax.[10] Note that the consumption of X is higher under the income tax than under the selective excise tax on X because the consumer has further opportunity to maximize in the region of the triangle DB_1B_2.

The analysis of an income subsidy versus a selective price subsidy is analogous. The individual consumer will be better off with an income subsidy rather than a selective price subsidy. An example of a price subsidy is where the government pays, say, 80 percent of the cost of medical care. This is like an 80 percent reduction in the price of medical care. Another example was the Food Stamp Program in the United States before 1979. Low-income families paid, say, $20 to buy $60 worth of food stamps. This is equivalent to a two-thirds' reduction in the price of food.

The above discussion is for a *price* subsidy. We will now discuss a *quantity* subsidy.

[9]Consider the horizontal distance DF between the lines AB_1 and AB. At the point D, the consumer has the same quantity of Y but less of X than at F. This reduction is (the amount of tax)/P_X. But this is also B_2B. Hence, the parallel line A_2B_2 must pass through D.

[10]As mentioned earlier, this conclusion does not follow when we consider the economy as a whole, but this point is beyond the scope of our discussion. For a discussion of this aspect of the problem see "Welfare Effects of Taxes," in M. Friedman, *Price Theory*, Aldine, Chicago, 1962, pp. 56–67.

4.9.2 Cash subsidy versus subsidy in kind: The Food Stamp Program

Consider a cash subsidy of amount M that can be spent on either of two goods X and Y, and an equal subsidy tied to good X. The latter is what we mean by an in-kind subsidy. An example of this is the Food Stamp Program in the United States (after 1979) under which eligible low-income families receive free food stamps which the family can use for the purchase of food only. These stamps are non-tradable (if they were tradable, then the program would be equivalent to a general cash subsidy).

We will assume that the prices P_X and P_Y of X and Y respectively do not change and neither does the consumer's other income.[11] The shifts in the budget line and the equilibrium of the consumer are shown in Figure 4.21. The budget lines are shown in Figure 4.21(a). AB is the budget line without the subsidy. If the subsidy is tied to good X and if AC is the amount of X than can be bought with the subsidy, then ACD will be the new budget line. CD will be parallel to AB, since the consumer has the same money income as before plus the extra quantity AC of X. Note that the consumer cannot purchase more units of good Y than before. With a cash subsidy the budget line is ECD because the consumer is now free to spend any part of the subsidy on good X or on good Y.

Now the consumer's equilibrium in the case of the in-kind subsidy will be on the line ACD, and in the case of the cash subsidy will be on the line ECD. We show three cases in Figure 4.21. In all cases F is the equilibrium without any subsidy.

In Figure 4.21(b) the consumer's equilibrium with a subsidy is at G. This lies on both the lines ACD and ECD. Hence, the consumer is indifferent between the two subsidies.

In Figure 4.21(c) the consumer's equilibrium with the subsidy is at the point C. This is a corner point for the budget line ACD and a point of tangency for the budget line ECD. But this difference is irrelevant. The equilibrium point is the same. Hence, again the consumer is indifferent between the two subsidies.

In Figure 4.21(d) the consumer's equilibrium occurs at the corner point C in the case of the in-kind subsidy. But in the case of the cash subsidy the consumer can get to a higher indifference curve, and thus the consumer will prefer a cash subsidy to an in-kind subsidy.

In summary the consumer will never be worse off and sometimes will be better off with a cash subsidy than an in-kind subsidy. Whether this conclusion carries over when we consider the economy as a whole is questionable, but we cannot answer this question with the tools of analysis we have studied until now. It is, of course, true that each consumer who takes the prices as given will prefer a cash subsidy to an in-kind subsidy except in circumstances considered in the next example.

4.9.3 Taxes on cash subsidy

The preceding analysis shows that the consumer would never prefer an in-kind subsidy to a cash subsidy. However, this conclusion will change if the cash subsidy

---

[11]Of course, if many individuals are given subsidies tied to X, the market price of X will change. In our analysis we are abstracting from this problem.

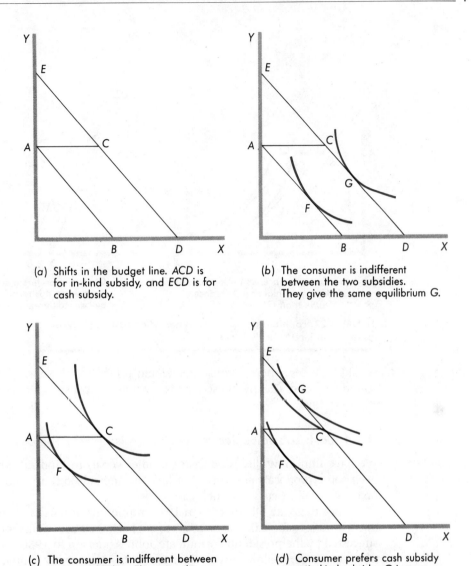

(a) Shifts in the budget line. *ACD* is for in-kind subsidy, and *ECD* is for cash subsidy.

(b) The consumer is indifferent between the two subsidies. They give the same equilibrium G.

(c) The consumer is indifferent between the two subsidies. They give the same equilibrium C.

(d) Consumer prefers cash subsidy to in-kind subsidy. G is on a higher indifference curve than C.

FIGURE 4.21 Shifts in the budget line and the equilibrium of the consumer under cash versus in-kind subsidies.

is taxed but the in-kind subsidy is not. This is, for instance, the case with several fringe benefits that employees get.

With the in-kind subsidy the budget line would still be *ACD* as shown in Figure 4.21. But with the cash subsidy, the budget line, *net of tax* would be a parallel line to the left of *ECD* in that figure. This is shown as *E'C'D'* in Figure 4.22. Now, it can be verified that the consumer may prefer the in-kind subsidy on good *X* to a cash subsidy, since he can attain a higher indifference curve. This is shown in Figure 4.22(*a*). However, this is not always the case, as is shown in Figure 4.22(*b*). There

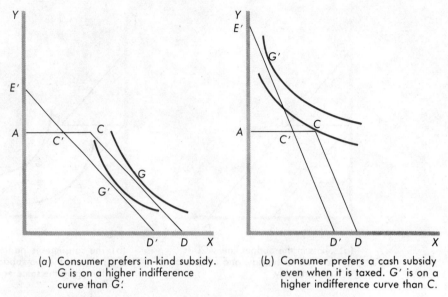

(a) Consumer prefers in-kind subsidy. G is on a higher indifference curve than G'.

(b) Consumer prefers a cash subsidy even when it is taxed. G' is on a higher indifference curve than C.

FIGURE 4.22 Equilibrium of the consumer when cash subsidy is taxed but in-kind subsidy is not.

would be cases where a consumer would prefer a cash subsidy even if the cash subsidy is taxed. Clearly, these are cases where the consumer's preference for good X is very low.

4.9.4 Cash subsidies tied to specific excise taxes: The case of gasoline

We have until now discussed cash subsidies versus in-kind subsidies. There have been some proposals put forth that link income subsidies to some specific excise taxes. We will discuss one such case.

Since the Arab oil embargo in 1973, numerous proposals have been designed to encourage or force U.S. consumers to cut back their use of oil. One such proposal, suggested by the presidential candidate John Anderson in 1980, was an excise tax of 50 cents per gallon on gasoline. Since this large a tax would place a heavy burden on poorer U.S. families, he recommended that the revenues collected be returned to customers in the form of a tax rebate. The revenues could also be used to reduce some other taxes such as the social security tax. One question that was raised by press reporters was that if the tax revenues were given back to consumers in the form of tax rebates, why would the consumption of gasoline fall? As we will show presently, this is not the important question. We will show that the consumption of gasoline could decline.

The gasoline tax with rebate may reduce the consumption of oil but does not get at the problem of the huge income transfers going from the oil-consuming nations to OPEC. Furthermore, why not have a similar tax on oil used by producers and give them rebates? Or a tax on natural gas and a rebate to consumers? The main objective of a gasoline tax with rebates is to shift consumers' purchases from gasoline to other goods. It provides no incentives on the supply side. In fact, it provides incentives for the production of the other goods. The proposal is exactly equivalent to an income tax and a subsidy for other goods (of course, the latter proposal is difficult to operate but the argument is made here to show the problems with the gasoline tax and tax-rebate proposal).

At any rate, we will now demonstrate the effect of the gasoline-tax and a tax rebate. Under the proposal, each consumer (or family) would receive a lump-sum rebate equal to the amount of tax paid by the average consumer. (Clearly, if each consumer received back exactly the amount paid in tax, nothing would change. This would be tantamount to paying an extra 50 cents per gallon and then receiving it in change.) As proposed, a consumer who purchased less gasoline than average would receive a rebate in excess of tax paid and an above-average consumer would receive a rebate less than the amount of tax paid.

Figure 4.23 presents the analysis in terms of indifference curves. Suppose the initial budget line is AB. Imposing the excise tax shifts the budget line to AC. Finally, the lump-sum rebate shifts the budget constraint outward to DE. Note that DE is parallel to AC because the rebate does not affect the price ratio.

Now, we must consider the behavior of the average consumer. We know that after the tax and rebate are imposed, the average consumer will purchase Q_3 units of gasoline where Q_3 corresponds to the intersection of AB and DE. How do we know this? Because AD is the amount of tax paid, expressed in terms of the value of other goods foregone. TS is also the amount of the lump-sum rebate expressed in terms of the amount of other goods which can be purchased. For the average consumer, these amounts must be equal. $AD = ST$ since $ADST$ is a parallelogram.

Now that we have identified the average consumer, we can examine the impact of the tax-rebate program on his, and hence, total, consumption of gasoline. With

FIGURE 4.23   Effects of excise tax and tax subsidy on gasoline consumption.

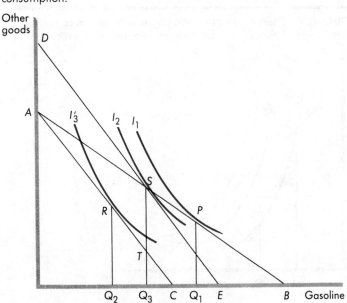

only the tax, this typical consumer would purchase commodity bundle R. Because he receives a subsidy as well, he chooses commodity bundle S which contains more gasoline. But with no intervention, he would purchase commodity bundle P which contains still more gasoline. So the tax-rebate program does reduce the consumption of gasoline. Note also that our average consumer is best off with no intervention, better off with both tax and rebate, and worst off with only the tax.

The rationale behind forcibly reducing the consumption of gasoline is to force consumers to make decisions that would reduce the demand for OPEC output and, thus, weaken the power of the cartel. But the proper way to do this is to take measures that stimulate domestic production and measures that cut OPEC's income subsidy. In Chapter 12 we discuss an import fee on oil as one such measure.

There is something interesting in the result we have derived. The effect of the tax rebate is to put the consumer on his original budget line. A quantity allotment (like gasoline coupons) does the same thing. With the gasoline tax and tax rebate, it is true the consumption of gasoline will fall, but it is hard to predict how much the decline will be. In Figure 4.23, if the objective is to reduce the consumption of gasoline from Q_1 to Q_3, a quantity allotment of Q_3 will put the consumer at the point S, precisely the same as the gasoline tax and tax rebate we considered, but this is a policy with predictable effect. Different rates of gasoline tax (with the corresponding tax rebate) will generate points of equilibrium along the line AB. Different levels of quantity allotments will do the same, but in a more predictable way. This is shown in Figure 4.24. Initially, the consumer's equilibrium is at P on indifference curve I_1. The quantity consumed is Q_1.

If the consumer's consumption of X is restricted to Q_2, she moves to the point R on a lower indifference curve I_2. If it is further restricted to Q_3, she moves to the point S on a still lower indifference curve I_3.

In summary, a quantity allotment scheme like the gasoline coupons achieves

FIGURE 4.24   Effect of quantity rationing is to leave the consumer on the original budget line but on lower indifference curves.

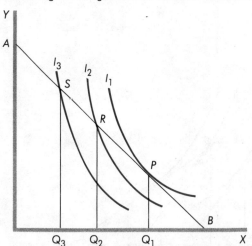

the same purpose as the Anderson proposal of a gasoline tax with tax rebates but in a more predictable fashion.

We will discuss the problems of price rationing versus quantity allotments in the next section.

EXAMPLE 4.1 The Economics of Christmas Gifts

Analysis of cash versus in-kind subsidies suggests that individuals would be better off with cash than in-kind gifts. This raises the question: Why do people ever give gifts in any other form than money? Surely individuals would be better off buying whatever they want with money instead of getting things that givers decide to buy. As far as the givers are concerned, it is much easier to send money than a gift. If both the givers and receivers are better off with money than with a gift, why do people buy so many gifts?

The answer is that giving money is considered by many as a thoughtless act. When you receive a Christmas gift, it is not just the item you receive but the satisfaction that the sender has spent some time thinking about you. Thus, you have to add another "good" to the analysis, a good you can label "thoughtfulness," whose money value is difficult to assess. The situation is similar to spending an expensive night out, or offering to send your date a check for half of the bill. Of course, with some of the individuals who send you Christmas gifts, you might not care whether they think about you, and thus their thoughtfulness is not a good for you, but in that case you should not expect any money from them either.

With some others who you know are thoughtful of you and show concern about you anyway (for instance, your parents, grandparents, children), the thoughtfulness in the Christmas gift is again not a "good." But here the reasons for the gift are different. Parents might feel they know your interests better and hence send you things that they feel you should have. With children, the good might be "sharing." They like to share the things that interest them with you—a book that they have read and liked, a new cooking gadget they have discovered and like very much, and so on. Or the good might be a feeling of "remembrance." They like to show that they remember your interests. In each case there is some good involved, other than the item sent to you as a gift, and the money value of each good is difficult to determine. Since it is a commodity that depends on personal relations, its money value can be determined only in those cases where personal relations are so close that explicit choices are offered.

4.10 APPLICATIONS: PRICE AND NONPRICE RATIONING AND BLACK MARKETS

If the consumption of any good is considered "too high" in the interest of society as a whole, then the government can cut down its consumption by *price rationing* or *nonprice rationing*. By price rationing we mean an excise tax, and by nonprice rationing we mean all types of controls on the quantity consumed. As an example of this, we considered in the previous section an excise tax on gasoline. This is rationing by price. An alternative would be the issuing of gasoline coupons.[12] The purpose of a coupon program would be to enable low-income families to obtain some gasoline at affordable prices, which they could not do if rationing were done by price increases alone. With the coupon scheme, there would develop a black market for coupons, and, in fact, this would result in a better allocation of gasoline than if such a black market did not exist. It would be better for the government to encourage trading of the coupons. Those for whom the marginal utility of gasoline is high would buy the coupons from those for whom the marginal utility was low. Those who sold the coupons would receive a money income. Thus, there would be an income redistribution, hopefully, from the rich to the poor.

In the following sections, we will analyze these problems step by step, first considering a single consumer, then two consumers with identical incomes but different tastes, and finally two consumers with different incomes. We will then discuss the situation of black markets.

4.10.1 Price rationing versus quantity allotment

Consider a consumer with the indifference map and budget constraint as shown in Figure 4.25. AB is the budget line and C the point of equilibrium, the quantity of gasoline consumed being Q_0. With quantity allotment the price does not change, only the consumer is constrained to limit consumption to Q_1. The consumer will then be at the point D on the budget line, and since it is to the left of the indifference curve passing through C, the consumer will be worse off.

The same restriction in consumption can be achieved, by imposing an excise tax.[13] With this the budget line shifts to AE, and the consumer's equilibrium is at F. The consumption of gasoline is again reduced to Q_1, but the consumer is worse off than at D, since D is a point above the indifference curve passing through F and so corresponds to a higher level of utility. Thus, the consumer is better off with quantity allotment than with price rationing.

Of course, the conclusion is fairly obvious without even looking at Figure 4.25, which is used here for only pedagogical reason. Under both scenarios, the quantity consumed of gasoline is the same. But with quantity allotment consumers can spend the money which they would previously have spent on gasoline on something else. With the excise tax, this same amount of money instead goes to the government as tax revenue. The government, of course, gets the tax revenue, but the question is, what does it do with it? It can waste the revenues on unproductive projects, in which case our analysis holds good. At the other extreme, it can give it back to consumers in the form of rebates. In which case, the equilibrium with excise tax and rebates will not be at Q_1 any more.

We have analyzed this case in Section 4.9.4 earlier, and looking at Figure 4.23 we see that the consumer's consumption under a gasoline tax and rebate policy gives equilibrium consumption at Q_3. With quantity allotment at Q_3, the consumer will be at the point S in that figure (on the budget line AB). But this is also the equilibrium with gasoline tax plus rebate. Thus, *price rationing with rebates and*

---

[12]In fact, during the Carter administration in the United States, the government had gasoline coupons printed, to be used in the event of a shortage in oil supplies. Such coupons were used during World War II.

[13]The magnitude of the excise tax is such that the consumer's optimum consumption of gasoline after the tax is exactly Q_1.

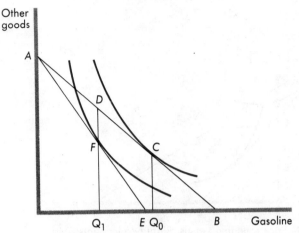

FIGURE 4.25 Proof that the consumers are better off with quantity allotments than with price rationing when government revenues from taxes are wasted.

quantity allotments are equivalent (with the particular rebate policy discussed in Section 4.9.4).

We will now consider the case of two consumers who differ in tastes (two is enough to analyze differences in tastes) and show that quantity allotments can make some consumers worse off as compared to price rationing. Actually, to analyze the problem completely, we need to know what the government does with the revenues from the excise tax. An analysis similar to that in Section 4.9.4 gets much too complicated for our purposes. Hence, we will make this simplifying assumption (not unreasonable) that the government wastes the revenues on some unproductive projects. Hence, the budget lines of the consumers do not change.

4.10.2 Price rationing versus quantity allotments: Consumers with different tastes but the same income

Consider two consumers with different tastes but both with the same budget line (Figure 4.26). AB is the budget line under quantity rationing (we assume that market prices do not change). With price rationing or an excise tax on commodity X, AE is the budget line. I_0 is the indifference curve of consumer 1, his equilibrium is at C with the consumption of X being x_1. J_0 is the indifference curve of consumer 2, her equilibrium is at D, and her consumption of X is x_2. Let the average of x_1 and x_2 be $\bar{x}$.

Now, let us say there is a quantity rationing scheme under which each of the consumers is allowed to purchase a quantity $\bar{x}$. The total consumption of good X under quantity rationing is then less than or equal to total consumption under the price rationing scheme. Quantity rationing allows the consumers to choose any bundle along AF. Consumer 1 is worse off with quantity rationing, as all feasible bundles lie on indifference curves lower than I_0. But consumer 2 is better off under quantity rationing, because she can purchase a commodity bundle on an indifference curve above J_0.

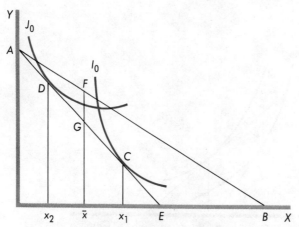

FIGURE 4.26   Price rationing versus quantity allotments: Two consumers with different tastes. (Consumer 1 is worse off at F than at C. Consumer 2 is better off at F than at D. Note that by making I_0 flatter so that F is to the right of I_0, we can show that consumer 1 is also better off.)

Of course, in our analysis we have not said anything about what the government does with the excise taxes it collects. We have implicitly assumed the revenue is wasted.

4.10.3 Price rationing versus quantity allotments: Differences in tastes and incomes among consumers

We will now extend the preceding analysis to the case of two individuals with different incomes. Since the prices of the commodities are the same for both, their budget lines will be parallel. We will also assume that in the case of price rationing, we consider a 100 percent excise tax, and that this is completely passed on to the consumers. This is a high rate, but we can easily discuss the results in our diagram without cluttering it up with close lines. The 100 percent tax implies that after the tax the consumer can buy only half the quantity of X that he could before the tax.

Figure 4.27 shows the situation: A_1B_1 and A_2B_2 are the budget lines of consumers 1 and 2, respectively, without any tax. A_1C_1 and A_2C_2 are the budget lines of the two consumers after the 100 percent excise tax on X. With the excise tax the equilibrium of consumer 1 is at D_1, with his consumption of X at x_1 and consumer 2's equilibrium is at D_2, with her consumption of X at x_2.

Let the average of x_1 and x_2 be $\bar{x}$. We will assume, as before, that under quantity rationing each of the consumers is alloted a quantity $\bar{x}$. So, the total consumption of X is at least as large under price rationing as under quantity rationing. This allotment puts both consumers on their original budget lines, but the portions of the budget lines below E_1 and E_2 are effectively eliminated.

As we have drawn the diagram, consumer 1 is definitely worse off. The point E_1 is to the left of the indifference curve I_0 that he was on under price rationing.[14]

---

[14]By making I_0 flatter we could have shown that consumer 1 is better off with quantity rationing. However, we want to illustrate some consequences of trading in the black market.

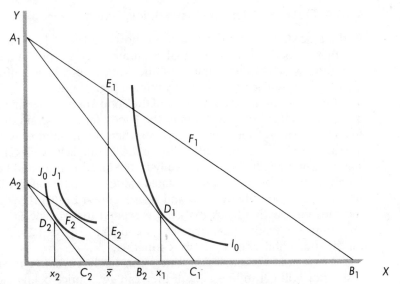

FIGURE 4.27 Quantity allotments with trading of coupons makes both consumers better off than under price rationing. (Consumer 2 is better off even without trade since she can move from E_2 to F_2 by buying less of X and more of Y. But consumer 1 is better off only after the trade.)

As for consumer 2, she can reach indifference curve J_1 by consuming F_2. Her consumption of gasoline will be greater than under price rationing but still less than her allotment. Consumer 2 is clearly better off.

If the allotments are controlled through the issuance of coupons (as during World War II), consumer 2 might give her unused coupons to consumer 1. In this case, consumer 1 moves to point F_1, and his situation improves. In fact, consumer 2 is now better off with quantity allotments than with price rationing. Actually, consumer 2 can sell the coupons that she does not need at some profit to consumer 1 and thus reach a higher indifference curve than J_1. In this case, not only is consumer 2 better off compared to her situation with price rationing, but she is better off even compared with her position before any quantity rationing was imposed. As for consumer 1, he would be willing to pay a price for the coupons so long as he can improve his position over I_0.

This example illustrates how a market (black or grey) will develop if something like a gasoline coupon scheme is instituted.

Finally, note that all this discussion of quantity allotments versus price rationing does not account for the following factors:

1. Costs to the government of implementing the quantity allocations
2. Alternative uses for the government revenues from excise taxation in the case of price rationing

To discuss these is beyond our scope at this stage. Our purpose here has been to illustrate the use of indifference curve analysis in comparing different policies.

4.10.4 Quantity allotments, subsidies, and black markets

In the preceding example, we showed how we get a black market with quantity allotments. As far as the individual consumer is concerned, if he gets an allotment of a good which is more than what he wants, he is better off trading the excess quantity in the black market and getting a higher price.

Consider, for instance, the case of the Food Stamp Program illustrated in Figure 4.21. The budget line is ACD under the Food Stamp Program. If the consumer can freely trade any of the stamps for cash, then the in-kind subsidy is equivalent to a cash subsidy, and the budget line is ECD. But if it is illegal to trade the food stamps, the individual can trade only in the black market and because of the risks involved, might get less than the stated value. Thus, the budget line could be E_1CD where E_1 is a point between E and A in Figure 4.21. To show the equilibrium of the consumer with a black market we expand the triangle ECA in Figure 4.21(d) and show it in Figure 4.28. In cases (b) and (c) in Figure 4.21, there is no incentive for the individual to go to the black market.

As we said earlier, if consumers can freely exchange their food stamps for cash, they will get to line ECD. If they can get a price below face value, they are still better off if they can get on the budget line E_1CD. But if consumers get a low price which puts them on the budget line E_2CD, they have no incentive to trade in the black market. There is no way they can get to a higher indifference curve.

In any case, the consumers will have greater opportunities to improve their position by the existence of the black market. A black market can develop even with government-provided housing. The consumer can take the government-provided housing, rent it, and live elsewhere. Of course, there are greater chances of being caught in this than in the case of trading food stamps or gasoline coupons.

The crucial issue in all these cases is whether the black market provides a desirable social function. In this respect a black market in housing or food stamps is different from a black market in gasoline coupons. To see this, we have to ask

FIGURE 4.28   A black market in food stamps. (Consumers are better off if they can get to the budget line such as E_1C by trading in the black market. Consumers will not trade in the black market if the low price received puts them on the line E_2C.)

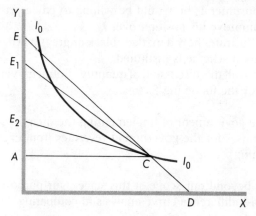

what the purpose of the program is. For instance, the purpose of the food stamp program is to ensure that low-income families have the minimum amount of food to eat. If trading in food stamps is allowed, it is equivalent to a cash subsidy. Then the question arises as to why the cash subsidy was not given instead of the food stamps. Presumably, the argument is that you do not want the family to waste the cash subsidy on alcohol, cigarettes, drugs, etc. In other words, you are afraid that individual consumers would make decisions about consumption that are not in their long-term interest or in society's interest. In this case, it is not desirable to permit trading in food stamps, and stiff penalties should be imposed for trading in them.

The case of a housing subsidy is similar, although in the case of housing things are a bit complicated. Buying housing is not like buying food. You buy the shelter but also all the "neighborhood effects." What if an individual wants to take the government-provided housing but cannot tolerate the neighborhood? Anyway, even in this case one can make a case that a black market should be discouraged, because a housing subsidy is in many ways like the food stamp program, designed to ensure a minimum necessity.

The case of gasoline coupons is different. First of all, the main purpose is to reduce the total consumption of gasoline. If price rationing is used, it is argued that this produces undue hardship on low-income families. To alleviate this it has been proposed that income rebates be given to low-income families. We have discussed this proposal in Section 4.9.4. We have also discussed an alternative scheme, that of quantity allotments. Whatever the relative merits of these proposals, suppose that the quantity allotment method is chosen. Then it might be better to permit the trading of coupons than to ban it. The reason is that gasoline is a consumer's commodity (luxury consumption like pleasure driving and necessary consumption like driving to the supermarket) as well as a producers' commodity (business travel). It is a resource that should be allocated to the most productive use. (In Chapter 19, we will discuss a similar problem of trading in pollution licenses.)

Of course, we saw in Figure 4.27 that allowing the trading of coupons might also increase overall consumption. So the benefits of improved allocative efficiency will have to be weighed against the cost of a potential increase in total consumption.

In any event, the case for allowing the trading of gasoline coupons is much stronger than for allowing the trading of, say, food stamps.[15]

4.11 SUMMARY AND CONCLUSIONS

The satisfaction that a consumer derives from the consumption of commodities is called utility. The extra satisfaction derived from an additional unit of a commodity is the marginal utility of that unit. Cardinal utility theory says that utility is measurable; the units of measurement are utils. Ordinal utility theory says that the utility of different commodities (or commodity bundles) can be ranked or ordered

---

[15]We are not, however, justifying either of these programs. All we are discussing is, given the existence of the program, whether trading in the coupons should be allowed.

but not measured. The law of diminishing marginal utility asserts that each additional unit consumed of a commodity yields less marginal utility than previous units.

An indifference curve consists of all the combinations of two commodities which provide equal utility to the consumer. When both commodities are valued by the consumer, indifference curves must be negatively sloped, with indifference curves farther from the origin denoting greater levels of utility. If preferences are transitive, then indifference curves cannot intersect.

The marginal rate of substitution is the rate at which one commodity can be substituted for the other, holding total utility constant. Mathematically, the marginal rate of substitution equals MU_X/MU_Y for commodities X and Y. Graphically, it is equal to the absolute value of the slope of the indifference curve. If the marginal rate of substitution declines as more X and less Y are consumed, then the indifference curves will be convex to the origin. Convexity can also be implied by observing that consumers do not specialize in the consumption of a single commodity.

A budget line consists of all the combinations of two commodities that the consumer can just afford with a given budget and given commodity prices. The slope of the budget line is $-P_X/P_Y$ for commodities X and Y. With convex indifference curves and positive marginal utility for both commodities, consumers will maximize their satisfaction by choosing the commodity bundle defined by the tangency between the budget line and an indifference curve. This tangency implies that the marginal utility to price ratio will be the same for all commodities.

A demand curve can be derived from a set of indifference curves by holding the budget (income) and the price of one good constant. One can then vary the price of the other commodity, rotating the budget line, and observe the optimal bundles. One can then simply plot the various prices against the quantities of the commodity contained in the corresponding optimal bundles.

A consumer is always better off with an income tax than with an excise tax on one commodity if the two taxes yield the same total tax payment. The consumer is also better off with a cash subsidy than with an in-kind subsidy except when the cash subsidy is taxable and the in-kind subsidy is not. An excise tax with rebate will reduce the consumption of the commodity on which the tax is levied. The average consumer will be worse off.

A consumer is better off with a quantity allotment than with an excise tax that yields an equal reduction in consumption. Consider two consumers with different incomes and/or preferences. Both consumers are at least as well off with a quantity allotment scheme under which coupons can be transferred than with a price-rationing scheme which yields the same total consumption.

KEY TERMS

Additive Utility
Budget Line
Cardinal Theory of Utility
Completeness of
   Preferences

Giffen Paradox
Indifference Curve
In-Kind Subsidy
Law of Diminishing
   Marginal Utility

Marginal Rate of
   Substitution
Marginal Utility
Ordinal Theory of
   Utility

Price Rationing	Selective Excise Tax	Transitivity of
Quantity	Specialization in	Preferences
Allotment	Consumption	Utility

QUESTIONS

1. Commodity bundle 1 contains 5 units of commodity X. Commodity bundle 2 contains 3 units of commodity Y. Suppose that a consumer derives 11 utils from bundle 1 and 6 utils from bundle 2, yet, when given both bundles, his total utility is only 14 utils. Is utility additive? How do goods X and Y appear to be related? Why?

2. Suppose that a consumer derives no utility or disutility from good X, whereas the marginal utility of good Y is strictly positive. Draw an indifference curve map with these two commodities. If the prices of both commodities are positive, what will the consumer purchase? Does this make sense?

3. We have stated that if preferences are transitive then indifference curves cannot intersect. Is tangency of indifference curves also ruled out? Why?

4. Suppose that we have constructed a budget line where the two commodities are apples and bananas. The slope of the budget line equals $-$(price of bananas/price of apples). Which commodity is measured on which axis? Why?

5. Graph the budget line for a consumer in a two-commodity world with an income of $100, $P_X = \$5$ and $P_Y = \$10$ where the two commodities are X and Y. Label both intercepts and compute the slope. Now graph her budget line if she is given a non-transferable coupon redeemable for three units of commodity Y.

6. A consumer suddenly realizes that $MU_X/P_X < MU_Y/P_Y$ with his current commodity bundle. Is he maximizing his utility? If not, which commodity should he consume more of, to improve utility, without increasing total expenditure? What happens to the MU/P ratio for each good as he begins to adjust consumption? Why?

7. Indicate graphically that members of the armed forces would be better off if the military closed post exchange stores and instead issued aftertax pay supplements equal to the individuals' current savings on items purchased at these stores.

8. A child with additive utility is given 50 cents to spend at the candy store. She likes three kinds of candy, and the utils associated with the quantities of each are listed below. The price of all candy is 10 cents per piece.

	Total Utils		
Quantity	Jaw Breakers	Licorice Sticks	Peanut Clusters
1	15	30	20
2	29	58	37
3	42	84	50
4	54	108	60
5	65	130	68

a. What combination of candy should the child purchase to maximize her utility? Would an indifference curve between peanut clusters and licorice be concave to the origin? If not, how do you explain your answer?

b. Today the store is out of licorice sticks. What should she now purchase? (Saving the money is out of the question.)

9. Consider the subsidized education program in many underdeveloped countries. An eligible student can go abroad to college at government expense, but if he accepts this offer, the quantity of education is beyond his control. Most commonly, he must complete 4 years and then return home. Of course, he is not forced to participate: He can forego higher education altogether. Or he can pay for it himself, in which case he can choose the quantity purchased.

Measuring education on one axis and other goods on the other axis, draw the budget lines for an eligible student who accepts the offer and for the student who rejects it. Using indifference curve analysis, demonstrate that it might be rational to purchase one's own education. Now demonstrate that such a program might actually induce the student to acquire less education. Why? What is the crucial difference between this program and the food stamp program?

10. Consider again the proposed tax rebate program for gasoline. We examined the behavior of the average consumer and explained why that consumer's consumption of gasoline would decline. But what about the below-average consumer? Can you conclude how her or his gasoline consumption will be affected? Why or why not?

11. Construct indifference curves for two goods which are:

a. Perfect complements

b. Perfect substitutes

Explain the nature of the two shapes.

12. Why is the convexity assumption so important in indifference curve analysis? In particular, would a consumer equilibrium exist if indifference curves were concave? Explain.

13. A student is first and foremost interested in beer and would be willing to forgo any quantity of milk for the smallest additional quantity of beer. However, if the beer consumption is given, the student prefers to have more milk rather than less. Draw an indifference curve to represent these preferences. If you are unable to draw such a curve, briefly explain. Why do you believe that in this case an indifference curve does not exist?

ANALYSIS OF CONSUMER DEMAND

   INTRODUCTION

In the previous chapter we studied consumer preferences and how they can be graphically depicted with indifference curves. We also examined the consumer's budget constraint, and we combined an indifference curve map with a budget constraint to determine the consumer's optimal consumption bundle.

In Chapter 5 we will further analyze the demand curves that we looked at in Chapter 2 and Chapter 3. Specifically, we are concerned with what happens to the quantity of a good demanded when (1) the consumer's income changes and prices of the goods remain constant and (2) the price of one good changes and the prices of other goods and the consumer's income remain constant. The answer to (1) also enables us to study the income elasticity of demand that we talked about in Section 3.6 of Chapter 3. Question (2) was discussed briefly in Section 4.7 of the previous chapter, where we derived the demand curve from indifference curves, but here we will examine the effects of a price change in greater detail. We will separate the impact of a price change into two components. When the price of one good declines, holding other prices and money income constant, the consumer generally purchases more of the now cheaper item. This is for two reasons: First, the consumer will substitute the good for other products because it has become relatively cheaper. This response is the *substitution effect*. Second, when the price of one good declines, ceteris paribus, the consumer's purchasing power or *real income* has increased. For a normal good, this increase in real income will also induce the consumer to buy more. This response to a larger real income is the *income effect*. It will be discussed in Section 5.4.

Finally, we will apply our analysis to several issues from the field of labor economics. We will consider how the quantity of labor supplied responds to a change in the wage rate. As the wage rate goes up, the cost of an hour of leisure goes up. However, the individual will receive higher income from the hours worked, and this will increase the demand for leisure. The net effect of an increase in the wage rate on hours worked is, therefore, not clear. Having studied the labor supply curve, we will then examine the impact of different income taxes and welfare programs on work effort.

We will conclude this chapter with several other applications: We will examine the consumer's consumption decision in a multiperiod context. We will look at how insurance deductibles affect the quantity of medical care received. And finally, we will compare and contrast two cost-of-living indexes.

   INCOME-CONSUMPTION AND ENGEL CURVES

In this section, we will examine the impact of a change in income on the quantity of good X demanded. We will confine our attention to two commodities by adopting the composite-good convention. Y will be all other goods. And again, the quantity of the other goods will be expressed in terms of expenditure on them.

If we hold all prices constant and increase the consumer's budget or money income, the budget line will shift outward in a parallel manner as shown in Figure

5.1. The vertical intercept is now equal to the amount of the budget. So M_1 is the income corresponding to the lowest budget line, M_2 is a higher income corresponding to the middle budget line, and so on.

For each budget line, we can locate the point of tangency with an indifference curve and thus observe the consumer's optimal consumption bundle. By connecting all these tangency points, we derive an *income-consumption curve*. From the points on the income-consumption curve, we can read off the quantities of X demanded at the different income levels.

Income	Quantity of X Demanded
M_1	X_1
M_2	X_2
M_3	X_3
.	.
.	.
.	.

These data can be plotted in a graph showing the quantity of X demanded for each income M. This graph, shown in Figure 5.2, is called an *Engel curve* after a German statistician Ernst Engel (1821–1896) who first studied the relationship between family incomes and quantities demanded of different goods. There is also *Engel's law*, which states that the lower a family's income, the greater is the proportion of it spent on food. Engel's conclusion was based on a budget study of 153 Belgian families and was later verified by a number of other statistical inquiries into consumer behavior.[1]

[1]Among Engel's other contributions was his examination of the relationship between the size of the Prussian rye harvest and the average price of rye over a number of years prior to 1860. This was perhaps the first empirical study of a supply function.

FIGURE 5.1 An income-consumption curve.

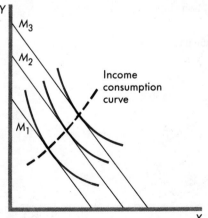

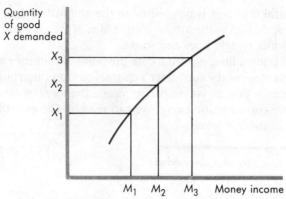

FIGURE 5.2   An Engel curve.

The Engel curve is very often positively sloped, so that the quantity of the good demanded rises with income. In this case the good is a *normal* good. The elasticity of the Engel curve is the income elasticity of demand (see Chapter 3, Section 3.6). We said earlier that if the income elasticity of demand for a good is greater than 1 we call it a *luxury* and if it is less than 1 we call it a *necessity*.

The Engel curve need not always be positively sloping. There are cases where it can be negatively sloped, so that an increase in income leads to a decrease in the quantity demanded. In this case the good is an *inferior good*. Figure 5.3 shows a set of indifference curves for which consumption of the good X declines as income rises. In this case the Engel curve will be downward sloping.

No good is an inferior good at all income levels. A good can be a luxury good at low income levels, a necessity at middle income levels and an inferior good at very high income levels (for example, compact cars). Figure 5.4 shows an Engel curve that exhibits these properties.

Examining Figure 5.4 we see that the Engel curve reaches a maximum at point B, corresponding to an income of M_2. To the left of B, income and quantity demanded vary directly indicating that X is a normal good for income levels below

FIGURE 5.3   Income-consumption curve for an inferior good.

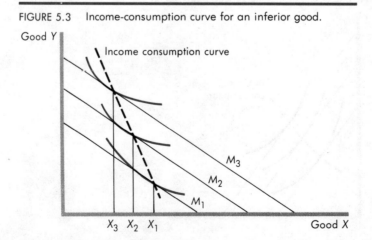

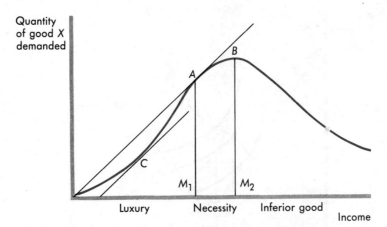

FIGURE 5.4   An Engel curve in its most general form.

M_2. To the right of B, income and quantity demanded vary inversely, indicating that X is an inferior good for income levels above M_2.

Now, recall from Chapter 3 that

$$|\text{Elasticity at a point}| = \frac{\text{distance from the } y \text{ axis}}{\text{distance from the } x \text{ axis}}$$

where both distances are measured along a line tangent to the curve of interest. We can, thus, draw a few tangent lines and further break down income elasticity. A line through the origin is tangent to the Engel curve at point A. This means that income elasticity of demand is 1 at an income level of M_1. To the left of M_1, at a point such as C, a tangent line will have a negative vertical intercept, indicating that elasticity exceeds 1. So good X is a luxury for income levels less than M_1. Finally, the student can verify that for income levels between M_1 and M_2, the income elasticity of demand for X is positive but less than 1. This, of course, implies that X is a necessity for income levels between M_1 and M_2.

5.3   PRICE-CONSUMPTION AND DEMAND CURVES

In the previous section we derived the income-consumption curve as the curve that joins the points of tangency of successive budget lines (given by different levels of income) with the indifference curves. Since the prices of goods X and Y were fixed, changes in income gave us a set of parallel budget lines.

Suppose, instead, that we hold money income and the price of good Y (or all other goods) constant and vary the price of X. We will again generate a set of budget lines. The curve joining the points of tangency of these budget lines with the indifference curves is called the *price-consumption curve* and is shown in Figure 5.5. Since the price of good Y and income are both fixed, maximum expenditure on Y is fixed at M. However, since the price of X changes, the amount of good X that can be bought changes. If M is the money income, and $P_1, P_2, P_3, \ldots$ are the

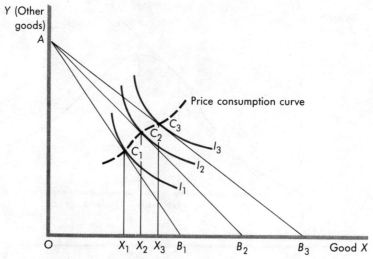

FIGURE 5.5 A price-consumption curve.

successive prices of good X, then the amounts of good X that can be bought are $OB_1 = M/P_1$, $OB_2 = M/P_2$, $OB_3 = M/P_3$, etc. The budget lines are thus, AB_1, AB_2, AB_3, etc., where $OA = M$, the money income. The points of tangency with the indifference curves are C_1, C_2, C_3, etc. The curve $C_1C_2C_3 \ldots$ is the price-consumption curve. Also from the points C_1, C_2, C_3, etc., we can read off the amounts of the good X that are demanded. As we can see in Figure 5.5, as the price of X falls, the quantity demanded of X rises. We thus get a downward-sloping demand curve.

However, there could be cases where the demand curve need not be downward sloping. We discussed this in the last chapter (Section 4.7) and illustrated it in Figure 4.18. Again, a good for which the quantity demanded falls as the price declines is a Giffen good.

5.4 INCOME AND SUBSTITUTION EFFECTS
OF A PRICE CHANGE

Earlier we said that, if the money income and the price of good Y stay the same but the price of good X rises, then the consumer will feel poorer, and if the price of good X falls, the consumer will feel richer. This observation has led economists to try to separate the impact of a price change on quantity demanded into two components:

1. The substitution effect, which involves the substitution of good X for good Y or vice-versa due to a change in the relative prices of the two goods
2. The income effect, which results from an increase or decrease in the consumer's real income or purchasing power as a result of the price change

The sum of these two effects is often called the total effect of a price change or just the *price effect*. The decomposition of the price effect into the substitution and income effect components can be done in several ways depending on what we would like to hold constant. There are two main methods suggested in the literature: (1) the Hicksian method[2] and (2) the Slutsky method.[3] We will first illustrate the two methods in figures using indifference-curve analysis and then discuss the relative merits of the two approaches.

The Hicksian method

Consider Figure 5.6. AB_1 is the original budget line, but then a fall in the price of good X shifts the budget line to AB_2. (Income and the prices of other goods remain constant.) Initially, the optimal bundle was E_1 on indifference curve I_1. After the decline in the price of X, the new consumer optimum becomes E_2 on indifference curve I_2. The total effect of the price change is thus a movement from E_1 to E_2, or an increase in the quantity demanded of X from X_1 to X_2.

Now we can ask the question: "What would the consumer's optimal bundle be if he or she faced the new lower price for X but experienced no change in real income?" The answer is E_3 with X_3 units of good X demanded. To see this, one must realize that holding consumers' real income constant amounts to keeping them on the same indifference curve. And with the new price ratio, the new optimum on I_1 is at E_3, where a line with the slope of the new budget line (or parallel to the new budget line) is tangent.

Thus, we argue that the movement from E_1 to E_3, or the increase in quantity

---

[2]This method is attributed to the famous British economist Sir John R. Hicks and is described in his book *Value and Capital: An Inquiry into Some Fundamental Principles of Economic Theory*, 2d ed., Oxford University Press, London, 1946, pp. 29–33.

[3]This is the method suggested by the Russian economist Eugene Slutsky (1880–1948) in his paper "On the Theory of the Budget of the Consumer," reprinted in Kenneth E. Boulding and George Stigler, eds., *Readings in Price Theory*, Richard D. Irwin, Homewood, Ill., 1952, pp. 27–56.

FIGURE 5.6   Substitution and income effects of a price change: The Hicksian method.

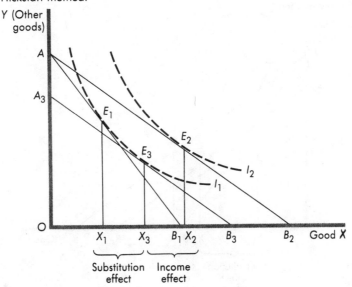

demanded from X_1 to X_3, is solely in response to a change in relative prices. This is the substitution effect.

The remainder of the total effect is due to a change in real income. The movement from E_3 to E_2, or the increase in quantity demanded from X_3 to X_2 is thus the income effect. The increase in real income is evidenced by the consumer's movement from I_1 to a higher indifference curve, I_2.

The Slutsky method

The Slutsky method is illustrated in Figure 5.7. The initial budget line is again AB_1. And again, a decline in the price of good X shifts the budget line to AB_2. The consumer moves from position E_1 on indifference curve I_1 to position E_2 on indifference curve I_2.

In an attempt to isolate the substitution effect, Slutsky suggests that as we change the price of X_1, we adjust the consumer's money income so that he can just afford his original consumption bundle. Doing so would lead to the budget line A_4B_4, which passes through E_1 but is parallel to AB_2, thus reflecting the new price for X. Slutsky then argues that the movement along this budget line from E_1 to E_4 is due to the change in the price of X or constitutes the substitution effect. Note that with the Slutsky method, the substitution effect involves a movement to a higher indifference curve.

This leaves the movement from E_4 to E_2, or the increase in consumption of good X from X_4 to X_2, as the income effect. And again, the substitution effect plus the income effect must equal the total effect.

The difference between the Hicksian method and the Slutsky method

The Hicksian method is theoretically the correct one, because with this method the substitution effect measures the effect of movement along an indifference curve

FIGURE 5.7 Substitution and income effects of a price change: The Slutsky method.

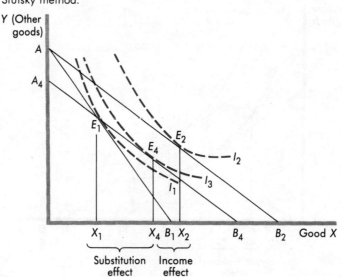

due to a change in relative prices, whereas the income effect measures the effect of a movement between indifference curves at unchanged relative prices. However, the problem with this method is that it is *nonoperational* in the sense that the point E_3 in Figure 5.6 cannot be observed in practice.

However, the Slutsky method is operational in the sense that we can do something to observe the point E_4 in Figure 5.7. What we do is adjust money income for the consumer to allow her to just afford the bundle of goods X and Y given by the point E_1. Then we observe what the consumer chooses, which is the point E_4.

As an example, suppose that initially the prices of goods X and Y are $P_X = 10 and $P_Y = 10. The consumer's income is $150. Suppose the consumer buys 7 units of X and 8 units of Y. Now P_X falls to $5. Then in the Slutsky method we take away $35 of the consumer's income. With the income of $115 the consumer can still buy 7 units of X and 8 units of Y as before. Actually, the consumer will choose another bundle, and this is what we observe (as E_4 in Figure 5.7). Note that a similar experiment cannot be performed under the Hicksian method, although one can talk theoretically about an income adjustment that will keep the consumer on the same indifference curve.

Although operational, the Slutsky method is not theoretically defensible, because the movement from E_1 to E_4 involves a movement between indifference curves and thus is not really a substitution effect. The method, in general, overestimates the substitution effect and underestimates the income effect. (This is true in the case of Figures 5.6 and 5.7 the way we have drawn them.)

In the following sections and in subsequent chapters, whenever we have to decompose the effect of a price change into substitution and income effects, we will use the Hicksian approach. This is the right approach for deriving theoretical conclusions.

Effects of a price increase

We have, so far, discussed the substitution and income effects of a decline in the price of X. The analysis of an increase in the price of X is similar. In this case the substitution effect results in a decrease in the consumption of X and so does the income effect in the case of a normal good. In the Slutsky method we now have to compensate the consumer with an income subsidy that will enable the consumer to buy the old combination of goods X and Y at the new prices. In the Hicksian method, we again can think of an income compensation (although it is difficult to implement) that will enable the consumer to stay on the same indifference curve as before the price rise. Since the analysis is symmetrical we will not present it here but will leave it as an exercise.

EXAMPLE 5.1 Shipping the Good Apples Out

Suppose that a good apple costs 20 cents and a poor apple costs 10 cents locally in Washington State. Then to eat two good apples it costs the same as eating four poor apples. Suppose that it costs 10 cents per apple to ship apples to the East Coast. The cost of a good apple there is 30 cents and the cost of a poor apple is 20 cents. Now eating two good apples costs the same as eating three poor apples (not four). Although the prices of apples are higher, good apples are *relatively* cheaper (relative to poor apples), and a higher percentage of good apples will be consumed in the East than in Washington. The good apples from Washington State are shipped to the East.

Although this was apparently a part of the UCLA oral doctrine for a long time, the proposition that, if the same fixed cost (for example, a transportation cost) is added to the prices of similar goods, the effect would be to raise the relative consumption of the higher-quality or premium good, first appeared in a textbook by Alchian and Allen in 1964.[4] Since then it has also appeared in other texts such as those by Stigler and Hirschleifer.[5]

One can use similar reasoning to explain why fine tailoring will be done on expensive fabric rather than on inexpensive fabric (because tailoring is *relatively* cheaper on expensive fabric, it is a smaller proportion of total cost). Similarly, houses situated on lots with high site value tend to be fancier than those situated in places with low site value (because site value is relatively cheaper for expensive houses). Most top-grade beef is sold to restaurants (because the cost of restaurant services is relatively cheaper for high-grade beef).

There has been some controversy over whether the Alchian-Allen proposition can be derived solely using the law of demand, although there is no question of its empirical validity. Also, although we quoted all the other examples as being similar to the example of apples, it should be acknowledged that transportation costs are different from tailoring services, site values, or restaurant services. However, the Alchian and Allen proposition holds even in these cases, but the reasoning may be different. (We will not get into the details here because this involves the use of consumer's surplus discussed in Chapter 9.)[6]

5.5 GIFFEN GOODS AND INFERIOR GOODS

In previous sections we defined Giffen goods and inferior goods. The distinction between the two can be made clearer by considering the substitution and income effects.

In Figure 5.6, note that the substitution effect and income effect both led to an increase of the consumption of X when the price P_X of X fell. This need not always be the case. The substitution effect will always be positive, that is, the decline in the relative price of X will lead to a substitution of X for Y. However, the income effect need not be positive.[7] It is negative for inferior goods. If the income effect is so strongly negative that it swamps the positive substitution effect, the total effect will be negative, and we thus have the result that a decline in the price of X results in a decrease in quantity of good X demanded. This is the case

---

[4]A. A. Alchian and W. R. Allen, *University Economics*, Wadsworth, Belmont, Calif., 1964, pp. 74–75.

[5]G. J. Stigler, *The Theory of Price*, 3d ed., Macmillan, New York, 1966, p. 103, and J. Hirshleifer, *Price Theory and Applications*, Prentice-Hall, Englewood Cliffs, N.J., 1976, p. 321.

[6]See John Umbeck, "Shipping the Good Apples Out: Some Ambiguities in the Interpretation of 'Fixed Charge,'" *Journal of Political Economy*, February 1980, pp. 199–208. This is a comment on T. E. Borcherding and E. Silberberg, "Shipping the Good Apples Out: The Alchian and Allen Theorem Reconsidered," *Journal of Political Economy*, February 1978, pp. 131–138.

[7]In fact, we will see this happening in the case of labor supply. This point is discussed in Section 5.7 later.

TABLE 5.1 Substitution and Income Effects of a Price Decline on Quantity Demanded

Type of Good	Substitution Effect	Income Effect	Total Effect
Normal	Increase	Increase	Increase
Inferior (but not Giffen)	Increase	Decrease	Increase
Giffen	Increase	Decrease	Decrease

with Giffen goods. Thus, Giffen goods are inferior goods, but not all inferior goods are Giffen goods. This point is set out in Table 5.1 and illustrated in Figures 5.8 and 5.9.

5.6 ORDINARY VERSUS COMPENSATED DEMAND FUNCTIONS

The separation of the effect of price changes into substitution and income effects also has led to the definition of two types of demand curves: (1) the *ordinary demand curve (OD)*, which includes the substitution and income effects, and (2) the *compensated demand curve (CD)*, which includes the substitution effect only. The compensated demand curve is so called because the consumer is compensated for any decline in real income due to a rise in the price of a good, or taxed (given negative compensation) for any increase in real income due to a decline in the price of a good.

FIGURE 5.8 Income and substitution effect for an inferior good (not a Giffen good).

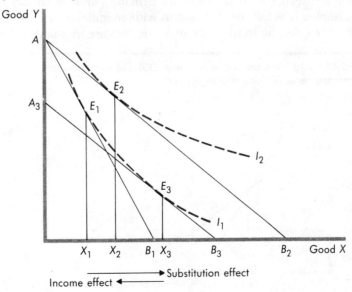

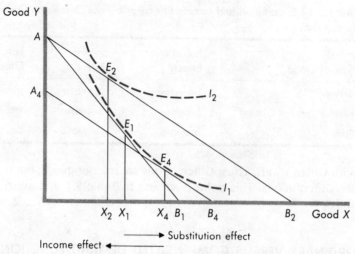

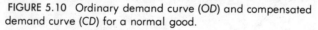

FIGURE 5.9 Income and substitution effects for a Giffen good (negative income effect dominates positive substitution effect).

Since there are two ways of compensating the consumer, the Hicksian method and the Slutsky method, we have two definitions of compensated demand curves. Recall that, in the Hicksian method, consumers are compensated (or taxed) to keep them on the initial indifference curve. In the Slutsky method, consumers are compensated (or taxed) to enable them to buy the original bundle of the goods X and Y.

The main difference between the ordinary demand and the compensated demand curve is that the ordinary demand curve can have an upward slope (as in the case of Giffen goods) but the compensated demand curve will always be downward sloping. Furthermore, for a normal good, the compensated demand curve will be steeper than the ordinary demand curve as shown in Figure 5.10. The reasoning is as follows: Let us start with an initial price P_0 and quantity demanded X_0. For a decline in the price of X, the increase in quantity demanded is higher if

FIGURE 5.10 Ordinary demand curve (OD) and compensated demand curve (CD) for a normal good.

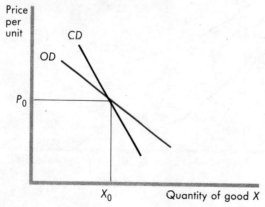

we consider both the income and substitution effects than if we consider the substitution effect alone. Thus, the *CD* curve will be to the left of the *OD* curve. Conversely, for an increase in price, the decrease in quantity demanded is higher if we consider both the substitution and income effects (they are both decreases) than when we consider substitution effects alone. Thus, *CD* will be to the right of *OD*. The *CD* curve is, therefore, steeper than the *OD* curve.

For an inferior good, the substitution and income effects have opposite signs. Hence, we get the *CD* and *OD* curves as shown in Figure 5.11(*a*). Also Figure 5.11(*b*) shows the *CD* and *OD* curves for a Giffen good. Since the reasoning is clear from Table 5.1, we will not elaborate on it here.

5.7 APPLICATIONS TO LABOR SUPPLY

The decomposition of the effects of a change in price into income and substitution effects has interesting applications in the theory of labor supply and in the analysis of different government policies on work effect. We will now discuss these applications. In the next section, we will discuss some applications of this theory in other areas.

5.7.1 Labor-leisure choice and backward-bending supply

There are some people with philanthropic motives who work for pleasure and not money. However, workers usually work for money and prefer to have leisure too. Thus, both income and leisure are "goods." As with any two goods we can draw the indifference curves between income and leisure. These are shown in Figure 5.12.

To find the equilibrium for the worker, we have to draw the budget line. The budget line will depend on the wage rate. If the wage rate is $3 per hour, the maximum income per day is $72. If the wage rate is $4 per hour, the maximum income per day is $96, and so on. Figure 5.13 shows the amount of leisure per

FIGURE 5.11 Ordinary and compensated demand curves for (non-Giffen) inferior goods and for Giffen goods.

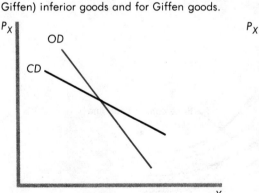

(a) Non-Giffen inferior goods.

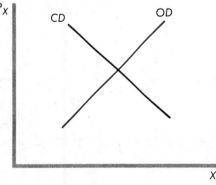

(b) Giffen Goods.

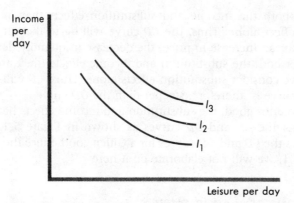

FIGURE 5.12   Indifference curves for income and leisure.

day demanded at different wage rates. Subtracting from 24 we get the number of hours of labor supplied per day at different wage rates. The supply curve is shown in Figure 5.14. Note that it is upward sloping for a while and then backward bending.

As we did in the theory of consumer behavior (Section 5.4), we can separate the effect of a change in the wage rate on the demand for leisure into a substitution effect and an income effect. Figure 5.15 shows this. Note that income effect and substitution effect work in opposite directions. As the wage rate goes up, the price of leisure increases and the worker reduces hours of leisure, thus increasing hours worked. This is the substitution effect. However, the increased income will make the worker demand more hours of leisure, since leisure is a normal good. This is the income effect. At low wage rates, the substitution effect dominates the income effect, and we get an upward-sloping supply curve for labor. But at high wage rates the income effect is larger than the substitution effect, and we get a backward-bending supply curve.

The backward-bending supply curve is not necessarily observed all the time

FIGURE 5.13   Determination of hours of leisure at different wage rates.

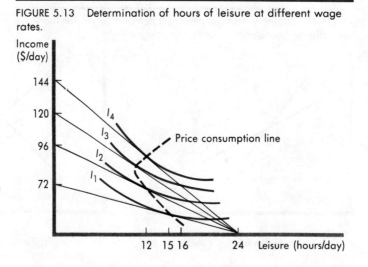

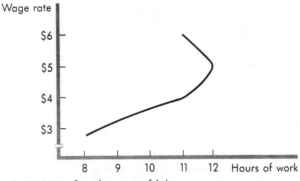

FIGURE 5.14   Supply curve of labor.

but there is substantial empirical evidence in its favor. Lucia Dunn[8] surveyed low-income textile workers in the southeastern United States. She found that workers would decrease their hours of work if the wage rate was raised from the current $2 per hour (1979) and increase their hours of work if the wage rate was reduced. The supply curve of labor is shown in Figure 5.16.

The phenomenon of the backward-bending supply curve for labor was also verified in experiments with rats and pigeons.[9] The animals were required to push levers a certain number of times to get a unit of food. The wage rate was changed by changing the number of times the lever had to be pushed. As this number was decreased, beyond a point the animals reduced the quantity of labor supplied as depicted in Figure 5.14.

5.7.2 Effects of welfare programs and negative income tax on work effort

Many welfare programs such as Food Stamps, Medicaid, local housing assistance, and AFDC (Aid to Families with Dependent Children) are intended to assist the

[8]Lucia Dunn, "Measurement of Internal Income-Leisure Trade-Offs," *The Quarterly Journal of Economics*, August 1979, pp. 373–393.

[9]Tom Alexander, "Economics According to the Rats," *Fortune*, December 1, 1980, pp. 127–132.

FIGURE 5.15   Income and substitution effects of changes in wage rates.

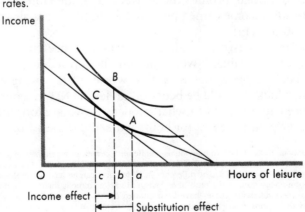

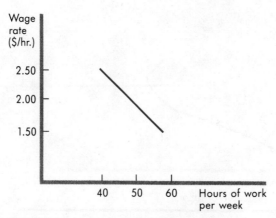

FIGURE 5.16   A backward-bending supply curve.

low-income population. However, many of these benefits are reduced dollar for dollar (and sometimes even more!) with an increase in the recipient's income. For instance, if a family member takes a part-time job, not only will AFDC payments be reduced but the housing assistance will as well. Thus, these programs may have a negative effect on work effort.

The welfare programs also suffer from other defects such as the disparity in payments to equally needy families because of differences in state laws, eligibility requirements, and so on. To solve these problems and eliminate the negative effect on work effort, one proposal that has been often made is the negative income tax (NIT). There are several versions of the NIT proposal. One version is to replace all existing welfare programs (except Medicaid) with a guaranteed minimum-income level (dependent on family size) and tax any earnings at the rate of 50 percent. The family can, at any time, opt to withdraw from the program. We can analyze the effects of NIT on work effort in a figure similar to Figure 5.13 except that the budget line under the NIT program will be different. The analysis is presented in Figure 5.17.

In Figure 5.17 *AB* is the budget line if the family is not in the NIT program. If the family is in the NIT program, it receives a guaranteed income of *BD* but only 50 percent of earned income. The budget line is, therefore, *CD*, which has a lower slope than *AB* (income earned by those not in the NIT is also taxed but at a lower rate than 50 percent).

Now consider two individuals with indifference curves given by I_1 and I_2, respectively.[10] Individual 2 would not find it worthwhile to participate in the NIT program because he or she would be worse off (I_2' being a lower indifference curve). Individual 1 would be better off under the NIT program (attaining a higher indifference curve I_1'). As to what happens to work effort, the amount of leisure for the participant increases (or hours worked declines) from what it would have

[10]These are only portions of the two individuals' indifference curves. Completeness of preferences requires that every commodity combination lie on some indifference curve for both individuals. For example, point E lies on some indifference curve for individual 1. The difference in preferences can be seen in the shapes of the two sets of curves. For a given commodity bundle, the ratio of *MU* leisure to *MU* income is higher for individual 2 than for individual 1. Portions of the indifference curves have been omitted merely for simplicity, since they are not needed for this analysis. Only the regions where tangencies occur are illustrated.

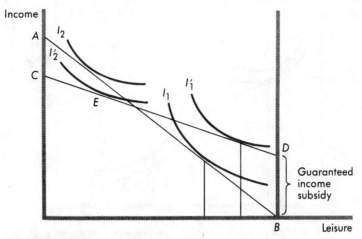

FIGURE 5.17 Effects of negative income tax on work effort.

been in the absence of any income assistance program. However, with the NIT program, the individual has a work incentive, and hours worked would not be 0 as in the case of the current welfare programs. Under the current welfare programs, since welfare payments go down dollar for dollar (in effect a 100 percent tax rate on earned income) the budget line would be essentially horizontal, and the optimal solution would be at the corner point D.

One can easily demonstrate that with a sufficiently high wage rate even individual 1 will find it worthwhile to leave the NIT program. We can show this by drawing the budget line AB steeper. We leave this as an exercise.

5.7.3 Effects of progressive income tax on work effort

In almost every country, the income tax is progressive. In other words, as income rises, a greater proportion of it is taken away as tax. It is easy to see, even by commonsense reasoning, that this discourages work effort because the worker gets a reduced share of the additional income at higher levels of work effort.

One can clearly argue that if we want to improve work effort then all income taxes should be eliminated. We will, however, address a different question. The question is "What is the effect of a proportional income tax on work effort as compared to that of a progressive income tax?" The answer to this question is not clear. In Figure 5.18 we show indifference curves for two types of workers: worker 1, who consumes a lot of leisure (indifference curves I_1 and I_1'), and worker 2, who works lots of hours (indifference curves I_2 and I_2').[11] The straight line A_1B is the budget line with a proportional income tax (everyone pays the same rate). The curved line A_2B is the budget line with a progressive income tax. They are drawn to cross each other because we are assuming that the government wants to collect the same tax revenue in both cases. Thus, the tax rate is higher (and, hence, income received is lower) at lower incomes with a proportional tax rate.

[11] Again we have illustrated only the relevant portion of the indifference curves.

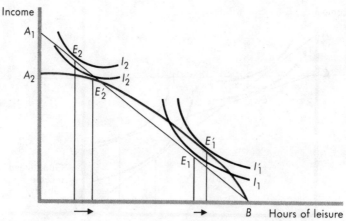

FIGURE 5.18   Comparative effect of a progressive income tax and proportional income tax on work effort.

With a proportional tax rate, worker 1 is at the point E_1 on indifference curve I_1, and worker 2 is at the point E_2 on indifference curve I_2. When the tax is changed to a progressive income tax, worker 1 moves to point E_1' on a higher indifference curve I_1', and consumption of leisure goes up so that work effort goes down. Worker 2 moves to the point E_2' on a lower indifference curve I_2', but this worker also increases consumption of leisure and so reduces work effort. Thus, both the workers reduce work effort except that worker 1 is better off and worker 2 is worse off with the progressive income tax.

It is possible to draw a set of indifference curves between the points E_1 and E_2 in Figure 5.18 where a worker moves to a higher indifference curve and, thus, is better off under a progressive income tax but also reduces consumption of leisure and, thus, increases hours of work. We will leave this as an exercise.

The impact on the economywide work effort of a switch from a progressive to a proportional income tax is unclear. First, we do not know what flat rate would provide the government with the same amount of revenue. Furthermore, we do not know what fraction of workers would increase or decrease hours worked.

5.8   OTHER APPLICATIONS

In the previous section we considered applications of the theoretical results we derived to three problems in labor supply. More applications in this area will be found in Chapter 15. We will now consider a few applications in other areas. In these applications we will not be considering the substitution and income effects. We will simply be applying the basic principles of indifference curve analysis. The three problems we will discuss are (1) consumption over time—borrowing and lending, (2) the effect of deductibles on the demand for medical care, and (3) use of cost-of-living indexes to measure changes in welfare.

5.8.1 Consumption over time: A two-period analysis

In this example we will use indifference curves to show the consumers' choices between current and future consumption. Consumers usually do not consume all their income during the period they receive it. Sometimes they save part of it for future periods. At other times they borrow to increase current consumption and pay off these debts from future income. In general, consumers try to maximize their utility or satisfaction over a number of time periods. In our example we will consider only two time periods: current and future. This may not sound very realistic, but it captures many important aspects of *intertemporal choice* or choice over time. These problems are discussed in greater detail in Chapter 20.

Consider a consumer with current income y_0 and future income y_1. We will denote current consumption by c_0 and future consumption by c_1. If the consumer does no saving or borrowing, we have

$$c_0 = y_0 \quad \text{and} \quad c_1 = y_1$$

Suppose, for simplicity, that the consumer can borrow or save at an interest rate r, so that \$1 today is the same as $(1 + r)$ dollars next period. Thus, borrowing on future income y_1 will enable the consumer to get a maximum loan of $y_1/(1 + r)$ this period. So, the consumer's total wealth in the current period, which we will denote by w_0, is given by $w_0 = y_0 + y_1/(1 + r)$. This is the maximum amount of consumption the consumer can afford during the current period. Similarly, the consumer can save the entire income y_0 for the next period and get $y_0(1 + r)$. The consumer's maximum wealth in the next period is $w_1 = y_0(1 + r) + y_1$. This is the maximum amount of consumption the consumer can afford during the next period. [Note that $w_1 = (1 + r)w_0$.]

There are, in essence, two goods we are considering: current consumption and future consumption. Since we know the maximum amounts of these two goods that the consumer can afford, we can draw the budget line. This is shown in Figure 5.19. The slope of the budget line is $-(1 + r)$. We can also interpret this in terms

FIGURE 5.19   Budget line for current and future consumption.

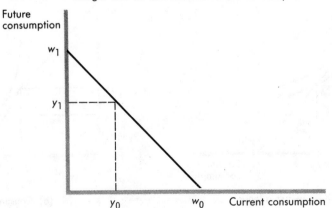

of the "prices" of current and future consumption. If the prices of current and future consumption are denoted respectively by p_0 and p_1, then, from our discussion (in Chapter 4, Section 4.6) we have:

$$\frac{p_0}{p_1} = (1 + r)$$

This relationship is just an alternative statement of the result that \$1 saved today gives us $(1 + r)$ dollars the next period.

To derive the consumer's equilibrium we now have to consider the point of tangency between the consumer's indifference curves and the budget line. This determines whether the consumer would be a lender (saver) or a borrower. The two cases are shown in Figures 5.20(a) and 5.20(b). Without any borrowing or lending the consumer's equilibrium would be at A. In Figure 5.20(a) the shape of the indifference curves is such that the tangency point is at C, which gives $c_1 > y_1$ and $c_0 < y_0$. Thus, the consumer would be saving current income to increase future consumption. In Figure 5.20(b) the shape of the indifference curves is such that the point of tangency indicates that $c_0 > y_0$ and $c_1 < y_1$. This consumer would be borrowing to increase current consumption over current income.

One can also show a case where the point of tangency is at the point A, in which case the consumer would be neither borrowing nor saving. We saw earlier in Chapter 4 (Section 4.5) that at the point of tangency, the slope of the indifference curve (in absolute value) is equal to the ratio of the marginal utilities of c_0 and c_1. Hence, we have the relationship, in equilibrium,

$$\frac{\text{Marginal utility of } c_0}{\text{Marginal utility of } c_1} = (1 + r)$$

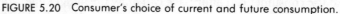

FIGURE 5.20   Consumer's choice of current and future consumption.

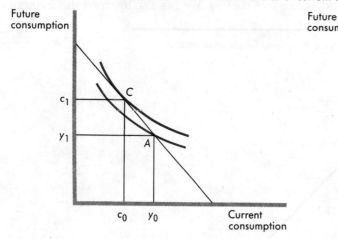

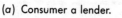

(a) Consumer a lender.

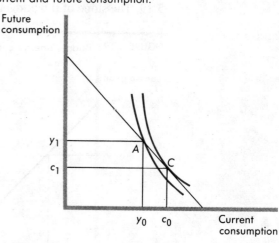

(b) Consumer a borrower.

We have illustrated the use of indifference curves in deriving the consumer's choice between current and future consumption. Further analysis of this problem can be found in Chapter 20.

5.8.2 Deductibles and the demand for medical care

With almost all health insurance plans, the patient pays the first $100 or $200 (called the "deductible") of the annual total cost of health services. Over and above that, the insurance company picks up all the expenses or a high proportion (say 80 percent) of the expenses. This arrangement produces a kink in the budget line. The absolute slope of the budget line is the market price of medical services until the deductible is reached. After that the slope is a fraction of the market price of medical services. We showed such a kinked budget line in Figure 4.12. The point B is where the deductible is reached and the slope of the budget line changes. The budget line is ABC. After the deductible is reached, if the insurance company pays all the expenses, the budget line would be horizontal beyond B. However, even if the insurance company pays all the expenses, some time costs are involved in transportation or waiting for the doctor and some psychic costs are involved, and, hence, it is not true that the individual pays no cost. Thus, we can argue that the budget line would look more like the kinked line in Figure 4.12 in Chapter 4.

To derive the consumer's equilibrium we need the indifference curves. The indifference curves, however, depend on the health of the individual. Figure 5.21 shows indifference curves of healthy and sick individuals. For the same individual, depending on the health status, the indifference curve may shift.

Now we are ready to study the equilibrium of the consumer. This is shown in Figures 5.22 and 5.23. In Figure 5.22 we show the situation with a healthy individual. There are two points of tangency: A and B. However, point A is on the higher indifference curve. Hence, the amount of health care demanded is OC. In Figure 5.23 we show the situation for a sick individual. Again, there are two points of tangency: A and B. However, point B is on the higher indifference curve. The

FIGURE 5.21   Indifference curves for healthy and sick individuals.

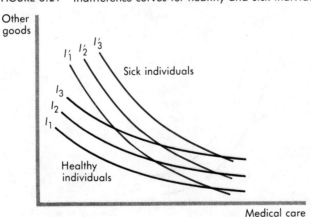

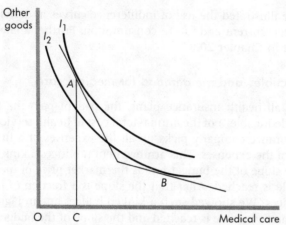

FIGURE 5.22   Effect of deductibles on demand for medical care:
Healthy individuals.

quantity of health care demanded is *OD*, which is much higher than *OC*. The
example illustrates multiple equilibria with kinky budget lines.

5.8.3 Cost-of-living indexes

One important use of indifference curve analysis is in the inferences we can make
regarding cost-of-living indexes. We will first explain the reasoning behind the
construction of two different cost-of-living indexes—the *Laspayre index* and the
Paasche index, and we will then illustrate the reasoning in terms of indifference
curves.

Index numbers are used to measure how much something has changed from
one time to another. Suppose the price of gasoline in 1981 was $1.32 a gallon and

FIGURE 5.23   Effect of deductibles on demand for medical care:
Sick individuals.

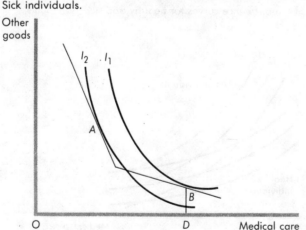

in 1980 it was $1.20 a gallon. Then the price index of gasoline in 1981 relative to the base year 1980 is $(1.32)/(1.20) \times 100 = 110$. This means that the price of gasoline has risen 10 percent. Note that the index is always for a certain year relative to the corresponding value for a *base year*. By taking the base year as a year of very low prices, we can show how prices have risen, and by taking the base year as one of high prices we can show how prices have fallen.

We can compute such price indexes for a great many commodities. But if we are considering an overall index such as the cost-of-living index or the wholesale price index, we have to find a way of weighing each of these component commodities.

Suppose that we have the following situation:

- Food costs went up 10 percent.
- Gasoline costs went down 10 percent.
- Cost of recreation went down 15 percent.
- Housing costs went up 5 percent.

From these data, can we compute by what percentage living costs went up? We could just average these $(+10, -10, -15, +5)$ and get a *decrease* of 2.5 percent. This is not correct, however, because the proportion of income spent on these items is different. A proper procedure is to compute a weighted average, the weights being the share of each category in total expenditure. If the fraction of income spent on food is 0.40, on gasoline is 0.10, on recreation is 0.10, and on housing is 0.40, we get the increase in cost of living as:

$$0.40(10) + 0.10(-10) + 0.10(-15) + 0.40(5)$$

which gives an *increase* of 3.5 percent.

A question arises as to what we should do if the shares of the different categories in total expenditure change over time. Suppose the share of total expenditure on food goes down from 0.40 in the base year (say 1980) to 0.35 in the current year (say 1985) and that of recreation rises from 0.10 to 0.15. What do we do?

The Laspayre index uses the base-period shares. The Paasche index uses current-year shares. In actual practice, almost all cost-of-living indexes are computed by a Laspayre formula, because data on the shares of the different categories in total expenditures come from studies of family budgets, and these are not done every year. Thus, the Laspayre index is cheaper to compute, particularly in view of the large number of commodities involved.[12]

We will illustrate the Laspayre and Paasche price indexes with reference to two commodities X and Y. The extension to the case of several commodities is straightforward, and since we want to discuss the meaning of the indexes in terms of indifference curves, we have to consider only two commodities.

[12]For instance, the *consumer price index* (CPI) constructed by the Bureau of Labor Statistics considers a "market basket" of over 400 consumption items such as meats, dairy products, residential rents, clothing, appliances, new and used cars, gasoline and oil, physicians' and dentists' services, drugs, liquor, and cigarettes.

Suppose we consider two years: year 1 (say 1980) and year 2 (say 1985). For these two years we have the following data for a representative family:

Year	Quantities	Prices	Total Expenditures	Shares of X and Y in Total Expenditures
1	X_1, Y_1	P_{1x}, P_{1y}	E_1	S_{1x}, S_{1y}
2	X_2, Y_2	P_{2x}, P_{2y}	E_2	S_{2x}, S_{2y}

Total expenditure $E_1 = X_1 P_{1x} + Y_1 P_{1y}$

Share of X in year 1 $= S_{1x} = \dfrac{X_1 P_{1x}}{E_1}$

The other quantities are defined similarly. We first consider the price changes for X and Y separately:

$I_x = \dfrac{P_{2x}}{P_{1x}}$ measures the change in the price of X

$I_y = \dfrac{P_{2y}}{P_{1y}}$ measures the change in the price of Y

These are called *price relatives* for X and Y.

To construct an overall index we have to somehow weight these price relatives. The Laspayre index L, as we said earlier, uses base-period shares:

$L = S_{1x} I_x + S_{1y} I_y$

The Paasche index P uses final-period shares as weights:

$P = S_{2x} I_x + S_{2y} I_y$

These formulas are usually written differently:

$$L = S_{1x} I_x + S_{1y} I_y$$
$$= \left(\frac{X_1 P_{1x}}{E_1} \cdot \frac{P_{2x}}{P_{1x}} \right) + \left(\frac{Y_1 P_{1y}}{E_1} \cdot \frac{P_{2y}}{P_{1y}} \right)$$
$$= \frac{X_1 P_{2x} + Y_1 P_{2y}}{E_1}$$

but

$$E_1 = X_1 P_{1x} + Y_1 P_{1y}$$

thus,

$$L = \frac{X_1 P_{2x} + Y_1 P_{2y}}{X_1 P_{1x} + Y_1 P_{1y}}$$

Similarly, we can show that

$$P = \frac{X_2 P_{2x} + Y_2 P_{2y}}{X_2 P_{1x} + Y_2 P_{1y}}$$

Thus, in the construction of the Laspayre's index we take base-period quantities and use these as weights for the respective *prices* (not price relatives). In the Paasche index we use final-period quantities as weights.[13] For example, consider the following situation:

Year	Quantities		Prices		Expenditure
	X	Y	P_x	P_y	E
1	50	100	$10	$3	$800
2	55	95	9	4	875

The Laspayre price index is

$$L = \frac{(50)(9) + (100)(4)}{(50)(10) + (100)(3)} = \frac{850}{800} = 1.0625$$

The Paasche price index is

$$P = \frac{(55)(9) + (95)(4)}{(55)(10) + (95)(3)} = \frac{875}{835} = 1.0479$$

The price index L compares the cost of obtaining the year 1 bundle of goods in the 2 years. The price index P compares the cost of obtaining the year 2 bundle of goods in the 2 years. Suppose that

$$X_1 P_{2x} + Y_1 P_{2y} < E_2 \qquad\qquad [5.1]$$

This means that cost of year 1 bundle at year 2 prices is less than year 2 expenditures. In other words, in year 2 the family could have bought the same bundle as in year 1 but chose not to do so. Thus, the family must be better off in year 2 than in year 1. Dividing both sides of equation [5.1] by E_1 we get

$$L < \frac{E_2}{E_1} \qquad\qquad [5.2]$$

---

[13]In practice, one can use any other set of quantity weights. This is, in fact, the case in the construction of the CPI. The weights are neither base-year nor final-year quantities. That is why it is called a fixed-quantity weighted index.

If this condition is satisfied, the family is better off. In our example we have $L = 1.0625$ and $E_2/E_1 = 1.094$. Thus, this condition is satisfied.

Consider another case,

$$X_2P_{1x} + Y_2P_{1y} < E_1 \qquad [5.3]$$

This means that the cost of year 2 bundle at year 1 prices is less than year 1 expenditures. Thus, the family could have bought year 2 bundle in year 1 but did not. Thus, the family was better off in year 1 than in year 2. Alternatively, the family is worse off in year 2 than in year 1.

Dividing both sides of equation [5.3] by E_2 we get

$$\frac{1}{P} < \frac{E_1}{E_2}$$

or

$$P > \frac{E_2}{E_1} \qquad [5.4]$$

Thus, if the Paasche index is $> E_2/E_1$ then the family is worse off in year 2 than in year 1. In our example this condition is not satisfied. Thus, condition [5.2] shows that the family is better off in year 2 than in year 1, and condition [5.4] shows that the family is not worse off in year 2 than in year 1. The two conditions give the same conclusions.

In our example, suppose the year 2 quantities were instead

$$X = 51, Y = 90$$

and year 2 prices were

$$P_x = 8, P_y = 6$$

Then, $E_2 = \$948$ and $E_2/E_1 = 948/800 = 1.185$. The Laspayre index is

$$L = \frac{50(8) + 100(6)}{800} = \frac{1000}{800} = 1.25$$

Thus, $L > E_2/E_1$ and condition [5.2] is not satisfied. The Paasche index is

$$P = \frac{51(8) + 90(6)}{51(10) + 90(3)} = \frac{948}{780} = 1.215$$

P is greater than E_2/E_1, and condition [5.4] is satisfied showing that the family is worse off in year 2 than in year 1.

What happens if L is greater than E_2/E_1 and P is less than E_2/E_1? In this case the first condition says that we cannot say whether the family was better off in year 2, and the second condition says that we cannot say whether the family was better off in year 1. In summary, we cannot say anything.

In our example, suppose the second-year quantities were:

$$X = 55, Y = 90 \ (P_x = 8 \text{ and } P_y = 6 \text{ in second year})$$

Now

$$E_2 = 980, E_2/E_1 = 980/800 = 1.225$$

$$L = 1000/800, P = 980/820$$

Thus, $L > E_2/E_1$ and $P < E_2/E_1$. Hence, we cannot say anything about the family's relative well-being in the 2 years.

These points can be illustrated graphically in terms of indifference curves. This is done in Figures 5.24(a) and (b). In Figure 5.24(a) the family is initially at point C_1 on indifference curve I_1. If the family is given just enough income to buy the year 1 bundle at the year 2 prices, the budget line will be the line A shown in Figure 5.24(a). This clearly enables the family to attain a higher indifference curve I_2. The situation $L < E_2/E_1$ or $E_2 > L \cdot E_1$ corresponds to a budget line higher than (and parallel to) line A. Thus, the family is definitely better off in year 2 than in year 1.

In Figure 5.24(b) we show another configuration of indifference curves. The year 2 budget line puts the family on indifference curve I_2 at the point C_2. If the family is given just enough income to buy the year 2 bundle at the year 1 prices,

FIGURE 5.24   Laspayre and Paasche indexes in terms of indifference curves.

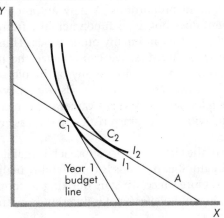

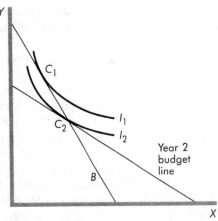

(a) Budget line A enables the family to buy year 1 bundle at year 2 prices. Family is better off in year 2.

(b) Budget line B enables the family to buy year 2 bundle at year 1 prices. Family is better off in year 1.

the budget line will be the line B shown in Figure 5.24(b). This clearly enables the family to attain a higher indifference curve I_1. The situation $P > E_2/E_1$ or $E_1 > E_2/P$ corresponds to a budget line higher than (and parallel to) line B. Thus, the family is definitely better off in year 1 than in year 2.

In actual practice, however, as we said earlier, most of the price indexes available are either Laspayre indexes or some other fixed-weight indexes. We are rarely given both the Laspayre and Paasche indexes. Thus, we are often unable to make any welfare comparisons. However, note that when some prices go up, the Laspayre index overstates the rise in the cost of living (i.e., the cost of maintaining a given level of utility), because it ignores the possibility of substitution.

5.9 A NEW APPROACH TO CONSUMER THEORY: THE DEMAND FOR CHARACTERISTICS

In the preceding discussion we have throughout considered two goods, X and Y. An alternative approach to the theory of consumer demand was pioneered by Lancaster; it argues that goods are demanded because of their characteristics and it is these characteristics that give utility.[14] Thus, we may consider three different goods: sugar, honey, and saccharine. But there may be only two characteristics: sweetness and calories. If a new sweetener is produced we analyze it, not as a new good, but as one more good that has the same characteristics. Thus, compared with the traditional analysis, the new approach has two advantages: (1) We can study the introduction of new goods and (2) we can study the effects of changes in quality.

In the traditional theory, the consumer's indifference curves are given in terms of the original set of goods, and if a new good is introduced, then we have to redefine a whole new set of indifference curves or surfaces. All the information on the preferences about the old set of goods is discarded.

Many of the so-called new goods are actually the same as the old goods with the characteristics in different proportions. A new automobile is not exactly the same as an old model but does not differ fundamentally from the old one either. Similar is the case of refrigerators and many other goods. Thus, if we consider the preferences in terms of characteristics, we can analyze the introduction of new goods very easily. We do not have to discard any of the old set of preferences.

Of course, there are always some new goods with new characteristics, for example, when a color television or a video camera and recorder are first introduced, we have a product with new characteristics. In this case we have to introduce a new set of preferences.

A major advantage of the characteristics approach is that it permits the analysis of many goods. Often the number of goods is considerably higher than the number of characteristics. Furthermore, once we start thinking in terms of characteristics, we have to consider a substitution effect that is different from the substitution effect we have considered earlier.

[14]This theory based on the demand for characteristics is discussed in: K. J. Lancaster, "Change and Innovation in the Technology of Consumption," *American Economic Review*, May 1966, pp. 14–23 and "A New Approach to Consumer Theory," *Journal of Political Economy*, 1966, pp. 132–157. The former paper is nontechnical.

For instance, suppose the consumer is interested in two characteristics: nutrition and warmth. Suppose that there are goods X_1, X_2, X_3, etc. that provide nutrition. The consumer will clearly choose the one with the lowest price per unit of nutrition. Let us say this is X_1. If the prices of these goods change and X_2 is now the one with the lowest price, an efficient consumer will substitute X_2 for X_1. Lancaster calls this the *efficiency substitution* effect. This substitution does not have anything to do with indifference curves. Similarly, if Y_1, Y_2, Y_3, etc. are goods that provide warmth, the consumer would choose the one with the lowest price per unit and will substitute some other good with the lowest price if the prices change.

The substitution and income effects we discussed still apply for a choice between the X good and Y good. But the intragroup substitution does not depend on any indifference curves.

In the above example X_1, X_2, X_3, etc. provide nutrition only and Y_1, Y_2, Y_3, etc. provide warmth only. Very often this is not the case. The characteristics are present in all the goods but in different proportions. To illustrate the analysis in this case let us consider the following example. There are two characteristics: carbohydrate denoted by C and protein denoted by P. Consider two foods with the following characteristics:

	Price
Food A: 2 units of C 0.25 units of P	$1/lb
Food B: 0.25 units of C 2 units of P	$1/lb

The budget line for a consumer with a budget of $8 is shown by the line *AB* in Figure 5.25. If the consumer spends all the money on food A, he gets 16 units of C and 2 units of P. If he spends all his income on food B he gets 2 units of C and 16 units of P. By superimposing the consumer's indifference curves, we can find the consumer's equilibrium and the amounts of the two foods A and B the consumer buys.

Suppose there is a new food D that comes on the market. It gives 3 units of C and 3 units of P per pound and costs $2 per pound. If the consumer spends all his income on the new food, he gets 12 units of C and 12 units of P. This is represented by the point D in Figure 5.25. The new budget line is now *ADB*. A consumer with indifference curves I_1, I_1' will now consume foods A and D only. A consumer with indifference curves I_2, I_2' will consume only foods B and D. Note the following points:

1. Every consumer will consume at most two foods.
2. If there is sufficient dispersion in the preferences of the consumers, we will find that all three foods are consumed.
3. Both the consumers of type 1 and type 2 are better off by the availability of food D.
4. No new good can be marketed unless it pushes the budget line of the consumer to the right.

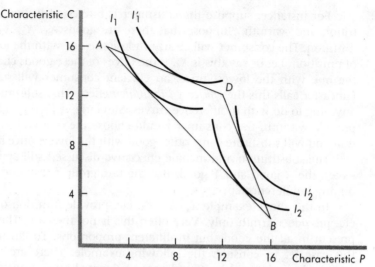

FIGURE 5.25   Analysis of consumer demand in terms of characteristics of goods.

5. The introduction of new goods with the same characteristics can be analyzed by just changing the budget line.

The important thing to note is that it is the budget line, not the indifference map, that changes with the introduction of new goods with a different proportion of the characteristics.

EXAMPLE 5.2   Will a Gasoline Tax Really Combat Air Pollution?

One interesting application of the theory that goods are demanded because of their attributes is in the study of the effects of taxes on goods. In an interesting paper, Barzel argues that since commodities as transacted are a complex combination of different attributes, the margins with respect to which optimization takes place are numerous.[15] Hence, a tax on a commodity will induce a resource reallocation not only from the taxed commodity to other commodities but also from the "quality" of the commodity, through a substitution of the taxed attribute for others.

For instance, a gasoline tax is often regarded as a good method of combatting air pollution because it would decrease gasoline consumption. However, since the tax is constant per gallon for all brands of gasoline, the high-octane gasoline will now be *relatively* cheaper (see Example 5.1) and consumers will tend to substitute high-octane gasoline for the other brands. But high-octane ratings are produced by lead, which is a major air pollutant, and the gasoline tax can even have a perverse effect of actually increasing air pollution.[16]

Other implications that Barzel derives from this theory (that taxes lead not

[15]Yoram Barzel, "An Alternative Approach to the Analysis of Taxation," *Journal of Political Economy*, December 1976, pp. 1177–1197.

[16]This argument was made by Barzel in 1976. Since then lead has been progressively eliminated. However, the argument that with a tax on a good, there would be substitution of attributes, not just goods, is the interesting point.

just to changes in quantities but also to changes in qualities of goods) are that (1) a per-unit tax will increase consumer price by more than what conventional analysis suggests and (2) an *ad valorem tax* (a tax on value such as a sales tax) will raise price by less than a comparable per-unit tax. Barzel used data on prices of cigarettes in different states for the years 1954 to 1972 to test these predictions. The state taxes on cigarettes varied considerably across states and over time. In 1972 they were 2 cents per pack in North Carolina and 21 cents in Connecticut. In 1954 they were 0 and 3 cents, respectively. New Hampshire had an ad valorem tax whereas the other states had a per-unit tax. Since the supply elasticities of cigarettes to a single state is high, a 1 cent per-unit difference in tax should lead close to a 1 cent per-unit difference in price. Barzel finds that the price differences were higher than 1 cent. Furthermore, in New Hampshire, the prices were significantly lower than in states with a similar per-unit tax. Thus, the two predictions of Barzel were confirmed in the case of cigarettes.

Although the theory is rather complex to be explained in detail here, the important points to note are

1. Each commodity is a complex combination of attributes.

2. Taxes are levied on commodities, not on attributes, but they affect various attributes differently.

3. Because consumers will substitute one attribute for another, taxes will affect not just quantities but also qualities of goods.

5.10 SUMMARY AND CONCLUSIONS

An income-consumption curve is the locus of tangencies between indifference curves and a series of parallel budget lines. An Engel curve can be derived from an income-consumption curve. It shows the quantities of a good demanded at various income levels, holding prices constant. For a normal good, the slope of the Engel curve will be positive, whereas for an inferior good the slope will be negative.

By holding the price of one good and money income constant while varying the price of another good, we can generate a set of budget lines. The locus of the tangencies between indifference curves and these budget lines is the price-consumption curve. From the price-consumption curve we can derive a demand curve.

The impact of a price change on quantity demanded can be separated into a substitution effect and an income effect. The substitution effect is the response to the change in relative prices. The income effect is the response to the change in real income.

There are two primary methods of decomposing the effect of a price change into an income effect and a substitution effect. The Hicksian method isolates the substitution effect by adjusting the consumer's money income to leave her on the same indifference curve. The Slutsky method isolates the substitution effect by adjusting the consumer's money income so that she can just afford her original consumption bundle. The Slutsky method is operational, but the Hicksian method is not. The latter, however, is theoretically the correct method.

All Giffen goods are inferior, but all inferior goods are not Giffen goods. For a Giffen good the income effect must outweigh the substitution effect. The uncompensated (or ordinary) demand curve for a Giffen good has a positive slope.

An ordinary demand curve reflects both the substitution effect and the income effect. A compensated demand curve reflects only the substitution effect.

A labor-supply curve can be derived from a price-consumption curve for leisure. The labor-supply curve is positively sloped as long as the substitution effect dominates the income effect. When the income effect becomes stronger than the substitution effect, the labor-supply curve will bend backward.

For an individual who opts to participate in a NIT program, work effort will be less than it would be in the absence of any income assistance. But work effort will be greater than it is with the current welfare system.

A worker may be better off or worse off with a progressive income tax as compared to a proportional income tax. Work effort could also be greater or smaller with a progressive income tax as compared to a proportional income tax.

The Laspayre index and the Paasche index both measure changes in the cost of living. The Laspayre index uses base-period shares of total expenditure for weighting the price changes of the various commodities. The Paasche index uses the current shares of total expenditure as weights for the various price changes. If we are given both these indexes and data on total expenditures in 2 years, we can make welfare comparisons and sometimes decide whether the consumer is better off or worse off in year 2 as compared to year 1.

The traditional theory of consumer behavior in terms of choices between goods has been extended by Lancaster to choices between characteristics. This theory enables us to study the effects of introduction of new goods as well as the effects of changes in quality.

KEY TERMS

Engel Curve	Laspayre Index	Real Income
Giffen Good	Negative Income Tax	Slutsky Method
Hicksian Method	Paasche Index	Substitution Effect
Income-Consumption Curve	Price-Consumption Curve	
Income Effect	Price Effect	

QUESTIONS

1. Explain the derivation of an Engel curve from an income-consumption curve. What does an Engel curve for an inferior good look like? Explain intuitively and graphically why both goods in a two-commodity world cannot be inferior.

2. Graphically decompose the impact of a price increase into the substitution effect and the income effect using both the Hicksian and the Slutsky methods. Assume the affected good is a normal good.

3. Repeat question 2 for an inferior good.

4. Can a good be inferior at all income levels? How would a dramatic reduction in income affect the demand for a Giffen good?

5. Graphically derive a price-consumption curve. Plot the corresponding compensated and ordinary demand curves. Use the Hicksian method in determining the compensated curve. How do these two demand curves compare? Why?

6. Using indifference curve analysis, examine the impact of a higher overtime wage rate on work effort. Consider the case of the worker who would typically work overtime without the higher wage rate as well as the worker who would not. Do your conclusions differ? Why? (Assume that leisure is a normal good.)

7. Using indifference curve analysis and a two-period framework, demonstrate how a proportional tax on interest income affects the consumer's choice between current and future consumption.

8. Explain the primary difference between the Hicksian and Slutsky methods of decomposing the substitution effect and the income effect.

9. If the demand for a product is perfectly inelastic, what does the corresponding price-consumption curve look like?

10. Suppose that the Jones family faced the following prices and purchased the corresponding quantities of the various goods listed below in 1980 and 1985.

Good	Price 1980	Quantity 1980	Price 1985	Quantity 1985
A	$ 2	20	$ 5	15
B	5	50	5	60
C	10	30	8	25
D	20	10	30	0
E	100	5	150	10

Assuming that these were the only items purchased and letting 1980 be the base year, compute both the Laspayre index and the Paasche index for 1985. Is the family better or worse off in 1985 compared to 1980? Why?

11. "I can't understand people who will fork over $5 or $10 to see a first-run movie when they can see it for about half that price a few months later, or see it on VCR much cheaper a year later, or even watch it on TV for free a few years later." Explain this using the theory of consumption choices over time.

12. "A main argument against the income tax is the way it affects incentives to work. Just what those effects are is controversial, because raising taxes may encourage people to work more rather than less to maintain their living standards. At some point, however, high taxes become demoralizing; people emigrate, or fiddle with their taxes, or decide that extra work is simply not worth the effort." Justify this statement.

13. Consider the following two housing schemes to help poor families to obtain better housing: (1) a cash-grant scheme and (2) a rent-subsidy program in which recipients locate and choose their own housing in the commercial market and the federal government pays 50 percent of the rental price. Draw indifference curves and budget line with income measured on the vertical axis and quantity of housing measured on the horizontal axis. Answer the following questions:

a. What is the economic interpretation of the slope of the budget line?

b. Show on the diagram the effect of a 50 percent rent subsidy. If the new quantity of housing purchased is H, how much would it have cost the individual to purchase H amount of housing without the rent subsidy? What is the amount of rent subsidy being paid for H?

c. Show on the diagram how much cash the government would have to give a recipient if he or she is to be made as well off as under the rent subsidy.

d. What is the amount of cash that the government would have to provide to the recipient to enable her or him to buy a quantity of housing H at market prices?

e. Using the results from a to d, compare the cost of providing H amount of housing under the two schemes. Present the results in a table as follows:

	Rent Subsidy	Cash Grant
Government cost		
Recipient cost		
Total cost		

f. Prepare a similar table for the case where the recipient is on the same indifference curve under both schemes (question c). Note that in this case the amount of housing purchased is different under the two schemes.

14. Suppose that the Congress passes a 10-cent per-gallon gasoline tax. Would this tend to increase or decrease the equilibrium *quality* of gasoline?

THEORY OF PRODUCTION

6.1   INTRODUCTION

In the previous two chapters we presented the theory of consumer behavior. This theory underlies the derivation of demand curves. We will now turn our attention to the supply side. On the supply side, things are a bit more complicated. We must consider several factors:

> *1. Theory of production:* How factors of production are combined to produce the outputs or commodities
> *2. The cost of production:* How the cost of production is determined
> *3. Theory of the firm:* How production is organized

The supply of different goods and services depends on all these factors.

In this chapter we will discuss the theory of production, and in Chapter 7 we will discuss the cost of production. Actually, the two are very interrelated and are really like two sides of the same coin. We are discussing them in separate chapters only because a single chapter would be very lengthy. Finally, in Chapter 8, we will discuss alternative models of the firm or how production is organized.

In the last chapter we assumed that the consumer had no control over the prices of the various commodities. Similarly, we will now assume that the firm has no control over the price of its output or the prices of its inputs.

These assumptions are only a matter of convenience. We just want to go step by step. The problem of pricing of output is discussed later in Chapters 10 to 14, and the problem of pricing of inputs is discussed in Chapters 15 to 17.

6.2   TECHNOLOGICAL RELATIONSHIP BETWEEN
OUTPUTS AND INPUTS

Suppose we want to produce oranges. We need land, fertilizer, water, workers, and some machinery. These are called *inputs* or *factors of production.* The output is oranges.

In general, a given output can be produced with many different combinations of inputs. A *production function* is a statement of the functional relationship between inputs and outputs. It shows the maximum output that can be produced from given inputs. It is a *technological relationship* and summarizes the latest technology for producing the output.

In abstract terms it is written as

$$Q = f(x_1, x_2, \ldots, x_r)$$

where Q is the maximum quantity of output and $x_1, x_2, \ldots, x_r$ are the quantities of the various inputs. If there are only two inputs, labor L and capital K, we write

$$Q = f(L, K)$$

Not all firms will be producing the maximum output Q that is possible from given inputs L and K at any point in time. There are two main reasons for this:

1. Some firms may be inefficient. We will discuss the problem of efficiency later in Chapter 9 (Section 9.3).

2. Different firms have machines and equipment of different vintages. Not everyone will utilize the latest technology.

Thus, the more efficient firms and those using the latest technology will be producing more output than other firms even for the same levels of measured inputs.

In view of these problems we cannot talk of a single production function for all firms. However, we need not worry about this complication here. We will assume that we are considering a typical firm and we want to study the relationship between its output and inputs. Also, we are talking of a *given state of technology*.

To fix these ideas, we will first consider a production process with a single variable input and then consider two inputs and substitution between inputs.

6.3 PRODUCTION WITH A SINGLE VARIABLE INPUT: TOTAL, AVERAGE, AND MARGINAL PRODUCTS

Let us say that in the example of production of oranges, we have land, fertilizer, water, machinery, etc., all fixed at certain quantities. The only input we can adjust is labor. Thus, labor is our only variable input. If labor input (measured in, say, worker-days) is 0, the output of oranges is, of course, 0. As we increase the labor input, we will increase the output of oranges. But a point will come where increasing labor will not increase the output of oranges at all and, in fact, might even decrease it. For example, in a very small orange grove where 10 workers can harvest the whole crop, if we employ a hundred workers, they will crowd the farm and they might even eat all the oranges!

As we did in the case of the individual consumer where we prepared a table of total utility and marginal utility (Table 4.1 in Chapter 4), we can prepare a hypothetical table of input and output for the producer of oranges. There is, however, one major difference. Output or product is measurable, whereas utility is really measurable only on an ordinal scale.

Total, marginal, and average products
Consider the data in Table 6.1, which gives the total output of oranges for different quantities of labor. Total output is usually called *total product* by economists and is denoted by *TP*. From this data we can derive the *marginal product MP*, which is the increase in total product due to a one-unit increase in labor or $\Delta TP/\Delta L$. We can also calculate average product which is simply output per unit of labor or *TP/L*.

Looking at the *MP* values, we see that initially *MP* is increasing. The second and third worker add more to output than the worker before them. This is intuitively plausible. With only one unit of labor, that worker must do everything. With more workers, they can divide the work and specialize, thus increasing productivity for each worker.

TABLE 6.1 Total Product, Marginal Product, and Average Product for Different Levels of Input (Labor)

Units of Input L	Total Product TP	Marginal Product MP	Average Product AP
1	100	100	100
2	220	120	110
3	360	140	120
4	460	100	115
5	530	70	106
6	570	40	95
7	595	25	85
8	600	5	75
9	594	−6	66
10	560	−34	56

Eventually, though, *MP* begins to decline. This is what is known as the *law of diminishing marginal productivity*. It is also sometimes called the *law of diminishing returns*. Formally, the law of diminishing returns states: Holding technology and the quantities of all other inputs constant, as equal increments of the variable input are employed, a point will eventually be reached where the increments to output begin to decline.

In the example in Table 6.1 there are increasing returns to labor for the first three units of labor employed. The law of diminishing returns sets in with the fourth worker. In some cases we might have constant returns to labor in between. The law of diminishing returns is also intuitively reasonable. Remember that capital, land, and so on are fixed. Eventually, additional workers will not have a tractor, shovel, or ladder to use. Hence, they will add less to output than earlier workers who had access to ample quantities of the other inputs.

Returning to our example, we see that *MP* becomes negative with the addition of the ninth worker. This point should not be confused with the point of diminishing returns. As we shall see, it is unlikely that firms would ever hire a unit of labor with a negative *MP*.

We will now examine some relationships between total product *TP*, average product *AP*, and marginal product *MP*.

Relationship between the MP and TP curves

MP is equal to $\Delta TP/\Delta L$. So graphically it is the slope of the *TP* curve.

   1. If $MP > 0$, *TP* will be rising as *L* increases. (The additional labor adds something to output.)

   2. If $MP = 0$, *TP* will be constant as *L* increases. (The additional labor does not affect output.)

3. If $MP < 0$, TP will be falling as L increases. (The additional labor actually reduces output.)

The law of diminishing returns refers to the decrease of MP—not its sign. What it says is that MP may rise or stay constant for a time, but as we keep increasing the units of the variable input, MP should start falling. It can keep falling and turn negative, or it can stay positive all the time.

Figure 6.1 shows TP curves where the slope is positive, so that $MP > 0$. In the first case the slope is increasing, whereas in the second it is decreasing. In both cases TP is increasing with an increase in the labor input. But in Figure 6.1(a) TP is increasing at an increasing rate (slope at B is higher than slope at A), and in Figure 6.1(b) TP is increasing at a decreasing rate (slope at B is lower than slope at A). So, although in both cases $MP > 0$, MP is increasing in Figure 6.1(a) but decreasing in Figure 6.1(b).

The total product curve reaches a maximum when $MP = 0$ and then starts declining when $MP < 0$.

In Figure 6.2 we show a typical curve that exhibits all these characteristics:

1. $MP > 0$ and increasing (from 0 to A)
2. $MP > 0$ but decreasing (from A to C)
3. $MP = 0$ at the point C
4. $MP < 0$ after the point C

The point A where MP stops increasing and starts decreasing is called an *inflection point* because the curvature of the TP curve changes at this point. It is here that diminishing returns set in.

The AP curve and its relationship to the MP and TP curves
The average product at each point on the TP curve is given by the slope of the line joining this point to the origin. This is illustrated in Figure 6.3(a). Consider the point A on the TP curve. Average product is output/labor input $= AB/OB =$ slope of the line OA.

FIGURE 6.1 Two cases of increasing total product.

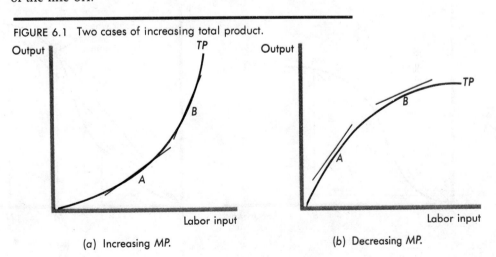

(a) Increasing MP.   (b) Decreasing MP.

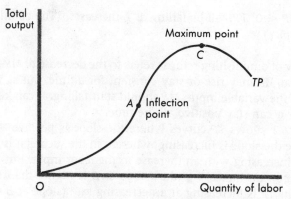

FIGURE 6.2 A typical total product curve.

We can graphically examine what happens to AP as we alter the labor input. This is illustrated in Figure 6.3(b). As we increase labor from 0 units to J units to K units and to M units, we see that lines from the origin to the corresponding points on the TP curve become steeper, that is, AP is increasing. For points on the TP curve beyond G, lines from the origin become successively flatter. So beyond M units of labor, AP is decreasing. Now if AP is increasing to the left of G and decreasing to the right of G, AP must reach its maximum at M units of labor corresponding to point G on the TP curve. G is the point where a line from the origin is just tangent to the TP curve. So AP is maximized at a quantity corresponding to the point of tangency between the TP curve and a line from the origin.

We also know that $MP = AP$ at the quantity of labor where AP is maximized. So in Figure 6.3(b), $AP = MP$ at M units of labor. How do we know this? MP is the slope of the TP curve, which, at a point, is the same as the slope of the tangent to the TP curve. At point G, the tangent line is also the line from the origin. So

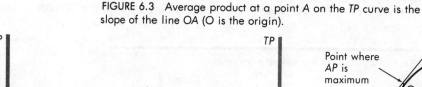

FIGURE 6.3 Average product at a point A on the TP curve is the slope of the line OA (O is the origin).

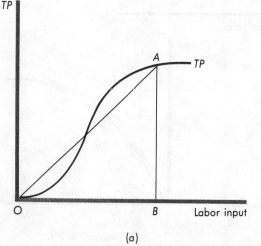

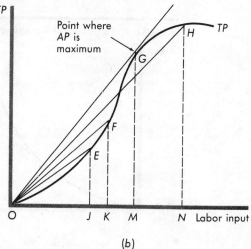

(a)

(b)

the slope of the tangent line (or MP) equals the slope of the line from the origin (or AP).

This result is also easy to see noting that if and only if $MP > AP$, AP will be rising as L increases and if and only if $MP < AP$, AP will be falling as L increases.[1] Thus, $MP = AP$ when AP is at a maximum.[2]

The three stages of production

Based on the behavior of MP and AP, economists have classified production into three stages:

Stage I: $MP > 0$, AP rising. Thus, $MP > AP$.

Stage II: $MP > 0$, but AP is falling. $MP < AP$ but TP is increasing (because $MP > 0$).

Stage III: $MP < 0$. In this case TP is falling.

No profit-maximizing producer would produce in Stages I or III. In Stage I by adding one more unit of labor, the producer can increase the average productivity of all the units. Thus, it would be unwise on the part of the producer to stop production in this stage. As for Stage III, it does not pay the producer to be in this region because by reducing the labor input she can increase total output and save the cost of a unit of labor.

Thus, the economically meaningful range is just that given by Stage II. All these results are shown in Figure 6.4. At the point of inflection A, we saw earlier that MP is maximized. At the point B, since AP is maximized, we have $AP = MP$. At the point C, total product reaches a maximum. Thus, $MP = 0$ at this point. The student should note that the relationships we have discussed do not hold exactly for the illustrative example in Table 6.1. For instance, TP is maximum when labor input is 8 units. However, at this point MP is not 0. It is 5. Similarly, AP is maximized for 3 units of labor. But at this point $AP \neq MP$.

These discrepancies result because the input increments are discrete. But the curves we have drawn are continuous. If we can vary the labor input in finer intervals (instead of worker-days, say, worker-hours or worker-minutes) and observe output in finer intervals, then the relationships we have talked about will hold true. As it stands, the TP, MP, and AP curves for the data in Table 6.1 are like steps and not continuous curves. Note, however, that even with discrete data, when AP is rising, $MP > AP$, and when AP is falling, $MP < AP$.

Another useful relationship is that TP is the area under the MP curve.[3] This is

---

[1] These relationships hold for all averages and marginals and should be intuitively plausible. Suppose that average height of students in a classroom is 5 feet 9 inches. Another student enters. If average height increases, what do we know about the height of the marginal student? Clearly, it is higher than the average.

Mathematically, $MP = \Delta TP/\Delta L$. But $TP = AP \cdot L$, and substituting yields $MP = \Delta(AP \cdot L)/\Delta L = \Delta L \cdot AP/\Delta L + L \cdot \Delta AP/\Delta L = AP + L \cdot \Delta AP/\Delta L$. Since AP and L are always positive, $MP > AP$ if and only if $\Delta AP/\Delta L > 0$. But the condition $\Delta AP/\Delta L > 0$ is merely a restatement of the requirement that AP increases with increases in L. Similarly, $MP < AP$ if and only if $\Delta AP/\Delta L < 0$.

[2] At maximum AP, the AP switches from increasing with increases in L to decreasing with increases in L. Thus the MP must switch from being greater than AP to being less than AP. So at the point of maximum AP, the two must be equal.

Mathematically, at maximum AP, $\Delta AP/\Delta L = 0$. Thus from note 1 we know that $MP = AP$.

[3] $MP = dTP/dL$, so TP is the integral of MP.

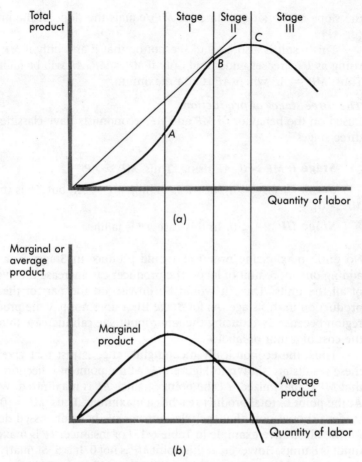

FIGURE 6.4 Relationship between *TP*, *MP*, and *AP* curves and the three stages of production.

shown in Figure 6.5. If we take a small change ΔL in labor input, then $MP \cdot \Delta L$ is the shaded area of the thin rectangle. But $MP = \Delta TP/\Delta L$, and multiplying both sides by ΔL, we see that this area is also ΔTP or the change in output. Adding all these rectangular areas we get the area under the *MP* curve. But this is equivalent to adding the small changes in total output. This addition gives us the total product.

To find the total product when using an amount of labor input equal to L^*, we just take the whole area under the *MP* curve from the origin up to the point $L = L^*$.

EXAMPLE 6.1   The Nobel Prize in Economics in 1979

In 1979 the Nobel prize in economics was shared by Professor T. W. Schultz of the University of Chicago and Professor (Sir) Arthur Lewis (a British citizen) of Princeton University. The interesting fact about these two economists is that Professor Lewis is famous for his theory of surplus labor, which essentially argues that the marginal product of labor in the agricultural sector in the less developed coun-

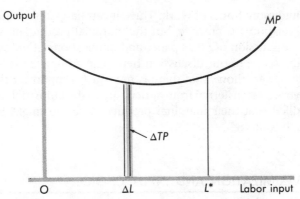

FIGURE 6.5 Total product is the area under the *MP* curve.

tries (LDCs) is 0 or even negative,[4] and Professor Schultz held exactly the opposite view—that the marginal product of labor in the agricultural sector of the LCDs is positive.[5] The theory of surplus labor argues that workers can be removed from the agricultural sector without decreasing agricultural output (because their marginal product is 0 or even negative), and these workers can be transferred to the industrial sector at very low wages and thus aid industrialization at very low cost. The emphasis in the economic development of the LDCs should, therefore, be on rapid industrialization ignoring the agricultural sector (or even taking away resources from it). This will improve the incomes of the people in the LDCs. This idea is also known as *industrial fundamentalism*.[6] The opposite view, that of *agricultural fundamentalism*, argues that the marginal product of labor in agriculture is positive, that transferring labor from there to the industrial sector will reduce agricultural output and that development of the industrial sector has not been hindered by lack of workers. In fact the major problem is finding employment for all the urban unemployed. According to this view increased agricultural production is a prerequisite to increased income and industrialization.

There is also the question of what is meant by saying that the marginal product of labor is 0. Sen distinguishes between the marginal product of a laborer in agriculture and the marginal product of a worker-hour.[7] He defines household labor L as the product of the number of working members N and the hours of work H contributed by each member. Thus $L = NH$. For output to decrease, the quantity of household labor L has to decrease after a decrease in the number of workers N. But this may not necessarily happen because the remaining workers

[4]W. A. Lewis, "Economic Development with Unlimited Supplies of Labor," *Manchester School of Economic and Social Studies*, May 1954, pp. 139–191. Also, W. A. Lewis, *The Theory of Economic Growth*, Allan & Unwin, London, 1955. This theory has also been propounded by Ragnar Nurkse, *Problems of Capital Formation in Underdeveloped Countries*, Oxford University Press, New York, 1953. Nurkse talks of "painless" or "up by the bootstraps" process of development. A more elaborate treatment of the surplus labor theory is in J. C. H. Fei and G. Ranis, *Development of the Labor Surplus Economy: Theory and Policy*, Irwin, Homewood, Ill., 1964.

[5]Schultz's views are expressed in T. W. Schultz, *Transforming Traditional Agriculture*, Yale University Press, New Haven, 1964.

[6]This view was also propounded by the Marxist economist Paul Baran. See P. H. Baran, "On the Political Economy of Backwardness," *Manchester School of Economic and Social Studies*, January 1952, pp. 66–84.

[7]A. K. Sen, "Peasants and Dualism: With or without Surplus Labor," *Journal of Political Economy*, October 1966, pp. 425–450.

can contribute more hours of work. Thus, it can happen that the marginal product of L (a worker-hour) is positive, but the marginal product of N (a worker) is 0.

Further discussion of Sen's paper and implications of the surplus labor theory is beyond the scope of our discussion here. The empirical evidence that has been gathered, however, shows that there is not much support for the theory. Furthermore, the workers transferred from agriculture to the industrial sector would usually be so unskilled that their marginal product there too might be 0 until they are given enough training.

6.4   PROFIT MAXIMIZATION AND INPUT CHOICE

Just as we said earlier, in our discussion on consumer behavior, that the consumers will maximize their utility, we will assume that producers will maximize their profit. If the input is free, then producers will increase the input until its marginal product is 0. (If TP is at a maximum, $MP = 0$.) In the case of the data with discrete jumps presented in Table 6.1, this maximum output occurs at 8 units of the labor input (just before MP turns negative).

But inputs are not free. In this case the input we are considering is labor, and the producer has to pay a price. Suppose the producer pays a price of $50 per unit of labor (worker-day). The producer hires labor, produces oranges, and sells them at a price. Let us assume that the price of a unit of output is $1. In this case the producer will keep on hiring units of labor as long as

(Price of a unit of output) $\times$ (Marginal product) $>$ (Price of a unit of labor)

The left side is the increase in revenue and the right side is the increase in cost from adding one more unit of labor. As long as the increment to revenues exceeds the increment to costs, the producer's profit will increase. As we increase the units of labor, we see that MP diminishes. We will assume that the price of output and the price of the labor input do not change. In this case, as MP declines, revenues will start falling, and a point will come when the increase in revenue equals the increase in cost. At this point the producer will stop adding any more units of input. With further addition, since MP declines, the additional revenues would be less than the added costs, and the producer's profit would decline.

Thus, profit maximization implies that a producer with no control over prices will increase the use of an input until

value of MP = price of a unit of input

But there are two complications to this rule. First, the optimal level of input usage assumes that some of the input will be employed. If the producer does not cover costs at this input usage, then the producer may produce nothing and, of course, hire no variable inputs. We will consider this possibility in future chapters.

Second, it is likely that value of MP will equal price of a unit of input at two levels of input usage. This should be clear by considering the shape of the typical

MP curve. But one of these levels of input usage will correspond to Stage I. And in this region, we said that it pays the producer to extend input usage since $MP >$ AP and so AP is rising.

In summary then, if the employer hires any of an input, he will hire until price of the input equals value of MP. Also, AP must exceed MP at optimal usage.

Let's consider some examples based on the data in Table 6.1. Since the price of a unit of input is \$1, what is shown as MP there is also the value of MP. If the price of a unit of labor is \$50, only 5 units of labor will be hired, because for the sixth unit the value of MP is \$40 but the labor cost is \$50 and thus the firm's profit falls by \$10 if the sixth unit of labor is hired.

Suppose that the price of a unit of labor is \$100, then the producer will hire 4 units of labor (not 1 unit). As we said in the previous section, the usage up to 3 units of labor input corresponds to Stage I of production. This is the usage where $MP > AP$, and it pays the producer to extend the usage of inputs.

6.5 TWO VARIABLE INPUTS: PRODUCTION ISOQUANTS AND THE ECONOMIC REGION OF PRODUCTION

We have until now analyzed a single variable factor of production: labor. Consider now the case of two variable factors of production, let us say labor and capital. The question "What is capital?" is difficult to answer (in our example it includes fertilizer as well as machinery). We will discuss this in Chapter 17. For the present capital is just another factor of production.

First, as an extension of the results for one factor of production derived in Section 6.3 earlier, we have the following results: (1) Output is maximum when marginal products of *both* labor and capital are 0. Denoting these by MP_L and MP_K, respectively, we have $MP_L = MP_K = 0$. Note that the definition of the MP of an input is essentially unchanged. MP_K is the increase in TP due to a 1-unit increase in K, holding labor constant. (2) Profit maximization implies that

Price of labor $=$ value of MP_L
Price of capital $=$ value of MP_K

Both factors will be increased to the point where the values of their marginal products are equal to their respective prices. Again, we are assuming that the producer has no control over output or input prices. As before, we have the law of diminishing marginal productivity applying to both labor and capital after a certain point.

The new things we have to add when we consider the two factors are

1. The production isoquants
2. The law of diminishing marginal rate of substitution in production
3. The effects of changes in input prices on input choice and output
4. The concept of returns to scale

These items will be discussed in order.

The production isoquants

The word "iso" is of Greek origin and means "equal" or "same." An *isoquant* is a curve along which quantity is the same. In this case, quantity refers to quantity of output or total product. With two inputs, labor and capital, the isoquant gives the different combinations of labor and capital that produce the same maximum total output.

Figure 6.6 shows two isoquants corresponding to two quantities of output Q_1 and Q_2 (we will explain soon why they are, like indifference curves, convex to the origin). The isoquants are similar to the indifference curves that we discussed in Chapter 4. Indifference curves are isoutility curves, that is, curves that show the different combinations of two goods that give the same utility. As with indifference curves, Q_2 corresponds to a higher level of output than Q_1. Also like indifference curves, isoquants corresponding to two levels of output do not intersect. We can show this as we did with indifference curves (Figure 4.4 in Chapter 4) by showing that if they intersect we have a contradiction.

The primary difference, as we mentioned earlier, between isoquants and indifference curves is that in the case of indifference curves, all we can talk about is higher or lower levels of utility. In the case of isoquants we can say *by how much* Q_2 exceeds Q_1 in Figure 6.6.

We also saw in the case of indifference curves that as more and more of a good is consumed the good may become "a bad" and the indifference curve turns backward and upward. A similar thing happens in production as well. As more and more units of an input are used, after a point the successive units will contribute negatively to production, and, hence, more of the other input would be needed to compensate for this and maintain output. Figure 6.7 shows production isoquants which are backward bending and upward sloping after a while. With more than K_2 units of capital, MP_K is negative. If we use more than K_2 units of capital, additional units of labor must also be hired to maintain constant output. Similarly, beyond L_2 units of labor, MP_L is negative.

We have said that it makes little sense to hire a unit of input whose MP is negative. Looking at the isoquant in Figure 6.7 should reinforce this idea. Both input bundle C and input bundle A produce the same total output. But input bundle C contains more capital and more labor. Input bundle C must therefore be more

FIGURE 6.6   Production isoquants.

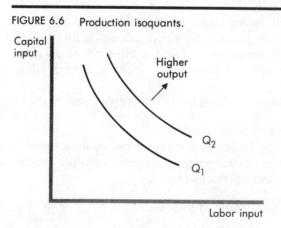

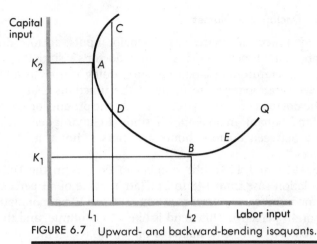

FIGURE 6.7   Upward- and backward-bending isoquants.

expensive and would not be chosen. The same argument can be made to rule out input bundle E or any other bundle lying on a portion of the isoquant where the slope is positive. Only the negatively sloped segment of the isoquant (AB) is economically feasible.

The economic region of production

In Figure 6.7 we saw that the segment AB is the economically feasible portion of the isoquant for Q. If we consider such feasible portions of all the isoquants, then the region comprised of these portions is called the *economic region of production*. This is the region in which a producer will operate. It is illustrated in Figure 6.8. The lines OA_1A_2 and OB_1B_2 are called *ridge lines*. They give the boundary of the economic region of production. We have drawn them as straight lines, but they need not always be.[8] The region between the lines OA_1A_2 and OB_1B_2 is the economic region of production.

[8]They will be straight lines if the isoquants are radial blowups of a single isoquant.

FIGURE 6.8   Ridge lines and the economic region of production.

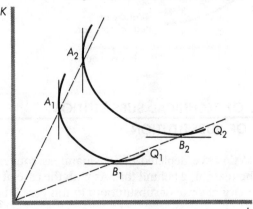

EXAMPLE 6.2   Doctors and Nurses

The production of medical services has two major inputs: doctors' time and nurses' time. There are many functions that go into a doctor's visit that a nurse can do as well. Taking temperature and blood pressure, doing urinalysis and blood count, getting the electrocardiogram are many of the functions that a nurse performs which save the doctor's time. Thus, we can show the production of medical services by a production isoquant. In an empirical study, Reinhardt demonstrates extensive substitutability between doctors' hours and nurses' hours in the production of medical services.[9]

Between 1971 and 1981, the number of doctors in the United States per 100,000 population rose from 148 to 211 (an increase of 43 percent). During the same period the numbers of nurses rose from 356 to 520 per population of 100,000 (an increase of 46 percent). This trend is likely to continue, and the nurse/doctor ratio is likely to keep rising. One main reason for this is that the federal government introduced in 1983 a "prospective payment" system for Medicare patients. It is designed to reduce health care costs. It requires hospitals to assign patients to one or more of 486 "diagnostically related groups" (DRG). Medicare then pays only a fixed amount for a particular diagnosis or DRG. Faced with a fixed payment, hospitals have tried to cut costs by limiting patient days and sending patients to home care and community clinics which make extensive use of nurses. This results in a movement from point *A* to point *B* on the production isoquant as shown in Exhibit 6.2*A*.

EXHIBIT 6.2A   A production isoquant for the production of medical services.

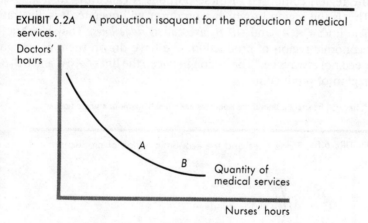

6.6   MARGINAL RATE OF TECHNICAL SUBSTITUTION
AND ELASTICITY OF SUBSTITUTION

In the preceding section we depicted the isoquants as convex to the origin. We will now explain the reasoning behind this. As with the case of indifference curves, we can define the marginal rate of substitution. In this case it is called the *marginal*

[9]U. E. Reinhardt, *Physician Productivity and the Demand for Health Manpower*, Ballinger, Cambridge, Mass., 1975.

rate of technical substitution (MRTS), since it is based on the technology of production. It is formally defined in the case of two inputs, labor and capital, as the amount of capital that can be replaced by an extra unit of labor, without affecting total output.

$$MRTS_{L \text{ for } K} = \left| \frac{\Delta K}{\Delta L} \right|$$

holding Q constant, where Q = output, ΔK is change in capital input, and ΔL is change in labor input. This is shown in Figure 6.9. Since $\Delta K/\Delta L$ is the slope of the isoquant, the $MRTS$ is given by the absolute slope to the isoquant.

There is a simple relationship between $MRTS_{L \text{ for } K}$ and the marginal products MP_L and MP_K of labor and capital, respectively. Since along an isoquant the level of output remains the same, if ΔL units of L are substituted for ΔK units of K, the increase in output due to ΔL units of L (namely, $\Delta L \cdot MP_L$) should match the decrease in output due to a decrease of ΔK units of K (namely, $\Delta K \cdot MP_K$). In other words, along an isoquant,

$$|\Delta L \cdot MP_L| = |\Delta K \cdot MP_K|$$

which is equivalent to

$$\left| \frac{\Delta K}{\Delta L} \right| = \frac{MP_L}{MP_K}$$

However, $|\Delta K/\Delta L|$ is equal to the $MRTS_{L \text{ for } K}$, and hence, we get the following expression for the marginal rate of technical substitution of L for K as the ratio of the corresponding marginal products:

$$MRTS_{L \text{ for } K} = \frac{MP_L}{MP_K}$$

FIGURE 6.9   Isoquant and the marginal rate of substitution.

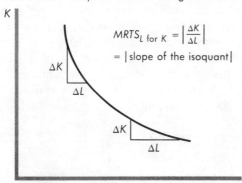

As in the theory of the consumer, we have also in the theory of the producer, the *law of diminishing marginal rate of substitution.* As we move down the isoquant, the producer has fewer units of capital and more units of labor. So the MP_L is decreasing while the MP_K is increasing. This, of course, implies that the slope of the isoquant, in absolute terms, is declining or that the isoquant is convex to the origin. An alternative explanation is similar to the one we gave for the convexity of indifference curves at the end of Section 4.5 of Chapter 4. If the isoquants were not convex but concave to the origin, then we would observe that the producer would use only one input, labor or capital, but not both. But this is contrary to our empirical observation. Since the argument is similar, we will not explain it in detail here.

Earlier we said that profit maximization implies

$$P_L = \text{value of } MP_L$$

and

$$P_K = \text{value of } MP_K$$

where P_L and P_K are the prices of a unit of labor and capital, respectively. Thus,

$$\frac{P_L}{P_K} = \frac{MP_L}{MP_K} = MRTS_{L \text{ for } K}$$

at the point of maximum profit, which is a condition similar to the one we derived in the theory of the consumer.

An alternative way of deriving this same condition is to look at the objective of the producer as one of *cost minimization.* Clearly, minimizing the cost of the chosen output level is necessary if profit is to be maximized.[10]

Given the prices P_L and P_K of the inputs labor and capital, we can draw an *isocost line* like the budget line in the theory of the consumer. The isocost line gives the combinations of L and K for which the total cost C is the same. The line's equation is given by

$$C = P_L \cdot L + P_K \cdot K$$

where L and K are the numbers of units of labor and capital, respectively.

The slope of this line is $-(P_L/P_K)$ or, if we consider it in absolute terms, P_L/P_K. A series of isocost lines is presented in Figure 6.10.

Suppose the producer wants to produce an output Q. Then by imposing the isoquant for Q on the isocost lines, we see that the minimum cost corresponds to the level of cost for which an isocost line is tangent to the isoquant, as shown in Figure 6.11. Thus, at this point, denoted by A in Figure 6.11, we have

$$\frac{P_L}{P_K} = \text{slope of the isoquant} = \frac{MP_L}{MP_K} = MRTS_{L \text{ for } K}$$

---

[10]Note that cost minimization refers to minimizing the cost of a chosen output. This is a constrained minimization. An unconstrained cost minimization would lead to the firing of all variable inputs and hence an output of 0.

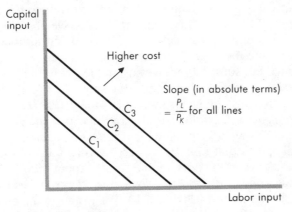

FIGURE 6.10 Isocost lines.

as derived earlier. Corresponding to A, L_1 gives the amount of labor input used and K_1 the amount of capital input used.

The elasticity of substitution

As the price ratio P_L/P_K of inputs changes, the slope of the isocost line changes, and we get a new point of tangency and a new level of input usage for labor and capital. Thus, the L/K ratio changes. If P_L/P_K rises, the isocost line is steeper and the L/K ratio falls. There is a measure of responsiveness of L/K to a change in P_L/P_K. This is called the *elasticity of substitution*. It is usually denoted by the letter σ (sigma) and is expressed in absolute terms. It is defined by

$$\sigma = \left| \frac{\text{Percent change in } L/K}{\text{Percent change in } P_L/P_K} \right|$$

holding Q constant. This concept will be useful in deriving elasticities of input demand. These are discussed in Chapter 15 and in Table 15.2, in which we present some estimates.

FIGURE 6.11 Input use under cost minimization.

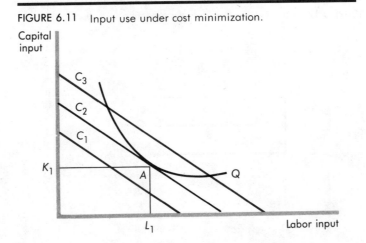

Note that we define σ holding Q constant, so we observe the changes in L/K as we change P_L/P_K for the same isoquant. That is, we observe points of tangency on a single isoquant. One can define elasticities of substitution holding different things constant, but these elasticities are of limited use.

The elasticity of substitution gives us an idea of how the shares of labor and capital in total cost behave, if input prices change. If $\sigma = 1$, the share of labor in total cost will be constant (labor's share is simply $(P_L \cdot L)/(P_L \cdot L + P_K \cdot K)$. If $\sigma > 1$ as P_L/P_K goes up, L/K declines by a greater percentage, and, hence, labor's share falls. If $\sigma < 1$ as P_L/P_K goes up, labor's share increases.

A special case is that of $\sigma = 0$ or zero elasticity of substitution. In this case whatever the change in the price ratio P_L/P_K, the input ratio L/K does not respond. This is what is known as *the case of fixed proportions*. In this case the production isoquants look like those in Figure 6.12. For instance, for producing output Q_1, the minimum quantities of the labor input and capital input needed are L_1 and K_1, respectively, but any additions of only one input, keeping the other input constant, does not increase the output at all. That is why isoquants are right angles. For the outputs Q_2 and Q_3 the situation is similar.

Similarities between consumer and producer behavior

Throughout this chapter, we have mentioned similarities between the theory of consumer behavior and the theory of producer behavior. A summary of these similarities is presented in Table 6.2.

6.7   THE EXPANSION PATH AND RETURNS TO SCALE

In Figure 6.11 we considered the optimal input combination and the minimum cost for producing an output Q. We can do this for various levels of output. Then the points of tangency give us the minimum cost and the optimal input usage for successive levels of output. The line joining these points of tangency is called the *long-run expansion path*. This is the dotted line in Figure 6.13. Note that we keep

---

FIGURE 6.12   Isoquants in the case of production with fixed

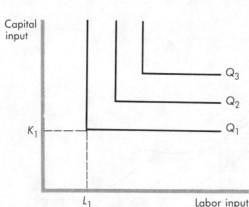

TABLE 6.2 Comparison between the Theories of the Consumer and the Producer

Theory of Consumer Behavior	Theory of Producer Behavior
1. Consumer	1. Producer
2. Goods X and Y	2. Inputs L and K
3. Tastes are represented by the utility function $U(X,Y)$	3. Technology is represented by the production function $f(L,K)$
4. MU_X and MU_Y	4. MP_L and MP_K
5. Indifference curve	5. Isoquant
6. $MRS_{X \text{ for } Y}$	6. $MRTS_{L \text{ for } K}$
7. (Absolute value of the) Slope of the indifference curve $= MRS_{X \text{ for } Y} = \|\Delta Y/\Delta X\| = MU_X/MU_Y$	7. (Absolute value of the) Slope of the isoquant $= MRTS_{L \text{ for } K} = \|\Delta K/\Delta L\| = MP_L/MP_K$
8. Consumers are price takers in the goods markets.	8. Producers are price takers in the input markets.
9. Budget line: $(P_X X) + (P_Y Y) = M$	9. Isocost line: $(P_L L) + (P_K K) = C$
10. Consumer *maximizes* the utility of a given money income.	10. Producer *minimizes* the cost of a given output.
11. At equilibrium, $MRS_{X \text{ for } Y} = P_X/P_Y = MU_X/MU_Y$	11. At equilibrium, $MRTS_{L \text{ for } K} = P_L/P_K = MP_L/MP_K$

the input price ratio P_L/P_K constant. It is only the output that is increased. Thus, the slopes of the isocost lines are all the same.

It is necessary at this time to distinguish between the *long run* and the *short run*. To economists, the long run is a period of time sufficient to alter the quantities of all inputs into the production process. Thus in the short run, some inputs are

FIGURE 6.13 The long-run and short-run expansion paths.

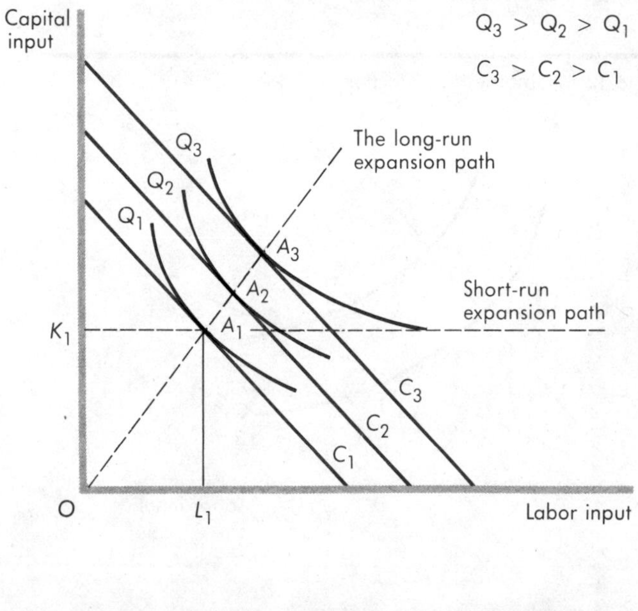

fixed in quantity. That is, the firm might be stuck with a particular capital stock or plant size in the short run, but these can be changed in the long run. The precise amount of time required for the adjustment of all input quantities will obviously depend on the nature of the product and the state of technology.

When we draw the long-run expansion path, we assume that there is enough time to adjust the quantities of all (both) inputs to the optimal levels for the given outputs. This long-run expansion path tells us how optimal input usage changes in response to a change (or expansion) in output.

In the short run, we may treat capital as fixed. In this case only the labor input can be changed. If the producer expands output from the level Q_1, assuming that the capital input is fixed at K_1, *the short-run expansion path* will be just a straight line with capital input equal to K_1.

In Figure 6.13 the long-run expansion path looks like a straight line. It need not always be. This depends on the shape of the isoquants, which depends on the form of the production function.

The long-run expansion path is a straight line if the production function is homothetic. A production function is *homothetic* if MP_L/MP_K does not change with any proportionate change in L and K. We will explain the concept of a homothetic production function in terms of two isoquants. In Figure 6.14 we have two iso-quants.[11] Draw any lines OA_1A_2 and OB_1B_2 through the origin. Then the production function is said to be homothetic if

slope of Q_1 at A_1 = slope of Q_2 at A_2

and

slope of Q_1 at B_1 = slope of Q_2 at B_2

Along OA_1A_2 or OB_1B_2, the ratio of L to K is constant so that a movement along such a ray represents a proportionate change in L and K. If the slopes of the

[11]The argument holds for any two isoquants.

FIGURE 6.14   Homothetic production functions.

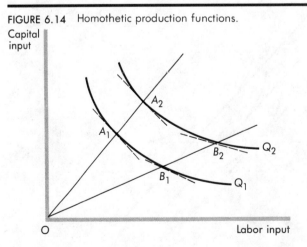

isoquants are equal along any ray, then MP_L/MP_K must not change with a proportionate change in L and K. But since the input price ratio is constant, all the isocost lines are parallel. Homotheticity now requires that all tangencies between the isocosts and isoquants lie along a single ray from the origin so that the long-run expansion path coincides with such a ray.

A special case of homothetic production function is the *homogeneous* production function. With reference to Figure 6.14, the production function is homogeneous if, in addition, $OA_2/OA_1 = OB_2/OB_1$.

Returns to scale

Another concept used in the theory of production is that of *returns to scale*. Returns to scale refer to how output responds to an equiproportionate change in all inputs. In our case, suppose labor and capital are both doubled, then if output doubles, we have *constant returns to scale*. If output less than doubles, we have *decreasing returns to scale*, and if output more than doubles, we have *increasing returns to scale*.

In the case of Figure 6.14, a proportionate change in inputs is a movement along a ray through the origin, such as a movement from OA_1 to OA_2 or from OB_1 to OB_2. The value of the proportion is OA_2/OA_1 or OB_2/OB_1. In other words, if $OA_2/OA_1 = 2$, then both inputs are doubled as we move from OA_1 to OA_2. For constant returns to scale, the change in output must be equal in proportion to the change in inputs. This requires that $Q_2/Q_1 = OA_2/OA_1$. For increasing returns $Q_2/Q_1 > OA_2/OA_1$. For decreasing returns $Q_2/Q_1 < OA_2/OA_1$.

EXAMPLE 6.3   A Cobb Douglas Function for the Production of Shakespearean Performances

One commonly used production function in applied work is the Cobb-Douglas production function suggested by Cobb and Douglas in 1928.[12] In its simplest form with output X and two inputs, labor L and capital K, it can be written as

$$X = CL^a K^b$$

(or taking logs, $\log X = \log C + a \log L + b \log K$). C is a constant that depends on the units of measurement of X, L, and K. The coefficients a and b can be interpreted as the elasticities of output with respect to the labor and capital inputs, respectively. Also $(a + b)$ measures returns to scale. For instance, suppose we double L and K. Then the new output X_1 is given by

$$X_1 = C(2L)^a(2K)^b = 2^{a+b}(CL^a K^b) = 2^{a+b} \text{ (old output)}$$

Thus, if $a + b = 1$, output is also doubled, and we have constant returns to scale. If $a + b < 1$, output is less than doubled, and we have decreasing returns to scale. If $a + b > 1$, then output more than doubles, and we have increasing returns to scale.

In 1948 Douglas[13] estimated the Cobb-Douglas production function for U.S.

---

[12]C. W. Cobb and P. H. Douglas, "A Theory of Production," *The American Economic Review*, 1928 supplement, pp. 139–165.

[13]P. H. Douglas, "Are There Laws of Production?" *The American Economic Review*, 1948, pp. 1–41.

manufacturing industries, based on time series as well as cross-section data, the former based on the period 1899 to 1922, and the latter based on a cross-section of industries (not firms) from the U.S. Census of 1919. The estimates he obtained were:

	Time series	Cross-section
a	0.73	0.76
b	0.25	0.25

In both cases $a + b \cong 1$, thus showing constant returns to scale. However, since the data referred to aggregates over industries or total manufacturing, it is questionable what "constant returns to scale" means.

Since then, a large number of studies have estimated the Cobb-Douglas function based on time series data and individual firm data in manufacturing, and based on individual farm data for agriculture.[14] However, during recent years other general functional forms are being used in empirical work.

Gapinski estimated a Cobb-Douglas production function for performances of Shakespeare by Britain's Royal Shakespeare Company from 1965 to 1980.[15] He estimates a different constant C for Stratford and Aldwych, but the same elasticities a and b for both the theaters. He gets $a = 0.62$ and $b = 0.33$. Thus $a + b = 0.95$, which is again close to 1. The measures of output and inputs were as follows:

X = output measured as paid attendance
L = labor input including services of everyone involved: designers, directors, players, program sellers, secretaries, and even carpenters
K = capital input measured by depreciation, rental, utilities, etc.

6.8   EFFECTS OF CHANGES IN INPUT PRICES ON OUTPUT

The analysis of the effects of changes in input prices on output proceeds exactly along the same lines as the analysis of effects of changes in the prices of goods in the theory of the consumer. If one of the prices, say, P_L, falls while the other price and total cost (or production budget) remain constant, then we can separate the effect of the price change into two components: (1) substitution effect—this will be a movement along the original isoquant—and (2) scale effect—this will be a movement to a higher isoquant.

[14]E. O. Heady and J. L. Dillon, *Agricultural Production Functions*, Iowa State University Press, Ames, 1961. A. A. Walters, "Production and Cost Functions: An Econometric Survey," *Econometrica*, January–April 1963, pp. 1–66.

[15]J. H. Gapinski, "The Economics of Performing Shakespeare," *The American Economic Review*, June 1984, pp. 458–466.

The impact of a decline in the price of labor is illustrated in Figure 6.15, which is essentially the same as Figure 5.6 with the following changes:

1. We are dealing with isoquants instead of indifference curves.
2. We are measuring inputs L and K on the axes instead of goods X and Y.
3. The movement to a higher curve is the scale effect instead of the income effect.

Suppose now that we instead want to analyze the impact of unequal changes in both input prices, holding total cost constant. For example, suppose that P_L increases by 20 percent and P_K increases by 50 percent. Thus, the new ratio of P_L/P_K = 1.20/1.50 times the old ratio, and we can analyze the effect in two steps:

1. Both P_L and P_K rise by 50 percent.
2. P_L falls 20 percent, P_K remaining constant. [Note that 1.20 = (0.80)(1.50).]

Step 1 can be analyzed by drawing a parallel but *lower* isocost line. This is pure scale effect. Step 2 can be analyzed as a decline in the price P_L, holding P_K constant. This will involve a scale effect and a substitution effect.

For labor, the scale effect is a decrease from step 1, but the substitution and scale effects are both increases from step 2. Thus, it is not clear whether the quantity of labor input used goes up or down.

For capital, the scale effect from step 1 is a decrease. The substitution effect from step 2 is a decrease. But the scale effect from step 2 is an increase. The net

FIGURE 6.15 Impact of a decline in the price of labor on output.

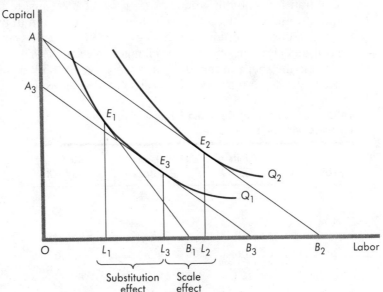

effect will in general be negative, because with both input prices going up it is virtually impossible for the usage of both inputs to go up.

In the theory of the consumer we mentioned that the income effect for a good is sometimes a decrease in quantity as income increases. In this case the good under consideration is called an inferior good. Similarly, in the case of the theory of production, the scale effect for an input can be a reduction in usage as output increases. In this case the input is called an *inferior input* or *regressive input*. In the above analysis we assumed that neither input was regressive.

6.9   MULTIPLE PRODUCTS: THE PRODUCTION TRANSFORMATION CURVE

In the previous sections we discussed the case of only one output. In actual practice, the same resources can be used to produce different products, and the producer has to choose between different product combinations. As with the production function, we will discuss the technological possibilities first. Again, we will consider only two outputs, X and Y (e.g., corn and potatoes). The curve that shows the different combinations of X and Y that the producer can produce with the given resources is called the *production transformation curve*.

As we did before, we will present a table of hypothetical outputs: Table 6.3 gives different combinations of corn and potatoes the producer can produce with given resources. Figure 6.16 shows the production transformation curve.

Just as we considered the concepts of MRS (marginal rate of substitution) in the theory of the consumer and MRTS (marginal rate of technical substitution) earlier, we will consider the *marginal rate of transformation* (MRT) in production. If we have two products X and Y, then we define MRT as follows: The marginal rate of transformation of product X for product Y is equal to the reduction in the output of product Y necessary to increase the production of product X by 1 unit, holding resources constant. It is denoted by $MRT_{X \text{ for } Y}$ and is equal to $|\Delta Y/\Delta X|$, since we consider absolute values of the changes. We show $MRT_{X \text{ for } Y}$ in Figure 6.16. To determine the shape of the MRT curve we have to think of what $|\Delta Y/\Delta X|$ will be as we move down the curve. We will show that as we move down the curve (so

TABLE 6.3   Outputs of Corn and Potatoes that Can be Produced with Given Resources

Combination	Units of Corn X	Units of Potatoes Y	$MRT_{XY} = |\Delta Y/\Delta X|$
1	0	140	–
2	30	135	5/30
3	60	120	15/30
4	90	105	15/30
5	120	65	40/30
6	140	0	65/20

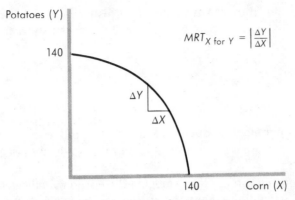

FIGURE 6.16 A production tranformation curve.

that we reduce the output of Y and increase the output of X), $|\Delta Y/\Delta X|$ will increase (see the last column in Table 6.3) and, hence, the MRT curve will have the concave shape as shown in Figure 6.16.

Intuitively, the reasoning behind this is: When output of potatoes is high and that of corn low, the marginal productivity of resources is low in the production of potatoes and high in the production of corn. Thus, if the producer reduces the production of potatoes by a small amount, the resources released will produce a lot of corn. Thus, (reduction in output of potatoes)/(increase in output of corn) will be low when potato output is higher and will progressively rise as potato output is reduced and corn output increased.

The formal relationship between the MRT and the marginal productivities of resources in the production of the two products can be derived as follows: Suppose we consider the labor input. Define

MP_{LX} = marginal product of labor in the production of $X = \Delta X/\Delta L$

MP_{LY} = marginal product of labor in the production of $Y = \Delta Y/\Delta L$

When we reduce output of Y by ΔY, some labor will be released, and this is $\Delta L = \Delta Y/MP_{LY}$. Now we can use this labor to produce X. The increase in the output of X is

$$\Delta X = \Delta L \cdot MP_{LX}$$
$$= \left(\frac{\Delta Y}{MP_{LY}}\right) \cdot MP_{LX}$$

Hence, we get

$$MRT_{X\,for\,Y} = \left|\frac{\Delta Y}{\Delta X}\right| = \frac{MP_{LY}}{MP_{LX}}$$

At high rates of output of Y and low rates of output of X, MP_{LY} is low and MP_{LX} is high. Hence, $|\Delta Y/\Delta X|$ is small. As we reduce the output of Y, MP_{LY} goes up, MP_{LX}

goes down, and, thus, $|\Delta Y/\Delta X|$ goes up. This explains the concave shape of the MRT curve. By a similar reasoning for capital, we can show that

$$MRT_{X \text{ for } Y} = \frac{MP_{KY}}{MP_{KX}}$$

where

MP_{KX} = marginal product of capital in the production of X

MP_{KY} = marginal product of capital in the production of Y

These relationships are useful in judging the economic efficiency of production, a topic which we will discuss in detail later in Chapter 9. For the present, we will show how the optimal levels of outputs of X and Y are determined.

Suppose that the prices of products X and Y are P_X and P_Y respectively. Then the producer's total revenues are

$$R = XP_X + YP_Y$$

where X and Y are the quantities produced of products X and Y respectively. We can plot *isorevenue lines* for different values of R as shown in Figure 6.17. For instance, to get revenues of R_1, if the producer produces output X only, the required output is $X_1 = R_1/P_X$. If the producer produces output Y only, the required output is $Y_1 = R_1/P_Y$. The producer can produce other combinations in between. The slope of the isorevenue line is (in absolute terms) $\Delta Y_1/\Delta X_1 = P_X/P_Y$.

Superimposing the isorevenue lines on the production transformation curve, we get the outputs of X and Y that give the highest revenue (we try to get the highest line possible). These outputs are given as X_0 and Y_0 in Figure 6.18. R_1, R_2, and R_3 are three typical isorevenue lines. R_3 cannot be attained. R_1 can be improved upon. The maximum revenue is R_2. The isorevenue line corresponding to R_2 is tangent to the product transformation curve at the point A. The output combination at A gives the maximum revenue. At this point the slopes of the transformation

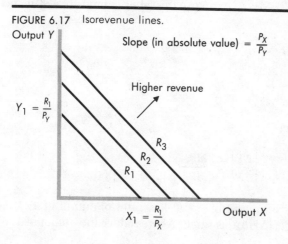

FIGURE 6.17 / Isorevenue lines.

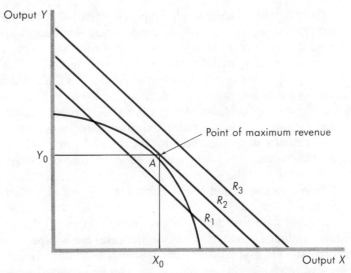

FIGURE 6.18 Optimal production of two outputs under revenue maximization.

curve and the isorevenue line are equal. Thus, revenue maximization implies $MRT_{X \text{ for } Y} = |\Delta Y/\Delta X| = MP_{LY}/MP_{LX} = MP_{KY}/MP_{KX} = P_X/P_Y$. Note that $MP_{LY}/MP_{LX} = P_X/P_Y$ can be rewritten as $MP_{LX} \cdot P_X = MP_{LY} \cdot P_Y$. What does this mean? The left side is the value of marginal product of labor in the production of X. The right side is the value of marginal product of labor in the production of Y. Thus, the producer will keep shifting labor between the production of the two products X and Y until the value of marginal product is the same in the production of X and Y. The producer will do the same with the capital input. Hence, we have

$$MP_{KX} \cdot P_X = MP_{KY} \cdot P_Y$$

for revenue maximization.

We have talked of revenue maximization; it is equivalent to profit maximization in this case because we have assumed that producers have given resources at their command. This means that the costs of inputs are given and fixed.

6.10 AN APPLICATION: PRICE CONTROLS
ON JOINTLY PRODUCED GOODS

Suppose that two goods X and Y are jointly produced. Examples are beef and leather, oil and natural gas. We will assume that the outputs are produced in a fixed proportion and we measure them in units such that 1 unit of the composite good is equal to 1 unit of X and 1 unit of Y. For instance, in the case of beef and leather the composite good is cattle, and we are measuring beef and leather in units such that one cow produces 1 unit of beef and 1 unit of leather. Similarly, 1 unit of petroleum product is equivalent to 1 unit of oil and 1 unit of natural gas.

There is, in this case, a single supply curve (supply of cattle, supply of petroleum products, and so on) but two demand curves—demand for leather and demand for beef if we are considering cattle. By a vertical summation of the two demand curves we get the demand curve for cattle. In Figure 6.19, SS is the supply curve of cattle, D_1D_1 is the demand for leather, and DD is the summation of two demand curves: demand for leather and demand for beef. (We have not shown D_2D_2, the demand curve for beef, separately.) For D_1D_1 the vertical axis measures the price of leather, and for DD the vertical axis measures the price of a cow which is equal to the price of a unit of leather plus the price of a unit of beef. (Note that we have defined the units so that one cow produces 1 unit of leather and 1 unit of beef.) The intersection of the demand and supply curves determines the output of cattle. In Figure 6.19 the output is OA. The price of a unit of leather is AC, and the price of a unit of beef is BC.

In some cases, we find that government imposes price controls on one of the jointly produced products. This was the case, for instance, with price controls on natural gas. Oil and natural gas are jointly produced. Hence, the analysis of the effects of price controls on natural gas can be analyzed within the framework of price determination of joint products which we have discussed. The result will, however, depend on whether X and Y are substitutes in consumption or whether they are independent. In the case of cattle, it is reasonable to assume that leather and beef are not substitutes in consumption. In the case of natural gas and oil there will be some substitution in consumption. Let us, however, start the analysis with the assumption that there is no substitution in consumption.

Suppose there is a price control on one commodity. What this does is to produce a kinked demand curve as shown in Figure 6.20. If the price is controlled at level OA, the demand curve becomes ABD (shown as a thick line in Figure 6.20).

Returning to the case of the joint products natural gas and oil, a price control on natural gas produces a kink in the demand curve for natural gas. Adding to this the demand curve for oil, we get the demand curve for petroleum products. This is shown in Figure 6.21. D_1D_1 is the demand curve for natural gas. With the price of natural gas controlled at level OA, the demand curve becomes ABD_1. To

FIGURE 6.19   Price and output determination with joint products.

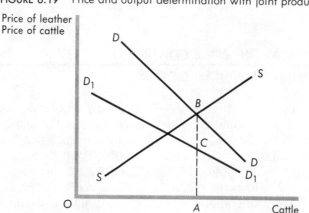

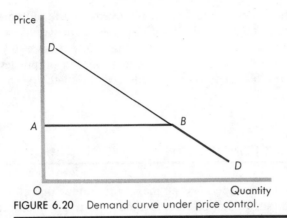

FIGURE 6.20   Demand curve under price control.

this we have to add (a vertical addition) the demand curve for oil. This is done by measuring the vertical distance from each point on AB, the distance between D_1D_1 and DD (DD is the demand for petroleum products without price controls). Note that the portion CD remains unaffected. Thus, we get $D'CD$ (shown by a thick line in Figure 6.21) as the demand curve for total petroleum products.

Without any price controls, the demand curve DD intersects the supply curve SS at the point E. Output is OQ_1. The price of natural gas if FQ_1 and the price of oil is EF. With the price of natural gas controlled at the level OA, the demand curve for petroleum output is $D'CD$. This intersects the supply curve at the point G. The output declines from OQ_1 and OQ_2. The price of natural gas is at the controlled level HQ_2. But the price of oil rises from EF to GH. Thus, the result is a decline in output and a rise in the price of oil.

We have until now assumed that the demand for oil and demand for natural gas are independent. However, this is not appropriate, since there is some substitution among the fuels. At the controlled price OA, there is an excess demand for

FIGURE 6.21   Effect of a natural gas price control on the price of oil.

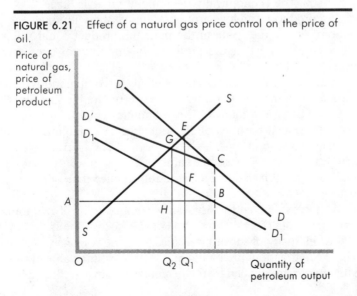

natural gas. This excess demand will spill over into the oil market and will push the demand curve for oil to the right. The net result would be a tilt upward (or clockwise) of the curve CD'. This would push output back towards Q_1 and raise the price of oil further. In fact, it is possible that the output level would remain unchanged at the level Q_1. Then the effect is completely seen in the rise in the price of oil.

6.11   SUMMARY AND CONCLUSIONS

A production function specifies the maximum output that can be produced with a given set of inputs. Total product is another term for total output. The average product of labor is equal to total product divided by the quantity of labor employed. The marginal product of labor is equal to the change in total product divided by the corresponding change in labor, holding all other inputs constant. Average product and marginal product can be similarly defined for any input into the production process.

The law of diminishing marginal productivity states that as equal increments of a variable input are added to fixed quantities of other inputs, a point will eventually be reached where the corresponding increments to output begin to decline. If $MP > 0$, then TP is rising. If $MP < 0$, then TP is falling. If $MP > AP$, then AP is rising. If $MP < AP$, then AP is falling. MP is the slope of the TP curve or the slope of a tangent to the TP curve. AP is the slope of a line from the origin to a point on the TP curve. TP reaches its maximum where $MP = 0$. AP reaches its maximum where $AP = MP$. MP reaches its maximum at the inflection point on the TP curve.

There are three stages of production. Stage I is characterized by $MP > 0$ and $MP > AP$. Stage II is characterized by $MP > 0$ and $MP < AP$. Stage III is characterized by $MP < 0$. The economically meaningful range is Stage II.

If a producer employs any of an input, she will maximize profit by hiring to the point where the value of the marginal product equals the price of the input. (We are assuming that the producer has no control over output price or input prices).

A production isoquant consists of all the combinations of two inputs that will yield the same maximum output. An upward-sloping isoquant implies that the MP of one input is less than 0. The economic region of production consists of the negatively sloped portions of all isoquants. The marginal rate of technical substitution is the absolute value of the ratio of ΔK to ΔL, holding output constant. Graphically, it is the absolute value of the slope of the isoquant. The law of diminishing marginal rate of substitution implies that isoquants are convex to the origin.

An isocost line consists of all the combinations of two inputs which have the same total cost. The absolute slope of the isocost line is the input price ratio.

The elasticity of substitution measures the responsiveness of the input ratio to a change in the input price ratio and is the absolute value of the percentage change in the input ratio divided by the percentage change in the input price ratio, holding output constant. The long-run expansion path demonstrates how the input ratio changes as output expands, holding input prices constant. The path consists of the tangency points between the isoquants and a series of parallel isocost lines. The long run is a period of time sufficient to alter the quantities of all inputs in the production process.

A production function is homothetic if the *MP* ratio remains the same as long as the input ratio remains constant. If doubling all inputs just doubles output, then the production process is characterized by constant returns to scale. If doubling all inputs more than doubles output, we have increasing returns to scale. If doubling all inputs less than doubles output, we have decreasing returns to scale.

The impact of a change in input price on input usage can be separated into a substitution effect and a scale effect.

The production transformation curve consists of all combinations of two outputs that can be produced from a given set of inputs. The marginal rate of transformation is the reduction in the output of one product required to increase the output of another product by 1 unit, holding inputs constant. The MRT is the absolute slope of the production transformation curve. To maximize profit, the value of the marginal product of each input must be identical in the production of each output.

KEY TERMS

Average Product
Constant Returns to Scale
Decreasing Returns to Scale
Economic Region of
    Production
Elasticity of Substitution
Fixed Proportions
    Production Process
Homogeneous Production
    Function
Homothetic Production
    Function
Increasing Returns to Scale

Inflection Point
Isocost Line
Isorevenue Line
Law of Diminishing
    Marginal Productivity
Law of Diminishing
    Marginal Rate of
    Substitution in Production
Long Run
Long-run Expansion Path
Marginal Product
Marginal Rate of
    Technical Substitution

Marginal Rate of
    Transformation
Production Function
Production Isoquant
Production Transformation
    Curve
Regressive or Inferior Input
Ridge Line
Scale Effect
Short Run
Substitution Effect
Stages of Production
Total Product

QUESTIONS

1. The production function for widgets is

$$Q = 100 \, L^{.6} \, K^{.4}$$

where Q is the total output, L is the quantity of labor employed, and K is the quantity of capital in place.

   a. Calculate *TP*, *AP*, and *MP* for the sixth, seventh, and eighth units of labor employed if capital is fixed at 240 units.

b. To which stage of production do these quantities of labor correspond? Why?

2. Herewego Corporation produces bicycles using only two variable inputs—bicycle frames and wheels. Draw the isoquants for 100 and 200 units of output. Why do they look like this?

3. Consider the production function $Q = 150L$, where Q is total output, and L is the quantity of labor employed. What does the total product curve look like? Describe the corresponding AP and MP curves. Why is it unlikely that a true production function would have this form?

4. Consider the production function

$$Q = 5L + 10K$$

where Q is total output, L is the quantity of labor employed, and K is the quantity of capital employed. Find two input bundles on the isoquant for $Q = 100$. What is the slope of this isoquant? What does the isoquant look like graphically? What law does it violate?

5. Explain why a profit maximizing firm using only one variable input will produce in Stage II.

6. XYZ Corporation has just completed a study of its production process for gadgets. It determined that 1 more unit of labor could increase output by 200 gadgets. However, an additional unit of capital could increase output by only 150 gadgets. What are the marginal products for capital and labor? If the current price of capital is $10 and the current price of labor is $25, is the firm employing the optimal input bundle for its current output? Why or why not? If not, which input's usage should be increased?

7. What does the long-run expansion path look like if one input is regressive? Can both inputs be regressive? Why?

8. Explain why an AP curve and the corresponding MP curve must intersect at the maximum point on the AP curve.

9. Is the production process in problem 4 characterized by constant, increasing, or decreasing returns to scale? Why?

10. Explain why profit maximization for a two-product firm requires that the marginal rate of transformation be equal to the product price ratio.

11. Suppose that the price of capital doubles while the price of labor triples. If the firm's total expenditure remains constant, can you ascertain whether capital usage will increase or decrease? Why? Does your answer change if capital is regressive? Why?

12. Suppose that you wake up tomorrow to discover that you have 12 hours of study time in which to prepare for three exams. For each hour of study you can expect your grades to be as follows:

Hour	Exam A	Exam B	Exam C
1	40	60	30
2	65	90	46
3	80	100	60
4	90	100	72
5	95	90	82
6	99	75	90

Hour	Exam A	Exam B	Exam C
7	100	55	96
8	100	33	100
9	99	8	100
10	95	0	100

You want to allocate your time to maximize your total numerical score on all three exams (each is weighted equally in your cumulative average).

a. Calculate the marginal product (score) of each hour of study for each exam.

b. State briefly the meaning of negative marginal product in this example.

c. State a general rule for dividing your time to maximize total score on all three exams. How many hours should be devoted to the preparation of exams A, B, and C?

COSTS OF PRODUCTION

7.1   INTRODUCTION

In the previous chapter we outlined the theory of production and concentrated more on the production side than on the cost side. As we said there, the problem of output maximization given a total cost and the problem of cost minimization given the total output are two sides of the same coin. We will, therefore, discuss the other side of the coin in this chapter. We did talk a little bit about isocost lines in Sections 6.6 and 6.7 of the previous chapter (see Figures 6.10, 6.11, and 6.13), but we will pursue the cost side in greater detail here.

The relationship between output maximization and cost minimization is as follows:

Output Maximization	Cost Minimization
Given: (1) Input prices (2) a budget or total cost	Given: (1) Input prices (2) total output to be produced
Find: Maximum output	Find: Minimum cost

In the last chapter we saw that

1. The production function gives information necessary to trace the isoquants.
2. The input prices determine the budget lines or isocost lines.
3. Production occurs at that combination of inputs for which $MRTS$ = ratio of input prices

Each position of tangency determines a level of output and the associated total cost. The similarity between output maximization given the budget or total cost and cost minimization given the total output to be produced is shown in Figure 7.1.

In Figure 7.1(*a*) we show output maximizaton given total cost. This procedure amounts to drawing the total cost line and moving to the highest isoquant to which we can get.

In Figure 7.1(*b*) we show cost minimization given total output. This procedure amounts to drawing the isoquant for the given output and moving to the lowest isocost line.

Note that both the procedures lead to the same level of input use and, hence, the same levels of total cost and output, because the cost lines have the same slope and the isoquants the same shape in the two figures.

7.2   DIFFERENT CONCEPTS OF COSTS

We have frequently used the word "cost" without explaining exactly what it means, because the word is in common usage. If we pay $5 per hour to a worker whom we employ for 20 hours, then our cost is clearly $100. This is the common usage

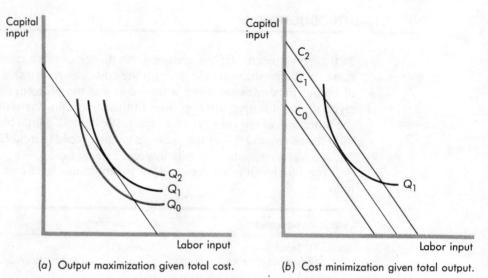

(a) Output maximization given total cost.   (b) Cost minimization given total output.

FIGURE 7.1   Output maximization versus cost minimization.

of cost, which in economics is called *accounting cost* (so called because accountants use this cost concept). The concept of cost in economics is somewhat different. *Opportunity cost* is the cost concept most relevant to economic decisions.

Opportunity cost is defined as the value of a resource in its next best use. Suppose that Mr. Smith quits his job making $50,000 per year and instead opens his own small business. Although the accounting cost of Mr. Smith's labor to his business is 0, the opportunity cost is $50,000 per year—the earnings he foregoes by working for his own firm. Is this opportunity cost meaningful? As we will see, it is very important. If Mr. Smith cannot cover this cost, then he will probably return to his old job.

Opportunity cost can similarly be defined for the other factors of production. For example, the opportunity cost of using a piece of machinery (or building, or land) is the value of the product generated in its next best use. If the machine is owned by the firm, this value could be realized by renting or selling the machine to someone else. The price at which the machine would rent is the opportunity cost of the machine to the producer. This opportunity cost could be less than or greater than the accounting cost which is likely to reflect only some estimated depreciation and not the market rental value at all.

Several other cost concepts are used in economics: sunk costs, user costs, shadow costs, private costs, social costs, and so on. We will define some of these concepts here and some others in later sections and chapters.

Sunk costs are costs only in the accounting sense. These are costs that the producer cannot recover by renting or selling the productive resource. Suppose that a firm purchases a custom-designed piece of specialized machinery with no alternative use. Once purchased, the price of the machine is a sunk cost. The concept of sunk cost is generally related to equipment (or even some labor) that is already in place and that has no alternative use. The opportunity cost of such resources is 0, and, hence, sunk costs are not relevant to economic decisions.

User cost is a concept that applies to capital equipment; we will explain it later in Chapter 17 (Section 17.4) when we discuss pricing of capital services taking into account depreciation, obsolescence, and capital gains.

Shadow cost is the scarcity value of a resource. This is a concept that arises in the evaluation of scarce resources (scarce foreign exchange, scarce skilled labor, and so forth). We will be discussing this in the next chapter when we discuss the linear programming model of production.

In making production decisions, the producer will generally calculate only his costs or the *private costs* of production. These are the opportunity costs of the resources employed in the course of production. But sometimes the producer will impose other costs on society that he will not consider. An example that is often used is that of a paper mill polluting a nearby river. The private costs of production combined with the cost of the pollution make up the full *social costs* of production. If the producer is benevolent, the producer may take account of the costs of cleaning up the pollution in making any production decisions. Otherwise, some measures may have to be taken to solve this problem of discrepancy between the private cost and social cost. We discuss this problem in greater detail in Chapter 19.

In the following sections we will ignore this discrepancy between private and social cost. We will assume that all costs that are relevant are private costs and that they are opportunity costs.

7.3 TOTAL, MARGINAL, AND AVERAGE COSTS

In the last chapter (Section 6.7) we considered the long-run expansion path for a producer. As we move the isocost line to higher and higher cost levels, we can produce greater and greater quantities of output. The line joining the successive points of tangency, as shown in Figure 6.13, is the long-run expansion path. All points on the expansion path correspond to the choice of the optimal combination of inputs, so that $MRTS = $ input price ratio. Thus, from the expansion path we can obtain the minimum total cost at which various quantities of output can be produced.

We can then construct a table showing total cost TC, marginal cost MC, and average cost AC. Table 7.1 presents such a (hypothetical) table. Marginal cost is the cost of the additional unit of output. Mathematically, it is equal to $\Delta TC/\Delta Q$. Graphically, it is the slope of the total cost curve. Looking at the values for MC, we see that it is first decreasing and then increasing. We will argue that this pattern is typical.

Average cost is simply cost per unit of output. Mathematically, it is equal to TC/Q. Graphically, it is the slope of a line from the origin to a point on the total cost curve. Looking at the values for AC, we see that it, too, initially decreases and later increases. Again, we will argue that this is a typical pattern.

A typical total cost curve, though not to the same scale as for the data in Table 7.1, is shown in Figure 7.2. At the point of minimum marginal cost, the total cost curve has an inflection point (change in curvature). Also, the point of minimum AC is found by drawing a tangent to the total cost curve from the origin (compare Figure 6.3 of Chapter 6).

TABLE 7.1 Total, Marginal, and Average Costs

Units of Output	Total Cost TC	Marginal Cost MC	Average Cost AC
0	0		
1	50	50	50
2	90	40	45
3	120	30	40
4	140	20	35
5	150	10	30
6	156	6	26
7	175	19	25
8	208	33	26
9	270	62	30
10	350	80	35

The same relationships that we considered between AP and MP in the previous chapter (Section 6.3) hold true for MC and AC:

1. If $MC < AC$, then AC will be falling as output increases.
2. If $MC > AC$, then AC will be rising as output increases.
3. At the point of minimum AC, we have $AC = MC$.

Typical MC and AC curves satisfying these relationships are shown in Figure 7.3.

Note that the first two conditions are clearly satisfied in the case of the numbers in Table 7.1. As for the third condition, we do not see it because of the discrete steps in the data. The minimum average cost occurs somewhere between 7 and 8 units of output. If output and costs were measured in finer units, this relationship would be satisfied. As it stands the minimum AC listed = 25 and occurs for

FIGURE 7.2 A typical total cost curve.

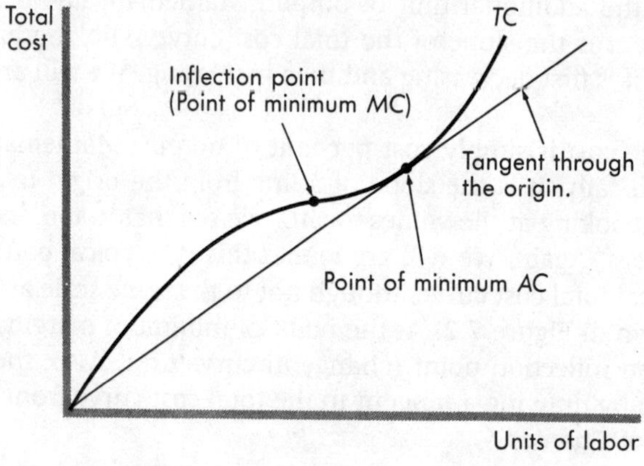

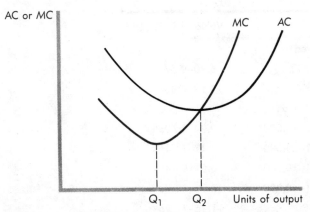

FIGURE 7.3   Typical MC and AC curves.

7 units of output, but $MC = 19$ for this level of output. Thus, it looks like $AC \neq MC$ at the minimum point on the AC curve. The problem is similar to the one we mentioned in the previous chapter with reference to the data in Table 6.1.

EXAMPLE 7.1   Rationing by Waiting

As a consequence of gasoline price controls in force in the spring of 1980, a number of Chevron stations in California were required to lower their gasoline price (only Chevron stations that were owned and operated by Standard Oil of California were involved). The resulting prices per gallon were 16 to 21 cents lower than those of other brand suppliers. As expected, long queues were found at Chevron stations. On April 9, 11, and 12, 1980, Deacon and Sonstelie surveyed customers at one low-priced Chevron station and at two neighboring stations (Mobil and Union) whose prices were not controlled.[1] They gathered data on the employment status and incomes of the customers. The customers in the sample faced a choice between the low-priced and regular stations. In their analysis, Deacon and Sonstelie allowed for two choices: choice of the station and choice of the quantity of gasoline bought. They found that (as expected) those who bought at the Chevron station bought more gasoline (on the average) than at the other stations because of the time costs involved in waiting in the queue. You would expect that consumers would try to average these time costs over more gallons purchased. After adjusting for these factors, the estimates of value of time (dollars per hour) that Deacon and Sonstelie obtained were as follows:

Category	Value of Time ($/hr)
Part-time workers	3.52–5.39
Students	7.15–10.96
Homemakers	6.32–9.70

[1] Robert T. Deacon and Jon Sonstelie, "Rationing by Waiting and the Value of Time: Results from a Natural Experiment," *Journal of Political Economy*, August 1985, pp. 627–647. For a theoretical analysis see Y. Barzel, "A Theory of Rationing by Waiting," *Journal of Law and Economics*, April 1974, pp. 73–95.

Category	Value of Time ($/hr)
Unemployed[a]	
$0–15,000	6.30–9.67
>$15,000	5.12–7.85
Fully employed[b]	
$ 0–10,000	9.94–15.25
$10,001–20,000	7.47–11.46
$20,001–30,000	6.51–9.44
$30,001–40,000	8.93–13.70
>$40,000	11.26–17.26

[a]Family income.
[b]Individual income.

The decline in the estimates of the value of time in the two categories for the unemployed as well as the first three categories of the employed is rather puzzling.

EXAMPLE 7.2 Costs of the 55-mph Speed Limit

In 1975 the U.S. government imposed the 55-mph speed limit on highways. (The restrictions were relaxed to 65 mph in late 1987.) Although the policy currently holds little interest, it is a good example to study the costs and benefits of government policies, and several studies have been done on the costs of driving at 55 mph. The aims of the policy were to save on the consumption of gasoline and to reduce the number of fatal accidents on highways and thus save lives. The major cost associated with the 55-mph speed limit is the enormous chunk of wasted time.

Examining the estimates of the decrease in the fatality rate and the increase in travel time with decreased speed, it was estimated that it costs about 102 worker-years of extra travel time to save one life.[2] Assuming an average working life of 50 years leads us to believe that the cost of saving a life is about twice the value of life. There are actually several other ways of saving life that cost substantially less, such as requiring smoke detectors in every home or adding more cardiac care units.[3]

As for saving gasoline, again there are other ways. It has been estimated that a gasoline tax of 3.4 percent would have the same effect as the 55-mph speed limit.[4] Since the fuel-efficient cars give twice (or even three times) the mileage of gas guzzlers, a policy of inducing people to switch to the fuel-efficient cars would

[2]J. Jondrow, M. Bowes, and R. Levy, in their paper, "The Optimal Speed Limit," *Economic Inquiry*, July 1983, pp. 325–336, list several estimates and give references. See also Charles A. Lave, "The Costs of Going 55," *Newsweek*, October 23, 1978, p. 37.

[3]J. Graham and J. Vaupel, in "The Value of Life: What Difference Does It Make?" *Risk Analysis*, March 1981, pp. 89–95, list the costs of saving life by 57 government safety efforts. The 55-mph speed limit is in the top quarter.

[4]R. D. Blair, D. Kaserman, and R. Tepel, "The Impact of Improved Mileage on Gasoline Consumption," *Economic Inquiry*, April 1984, pp. 209–217.

be to impose different speed limits: 55 mph for gas guzzlers and 65 mph for fuel-efficient cars. Issuing two kinds of license plates would enable the police to distinguish them.[5] The saving in travel time would be a sufficient incentive for travellers to switch to fuel-efficient cars.

7.4   FIXED COSTS AND VARIABLE COSTS:
SHORT AND LONG RUN

In the previous chapter we distinguished between the short run and the long run. We said that the short run is a period insufficient to alter the quantities of all inputs. So some factors are fixed in the short run. The costs of these fixed factors are called *fixed costs* or sometimes *sunk costs*. Since the quantities of the fixed inputs cannot be changed as output varies, fixed costs do not change with the level of output. Common examples of fixed costs are the costs of land, factory buildings, or even labor under long-time contracts.

The quantities of some other inputs can be altered even in the short run. These inputs are called variable inputs, and their costs are called variable costs. Since the usage of these inputs varies with the level of output, variable costs also vary with the level of output. It is often customary to consider the costs of labor input, materials and energy inputs, and so on as *variable costs*, that is, their amount can be changed depending on the level of production.

What is fixed and what is variable depends on the time horizon. For instance, a factory owner can, over the course of 5 or 10 years, either sell her factory building and equipment or expand it by enlarging it and adding more equipment. Thus, what we considered as fixed becomes variable if the time horizon we are considering is large enough. So, for long time horizons, or in the long run, all costs are variable and nothing is fixed.

We will now formally define the terms:

- *Fixed costs:* Costs that do not change with output.

- *Variable costs:* Costs that change with changes in output.

- *Short run:* A period over which the quantities of some inputs (fixed inputs) cannot be changed as output is changed.

- *Long run:* A period long enough for all inputs to be changed with changes in output.

How short is the short run and how long is the long run? This depends on the industry and production techniques used. Period length will vary from firm to firm. If there are no transactions costs and no specialized inputs, then all inputs can be quickly adjusted, and the long run is not very long. Also, although one can talk of intermediate runs, for our analysis a classification into two categories is enough.

[5]See Lave, "Costs of Going 55."

Corresponding to our discussion we can define the total, marginal, and average costs for the short run:

TFC = total fixed costs
TVC = total variable costs
TC = total cost   = $TFC + TVC$
AFC = average fixed costs   = TFC/Q where Q = output
AVC = average variable costs = TVC/Q
ATC = average total costs   = $AFC + AVC = TC/Q$
MC = marginal cost   = $\Delta TC/\Delta Q = \Delta TVC/\Delta Q$

Note that marginal cost can be expressed either as the ratio of change in total cost to a change in output or as the ratio of change in total variable cost to a change in output. This is because fixed costs do not vary with output so that any change in the total cost must result from a change in the cost of the variable inputs.

Consider the data in Table 7.1. We see that the total costs when nothing is produced are 0. Since fixed costs would remain constant even for this level of output, we can deduce that there are no fixed costs. These data must correspond to the long-run situation. We know this to be true because the data were derived from the long-run expansion path. This is also the reason that a single column for average cost is presented.

The data presented in Table 7.2 correspond to the short run. This is evident from the presence of fixed costs. Figure 7.4 illustrates the various total cost curves. Since total fixed costs are constant, the TFC curve is simply a horizontal line at 200. And because total cost is the sum of total variable costs and total fixed costs, the TC curve has the same shape as the TVC curve but lies above it by a vertical distance of 200.

Before presenting the AFC, AVC, ATC, and MC curves graphically, we will examine the relationships between them. The AFC curve will be steadily declining.

TABLE 7.2 Total, Marginal, and Average Costs in the Short Run

Output Q	TFC	TVC	TC	MC	AFC	AVC	ATC
0	200	0	200				
1	200	50	250	50	200.0	50	250.0
2	200	90	290	40	100.0	45	145.0
3	200	120	320	30	66.7	40	106.7
4	200	140	340	20	50.0	35	85.0
5	200	150	350	10	40.0	30	70.0
6	200	156	356	6	33.3	26	59.3
7	200	175	375	19	28.6	25	53.6
8	200	208	408	33	25.0	26	51.0
9	200	270	470	62	22.2	30	52.2
10	200	350	550	80	20.0	35	55.0

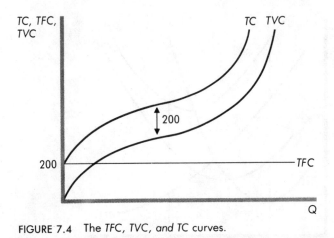

FIGURE 7.4 The TFC, TVC, and TC curves.

Recall that $AFC = TFC/Q$. As Q increases, TFC remains constant so that AFC clearly falls.

We also know that ATC always exceeds AVC. This is because ATC is the sum of AVC and AFC. Furthermore, since AFC falls as output increases, AVC and ATC get closer as output rises.

Our now familiar relationships between marginals and averages hold for both ATC and AVC. That is, if $MC < ATC$, then ATC is falling; if $MC > ATC$, then ATC is rising. And if $MC < AVC$, then AVC is falling, whereas if $MC > AVC$, then AVC is rising.[6] This implies that MC must intersect ATC at its minimum point and that MC must also intersect AVC at its minimum point.[7] Looking at our data, we see that the lowest ATC listed occurs at 8 units of output. But at this output, $ATC \neq MC$ as one might think it should be. However, the minimum ATC actually occurs between 8 and 9 units of output, and we would have gotten $MC = ATC$ at the minimum ATC if we observed our data in finer intervals. The same thing is true with respect to MC and AVC.

Note also that ATC will reach its minimum at an output larger than that at which AVC reaches its minimum. This is because $ATC = AVC + AFC$. And even though AVC has begun to rise, AFC is still declining, pulling ATC down. Eventually, the increase in AVC will offset the decrease in AFC and ATC, too, will begin to increase.[8]

The relationships between the various average and marginal curves are illustrated in Figure 7.5. The figure shows typical AFC, AVC, ATC, and MC curves but is not drawn to scale for the data in Table 7.2

---

[6]$MC = \Delta TC/\Delta Q$. But $TC = ATC \cdot Q$. Substitution yields $MC = \Delta(ATC \cdot Q)/\Delta Q = [(\Delta ATC/\Delta Q) \cdot Q] + [ATC \cdot (\Delta Q/\Delta Q)]$. Since ATC and Q are nonnegative, $MC > ATC$ if and only if $\Delta ATC/\Delta Q > 0$ which means that ATC increases as Q increases. Also, $MC < ATC$ if and only if $\Delta ATC/\Delta Q < 0$ which means that ATC decreases as Q increases.

Since $TC = TVC + TFC$ and $\Delta TFC/\Delta Q = 0$, MC is also equal to $\Delta TVC/\Delta Q$. But $TVC = AVC \cdot Q$. We can follow the procedure above to get $MC = [(\Delta AVC/\Delta Q) \cdot Q] + AVC$ which indicates that $MC > AVC$ if and only if $\Delta AVC/\Delta Q > 0$, and $MC < AVC$ if and only if $\Delta AVC/\Delta Q < 0$.

[7]At minimum ATC, the ATC curve switches from falling to rising. Thus the MC curve must switch from lying below the ATC curve to lying above it. This means that ATC and MC must intersect at minimum ATC. We can similarly argue that AVC and MC must intersect at minimum AVC.

[8]Mathematically $ATC = AVC + AFC$. $\Delta ATC/\Delta Q = (\Delta AVC/\Delta Q) + \Delta AFC/\Delta Q$. ΔAFC equals zero.

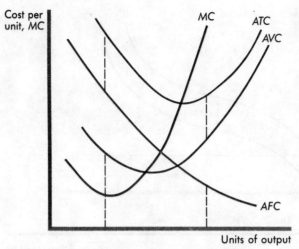

FIGURE 7.5   The AFC, AVC, ATC, and MC curves.

There is also an important relationship between *MC* and *TVC*. Since *MC* is the change in *TVC* for a unit change in output, *TVC* is the area under the *MC* curve. This, of course, means that *TC* is the area under the *MC* curve plus *TFC*.

There is a straightforward relationship between factor productivity and output costs. To see this, let us consider a single variable factor, labor. All other inputs are fixed. *AP* and *MP* will denote the average and marginal products of labor, respectively. If *W* is the wage rate and *L* is the quantity of labor, then

$$TVC = W \cdot L$$

Hence, if *Q* is the output,

$$AVC = \frac{TVC}{Q} = W \cdot \left(\frac{L}{Q}\right)$$

But $Q/L = AP$. Hence, $AVC = W/AP$. Also, $\Delta TVC = W \cdot \Delta L$. (*W* does not change. It is assumed given.) Dividing by ΔQ we get

$$MC = \frac{\Delta TVC}{\Delta Q} = W \cdot \frac{\Delta L}{\Delta Q}$$

But $\Delta Q/\Delta L$ = marginal product *MP*.

Hence, we have $MC = W/MP$. The relationships $AVC = W/AP$ and $MC = W/MP$ show that *MC* is at a minimum when *MP* is at a maximum, and *AVC* is at a minimum when *AP* is at a maximum. Also, when *AP* is at a maximum, $AP = MP$. Hence, when *AVC* is at a minimum, $AVC = MC$. These relationships are illustrated in Figure 7.6.

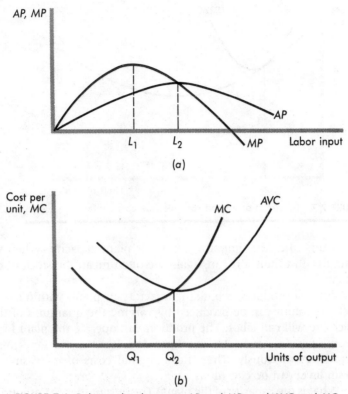

FIGURE 7.6 Relationship between AP and MP, and AVC and MC.

7.5   LONG-RUN AND SHORT-RUN AVERAGE COST CURVES

In the long run all factors are variable. Thus, the producer has an opportunity of minimizing the costs of the chosen output with respect to *all* factors. This accounts for the fact that the short-run average total cost curve (which we will denote by *SRAC*), cannot be below the long-run average cost curve (which we will denote by *LRAC*). In the short run there are more constraints than in the long-run (capacity constraint and constraints imposed by other fixed factors), and the constrained minimum is never less than the unconstrained minimum.

Another thing to note is that the *SRAC* curve and the *LRAC* curve touch each other as illustrated in Figure 7.7. The point of tangency corresponds to an output of Q_s. The producer will be unable to reduce the cost of this output even in the long run when fixed inputs can be varied. This implies that the quantities of the fixed factors are optimal for this output.

To understand why the point of tangency is at Q_s and not at the lowest point of the *SRAC* curve, we have to digress a bit to discuss what is commonly known as *plant capacity*.

We have frequently talked of some factors of production being fixed in the

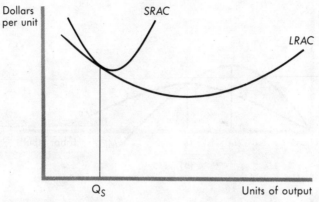

FIGURE 7.7   Long-run and short-run average cost curves.

short run. One such important factor is plant capacity. When we talk of capital being fixed in the short run, again we often mean the stock of capital equipment or plant.

When a producer is building a factory or plant, within some limits, different levels of output can be produced by varying the quantities of the variable input, which we will call labor. The producer can operate the plant for 4 hours per day, 8 hours per day, even 24 hours per day. But the machines may break down if operated continuously. Thus, the marginal costs of increasing output beyond a certain level can be enormous.

What is the capacity of the plant? The output that corresponds to the minimum average total cost is often called by economists and business people, the *capacity* of the plant. Capacity is *not* the maximum possible output. Instead, by this definition, it is the largest output that can be produced without encountering rising average or per-unit costs.

A producer producing an output smaller than that given by the minimum average total cost is said to be operating with *excess capacity*. A producer may also be producing an output greater than that corresponding to the minimum average total cost. In this case the producer is said to be operating *above capacity*.

Why would a producer operate with excess capacity? One reason is that there are alternative ways of producing a given output. The producer can build a smaller plant and operate it at capacity (that is, at the point of minimum average total cost). Alternatively, the producer can build a larger plant and operate it below capacity. The producer will choose whichever is cheaper. If the long-run average cost curve is downward sloping, the latter course will be cheaper because the short-run average costs will be decreasing with increases in capacity. This point is illustrated in Figure 7.8.

The producer wants to produce output Q_s. He can build the plant size so that Q_s is the output at which SRAC is minimized. The SRAC curve for this plant size is shown as $SRAC_1$ in Figure 7.8. Alternatively, the producer can build a bigger plant, the SRAC curve for which is shown as $SRAC_2$ in Figure 7.8, and operate it below capacity. Clearly, the larger plant results in lower average costs and will be chosen.

Note that operating a given plant at the minimum point on the average cost

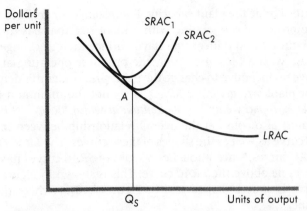

FIGURE 7.8   Short-run average cost curves for increasing plant sizes when long-run average cost is decreasing.

curve and producing a given output at minimum average cost are two different things. A profit-maximizing producer is interested in the latter. The two objectives would be the same only at one point on the *LRAC* curve. This is the minimum point of the *LRAC* curve.

The reverse case, the producer operating above capacity, occurs if the *LRAC* is increasing with increases in plant size or output. This is shown in Figure 7.9. In this case, to produce output Q_s the producer can operate at the point of minimum average cost on the bigger plant, whose *SRAC* is given by $SRAC_1$, or operate above capacity with a smaller plant, whose *SRAC* curve is given by $SRAC_2$. Clearly, the latter method leads to lower average costs for producing output Q_s.

Some economists find all this puzzling and would like to redefine the phrase "capacity output."[9] Instead of defining it as the output for which average costs are minimum they would define it as a rate of output at which the producer has no

[9]For example, Milton Friedman. The references are given in Chapter 13 when we discuss the problem of "excess capacity" in monopolistic competition.

FIGURE 7.9   Short-run average cost curves for increasing plant sizes when long-run average cost is increasing.

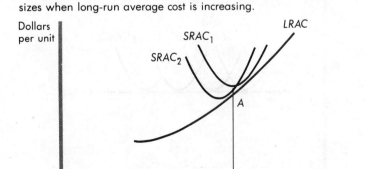

incentive to change the plant capacity. For instance, to produce output Q_s, in Figure 7.8, if the producer is operating with a plant size that has the SRAC curve given by $SRAC_1$, then the producer will have an incentive to change the plant capacity and operate with $SRAC_2$. However, the producer operating at point A on $SRAC_2$ would have no incentive to change the plant size. Under this definition, the capacity output for plant size given by $SRAC_2$ is Q_s, not the minimum point of the $SRAC_2$ curve, that is, *capacity output is that output at which SRAC = LRAC.*

We must also consider the overall relationship between the SRAC curves and the LRAC curve as well as the shapes of these curves. The LRAC curve is an envelope of the SRAC curves, since it touches a series of SRAC curves in such a way that the SRAC curves lie above the LRAC curve. This is shown in Figure 7.10(*a*) where the LRAC curve is saucer-shaped and in Figure 7.10(*b*) where the LRAC curve is a straight line.

In the case where the LRAC curve is a straight line, the LRAC curve consists of the minimum points of the SRAC curves. This is not so in the case where the LRAC curve is downward sloping, upward sloping, or saucer-shaped. The LRAC curve includes the minimum point of only one SRAC curve. This is where the

FIGURE 7.10 The long-run average cost curve is an envelope of short-run average cost curves.

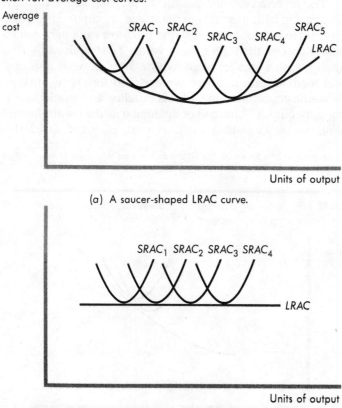

(a) A saucer-shaped LRAC curve.

(b) The LRAC curve is a straight line.

minimum points of the *SRAC* and *LRAC* curves coincide. Otherwise, as shown in Figures 7.8 and 7.9, the minimum point of the *SRAC* curve will be above the *LRAC* curve. The *SRAC* curve touches the *LRAC* curve at a point other than its minimum point for the reason (as explained earlier) that the minimum average cost attainable with a given plant is not the same thing as minimum average cost of producing a given output.

The relationship between long-run and short-run cost curves was introduced by the economist Jacob Viner (1892 to 1970) in a famous article in 1931.[10] Viner was confused between minimum short-run average cost for a given plant, as given by the minimum of $SRAC_1$ in Figures 7.8 and 7.9, and minimum long-run average cost of producing a given output (such as point *A*). He therefore instructed his draftsman to draw a smooth curve of *LRAC* as in Figure 7.10(*a*). The curve was to pass through the minimum points of all the *SRAC* curves and still be below all of them. The draftsman, who was a mathematician, objected that this could not be done. However, Professor Viner insisted, and the result was an impossible figure. Later when the article was reprinted in 1950, Professor Viner refused the opportunity to revise it, saying that he did not want to deprive future teachers and students of the pleasure of discovering the error.

7.6 LONG-RUN AND SHORT-RUN MARGINAL COST CURVES

In the previous secton we discussed the long-run and short-run average cost curves. We will now talk of the corresponding marginal cost curves. We will denote the long-run and short-run marginal cost curves respectively by *LRMC* and *SRMC*. We need to study the relationships between (1) *LRMC* and *LRAC*, (2) *SRMC* and *SRAC*, and (3) *LRMC* and *SRMC*. Note that the relationship between *LRAC* and *SRAC* has been discussed in the previous section.

In Section 7.3, we discussed the relationship between *AC* and *MC*. Those relationships hold good separately both for *LRAC* and *LRMC* and for *SRAC* and *SRMC*. These relationships, as we recall, are (1) If $MC < AC$, *AC* will be falling. (2) If $MC > AC$, *AC* will be rising. (3) At the point of minimum *AC*, we have $AC = MC$. Figure 7.3 thus holds good for both the long-run and short-run cost curves.

The more important relationship is between *LRMC* and *SRMC*. For this we have the relationship:

$$SRMC = LRMC \text{ when } SRAC = LRAC$$

Thus, at the rate of output Q_s given in Figures 7.8 and 7.9 we will have $SRMC_2 = LRMC$. Note that there is only one *LRMC* curve. But corresponding to each of the *SRAC* curves (or to each plant size), there is a *SRMC* curve.

It is not difficult to see that $LRMC = SRMC$ at the point where $LRAC = SRAC$. Consider the firm operating where $LRAC = SRAC$ or at Q_s in Figure 7.7. Currently,

---

[10]Jacob Viner, "Cost Curves and Supply Curves," American Economic Association, *Reading in Price Theory*, Irwin, Chicago, 1952, chap. 10. A reprint of the famous article of 1931 with a supplementary note in 1950.

its fixed inputs (as well as its variable inputs) are at the optimal levels. Now what will it cost to produce one more unit of output? It will cost more in the short run because the quantities of the fixed inputs cannot be adjusted. Thus, for outputs greater than Q_s, SRMC must exceed LRMC. But how much can be saved if output is reduced to one unit less than Q_s? More can be saved in the long run because we can get rid of some fixed inputs. And since our savings is simply the MC of the unit not produced, we conclude that $LRMC > SRMC$ for outputs less than Q_s. Now, combining these two pieces of information, we know that at Q_s, the SRMC curve must switch from lying below the LRMC curve to lying above it. And this, of course, implies that $SRMC = LRMC$ where $SRAC = LRAC$. This is illustrated in Figure 7.11.

The LRMC curve intersects the LRAC curve at its minimum point. Similarly, each SRMC curve intersects the corresponding SRAC curve at its minimum point. For the output Q_1, the tangent SRAC curve is $SRAC_1$ and the corresponding marginal cost curve is $SRMC_1$. Since, as we have shown at the output level Q_1, $SRMC_1 = LRMC$, the intersection of these curves is shown at the point B.

Another point we show in Figure 7.11 is the output Q^* at which the LRAC is minimum. Let $SRAC^*$ and $SRMC^*$ be the corresponding short-run average and marginal cost curves. As we discussed earlier, at this point the $SRAC^*$ curve also has it minimum, and, hence, at Q^* we have $SRAC^* = SRMC^*$. Thus, at this point

$$LRAC = LRMC = SRAC^* = SRMC^*$$

This relationship will be used later in Chapter 10 when we discuss long-run equilibrium in a competitive industry.

Note that at output levels less than Q^*, the intersection points of the LRMC curves with the SRMC curves will lie below the LRAC curve. For output levels greater than Q^*, the intersection points have to lie above the LRAC curve. The student may find it instructive to draw them.

FIGURE 7.11   Long-run and short-run average cost and marginal cost curves.

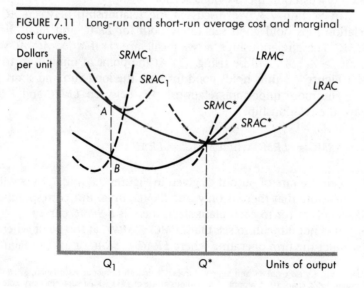

EXAMPLE 7.3   Why Are Medical Costs out of Control?

Outside of government itself, the United State's largest public industry is the health care industry. The cost of health care has been increasing over the last two decades at a much faster rate than inflation in general. Why? The main reason is the system of third-party payment in which neither the physicians nor the patients have any incentive to cut costs. Although all of us collectively do bear the costs, there is no incentive for any individual to cut costs.[11]

If a test is needed, doctors put patients into the hospital overnight because they know that insurance pays the bill. They order a number of tests, again because the insurance pays for them. Their attitude is: "When in doubt, order." The patients, all covered by Blue Cross, Medicare, and Medicaid, do not object to what the physicians order because they do not pay the expenses. If the health insurance pays, why take the risk? Many have health insurance through their employers who can write off the cost of insurance as a business expense. Of course, eventually all employees bear the cost through a decrease in salary and through increased taxes as taxpayers. The hospitals have no incentives to cut costs because again they get reimbursed by the insurance companies. The situation is similar to the one in the late 1960s when the Pentagon used to reimburse all its contractors at cost-plus, thus destroying any incentive to cut costs.

Suppose we all had an insurance for our lunch—the cost of whatever we ate would be reimbursed by the insurance company. Then each of us would buy the best food, and a number of fancy restaurants would spring up. The insurance company would charge each of us a "premium" equal to the average price of a lunch. If the premium is $25 per day, many of us would not want to buy this insurance. But suppose our employer paid the insurance. Then we would not know the hidden costs. The employer would deduct the insurance as a business expense for tax purposes and might also reduce our salaries by an amount equal to the after-tax cost of the insurance. Since none of us would have any incentive to cut the cost of the lunch, the price of lunch would keep going up and so would the premiums we pay for our lunch. The only way to stop this "lunch inflation" would be to abolish the third-party payment.

In the case of health care the situation is not that simple because health insurance cannot be easily abolished. There is always a chance that any individual can get struck by a catastrophic illness and go bankrupt. One way to cut costs is to let individuals bear part of the cost through deductibility and coinsurance. To face the equity issue, every individual (or better still household) can be given a ceiling on out-of-pocket expense, the ceiling being dependent on income, and expenses over the ceiling would be fully reimbursed. Thus, there would be an income-related cost-sharing scheme, and serious illnesses would be completely covered. Doctors, knowing that the patient has to bear part of the costs, would not be as irresponsible as at present and would be more cost conscious in prescribing treatments. This would make hospitals also more cost conscious instead of pursuing a policy of pleasing the doctors. (Many current plans have these provisions, except that the ceiling is not typically tied to income.)

[11]This problem is known as "moral hazard" and discussed in greater detail in Chapter 21.

7.7 RETURNS TO SCALE, ECONOMIES OF SCALE, AND COST CURVES

What determines the shape of the *LRAC* curve? And why do we argue that it is typically saucer-shaped? We will now consider these questions.

First, we must define a couple of terms. If *LRAC* declines as output increases, then we say that the cost structure is characterized by *economies of scale*. If, instead, the *LRAC* increases as output increases, then we have *diseconomies of scale*. Finally, if *LRAC* is constant, we have neither economies nor diseconomies of scale.

A firm's costs are determined by its production function, which dictates the quantities of the various inputs which can be used to produce a chosen output, and by the prices of those inputs. Both factors must be considered in analyzing costs.

In the last chapter we defined constant, increasing, and decreasing returns to scale. These terms deal with how output responds to a proportionate change in all inputs. Returns to scale in production tell us something about the shape of the *LRAC* curve, but the link is not as straightforward as many students first believe.[12] For example, constant returns to scale in production do not necessarily imply that the *LRAC* curve is horizontal. Why? First, firms do not usually vary their inputs in fixed proportions.[13] In fact, a firm producing a large output may employ inputs that the small producer does not find profitable to use. Second, even if the firm did opt to expand all inputs proportionately, it is quite possible that the prices of those inputs would vary (for instance, quantity discounts). So constant or even decreasing returns to scale in production could be associated with economies of scale in costs. What about increasing returns to scale in production? (To double output, inputs must be less than doubled.) Are scale economies present? This time we can answer yes only if input prices do not rise significantly as the firm expands their usage.

Economies of scale might result from increasing returns to scale in production, access to more efficient capital equipment, quantity discounts for inputs, or other factors. Diseconomies of scale could result from decreasing returns to scale in production, increases in input prices resulting from increases in usage by the firm, or managerial limitations.

In this section we examined the shape of the *LRAC* curve or the relationship between a firm's output and its long-run per-unit costs. The scale economies that we have discussed are sometimes called *internal economies* and *internal diseconomies* of scale, because the changes in long-run average costs result solely from the individual firm's adjustment of its output.

Economists generally argue that economies of scale are present over smaller outputs but that eventually diseconomies of scale set in. We will consider some empirical evidence in Section 7.9.2.

---

[12] For a nice discussion on the source of this confusion see Christopher Ross Bell, "Economies of vs. Returns to Scale," *Journal of Economic Education*, Fall 1988.

[13] An exception occurs in the case of a homothetic production function with constant input prices.

7.8 SHIFTS IN COST CURVES

Cost curves shift if there are changes in the firm's input supply curves or changes in technology:

1. A decrease in the supply of inputs to the firm causes the family of short-run and long-run cost curves to shift upward. An increase in the supply of inputs to the firm will cause these cost curves to shift downward.

2. An improvement in technology or technological progress shifts the family of short-run and long-run cost curves downward because with the same level of inputs (and, hence, total cost), we get more output.

As with demand functions, we have to be careful in distinguishing between movements along a given cost function and shifts in the cost function. In Figure 7.12 we show the *LRAC,* shifting down from $LRAC_1$ to $LRAC_2$ either due to technological change or due to an increase in factor supply. If a producer operating at point *A* switches to the output level corresponding to point *B*, then the observations *A* and *B* would give a mistaken impression that the long-run average cost curve is downward sloping. Actually, each *LRAC* curve is upward sloping, but there has been a downward shift in the *LRAC* curve.

Changes in input supply
A change in the firm's input supply could result from a change in the market supply for the input. Such a shift in the market supply curve for the input could be the result of any of the factors we discussed in Chapter 2.

But a change in the firm's input supply could also be the result of an adjustment of output by several firms in the industry. For example, even if a single firm has no control over input price (the firm's input supply curve is horizontal), as all firms increase output, increasing market demand, the input price increases. The individual firm's input supply decreases, and its average cost curves shift upward.

A change in a firm's average cost curves resulting from an overall increase or decrease in output by several firms is sometimes said to be the result of *external*

FIGURE 7.12   Shifts in cost curves and the apparent downward-sloping *LRAC*.

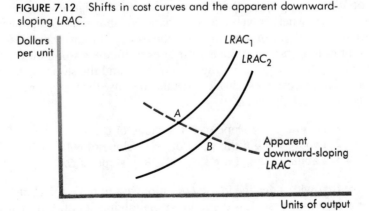

economies or *external diseconomies* of scale. An external economy of scale occurs when a general expansion of output results in a downward shift of each firm's average cost curves—an economy because the curves shift downward, and external because the individual firm has no control over it. External diseconomies of scale cause each firm's average cost curves to shift upward as all firms expand their output.

External economies and diseconomies do not occur solely as the result of shifts in firms' input supply curves. An overall expansion of output could cause congestion in the transportation of output or extensive pollution that must be cleaned up (external diseconomies). However, new transportation terminals or improved roads might come into existence as overall output is expanded (external economy). The important thing to remember is that *internal* economies and diseconomies determine the shape of a single firm's *LRAC* curve, whereas *external* economies and diseconomies cause each firm's average cost curves to shift as several or all firms expand or contract output.

Types of technological change

Technological change consists of discovering better and improved methods of producing old products; of introducing better techniques of marketing, organization, and management; and of developing new products. From the purely business point of view all forms of technological change enable the producer to produce more output with the same inputs as before and, thus, reduce costs. However, economists like to classify technological change into three categories: (1) labor saving, (2) capital saving, and (3) neutral. Technological change can be depicted as a shift in the production function and, thus, the production isoquants. The type of shift, however, is different for the three categories.

If the production isoquants shift so that the optimal capital-labor ratio remains unchanged at the same factor-price ratio and the same output, then technological change is said to be *neutral*. If the isoquants shift in such a way that the optimal K/L rises or the L/K ratio falls, at unchanged factor prices, then the technological change is said to be *labor saving*. Since a decline in L/K is the same as a rise in K/L, it can also be called *capital using*. If the isoquants shift in such a way that optimal K/L declines at unchanged factor prices, technological change is called *capital saving* (or *labor using*). These three cases are shown in Figure 7.13.

To see whether technological change is labor saving, capital saving, or neutral, we find the point of tangency A of the isocost lines to the old isoquant Q, and the point of tangency B of the isocost lines to the new isoquant Q'. If O is the origin, then the slope of OA gives the old K/L ratio and the slope of OB gives the new K/L ratio. The isocost lines will all be parallel because the factor-price ratio is unchanged. Technological change is

1. Neutral if the slope of OB = slope of OA
2. Labor saving if the slope of OB > slope of OA
3. Capital saving if the slope of OB < slope of OA

Note that with a decline in the L/K ratio, we can have a decline in the capital input or even an increase. It is the ratio we are talking about. But in any case, total costs will be lower. We are on a lower isocost line.

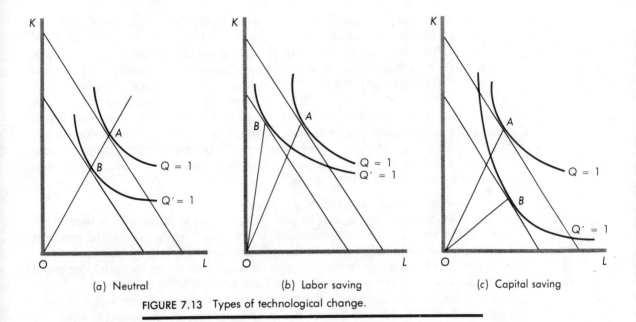

(a) Neutral   (b) Labor saving   (c) Capital saving

FIGURE 7.13   Types of technological change.

One important thing to note is that technological change can be labor saving at one factor-price ratio and capital saving at another factor-price ratio. Consider the isoquants Q and Q' in Figure 7.14, both corresponding to the same levels of output. Q is the old isoquant, and Q' is the new isoquant after technological change. Consider a factor-price ratio that gives A as the point of tangency for Q. Drawing a parallel tangent to Q' we get the point of tangency A'. The slope OA' is higher than the slope of OA, and thus the technological change is labor saving. Suppose the price of labor falls relative to the price of capital. The slope of the isocost line

FIGURE 7.14   Technological change that is labor saving and capital saving at different factor-price ratios.

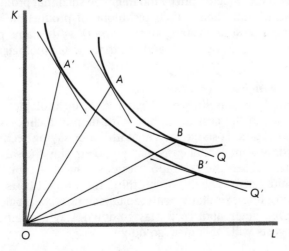

(in absolute value) is now lower. The point of tangency to Q is now at B, and drawing a parallel tangent to Q' we find the point of tangency B'. The slope of OB' is lower than the slope OB and thus the technological change is capital saving. Thus, at a high P_L/P_K ratio the technological change is labor saving, and at a low P_L/P_K ratio technological change is capital saving. Of course, this need not be always the case. We can come to the reverse conclusion by drawing the isoquant Q rather flat and Q' with a lot of curvature. The important point to note, however, is that whether technological change is labor saving or capital saving refers to the factor-price ratio we consider. Of course, we can define a technological change as labor saving if the L/K ratio declines for *all* factor-price ratios, with similar definitions for capital-saving and neutral technological change.

Technological change and change in technique

One other point to note is that we should be careful to distinguish between *technological change* and *change in technique*. When factor prices change, the producer changes the capital-labor ratio (unless production takes place under fixed proportions). This is a change in technique. Suppose, for example, the producer might use a mechanical reaper instead of hand harvesting if labor costs go up.

Is the shift to a mechanical reaper a change in technique or technological change? The answer depends on whether the mechanical reaper was available when the producer was using hand harvesting. If it was available but the producer switched to it only when labor costs went up, then it is just a change in technique. This is a movement along a given isoquant. The isoquant which gives the different combinations of capital and labor to produce the same output has as its points the mechanical reaper with small labor input or hand harvesting with large labor input.

However, if the mechanical reaper became available at the same time that labor costs went up, we have to view this as a combination of both technological change and change in technique. The availability of the mechanical reaper has shifted the isoquants.

Usually, technological change is accompanied by a change in technique. But this need not always be the case. For instance, in the case of the mechanical reaper, the availability of the reaper is technological change and, thus, shifts the production isoquant. However, the factor-price ratio might be such that producers do not make any switch and do not change their technique of production. This is shown in Figure 7.15. The isocost line is tangent to Q and Q' at the same point A. At higher prices of labor we would be on Q' and see that the technological change is labor saving.

Technological change and cost functions

Except in the odd cases as shown in Figure 7.15, technological change results in a downward shift in the cost functions. With neutral technological change both labor costs and capital costs go down. With labor-saving technological change, labor costs go down but capital costs may go down, stay the same, or even go up. As we explained earlier, the L/K ratio goes down but the capital input may even go up in absolute terms. The important thing is that total costs go down (we are on a lower isocost line). Similarly, with capital-saving technological change, capital costs go down although labor costs may go down, stay the same, or even rise. In all cases, total costs will, of course, go down.

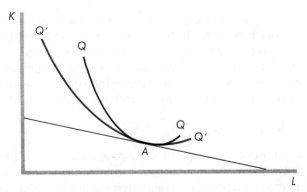

FIGURE 7.15 Technological change that does not result in a change in technique of production.

The impact of a change in factor prices on the position of the cost curves is somewhat different. A decline in the price of labor P_L, the price of capital P_K unchanged, will result in a reduction in total costs. As to whether labor costs will go down, stay the same, or go up will depend on the elasticity of demand for labor (this is discussed in detail in Chapter 15). If this elasticity is greater than 1 (in absolute value), the decline in P_L results in a more than proportionate increase in the labor input, and, thus, labor costs will actually go up. If this elasticity is 1, the labor costs will remain unchanged, and if this elasticity is less than 1, labor costs will go down. As for capital costs, they will go down in any case.[14] Thus, a reduction in the price of labor, when the price of capital remains unchanged, is similar in its effects to capital-saving technological change. Similarly, a reduction in the price of capital when the price of labor remains unchanged is similar in its effect to a labor-saving technological change.

7.9 APPLICATIONS

In the previous sections we discussed total, marginal, and average cost curves, for both the short run and long run. The relationships between these cost curves will be used often in discussions of pricing in product markets (Chapters 10 to 14) and pricing in factor markets (Chapters 15 to 17). Here we will discuss a few applications of these concepts. Before we proceed with a discussion of cost curves in several industries, let us first ask: Are average cost curves really U-shaped?

7.9.1 Are average cost curves really U-shaped?

In our discussion of cost curves, we have drawn the average cost curves as U-shaped or at least saucer-shaped (in the case of long-run cost curves). One question that some economists examining empirical evidence have raised is whether curves are really shaped so.[15] They argue that over a wide range of output, average

[14]Unless the scale effect dominates the substitution effect.

[15]As in J. Johnston, *Statistical Cost Analysis*, McGraw-Hill, New York, 1960.

variable costs and, hence, marginal costs are constant and then rise sharply when the plant capacity is reached. If this is the case, the shape of the *LRAC* is like that in Figure 7.8, that is, steadily declining. This implies, of course, that the *MC* curve lies below the *LRAC* curve, and this will have serious implications when we talk of market structure. Examples of this type of industry are electricity generation and steel production. They are industries with large equipment costs.

7.9.2 The survivor principle

The determination of the shape of the average cost curves from actual data is a very difficult task. There are several problems of measurement of output and inputs, but the most important problem is measurement of cost.[16] The costs that are usually measured are accounting costs which do not account for the opportunity costs of managerial skills. Further, different producers would be at different stages of adjustment to their long-run equilibrium. Friedman, in fact, argued that one cannot infer anything about the nature of cost curves in an industry by observing different firms at a single point in time.[17]

To avoid these problems of measurement, Stigler suggested an indirect method called the "survivorship method."[18] His idea is that competition among different sizes of firms in an industry will, in the long run, allow only the most technically efficient firms to survive. Thus, the nature of the industry's long-run cost function will be revealed by the characteristics of the surviving firms.

According to Stigler, if firms of many different sizes in the industry survive in the long run, then we can assume that there are no economies or diseconomies of scale. If only large firms survive, we can say that there are economies of scale. If only small firms survive, we can say that there are diseconomies of scale.

One example Stigler studied is that of firms making steel ingots by open hearth process. Stigler classified the firms involved into size classes and observed the trends in the number of firms as well as in their total market shares. The results are shown in Table 7.3. Stigler concluded that there appear to be economies of scale until an output of about 2.5 percent of industry output is reached. Then, there are neither economies nor diseconomies of scale over a wide range of output (2.5 to 25 percent of industry capacity). The decline in the market share in the largest class indicates diseconomies of scale thereafter.

7.9.3 Plant closing and concentration of output in the short run

This is an example of the use of opportunity costs that we discussed earlier (Section 7.2). Consider a producer who owns two identical plants. Because of a decline in available raw materials, the producer has to cut the output by half. Should the producer operate both plants and produce equal output from each or produce the entire output with a single plant? The problem is illustrated in Figure 7.16. The

---

[16]Several of these problems with a critical review of earlier studies of cost functions are in Johnston, op. cit.

[17]Milton Friedman, "Comment" on a paper by Caleb Smith in *Business Concentration and Price Policy*, NBER, Princeton University Press, Princeton, N.J., 1955, pp. 230–238.

[18]George Stigler, "The Economies of Scale," *The Journal of Law and Economics*, October 1958, pp. 54–71. A criticism of this method is in William G. Shepherd, "What Does the Survivor Technique Show about Economies of Scale?" *The Southern Economic Journal*, July 1967, pp. 113–122.

TABLE 7.3 Trends in the Number of Firms and Their Market Shares in the Steel Ingot Industry

Percentage of Industry Output	Number of Firms			Total Market Share		
	1930	1938	1951	1930	1938	1951
<0.5	39	29	22	7.2	6.1	4.6
0.5–1.0	9	7	7	5.9	5.1	5.4
1.0–2.5	9	6	6	13.2	8.3	9.1
2.5–5.0	3	4	5	10.6	16.6	22.2
5.0–10.0	2	2	1	11.2	14.0	8.1
10.0–25.0	1	1	1	13.2	14.0	16.1
>25.0	1	1	1	38.7	35.9	34.5

total output is *OD*. Let *OB* = ½*OD*. If the output is all produced in a single plant, the total cost would be *CD* × *OD*. However, if half the output is produced in each of the two plants, the total costs would be twice *AB* × *OB* or *AB* × *OD*. Since *AB* > *CD*, it would appear that the total costs are lower if all the output is produced in a single plant.

But this reasoning is incorrect. In the short run, producers cannot do anything else with the equipment they have. Thus, the fixed costs are incurred whether or not the plant is under production. Thus, all that is relevant is total variable costs.

We noted earlier (in Section 7.4) that the area under the *MC* curve measures total variable costs. Thus, the total variable costs of producing the entire output in a single plant is *OECD*. The total variable cost of producing half the output in each plant is twice the area *OEFB*. If area *OEFB* is less than area *BFCD*, then it would be better to produce half the output in each plant, which is the case in Figure 7.16. If area *OEBF* is greater than *BFCD*, then it would be better to produce the entire output in a single plant. This would be the case if the *MC* curve intersected the *y*

FIGURE 7.16 Production from a single plant versus production from two plants.

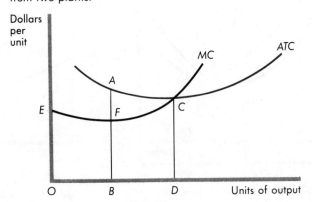

axis at a point much higher than the point E in Figure 7.16, that is, if the marginal costs were very high at low levels of output.[19]

In the preceding analysis we assumed that the marginal costs for the two plants are identical. If they are not, the proper allocation of output between the two plants requires that we equate the marginal costs of the two plants, as shown in Figure 7.17(a) if both the plants are used. We measure the output of plant 1 from left to right and the output of plant 2 from right to left. Thus, the MC curve for the second plant has to be plotted as a mirror image of what it would be if drawn normally (with output measured from left to right).

Since the total variable cost is the area under the marginal cost curves, the minimum total variable cost occurs at the point of intersection A of the marginal cost curves MC_1 and MC_2 of the two plants. This point gives the division of output between the two plants as shown in Figure 7.17(a).

However, note that the point of intersection of the marginal cost curves is not always the optimal point. This is illustrated in Figure 7.17(b), where the MC curve is steep for low levels of output. In this case note that the total variable costs are maximum, not minimum, at the point of intersection A of MC_1 and M_2 (note total variable cost is the area under the MC curve). In this case it is optimal to produce the total output from only one plant. Whether plant 1 or plant 2 will be chosen depends on whether the area under MC_1 is less or greater than the area under MC_2. The way we have drawn the figure, it would be the second plant that will be operated.

This example illustrates the problem of how best to distribute a given output

[19]George Stigler in his book, *The Theory of Price*, Macmillan, New York, 1952, p. 126, gives an example of this problem. During World War II the British government embarked upon a program called "concentration of production." Because of shortage of raw materials, the British fabricating industries were operating at low rates of output. The Board of Trade argued that it was inefficient for all plants to operate at half the output and that it would be better if half the plants operated at full output, thus, concentrating production. Clearly, this argument is not always correct.

FIGURE 7.17 Choice between one and two plants and distribution of output between two plants in the short run.

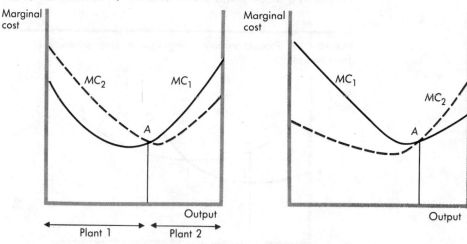

(a) Use both plants for production.

(b) Choose only one plant.

between two plants in the short run and when it is optimal to close down one of the plants.

7.9.4 Cost curves for products that are likely to be fads

Suppose that a producer has two types of plants available for which the average cost curves are shown in Figure 7.18 as ATC_1 and ATC_2. Which plant the producer will choose will depend on the type of variation in output the producer expects. If the output variation is between Q_1 and Q_2, the plant corresponding to ATC_1 is better. If the output variation is between Q_3 and Q_4, then the plant corresponding to ATC_2 is better.

This sort of choice occurs in the production of products with unstable demand (output variation between Q_3 and Q_4). The latter are products which are fads, such as some toys (Cabbage Patch dolls, for instance) or some gaming equipment. The demand for these products may slowly pick up, accelerate, and then suddenly fade away. The producer anticipating the cycle would not invest in long-lasting equipment even though the average cost might be lower at certain ranges of output (such as Q_1 and Q_2 in Figure 7.18) with such equipment.

7.9.5 How important are constraints due to fixity of capital in the short run?

We have frequently referred to capital as the fixed factor and labor as the variable factor. In practice this distinction is not quite so rigid. In fact, one can cite many instances where firms got rid of their capital equipment or acquired some from another firm at short notice. An example of this is the sale of a six-cylinder engine-manufacturing assembly line by General Motors to American Motors in 1968 and a repurchase of the same by General Motors in 1974. Many big corporations buy up small companies when they want to acquire capital equipment in a short time. All this suggests that in some cases capital may not be fixed even in the short run as we have said frequently.

The case of labor is similar. It also is not as variable a factor as we have often said. There are many "sunk costs" associated with labor too, particularly at the higher end of the skill level. These sunk costs are search, hiring, and training costs.

FIGURE 7.18 Average cost curves for two types of plants.

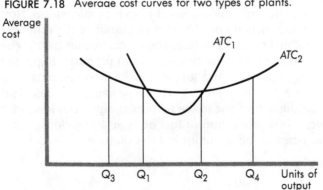

In this case the producer or firm will not fire the employee whenever there is a reduction in output. In the short run, all these employment costs have to be treated as fixed costs. It is only the costs of unskilled workers, who can be hired or fired at short notice, that can be treated as variable costs. The consequences of treating labor as a quasi-fixed factor are discussed in greater detail in Chapter 15.

Another point to note is that in the process of expansion of a producer's output, capital (and other "fixed" factors) may appear as constraints in the short run but may not indeed be. The producer would like to buy more equipment and hire and train more skilled labor only if the output expansion is going to be permanent. For something that is a fad (such as Cabbage Patch dolls) the producer would realize that the demand is temporary and would operate within the constraints of the existing capital equipment and skilled labor but would not expand these factors even in the long run.

7.9.6 Cost curves for multiproduct firms

In the previous sections, we assumed that the producer produces only one product. This assumption was made for the sake of convenience, so as to understand the basic principles. In actual practice, we encounter many cases where the producer produces several products. In this case we have to allocate the total costs to the different products to use the cost data for pricing purposes.

The case of multiple products can be classified into three categories: (1) joint products, (2) independent products, and (3) products whose proportions can be varied. For simplicity, we will consider the case of two products. The theory is similar when we have more than two products.

In the case of *joint products*, the increase or decrease in the production of one of the products results in an automatic proportionate increase or decrease in the production of the other product. The producer has no choice in this case. Examples of joint products are: meat and leather from cows, meat and by-products from livestock, cottonseed and lint. In the case of joint products, since the different products are produced in the same proportion, we can just as well consider one product. Thus, the total costs, variable costs, marginal costs, and so on can be calculated using one of the products. There are no additional problems here.

In the case of *independent products* the costs of the different products are independent and, hence, again there are no problems. We just consider each product separately.

In the third case, calculation of costs is problematical. Now the marginal costs of each output depend on the level of output of the other product. Consider the example of fuel oil and gasoline. The oil companies have a choice of changing the mix of production of these two petroleum products. Suppose the total cost of the production of gasoline and fuel oil for different combinations of these outputs is given by the data in Table 7.4. Then one can easily calculate the marginal costs for the production of one of the outputs at any given level of the other output; for example, when production of fuel oil is at 400 gallons, the *MC* of production of gasoline when gasoline output is 440 gallons is

$$\frac{\$84 - 70}{40} = \frac{\$14}{40} = \$0.35$$

TABLE 7.4 Total Costs of Producing Two Petroleum Products

Output of Fuel Oil (gallons)	Output of Gasoline (gallons)				
	400	440	480	520	560
320	$ 48	$ 60	$ 74	$ 90	$108
360	58	71	86	103	122
400	70	84	100	118	138
440	84	99	116	135	156
480	100	116	134	154	176

We can calculate such marginal costs for different levels of gasoline output, that is, we have:

MC of Gasoline When Output of Gasoline Is	Output of Fuel Oil		
	320	400	480
440	0.30	0.35	0.40
480	0.35	0.40	0.45
520	0.40	0.45	0.50
560	0.45	0.50	0.55

Of course, we can plot these data as a series of *MC* curves. If we wanted to plot the total cost curve from the data in Table 7.4, we would need a three-dimensional diagram with the two outputs being measured on two axes and total cost being measured on the third. Thus, we will get a *cost mountain*. It is to avoid these three-dimensional diagrams that we avoid the discussion of multiple products.

7.10 SUMMARY AND CONCLUSIONS

Minimizing cost for a given output will yield the same optimal input bundle as maximizing output for that given total cost. The concept of opportunity cost is the cost concept most relevant to economic decisions. It is defined as the value of a resource in its next best use.

Long-run average cost equals long-run total cost divided by output. Long-run marginal cost equals the change in total cost divided by the corresponding change in output. Marginal cost reaches a minimum at an output corresponding to the inflection point on the total cost curve. Average cost reaches a minimum at an output corresponding to the point of tangency between the total cost curve and a ray from the origin.

In the short run, the quantities of some inputs are fixed. The cost of these fixed inputs is called fixed cost. In the short run, total cost equals total variable cost plus total fixed cost. And average total cost equals average fixed cost plus average variable cost. Each average cost is equal to the corresponding total cost divided by output.

When MC is greater than ATC, ATC is rising, and when MC is less than ATC, ATC is falling. Similarly, when MC is greater than AVC, AVC is rising, and when MC is less than AVC, AVC is falling. Thus, MC must intersect both of these average curves at their minimum points. Total variable cost is the area under the MC curve.

In the case of a single variable input, if average product is rising then AVC is falling. And if marginal product is rising, MC is falling.

The long-run average cost curve is the envelope of the short-run average total cost curves. Short-run average total cost is always greater than or equal to long-run average cost.

Plant capacity is defined as the output corresponding to the minimum point on the short-run average total cost curve. At the point of tangency between a short-run average total cost curve and the long-run average cost curve, short-run marginal cost equals long-run marginal cost. Economies of scale cause the $LRAC$ curve to slope downward, whereas diseconomies of scale cause the $LRAC$ curve to slope upward. External economies of scale cause the $LRAC$ curve to shift downward, and external diseconomies cause it to shift upward.

Holding the input-price ratio and output constant, technological change is classified as labor saving if the optimal capital-labor ratio increases. It is capital saving if the capital-labor ratio falls. And the technological change is neutral if the optimal capital-labor ratio is unaffected. All forms of technological change cause a downward shift in the cost functions.

For industries with large fixed input requirements, the $LRAC$ curve may be strictly downward sloping. This implies that MC is strictly less than $LRAC$. According to the survivor principle, we can infer the shape of the $LRAC$ curve from changes in the size distribution of firms over time.

In the short run, the proper allocation of output between plants requires that we equate the marginal cost of the two plants if both plants are to be used. The producer of products likely to be fads will not invest in long-lasting equipment even though the average cost can be lowered at certain ranges of output.

We frequently refer to capital as a fixed input and labor as a variable input. In the real world, this is frequently not the case.

If two or more products are produced in fixed proportion, the cost curves can be constructed with reference to a single product. In the case of independent products, each product can be considered separately. In the case of multiple products with variable proportions, two-dimensional cost curves are infeasible.

KEY TERMS

Accounting Cost
Average Cost
Capital-saving Technological
   Change
Change in Technique

Excess Capacity
External Economies of Scale
Fixed Costs
Independent Products
Internal Economies of Scale

Joint Products
Labor-saving Technological
   Change
Long Run
Marginal Cost

Neutral Technological Change	Short Run	Survivor Principle
Opportunity Cost	Social Cost	Technological Change
Plant Capacity	Sunk Cost	Variable Costs
Private Cost		

QUESTIONS

1. What are the accounting costs of your college education? What are the economic costs? How do they compare?

2. Explain why short-run MC is equal to the slope of both the TC and the TVC curves.

3. How is the law of diminishing marginal returns related to the shape of the short-run marginal cost curve?

4. Draw the relationship between the long-run and short-run average and marginal cost curves when the LRAC is rising.

5. How does the change in an input's price affect the various short-run cost curves? Consider the case of both a fixed input's price and a variable input's price.

6. According to the survivorship principle, what might the plight of the family farm tell us about returns to scale in agriculture? What are some of the problems with this analysis?

7. How do external economies and diseconomies of scale affect the firm's long-run marginal cost curve? Why?

8. Using an isoquant map and a given input-price ratio, explain how one would derive the long-run and short-run total cost curves.

9. Suppose that a widget producer's total cost function is as follows:

$$TC = 300 + 3Q + 0.02Q^2$$

where TC is total cost in dollars and Q is the number of cases of widgets produced. What is the corresponding TFC function? The AFC function? The TVC function? The AVC function? Plot these curves as well as the MC curve for the first six units of output.

10. If the long-run total cost curve is linear, what do the corresponding average and marginal cost curves look like?

11. Why is a typical short-run average total cost curve more U-shaped than the long-run average total cost curve?

12. Examine whether the following statements are true or false. Explain your answer.

    a. Short-run average total cost is never less than long-run average total cost.

    b. Short-run marginal cost is never less than long-run marginal cost.

    c. If the production function exhibits increasing returns to scale everywhere, a firm's long-run average cost curve must be declining.

    d. Hospital costs are high because, although the case load of a hospital varies widely over time, the hospital has to maintain its nursing staff at a constant level and nursing costs account for over 60 percent of total hospital costs.

13. A firm providing food services provides you with the following results from past operations: Q is meals sold per day, P is price per meal, TFC is total fixed cost, and TVC is total variable cost.

Q	P	TFC	TVC
0	$3.50	$150	$ 0
100	3.25	150	300
200	3.00	150	500
300	2.75	150	650
400	2.50	150	750
500	2.25	150	830
600	2.00	150	905
700	1.75	150	995
800	1.50	150	1110
900	1.25	150	1260
1000	1.00	150	1460

a. Calculate *TR, MR, TC, MC, AFC, AVC, ATC,* and profit for each level of output *Q*.

b. Determine the optimal output and price for maximization of profit. What is the total profit?

c. Draw the following graphs: price against quantity—the demand curve; *TR, TC,* and profit against quantity; *TFC, TVC, TC* against quantity; *AFC, AVC, TC* against quantity; *MC, MR,* profit against quantity.

d. What does profit maximization imply about *MC* and *MR?*

14. The following are hypothetical costs for an airline for a single flight from New York to Los Angeles on a Boeing 707 with 180 seats:

- Maintenance and depreciation　　$2400
- Fuel　　$5200
- Salary for crew　　$7200
- Administrative salaries　　$4200
- Cost of sales and publicity　　$2200
- Office rent　　$5600
- Interest on debt　　$7060

a. What are the total fixed costs of the flight? What are the total variable costs of the flight?

b. If the fare is set at a level that covers total costs at 50 percent of the capacity, what will the fare be? What then is the marginal cost to the airline of carrying the ninety-first passenger?

c. Should the airline agree to supply a charter flight for a group that offers to guarantee the sale of 150 tickets at a price of $225 per ticket? Explain your reasoning. Assume that the charter would use the same equipment with the same costs of operation as the scheduled service.

d. Now the airline buys a new wide-bodied 747 that holds 400 passengers and operates with essentially the same costs as the 707 except that the fuel costs and salary for crew double. If the airline follows the same pricing policy as before, by how much will the New York-Los Angeles fare decline for a traveler on a regularly scheduled flight?

15. The following is a production function for a firm that employs two inputs: capital K and labor L to produce output X. Assume that $X = 0$ if $K = 0$ and $L = 0$.

L \ K	1	2	3	4
1	50	60	70	75
2	60	100	115	135
3	70	115	150	160
4	75	135	160	200

Assume that the wage rate is $10 per unit of labor and the rental price is $15 per unit of capital. Sketch the *LRTC, LRAC,* and *LRMC* curves on the basis of the corresponding short-run curves for $K = 1, 2, 3,$ and 4.

CHAPTER 8

THEORY OF THE FIRM AND PRODUCTION:
SOME ALTERNATIVE MODELS

8.1 INTRODUCTION

In the previous two chapters we considered the technology of production. In practice, production is organized within a firm. The term "firm" is an analytical label for an organization that transforms inputs into goods and services. A firm can consist of a sole proprietor or several thousands of employees (IBM, General Motors, AT&T, and so on). The common feature of all firms is that inputs are purchased and transformed into outputs of goods and services.

The *theory of the firm* is an important topic in microeconomics and is concerned with explaining and predicting the behavior of firms particularly with respect to pricing and output decisions. The topic also includes choice of production processes, promotion of sales through advertising, introduction of new products (product innovation), investment decisions, and dividend policy. Traditional theories of the firm are based on the assumption of profit maximization. This is the assumption we have made in the previous two chapters. Modern theories of the firm emphasize the separation of ownership and control. The managers of the firm control the operations, and the ownership is dispersed among a large number of shareholders. Since output and pricing decisions are made by managers rather than the owners, the new theories are called *managerial theories of the firm*. We shall consider three such models: those based on sales maximization, growth maximization, and utility maximization. Another set of theories is the *behavioral theories of the firm* where the assumption that something is maximized is replaced with one of satisficing behavior. Principal proponents of this approach are H. Simon, R. M. Cyert, and J. G. March.[1] A significant contribution of their work has been to focus attention on the internal organization of the firm. We will not be discussing the behavioral theories because they depend on psychology and organizational theory.

Why do firms exist?

In a classic paper published in 1937, Ronald Coase raised the question: "How can economists explain the existence of firms?"[2] In principle, firms are not really necessary. One could imagine separate contracts for each function of a firm. For instance, consider car assembly. One individual could manufacture part of the car and then sell it to another individual who would add another part and sell it to a third individual who would add another part and so on. The assembly line would be replaced by a series of individual contracts. The activities of car production would be done individually and coordinated through prices.

There are two reasons that production is organized through firms rather than through a series of individual contracts: transactions costs and higher productivity under teamwork.

Transactions and exchange are not costless. Firms economize on transactions. In the absence of firms we have to deal with multilateral contracts. Each individual would have to negotiate a contract with the person supplying the materials and with the person buying the goods. In the example of car assembly, every individual in the chain would have to enter into two contracts. Such a complex set of contracts

---

[1]See R. Cyert and J. March, *Behavioral Theory of the Firm*, Prentice-Hall, Englewood Cliffs, N.J., 1963.

[2]Ronald H. Coase, "The Nature of the Firm," *Economica* vol. 4, November 1937, pp. 386–405.

would be costly to negotiate. Firms reduce these costs by the method of bilateral contracts. Each individual deals with the firm on a bilateral basis rather than with other individuals on a multilateral basis.

In many activities a larger output can be obtained from a team than from the separate individuals working independently.[3] Group production yields the benefits of specialization. However, group production has some costs. Problems arise because there can be shirking and "free riding." Under group production, it is often difficult to assess the separate contribution of each individual. The costs of an individual's preference for on-the-job leisure are shifted to the group. By contrast, under independent production the individual bears all the costs of leisure. This free-riding problem can be solved by hiring a monitor to discipline the team. This implies that the costs of monitoring have to be weighed against the benefits of the greater productivity arising from group production.

Agency theory of the firm

An alternative to the managerial and behavioral theories we have mentioned is the agency theory suggested by Jensen and Meckling.[4] This is also a managerial theory but with a different emphasis which we will explain. Economists have long been concerned with the incentive problems that arise when decision making in the firm is in the hands of managers who do not own a major share of the firm. The managerial and behavioral theories that were suggested in the 1960s (which we discuss in the following section) reject the classical model of an entrepreneur who single-mindedly operates the firm to maximize profits, in favor of different motivations for the managers (sales maximization, growth maximization, utility maximization, satisficing, and so on). The agency theory also rejects the classical model of the firm (an entrepreneur maximizing profits) but assumes classical forms of economic behavior on the part of agents of the firm. Alchian and Demsetz, and Jensen and Meckling view the firm as a set of contracts among factors of production. In effect the firm is viewed as a team, and the members act in self-interest because their survival depends on how best they compete with the other teams. The agency theory has attracted quite a bit of attention during recent years.[5]

In the following sections (sections 8.2 to 8.5) we discuss the different managerial theories of the firm that were proposed in the 1960s (the sales maximization, growth maximization, and utility maximization models). They have been superceded by the new theories of the 1970s and 1980s, but since they form the basis of the new theories, we discuss them here.

In Sections 8.6 and 8.7 we consider the special theory of production when inputs have to be combined in fixed proportions. This model gives rise to the concepts of shadow prices and shadow costs, which are often used in models of central planning. Actually, we could have discussed this model in Chapter 6, but

---

[3]The advantages of group production are discussed in Armen Alchian and Harold Demsetz, "Production, Information Costs and Economic Organization," *American Economic Review*, vol. 62, December 1972, pp. 777–795.

[4]M. C. Jensen and W. J. Meckling, "Theory of the Firm: Managerial Behavior, Agency Costs and Ownership Structure," *Journal of Financial Economics*, October 1976, pp. 305–360. See also Alchian and Demsetz, op. cit..

[5]Interested students can refer to the papers in the June 1983 issue of the *Journal of Law and Economics*: E. F. Fama and M. C. Jensen, "Separation of Ownership and Control," pp. 301–325 and "Agency Problems and Residual Claims," pp. 327–349; O. E. Williamson, "Organizational Form, Residual Claimants and Corporate Control," pp. 351–366; Benjamin Klein, "Contracting Costs and Residual Claims: The Separation of Ownership and Control," pp. 367–374; and H. Demsetz, "The Structure of Ownership and the Theory of the Firm," pp. 375–390.

we have included its discussion in this chapter because it is ideally suited for solving managerial problems.

EXAMPLE 8.1   How Separate Are Ownership and Control?

The following table gives an idea of the extent of ownership interest of corporate directors and management in U.S. corporations. The data are based on an un-weighted average for the period 1973 to 1982.

	Percentage of shares
Manufacturing firms:	
Ten largest on 1975 Fortune 500	2.1
Middle 10 on 1975 Fortune 500	19.3
Last 10 on 1975 Fortune 500	20.4
Ten too small for 1975 Fortune 500 (randomly selected)	32.5
Ten public utility firms (randomly selected)	32.5
Average over all 50 firms	17.5

Source: H. Demsetz, ''The Structure of Ownership and the Theory of the Firm,'' Journal of Law and Economics, June 1983, p. 388, table 1.

Demsetz, however, argues that the numbers underestimate the degree of ownership representation because corporate executives, although often not among the largest shareholders, receive incomes (salaries and bonuses) that are highly correlated with stock performance. Thus, ownership and control are not so separate as is often supposed.

8.2   THE SALES MAXIMIZATION MODEL

The sales maximization model developed by Baumol is a managerial theory of the firm.[6] It suggests that firms maximize sales revenue subject to a minimum profit contraint. Larger sales might give managers satisfaction from greater firm size and the associated prestige. Their salaries and benefits might also be related to sales performance rather than profits. The profit constraint is specified as that minimum level that is necessary to secure shareholder acquiescence. Baumol suggested that this model is typical of oligopoly behavior.

If this constrained maximization problem is solved by the choice of output level, we can show that output is higher under the sales maximization model than under the profit maximization model. This is shown in Figures 8.1 and 8.2. In Figure 8.1 we show the derivation of the profit curve Π from the TR (total revenue)

[6]W. J. Baumol, *Business Behavior, Value and Growth,* Macmillan, New York, 1959. Review by F. M. Fisher in *Journal of Political Economy,* vol. 68, June 1960, pp. 314–315.

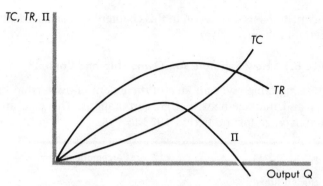

FIGURE 8.1   Total cost (TC), total revenue (TR), and profits (Π) curves.

and TC (total cost) curves. Profits $\Pi = TR - TC$ are maximum at the output level where the slopes of the TR and TC curves are equal (or where $MR = MC$).

In Figure 8.2 we show the constrained maximization. Q_1 is the level of output at which profits are maximum. Q_2 is the maximum level of output which satisfies the profit constraint. The sales-maximizing firm chooses the output level in the range Q_1 to Q_2 that maximizes total revenue TR. This is the output level QS in Figure 8.2. Note that at the profit-maximizing output level Q_1, TR cannot reach a maximum since at this point $MR = MC$ and, since MC must always be positive, MR has to be positive, so that TR is increasing.

We have assumed that the output level is the only choice variable. Suppose that we include advertising also as a choice variable. Then it can be shown that either advertising *or* output level must be higher than the profit-maximizing levels but not necessarily both.[7]

8.3   THE GROWTH MAXIMIZATION MODEL

The growth maximization model is another managerial theory of the firm and was suggested by Penrose and Marris.[8] This theory is considered appropriate to a corporate economy and is concerned with the time path of expansion of the firm. Managers are assumed to satisfy instincts of power dominance and prestige (and possibly higher salary) by pursuing growth as an objective. They also take account of the valuation ratio, which is the ratio of the stock market value of the firm to its accounting or book value.

The relationship between the valuation ratio and the growth rate is described by the *valuation curve* shown in Figure 8.3. The valuation curve takes into account the relationship between growth and profitability and the present value of shareholders' dividends and capital gains. After a point the valuation ratio declines. If it is substantially below 1, then the firm is threatened by a takeover. The managers'

[7]This can be proved algebraically but we will omit the proof. A geometric illustration is cumbersome.

[8]E. T. Penrose, *The Theory of the Growth of the Firm*, Blackwell, Oxford, 1959, and R. L. Marris, *The Economic Theory of Managerial Capitalism*, Macmillan, London, 1964.

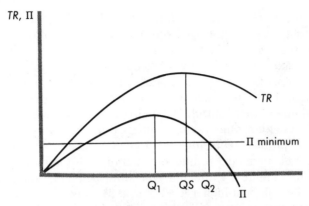

FIGURE 8.2   Output determination under sales maximization.

preferences for valuation and growth can be depicted by indifference curves as shown in Figure 8.3. The maximum satisfaction obtained by the managers occurs at the growth rate g_1 with the corresponding valuation ratio V_1. The growth rate that maximizes stockholders' equity (which is also the profit-maximizing point) is at the growth rate g_0 with the corresponding valuation ratio V_0. The growth maximization model results in a higher growth rate and lower valuation ratio than the profit maximization model. Note that the maximum growth rate the managers can pursue is g_2 corresponding to a valuation ratio of 1. Any higher growth rate will result in a threat of the firm being taken over.

8.4   THE UTILITY MAXIMIZATION MODEL

A more general model in the managerial theory of the firm is the utility maximization model by Williamson.[9] In this model the utility function of the managers

[9]O. Williamson, *The Economics of Discretionary Behavior: Management Objectives in a Theory of the Firm*, Prentice-Hall, Englewood Cliffs, N.J., 1964.

FIGURE 8.3   Growth maximization model.

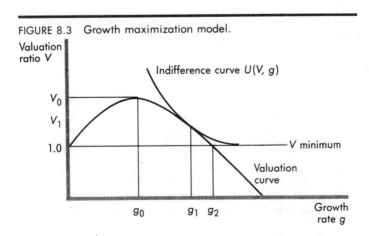

depends on expenditures on staff, managerial emoluments, and so on. Managers obtain satisfaction and prestige from the number of staff under their control and from the luxury offices, company cars, expense accounts, and bonuses they get. Managers maximize their utility subject to a minimum profit constraint. There are several other variations of this model, but we will illustrate a few simple ones. Suppose that the utility function of the managers depends on profits and the size of the staff under their control. The indifference curves are as shown in Figure 8.4. Profits increase for a while as the number of staff increases, but after a point profits decline. The profit-maximizing model gives S_0 as the optimum level of staff. The utility maximizing model results in a staff of S_1. If the minimum profit constraint is as shown in Figure 8.4, the utility-maximizing model results in a staff of S_2. The final solution will be a higher level of staff and lower total profits than under the profit-maximizing model. A similar conclusion holds when we consider other objectives in the utility function.

8.5 EFFECTS OF PROFIT TAXES IN THE ALTERNATIVE MODELS OF FIRM BEHAVIOR

We have presented three alternatives to the profit maximization model. There is, however, a fundamental debate over whether we should choose between the alternative models on the basis of realism of assumptions or their predictive accuracy. Milton Friedman argued that it is not meaningful to talk of realism of assumptions on which a theory is based, because theories, being abstractions, cannot exhibit complete realism and the question of whether a theory is realistic enough can only be settled by seeing whether it yields predictions that are good enough for the purpose at hand or that are better than predictions from alternative theories.[10] Thus, the assumption of profit maximization can only be tested by the theory's predictions and not by any measure of the "realism" of the profit-maximizing "firm."

How are predictions to be tested? They are to be tested by studying the effects

[10]M. Friedman, "The Methodology of Positive Economics," in *Essays in Positive Economics*, University of Chicago Press, Chicago, 1953.

FIGURE 8.4 Utility maximization model (utility is a function of profits and staff size).

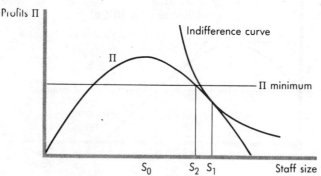

of different policies (taxes, subsidies) or changes in economic conditions on prices and outputs. Machlup argues that the models of the firm are not designed to explain and predict the behavior of real firms.[11] Instead, he believes that the models are designed to explain and predict changes in observed prices as effects of particular changes in conditions (wage rates, interest rates, import duties, excise taxes, and so on). "In this causal connection, the firm is only a theoretical link, a mental construct helping to explain how one gets from the cause to the effect. This is altogether different from explaining the behavior of a firm."

Instead of a detailed analysis of the impact of different policies or changes in economic conditions on output and prices in the different models, we will consider one policy: that of a profits tax. First consider a lump-sum profits tax. It is clear that in Figure 8.2, the profit curve will shift vertically downward with such a tax. The profit-maximizing output Q_1 will remain unaltered. But Q_2 will now be closer to Q_1, and thus we conclude that although output will remain unchanged under profit maximization, output may decline under sales maximization.

What will be the effect of a percentage tax on profits? Now the profit curve will be flatter than before but will have the maximum at the same output level as before. Thus, the profit-maximizing output will remain unchanged at Q_1. However, since the profit curve is flatter, output will decline under sales maximization (with a binding profit constraint).

What about the utility maximization model? With a lump-sum tax, since the profit curve shifts downward vertically in Figure 8.4, we can conclude that output will decline. With a percentage tax (which makes the profit curve flatter) we cannot say whether output will rise, fall, or remain unchanged. It depends on the shape of the indifference curves. (Drawing the appropriate diagrams is left as an exercise.)

The above cases illustrate how we can analyze the effects of different policies in the alternative models.

8.6 LINEAR PROGRAMMING

Linear programming is a mathematical technique for solving maximization or minimization problems where the constraints and the functions to be maximized or minimized are linear and, thus, can be represented by straight lines. We discuss this technique here because it is an important development in the theory of the firm, and managers must often solve constrained optimization problems. Linear programming was developed by the Russian mathematician L. V. Kantorovich in 1939 and extended by the U.S. mathematician G. B. Dantzig in 1947. There are now computer programs available to solve complex optimization problems.

Choice of production processes
Although linear programming can be used to solve a variety of managerial problems, it is used most frequently in production decisions. Often managers need to determine the least-cost input bundle that will yield a specified output, or they

---

[11]F. Machlup, "Theories of the Firm: Marginalist, Behavioral, Managerial," *American Economic Review*, vol. 57, March 1967, p. 9.

might want to determine the maximum output obtainable from specified quantities of inputs.

We will first examine these problems in a simple setting: We will consider the firm which produces only one output but has several production processes available to it. The linear programming approach is based on the assumptions of (1) constant input and output prices, (2) constant returns to scale, and (3) the existence of several technologically fixed input proportions (called "processes") with which to

FIGURE 8.5   Isoquants when production takes place under fixed input proportions.

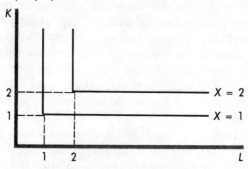

(a) Single production process.

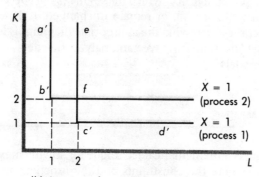

(b) Isoquants for each production process.

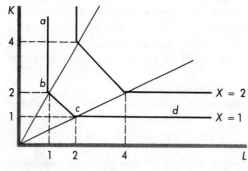

(c) Two production processes.

produce the single output. These assumptions imply that long-run average cost curves are horizontal. Assumption (3) implies that the isoquants are not smooth (as we discussed in Chapter 6) but are made up of straight line segments.

To see what the isoquants look like under fixed input proportions, let us consider two inputs: capital K and labor L. Suppose it requires 1 unit of L and 1 unit of K to produce 1 unit of output X. Then the isoquants will be as in Figure 8.5(a). If we have 1 unit of L and 2 units of K, the extra unit of K is a waste. All we can produce is 1 unit of output. In this case K is called a *slack* variable.

In the preceding example the output X can be produced by a single production process. Consider now the case of two processes. (The case of more processes is similar.) Suppose that to produce 1 unit of X, process 1 requires 2 units of L and 1 unit of K and process 2 requires 1 unit of L and 2 units of K. These isoquants are shown in Figure 8.5(b). If a firm can produce using process 1 or process 2 or both, then its isoquants are as shown in Figure 8.5(c). The portion ab of the isoquant for 1 unit of output X is the portion $a'b'$ of the isoquant for 1 unit of output using process 2. For these input bundles, process 2 yields a larger output. Similarly, the portion cd of the isoquant for 1 unit of output corresponds to the portion $c'd'$ of the isoquant for 1 unit of output using process 1. For the input bundles along cd, process 1 yields a larger output. The segment bc is a linear combination of the points b' and c' in panel (b). The input bundles along bc will produce 1 unit of output only if both production processes are used. For example, one point on the segment bc represents the bundle $L = K = 1\frac{1}{2}$. This bundle does not contain enough K to produce 1 unit of output with process 2 and does not contain enough L to produce 1 unit using process 1. But to product $\frac{1}{2}$ unit of output using process 1 requires $K = \frac{1}{2}$ and $L = 1$, whereas producing $\frac{1}{2}$ unit using process 2 requires $K = 1$ and $L = \frac{1}{2}$. Thus, 1 unit of output can be produced by combining the two processes.

Suppose now that we specify the amounts of L and K that the producer has at her disposal, and determine the maximum output the producer can produce and the production processes used. We can draw the isoquants and locate the highest isoquant feasible for the given input combination. This is shown in Figure 8.6. We get the following results:

Input Combination	Result
1 unit of L, 3 units of K (point e)	1 unit of X; process 2 used; 1 unit of K wasted.
6 units of L, 2 units of K (point f)	2 units of X; process 1 used; 2 units of L wasted.
5 units of L, 4 units of K (point g)	3 units of X; process 1 produces 2 units; process 2 produces 1 unit; no inputs wasted.

We can also determine the production process (or processes) which will be chosen from input prices. This is shown in Figure 8.7: $abcd$ is our isoquant. Note that the slope of segment bc equals -1. Now as we know, for a given total cost the producer will try to reach the highest possible isoquant. If $P_L = P_K$, then the

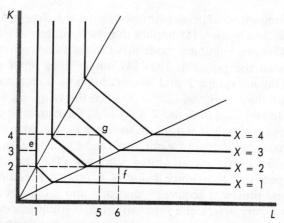

FIGURE 8.6   Maximum output obtainable from given input quantities.

isocost lines will be parallel to segment *bc,* and both production processes will be used. If $P_L > P_K$, then process 2, which uses less of L and more of K, will be used. And if $P_L < P_K$, then process 1, which uses more of L and less of K, will be used.

Until now we have illustrated the nature of isoquants when production is carried under fixed input combinations and the determination of the output level and choice of production processes when (1) input prices are given or (2) input quantities are given. In both cases we simplified the analysis by considering a single-product firm. We are now ready to apply linear programming to the production problems of a multiproduct firm.

Profit-maximizing output mix

Suppose that a firm produces two commodities X and Y and has at its disposal 8 units of labor L, 5 units of capital K, and 3 units of raw materials R. Suppose that each unit of output X requires 1 L, 1 K and 1 R, and each unit of output Y requires

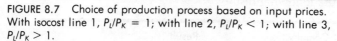

FIGURE 8.7   Choice of production process based on input prices. With isocost line 1, $P_L/P_K = 1$; with line 2, $P_L/P_K < 1$; with line 3, $P_L/P_K > 1$.

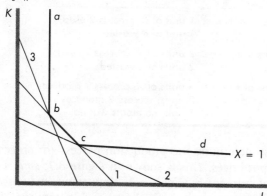

2 L and 1 K and no R. The firm earns \$15 on each unit of X it sells and \$10 on each unit of Y it sells. Since input quantities are given, we take total revenues as total profits.

What we want to know is how many units of X and Y are produced. We follow these steps:

1. First we formulate the objective function and state the constraints. The objective function is (assuming no fixed costs)

Total profits $\Pi = 15X + 10Y$

The input constraints are

L: $1X + 2Y \le 8$
K: $1X + 1Y \le 5$
R: $1X \quad\quad \le 3$

The nonnegativity constraints are

$X \ge 0, Y \ge 0$

The last constraints merely state that outputs cannot be negative.

2. The second step is to plot the *feasible* region of production. We plot a line corresponding to each constraint and the feasible region is shown in Figure 8.8 as the shaded area.

3. The third step is to superimpose the isoprofit lines and see the maximum level of profit that can be reached. This is shown in Figure 8.9. We see that the maximum profit occurs when $X = 3$ and $Y = 2$. Profits are $\Pi = \$65$. Also, for this level of production both K and R are completely utilized, but an extra unit of

FIGURE 8.8   Feasible region implied by the input constraints.

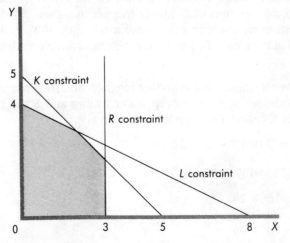

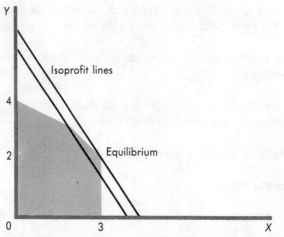

FIGURE 8.9 Determination of the optimal production levels.

L is left over. In the next section when we discuss shadow prices, we will see that the shadow prices are $0 for L, $10 for K, and $5 for R. Note that the total value of the resources of the firm is $65, which is exactly equal to the maximum profit. This is indeed the way shadow prices are supposed to be.

Cost minimization

Linear programming can also be used to determine the cost-minimizing input mix when products are produced in fixed proportions and output requirements are given. For example, consider Caughtone Inc., a firm in the commercial fishing business. The firm has a deep water and a shallow water fleet. The cost of one day of deep water fishing is $3,000, whereas the cost of a day's shallow water fishing is only $2,000. The firm has a contract to supply a packing plant with three qualities of fish: X, Y, and Z. A day of deep water fishing will produce 1 ton of X-quality fish, 1 ton of Y-quality fish, and 2 tons of Z-quality fish. A day of shallow water fishing will yield 1 ton of X-quality fish, 2 tons of Y-quality fish, and 1 ton of Z-quality fish. The firm's contract calls for 28 tons of X-quality fish, 36 tons of Y-quality fish, and 36 tons of Z-quality fish per month.

The question we want to ask is how many tons of X, Y, and Z fish the firm produces and at what cost. To solve this problem, again we go through the following steps:

1. First we formulate the objective function and state the constraints. (Define D to be the number of days of deep water fishing and B the number of days of shallow water fishing.) The objective function is

Costs $C = 3,000D + 2,000B$

The output constraints are

X: $1D + 1B \geq 28$
Y: $1D + 2B \geq 36$
Z: $2D + 1B \geq 36$

The nonnegativity constraints are

$D, B \geq 0$

2. The second step is to plot the feasible region of production. We plot a line corresponding to each constraint and the feasible region is shown as the shaded area in Figure 8.10.

3. The third step is to superimpose the isocost lines and see the minimum level of cost reached. This is shown in Figure 8.11. We see that the minimum cost occurs when $D = 8$ and $B = 20$, so that $C = \$64,000$. For these inputs the outputs are $X = 28$, $Y = 48$, and $Z = 36$. The firm produces the minimum required amounts of X and Z but overproduces 12 units of Y. In the next section when we discuss shadow prices, we will see that since there is surplus output of Y, its shadow price is 0. The shadow prices of X and Y, we will see are $\$1,000$ for X and $\$1,000$ for Z. The shadow price of total output is, thus, $\$64,000$, which is exactly the minimum cost of production.

Applications of linear programming

We have given very simple illustrations of two types of linear programming problems: profit maximization and cost minimization. There are several applications of the linear programming methods. One prominent example is that of the petroleum industry, of which there were many studies in the 1950s.[12]

For profit maximization problems we are interested in determining the optimum product mix given the input constraints. In the case of the petroleum industry we can consider the product mix as consisting of gasoline (leaded and unleaded),

[12]A. Charnes, W. Cooper, and B. Mellon, "Blending Aviation Gasolines," *Econometrica*, April 1952, pp. 135–159, and "A Model for Programming and Sensitivity Analysis in an Integrated Oil Company," *Econometrica*, April 1954, pp. 193–217. Another study is A. Manne, *Scheduling of Petroleum Refinery Operations*, Harvard University Press, Cambridge, Mass., 1956.

FIGURE 8.10   Feasible region implied by the output constraints.

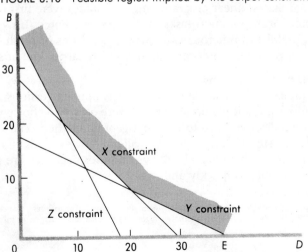

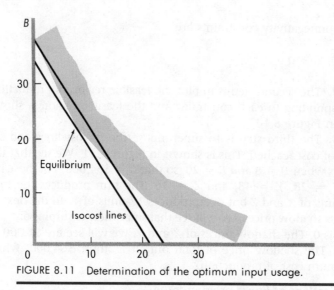

FIGURE 8.11   Determination of the optimum input usage.

heating oil, diesel fuel, kerosene, and lubricants. The input constraints are limited crude supplies and refining capacity. Another example is that of forest products. The product mix consists of lumber, plywood, and paper. The input constraints are the given supply of logs and fixed milling capacity.

For cost minimization problems we are interested in determining the amounts of inputs used subject to the minimum requirements of the different outputs. One prominent example of this is the computation of a minimum-cost diet. The inputs here are different foods: milk, bread, eggs, meats, vegetables, and so on. The output constraints are minimum levels of carbohydrate, protein, minerals, and so forth. Another application of linear programming techniques is for the determination of least-cost transportation systems. If we have a number of warehouses with given supplies and a number of consumption centers with specified demands, then the task is to devise a scheme of shipments that can be done with minimum cost. In the United States, linear programming techniques were first used to help with the complicated transportation tasks of the U.S. Air Force. However, the procedures are also useful in numerous cases where deliveries of products have to be made at different retailing centers and production is carried out at some other centers.

Computational problems

The examples we have illustrated are very simplified versions, and we could obtain the solutions graphically because there were only two choice variables. With more choice variables, we have to use an algebraic method. The commonly suggested method is the simplex method.[13] We will not, however, discuss it because it involves quite a bit of algebraic detail. Many computer packages are available which will solve such problems quickly and easily.

[13]See G. Dantzig, *Linear Programming and Extensions,* Princeton University Press, Princeton, N.J., 1963. In 1984 N. Karmarkar of Bell Labs suggested an alternative algorithm that permits much faster solutions of linear programming problems.

8.7 SHADOW PRICES

One of the most important economic applications of the linear programming method is the derivation of shadow prices.[14] In the profit maximization problem that we discussed in the last section, we specified output prices, and the firm had given quantities of inputs at its disposal. The firm was not purchasing the inputs. Based on the constraints the firm faces, it can assign some imputed prices to the inputs (based on their scarcity value). These imputed prices are called "shadow prices" of the inputs. Similarly, in the cost minimization problem, we are given input prices but not output prices. Again, the firm can assign some imputed prices to the outputs. These prices are called "shadow prices" of outputs. The term "shadow price" is used in other contexts as well, particularly in the planning of investment projects when market prices do not reflect social values. This will be the case when a project uses inputs that are purchased on a distorted market where the distortion takes the form of a divergence between the demand price and marginal cost. The problems of private versus social costs are discussed in Chapter 19. For the present we will use the term "shadow price" as it relates to the linear programming models.

The shadow prices are derived by considering an alternative linear programming problem called the "dual problem." Every linear programming problem has a corresponding problem called its dual; the original problem is called the "primal problem." If the primal is a maximization problem, the dual is a minimization problem, and if the primal is a minimization problem, the dual is a maximization problem. In the profit maximization problem in the previous section, we considered the production of two outputs X and Y given 8 units of L, 5 units of K, and 3 units of R. The dual for this problem is a cost minimization problem. Let P_1, P_2, P_3 be the (shadow) prices or imputed values of a unit of L, K, and R, respectively. Then total cost is

$$C = 8P_1 + 5P_2 + 3P_3$$

The imputed value of a unit of X is $P_1 + P_2 + P_3$ and that of a unit of Y is $2P_1 + P_2$. The market prices were given to be \$15 for a unit of X and \$10 for a unit of Y. Thus, we minimize C subject to the constraints

$$P_1 + P_2 + P_3 \geq 15$$
$$2P_1 + P_2 \geq 10$$

This is the dual cost-minimization problem to the profit maximization problem discussed in the previous section. We can solve this linear programming problem and get the shadow prices P_1, P_2, P_3.

We will first reduce the problem to one of two choice variables (otherwise, we cannot use the geometric method). There is an alternative way of looking at shadow prices. The shadow price of labor L is obtained by asking the question:

[14]Many other economic applications are discussed in R. Dorfman, P. Samuelson, and R. Solow, *Linear Programming and Economic Analysis*, McGraw-Hill, New York, 1958.

"How much would profits rise if we increase L by one unit?" The shadow prices of the other inputs are obtained by asking a similar question. Now we saw already that there were surplus units of L. Thus, increasing L by one unit, keeping other inputs constraints constant, does not increase profits at all. Thus, the shadow price of L, which is P_1, is 0. So the cost minimization problem becomes:

$$\text{Minimize } C = 5P_2 + 3P_3$$
$$\text{Subject to } P_2 + P_3 \geq 15$$
$$P_2 \geq 10$$
$$P_2, P_3 \geq 0$$

The solution is $P_2 = \$10$, $P_3 = \$5$, and minimum $C = \$65$, which is the result we stated earlier. It can be checked (this is left as an exercise) that if K is increased by 1 unit (other inputs remaining constant), total profits will go up by $10, and if R is increased 1 unit, total profits will go up by $5.

Returning to the cost minimization problem considered in the previous section, the dual would be a revenue maximization problem. Let P_1, P_2, P_3 be the imputed prices of the outputs of X, Y, and Z, respectively. Then total revenues are

$$TR = 28P_1 + 36P_2 + 36P_3$$

We maximize this subject to the constraints

$$P_1 + P_2 + 2P_3 \leq 3{,}000$$
$$P_1 + 2P_2 + P_3 \leq 2{,}000$$

Again, we can look at the shadow prices another way. We ask the question: "How much would costs increase if we were required to produce an extra unit of X, other output constraints remaining the same?" This extra cost is the shadow price or imputed value of a unit of X. The shadow prices of the other outputs are obtained by asking a similar question. Now we saw that the firm, in trying to meet the minimum requirements for X and Z, was already overproducing Y. Thus, increasing the requirement for Y by 1 unit does not increase costs. The shadow price of Y, which is P_2, is 0. Thus, the maximization problem reduces to

$$\text{Maximize } TR = 28P_1 + 36P_3$$
$$\text{Subject to } P_1 + 2P_3 \leq 3{,}000$$
$$P_1 + P_3 \leq 2{,}000$$

This gives $P_2 = 1000$, $P_3 = 1000$, and $TR = 64{,}000$ as we stated earlier in the previous section.

To answer questions such as "How much would costs rise if one output requirement is increased by 1 unit?" involves solving the linear programming problem with the new output constraint. In practice, linear programming problems involve several constraints. Instead of solving so many linear programming problems, one solves a single dual problem. This gives us the required shadow prices.

In summary, in a profit maximization problem with given quantities of inputs, the shadow price of each input is the increase in profits that will result if an extra unit of this input is made available. Similarly, in a cost minimization problem with minimum output requirements, the shadow price of each output is the extra cost of production if the requirement for that output is increased by 1 unit. We can obtain these shadow prices by increasing each input or output constraint one at a time by 1 unit, and solving the resulting linear programming problem. However, an easier way of obtaining all the shadow prices simultaneously is to solve the dual problem.

8.8   SUMMARY AND CONCLUSIONS

Production is organized through firms, rather than through a series of individual contracts, in order to economize on transactions costs and to enjoy the benefits of specialization. The sales maximization model suggests that the goal of the firm is the maximization of sales revenue subject to a minimum profit constraint. This model predicts a larger output than under profit maximization.

The growth maximization model stresses the trade-off between the growth rate and the valuation ratio for the firm. According to this model, managers maximize their satisfaction by choosing a higher growth rate and lower valuation ratio when compared to profit maximization.

The utility maximization model suggests that the manager's utility is a function of staff size and other like considerations. The manager will maximize utility subject to a minimum profit constraint by employing a larger staff than would be consistent with profit maximization.

A lump-sum profits tax will not affect output under profit maximization, but may reduce output under sales maximization. The same is true for a percentage profits tax. Output will decline under utility maximization with a lump-sum tax, but the result is unclear with a percentage tax.

Linear programming is a technique for solving constrained optimization problems when the objective function and constraints are linear. There are two common types of problems: output or profit maximization and cost minimization. Under the profit maximization problem, the firm solves for the profit-maximizing output mix given fixed quantities of inputs available. In the cost minimization problem, the firm solves for the cost-minimizing input bundle, given minimum output requirements.

Shadow prices tell us how the maximum (or minimum) value of the objective function responds to a unit change in a constraint. In the profit maximization problem, the shadow price of an input is the increase in maximum profit which will result if 1 more unit of the input is made available. In the cost minimization problem, the shadow price of an output is the increase in minimum cost if 1 more unit of an output is required. Shadow prices can be found by solving the dual problem.

KEY TERMS

Behavioral Theories of the Firm	Managerial Theories of the Firm	Utility Maximization Model
Dual Problem	Sales Maximization Model	Valuation Ratio
Growth Maximization Model	Shadow Price	
Linear Programming	Transaction Costs	

QUESTIONS

1. Why is the profit maximization model more realistic when ownership is concentrated? Can well-informed owners force the managers to behave as profit maximizers? What information do they need?

2. Suppose that to produce one widget requires 2 units of K and 3 units of L using process 1. Process 2 requires 1 unit of K and 4 units of L to produce one widget. Draw the isoquant for one widget if the firm can utilize either or both processes.

3. If the price of capital is $5 and the price of labor is $3, which production process will the widget producer in problem 2 utilize? Support your answer graphically.

4. Suppose the firm has 10 units of labor, 20 units of materials, and 8 units of capital available in the short run. A unit of output X requires 2 units of labor, 4 units of materials, and 1 unit of capital. A unit of output Y requires 1 unit of labor, 5 units of materials, and 4 units of capital. Graph the feasible region of production. If the price of Y is $2 and the price of X is $3, what output combination maximizes profit?

5. If the shadow price of capital is $100, but capital can be purchased for $20 per unit in the long run, what can you recommend to this firm?

CHAPTER 9

ECONOMIC EFFICIENCY
AND ECONOMIC SURPLUS

9.1   INTRODUCTION

The purpose of an economic system is to allocate the scarce resources of the economy to the production of goods and services for the use of individuals. This allocation should be done efficiently. We already have a general idea of what efficiency means. Suppose initially that 1,000 cars and 1 million loaves of bread were being manufactured. If by reshuffling the resources we can produce 1,001 cars and 1 million loaves of bread, then obviously the original allocation of resources was inefficient.

The Italian economist Vilfredo Pareto (1848–1923) laid down some marginal conditions that must be satisfied if economic inefficiency is to be avoided. The basic idea of Pareto's conditions is that if, starting from the existing allocation of resources and goods, we can find a new allocation that will make someone better off without making anyone worse off, then obviously the original allocation is inefficient. We will first give some definitions and then some examples.

A *Pareto optimum* is defined as a state of affairs such that no one can be made better off without at least one other person being made worse off. A change in the allocation of resources or goods is said to constitute a *Pareto improvement* if at least one person is made better off without anyone being made worse off. Thus, a Pareto optimum is a situation from which no Pareto improvement is possible. Also, according to Pareto, a policy is said to improve economic welfare only if it results in a Pareto improvement, that is, at least one person is made better off without anyone else being made worse off. A study of economic welfare based on Pareto's conditions is known as *Paretian welfare economics.*

Clearly, Pareto's conditions are very stringent and can hardly be satisfied in practice. Suppose an economic policy makes 1 million people better off and only 1 person worse off. According to Pareto, this policy is not considered to be an improvement! The reason for this argument is that it is hard to compare or weigh the utilities of two individuals. Suppose I buy a dog for protection against burglary. I am better off. But my neighbor cannot stand the dog's barking. My neighbor is worse off. How can we judge whether my neighbor is worse off by more than I am better off? This is the problem of *interpersonal comparison of utilities.* Pareto's method treats this problem as impossible to solve and tries to make judgments in only those situations where such comparisons are not needed.

One suggested solution to the problem of interpersonal utility comparisons is that we determine whether the person who is made better off can compensate the person who is made worse off and still come out ahead. If this is so, then the new situation is better than the old one. For instance, in the above example, suppose that having the dog is worth $700 to me. The neighbor feels that the barking damages him to the tune of $400. The value to me is greater than the cost to him. I could compensate him fully for damages and still be better off by $300. In this case my having the dog is justifiable. This method of compensating those who are made worse off and judging whether there is a net increase in welfare is known as the *compensation criterion.* We will be discussing compensation criteria later in Chapter 18. For the present we will first discuss Pareto's criteria of economic efficiency. We will see later in Chapters 10, 11, and 12 that under a competitive system Pareto's criteria are satisfied whereas under monopoly they are not. Thus, there is an inefficient allocation of resources under monopoly, and this results in a loss of social welfare.

Three basic conditions must be satisfied if Pareto efficiency is to be attained. The economy must achieve:

1. Efficiency in the use of outputs in consumption (Section 9.2).
2. Efficiency in the use of inputs in production (Section 9.3).
3. Efficiency in matching production to consumption (Section 9.4).

After discussing each of these we will briefly review criticisms of Pareto's conditions and discuss applied welfare economics based on the concepts of consumers' surplus and producers' surplus. The final section presents some applications of these concepts.

9.2   EFFICIENCY IN CONSUMPTION

Efficiency in consumption requires that it be impossible to redistribute a given set of goods among consumers in a manner that would improve one person's welfare at nobody's expense. In economic terms this requirement says that if X and Y are two goods, then the marginal rate of substitution of X for Y ($MRS_{X \text{ for } Y}$) should be the same for all individuals consuming both of the goods.

For example, suppose that X = apples and Y = oranges:

For individual A, $MRS_{X \text{ for } Y} = 2$
For individual B, $MRS_{X \text{ for } Y} = 1$

This means that individual A is willing to exchange 2 oranges for 1 apple. Individual B is willing to exchange 1 orange for 1 apple. We can now reallocate apples and oranges between them to make at least one of them better off, without making the other one worse off. What we do is take away 1 apple from B and give it to A. He will give us 2 oranges. Now we give one of these to B. He is no worse off because he is willing to exchange 1 apple for 1 orange. But we have 1 orange left. We can give it to either A (or B) and, thus, make A (or B) better off without making the other person worse off. Thus, the initial allocation was not efficient.

We cannot make any such redistribution if (and only if) the $MRS_{X \text{ for } Y}$ is the same for all consumers. In that case, we could make one person better off only by making another worse off. In other words, if the $MRS_{X \text{ for } Y}$ is the same for everybody, then there are no redistributions of goods that would constitute Pareto improvements. Efficiency in consumption has been attained.

9.3   EFFICIENCY IN PRODUCTION

Production efficiency requires that it be impossible to redistribute inputs to produce more of one product without reducing the output of another product. Clearly, such an increase in one product could make someone better off at nobody's expense. If this is possible, then the old allocation of inputs was not efficient.

Production efficiency requires that the marginal rate of technical substitution of L for K ($MRTS_{L \text{ for } K}$) must be the same for (1) all products that a single firm produces using these two inputs and (2) all producers producing the same output.

The first condition is sometimes referred to as the requirement for *managerial efficiency*, because it deals with input allocation within a single firm. If this condition is not satisfied and two products have different $MRTS_{L \text{ for } K}$, then we can redistribute the inputs so that this firm can produce more of one good without reducing the production of the other good. Suppose that the two products are corn and potatoes, and suppose the $MRTS_{L \text{ for } K}$ is 2 for corn and 1 for potatoes. This means that we can substitute 1 unit of labor for 2 units of capital and keep corn output constant. Similarly, we can substitute 1 unit of labor for 1 unit of capital and keep potato output constant. So, all we do is take 1 unit of labor out of potato production and switch to corn production. This releases 2 units of capital from corn production, 1 unit of which is transferred to the production of potatoes. Now the output of corn and potatoes is unaltered, but we are left with an extra unit of capital. We can allocate this to corn (or potatoes) and get more corn (or potatoes). Thus, one output is increased without reducing the other output.

The second condition deals with the efficient allocation of inputs between firms. If the condition is not satisfied then a redistribution of inputs between firms will produce an increase in at least one output with no reduction in the other.

As an example, consider two producers A and B both producing corn and potatoes. Let us call the two factors of production labor and capital. Suppose the marginal products of the two factors are as follows:

	Producer A		Producer B	
	Labor	Capital	Labor	Capital
Corn	160	40	100	120
Potatoes	360	90	150	180

For producer A, $MRTS_{L \text{ for } K}$ is 4 in both corn production and potato production. Similar is the case of producer B. The $MRTS_{L \text{ for } K}$ is $\frac{5}{6}$ for both outputs. Thus, the managerial efficiency condition is satisfied for both producers.

However, since $MRTS_{L \text{ for } K}$ is not the same for both producers, we can increase output by moving labor from producer B to producer A. Now for producer A the marginal product of labor will fall (there are more units of labor per unit of capital), and the marginal product of capital will rise (since there are fewer units of capital per unit of labor). For producer B the reverse will happen, the marginal product of labor will rise, and the marginal product of capital will fall. We continue this transfer of labor until the marginal product of labor and capital are the same for both producers. We can do the same for each of the two outputs: corn and potatoes. Finally, after the transfer of labor from producer A to producer B, we could end up with a situation where the marginal products are as follows:

	Producer A		Producer B	
	Labor	Capital	Labor	Capital
Corn	140	70	140	70
Potatoes	280	140	280	140

Now the $MRTS_{L \text{ for } K}$ is 2 for both outputs as well as both producers.

9.4 EFFICIENCY IN MATCHING PRODUCTION AND CONSUMPTION

This efficiency concept requires that we produce the correct mix of outputs. The condition for efficiency in the matching of production and consumption is that it be impossible to rearrange outputs in a manner that would constitute a Pareto improvement. This type of efficiency necessitates that for two goods X and Y the marginal rate of transformation (in production) of X for Y ($MRT_{X \text{ for } Y}$) is the same as the marginal rate of substitution (in consumption) of X for Y ($MRS_{X \text{ for } Y}$). That is,

$$MRT_{X \text{ for } Y} \text{ for all producers} = MRS_{X \text{ for } Y} \text{ for all consumers}$$

Suppose this condition is not satisfied and for a producer A we have $MRT_{X \text{ for } Y} = 2$ and for a consumer B we have $MRS_{X \text{ for } Y} = 1$. Suppose

$X =$ pounds of potatoes
$Y =$ pounds of corn

Then, since $MRT_{X \text{ for } Y} = 2$, the producer can decrease production of potatoes by 1 lb and increase production of corn by 2 lbs (with the same total inputs). Now the producer can give the consumers 1 lb less of potatoes and 1 lb more of corn. Since $MRS_{X \text{ for } Y} = 1$ for consumers, they are neither better off nor worse off. But the producer is better off—she has 1 lb of corn left. If she gives it away to the consumer, the consumer is better off and the producer is not worse off. Thus, at least one of the two can be made better off without the other being made worse off, by the change. Thus, the original situation is not Pareto optimal.

One can state many other conditions for efficiency but they all boil down to two basic principles: (1) Any *MRT* must equal any corresponding *MRS*. (2) Any *MRT* must equal anybody else's *MRT*, and any *MRS* must equal anybody else's *MRS*.

When all the conditions of economic efficiency are fulfilled simultaneously, a society is said to have achieved a *Pareto optimum*. As long as these conditions are not fulfilled and inequalities persist, a reallocation of resources or goods can be made that will increase total economic welfare.

Pareto's conditions for efficiency would be satisfied if profit-maximizing firms and utility-maximizing households were to determine the optimum quantities of goods and services that they wish to trade with the help of equilibrium prices established in perfectly competitive markets. In this case

$$MRS_{X \text{ for } Y} = \frac{P_x}{P_y} \text{ is the same for all consumers}$$

$$MRTS_{L \text{ for } K} = \frac{P_L}{P_K} \text{ is the same for all producers}$$

$$MRT_{X \text{ for } Y} = \frac{P_x}{P_y} \text{ for all producers}$$

$$= \frac{P_x}{P_y} \text{ for all consumers}$$

$$= MRS_{X \text{ for } Y}$$

EXAMPLE 9.1   The Allocative Efficiency of Traditional Agriculture

It is frequently assumed that farmers in poor agricultural communities do badly in using the factors of production they have, that they do not allocate their resources efficiently. Schultz[1] disputes this claim and presents evidence to the contrary. In his discussion of empirical evidence Schultz excluded poor agricultural communities in transition or those adjusting their production to outside circumstances such as large political changes such as civil wars and partition of a country, large changes in relative prices of agricultural commodities, and technical advances in agricultural production.

The first study Schultz cites is that by Sol Tax[2] which covered Panajachel, a small community of 800 in Guatemala over the period 1936 to 1941. It was a society which was "capitalist" on a microscopic scale. There were no machines, no factories, and no co-ops or corporations. Each individual was his or her own firm and worked ruggedly alone. There was money, and there was trade. After a careful analysis of the way transactions took place in this small community, Sol Tax concluded that the village economy could be characterized as a "money economy organized in single households as both consumption and production units, with a strongly developed market which tends to be perfectly competitive."

Another study Schultz cites is that of a village Senapur in India by W. David Hopper. He estimated the relative prices of factors of production implicit in the allocation decisions of the farmers. He found the following:

Factors of Production	Crop			
	Barley	Wheat	Peas	Gram
Land (acres)	4.42	4.03	4.41	4.84
Bullock time (hours)	0.070	0.072	0.082	0.083

[1] T. W. Schultz, *Transforming Traditional Agriculture*, University of Chicago Press, Chicago, 1983, chap. 3.
[2] Sol Tax, *Penny Capitalism*, University of Chicago Press, Chicago, 1963.

Labor (hours)	0.0086	0.0097	0.0087	0.0076
Irrigation water (750 gallons)	0.036	0.033	0.031	0.032

Hopper concluded that the average allocation made by the sample of farmers he studied was efficient within the context of the prevailing technical relationships.

Bauer and Yamey[3] cite many similar examples. Based on all this evidence Schultz contends that the farmers (although illiterate) do know how to allocate resources efficiently. He concludes, "Although schooling may increase greatly the productivity of the human agent, it is not a pre-requisite to an efficient allocation of the existing stock of factors. The notion that these poor agricultural communities do not have enough competent entrepreneurs is in all probability mistaken."[4]

9.5   THE EDGEWORTH BOX DIAGRAM

The Edgeworth box diagram is a graphic way of describing the efficiency conditions discussed in the previous sections and showing how the allocations of some goods and resources can be improved upon by exchange. The box diagram is named after a famous British economist Francis Y. Edgeworth (1845–1926). Although named after him, this box diagram does not appear in any of Edgeworth's writings and apparently was first used by Pareto in 1893.[5]

To illustrate the use of the box diagram consider the following:

1. There are two individuals A and B and two goods X and Y.

2. Each individual has an initial stock of the goods (called *initial endowments*) but not in the proportion that gives the individual the greatest satisfaction.

3. There is no new production but the individuals can exchange the goods among themselves.

Let the initial endowments of X and Y held by A and B be denoted by (X_a, Y_a) and (X_b, Y_b) respectively. Then,

$\overline{X} = X_a + X_b$ is the total quantity of X available for exchange

$\overline{Y} = Y_a + Y_b$ is the total quantity of Y available for exchange

The Edgeworth box is a rectangle where the horizontal side measures $\overline{X}$ and the vertical side measures $\overline{Y}$. This is shown in Figure 9.1. The lower left corner is denoted O_A and the endowments of X and Y held by individual A are measured horizontally left to right and vertically from bottom to top. For individual B, however, the graph is inverted. The origin is 0_B, and her endowment of X is measured

[3]P. T. Bauer and B. S. Yamey, *The Economics of Underdeveloped Countries*, University of Chicago Press, Chicago, 1957, chap. 6.

[4]Schultz, *Transforming Traditional Agriculture*, p. 49.

[5]See Vincent J. Tarascio, "A Correction: On the Genealogy of the So-Called Edgeworth-Bowley Diagram," *Western Economic Journal*, June 1972, pp. 193–197. A more extensive discussion is in William Jaffe, "Edgeworth's Contract Curve," parts I and II, *History of Political Economy*, Fall and Winter 1974, pp. 343–359 and 381–404.

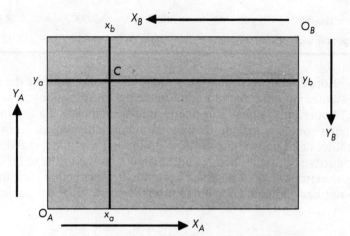

FIGURE 9.1   Initial endowments of A and B shown in a box diagram.

horizontally but right to left, and her endowment of Y is measured vertically but from top to bottom. The initial endowments are, therefore, shown by the point C in Figure 9.1.

Now consider the indifference curves for A and B. We have to again note that the origin for B is the right top corner (the graph for B is inverted). The indifference curves for A and B are shown in Figure 9.2.

The next thing to consider is the curve consisting of the points of tangency of the indifference curves for A and B. This curve is called the *Edgeworth contract curve*. It is called a "contract curve" because, as we will presently see, the points on the curve are equilibrium positions that A and B can eventually reach through exchange contracts. This curve is shown in Figure 9.3. The indifference curves for A are denoted by A_1, A_2, A_3, . . ., and the indifference curves for B are denoted by B_1, B_2, B_3, ... Note that the indifference curves for B are convex to the origin O_B and higher utility means moving southwest, as shown in Figure 9.2(b).

FIGURE 9.2   Indifference curves in the box diagram.

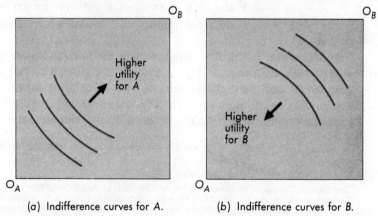

(a) Indifference curves for A.   (b) Indifference curves for B.

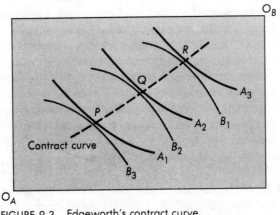

FIGURE 9.3   Edgeworth's contract curve.

Now consider points *P, Q, R* on the contract curve. Let us compare *P* and *Q*. At *P*, *A* is on indifference curve A_1, and *B* is on indifference curve B_3; at *Q*, *A* is on indifference curve A_2, and *B* is on indifference curve B_2. Thus, a movement from *P* to *Q* makes *A* better off but *B* worse off. Similar is a movement from *Q* to *R*. Thus, no point on the contract curve is a Pareto improvement over another point. In other words, every point on the contract curve is Pareto optimal. At each point on the contract curve MRS_{xy} is the same for both *A* and *B*.

Which of these points will be reached by *A* and *B*? To answer this question we start with the initial endowment of *A* and *B* and their preferences. Thus, we have to superimpose Figures 9.1 and 9.3. The picture is shown in Figure 9.4. *C* is the point that shows the initial endowments of both *A* and *B*. Now draw the indifference curves for *A* and *B* passing through the point *C*. Label these as A_1 and B_1. Next consider the indifference curve A_2 that is tangent to B_1 and the indifference curve B_2 that is tangent to A_1. The points of tangency *S* and *T* are on the contract curve. Both *A* and *B* could move to *S* or *T* or a point in between. At *S*, *A* is on indifference curve A_1, and *B* is on indifference curve B_2.

FIGURE 9.4   Movement from initial endowment to the contract curve through exchange.

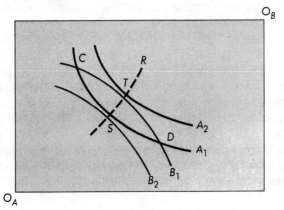

Thus, compared with the point C where A and B both started, B is better off (moving to a higher indifference curve) and A is no worse off. Thus, S is a Pareto improvement over C. Similarly, T is also a Pareto improvement over C, since A is made better off (moving to a higher indifference curve) and B is no worse off (staying on the same indifference curve). If A is very powerful in bargaining he might be able to make B move to the point T from the point C. If B is very powerful in bargaining, she might be able to make A move to the point S. More likely, both would move to a point between T and S. In this case, they both move to a higher indifference curve than at C.

In summary, we should note the following:

1. A and B can, by exchanging X and Y, reach any point in the box.

2. If the initial point is off the contract curve, they can both be made better off by moving to certain points on the contract curve.

3. Any points outside area CTDS, even on the contract curve, are not attainable through voluntary exchange when starting from C. Take, for instance, a point like R: A is made better off but B is worse off. Thus, B would not want to move to the point R from the point C. Thus, the only feasible final points are on the segment ST. In between S and T, both A and B are made better off. Which point will be reached will depend on the bargaining power of A and B.

4. Any point on the contract curve is efficient with respect to consumption, or is Pareto optimal.

The Edgeworth box for production

The Edgeworth box for examining efficiency in production is similar. We consider two factors of production labor (L) and capital (K). There are two outputs X and Y. The total amount of labor available is $\overline{L}$ and of capital $\overline{K}$. L_x and K_x are the amounts of labor and capital used in the production of X, and L_y and K_y are the amounts of labor and capital used in the production of Y.

The analysis is the same as before. We construct a figure like Figure 9.1. The length of the rectangle is $\overline{L}$ and the height is $\overline{K}$. The point C shows the initial allocation of inputs L and K to the production of X and Y. Since the analogy is direct, we will not present another diagram.

Next we consider Figure 9.2. Instead of indifference curves for A, we have production isoquants for output X. Similarly, instead of indifference curves for B, we have production isoquants for Y.

We now come to Figure 9.3. Label O_A as O_X, O_B as O_Y. Now A_1, A_2, A_3, ..., are isoquants X_1, X_2, X_3, ..., and B_1, B_2, B_3, ..., are now isoquants Y_1, Y_2, Y_3, ... The curve PQR is now the contract curve for production. Since the slope of a production isoquant is $MRTS_{LK}$, $MRTS_{LK}$ is the same in the production of X and Y at each point on the contract curve. As before we can show that each point on the contract curve is Pareto optimal, or satisfies the conditions for efficiency in production.

Since the analysis is so similar we have avoided the repetition of Figures 9.1 to 9.3. We will, however, replicate Figure 9.4. This is shown in Figure 9.5. O_X is the origin from which we measure production isoquants for X, increasing in the

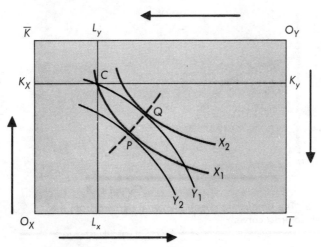

FIGURE 9.5 Movement from initial allocation to optimal allocation along a contract curve.

usual northeast direction, and O_Y is the origin from which we measure the production isoquants for Y (going southwest). C is the point of initial allocation. L_x units of labor and K_x units of capital are used in the production of X to produce output X_1. Similarly, L_y units of labor and K_y units of capital are used in the production of Y to produce output Y_1.

Now draw production isoquant Y_2 which is tangent to production isoquant X_1 (the point of tangency being P). Also draw production isoquant X_2 which is tangent to production isoquant Y_1 (the point of tangency being Q).

Compared with C, the point P is better because we have the same output X_1 of X but an output Y_2 for Y that is higher than the earlier output Y_1. Thus, a reallocation of inputs produces more of the output of Y without reducing the output of X. Similar is the point Q. We have more of X and the same output of Y as compared with the situation at the point C. As before, we can show that all points along PQ on the contract curve are better allocations of the given inputs compared with the initial allocation at C because they yield more of both X and Y. Which of these points will be reached depends on the prices of X and Y.

The production possibility curve

From the Edgeworth box for given labor input $\bar{L}$ and capital input $\bar{K}$ and the production isoquants for X and Y, we get a contract curve that gives the combinations of the outputs of X and Y that result from an efficient allocation of the inputs. The curve showing these combinations is called the *production possibility curve* and is illustrated in Figure 9.6.

The absolute value of the slope of the production possibilities curve is the marginal rate of transformation of X for Y. And efficiency in the matching of production and consumption requires the MRT to be equal to the $MRS_{X \text{ for } Y}$ in consumption. So for any output bundle on the production possibilities curve, we can determine the corresponding $MRS_{X \text{ for } Y}$ that results in full economic efficiency.

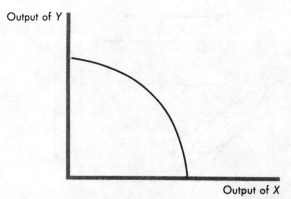

Output of Y

Output of X

FIGURE 9.6 The production possibility curve derived from the Edgeworth contract curve.

9.6   EFFICIENCY IN CONSUMPTION AND PRODUCTION OVER TIME

The conditions derived earlier in Sections 9.2 to 9.4 can be easily extended to consumption and production over time. In the case of consumption, instead of two goods X and Y, we have C_p and C_f, which are present and future consumption, respectively. As we did earlier in Secton 5.8.1, we can draw indifference curves between current and future consumption for each of two individuals A and B. Then, instead of apples and oranges, we talk of C_p and C_f.

If we denote the marginal rate of substitution between C_p and C_f by MRS_{pf}, then we have

$$MRS_{pf} = \frac{\Delta C_f}{\Delta C_p}$$

where $\Delta C_f / \Delta C_p$ is the slope of the indifference curve at the point under consideration.

Again, if two individuals have different values of MRS_{pf}, then we can redistribute present and future goods between the two individuals so that no one is worse off and at least one is better off. The reasoning is exactly the same as in Section 9.2 except that instead of oranges and apples we have present and future goods.

Thus, the condition for efficiency in consumption over time is that MRS_{pf} is the same for all individuals. Note that we showed in Section 5.8.1 that

$$MRS_{pf} = \frac{\Delta C_f}{\Delta C_p} = 1 + r$$

where r is the rate of interest. Thus, if the rate of interest is the same for all individuals, the efficiency condition will be satisfied. However, if the borrowing and lending rates are different then MRS_{pf} is different for borrowers and lenders, and, thus, the efficiency condition is not satisfied.

The situation with production over time is similar. Instead of corn and potatoes we have present and future production. This could be interpreted as present consumption goods and investment goods or future consumption goods. Now we define MRT_{pf} as the marginal rate of transformation of present goods for future goods. Again, the equilibrium for any producer is attained when:

$$MRT_{pf} = 1 + r$$

where r is the rate of interest.

If MRT_{pf} is different for different producers, we can reallocate the inputs among the producers so that no one is worse off and at least one is better off. The argument is exactly the same as in Section 9.3 earlier with corn replaced by present production and potatoes by future production. Thus, the condition for efficiency is that MRT_{pf} is the same for all producers. If the rate of interest r is the same for all producers, this condition will be satisfied.

The conditions for overall efficiency are that MRS_{pf} is the same for all consumers, MRT_{pf} is the same for all producers, and

$$MRS_{pf} = MRT_{pf} = 1 + r$$

9.7 X-INEFFICIENCY

In the previous sections we discussed the marginal conditions required for economic efficiency. How often are these conditions satisfied in reality? Some economists such as Harvey Leibenstein argue that these conditions are not usually satisfied in practice because people are not always fully motivated toward maximization or minimization (profit maximization, cost minimization, utility maximization, and so on). Leibenstein coined the word *X-inefficiency* to describe this inefficiency.[6]

If there are two firms with identical production conditions and identical measured inputs, the one with the lower X-factor would have lower output. What is this X-factor? The X-factor is the "APQ bundle": activity type, pace, and quality.

Leibenstein distinguishes between what he calls *principals* (owners) and *agents* (those who work for others). Most Americans work for others in relatively large establishments. The largest 100 corporations in manufacturing employ more than half the total employees in the field. In a small firm, activities and pace of work can be closely supervised, but in large organizations with several managers, many of whom have predetermined labor contracts, owners cannot supervise everything. (Moreover, the owners are a group of diffuse stockholders.) The managers have discretionary choices regarding (1) some of their activities, (2) the rate at which they carry out these activities, and (3) the quality of their efforts. This is the APQ bundle.

[6]Harvey Leibenstein, "Allocative Efficiency vs. X-Efficiency," *The American Economic Review*, June 1966, pp. 392–415.

Leibenstein's theory is not well accepted by mainstream economists. For instance, George Stigler argued that X-inefficiency is a result of ignorance, mistakes, or differences in production techniques.[7] Firms that are seemingly identical could be operating under different constraints. Businesspeople, however, would not question the existence of X-inefficiency. In fact, organizational behavior studies address the motivational factors that Leibenstein was talking about.

Leibenstein and those following his theory have produced a number of case studies from different parts of the world to show that managers do not minimize costs, or productivity could be higher than what it actually is, or consumers do not maximize their utility, and so on. Some of the examples are as follows:

1. A study by John Shelton (*The American Economic Review,* December 1967) compared manager-operated and franchised fast food restaurants. Menus, raw materials, accounting systems, and so on were similar or identical. But owner-operated units averaged a 9.5 percent profit margin versus an average of 1.8 percent profit margin for manager-operated units. This illustrates the importance of the principal versus agent distinction mentioned earlier.

2. In the Fall 1979 issue of *The Public Interest,* Richard L. Freeman and James L. Medoff argued that although unionization resulted in increased wages, in 75 percent of the cases unionization also resulted in a 20 to 25 percent increase in productivity per worker. Increases in the price of the input did not result in an increase in the cost of the output. Leibenstein's argument is that if there is considerable X-inefficiency then the increase in the price of the input will exert pressure on managers to be more effective in their effort at cost minimization and the resulting decrease in X-inefficiency might actually compensate for the increase in the price of the input.

3. Walter Primeux, Jr. (*Review of Economics and Statistics,* 1977) compared 49 cities with two or more electric companies to cities with only one. The former, he found, had costs of production which were, on the average, 11 percent less than the latter (after adjusting for economies of scale). Note that this is not an inefficiency resulting from monopoly. According to theory, monopolies have as much incentive to minimize costs as do competitive firms. Leibenstein uses this example to argue that the X-inefficiency is a consequence of "sheltering" from competition.

All these are scattered examples. There are two questions one might raise: (1) How important is X-inefficiency for the economy as a whole? (2) What can one do about it?

The answer to the second question is simple. Devote more attention to a study of how individuals and firms *do* behave rather than to how they *ought to* behave as is done by many economists. This will help us to see how motivation can be increased.

Regarding the first question, no one has done a careful assessment. Leibenstein says that a "back of the envelope" calculation suggests that the production sector

---

[7]See George J. Stigler, "The Xistence of X-Efficiency," *The American Economic Review,* March 1976, pp. 213–216. For a reply, see Harvey Leibenstein, "X-Inefficiency Xists—Reply to an Xorcist," *The American Economic Review,* March 1978, pp. 203–211.

is only 70 percent as efficient as could be.[8] But if households are also X-inefficient, then the whole economy is only 60 percent X-efficient. That is 40 percent inefficiency! Forty percent of $2 trillion is a huge sum!

Much of what Leibenstein calls X-inefficiency may, in fact, be consumption of leisure and relaxation, and these have a value too. Instead of constantly driving themselves and getting heart attacks or neurosis, individuals might like to just take things easy. This does not rule out the existence of X-inefficiency, but Leibenstein's estimates are perhaps grossly exaggerated.

The most important criticism of the X-inefficiency theory is that it does not provide a systematic framework for predicting when and how firms will fail to minimize costs, that the theory is just a label given to ignorance regarding why firms and individuals behave in certain ways, and that giving different names for ignorance does not dispel ignorance. Some of the examples cited in support of the X-inefficiency theory can be explained by accounting for the institutional restrictions and transaction costs in addition to the usual constraints.[9] For instance, high monitoring costs encourage profit-sharing arrangements. This explains the finding of Shelton quoted earlier that the same franchises are more profitable when operated by owner managers than by employees of the parent company. Similarly, transaction costs and the weakening of property rights associated with explicit or implicit regulation would account for the higher costs reported by Primeaux for electric utilities which have a monopoly. Thus, in the examples of Shelton and Primeaux we can explain why firms behaved that way. In some other examples, however, De Alessi argues that the evidence provided by the proponents of the X-inefficiency theory is insufficient to determine why firms behaved the way they did but because of insufficient evidence we cannot argue either that the traditional theories are useless.

9.8 PARETO'S CONDITIONS AND APPLIED WELFARE ECONOMICS

According to Pareto, total economic welfare is the sum of individuals' welfare. But one individual's welfare cannot be compared with another individual's welfare, so *interpersonal comparisons* are ruled out. Thus, only those policies that make at least one person better off without making anyone else worse off are considered to increase total welfare. As mentioned earlier, even if a million people are made substantially better off and one individual made slightly worse off by a policy, the policy does not increase welfare by Pareto's definition.

Very few economists find Pareto's conditions satisfactory, so some modifications have been suggested (these are discussed in Chapter 18). Even these modifications, however, do not help us in practical applications. All the modifications

[8]Harvey Leibenstein, "Microeconomics and X-Efficiency Theory: If There Is No Crisis, There Ought to Be," *The Public Interest Special Issue 1980: The Crisis in Economic Theory*, pp. 97–110.

[9]For a detailed discussion of this, see Louis De Alessi, "Property Rights, Transaction Costs, and X-Efficiency: An Essay in Economic Theory," *The American Economic Review*, March 1983, pp. 64–81. For a discussion of empirical evidence on property rights, see Louis De Alessi, "The Economics of Property Rights: A Review of the Evidence," *Research in Law and Economics*, Spring 1980, pp. 1–47.

are theoretical exercises, and as Kenneth Boulding once said, the best that can be said about this whole area is that "it is virtually impossible to study it without learning a good deal of economics in the process."

One method that is widely used to evaluate economic policies is based on the concepts of *consumers' surplus* and *producers' surplus*. These concepts are defined in the next section. Using this approach, the problem of interpersonal comparison of utilities is essentially swept under the rug, and benefits and costs are added without regard to whom they accrue. This method of applied welfare economics does not appeal to some economists because it involves the simple addition of benefits and costs across all individuals. For instance, suppose a theft is committed, and the thief walks alway with $1,000 from Mr. X's house. The thief is better off by $1,000. Mr. X is worse off by $1,000. Adding up the total benefits and costs, the net effect is 0, and we might say there is no social cost. Of course, there are other social costs if Mr. X has to install a burglar alarm system for his house, spends sleepless nights, and the neighbors, too, install burgular alarm systems. There is also the cost of police investigation of the crime. All this involves a waste of otherwise productive resources. But if none of these other things happens, then all we have is the thief's benefit of $1,000 and Mr. X's loss of $1,000, and, adding the two, we have a net cost of 0.

On the face of it, this procedure does not sound very reasonable. However, the method of consumers' surplus and producers' surplus does give us some means for evaluating the comparative merits of different economic policies. It is a method of great pedagogical value, and it gives us some insight into the factors that should be taken into account when analyzing different economic proposals. We will illustrate the application of the surplus approach with a number of practical problems such as: welfare costs of price controls, effects of medical insurance, welfare cost of the Medicaid program, and effects of highway construction on land values.

Arnold Harberger[10] was a strong advocate of the use of surpluses to evaluate the impact of various economic policies on social welfare. In fact, this method is sometimes called the Harberger triangle method after him. It is called the triangle method because, as we will see, it involves the measurement of various triangles.

9.9   CONSUMERS' SURPLUS AND PRODUCERS' SURPLUS

Suppose you go to a store and like a suit so much that you are willing to pay $200 for it. If the suit actually costs $160 then you are said to have a consumers' surplus of $200 − 160 = $40.

The concept of consumer's surplus was first formulated in 1844 by the French engineer J. Dupuit, who was concerned with evaluating the worthiness of a subsidy toward the cost of constructing a bridge.[11] He was aware that a consumer might be willing to pay more for a good than he actually has to pay. The "excess satisfaction" the consumer gets is the "consumer's surplus."

---

[10] A. C. Harberger, "Three Basic Postulates for Applied Welfare Economics: An Interpretive Essay," *Journal of Economic Literature,* September 1971, pp. 785–797.

[11] An English translation of Dupuit's famous article is: Jules Dupuit, "On the Measurement of the Utility of Public Works," in American Economic Association's *Readings in Welfare Economics,* Irwin, Homewood, Ill., 1969, pp. 255–283.

The concept of consumer's surplus gained prominence after Marshall's *Principles of Economics* was published. Marshall defined consumer's surplus as "the excess of the price which the consumer would be willing to pay rather than go without the thing over what the consumer does actually pay." The way Marshall measured consumer's surplus is shown in Figure 9.7.

Let *DD* be the demand curve. Suppose the individual buys 5 units and pays a price per unit of $5. If the consumer is given the choice of buying a certain quantity of the good or going without it, she might be willing to pay $9 for the first unit, $8 for the second unit, $7 for the third unit, $6 for the fourth unit, and $5 for the fifth unit. Thus, when the actual price is $5, the consumer's surplus is $4 + $3 + $2 + $1 + $0 = $10. As an approximation to this, we take the area of the triangle *BCF*. The area under the demand curve *DD* up to the output level *OA* measures the amount the consumer is *willing to pay*. This is the area *OABF*. The amount the consumer *actually pays* is given by the area *OABC*. Hence, consumer's surplus is given by the area of the triangle *BCF* which is equal to *OABF* − *OABC*.

One can define a similar concept for producers. The analogous concept, called the producer's surplus, is the amount that the producer receives over and above what he is willing to sell for rather than forgo a sale. This is illustrated in Figure 9.8.

The producer sells *OA* units at a price *OC*. His revenues are given by the area *OABC*. However, the prices at which the producer would be willing to sell each successive unit rather than go without selling the unit are given by the points on the supply curve. (The points on the supply curve give the producer's marginal cost of production and, hence, his reservation price—the minimum price at which he is willing to sell.) Thus, the area under the supply curve up to output *OA*, which is equal to the area *OABE*, measures the minimum amount at which the producer is willing to sell the output *OA*. The difference *OABC* − *OABE* = *CBE* measures the producer's surplus.

Figure 9.9 illustrates the concept of consumers' surplus and producers' surplus together. *DD* is the demand curve, and *SS* is the supply curve. The equilibrium price is *OC*, and the equilibrium quantity is *OA*. The area of the triangle *BCF*

FIGURE 9.7   Consumers' surplus.

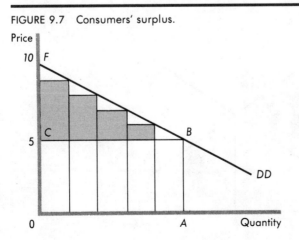

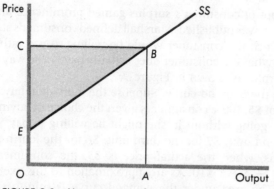

FIGURE 9.8   Measurement of producers' surplus.

measures consumer's surplus, and the area of the triangle *BCE* measures producer's surplus.

Alfred Marshall popularized the notions of consumers' surplus and producers' surplus and had high hopes for their use as a tool of public policy. However, the concepts were widely criticized. Consider, for instance, the case of consumers' surplus. Let us examine the effect of a fall in the market price of the good. This is shown in Figure 9.10. Let *DD* be the demand curve. Suppose initially that the price is *OC*. Then the consumers' surplus is given by the area of the triangle *BCF*. Now if the price falls to *OC'*, then the consumers' surplus is given by the area of the triangle *B'C'F*. Thus, the increase in the consumers' surplus is given by the shaded area *BB'C'C*.

However, a fall in the price of the good has an income effect as well. This would change the answer to the question of "what the consumer is willing to pay rather than go without." Marshall realized this problem and, hence, confined his discussion to small changes in price and goods with negligible income effects. To take care of the income effects, it is customary to say that the demand curve *DD*

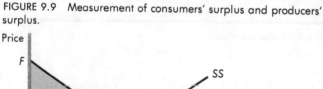

FIGURE 9.9   Measurement of consumers' surplus and producers' surplus.

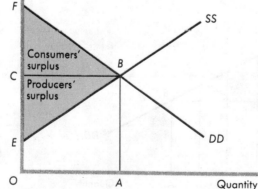

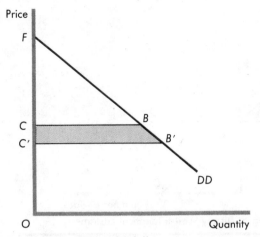

FIGURE 9.10   Effect of a fall in price on consumers' surplus.

that we consider in Figure 9.10 is the *income-compensated demand curve* (this concept was explained earlier in Chapter 5). In our discussions of consumers' surplus we will be assuming that income effects are small or else that the demand curve we are considering is the income-compensated demand curve.

There have also been criticisms concerning the usefulness of the concept of consumers' surplus. Some economists have dismissed it as completely useless. For instance, Paul Samuelson said, "It is a tool which can be used only by one who can get along without its use and not by all such." I. M. D. Little described it as a "totally useless theoretical toy." However, Abba Lerner considered it of great use as a heuristic device for showing students of economics the social benefits or costs of policy decisions.[12] Many other economists have argued in its favor because, they say, there is no alternative computable measure of the welfare loss (or gain) from different economic policies.[13] For the purpose of this book, we will use it as a pedagogical device to evaluate economic policies.

EXAMPLE 9.2   Pricing Admissions to Disney World

The concept of consumers' surplus can be used to analyze the pricing of entrance to Disney World (or Disneyland). Individuals going to Disney World are interested in going on the different amusement rides. The question we are interested in is how much Disney World should charge for entrance and how much for each ride.

For simplicity, let us initially assume that all customers are identical and that the demand curve is linear as shown by *AD* in the accompanying Exhibit 9.2A. Let us also assume that the marginal cost (for Disney World) of offering a ride to

[12]These and many other quotations, and some criticisms and applications of the consumers' and producers' surplus can be found in: J. M. Currie, J. A. Murphy, and A. Schmitz, "The Concept of Economic Surplus and Its Use in Economic Analysis," *The Economic Journal*, December 1971, pp. 741–799. An opposing view, recalling earlier criticisms can be found in E. R. Morey, "Confuser Surplus," *American Economic Review*, March 1984, pp. 163–173.

[13]A recent book by G. W. McKenzie, *A New Approach to the Measurement of Welfare*, Cambridge University Press, Cambridge, 1983, suggests an alternative measure that is free of the usual defects of measures of consumers' surplus, is operational, and can be calculated from observable information. However, a discussion of this measure is beyond the scope of this book.

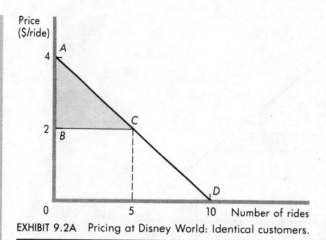

EXHIBIT 9.2A   Pricing at Disney World: Identical customers.

any individual is 0. The demand curve shows that at 0 price 10 rides are taken, whereas at a price of $4 no rides are taken. (This latter number is unrealistic but is a consequence of the linear demand curve. However, for the purpose of illustration it is all right.)

Suppose that Disney World charges a price of $2 per ride. Since 5 rides are taken, it gets $10 in revenues from the rides. The consumer reaps a consumer's surplus given by the shaded triangle *ABC*. Since this is the amount that the consumer is willing to pay rather than go without the rides, Disney World can charge an admission fee equal to the area of this triangle which in this case is $5. Thus Disney World gets $10 on rides and $5 on admission fee which is a total of $15. However, it can do better than that. Suppose all rides are free. The consumer takes 10 rides and reaps a consumer's surplus equal to the area of the bigger triangle *AOD*. Disney World can extract this consumer's surplus by charging an entrance fee equal to the area of this triangle, that is, $20. Thus Disney World would charge nothing for rides and just charge an entrance fee of $20. (This is, in fact, what Disney World did around 1980 when it abolished the tickets for rides and raised the entrance fee.)

We have until now assumed that all customers are identical. Suppose that we have two types of customers with their demand functions given by *AD* and *A'D'* shown in Exhibit 9.2B. Individual 1 takes 10 rides at 0 price and no rides at a price of $5. Individual 2 takes 15 rides at 0 price and no rides at a price of $6.

Disney World has to charge the same price for all customers. Suppose it tries to capture the consumer's surplus of individual 1 and charges an entrance fee equal to the area *AOD*. This entrance fee will be $25. Then it gets a revenue of $50 from the two customers. Alternatively, it can try to capture the entire consumer's surplus of indivudal 2, which is given by the area *A'OD'*. The entrance fee is then $45, but at this high entrance fee individual 1 will not go to Disney World, and Disney World's revenues fall to $45.

Suppose Disney World charges $1 per ride. The consumer's surplus for individual 1 is given by the area of the triangle *ABC*. This will be the entrance fee, and it is $16. At the price of $1 per ride, individual 1 takes 8 rides and individual 2 takes 12 rides (actually 12½, but there is no half ride). The revenues for Disney

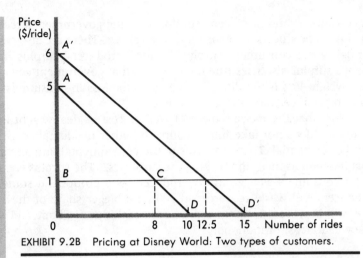

EXHIBIT 9.2B   Pricing at Disney World: Two types of customers.

World are $32 from entrance fees and $20 from tickets and are thus higher than with a scheme of entrance fee only. Thus, with two types of customers Disney World could increase its revenues by charging an entrance fee plus tickets for rides. This procedure of charging an entrance fee to the park and tickets for rides is known as a two-part tarriff.[14]

What would be the price that maximizes the revenue for Disney World? By considering similar triangles we get: If p is the price per ride, the entrance fee (area of triangle ABC) is: $(5 - p)^2$. The number of rides taken by individuals 1 and 2 are, respectively, $2(5 - p)$ and $\frac{5}{2}(6 - p)$. The total revenue is

$$2(5 - p)^2 + 2p(5 - p) + \tfrac{5}{2}p(6 - p)$$

(entrance fees plus rides). The profit maximizing price is $1 per ride, which is the price we considered.[15]

For comparison, at a price of $2 per ride, the entrance fee is $9. Individual 1 takes 6 rides and indivudal 2 takes 10 rides. Total revenues are 2($9) + 16($2) = $50, which is the same as with an entrance fee of $25 with free rides.

9.10   APPLICATIONS

The concepts of consumers' and producers' surplus have been used in a number of practical problems to judge the desirability or undesirability of economic policies. In this analysis the change in the sum of consumers' and producers' surpluses and government's surplus (or deficit) is defined as the *deadweight loss (or gain)* to society. This is the amount by which the government's expenditures exceed the increase

[14]Walter Y. Oi, "A Disneyland Dilemma: Two-Part Tarriffs for a Mickey-Mouse Monopoly," *Quarterly Journal of Economics*, February 1971, pp. 77–96. Monopoly is discussed in Chap. 11 but we have explained the principle here using just the idea of consumers' surplus.

[15]This can be determined by graphing the total revenue function or mathematically by differentiating total revenue with respect to price, equating the derivative to zero, and solving for price.

in consumers' and producers' surpluses, or the government's receipts fall short of the loss in producers' and consumers' surpluses. There are also cases (for example, tariffs) where consumers' surplus declines, producers' surplus rises, and government's surplus also rises (the tax revenues that government gets). In this case, the deadweight loss is the difference between the loss in consumers' surplus and the gain to producers and the government.

Note that the measurement of welfare cost or deadweight loss we are going to discuss does not take into account the other incidental costs involved, which can be substantial. These are costs of the governmental bureaucracy and the costs that individuals incur in "seeking the surpluses." The surplus we are talking about is for consumers as a group or producers as a group. But some consumers and producers will waste resources in getting a bigger share of these total surpluses. We will, however, postpone a discussion of this until Chapter 11 when we discuss the welfare cost of monopoly.[16]

9.10.1 Price controls

The first application we will consider is that of price controls. We already know that if a price is set below the equilibrium price, then output will fall and a shortage will result. As we shall see, there is a social cost associated with the reduction in output and there may also be a social cost associated with the allocation of the product.

In Figure 9.11 we present an analysis of welfare costs of price controls. *DD* is the demand curve, and *SS* is the supply curve. The equilibrium price is *OB* with equilibrium quantity *OA*. In equilibrium, the sum of consumers' and producers' surpluses is the area of triangle *NKC*. Now suppose that price is controlled at the level *OE*. The quantity supplied and, hence, the quantity consumed is *OF*. However, at the controlled price there is an excess demand of *FJ* or *GH*. The welfare cost of the price control depends on how this excess demand is handled and on which

---

[16]This phenomenon called "rent seeking" has been discussed by Tullock, Kreuger, Buchanan, and others. See Chapter 11, Section 11.9.

FIGURE 9.11   Welfare costs of price controls.

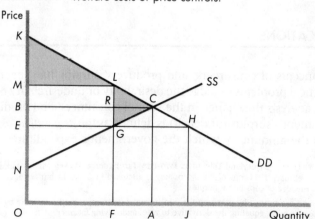

consumers along the segment KH of the demand curve receive the output. If the available quantity OF is allocated to those who obtain the highest satisfaction (how this could be done is a question which will be discussed later), then the consumer satisfaction is measured by the area $OKLF$. The consumers pay $OEGF$, and, hence, the consumers' surplus is $EKLG$. Producers' surplus becomes the area of triangle EGN under the price controls. Thus, the sum of the producers' and consumers' surpluses is $NKLG$. And the deadweight loss to society or the reduction in the sum of the surpluses is given by the triangle LCG. This deadweight loss is the excess of consumers' value over production costs for the units FA which are no longer produced due to the price controls. Note that the rectangle $BRGE$ was producers' surplus before the price controls were imposed but became consumers' surplus with the controls. Thus, this area merely represents a transfer from producers to consumers. Such a transfer does not affect total social welfare.

Now let's consider the impact on social welfare when the same available output (OF) is allocated at random among consumers willing to pay the regulated price. With random allocation, some consumers along the LH segment will receive output. But these consumers value the output less than those along the KL segment. In fact, at the price OE, total consumer surplus for the consumers along LH is equal to the area of triangle LGH which is $(LG \cdot GH)/2$. Average consumer surplus for this group is, thus, $(LG \cdot GH)/(2FJ)$. But $FJ = GH$, so this becomes $\frac{1}{2}LG$. Total consumer surplus for the consumers along KL is equal to the area of triangle KLM plus the area of rectangle $EMLG$. This sum is equal to $(KM \cdot ML)/2 + (EM \cdot EG)$. Average consumer surplus for this group is obtained by dividing by OF (which equals EG and ML). Thus, average consumer surplus for this group is $\frac{1}{2}KM + EM$.

The amount by which average consumer surplus for consumers along KL exceeds average consumer surplus for consumers along LH can now be expressed as $(KM/2) + EM - (LG/2)$. Since LG equals EM, this becomes $(KM + EM)/2$. This is the expected loss in consumer surplus for each unit of output that goes to a consumer along LH rather than to a consumer along KL. What fraction of output is expected to go to consumers along LH? With random allocation this depends on the number of consumers along this region relative to the total number willing to purchase at a price OE, which is FJ/OJ. The corresponding number of units of output expected to go to the consumers along LH is, thus, $(FJ/OJ) \cdot OF$. And the total expected loss in consumer surplus due to random allocation is $(FJ/OJ) \cdot OF \cdot \frac{1}{2}(KM + EM)$. If FJ/OJ is $\frac{1}{2}$ (as drawn), then $KM = EM$ and the total expected loss due to random allocation becomes $\frac{1}{2} \cdot OF \cdot KM$ which is the area of triangle KML.

The area of triangle KML, it should be noted, is only the expected loss in consumer surplus due to the fact that the output is randomly allocated. The total loss in social welfare due to the price control coupled with random allocation is the sum of triangles LCG and KML. Thus, triangle LCG can be thought of as the cost of the output reduction and triangle KML as the cost of the random allocation process.

Suppose the available output OF is distributed at random to the total number of customers OJ, but those who obtain any of the output can resell it to others who are willing to pay a higher price. Then the output will be consumed by individuals on the demand curve in the segment KL, and the welfare cost is given by the area of the triangle LCG as we derived earlier. Thus, with price controls and a situation of excess demand, it is best to distribute the available output at random and permit a resale to others. If the resale is not permitted, the welfare cost will be higher, as we have shown.

9.10.2 Applications in health economics

There are many applications of microeconomics in the area of health services. It is common knowledge that health expenditures have been steadily increasing over time even after adjusting for changes in the general price level. Between 1950 and 1980 health costs increased from 4 percent of national income to 9 percent of national income. The projected rates of increase for the next two decades are much higher. One can say that the demand for medical care will increase with a rise in per-capita income and increased health consciousness. However, the phenomenal increases in health care costs cannot be explained by these factors alone. On the supply side, the American Medical Association restricts the supply of physicians through strict barriers to entry. It is one of the strongest cartels in the world. However, one cannot say that the monopoly power exercised by the AMA has increased much during this period.

The major contributory factor in the enormous increase in health care costs is the growth in third-party payments (payments by insurance companies and government). Less than 30 percent of health care costs are currently paid directly by the patients. Since 1966 the Medicare and Medicaid programs have expanded rapidly. These benefits are directly paid by the government. The Medicare program covers the major costs of hospital and physician services provided to the aged under social security. Medicaid pays the costs of hospital and physician services provided to the poor. The combined expenditures of the Medicare and Medicaid programs in fiscal 1981 were $56.6 billion. Between 1970 and 1980 about one-fourth of the $181.3 billion growth in personal health costs was due to the growth in the Medicare and Medicaid expenditures. These expenditures are projected to grow at an ever-increasing rate over the next two decades.

In this section we will analyze the effect of medical insurance on the demand for medical care. We will also analyze the effect of government-paid insurance programs such as Medicare and Medicaid on the demand for medical care and on the price of medical care. We also show that there is a net welfare cost resulting from these programs and that doctors are clearly beneficiaries of these programs.

Effect of medical insurance

In Figure 9.12 SS' is the supply curve, D_0D_0' is the demand curve in the absence of insurance, and D_1D_0' is the demand curve if the insurance company pays half of total expenses. Q_0 and P_0 are the quantity and price without insurance; Q_1 and P_1 are the quantity and price with insurance.

The doctors' surplus is initially P_0AS. With the insurance program it is P_1BS. Thus, doctors' profits increase by P_1BAP_0. The consumers' surplus initially is D_0AP_0. With insurance it increases to D_1BP_1. But we have not considered the insurance payments that consumers have to make. Thus, we cannot say whether they are better off or worse off. Of course, to analyze the effects on consumers, we also have to consider the risks that consumers are insuring against. A simple analysis such as this, in terms of consumers' and producers' surpluses, will not be enough.

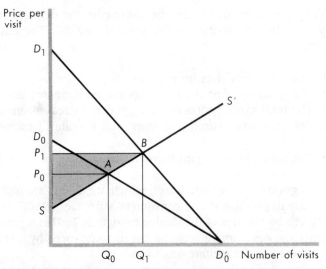

FIGURE 9.12 Effects of medical insurance.

However, this simple analysis does show that prices, number of visits, and doctors' profits all rise in the presence of medical insurance.

Medicare and Medicaid

In the previous example we discussed the effects of private health insurance. We will now discuss the effect of government-paid insurance. Let us assume for simplicity that the government pays all the expenses for medical care for everyone. The effects we are likely to observe are shown in Figure 9.13.

Let AB be the demand curve if there is no government insurance. Let HC be the supply curve of medical services. Initially, the price is OD, the quantity of medical care is OF, and total consumers' expenditures are $ODEF$. The consumers' surplus is ADE, and the producers' surplus (doctors' and hospitals') is DEH.

FIGURE 9.13 Government-paid insurance for all.

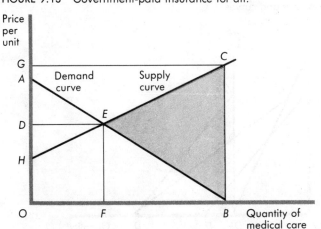

When the government pays the entire cost, the demand curve becomes completely inelastic and swings to the vertical line *BC*. The effects of this are the following:

1. The price now rises from *OD* to *OG*.
2. The quantity of medical care consumed increases from *OF* to *OB*.
3. The total expenditures on medical care increase from *ODEF* to *OBCG*.
4. The producers' surplus (doctors' and hospitals') increases by the amount *DECG*.
5. The consumers' surplus increases by *ODEB*.

However, government expenditures, which are *OBCG*, are higher than the sum of the increase in producers' and consumers' surpluses (*DECG* + *OBED*). The difference is given by the area of the shaded triangle *BCE*. This represents the net welfare loss. Since the government revenue has to be financed by taxes which society has to bear, there is a net welfare loss to society.

We can now analyze the case where the government pays for the expenses of only a particular group (this is the case with the Medicare and Medicaid program). We will first derive the aggregate demand curve for medical care from the demand curves of those covered under Medicare and Medicaid and those that are not covered. This is shown in Figure 9.14. Let D_1D_1' be the demand curve of one group and D_2D_2' be the demand curve of another group. The two demand curves have different slopes and intercepts. We have drawn D_2D_2' so that at high prices the quanity demanded by this group is larger than that demanded by the first group. This may be justifiable if we assume that the second group consists of more sick people than the first group. Anyway, the different curves are drawn for illustrative purposes only.

We first want to derive the total demand curve which can be obtained by adding the quantities demanded by the two groups at each price. Above the price OD_1, the demand by the first group is 0. Hence, the total demand curve is given

FIGURE 9.14   Derivation of aggregate demand curve from two individual demand curves.

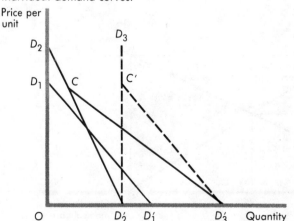

by the portion D_2C of D_2D_2'. After this, the total demand curve is obtained by a horizontal addition of D_1D_1' and D_2D_2'. Since the demand curves we have drawn are straight lines, this is easy to derive. From D_1' measure $D_1'D_3' = OD_2'$. Then OD_3' is the total demand at 0 price. Hence, the total demand curve is given by D_2CD_3'.

Now if the government pays the entire medical expenses of group 2, the demand curve for this group will be completely inelastic, and it will be the vertical line $D_2'D_3$ in Figure 9.14. The aggregate demand curve is then given by the horizontal summation of the two demand curves and becomes the dotted line $D_3C'D_3'$.

We can now analyze the effects of the Medicare and Medicaid program. This is done in Figure 9.15. The demand curve for the noncovered group is D_1D_1'. Without the program, the aggregate demand curve is D_2CD_3'. SS is the supply curve. Then OA is the price. OK is the quantity consumed by the noncovered group, and KL is the quantity consumed by the group that will soon be covered by the Medicare or Medicaid program.

Now with the program, the aggregate demand curve shifts to $D_3C'D_3'$. This intersects the supply curve SS at the point F. We now observe the following changes.

1. The price rises from OA to OD, and the total consumption of medical care rises from OL to OH.

2. Consumption for the noncovered group falls from OK to OG. There is a loss in consumers' surplus for this group. This loss is measured by the area $ABED$.

3. Consumption for the covered group rises from KL to GH. Since GH is the same as $D_1'D_3'$, and this group does not pay any expenses, the increase in consumers' surplus is the area between the demand curves $BJD_3'D_1'$. But since $D_1'D_3' = EF =$

FIGURE 9.15   Net welfare cost of the Medicare and Medicaid programs.

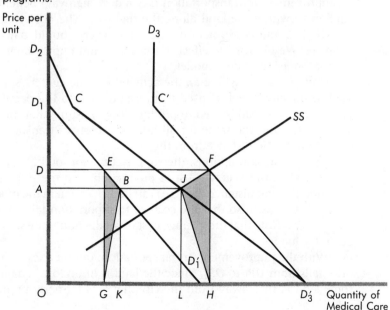

HG, this area is the same as $BJHG$. This is also the sum of rectangle $BJKL$ (previous medical expenditure by the covered group) and triangles GBK and JHL (the value to the covered group of the additional units consumed).

4. The producers' surplus of the medical profession increases by $AJFD$.

5. Finally the government's expenditures on the Medicare and Medicaid program are given by $EFHG$.

Thus, we have the following gains and losses:

1. The noncovered group loses—their loss in consumers' surplus is $ABED$.
2. The medical profession gains—their gain is $AJFD$.
3. The covered group gains—the gain is $BJHG$.

The net gain so far is $BJHG + AJFD - ABED = BJHG + BJFE$. But this gain is less than the government expenditure on the Medicare-Medicaid program, which is $EFGH$. Thus, we are left with a net loss given by the shaded triangles EBG and FJH. This measures the net welfare loss to society from the program.

The group that is not covered by the program suffers most. There is a loss in consumers' surplus as well as the tax burden arising from the program. The medical profession is a beneficiary of the program and so is the covered group, since their increase in consumers' surplus $BJHG$ will most likely be higher than their increased tax burden.

9.10.3 Transportation improvement and land values

In the area of transportation economics, one question that is often raised is whether an improvement in transportation (say a new highway) benefits consumers or the landlords owning the land along the highway. The answer to this question will tell whether the consumers or the landowners should pay for the cost of the highway. We discuss the effect of transportation improvement on land values by using a rather simplified model.

Consider a city where all the activity is at the center. Suppose that there is a road to the city which is used to transport food to the people living in the city. Land along this road is used to produce food. Assume that the costs of production are constant and the same for all land and costs of transportation vary in direct proportion to the distance from the city.

With these assumptions, the supply curve for food is SS_1 in Figure 9.16. The intercept gives the average cost of production, and the slope is the cost of transportation per unit distance. If there is an improvement in the mode of transportation (say a better road), so that the costs of transportation fall, the supply curve shifts down to SS_2. Note that the average cost of production is the same. DD is the demand curve for food.

With the improvement in transportation, output rises from OQ_1 and OQ_2, and price falls from OP_1 to OP_2. Since the land is of uniform quality and productivity, some land farther away from the city that was formerly unprofitable to cultivate

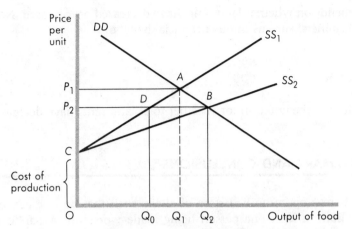

FIGURE 9.16   Effect of transportation improvement on land values.

now can be used to grow food and, hence, command some price. Before the improvement, land closest to the city commanded a rent of CP_1 (cost of production was OC and price OP_1; hence, rent was CP_1).[17] After the improvement in transportation, this rent falls to CP_2. Thus, land values closer to the city would fall. For land at Q_1, previously there was no rent. It was the marginal land for which the market price of output was equal to the cost of production plus the cost of transportation. After the improvement in transportation, the land at Q_2 is the marginal land. Thus, all land between Q_1 and Q_2, which earlier had no rent, now has some rent. Thus, the land values between Q_1 and Q_2 have definitely increased.

To see who gains and who loses we have to compare the vertical distance between P_1A and SS_1 (the rent before improvement) with the distance between P_2B and SS_2 (the rent after improvement). At some point Q_0, the land rents start increasing. For points between 0 and Q_0 the land rents fall. Thus, land values fall for land located between 0 and Q_0, and land values rise for land located between Q_0 and Q_2. Thus, landowners in the range 0 to Q_0 will oppose the transportation improvement. Landowners in the range Q_0 to Q_2 will support it.

The consumers in the city will definitely benefit from the improvement in transportation. The consumers' surplus increases by the amount P_1ABP_2. The total rent to landowners changes from P_1AC to P_2BC. It is difficult to tell whether landowners as a whole gain. Since the common area is P_2DC, the landowners gain as a whole if CDB is greater than P_1ADP_2. If CDB is less than P_2ADP_2, they lose.

The net social benefit is the increase in consumers' surplus plus the change in land rents. This is

$$P_1ABP_2 + P_2BC - P_1AC = P_1ABC - P_1AC = ABC$$

Whether the consumers' benefit is greater than or less than the net social benefit

[17]We will discuss the concept of rent in much greater detail in Chapter 17. For now it will suffice to define rent as the return to a factor which is in short supply. In this case it is land of a particular location which is in short supply.

depends on whether land rents have decreased or increased. Note that increase in consumers' surplus minus net social benefit

$$= P_1ABP_2 - ABC$$
$$= P_1ADP_2 - CDB$$

which is the criterion for whether total land rents have decreased or increased.

9.11   SUMMARY AND CONCLUSIONS

A Pareto optimum is a state of affairs such that no one can be made better off without at least one person being made worse off. A Pareto improvement is a change in the allocation of resources or goods which makes someone better off and nobody worse off. The designation of a change as a Pareto improvement does not require an interpersonal comparison of utilities. A suggested method for evaluating a change in the allocation of goods which makes one person better off at someone else's expense is the compensation criterion.

Efficiency in consumption requires the marginal rate of substitution for any pair of goods to be the same for all individuals consuming that pair of goods. Production efficiency requires the marginal rate of technical substitution for any pair of inputs to be the same for: (1) all products that a single firm produces using these two inputs and (2) all producers producing the same output. Efficiency in the matching of production and consumption requires the marginal rate of transformation in production to equal the marginal rate of substitution in consumption.

The Edgeworth box diagram can be used to illustrate efficiency conditions or to examine when and how voluntary exchange can improve the allocation of goods. The contract curve consists of all Pareto optimal allocations of goods or factors of production. The production possibilities curve consists of all combinations of two products that could be produced with an efficient allocation of inputs.

Efficiency in consumption over time requires the marginal rate of substitution of present consumption for future consumption to be the same for all consumers. Efficiency in production over time requires the marginal rate of transformation of present goods for future goods to be the same for all producers.

Consider two firms using the same technology and the same quantities of all inputs but producing different quantities of output. The X-factor accounts for the output difference. The X-factor encompasses activity type and rate and quality of effort.

Consumers' surplus is the excess of the amount that consumers would be willing to pay over the amount that they actually do pay. Producers' surplus is the excess of the amount actually received by producers over the amount required to induce them to sell. Consumer surplus can be measured as the area below the demand curve and above the price line. But the demand curve must be income-compensated or the income effect must be negligible. Producer surplus can be measured as the area under the price line and above the supply curve.

Price ceilings reduce output and create a shortage. The welfare cost due to the reduction in output is the amount by which society values the lost units over their production costs. The total cost of the price controls can exceed this amount if the product is not optimally allocated.

Health insurance increases the demand for medical care. Hence, both price and quantity consumed rise. Physicians' revenues and profits increase. The Medicare and Medicaid programs cover only some consumers, but the quantity of medical services consumed by the covered group rises. The quantity of medical care consumed by the noncovered group falls. Covered consumers gain and physicians gain. Noncovered consumers lose. And since the cost of the program exceeds the net gain (gain to covered consumers and physicians minus loss to noncovered consumers), there is a net social loss.

Improved transportation increases the land values for more distant land and reduces the value for land closest to the market. Consumers benefit because transportation costs fall, the supply curve shifts downward, and, thus, prices fall.

KEY TERMS

Compensation Criterion
Consumers' Surplus
Consumption Efficiency
Contract Curve
Deadweight Loss
Edgeworth Box Diagram

Initial Endowment
Interpersonal Utility
  Comparison
Pareto Improvement
Pareto Optimum
Producers' Surplus

Production Efficiency
Production Possibility
  Curve
Welfare Cost
X-inefficiency

QUESTIONS

1. Consider John and Mary who consume both hamburgers H and cokes C. Currently, for John the $MRS_{H \text{ for } C}$ equals 3, whereas for Mary, the $MRS_{H \text{ for } C}$ equals 5. Explain numerically how John and Mary could trade these items so that both of them would be better off.

2. Do welfare programs result in an allocation of resources which constitutes a Pareto improvement over the allocation that would prevail without such programs? Why or why not?

3. If a reallocation of goods satisfies the compensation criterion and the necessary compensation actually occurs, does the resulting allocation constitute a Pareto improvement? Why or why not?

4. In the case of consumption, does every point on the Edgeworth contract curve represent a Pareto improvement over a point not on the curve? Why or why not?

5. In the case of consumption, will the Edgeworth contract curve go through O_A and O_B? Why or why not?

6. In the Edgeworth box diagram for consumption, what would a vertical movement involve? Could such a movement result from voluntary exchange? What about a horizontal movement?

7. Using an Edgeworth box diagram, demonstrate that an equal division of two goods between two people might not be Pareto optimal.

8. Consider two firms, A and Z, which are almost identical. But suppose that the output of firm Z is of a slightly higher quality. If efficiency is evaluated without considering this quality difference, which firm will appear to have a higher X-factor? Suppose instead, the labor at A is a little better educated than at Z. If efficiency is again evaluated without considering the difference in labor quality, which firm will now appear to have a higher X-factor? Why? What other measurement problems might X-factors pick up?

9. Will the welfare cost of a price control be larger when the demand curve is flatter or steeper? Why? When will the loss associated with random allocation be larger?

10. Will measuring consumers' surplus with an uncompensated demand curve cause the true value to be overstated or understated? Why? Does it matter whether the good is normal or inferior?

11. Suppose that the demand for whatnots is $Q = 100 - 20P$. If the price of whatnots is $2, calculate consumer expenditure and consumers' surplus. If the price of whatnots increases to $3, what is the reduction in consumer surplus? What is the total value of the associated quantity of whatnots to consumers?

12. Draw an Edgeworth box diagram reflecting preferences between yourself and your neighbor for pizza and beer. Suppose initially that you have all the beer and your neighbor has all the pizza. By constructing the relevant indifference curves, determine the maximum utility level that you can reach through exchange and that your neighbor can reach through exchange. In practice, where is the final allocation of pizza and beer likely to be and what determines this allocation? Suppose your neighbor who is allergic to fish discovers that the pizza has anchovies on it. How would this affect the analysis?

13. During most market periods fishers catch Q_1 fish and offer it for sale in the marketplace. Suppose that in the current period, the catch is unusually large, resulting in Q_2 fish offered for sale.

   a. What is the effect on fishers' incomes? Would they gain or lose? Would the fishers hold back some fish from the market?

   b. What is the effect on consumers?

   c. What is the net effect on society?

   d. If it pays fishers to destroy some fish, what measures could be taken to prevent this?

14. Consider the market for a good in which no consumer would ever buy more than 1 unit of the good over the market period (for example, season tickets to a theater, football games).

   a. What will an individual's demand curve look like?

   b What will the market demand curve look like? Explain why the market quantity demanded increases as price falls.

   c. Show in a graph the consumer surplus a consumer obtains if the consumer purchases the good. Show how it would change should price fall.

   d. In such cases, is the law of diminishing marginal utility violated? Explain.

15. Explain how the loss in consumer surplus resulting from an increase in price can be broken down into:

   a. The loss in benefit on the units no longer consumed

   b. Increased expenditure on the units still consumed

   c. Decreased expenditure on the units not consumed

16. "The individual's marginal benefit curve is the same as the individual's demand curve." Explain the meaning of this statement.

PART THREE
PRICING IN PRODUCT MARKETS

Part Three (chapters 10 to 14) examines the problem of pricing of output. In Part Two we presented the theory of consumer and producer behavior, the driving forces behind demand and supply. But the way in which these two factors determine the price of output depends on how firms are organized (that is, market structure). Chapter 10 discusses how price and output are determined under perfect competition. Chapter 11 discusses price and output determination under monopoly. Chapter 12 contains a more detailed discussion of regulation of monopoly. Chapter 13 discusses the determination of output and price under monopolistic competition and oligopoly. Finally, Chapter 14 contains some extensions of the previous theories of output and price determination. It discusses the role of product differentiation and advertising. An outline of a new theory, the theory of contestable markets, is also presented.

CHAPTER 10

PRICING IN PRODUCT MARKETS:
COMPETITIVE MARKETS

There is no "invisible hand" in the market place, there are so many hands that most of them cannot be observed at any instant.

George Bernard Shaw

10.1   INTRODUCTION

In the previous chapters we considered the theory of the consumer and the theory of the producer. We will now explain how prices of output and inputs are determined. This chapter and the next three chapters will consider pricing in the product market. Chapters 15 to 17 will consider pricing in markets for inputs. In Chapter 2 we said that the market price is determined by the intersection of the market demand and supply curves, but we did not go into detail on how the market supply is determined. This is what will be done in this and the next three chapters. Furthermore, the pricing of output will depend on how the product markets are organized, that is, whether there are one, two, or many producers, whether the product is homogeneous, and so on. Thus, we have to start with a classification of the markets.

From the point of view of an individual, the *market* consists of those firms from which the individual can buy a well-defined product. From the point of view of a firm, the market consists of those buyers to whom it can sell a well-defined product. For example, for an individual buying skimmed milk, the market for skimmed milk consists of all firms from which the individual can buy skimmed milk; and for the firm supplying skimmed milk, the market consists of all buyers of skimmed milk. How many of these buyers the particular firm can attract will depend upon how many other firms are operating and how they price skimmed milk relative to this firm. These factors will fall under the title of *market structure* and will be discussed in this and the following chapters.

A group of firms that sells a well-defined product or closely related set of products is said to constitute an *industry*, for example, a group of firms that sells skimmed milk (and other milk products such as homogenized milk, cheese, and butter) is called the dairy industry. The industry can sell its products in different markets (markets in Wisconsin, Florida, California, and so on). The branch of economics that deals with how an industry is organized is called the *economics of industrial organization*. In actual practice an industry can be organized in a large number of forms depending on: (1) the number of firms in the industry, (2) whether the firms produce identical products or similar (but not identical) products, (3) whether entry into the industry is easy or difficult, (4) whether the markets are closely clustered or widely dispersed, (5) whether firms do a lot of advertising, and so on.

However, to make the analysis manageable economists have concentrated on a few models of industrial organization: (1) perfect competition, (2) monopoly, (3) monopolistic competition, and (4) oligopoly. Model 1 is discussed in this chapter, model 2 is discussed in Chapters 11 and 12. Models 3 and 4 are discussed in Chapter 13.

All of these are idealized models, and many industries fall in between. The reason we consider these idealized models is that they are manageable and enable us to study some basic principles in the pricing of output. Since many industries fall between the different models, some economists use terms such as "workably competitive," "effectively monopolistic," and so on. The question here is which of these different models does the industry we are considering closely approximate?

Agriculture is often cited as closely approximating the model of perfect competition, but even here only half of this sector can be considered competitive. Other examples of competitive industries are the construction industry and many of the service industries. As for manufacturing, it depends on the product. The shoe industry can be considered competitive but the steel industry not. As a rough rule of thumb we can say that about one-half of the U.S. economy can be considered competitive, about one-fourth monopolistic (or oligopolistic), and the remaining government-controlled.

Although we will be discussing the different models in detail as we proceed, we will first give a brief outline of the different characteristics of these four models. This is shown in Table 10.1. In this chapter we will consider perfect competition.

10.2 THE PROFIT MAXIMIZATION RULE

Before we begin analyzing the different forms of industrial organization, we need to lay down some ground rules by which firms operate. We will assume that the goal of the firm is profit maximization.

This assumption generally implies that output will be expanded to the point where $MR = MC$ (marginal revenue equals marginal cost). Figure 10.1 demonstrates this implication for two cases: (a) increasing MC and (b) decreasing MC. (Recall that as long as the demand curve is downward sloping, the MR curve will also be downward sloping.)

Consider an output level less than X^*. For any such output, $MR > MC$. This means that if the firm expands output, it will add more to its revenues than to its costs, thus increasing profit. But once the firm reaches X^*, it has no further incentive to increase output. This is because beyond X^*, $MR < MC$. Thus, by increasing output past X^*, the firm will add more to its costs than to its revenues, thus reducing profit. Hence, the profit-maximizing output occurs at X^* where $MR = MC$.

But let's consider the case of declining MC a bit further. In order that there be a determinate level of profit-maximizing output, we must also have the MR curve steeper than the MC curve as in Figure 10.1(b). The opposite case is illustrated in

TABLE 10.1 Different Models of Industrial Organization

Market Type	Number of Sellers	Entry Barriers to Sellers	Nature of Product
Perfect competition	Many, small, independent	None	Homogeneous
Monopoly	One	Insurmountable	Homogeneous
Monopolistic competition	Many, small, virtually independent	None	Differentiated
Oligopoly	Few, interdependent	Substantial	Homogeneous or differentiated

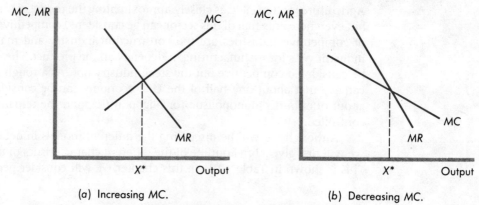

(a) Increasing MC.   (b) Decreasing MC.

FIGURE 10.1   Determination of the optimum level of output.

Figure 10.2 where the condition $MC = MR$ does not give the profit-maximizing output. In fact, in Figure 10.2 the firm can increase profit by increasing output beyond X^*, since $MR > MC$ for levels of output beyond X^*. Unless MC rises above MR, the profits of the firm will keep on increasing as output increases. If MC eventually does rise above MR, then the second point of intersection of these two curves gives the profit-maximizing output. This is shown in Figure 10.3. For both X_1^* and X_2^* we have $MR = MC$. But it is X_2^*, not X_1^*, that gives the profit-maximizing level of output.[1]

[1]The result is easily derived mathematically. Let x be the output, TR the revenue, and TC the cost. Profits are $\Pi = TR - TC$. To maximize profits we need

$$d\Pi/dx = \frac{d\,TR}{dx} - \frac{d\,TC}{dx} = 0$$

that is, $MR = MC$, and

$$\frac{d^2\,TR}{dx^2} - \frac{d^2\,TC}{dx^2} < 0$$

i.e., slope of MR curve $<$ slope of MC curve algebraically.

FIGURE 10.2   Optimum level of output unbounded.

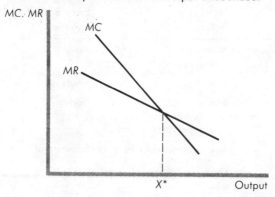

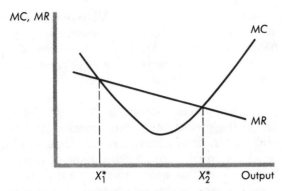

FIGURE 10.3   Multiple intersections of MR and MC curves.

Before continuing, it is certainly worth mentioning that many economists argue that the assumption of profit maximization as the goal of the firm is unrealistic. This might be particularly so in large corporations where there is a split between ownership by stockholders and control by managers. In this case, the profit maximization approach represents only the interests of owners and is probably not applicable. Since the alternative theories have been discussed in Sections 8.1 to 8.4 (Chapter 8), we will not repeat them here.

10.3   WHAT IS PERFECT COMPETITION?

"Perfect competition" is a phrase used often in everyday discussions, and many people have an intuitive and vague understanding of what it means. The concept of perfect competition is very old and was discussed in a casual way by Adam Smith in his *Wealth of Nations*. Edgeworth was the first to attempt (in his book, *Mathematical Psychics*, 1881) a systematic and rigorous definition of perfect competition. The concept received its complete formulation in Frank Knight's book, *Risk, Uncertainty and Profit* (1921).[2]

The concept of perfect competition is based on a large number of assumptions but the following are the most important:

1. Every firm in the market is so small relative to the market that it cannot exert any perceptible influence on price. Thus, the firm is a *price taker*.

2. The *product is homogeneous*. In the eyes of the consumer, the product of one seller is identical to that of another seller. This ensures that buyers are indifferent as to the firm from which they purchase. If a firm could differentiate its product from that of others, it would have at least a partial control over price.

3. The industry is characterized by *freedom of entry and exit*. Any new firm is free to set up production if it so wishes, and any existing firm can stop production and leave the industry if it so wishes.

[2]See George J. Stigler, "Perfect Competition Historically Contemplated," *The Journal of Political Economy*, February 1957, pp. 1–17.

4. There is also *free mobility of resources*. All resources are perfectly mobile. For instance, labor is mobile geographically and among jobs.

5. The participants in the market have *perfect knowledge*. Consumers know prices; producers know costs; workers know wage rates; and so on. In addition, everyone has complete knowledge of the future.

No industry, in actual practice, satisfies all these conditions. But the usefulness of any theory lies in the predictions it can generate. And the accuracy of such predictions depends in part on whether there are industries that come close to the theoretical model. An industry with 20 firms, none of which is dominant in the market, might be considered closer to competitiveness than another industry with only 2 or 3 firms. Thus, the automobile industry is not a perfectly competitive industry, but the vegetable industry might be considered competitive. Whether an industry is perfectly competitive depends on the demand curve *facing the individual firms*. If the demand curve is downward sloping, then the firm can change price by changing its output and the industry is not perfectly competitive (the firm is not a price taker).

Sometimes a distinction is made between "pure" and "perfect" competition— "pure" being a shade less perfect than "perfect." Chamberlain defined *pure competition* as "competition unalloyed with monopoly elements."[3] The only conditions required for this are a large number of traders and a standardized commodity. Thus, of the five requirements of perfect competition, Chamberlain's concept of pure competition requires only the first two.

George Stigler defines an alternative concept, *market competition*, which includes the fifth requirement but not the third and fourth. Thus, market competition can exist even though resources or traders cannot enter or leave the market in question. The industry will not be in long-run equilibrium, but market competition can still operate.

Note that the assumption of perfect knowledge is not special to the concept of perfect competition. In fact, one can argue that full knowledge of prices is easier to achieve under monopoly than under a system with a larger number of firms.

The preceding discussion was intended to point out that there are weaker definitions of competition than perfect competition, and each definition is obtained by relaxing a few of the assumptions underlying the concept of perfect competition. We will now discuss the problem of pricing.

10.4 SHORT-RUN EQUILIBRIUM IN A COMPETITIVE INDUSTRY

We will first discuss the determination of price and output in a competitive industry in the short run. By short run we mean a length of time during which (1) no new firms enter the industry, (2) no existing firms exit the industry, and (3) the individual firms cannot make any adjustments to fixed inputs.

The price and output in a competitive industry in the short run are determined

---

[3]Edward H. Chamberlain, *The Theory of Monopolistic Competition*, Harvard University Press, Cambridge, Mass., 1933, p. 6.

by the short-run supply and demand curves for the industry. We examined the demand side in earlier chapters. Now we have to examine where the short-run supply curve for the industry comes from. To do this we must derive the short-run supply curve of an individual firm and then aggregate the supply curves of all the firms to get the industry supply curve.

The demand curve facing the competitive firm

Consider a homogeneous product like wheat. The price of the product is determined by the interaction of the total market demand for and supply of the product. But, as we discussed earlier in Sections 10.1 and 10.3, the essential feature of a competitive industry is that there is a large number of firms selling the same homogeneous product. Since each individual firm produces such a small portion of the total, it has a very small or negligible effect on the price of the product. For simplicity we say that the firm has a zero effect on the price. Alternatively, we say that the competitive firm is a *price taker*. It takes the market price as given and can sell any amount it wants to at that price. The firm can sell nothing above that price and has no reason to sell below it. Thus, the demand curve that a competitive firm faces for *its* output is depicted as a horizontal line as shown in Figure 10.4. The elasticity is, therefore, infinity. In reality, the elasticity is very high, and the demand curve is almost horizontal as shown by the dotted line in Figure 10.4 (with a very small downward slope), but for convenience we take it to be horizontal.

Equilibrium of a competitive firm

Since the competitive firm is a price taker, the competitive firm calculates its revenues taking price as given. The firm's profit is $TR - TC$ (TR is total revenue and TC is total cost), and the firm will produce that output which yields the maximum profit. In Section 10.2 we argued that the condition for profit maximization is $MC = MR$. But, for the competitive firm, the price is constant and, hence, marginal revenue and average revenue are constant and equal to price. Thus, for the competitive firm that is maximizing profit we have

$$AR = P = MR = MC$$

The equilibrium output is shown in Figure 10.5. Note that the firm does not necessarily produce at the point where its average variable cost AVC is minimum.

FIGURE 10.4   The demand curve facing a competitive firm.

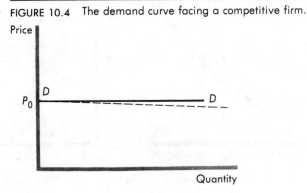

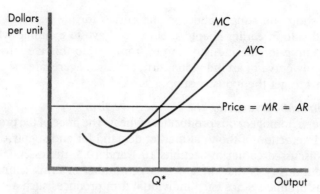

FIGURE 10.5 Equilibrium of a competitive firm.

The optimal level of output is Q^* where price is MC. It is not necessarily true that the firm makes a profit at this level of output. Since $AR > AVC$, the revenues of the firm will more than cover the variable costs. Whether they cover total costs depends on what the fixed costs are. In the short run the firm will continue to produce as long as the revenues cover variable costs. But, in the long run, the firm's revenues have to cover fixed costs as well to enable the firm to stay in production. In the short run the firm must pay the fixed costs even if it chooses not to produce, but in the long run, the fixed inputs and, hence, the fixed costs can be eliminated if the firm exits the industry.

Figure 10.5 shows how much output the competitive firm produces at a given price. By varying the price, we get different levels of output, and this gives the short-run supply curve of the competitive firm. This is shown in Figure 10.6. The minimum output the firm will produce is Q_0 where price P_0 is equal to the minimum point on the AVC curve. For any price below P_0, the firm's revenues do not even cover variable costs, and it does not pay for the firm to produce any output.

FIGURE 10.6 Short-run supply curve of a competitive firm.

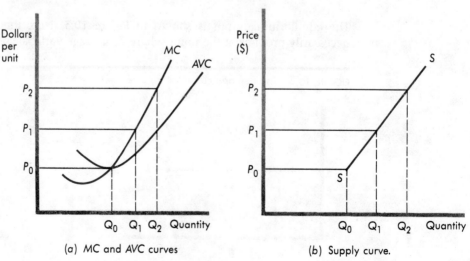

(a) MC and AVC curves

(b) Supply curve.

In Figure 10.6(a) we plot the MC and AVC curves. For different levels of the price, we get different quantities supplied by equating price to MC. In Figure 10.6(b) we plot these prices and quantities to get the supply curve.

The supply curve we have obtained is a *firm's short-run supply curve* because we have assumed that the minimum price P_0 is equal to the minimum AVC. That is, we have assumed that the revenues of the firm must cover variable costs. In the long run, unless the revenues cover fixed costs as well, the firm cannot stay in production.

In summary, we have until now discussed the short-run supply curve for a competitive firm. We have said that

1. If price < the minimum AVC the firm will not produce. Note that this does not mean the firm will exit the industry. It only means a temporary halt in production.

2. If price ≥ minimum AVC, then the firm will produce in the short run. And it will maximize its profit by producing where $P = MC$.

3. The firm will make a profit only if P exceeds minimum ATC. In all of this discussion, the MC, AVC, and ATC we are considering are the short-run values. That is,

MC = short-run marginal cost
AVC = short-run average variable cost
ATC = short-run average total cost

Industry supply

We must now consider the short-run market supply curve for the competitive industry. In Chapter 2 we obtained the *short-run industry supply curve* by adding the supplies of all the individual firms in the industry. It was based on the marginal costs of the individual firms. The minimum amount supplied by each firm will be the level of output where its AVC reaches a minimum. Suppose, for the sake of illustration, that there are three firms in the industry. Table 10.2 shows the individual supply curves and the total industry supply. Of course, in a competitive

TABLE 10.2 The Industry Supply Curve Derived as the Sum of the Supply Curves of Individual Firms: A Simplified Case

| | Output Supplied By | | | Total Output |
Price	Firm 1	Firm 2	Firm 3	Supplied
10	100	90	0	190
15	120	105	100	325
20	130	120	120	370
25	140	135	140	415
30	150	150	160	460
Minimum AVC	10	10	15	

industry there will be a large number of firms. But the industry supply curve is obtained in a similar fashion.

It is important to note that we have made a simplifying assumption in deriving the short-run industry supply curve as the horizontal sum of the individual firms' short-run supply curves. We implicitly assumed that all the firms move along their individual supply curves without affecting the cost structure of the other firms. In many cases this assumption is unrealistic. For example, the expansion of output by all firms might drive up the price of a specialized input. If this happens, then as product price rises and firms attempt to move upward along their individual supply curves, their marginal cost curves (hence their supply curves) shift upward. Thus firms do not increase output to the extent predicted by their original marginal cost curves. What does all this mean? It means that the market or industry short-run supply curve will be steeper than the sum of the individual firms' supply curves. Similarly, if the short-run expansion of output by all firms favorably affects the costs of the individual firms, then the short-run industry supply curve will be flatter than the sum of the individual firms' short-run supply curves.

Industry equilibrium
In Chapter 2 we discussed how market demand curves are obtained by aggregating the demand curves for individual consumers. The short-run industry supply curve that we have derived and the short-run demand curve together determine the equilibrium market price. This is shown in Figure 10.7. Note that though no firm can exert any influence on price, the *collective* action of suppliers and demanders determines the price.

At the price P^*, the industry output is Q^*. This is made up of all the outputs supplied by firms for which P^* exceeds minimum AVC. Firms for whom minimum $AVC > P^*$ will not produce anything. At the price P^*, some firms might be enjoying a short-run profit. These are the firms where P^* exceeds minimum ATC. Still other firms might be suffering a short-run loss. These are the firms where P^* is less than minimum ATC. And finally, the market clears because quantity demanded equals quantity supplied. Hence, there is no upward or downward pressure on price.

FIGURE 10.7   Determination of equilibrium price in a competitive market.

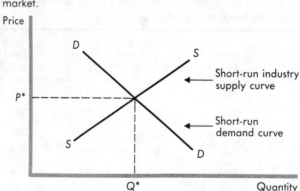

10.5   LONG-RUN EQUILIBRIUM IN A COMPETITIVE INDUSTRY

We defined one of the characteristics of perfect competition as easy entry into and exit out of the industry. But such entry and exit can occur only in the long run. This is because potential firms cannot acquire the necessary fixed inputs in the short run, and existing firms cannot get rid of their fixed inputs in the short run.

Also, existing firms have the option of adjusting the quantities of their fixed inputs in the long run. Thus, in the long run we expect two things to happen: (1) Existing firms will make adjustments in their output and costs. (2) If after these adjustments, a firm is still unable to cover its total costs, it will exit the industry. And if existing firms are earning profits, then new firms will be lured into the industry.

Let us first consider existing firms. These firms will adjust their output to maximize profit. They will produce where $LRMC = P$. And each firm will adjust its plant size to minimize the cost of producing its chosen output. Thus, each firm will move to a point on the $LRAC$ curve.

Figure 10.8 illustrates the adjustment process for an existing firm. In the short run, the firm might be stuck with plant 1 and short-run average and marginal cost curves $SRAC_1$ and $SRMC_1$, respectively. If the price of the product is P, the firm will maximize its short-run profit by producing Q_1 units of output so that $MR = SRMC_1$. The firm will enjoy a profit equal to the area of the rectangle $abcd$ or $(P\text{-}SRAC_1)Q_1$.

But this firm can do better in the long run. If price remains at P, then the firm will improve its profit by expanding output to Q_2, where $MR = LRMC$. It must also adjust its plant size to minimize the cost of its output. Thus, plant size will be increased to plant size 2 with cost curves $SRAC_2$ and $SRMC_2$. Its profit will now be equal to the area of rectangle $aefg$.

In the situation depicted in Figure 10.8, the firm is profitable in both the short run and the long run. In Figure 10.9, we consider a firm that may not operate in

FIGURE 10.8   Increase in profit for a competitive firm by adjusting output and plant size.

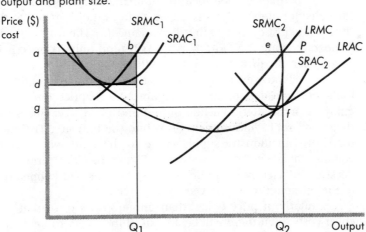

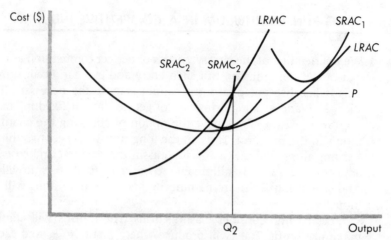

FIGURE 10.9 Short-run losses but long-run profits.

the short run but will be profitable in the long run. In the short run the firm has plant size 1 with short-run average total cost curve $SRAC_1$. If price is equal to P, the firm cannot cover its total costs. If P exceeds minimum average variable cost, then the firm will continue to operate at a loss in the short run. But if P is less than minimum AVC then the firm will minimize its losses by shutting down in the short run. In either case, the firm will suffer a short-run loss.

But if price remains at P, the firm can scale down its plant and operate at a profit in the long run. It will produce Q_2, where $LRMC = MR$. And it must also reduce its plant size to minimize the cost of producing Q_2. The plant size will be reduced to plant size 2 with cost curves $SRAC_2$ and $SRMC_2$.

In the previous example, the firm was able to eliminate short-run losses by adjusting output and plant size. If price is below the minimum point on the long-run average cost curve, no such adjustment can eliminate losses, and the firm will exit the industry in the long run.

It is perhaps a good idea to summarize what we have said until now about the behavior of existing firms as we go from the short run to the long run: (1) the firm will adjust output so that $P = LRMC$. (2) The firm will adjust plant size so as to operate along the $LRAC$ curve. (3) If (and only if) price is less than minimum $LRAC$, then the firm will exit the industry.

We will now examine the impact of entry and exit of firms on the competitive industry. Consider the firm in Figure 10.9. If price remains at P, then the firm enjoys a profit after adjusting output and plant size. But if this is a typical firm, then this profit will lure new firms into the industry. The effect of this is to shift the short-run industry supply curve to the right with a consequent decline in equilibrium price. This is shown in Figure 10.10(a). Entry will occur until price declines sufficiently to eliminate all profit. This will happen only when price falls to the minimum point on the $LRAC$ curve.

Similarly, if price is less than minimum $LRAC$ so that a typical firm cannot cover costs, then there will be an exit of the least profitable firms. This will result in a leftward shift of the short-run industry supply curve and a consequent increase

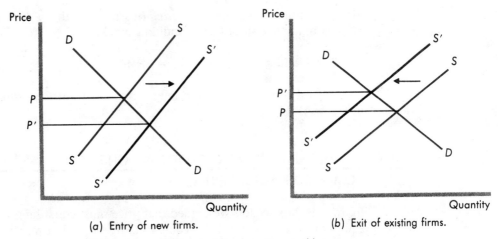

FIGURE 10.10   Effect of entry and exit of firms on the equilibrium
price of a competitive industry.

in equilibrium price. This is shown in Figure 10.10(b). Firms will continue to exit
the industry, shifting supply leftward until losses are eliminated for a typical firm
or until price increases to minimum *LRAC*. At that price, the surviving firms can
cover their full opportunity costs.

We have said that entry or exit of firms will occur until price is equal to
minimum *LRAC* for the typical firm. But entry and exit of firms is not the only
factor responsible for the adjustment in price.

In Figure 10.8, we assumed that the market price remained constant while
the particular firm we were considering adjusted its output and plant size. But if
several firms expanded plant size, then the short-run industry supply curve would
shift rightward and price would fall.[4] In fact, there might not even be an increase
in profit as shown in Figure 10.8. The effect is similar to that of new firm entry
into the industry. Thus, increase in industry short-run supply can occur through
expansion of plant size by existing firms or by the entry of new firms. Similarly,
decrease in industry supply can occur through contraction of plant size by existing
firms or through exit.

In summary, in the long run, a competitive industry undergoes two sorts of
adjustment. Existing firms are adjusting their outputs so that $P = LRMC$ to maximize
profit. Existing firms are also adjusting their plant sizes so that $SRAC = LRAC$, to
minimize the cost of their output. At the same time, new firms may be entering
or unprofitable firms may be exiting. All these adjustments cause changes in price
which trigger still more adjustments. So when will the industry settle down or
reach an equilibrium state?

Long-run equilibrium in a competitive industry requires that all incentives for
entry or exit be eliminated. This means that price must equal minimum *LRAC* for
a typical firm. The typical firm must also be in equilibrium so that it has no incentive

[4]As the firm adjusts plant size, it faces a new *SRMC* curve and hence a new firm supply curve. Thus the short-run
industry supply curve, which is derived from the individual firm supply curves, shifts.

to adjust either output or plant size. This requires that $P = LRMC$ and $SRAC = LRAC$. Combining all of these conditions we have

$$P = LRMC = LRAC = SRAC = SRMC$$

for a typical competitive firm in long-run equilibrium. This situation is illustrated in Figure 10.11.

10.6   THE MEANING OF ZERO PROFIT IN LONG-RUN COMPETITIVE EQUILIBRIUM

In the previous section we argued that price must equal long-run average cost in equilibrium. Clearly, if price is equal to $LRAC$ for each firm, then profit is equal to 0 for every firm. What does this zero profit mean? It means that firms are just covering their total costs. But these total costs are economic costs. The zero profit is an *economic profit*, so that the zero profit means that firms are just able to cover their full opportunity costs. This implies that all factors of production are earning what they could in their next best use.

A zero economic profit for all firms does not imply that *accounting profit* will be 0 or even equal for all firms. To illustrate these points, consider the following example: Suppose there are two firms, say A and B. For A, total revenues are $200,000, and its tangible costs (hired labor, materials bought, rental on equipment, and so on) are $140,000. So the firm will show an accounting profit of $60,000. For firm B, total revenues are $200,000 and tangible costs are $100,000. Thus, the firm will show an accounting profit of $100,000. For these two firms the accounting profits are positive and different. How can they coexist in a competitive industry over a period of time?

The so-called profit of $60,000 for firm A is the return to the specialized skills of the entrepreneurs operating firm A. (We are ignoring other intangibles such as

FIGURE 10.11   Competitive firm in long-run equilibrium.

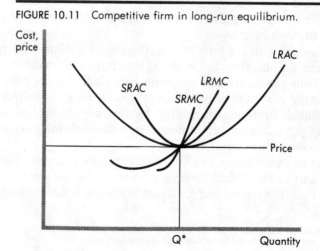

goodwill). The so-called profit of $100,000 for firm B is the return to the specialized skills of the entrepreneurs operating firm B. These profits are profits only in an accounting sense. In economic terms they are costs—opportunity costs that these entrepreneurs need to be paid for their specialized skills. In the short run, these entrepreneurs might receive more or less than their opportunity costs. But in the long run, in a competitive industry the entrepreneurs receive their opportunity cost. Thus, what appear as profits for the different firms are actually opportunity costs for the specialized skills for the entrepreneurs of these firms. Such profits can exist even in the long run in a competitive industry. Since in economic terms they are not profits but just opportunity costs, Friedman argues that in a competitive industry, in the long run, we should define total costs as identically equal to total revenues.[5] Here total costs are just the total explicit costs plus the total implicit costs (costs of goodwill and entrepreneurial skills).

The concept of long-run equilibrium we have discussed is an idealized one. No industry is ever characterized by a situation where no firm is making a profit (economic profit) and all firms are operating at the minimum point of their $LRAC$ curves. In actual practice there is continuous technological progress, and those firms using newer equipment and the latest technology will have lower costs than others and will be making a profit (economic profit). This, in turn, will prompt new firms to enter, or existing firms to change their technology, and the profits will disappear. Those with the old equipment will continue their operations so long as price covers AVC. If the equipment is so old that price does not cover even AVC, the equipment is junked. Thus, there will be a continuous process of entry and exit, and a continuous modernization of equipment going on.

Some industries, however, are characterized by exit only and no entry. These are the *declining industries,* where, because of some new developments, the demand for the industry's product is continuously declining. Examples of this are the cotton textile industry after the advent of synthetic fibers and the railroad industry in the United States after the advent of the automobile and highway construction. As demand declines, price falls, and firms that were previously covering ATC will not be able to do so. But it takes time for the firms to exit. With declining demand the firms do not undertake any investment in new equipment, but they can continue to operate with existing equipment as long as the price covers AVC. Of course, firms with minimum AVC > price will shut down immediately. Eventually, the industry looks "sick" with only antiquated equipment. But the antiquated equipment is a result of the industry's decline due to declining demand. It does not pay for new firms to enter or the old firms to modernize the equipment. The railroad industry is a case in point. Railroads in the United States do not function as a major means of transportation as they do in Europe or several Asian countries. One can blame this on the railroad industry for not modernizing their system of operation. However, the reason the industry is in bad shape is the decline in demand.

The manner by which entry of new firms drives down the profits of existing firms in a competitive industry can be seen clearly by looking at the recent experience of the minicomputer and microcomputer manufacturers as well as the manufacturers of electronic games. Initially, some of these firms made huge profits,

[5]M. Friedman, "Comment" on a paper by Caleb Smith in *Business Concentration and Price Policy,* National Bureau of Economic Research, Princeton University Press, Princeton, N.J., 1955, pp. 230–238.

but this induced many new firms to enter the field, and soon the field became so crowded that many companies were suffering losses and some were on the verge of bankruptcy. Eventually, this process results in an industry shake-up, and only the fittest survive, with the rest going under.

10.7   THE LONG-RUN SUPPLY CURVE IN CONSTANT-, INCREASING-, AND DECREASING-COST INDUSTRIES

Earlier, in Section 10.5, we discussed the response of individual firms in the long run. Each individual firm will adjust its plant size until it is producing at the minimum cost for its chosen output. Furthermore, new firms will enter if existing firms are making a profit and existing firms that are suffering losses will exit. In Figure 10.10 we showed the effect of this entry and exit of firms on the short-run industry supply curve, and in Figure 10.11 we illustrated long-run equilibrium. One interesting question that we will now ask is what the long-run supply curve of the competitive industry looks like and how it is obtained.

One important point to note is that the long-run supply curve is *not* obtained by the same procedure as the short-run supply curve. Earlier in Section 10.4 we obtained the short-run supply curve of a competitive firm as a portion of its short-run marginal cost curve (see Figure 10.6) and the short-run industry supply curve as an aggregation of the individual firms' supply curves (or short-run marginal cost curves). We *cannot* do this to obtain the long-run supply curve. That is, we cannot get the long-run industry supply curve by aggregating the individual firms' long-run marginal cost curves. This is because we have to account for exit from and entry into the industry.

To obtain the long-run industry supply curve we will make use of the fact that in long-run equilibrium all firms will be operating at the minimum point of their long-run average cost curves and this minimum value is equal to the market price for every firm. Thus, to obtain the long-run industry supply curve, we have to ask what happens to the individual firms' average cost curves when the industry output expands. The answer depends on whether the industry is a constant-cost industry, an increasing-cost industry, or a decreasing-cost industry. Thus, we have to consider the following three cases:

1. Constant-cost industries: These are industries where the individual firm's long-run average cost curve remains stable as the industry expands its output. An example of this is the restaurant industry, an industry which employs no specialized inputs.

2. Increasing-cost industries: These are industries where the individual firm's long-run average cost curve shifts upward as the industry expands its output. This situation arises if some of the productive resources are in limited supply. For example, if there is a limited supply of specific skilled labor, as the industry expands its output, each individual firm will have to pay a higher price for a unit of this skilled labor. There are several other sources of increasing costs. One such source is increased cost due to congestion in a manufacturing area or in a transportation and distribution area. The result is a slowing down of traffic and distribution. All these sources of increasing costs to the individual firms are called *external diseconomies of scale*. They are external because the firm has no control over them. They are called "diseconomies" of scale because as the scale or level of industry output rises, each firm's long-run average cost curve shifts up.

3. Decreasing-cost industries: These are industries where the long-run average cost curve of the individual firm shifts downward as the industry expands its output. One source of decreasing costs is the growth of auxiliary facilities or services. As the industry grows, transportation terminals might become available. Information processing equipment tailored especially for the industry's needs could be provided. Firms supplying inputs to the industry might begin to specialize in serving only that industry, improving service and efficiency. None of this would have happened in response to a single firm's expansion of output, so we say the resulting decrease in the individual firm's long-run average cost curve is due to *external economies of scale*. Again, they are called "external" because the individual firm has no control over them. They are "economies" because as the scale of industry output increases, each firm's long-run average cost curve shifts downward.

The long-run industry supply curve

We will now consider what the long-run industry supply curve looks like in each of these cases. We really need only to remember that in long-run equilibrium, price will be equal to minimum long-run average cost.

In the case of constant cost industries, as the industry expands its output, the *LRAC* curve for each individual firm stays the same. Hence, price, which is the minimum point on the *LRAC* curve, does not change in the long run. The long-run industry supply curve is horizontal. This is shown in Figure 10.12(*a*).

In the case of increasing cost industries, the *LRAC* curve of each firm shifts upward as the industry expands its output. Thus, the market price, which is the minimum point on the *LRAC* curve, has to rise in order that the industry expand its output. Thus, the long-run industry supply curve is upward sloping as shown in Figure 10.12(*b*).

Finally, in decreasing-cost industries, the *LRAC* curve shifts downward as the industry expands its output. In this case the long-run industry supply curve will be downward sloping as shown in Figure 10.12(*c*).

FIGURE 10.12   The long-run supply curve for a competitive industry.

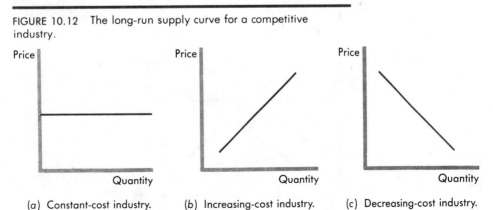

(a) Constant-cost industry.   (b) Increasing-cost industry.   (c) Decreasing-cost industry.

Effect of changes in demand

Now that we know the shape of the long-run supply curve of the competitive industry, we can study the effect of changes in demand on the output of the industry and the price level.

In Figure 10.13, SS is the long-run industry supply curve. ΣMC_1 is the initial sum of the marginal cost curves or the initial short-run industry supply curve. D_1D_1 is the initial demand curve. Now suppose that demand increases to D_2D_2. Immediately, there is a shortage at the initial price of P. This causes price to rise to P_1. As price rises, existing firms expand their output along their short-run supply curves so that industry output increases from Q to Q_1. But at a price of P_1, firms can earn a pure economic profit as $P_1 >$ minimum $LRAC$. Thus, new firms are drawn into the industry. As new firms enter, the industry short-run supply curve shifts to the right, putting downward pressure on price. Price will continue to fall until it again equals minimum $LRAC$, or until it returns to P. Thus, in the long run, an increase in demand brings about an increase in industry output with no change in price. A decrease in demand has the opposite effect.

The situation with an increasing cost industry is shown in Figure 10.14. Again SS is the long-run industry supply curve, and D_1D_1 is the initial demand curve. Now the demand curve increases to D_2D_2. It is clear that once the industry settles back to a long-run equilibrium, the equilibrium quantity will have increased to Q_2 and the equilibrium price will have increased to P_2. The effect of a decrease in demand would be the opposite. Both the long-run equilibrium price and quantity would decline.

Decreasing-cost industries

The case of decreasing-cost industries is a bit complicated. Now both the demand and long-run supply curves are downward sloping. To analyze the effects of changes in demand we have to decide which one of these two curves is steeper. The two cases are shown in Figure 10.15. In Figure 10.15(a) the supply curve is steeper than the demand curve. p^* is the equilibrium price. Suppose the equilibrium is disturbed and the price rises temporarily to p_1. At this price the quantity supplied

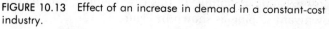

FIGURE 10.13   Effect of an increase in demand in a constant-cost industry.

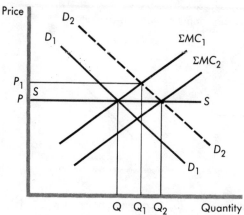

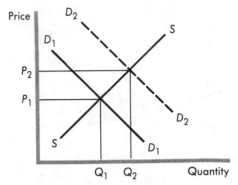

FIGURE 10.14   Effect of an increase in demand in an increasing-cost industry.

is greater than the quantity demanded, and the price has a tendency to fall. Thus, the market price will get back to the equilibrium level p^*. Similarly, with a temporary decline in price, quantity demanded is higher than quantity supplied and, hence, price will rise back to the equilibrium level. Thus, the equilibrium is said to be *stable*.

The reverse appears to be the case in case (*b*). It would appear from Figure 10.15(*b*) that with a disturbance that raises the price to p_1, we have quantity demanded greater than quantity supplied and, hence, price has a tendency to rise further and, thus, deviate more and more from the equilibrium level p^*. This is indeed not so. Note that even when the long-run industry supply curve is downward sloping, at each point on this curve the short-run supply curve will be upward sloping. This is shown in Figure 10.16. The short-run supply curves are shown as broken lines. They are denoted by S_1, S_2, and so on.

Now with a disturbance that results in a rise in price from the equilibrium level p^* to p_1, each firm will try to increase its output and, thus, there is an increase in the quantity supplied and a consequent excess supply. This will push price down

FIGURE 10.15   Equilibrium in a decreasing-cost industry.

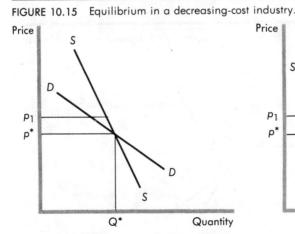

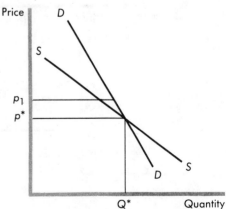

(a) Supply curve steeper than demand curve.   (b) Demand curve steeper than supply curve.

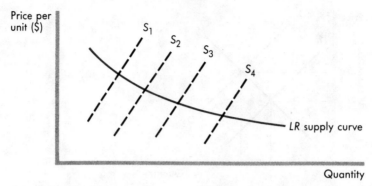

FIGURE 10.16   Short-run industry supply curves in a decreasing-cost industry.

to the equilibrium level p^*. This is shown in Figure 10.17. The initial equilibrium price is p^*, and the short-run supply curve is S_1. With the price rising to p_1 we see that there is an excess supply, and this pushes the price back to the equilibrium level p^*.

There are not many industries that one can think of which are decreasing-cost industries. One example that is often cited is the railroad industry. One can think of computers and electronics industries, but as we will discuss in the next section, it is hard to distinguish in practice between decreasing-cost industries and industries with rapid technological progress.

Even when there are decreasing costs, it will be after the industry has reached a certain scale of output so that the long-run industry supply curve will be forward bending at higher levels of output. This is shown in Figure 10.18. The industry is an increasing cost industry until the output level reaches Q_1 and a decreasing cost industry thereafter.

Since the supply curve is more likely to be only slightly forward bending for a decreasing-cost industry, we will use Figure 10.15(b) to analyze the effects of changes in demand. In this case the demand curve is steeper than the long-run

FIGURE 10.17   Effect of a rise in price in a decreasing-cost industry.

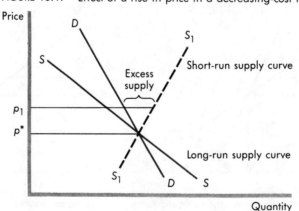

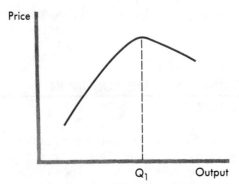

FIGURE 10.18   A forward-bending long-run industry supply curve.

supply curve, and the effect of an increase in demand is that the long-run equilibrium price declines and the equilibrium output rises. This is shown in Figure 10.19. SS is the long-run supply curve and D_1D_1 the initial demand curve. The initial equilibrium price level is p_1 and output level is Q_1. With an increase in demand the demand curve shifts to D_2D_2. In the long run, the equilibrium price level falls to p_2 and the quantity rises to Q_2.

Decreasing-cost industries and government intervention

With decreasing-cost industries, it is often argued that government should intervene to force firms to expand their output so that the benefits of external economies of scale can be realized. It is argued that each firm would have no incentive to expand its output because it would not know the benefits of the external economies of scale that would accrue to it from the expansion of the industry output. However, this argument is valid only if we assume that the entrepreneurs of the individual firms have no foresight at all. In the case of the U.S. railroad industry, economic historians have found that railroad investment (before the Civil War) was based on optimistic expectations about the benefits that came from an expansion of the

FIGURE 10.19   Effect of an increase in demand in a decreasing-cost industry.

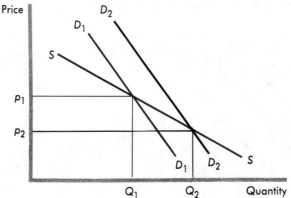

industry output. Thus, there was no deficiency of private investment and no need for government coercion.[6]

10.8   TECHNOLOGICAL CHANGE AND THE LONG-RUN INDUSTRY SUPPLY CURVE

Suppose that over time we observe an industry where price per unit of output has declined while quantity produced has risen. This has been the case with computers, electronic games, pocket calculators, and so on. Then can we say, using the conclusions in Figure 10.19, that the industry is a decreasing-cost industry? Not necessarily. To see this we have to consider the effects of technological change on the industry supply curves.

The term *technological change* refers to all those commercially applicable scientific discoveries that enable us to produce more of a particular output from the same given sets of inputs. For example, more potent fertilizer will enable us to produce more wheat on the same land with the same amount of labor as before. Some hybrid seeds have been found to increase output several times. Advances in computer technology have enabled us to perform calculations much faster than in earlier years. The effect of technological change is to shift the long-run average cost curves of firms lower and, hence, to shift the long-run supply curves to the right. Thus, even with an unchanging demand and an increasing-cost industry (so that the supply curve is positively sloped), we can have declining prices and increasing output, as the supply curve shifts to the right due to technological change. This is shown in Figure 10.20. As the supply curve shifts to the right we note that the equilibrium price falls but the equilibrium quantity rises. Thus, the long-run behavior of price and quantity is the same in the cases of both Figures 10.19 and 10.20. But the interpretation of the results is different: (1) Figure 10.19 refers to an industry with a downward-sloping supply curve and a shifting demand curve.

[6]See Albert Fishlow, *American Railroads and the Transformation of the Ante-bellum Economy*, Harvard University Press, Cambridge, Mass., 1965.

FIGURE 10.20   Shifts in supply curves produced by technological change.

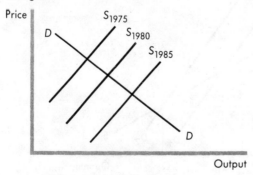

(2) Figure 10.20 refers to a stable demand but an upward-sloping supply curve that is shifting over time.

Earlier we said that in decreasing-cost industries there are external economies of scale. And these economies can be technological as well. In this case what we have in Figure 10.19 are external technological economies of scale, and what we have in Figure 10.20 is technological change. We have to distinguish between these two terms. For example, availability of better computers, availability of better production equipment, and so on constitute technological change. These result in shifts of the supply curve as shown in Figure 10.20. However, availability of computer services at a cheaper rate when the industry output expands comes under technological economies of scale. This would cause the long-run industry supply curve to slope downward.

10.9 SOME APPLICATIONS OF THE COMPETITIVE MODEL

In the previous sections we discussed the short-run and long-run supply curves of the competitive industry. In the policy questions we analyze using the competitive model, we should note that it is the long-run supply curve that is often considered. Thus, the conclusions we draw refer to the long-run equilibrium values after all the adjustments have taken place. To derive these long-run conclusions all we need is the demand and supply analysis that we discussed in Chapter 2. However, what is interesting is the process by which the new long-run equilibrium is established and what happens in between. We will illustrate this process with some examples. How long this adjustment process takes depends on the particular problem under consideration. The process depends on how many months or years it takes for firms to enter into or exit from the industry under consideration and how fast existing firms can expand or reduce their plant size.

10.9.1 Taxes and subsidies

We discussed the effect of a per-unit tax earlier in Chapter 2. In Figure 2.10 we showed it as a shift in the supply curve. What we have there is the long-run supply curve of the competitive industry. The final effect of the per-unit tax is to increase the price and reduce the quantity consumed. The effect of a per-unit subsidy can be analyzed similarly. The effect would be a decline in price and an increase in the quantity consumed.

The mechanism by which these shifts in the supply curves take place is the one we discussed in earlier sections of this chapter: (1) expansion (in the case of subsidies) and contraction (in the case of taxes) of the output by the individual firms and (2) entry (in the case of subsidies) and exit (in the case of taxes) of some of the existing firms.

In the case of subsidies, there will be short-run profits made by firms which will disappear as the industry output expands. The reverse is the case with taxes.

We will not analyze this problem in great detail, since it is quite straightforward. We will discuss the effects of rent controls in greater detail because the process by which the new long-run equilibrium is established is quite interesting.

10.9.2 Effects of price control: Rent control

In many countries during and after World War II, price controls were imposed on rental dwelling units with the purpose of protecting renters from avaricious landlords. These price controls, known as rent controls, were abolished later, although they still continue in New York City. During the 1970s, however, some localities in Los Angeles, Washington, D.C., and Boston instituted some new form of rent controls.[7] In many countries rent controls initiated during World War II persisted for many years after the war.[8] In Sweden, for instance, rent controls which were introduced in 1942 survived until 1975. But again, a new rent regulation system was introduced in 1978. In the United Kingdom rent control was first introduced as an emergency measure during World War I but then continued on until 1957, when an element of decontrol was permitted. But in 1965 rent controls were imposed again. All these examples show how rent controls are difficult to abolish. In fact, some of the rent controls in Europe can apparently be traced to the time of the Napoleonic wars.

The consequences of rent controls can be easily demonstrated with a simple demand and supply analysis like we did in Chapter 2. But as we will presently see, this analysis conceals a lot of complications and detail. This simple analysis is shown in Figure 10.21.

DD is the demand curve and SS the long-run supply curve (the industry supplying rental housing is assumed to be an increasing cost industry and, hence, we have drawn the supply curve to be positively sloping); p_0 is the initial equilibrium price, and Q_0 is the equilibrium quantity. If price is controlled at the level p_c, the quantity supplied falls to Q_1 and the quantity demanded rises to Q_2 and a "shortage" develops.

This simple analysis, however, leaves a number of questions unanswered:

1. How does the quantity of rental housing services decline from Q_0 to Q_1?

[7]See Monica Lett, *Rent Control: Concepts, Realities and Mechanisms*, Center for Urban Policy Research, Rutgers University, New Brunswick, 1976.

[8]The experience of many foreign countries is analyzed by several authors in M. Walker, ed., *Rent Control: A Popular Paradox*, The Fraser Institute, Vancouver, 1975, and Robert Albon, ed., *Rent Control: Costs and Consequences*, The Centre for Independent Studies, St. Leonards, Australia, 1980.

FIGURE 10.21   Consequences of rent control.

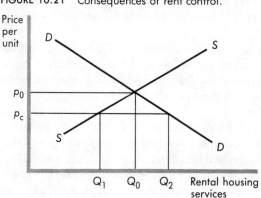

2. What happens to the excess demand $Q_2 - Q_1$?

3. Who benefits and who loses from the rent controls?

4. Why do rent controls persist if they are harmful?

We will answer these questions in turn, but before we proceed, we have to realize that the simple demand and supply analysis shown in Figure 10.21 also conceals several institutional arrangements involved in rent control legislation. We cannot go through all these in detail here, but for the sake of illustration we will point out a few of the issues.

Does the landlord have a right to evict the tenant? Suppose he does but can rent the housing unit only at the controlled price. Then the landlord can evict the existing tenant and do one of two things. He can either convert the rental unit into a condominium or rent it again but make the tenant buy some furniture at an exorbitant price. This has been the experience in the case of many rental arrangements in New York City.

Does the rent control apply only to the existing units or to the newly constructed units as well? If rent control applies only to the existing units, it should not affect the construction of new rental housing. If there is an expectation that rent control will be imposed on the newly constructed units as well, at a future date, then the suppliers of new rental units will take this into account in their investment decisions and in setting the current rental rates on the new units. In fact, in 1969 a mild form of rent control was extended to more than half of the uncontrolled rental units in New York City. Thus, even if there is no rent control on newly constructed units, the expectation of rent control being imposed at a later date would reduce the supply of new rental units below what it would be in the absence of rent control.

If rent control does not apply to newly constructed units, and if landlords can evict tenants for the purpose of reconstruction, then they might find it profitable to demolish buildings that are still in good shape and reconstruct the rental units to rent them at a higher rate. This seems to have happened in Hong Kong following rent control legislation in 1921. During the next 5 years there was a "reconstruction craze."[9]

These complications suggest that the quantity of rental housing supplied under rent control could be greater than the amount Q_1 shown in Figure 10.21, but to analyze the exact nature of the supply of rental housing under rent-control legislation we have to make a detailed analysis of the institutional arrangements that are permitted. Since this is quite beyond our scope, we will confine our analysis to that given in the simplified diagram in Figure 10.21 and answer the four questions we raised earlier.[10]

[9]This is described in an analysis of the effects of rent control in Hong Kong by Steve N. S. Cheung. See his paper: "Rush or Delay? The Effects of Rent Control on Urban Renewal in Hong Kong" in Albon, *Rent Control.*

[10]Some advanced students might find it interesting to study this problem in detail with special reference to a particular country or locale. One example is that of the Los Angeles housing market. References on this can be found in the paper: George Fallis and Lawrence B. Smith, "Uncontrolled Prices in a Controlled Market: The Case of Rent Controls," *American Economic Review*, March 1984, pp. 193–200. Fallis and Smith analyze the problem that in many instances of rent control, newly constructed units, vacated units, and high priced units are exempt from rent controls. They show that the rents on the uncontrolled market are likely to be higher (if there are rent controls on some units) than if there were no rent controls at all. The paper also discusses some earlier papers on the effects of price control on a related market.

Decline in the quantity of rental housing services

If landlords are prevented from raising the rents and they cannot evict the existing tenants, they will simply let the rental units deteriorate in quality over time. They will not undertake any maintenance expenditures, and rent-control breeds slums. Thus, the decline in the quantity of housing services shown as a decline from Q_0 to Q_1 in Figure 10.21 comes about through (1) a progressive decay of the quality of rental units and (2) where possible, a conversion of rental units into condominiums.

What happens to the excess demand?

Figure 10.21 shows an excess demand at the controlled price of p_c. This excess demand results in a queue for rental units at the controlled price. But people have to find a place to live even while they are in the queue. Some of the people will switch over to the owner-occupied housing market. Some others will have their demand satisfied at higher effective rents (payment of "key money," or buying up of furniture at exorbitant prices which the landlord requires to obtain the rental unit at the controlled price). The switch to owner-occupied housing implies that the demand curve shifts to the left, and the availability of some housing at the controlled price (but with the payment of key money or purchase of furniture) implies that there is a black market supply. These two factors result in a new equilibrium being established where the quantity of rental housing services supplied is greater than Q_1 (although still less than Q_0), and the equilibrium price is higher than the controlled price p_c. This is shown in Figure 10.22. $S'S'$ is the black market supply curve, and $D'D'$ is the new demand curve. The equilibrium quantity is now Q', which is greater than Q_1 although less than Q_0. The equilibrium price is p' which is higher than the controlled price p_c.

Who benefits and who loses from rent control?

In the short run, immediately after the imposition of rent control, the owners of rental units are made worse off. They find the return to their investment reduced

FIGURE 10.22   A black market in rental housing under rent controls.

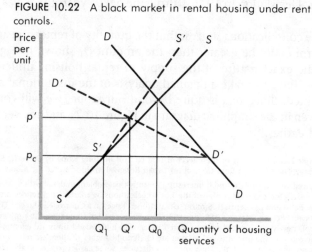

by law. Over time, however, they would be able to reduce their losses because they would not incur as many expenses for maintenance and repair.

As far as tenants are concerned, in the short run they are made better off. In fact, the purpose of rent control is precisely to benefit tenants. However, in the long run tenants as a group are made worse off because of the adverse effects rent control has on the long-run quantity supplied. Those tenants who cannot get rental units have to go to the owner-occupied housing market or pay much higher effective rent in the black market (through the purchase of useless furniture or payment of key money).[11] Even those who are fortunate enough to obtain rental housing at the controlled price will find the quality of their rental unit deteriorate over time and their neighborhood turn into a slum area.

One of the primary arguments used on behalf of rent control is that landlords are richer than tenants and, hence, rent control has a desirable redistributive effect. There is, however, no empirical evidence supporting this claim. Many of the owners of rental housing have lower incomes than the tenants, and it is not necessarily true that it is the low-income tenants who benefit by rent control. Many of the families living in housing with controlled rents have been found to have higher incomes than families that are not able to find any rental housing. Rent control can produce a highly random redistribution of wealth.[12]

Finally, in the case of housing, the needs of families change over time with the increase or decrease in family size. But many families cannot make the necessary changes, because the costs of moving from a unit with controlled rent are very high. Thus, older couples with all children gone would be occupying large rental units and younger couples with their family size increasing would be stuck in small rental units.

Why do rent controls persist?

If, as we have argued, rent controls are harmful to tenants, one interesting question to ask is: Why do rent controls persist? The answer is that, in the short run, rent control may be a rational choice of consumers. And, in fact, the likelihood of finding rent control in a jurisdiction increases with the size of the rental sector of the housing market.[13]

To see why consumers are likely to opt for rent control, we can use the analysis of consumers' surplus. Consider Figure 10.23. Let DD and SS be the initial demand curve and supply curve, respectively, with the equilibrium price p. Now a sudden change occurs that leads to an increase in equilibrium price. This could be a shift of the supply curve to the left or of the demand curve to the right. Examples of causes of a shift of the supply curve to the left are (1) the destruction of more than half the housing stock in San Francisco following the earthquake of 1906 and (2) the destruction of large portions of the housing stocks in several European cities

---

[11]Rent controls may be especially harmful to single mothers and members of minority groups because the excess demand creates a waiting list which allows landlords to discriminate at zero cost.

[12]See D. Gale Johnson, "Rent Control and the Distribution of Income," *American Economic Review,* May 1951, pp. 31–41.

[13]See Denton Marks, "Public Choice and Rent Control," *Atlantic Economic Journal,* September 1983, pp. 63–69. This paper is an application to rent control of a model developed in J. M. Buchanan and T. N. Tideman, "Gasoline Rationing and Market Pricing: Public Choice in Political Economy," *Atlantic Economic Journal,* November 1974.

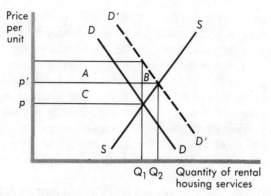

FIGURE 10.23   Consumers' preference for rent control under an exogenous increase in demand.

in World War II. Some causes of a shift of the demand curve to the right are (1) the heavy influx of immigrants into Hong Kong in the 1920s and (2) the heavy migration of population into California. Since the analysis is similar, we have shown the latter case in Figure 10.23.

In all these cases the result is a rise in the eqilibrium price. Suppose the consumers have a choice of allowing the market price to rise to the new equilibrium level or of having rent controls. What would they choose?

In Figure 10.23 $D'D'$ is the new demand curve and p' the new equilibrium price. If the price is controlled at the old price p, then consumer surplus will be the area under $D'D'$, above p and up to Q_1. If, however, price is allowed to rise to p', then consumer surplus will be the area under $D'D'$, above p' and up to Q_2. Thus, consumer surplus will be larger with the price control if the area of rectangle C is larger than the area of triangle B. Thus, in many practical cases, particularly if the supply curve is steep, consumers gain, and they have an incentive to vote for price controls. (Consumers' surplus is defined in Chapter 9).

We have discussed the problem of rent control at great length, since it has several fascinating aspects to it. We have seen that the simple analysis in Figure 10.21 is useful to merely give us a rough idea of the consequences of rent control. Unlike the case of the market for apples and oranges, the rental housing market involves different contractual arrangements between owners of the rental units and the tenants, and the consequences of rent control on the supply of and demand for rental housing depend on how rent control legislation affects these contractual arrangements. Thus, one needs a more detailed analysis than that in Figure 10.21.

10.9.3 Price control in decreasing-cost industries

In the preceding section we considered rent control, an example of price control in an industry which we said was an increasing-cost industry (we drew the long-run industry supply curve as upward sloping). We also saw the adverse effects such price control had. Price controls have even worse effects in decreasing-cost industries. In fact, as we will presently see, the output can decline to 0. The situation is shown in Figure 10.24. DD is the demand curve and SS the downward-sloping

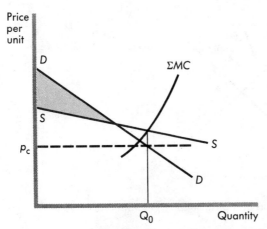

FIGURE 10.24 Effects of price control in a decreasing-cost industry.

long-run supply curve. Suppose that price controls are initiated with price at p_c, below the equilibrium price. Then, since at the old equilibrium output Q_0 price does not equal marginal cost, firms will try to curtail output and move down their marginal cost curves (shown as ΣMC curve in Figure 10.24). However, as the industry output goes down, the marginal costs of each firm rise, and then each firm tries to curtail its output further. This process goes on until the output of the industry is reduced to 0 (or if the decreasing costs start after a level of output Q_1 as in Figure 10.18, then the process continues until output contracts to Q_1).

It is also easy to see this by noting that points under the SS curve are not feasible (the suppliers suffer losses), and points above the DD curve are also not feasible (since the demand curve shows the *maximum* quantity demanded at each price). Thus, if we consider points above the supply curve and below the demand curve, the feasible region is given by the shaded portion in Figure 10.24, and the price level p_c is not in this region. However, we can easily see that a price support program (where prices are supported at a level higher than the equilibrium price) is feasible even in a declining-cost industry. Thus, whereas price controls are harmful in an increasing-cost industry, they are potentially disastrous in a decreasing-cost industry.

10.9.4 Price support programs: In agriculture

In the previous two sections we considered price controls by which we meant situations where prices had ceilings or limits above which they were prevented from rising. These price ceilings were below the market equilibrium price. There is another form of price control—price floors or price supports. In this case prices are not allowed to fall below a certain level, that is, they are "supported" at a level higher than the market equilibrating level.

There are many agricultural commodities in the United States that are guaranteed a minimum price by the government. The consequences of setting the minimum price are shown in Figure 10.25. At the supported price p_s, there is an excess supply. The question is: What happens to this excess supply? Since the

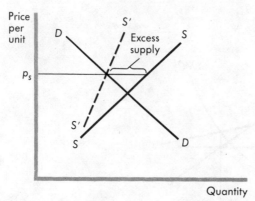

FIGURE 10.25   Effects of a price support program and acreage restriction.

government guarantees a minimum price, it is obligated to purchase whatever output is not sold in the market. If the government does not intend to buy up the excess supply, it can resort to other regulations that make the excess supply disappear. One such regulation is that of acreage control whereby farmers are paid to reduce acreage under cultivation. The effect of this would be to tilt the supply curve to $S'S'$ shown as a dotted line in Figure 10.25 so that the supported price is now a market equilibrium price.

Who benefits and who loses from these programs? Clearly the consumers lose. They have to pay the costs of implementation of the support programs and higher prices for agricultural products. The farmers are supposed to benefit because of the agricultural programs. The evidence, however, shows that it is actually the richest farmers and the biggest agribusinesses that receive the great bulk of farm subsidies.[14] Some of these subsidies have been so enormous that upper limits have been set on the amount of any one subsidy payment. However, these limits may not be of any consequence in practice because farmers can evade them by dividing the formal ownership among different individuals. The amount of the subsidy varies from year to year depending on world supply and demand. During periods of bumper crops the amounts of the subsidies run very high. In 1980 about $2.7 billion was spent for price supports. But because of bumper crops, this amount went up to $4 billion in 1981 and more than $6 billion in 1982.

The purpose of the price support program is to protect farmers from instability in income arising from widely fluctuating output and prices which depend to a large extent on changing weather conditions and pests. But the proper solution to this problem is the provision of loans and crop insurance. The government does this to some extent through the Federal Crop Insurance Corporation.

The price support program has not only served to stabilize farm prices but it has also served to subsidize farm incomes. The farm price support program is an example of an attempt to solve an income problem by manipulating the market price. The proper solution to an income problem is an income subsidy (in this case loans to farmers, crop insurance, and such), not a manipulation of the market

[14]See Charles L. Schultze, *The Distribution of Farm Subsidies: Who Gets the Benefits*, Brookings Institution, Washington, D.C., 1971.

price. Manipulation of the price introduces a divergence between *MC* and price, causing inefficiencies in the allocation of resources which would not result from a simple income subsidy program.

It is interesting to note the similarities and differences between the case of rent control we discussed earlier and the farm price support programs. There is an income distribution aspect to both the problems. The presumed aim of rent control is to "protect poor tenants from the exploitation of rich landlords." There is some question as to whether tenants are poorer or richer than landlords and what "exploitation" means, but one cannot question the fact that there are many poor tenants that do benefit from rent control. Furthermore, the income subsidy plan that one can devise for poor tenants is not very clear-cut (apart from a general negative income tax). One can think of a housing stamp program (like the food stamp program) for poor families, but the problems of such a program would be similar to those of the food stamp program.

In the case of farm programs the aim is one of protecting the incomes of poor farmers from wide fluctuations. The income distribution consequences here are more clear-cut than in the case of rent control. A major portion of the subsidies have gone to the richest farmers. The alternative solutions to price supports—loans to farmers and crop insurance—are also more easily implemented than in the rent control case.

There is one other important difference between the two cases. The sole aim of rent control is income redistribution. The purpose of the price support program is also to reduce the fluctuations in price that farmers can receive. To the extent that farmers' supply decisions are based on expected prices and the price supports reduce the uncertainty about expected prices, price supports have some beneficial effect. That there are other ways of reducing uncertainty about expected prices is another story. To analyze this aspect of uncertainty is beyond the scope of our analysis here, and so we will not go through it, but what this argument suggests is that in Figure 10.25, the existence of price supports will shift the supply curve (through the effect on supply decisions of farmers).

Thus, we see that the analysis in Figure 10.25 is a very simplified analysis of the farm price support program, although it is enough for the purpose of our discussion. In actual practice, the farm price support program is complicated by other problems—crop loans (that may not be repaid), subsidies, acreage restrictions, uncertainty, and so on.

10.9.5 Nonprice competition: The case of the airline industry

In the previous section we discussed a situation where the government supported the price at a level higher than the market equilibrating level. In this case the government had to absorb the excess supply in some form or another. Suppose the government regulates a price above the market equilibrium level and lets the firms take care of the excess supply. Then what can the firms do? Since they cannot compete with each other on price, they have to compete in other ways (by providing other accessory benefits). This will continue to the point where the excess supply disappears. This type of competition is called *nonprice competition*, and the airline industry is an example.

Before the Air Deregulation Act of 1978, the airline industry in the United States was regulated by the Civil Aeronautics Board (CAB) for over 40 years. The CAB was established in 1938 under the Civic Aeronautics Act. The 1938 Act, amended later by another act in 1958, gave the CAB absolute authority to set maximum as well as minimum rates. We cannot go through the details of all the objectives of the CAB and the means by which CAB intended to achieve them. What we will discuss is the pricing scheme adopted by the CAB.

Broadly speaking, the rates that the CAB set were such that they subsidized short-distance traffic and taxed long-distance traffic. The purpose of the rate structure was to see that air transport was provided to smaller communities that otherwise would not have the benefit of air transportation.

If price competition is allowed and there are no barriers to entry, we saw that price would be equal to marginal cost in the short run and to average total cost in the long run. Thus, if we have two destinations, say one 250 miles away and another 1,000 miles, and we equate price per mile to the average cost per mile, we have a higher price per mile for the short-distance destination than for the long-distance destination. This is because air transportation involves a large amount of fixed costs (capital equipment, salaried personnel, cost of airport terminals, and so on), and the averge variable costs (fuel costs) are fairly constant. This clearly implies that since average fixed costs decline with distance, average total costs would be declining with distance. This is shown in Figure 10.26. ATC is the declining average total cost curve; p_s is the price that would be charged for the shorter distance, and p_L is the price that would be charged for the longer distance under price competition. The CAB would require airlines to charge a uniform price shown as p_{CAB}. This would amount to a subsidy of $(p_s - p_{CAB})$ per mile for the short-haul traffic and a tax of $(p_{CAB} - p_L)$ per mile for the long haul traffic.

At the prices p_s and p_L for the short-haul and the long-haul traffic, respectively, the airline would not be making a profit. At the CAB price the airline would be losing money on the short-haul traffic but making a profit on the long-haul traffic.

FIGURE 10.26 Determination of air fares and profits under price competition and under CAB rules.

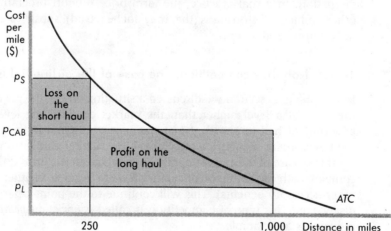

The CAB fixed the price in such a way that the profit on the long haul was considerably greater than the loss on the short-haul traffic as shown in Figure 10.26. This should have resulted in high profits for the airline industry. But this did not, however, happen, and we will explain why.

Since the CAB determined the rates, the airlines could not compete on price. They, therefore, began competing on service. This *nonprice* or *service competition* took several forms such as greater frequency of flights, attractive flight attendants, free drinks, free movies. This service competition increased the average costs for the airlines to the point where they earned just the normal profits. It is easy to see in Figure 10.26 that as the *ATC* curve shifts upward, the profit on the long haul decreases (and the loss on the short haul might also increase), and the net profit will disappear.

Thus, the effect of the price regulation by the CAB was that the airlines did not benefit and the consumers had to pay higher average fares than they would have without the regulations. They were provided some frills that many perhaps did not need or care about. The only beneficiaries were the communities that would not have had air service without the subsidy provided by the CAB rate structure.

10.10 SUMMARY AND CONCLUSIONS

With an upward-sloping *MC* curve, profit maximization occurs where $MR = MC$. With a downward-sloping *MC* curve, the output where $MR = MC$ will correspond to a profit maximum if the *MR* curve is steeper than the *MC* curve but to a profit minimum if the *MC* curve is steeper than the *MR* curve.

Perfect competition involves many relatively small firms producing a homogeneous product in an industry characterized by freedom of entry and exit. Resources must be mobile, and all participants must have perfect knowledge of present and future market conditions. There are several weaker definitions of competition.

The market price, under competition, is determined by the intersection of the industry supply curve and the market demand curve. The demand curve facing the individual firm is horizontal at the market price. Equilibrium for the competitive firm requires $MC = MR = AR = P$. MC must equal MR for profit maximization. And $MR = AR = P$ because the firm is a price taker. In the short run, the firm will continue to produce as long as price exceeds minimum *AVC*. The firm's short-run supply curve is its *MC* curve above its *AVC* curve. The industry short-run supply curve can be equal to, steeper than, or flatter than the horizontal sum of the individual firms' short-run supply curves.

In the long run, existing firms will make adjustments to their outputs and costs. If after these adjustments, a firm is still unable to cover its total costs, it will exit the industry. And if existing firms are earning a profit, new firms will enter the industry. Long-run profit maximization requires that output be expanded to the point where $P = LRMC$. The firm must also be producing that output at the lowest possible cost, which requires the firm to be operating on the *LRAC* curve. If price is less than minimum *LRAC*, then the firm will exit the industry. If price exceeds minimum *LRAC*, then profits can be made. Firms will enter the industry, shifting the short-run industry supply curve to the right and pushing price down until P = minimum $LRAC$. The opposite adjustment will occur if price is less than minimum $LRAC$.

Long-run equilibrium for a competitive industry requires that $P = LRAC = LRMC = SRAC = SRMC$. In long-run competitive equilibrium, a firm must be earning a zero economic profit. This implies that all factors of production are receiving their full opportunity cost. This does not imply that accounting profits will be 0 or that they will be equal for all firms.

In a constant-cost industry, each firm's $LRAC$ curve remains stable as firms enter or exit or as the output of the existing firms expands. The long-run supply curve for a constant-cost industry is horizontal. In an increasing-cost industry, each firm's $LRAC$ curve shifts upward as firms enter the industry. The long-run supply curve for an increasing-cost industry is positively sloped. In a decreasing-cost industry, each firm's $LRAC$ curve shifts downward as firms enter the industry. The long-run supply curve for a decreasing cost industry is negatively sloped.

Technological change shifts the firms' long-run average cost curves downward and, hence, shifts the long-run industry supply curve to the right. Taxes result in a decrease in output by existing firms and an exit of firms from the industry in the process of adjustment to a new long-run equilibrium. Subsidies have the opposite effects. Rent controls establish a price ceiling below the equilibrium price. In the long run, they result in a decrease in rental housing services and an excess demand for rental housing. It is still likely, however, that consumers would vote for rent control programs.

The imposition of price ceilings (set below the equilibrium price) in decreasing-cost industries can be to reduce industry output to 0. Support prices on agricultural commodities result in an excess supply which is sometimes eliminated through acreage reductions. Price support programs serve to stabilize and supplement the incomes of farmers, but at a high social cost. The imposition of a support price (or a price set above equilibrium) can result in nonprice competition. An example of this was the airline industry. Such nonprice competition may cause costs to increase until all economic profit is eliminated.

KEY TERMS

Accounting Profit	Free Mobility of Resources	Oligopoly
Constant-Cost Industry	Homogeneous Product	Perfect Competition
Declining Industry	Increasing-Cost Industry	Perfect Knowledge
Decreasing-Cost Industry	Industry	Price Control
Economic Profit	Long-run Equilibrium	Price Taker
External Diseconomies	Market	Pure Competition
of Scale	Market Competition	Short-run Equilibrium
External Economies of	Market Structure	Support Price
Scale	Monopoly	Technological Change
Freedom of Entry	Monopolistic Competition	Technological Economies
and Exit	Nonprice Competition	of Scale

QUESTIONS

1. Graph the total revenue curve for a competitive firm with a price of $5. Demonstrate graphically and mathematically that $MR = AR = P$.

2. Graph a total revenue curve and a short-run total cost curve for a competitive firm. Identify the point of profit maximization. Now graph the corresponding MR, MC, $SRAVC$, and $SRATC$ curves. How do the two sets of curves correspond? What does the profit curve look like?

3. Can a perfectly competitive firm ever maximize profit by operating on the downward-sloping portion of its MC curve? Why?

4. Must short-run supply curves for competitive industries satisfy the law of supply? Why?

5. In a constant-cost industry, if demand increases, must firms enter the industry to restore long-run equilibrium? Answer the same question for an increasing-cost industry.

6. Convenience stores typically charge a higher price for milk than grocery stores do. Does this mean that the retail milk market is not competitive? How do you explain this phenomenon?

7. In a constant-cost industry, the equilibrium number of firms can be determined if one knows only the position of the demand curve and the typical firm's $LRAC$ curve. Explain how. Can the number of firms be determined for an increasing-cost industry? Why?

8. Draw the firm's $LRAC$, $SRAC$, $LRMC$, and $SRMC$ curves which would correspond to the adjustment process depicted in Figure 10.14, and explain what is happening at a price of p_1 and p_2.

9. Assuming that demand is stable, will technological change affect the equilibrium number of firms in a competitive constant-cost industry? Why? Will it affect the size of the firm? Why?

10. Give an example of technological change and an example of a technological economy of scale. How does each relate to the $LRAC$ curve?

11. The farm support programs were designed in part to stabilize farm prices and in this way aid farmers. But stabilizing prices destabilizes both revenue and profit, and thus it is not clear that the farmer will benefit. Evaluate this statement.

12. In recent years, many low-income Mexicans have immigrated to small border towns in the United States. Evaluate the chances of a rent control program being approved in such a town. Remember that most of these new immigrants cannot vote.

13. In a perfectly competitive industry, under what circumstances would you expect a rise in demand for an industry's product to be met primarily by a short-run output response on the part of existing firms? By a long-run response on the part of existing firms? By entry of new firms?

14. In a perfectly competitive industry, if there are N identical firms and no "external" effects on factor prices, is the industry supply curve more or less steep than the firm supply curve? More or less elastic?

CHAPTER 11

PRICING IN PRODUCT MARKETS:
MONOPOLY

11.1 INTRODUCTION

In the previous chapter we discussed perfect competition, which is characterized by a large number of sellers each of whom is a *price taker*. The other extreme is the case of *monopoly*, which is characterized by a single seller (or group of sellers) who acts as a *price setter*. The word "monopoly" comes from the Greek words *monos polein*, which mean "alone to sell." This single seller is called a *monopolist*. The term is also sometimes used for a single group of sellers that acts as a price setter, although often a group is called a *cartel*.

Monopolists are called price setters because they select their own price and supply the entire quantity demanded. For a monopolist to have effective control over the pricing of a product, the monopolized product should have no close substitutes. Otherwise, when the monopolist raises the product's price, consumers can switch to other products. The pricing policies of a profitable monopolist may be constrained by the threat of potential competition if market entry is at all possible. Thus, in order that such a monopoly persists in an industry, there must be *barriers to entry*. As we shall see later, a monopolist need not always make a profit. All monopoly implies is that the monopolist can make the best of the demand conditions.

We should also note that monopoly does not imply that there is a single producer, because monopolists need not produce their own product. There can be many producers that supply the product to the monopolist. The essence of monopoly is that there is a single seller (or group of sellers) that sets the price. The number of producers is not relevant. As an example we can cite OPEC (Organization of Petroleum Exporting Countries) that consists of eleven major producers that collectively set the price of oil.

A monopolist setting prices may set a *single price* for all customers or may practice price discrimination, that is, set different prices for different customers. We will be discussing both these cases in Section 11.6.

The type of monopoly we have been discussing is called *pure monopoly*. Just as the concept of perfect competition is an ideal one, so is that of monopoly. Ideally, the monopolist should be able to control 100 percent of the market. In practice, that is not usually the case. Suppose a particular firm has 80 percent of the market. Is this a monopoly? To answer such questions, economists have devised measures of what is known as "monopoly power." We will be discussing these later in Chapter 12. Some economists use a weaker definition of monopoly and monopolist. If a seller (or group of sellers) can change the price of a product by changing the quantity sold, then the seller is a monopolist.[1]

In the following sections, unless stated otherwise, what we will be talking about is always pure monopoly. Furthermore, since the pricing policies of a single seller (monopolist) and a single group of sellers (cartel) are similar, when we talk of monopoly, our discussion applies to both a monopolist and a cartel.

We will also be discussing *natural monopoly*. A natural monopoly is a special type of monopoly that arises from economies of scale. Examples of this are a gas pipeline company, a telephone company, and an electric utility. In these cases, the

[1]See Richard A. Posner, *Antitrust Law: An Economic Perspective*, University of Chicago Press, Chicago, 1976.

average cost of production declines over a large range of output, and, hence, a single firm can supply the output at a lower price than two or more smaller firms. This monopoly is called "natural" because it arises naturally from the type of product being sold. Here monopoly has advantages over competition. We will discuss natural monopoly later in Sections 12.5 and 12.6 of Chapter 12.

Examples of monopolies and cartels

1. OPEC. One of the best known cartels is OPEC (Organization of Petroleum Exporting Countries). OPEC was formed in 1960 by the governments of Iran, Iraq, Kuwait, Saudi Arabia, and Venezuela. By 1980 there were eight additional members. The cartel did not really wield any power until 1973. On January 1, 1973, the price of oil was around $2 a barrel. By year's end and after the Yom Kippur War, OPEC, by restricting production, raised the price to nearly $12 a barrel. In the mid-1980s prices reached close to $40 a barrel. Since then, because of internal dissension in the cartel and decline in world demand for oil, the oil price has been falling. The price was around $27 a barrel at the beginning of 1985 with the cartel much weaker but still alive. Many famous economists (particularly Milton Friedman) predicted that the demise of the cartel would occur much earlier.

2. The American Medical Association (AMA). Although not as often mentioned as OPEC, the AMA is perhaps the strongest and the longest-lasting cartel that exists today. The AMA has been very effective in preventing individual doctors from cutting prices. With the help of state legislatures, the AMA has been able to restrict the supply of doctors, and, thus, restrict the output of medical services. Since the Flexner report of 1910, which recommended that the number of medical schools be reduced, and several other regulations giving AMA the responsibility for this restriction, the number of doctors relative to population has fallen. The demand for health care has increased because of an increase in per-capita income and the various insurance schemes (Blue Cross and Blue Shield, for example), and the incomes of doctors have grown much faster than incomes in the rest of the professions.

3. The dental cartel. State dental boards restrict movement of dentists between states by insisting that dentists practicing in some states must pass local examinations regardless of their previous experience. Thirty-five states in the United States do not honor licenses issued by other states, and usually a large percentage of out-of-state applicants are denied licenses, although most in-state applicants are granted licenses. Some states, called "reciprocity" states, honor another state's license on a reciprocal basis. Shepard did a study of the prices charged by dental practitioners and found that prices are in general higher in "nonreciprocity" states than in "reciprocity" states.[2] This is another case of increasing prices and incomes by the creation of entry barriers.

4. Taxis in New York City. This is an example of a monopoly (not a pure monopoly) created by licensing. In New York City (and many other cities) one cannot drive a cab without a license. In New York City this license is called a "medallion." Until 1937, any qualified taxi driver could get a medallion by paying a nominal licensing fee. Since then, the city has put a limit on the number of

---

[2]Lawrence Shepard, "Licensing Restrictions and Cost of Dental Care," *The Journal of Law and Economics*, April 1978, pp. 187–201.

medallions issued, thus effectively fixing the total supply of medallions. Current owners of medallions can sell them to others wanting to operate a taxicab. Because of the limited supply and a growing demand over time, the price of medallions has increased substantially over the years. Some have sold for over $50,000—a 10,000-fold increase over the initial licensing fee of $5.

5. *Input monopolies.* These are monopolies that come into existence through ownership of a key resource. The Aluminum Company of America (ALCOA) once controlled most domestic bauxite deposits from which aluminum is made. The International Nickel Company once owned about 90 percent of the world's nickel. American Metal Climax company similarly owned almost all the world's molybdenum. These monopolies usually break up when new sources of the supply are found. Another company that has a virtual monopoly through its control of natural resources is the DeBeers Consolidated Mines, Ltd. of South Africa, which handles about 80 percent of the world's uncut diamonds. This company has run a worldwide cartel for more than a century.

Questions to be discussed.

In this chapter we will be discussing product pricing under monopoly. In the next chapter we will discuss the regulation of monopoly.

There are many questions we need to ask regarding pricing under monopoly. These are:

1. How does the monopolist determine the output to be produced and the price to be charged (Section 11.2)?

2. How do the output and price under monopoly compare with those under perfect competition (Section 11.3)?

3. What is markup pricing (Section 11.4)?

4. How do monopolists prevent others from entering the market (Section 11.5)?

5. Do monopolists charge different prices to different customers and, if so, how do the monopolists determine these prices (Sections 11.6 and 11.7)?

6. What is the welfare cost of monopoly (Section 11.8)?

7. What are multiplant and bilateral monopolies (Sections 11.9 and 11.10)?

After answering these basic questions, we will consider an application of the theory.

11.2 A MONOPOLIST SETTING A SINGLE MARKET PRICE

The demand curve facing the monopolist is the market demand curve which is downward sloping. In Section 3.7 we examined the relationship between total revenue *TR*, average revenue *AR*, and marginal revenue *MR* for a downward-sloping demand curve. The average revenue curve coincides with the demand curve. Because the demand curve slopes downward, the *MR* curve must also slope downward. (Each unit of output adds less to revenue than the unit before it.) And because the monopolist charges a single price on all the units sold, *MR* is less than price. (In order to sell one more unit of output, the monopolist must reduce price on all previous units.)

As the monopolist expands output, TR (which equals price $\times$ quantity), can increase or decrease. This depends on whether marginal revenue is positive or negative, which in turn depends on whether demand is elastic or inelastic.

We have three possible cases:

1. If $\eta > 1$, the percentage increase in quantity demanded is greater than the percentage decrease in price. Hence, revenues go up as output is increased and $MR > 0$ (η is the absolute value of the elasticity of demand).

2. If $\eta = 1$, the percentage increase in quantity demanded is equal to the percentage decrease in price. Hence, revenues are constant and $MR = 0$.

3. If $\eta < 1$, the percentage increase in quantity demanded is less than the percentage decrease in price. Hence, revenues decline as output is increased, and $MR < 0$.

The TR curve for the monopolist is shown in Figure 11.1. The demand and MR curves are illustrated in Figure 11.2. The monopolist would never expand into the inelastic region of the demand curve: If he did, the TR would fall. At the same time, the increased output would cause total cost to rise. With revenues falling and costs rising, clearly profit would decline. We can, thus, conclude that the monopolist will always operate in the elastic region of the demand curve. This region is the thick line in Figure 11.2.

Figure 11.2 also points out a key difference between monopoly and perfect competition. The competitive firm faces a perfectly elastic demand curve so that $MR = P$ and both are viewed as constant. This is not the case for a monopolist. Because the monopolist faces the downward-sloping market demand curve, the MR curve will slope downward and MR will be less than price.

Earlier in Section 10.2 in Chapter 10, we said that profit maximization requires setting output where $MR = MC$. Thus, the monopolist selects the output at the point where $MR = MC$. He then charges the highest price that he can get for this output, according to the demand curve. Note that this does not imply that the monopolist can earn a profit. This depends on the cost structure of the firm.

The monopolist's profit-maximization point is illustrated in Figure 11.3. $SRMC$

FIGURE 11.1 Total revenue curve for a monopolist.

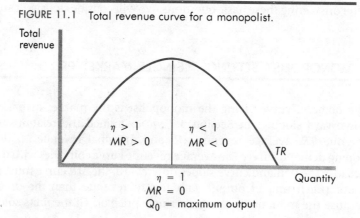

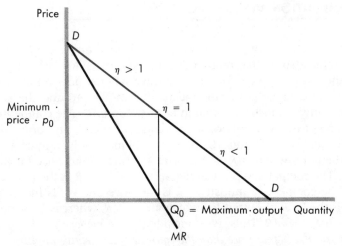

FIGURE 11.2   Range of monopoly output and price.

is the short-run marginal cost curve, and *SRAC* is the short-run average total cost curve. This monopolist equates *MR* to *MC* and produces ouput Q_m. He charges a per unit price of P_m. However, since *AR* (or price) is less than the average cost of this output, the monopolist suffers short-run losses. Like the competitive firm, the monopolist will continue to operate in the short run as long as variable costs are covered.

Whether the monopolist stays in business in the long run will depend on the long-run average cost curve. A monopolist will exit in the long run unless all costs can be covered. Long-run equilibrium for the monopolist requires that $LRMC = SRMC = MR$ so that profit is maximized, and $P \geq LRAC$ so that full opportunity cost is covered.

FIGURE 11.3   A monopolist suffering losses in the short run.

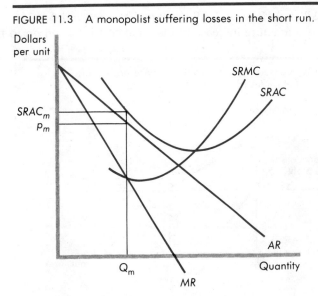

11.3   COMPETITION VERSUS MONOPOLY

Before we can compare the output and price under competition and monopoly, we must assume that market demand and costs do not change with the structure of the industry. Also, for simplicity, we will consider a long-run equilibrium in a constant average cost. This means that $MC = AC$ and the supply curve for the competitive industry is equal to both MC and AC. The competitive industry output will be at the level where supply equals demand, and price, or average revenue, will equal both MC and AC. In the case of monopoly, output will be expanded only to the point where $MR = MC$. And MR is less than price for the monopolist.

The comparison is illustrated in Figure 11.4. P_c is the price and Q_c is the output for the competitive industry. P_m is the price and Q_m is the output for monopoly. Q_m is the level of output for which $MC = MR$, whereas Q_c is the level of output for which $MC = AR$. Thus, we conclude that: *A monopoly will produce a smaller output and sell at a higher price than the equivalent competitive industry.*

The monopolist's per unit costs are P_c but the price he charges is P_m. The difference $P_m - P_c$ is called the monopolist's *markup*. The shaded area in Figure 11.4 gives the monopolist's profit.

There is another important difference between competition and monopoly that is often not noticed. Suppose there are some events that increase the monopolist's marginal costs. In the case of the steel industry, it might be an increase in energy costs (due to an oil embargo). In this case the popular conception of a monopolist as an "exploiter" might suggest that the monopolist would pass on all the increase in costs to the customers whereas this would not happen in a competitive industry. In fact, quite the opposite is the case. To see this note that the equilibrium condition under competition is

$$P = MC$$

Hence, $\Delta P = \Delta MC$ where ΔP is change in price and ΔMC is change in marginal cost. Thus, the entire increase in marginal cost is passed on to the consumer.

FIGURE 11.4   Comparison of output and price under perfect competition and under monopoly.

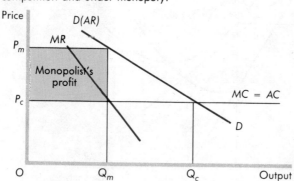

Under monopoly, the equilibrium condition is

$$MR = MC$$

Thus, $\Delta MR = \Delta MC$, or change in marginal revenue equals change in marginal cost. But we know that

$$MR = \text{price} \left(1 - \frac{1}{\eta} \right)$$

where η is the elasticity of demand. As MR goes up, we move up the demand curve. With a linear curve as in Figure 11.2, as we move up the demand curve, the elasticity η increases. Thus, the factor $(1 - 1/\eta)$ increases. Hence, the increase in price is *less than* the increase in marginal cost. Thus, the monopolist would not be able to pass on all of the increased costs to the consumers.

We can easily show this in a diagram, but it will be left as an exercise at this stage. We will see later, in Section 12.3, how we can use taxes to regulate the monopolist's profits. A lump-sum tax would change the monopolist's average cost without affecting marginal cost. A per-unit tax, however, would increase the monopolist's marginal cost, which is what we have been discussing here.

Is there a supply curve for the monopolist? In the case of the competitive firm, we discussed its supply curve. It gives us the quantities of output that the firm is willing and able to provide at various prices. There is no comparable curve for the monopolist. The concept of supply is meaningless because the monopolist is a price setter rather than a price taker. The monopolist determines a single price and quantity based on the entire demand curve and the cost structure.

11.4 MARKUP PRICING

Several studies on pricing in noncompetitive markets have suggested that the manager of a firm typically arrives at a price by adding a *markup* over costs. The markups differ from industry to industry, from firm to firm, and from product to product. Further, the markup can be calculated as a difference between price and average cost or as a percentage increase of price over average cost.

For a monopolist we saw that (see Section 11.3) the profit-maximizing price is given by

$$\text{Price} = MC \cdot \frac{\eta}{\eta - 1}$$

where η is the elasticity of demand. This is the optimum markup formula for a monopolist; $\eta/(\eta - 1)$ is called the markup factor. For a price elasticity of 1.5, price is three times the marginal cost. For a price elasticity of 11, price is 10 percent above marginal cost.

But markup pricing has been observed in other markets as well where the markup is based on average cost. In their 1939 article, Hall and Hitch report results from a survey they conducted.[3] They questioned 38 firms to discover what methods of price setting were actually applied and what motivated them to adjust prices. Their results reveal practices which appear to be at variance with widely accepted theories. Businesses typically set prices by calculating average costs of production and adding a markup for profit. Further, they do not habitually vary the markup with variations in demand. These findings were confirmed in other studies such as the one by Andrews[4] in the United Kingdom and another by Kaplan, Dirlam, and Lanzillotti in the United States.[5]

Theory suggests that price should be set by equating marginal revenue to marginal cost. The markup pricing adjustments conflict with this theory. Machlup suggests that the markup pricing adjustment can be interpreted as a rule of thumb by which profits might be maximized by trial and error.[6] Another explanation for the markup pricing method is the one by Okun, who argues that the markets for most industrial products require that firms cultivate relations with their customers to encourage repeat sales.[7] Prices convey only limited information about the products. Okun calls these "customer markets." In these markets prices are largely determined by costs. The needs of producers to promote goodwill makes them forgo any short-run advantage in raising prices when demand strengthens. Thus, customers are offered a stable price and prices are raised only when costs increase. These ideas of Okun are explored further by Carlton who analyzes a large amount of evidence on price rigidity in markets and concludes that price alone may not be clearing markets but that price, in conjunction with other mechanisms, such as seller's knowledge of buyers' needs, is performing that function.[8]

Markup pricing implies that firms do not behave as if they were maximizing short-run profits, although they may have this objective among others over a long horizon. The large amount of empirical evidence on markup pricing demonstrates that current microeconomic theory needs to be expanded to explain this behavior. We discuss the issue of price rigidity again in Section 13.9 after discussing oligopoly.

11.5   BARRIERS TO ENTRY AND LONG-RUN MONOPOLY

Earlier we saw that the condition $MR = MC$ does not necessarily imply that the monopolist enjoys a profit. But if the monopolist is making a profit, this profit provides an incentive for new firms to enter the industry. If entry occurs, the equilibrium position will change, and since there are more firms than one, there

[3]R. E. Hall and C. Hitch, "Price Theory and Business Behavior," *Oxford Economic Papers*, May 1939, pp. 12–45.

[4]P. W. S. Andrews, *Manufacturing Business*, Macmillan, London, 1949.

[5]A. Kaplan, J. Dirlam, and R. F. Lanzillotti, *Pricing in Big Business*, Brookings, Washington, D.C., 1958.

[6]F. Machlup, "Marginal Analysis and Empirical Research," *American Economic Review*, September 1946, pp. 519–554.

[7]A. Okun, *Prices and Quantities*, Brookings, Washington, D.C., 1981.

[8]Dennis W. Carlton, "The Theory and Facts of How Markets Clear," in R. Schmalensee and R. Willig, eds., *Handbook of Industrial Organization*, North Holland Publishing, Amsterdam, 1987.

will no longer be a monopoly. Thus, for a profitable monopoly to survive, we need *barriers to entry*.[9] Sometimes the barriers or impediments to entry are created at the time the monopoly is established. For example, the firm may be given the sole franchise or charter by law. In other cases the barriers are created by the monopolist through threats and coercion. If a monopolist has a cost advantage over its rivals then it can do *preemptive price cutting* to deter rivals from entering the market.

Whether a monopoly is sustainable or not (in the long run) depends on how the monopoly came about. The following are some factors that give rise to monopolies:

1. *Control over raw materials needed for the production of the good.* For instance, the Aluminum Company of America (ALCOA) once controlled most domestic bauxite deposits from which aluminum is made. American Metal Climax once controlled 90 percent of the world's molybdenum. DeBeers Company of South Africa owns most of the diamond mines there and controls the prices of diamonds by restricting production.

2. *Patents over new inventions.* Patents are exclusive rights to the production of an innovative product. Patents are granted because they encourage inventions. Without patents many firms (and individuals) would not have much incentive to invest money and resources in research. However, if an important discovery is made, the owner of the patent has a monopoly over that product. Over time, other firms will develop close substitutes and break this monopoly power or the patent will expire. For example, Xerox Corporation, by virtue of its patent on xerography had almost a monopoly over the copying industry. But as time went on, many firms (domestic and foreign) produced close substitutes.

3. *Cost of establishing an efficient plant, especially in relation to the market.* This is the case of natural monopoly we talked about earlier. Examples of this are electric and gas utilities, telephone companies, and so on. It does not make sense to have two electric, gas, or telephone companies in the same area. This problem is discussed later in Section 12.5 of Chapter 12.

4. *Market franchises.* The government gives exclusive rights to a firm to sell a certain good or service in a certain area. Usually, this is done with taxi companies, garbage collection, television cable companies, and so on. These franchises create monopoly profits for the holders of the franchises.

Monopolists can create barriers to entry by preemptive price cutting if they have a cost advantage over their rivals. This is shown in Figure 11.5. The average cost curve of the monopolist is denoted by AC_m, and the average cost curve of the rival is denoted by AC_r. To show that the monopolist has a cost advantage we have drawn the AC_r curve above the AC_m curve.

In the absence of any potential rival, the monopolist would produce output Q_m and charge the price p_m. However, when a rival with average costs given by AC_r threatens to enter, the monopolist lowers the price to p^* and produces the

---

[9]We are talking loosely of barriers to entry as impediments to entry. For the exact definition of this term as given by Joe Bain, George Stigler, and James Ferguson and a criticism of these definitions, see Harold Demsetz, "Barriers to Entry," *The American Economic Review*, March 1982, pp. 47–57.

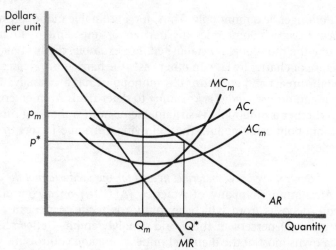

FIGURE 11.5   Preemptive price cutting by a monopolist to restrict entry by a rival.

output Q^*. At the price p^* the rival cannot cover average cost and, hence, does not enter. This price cutting by the monopolist is called preemptive price cutting. As a consequence the output expands from Q_m to Q^*.

11.6   THE PRICE-DISCRIMINATING MONOPOLIST

We have, until now, discussed the case of a monopolist setting a single price. We shall now discuss the case of a monopolist charging different prices to different customers or a price discriminating monopolist. Price discrimination is said to exist if a producer is selling the same good at different prices for reasons not associated with differences in cost.

For instance, if a producer has a manufacturing plant in Chicago and she sells the commodity at $5 per unit in Chicago and $6 per unit in Miami, but it costs $1 per-unit transportation costs from Chicago to Miami, then the different prices charged are due to transportation costs, and we cannot call this discrimination. However, if the producer sells the product for $4 in Miami, then this is called price discrimination. Note that a customer cannot buy the product in Miami and profitably resell it in Chicago.

Price discrimination can occur between markets and between individuals in the same market. *Perfect price discrimination* involves charging a different price (the maximum possible price) for each unit of output. This type of discrimination is difficult to achieve. But there are many cases of price discrimination in practice which are much simpler. Theaters charge lower prices for students, children, and senior citizens. This is price discrimination. The costs to the theater owner are the same whether the seat is filled by a student, a child, or a nonstudent adult.

Why would a monopolist price-discriminate? Clearly, the incentive is to increase profit. But not all monopolists can profitably price-discriminate. We will examine several conditions which must be met before the monopolist can successfully discriminate. One condition is the ability to prevent resale of the product. Otherwise, low-price buyers will re-sell to high-price buyers, and the monopolist will be unable to sell at the higher price. In the case of theater tickets, one can check that the person buying the ticket with a student identification card is the person that enters the theater. When electric companies charge lower rates to industrial users than to households, it is not possible for the industrial users to resell electricity to households. The main items that are not readily resalable are personal services (medical care, admission to educational institutions, theaters) and utilities involving expensive connections (gas, water, electric, telephone). But ordinary capital goods can also be made nonresalable. For instance, for a long time Xerox corporation did not sell its machines. It leased them.

11.7 DEGREES OF PRICE DISCRIMINATION

In his book, *The Economics of Welfare* (1920), the British economist A. C. Pigou presents what is perhaps still the most penetrating analysis of price discrimination. He identifies three degrees of discriminating power leading to three types of price discrimination.

First-degree price discrimination or perfect price discrimination is said to occur when the seller charges a different price for each unit of output. This involves charging different prices to different consumers as well as charging different prices for different units sold to the same consumer. The maximum price that someone is willing to pay for a unit of output is called the *reservation price*. The perfectly discriminating monopolist charges the reservation price for each unit of output. Thus, the *MR* curve for the monopolist becomes the demand curve. In this case, the equilibrium level of output, which is given by the intersection of the demand curve and the *MC* curve, is the same as the output under perfect competition. This is shown in Figure 11.6. The monopolist's output is *OC* and revenues are given by the area *OABC*, since the monopolist charges a different price (the maximum pos-

FIGURE 11.6   First-degree discrimination.

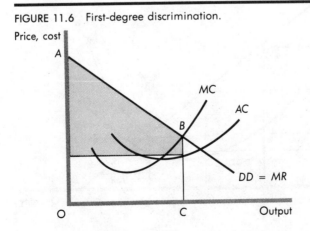

sible price) for each unit. Subtracting from this the costs (which are OC multiplied by the average cost), we get the monopolist's profit which is the shaded area in Figure 11.6.

Perfect discrimination is rather difficult to implement in practice. It can be used only for services for which no resale is possible and even then a negotiation with each customer can be costly.

Second-degree price discrimination occurs when the monopolist is able to charge several different prices for different ranges or groups of output. For example, in Figure 11.7, the first Q_1 units of output are each sold at a price of P_1. Units between Q_1 and Q_2 are each sold at a price of P_2, and so on. Each additional unit sold from 1 through Q_1 adds P_1 to revenues. Similarly, each additional unit sold between Q_1 and Q_2 adds P_2 to revenues. Thus, the MR curve is the step function shown by the thick line in Figure 11.7. The output produced, Q_3, is given by the intersection of the MC and MR curves. Reading off the average cost for that output and multiplying by Q_3, we get the total costs. Since the revenues are given by the total area under the MR curve up to output Q_3, the profits of the monopolist are given by the shaded area in Figure 11.7.

There are many examples of second-degree price discrimination. In the pricing of electricity, natural gas, or telephone calls, something called a *declining block price* is used. For instance, the first 200 kwh of electricity or 1,000 ft³ of natural gas or 3 minutes of a long distance call might cost a certain amount, but for subsequent units the price is lower. Magazine subscriptions also frequently cost a certain amount for a one-year subscription but a lower average for a two-year subscription and a still lower average for a three-year subscription.

Third-degree price discrimination occurs when the monopolist partitions market demand into two or more groups of customers and then charges different prices to the different groups (the price is uniform for members within a group). What the monopolist is trying to exploit is the different price elasticities of demand for

FIGURE 11.7   Second-degree price discrimination.

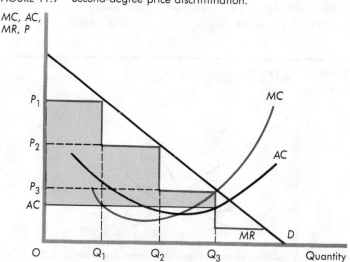

the different groups. Third-degree discrimination is profitable only if the customer groups that can be separated have different elasticities of demand.

Consider the monopolist with two separable customer groups. For each group he can compute total revenue and marginal revenue based on the group's demand curve. Let MR_1 be marginal revenue for the first group and MR_2 be marginal revenue for the second group. The monopolist will allocate his output to the two markets so that

$$MR_1 = MR_2$$

and he will choose his total output so that

$$MR_1 = MR_2 = MC$$

These conditions are intuitively plausible. MR_1 must equal MR_2 because otherwise the monopolist can improve his profit by shifting the output between the two groups. If $MR_1 > MR_2$, then revenues and profit will increase as the monopolist shifts a unit of output from group 2 to group 1. If $MR_2 > MR_1$, then the monopolist can increase profit by shifting output from group 1 to group 2. It is also clear that the common MR must equal MC. If $MR > MC$, then we saw in Chapter 10 that the firm will have an incentive to expand output, and if $MR < MC$, the firm will improve profit by reducing output.

We are now ready to compare the prices that will be set for the two customer groups. We know that $MR = P(1 - 1/\eta)$, and, since $MR_1 = MR_2$, we get

$$P_1 \left(1 - \frac{1}{\eta_1} \right) = P_2 \left(1 - \frac{1}{\eta_2} \right)$$

where P_1 and P_2 are the prices for group 1 and group 2, respectively, and η_1 and η_2 are demand elasticities for the two groups. If $\eta_1 < \eta_2$, then $1/\eta_1 > 1/\eta_2$ and $(1 - 1/\eta_1) < (1 - 1/\eta_2)$. Hence, P_1 must exceed P_2. So we see that *a discriminating monopolist will charge a higher price to the group with the less elastic demand*. Finally, if $\eta_1 = \eta_2$, the profit-maximizing price will be the same for the two groups, and thus there should be no price discrimination, since it is not profitable.

The separation of markets can take place on the basis of age and income as in the case of theater tickets (lower prices for children, students, and senior citizens) or sex (lower prices for ladies on "ladies day"). Very often the partitioning of markets is done on the basis of geographic location (domestic and foreign markets). Sometimes products are sold at a higher price domestically than abroad. Many international corporations are accused of such *dumping* tactics. They are said to "dump" their products in foreign markets (supposedly below cost). Of course, the firm would not be selling below cost but could charge a lower price abroad than domestically if the elasticity of demand is higher abroad than domestically. Examples of this are Kodak selling its film at a higher price in the United States than in some foreign countries, or Sony selling its televisions for a lower price in the United States than in Japan.

How desirable is price discrimination (of the third degree) from a social point of view? There are many who argue that price discrimination results in a more efficient allocation of resources. The general argument in several papers published in the 1950s and 1960s was that the objection to monopoly is not that some people make too much money, it is that monopoly leads to a misallocation of society's resources through a restriction of output. Price discrimination very often results in more output and, thus, should lead to increased welfare. This argument was challenged by Yamey, who showed with a special example that a profitable increase in output associated with price discrimination *need not* increase economic welfare but *can* reduce it.[10] An increase in output is a necessary condition but not a sufficient condition. Schmalensee[11] and Varian[12] also show that a necessary condition for price discrimination to lead to an increase in welfare is that there be an increase in output delivered. In all these discussions, social welfare is measured by the sum of consumers' and producers' surpluses.

11.8   WELFARE COSTS OF MONOPOLY

We know that monopoly restricts output and charges a price higher than what would prevail under perfect competition. This restriction of output results in a loss of consumers' and producers' surplus. By examining these losses, we can determine the net welfare cost to society from the monopoly.

Consider Figure 11.8. *DD* is the demand curve, *SS* is the monopolist's *MC* curve, and the competitive short-run supply curve. *MR* is the monopolist's *MR* curve. The competitive price is *OB*, and the quantity supplied and consumed is *OA*. The monopoly price is *OE*, and the monopolist's output is *OF*.

[10]B. S. Yamey, "Monopolistic Price Discrimination and Economic Welfare," *Journal of Law and Economics,* October 1974, pp. 377–380. Yamey's paper contains references to several papers that argue in favor of price discrimination.

[11]R. Schmalensee, "Output and Welfare Implications of Monopolistic Third-Degree Price Discrimination," *American Economic Review,* March 1981, pp. 870–875.

[12]H. Varian, "Price Discrimination and Social Welfare," *American Economic Review,* September 1985, pp. 870–875.

FIGURE 11.8   Welfare loss due to monopoly.

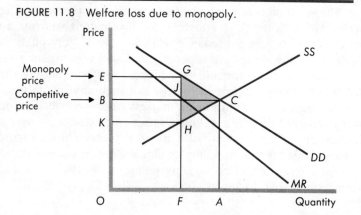

As we reduce output and increase price in going from perfect competition to monopoly, the loss in consumer surplus is equal to the area *EGCB*. But the rectangle *EGJB* becomes part of revenue for the monopolist. Thus, this rectangle represents a transfer from consumers to the monopolist and not a net loss to society. Economists do not attempt to evaluate this transfer because such an evaluation is normative or based on principles of equity. The final area to account for is the triangle *JCH*, which represents the loss in producer surplus. The total net welfare loss to society is the sum of triangles *GJC* and *JCH*, or the shaded area in Figure 11.8. This area represents the excess of the value to society (as reflected in the demand curve) over the cost to society (as reflected in the supply curve) for the units of output lost because of monopolization.

Harberger used this theory to empirically measure the welfare costs of monopoly.[13] In doing so he made some simplifying assumptions. He assumed that the elasticity of demand is equal to 1, that producers do not engage in price discrimination, and that long-run average total cost is constant (and, therefore, equal to long-run marginal cost) for both firms and industries. The supply curve is, thus, horizontal as shown in Figure 11.9. The welfare cost is given by the area of shaded right triangle *GCH*. This area is equal to $\frac{1}{2}(\Delta P)(\Delta Q)$. Harberger thus proceeded to measure this area by computing ΔQ and ΔP.

Harberger used data on manufacturing industries for 1924 to 1928. He used this period arguing that it was reasonably close to a long-run equilibrium period with no violent shifts in demand or economic structure. Furthermore, data on industrial profits for this period were readily available in a National Bureau study. Harberger computed the average rate of profit on capital for each industry for 1924 to 1928 and subtracted from it the average rate of profit on capital for the whole manufacturing sector. This difference he took as ΔP. Next, ΔQ was obtained from the assumption of unitary elasticity of demand (and values of P and Q). Note that $\eta = (\Delta Q/\Delta P) \cdot (P/Q)$. Using this procedure, Harberger estimated the total welfare loss to be about $59 million or about 0.1 percent of GNP.

[13]See Arnold C. Harberger, "Monopoly and Resource Allocation," *The American Economic Review*, May 1954, pp. 77–87.

FIGURE 11.9   Harberger's measurement of the welfare cost of monopoly.

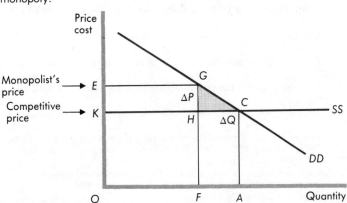

Harberger's method for computing the welfare loss of monopoly was used by others to compute welfare loss of trade restrictions like tariffs and quotas, and the estimates were often surprisingly low. Harberger himself obtained estimates of 2.5 percent of national income for the costs of trade restrictions in Chile and a number of Latin American countries.[14]

An important criticism of this method of evaluating the welfare losses due to monopoly is that the presence of monopoly profit induces others to waste resources in trying to capture part of this pie. Tullock[15] and Posner[16] pointed out that this wastage of resources is not captured in the Harberger method of computing welfare losses shown in Figures 11.8 and 11.9. For instance, Polaroid, by having a monopoly over instant photography, was earning monopoly profits, and Kodak spent a lot of resources trying to compete in the same area. From the social point of view this is a wastage. Similarly, if licenses were issued for the importation of some products or for the monopolistic production of some products, many firms would spend resources in hiring lawyers, lobbying with representatives, and so on. These resources could be employed elsewhere more productively and, hence, are a wastage from the social point of view. These activities of trying to capture profits from monopolies, tariffs, quotas, and so on have been termed "rent-seeking activities" by Kreuger[17] and "DUP (directly unproductive profit-seeking) activities" by Bhagwati.[18]

How important are these activities and what is their social cost? Ann Kreuger and Richard Posner both estimate these losses. Kreuger estimates a loss of 7.3 percent of national income for India and 15 percent of national income for Turkey from import licenses. Posner estimates welfare losses in the United States from regulatory actions at 3 percent of gross national product. The implicit assumption is that the welfare loss due to these DUP activities is equal to the monopoly profit. Tullock, however, questions this assumption. [19]

Of course, unproductive activities are not confined to seeking monopoly profits or benefits from import licenses alone. There are a host of activities individuals engage in to seek special favors or privileges. Taking account of all these, Mishan[20] has estimated the losses from "non-productive activities" in society at 50 percent of our GNP. This merely shows that there is no end to all these estimates.

In Figure 11.9 the rectangle *EGHK* measures the monopoly profits. The mere fact that the profits exist will induce firms to invest resources in seeking and preserving monopoly power. This resource cost is likely to take up a major portion

[14]See Arnold C. Harberger, "Using the Resources at Hand More Effectively," *The American Economic Review*, May 1959, pp. 134–146.

[15]Gordon Tullock, "The Welfare Costs of Tariffs, Monopolies and Theft," *Western Economic Journal*, June 1967, pp. 224–232.

[16]Richard A. Posner, "The Welfare Costs of Monopoly and Regulation," *Journal of Political Economy*, August 1975, pp. 807–828.

[17]Anne O. Kreuger, "The Political Economy of the Rent-Seeking Society," *American Economic Review*, June 1974, pp. 291–303.

[18]J. N. Bhagwati, "Directly Unproductive Profit-Seeking (DUP) Activities," *Journal of Political Economy*, October 1982, pp. 988–1002. "Lobbying, DUP Activities and Welfare: A Response to Tullock," *Journal of Public Economics*, December 1982, pp. 395–398.

[19]Gordon Tullock's paper in *Toward a Theory of Rent-Seeking Society*, edited by J. M. Buchanan, R. Tollison, and G. Tullock, Texas A & M University Press, College Station, Texas, 1980.

[20]Ezra Mishan, *Economic Efficiency and Social Welfare*, Allen and Unwin, London, 1981.

of the rectangle *EGHK*, and, thus, the welfare cost of monopoly is likely to be much higher than that given by the area of the triangle *GCH*. An alternative way of looking at the problem is to argue that because of the investments designed to secure and defend a monopoly position, the average costs for the monopolist are likely to be higher than for the competitive firm (Harberger assumed them to be equal). Yet another argument as to why the monopolist's average costs are likely to be higher than for a competitive firm is given by Comanor and Leibenstein who attribute it to X-inefficiency or the failure of the monopolist to minimize costs because of the absence of the "competitive stick."[21] The analysis of welfare cost of monopoly when the average costs of the monopolist are higher than under perfect competition is shown in Figure 11.10. *DD* is the demand curve, P_m the monopoly price, AC_1 the average cost of the monopolist (we are assuming $AC = MC$), and AC_2 the average cost under competition. By assuming that AC_1 is also the average cost for the competitive firm, the output under competition is also expected to be Q_1, and the welfare cost of monopoly is estimated to be the area of the triangle *A*. However, if the true average cost under competition is AC_2, the output under competition is Q_2. The total loss in consumers' surplus is $A + B + C + E + F$, and the monopolist's profits are *F*. Hence, the net welfare cost is given by $A + B + C + E$, which is substantially larger than the area *A*.

Harberger's measure of the welfare costs of monopoly (which was about 0.1 percent of GNP) has been criticized as being too low, and other investigators have started correcting for various factors ignored by Harberger. In commenting on Harberger's study, Stigler wrote: "If the estimate is correct, economists might serve a more useful purpose if they fought fires or termites instead of monopoly."[22] Stigler, however, argued that Harberger's estimate may well be low because of his method of estimating monopoly profit, his assumption of unitary elasticity of demand, and his neglect of rents to factors of production employed by the monopolist.

[21] W. S. Comanor and Harvey Leibenstein, "Allocative Efficiency, X-Efficiency and the Measurement of Welfare Losses," *Economica*, August 1969, pp. 304–309.

[22] George J. Stigler, "The Statistics of Monopoly and Merger," *Journal of Political Economy*, February 1956, p. 34.

FIGURE 11.10 Welfare comparison between monopoly and competition.

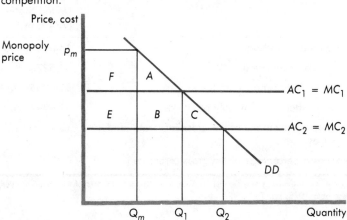

Kamerschen estimated the welfare cost of monopoly to be as high as 6 percent of GNP, although his estimates were later criticized as too high.[23]

Cowling and Mueller measured the social costs of the monopoly power of large firms in the United States and Great Britain and came up with quite high estimates.[24] Their sample consisted of 734 firms from 1963 to 1966 in the United States and 102 firms during 1968 and 1969 in Great Britain. In addition to making corrections in Harberger's analysis based on the criticism mentioned earlier, they added two more items: (1) advertising expenditures, which they view as a social waste, and (2) monopoly after tax profits, which they argue are an indication of resources wasted in the process of gaining monopoly power. In effect, Cowling and Mueller estimated the welfare cost of monopoly as $A + B + C + E + F$ in Figure 11.10. The results obtained by Cowling and Mueller are shown in Table 11.1. The results show that Harberger's estimates are substantially low. Even without adding the after tax monopoly profits, the percentages are 12.3 percent (of gross corporate product for those firms) for the United States and 5.4 percent for Great Britain.

Apart from these calculations, there are several papers arguing that the welfare costs of monopoly are quite substantial. Many studies have tried to refine the arguments. Posner's argument, for instance, was that firms contest for monopoly profits, that this "rent-seeking" activity will dissipate the monopoly profits, and, hence, monopoly profits should be added to the welfare cost triangle. This argument implies two things:

1. Rent dissipation. The total expenditure by firms to obtain monopoly profit is equal to the level of this profit.

2. Wastefulness. This expenditure has no socially valuable byproducts.

[23]David R. Kamerschen, "An Estimation of 'Welfare Losses' from Monopoly in the American Economy," *Western Economic Journal,* Summer 1966, pp. 221–236.

[24]Keith Cowling and Dennis C. Mueller, "The Social Costs of Monopoly Power," *The Economic Journal,* December 1978, pp. 727–748.

TABLE 11.1   Estimates of the Welfare Costs of Monopoly

	United States (734 firms)	Great Britian (102 firms)
1. Harberger's estimate	$448.2 million	£21.4 million
2. Harberger corrected	$4,527.1 million	£385.8 million
3. (2) + advertising expenditures	$14,005.4 million	£537.4 million
4. (3) + after tax monopoly profit	$14,997.6 million	£719.3 million
5. (4) as a percentage of the gross corporate product of *these* firms	13.1%	7.2%
6. (1) as a percentage of the gross corporate product	0.4%	0.2%

Source: Keith Cowling and Dennis C. Mueller, "The Social Costs of Monopoly Power," The Economic Journal, December 1978, pp. 740–742.

Fisher discusses these two arguments and points out that from the practical point of view, these arguments need to be qualified in several respects.[25] The monopoly profit need not be completely dissipated. The activity of rent seeking cannot be considered competitive. Competition involves free entry, but monopolies are characterized by barriers to entry with incumbents enjoying advantages over potential entrants.[26] A firm that is farsighted enough to enter a monopolizable area early will be able to monopolize at a cost lower than that which latecomers would have to expend to wrest monopoly power.

The Aluminum Corporation of America was, for instance, well placed to monopolize because of the patents it had obtained, and, furthermore, it was in an industry requiring particular mineral resources and a cheap energy supply. It might have been drawn into patent research in aluminum by the possibility of monopoly profits, but once it was in, no further entry into the aluminum industry was possible without substantial cost.

Monopolies can also be obtained through luck rather than foresight, and luck can go either way. In some cases, more will be expended on the rent-seeking activity than the actual amount that the rents turn out to be. In many cases the expenditure on rent seeking would be much less than that given by the monopoly rent rectangle (*EGHK* in Figure 11.9). Jadlow argues that, in practice, the profits from the monopoly accrue over a time period rather than a single period, as we have been assuming (for simplicity, of course).[27] During this time period rent seekers continue to compete for the valued monopoly prize, while consumers and regulators continue their efforts to eliminate the monopoly profits. Therefore, instead of a one-period prize, what the rent seeker has to calculate is the present value of a stream of future monopoly profits, most of which are uncertain. This would result in a significant reduction in rent-seeking activities, and, thus, the social costs are not as high as was suggested by others.

However, Wenders argues that the social costs of monopoly are much higher than what Posner suggests (maybe more than double), because we have to take into account not only rent-seeking costs but also *rent-defending costs*.[28] The monopolist would also expend a lot of resources to *defend* the monopoly profits. What we have been considering until now are only the expenditures of others to capture a share of the pie. Since we have presented enough triangles and rectangles, we will not present the details of Wenders' arguments here. The purpose of all this discussion is to show that there are large (social) gains to be achieved by deregulating monopolies.

In summary, the welfare costs of monopoly are substantial. In the next chapter we will discuss policies followed by the U.S. government to break up monopolies. Whether they have succeeded in their purpose and at what costs is a different story.

[25]F. M. Fisher, "The Social Costs of Monopoly and Regulation: Posner Reconsidered," *Journal of Political Economy*, April 1985, pp. 410–416.

[26]D. Fudenberg and J. Tirole, "Understanding Rent Dissipation: On the Use of Game Theory in Industrial Organization," *American Economic Review*, May 1987, pp. 176–183, show, using game theory, that extreme incumbency advantages may allow established firms to blockade entry and appropriate the entire rent (monopoly profit).

[27]J. M. Jadlow, "Monopoly Rent-Seeking Under Conditions of Uncertainty," *Public Choice*, vol. 45, no. 1, 1985, pp. 73–87. See also G. Tullock, "Back to the Bog," *Public Choice*, vol. 46, no. 3, 1985, pp. 259–263.

[28]J. T. Wenders, "On Perfect Rent Dissipation," *American Economic Review*, June 1987, pp. 456–459.

11.9   MULTIPLANT MONOPOLY

The monopolist may operate more than one plant, and the cost conditions may differ from one plant to the other. As an illustration we shall consider the case of two plants. In Table 11.2, MC_1 and MC_2 are the marginal costs of the first and second plant. The combined marginal cost, shown in the last column of Table 11.2 is obtained as follows. The monopolist produces the first two units of output from plant 1 because the marginal costs there are lower. Thus, MC for the first two units is 2.3 and 2.4, respectively. For the third unit of output, the MC is 2.5 in plant 1, but the monopolist can produce the unit with MC of 2.45 from plant 2. (It is the first unit for plant 2.) Hence, the overall MC is 2.45 for the third unit. For each successive unit of output the monopolist looks at whether it can be produced at a lower marginal cost in plant 1 or plant 2 and chooses the plant with the lower MC. The overall MC and the plant from which the unit of output comes are shown in the last two columns of Table 11.2. Now we equate MC to MR and get 9 units of output as the optimal level. Of these 9 units, 5 are produced in plant 1 and 4 in plant 2.

The above analysis applies to short-run equilibrium. We have considered only marginal costs but not average total costs for the two plants. If the fixed costs of plant 1 are very high, the monopolist could be suffering losses in this plant. In the long run the monopolist will close down unprofitable plants.

In the long run, the monopolist with a single plant adjusts the plant size and produces output where $LRMC = MR$. Note that this position is not the minimum point of the $LRAC$ curve as in the case of perfect competition.

For perfect competition the long-run equilibrium is given by

$$LRAC = SRAC = LRMC = SRMC = MR = AR = P$$

TABLE 11.2   MR and MC of a Two-Plant Monopolist

Units of Output	Price	Total Revenue	MR	MC_1	MC_2	MC	Produced from
1	6.00	6.00	6.00	2.30	2.45	2.30	Plant 1
2	5.50	11.00	5.00	2.40	2.55	2.40	Plant 1
3	5.10	15.30	4.30	2.50	2.65	2.45	Plant 2
4	4.80	19.20	3.90	2.60	2.75	2.50	Plant 1
5	4.56	22.80	3.60	2.70	2.85	2.55	Plant 2
6	4.35	26.10	3.30	2.80	2.95	2.60	Plant 1
7	4.17	29.19	3.09	2.90	3.05	2.65	Plant 2
8	4.01	32.08	2.89	3.00	3.15	2.70	Plant 1
9	3.87	34.83	2.75	3.10	3.25	2.75	Plant 2
10	3.73	37.30	2.47	3.20	3.35	2.80	Plant 1

For monopoly the long-run equilibrium is given by

$$LRMC = SRMC = MR \qquad \text{and} \qquad LRAC \leq \text{price}$$

For the multiplant monopolist the long-run equilibrium condition is the same except that the multiplant monopolist might adjust not only the plant size but the number of plants as well. She might close down unprofitable plants and open new ones. The overall marginal costs and total costs are derived as we did earlier in Table 11.2.

11.10 BILATERAL MONOPOLY

A bilateral monopoly is said to exist when one producer has an output monopoly and there is only one buyer for the product. The following distinctions make things clear:

- *Perfect competition:* Many buyers, many sellers
- *Monopoly:* Many buyers, single seller
- *Bilateral monopoly:* Single buyer, single seller

Since there is only one demander and one seller, the price and quantity will be determined by negotiation. However, we can find the upper and lower limits for prices and quantities, by considering alternately the single seller as all-powerful and the single buyer as all-powerful. The situation is described in Figure 11.11. DD is the demand curve, MR the marginal revenue curve, and MC_S the marginal

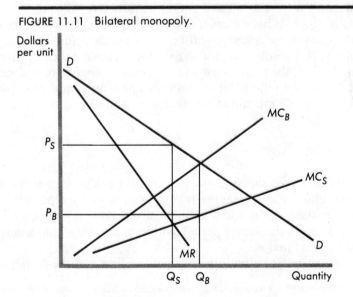

FIGURE 11.11 Bilateral monopoly.

cost curve of the single seller. If the monopolist is all-powerful, she will make the buyer behave as if there were many buyers. She will equate her MC to MR, produce output Q_S, and charge price P_S.

However, if the single buyer is all-powerful, he can make the monopolist behave like a perfect competitor. Thus, MC_S will be the monopolist's supply curve. Corresponding to this supply curve, we can construct the MC_B curve, which shows the marginal cost of buying an additional unit. MC_B exceeds price because in order to purchase an additional unit, the buyer must pay a higher price. And that higher price will pertain to all units purchased. The buyer equates his marginal cost of buying an additional unit with the marginal value of an additional unit (as given by the demand curve) and purchases Q_B units. Since the seller is behaving like a competitor with supply curve MC_S, he will sell the Q_B units at a per-unit price of P_B.

Thus, if the seller has all the power, the quantity supplied Q_S is given by the intersection of the MR and MC_S curves with the corresponding price P_S read off from the demand curve. If the buyer has all the power, the quantity demanded Q_B is given by the intersection of the DD and MC_B curves with the corresponding price P_B read off the MC_S curve.

The actual solution for the bilateral monopoly problem is indeterminate, depending on the respective bargaining powers of the buyer and the seller.

11.11 APPLICATION—ENERGY CONSERVATION: COMPETITION VERSUS MONOPOLY

There are many resources that are considered "nonrenewable" or "exhaustible." The idea is that there is a limited amount and if we do not use them carefully, they will be exhausted, with nothing left for the future. This argument has been made with respect to oil and energy sources. We will not debate the validity of this argument. What we are interested in showing is that under monopoly, more of the exhaustible resource will be saved for the future than under perfect competition. This result was first derived in a classic paper by Harold Hotelling in 1931.[29] Thus, the monopolist and the conservationist are strange bedfellows.

To illustrate the point we will present a numerical example. This approach will be more illuminating than discussion and diagrams. Let the market demand function be

$$P = 50 - Q \qquad [11.1]$$

Let the total fixed supply of the resource in question be $S = 56$. We consider two periods and the total quantity is consumed in the two periods. Our questions is: What are the quantity and price in the first period? If we know this, then we know the quantity in the second period, and from the demand function we get the price in the second period.

We assume that both the competitive firm and the monopolist discount the

[29] Harold Hotelling, "The Economics of Exhaustible Resources," *Journal of Political Economy*, April 1931, pp. 137–175.

future profits at a discount rate equal to the market rate of interest. For example, if the profits next year are \$110, and the interest rate is 10 percent, then they consider next year's \$110 profit as equivalent to \$110/1.1 = \$100 of profit this year. We will also assume that they try to maximize the present value of their total profits.[30] Let

p_1 = price in the first period
p_2 = price in the second period
Q_1 = quantity sold in the first period
Q_2 = quantity sold in the second period

We are given $Q_1 + Q_2$ is total supply, which equals 56.

The competitive solution

The competitive firm takes the market price as given. The total supply is in the hands of a large number of firms. The prices at which the competitive firm can sell are determined by the market demand function (11.1). Thus, we have

$p_1 = 50 - Q_1$
$p_2 = 50 - Q_2$

hence,

$p_1 + p_2 = 100 - (Q_1 + Q_2) = 100 - 56 = 44$

However, for each firm, a price p_2 received in the second period is the same as a price $p_1(1 + d)$ received in the first period, where d is the interest rate. Hence, in equilibrium, we have

$p_2 = p_1(1 + d)$

Thus, we get

$p_1 + p_2 = p_1 + p_1(1 + d) = p_1(2 + d)$

or

$$p_1 = 44/(2 + d) \qquad [11.2]$$

For different discount rates, we can now calculate the prices and outputs in the two periods.

For $d = 0$ we get

$p_1 = p_2 = 22$
$Q_1 = Q_2 = 28$

[30]More discussion of discounting and present values is in Section 20.2 of Chapter 20.

For $d = 0.2$ (20 percent rate of interest), we have

$$p_1 = \frac{44}{2.2} = 20 \qquad p_2 = p_1(1 + d) = 24$$

thus,

$$p_1 = 20, \; Q_1 = 30$$
$$p_2 = 24, \; Q_2 = 26$$

As the discount rate goes up, the first period's output goes up. We will now contrast this solution with the solution under monopoly.

Solution under monopoly

The monopolist will maximize the present value of her profits. Since the total supply is given, this amounts to maximizing the present value of her revenues, which requires that $MR_1(1 + d) = MR_2$. Substituting in the marginal revenue functions (remember that demand is linear), yields

$$(50 - 2Q_1)(1 + d) = 50 - 2Q_2$$

But since $Q_2 = 56 - Q_1$ we can again substitute to get

$$(50 - 2Q_1)(1 + d) = 50 - 2(56 - Q_1)$$

Solving for Q_1 now yields

$$Q_1 = \frac{112 + 50d}{4 + 2d} = \frac{56 + 25d}{2 + d} \qquad\qquad [11.3]$$

We can use this formula to get the prices and quantities for different rates of discount. But one interesting thing to note is that for $d = 0$ we get

$$Q_1 = 28, \; p_1 = 22$$
$$Q_2 = 28, \; p_2 = 22$$

which is the same as the competitive solution. For positive rates of discount, Q_1 will be lower under monopoly than under competition. To see this, note that under perfect competition

$$Q_1 = 50 - p_1 = 50 - \frac{44}{2 + d} = \frac{56 + 50d}{2 + d}$$

Under monopoly

$$Q_1 = \frac{56 + 25d}{2 + d}$$

For $d > 0$, since $25d < 50d$, output under monopoly is always lower in the first period than in the second period. As $d \to \infty$ note that $Q_1 \to 50$ under perfect competition and $Q_1 \to 25$ under monopoly.

Note the important result that the restriction of current output under monopoly is a function of the interest rate or discount rate. With low interest rates there is not much difference between the two.

The monopolist can claim that he is serving the society by conserving scarce resources. In fact, when OPEC was raising petroleum prices, Sheikh Yamani of Saudi Arabia often argued that he was serving the interests of the industrialized world by conserving scarce resources for the future!

11.12   SUMMARY AND CONCLUSIONS

Pure monopoly is characterized by a single seller of a product with no close substitutes. The monopolist is a price setter. The monopolist faces the downward-sloping market demand curve. Because the demand curve slopes downward, the MR curve must also slope downward. If the monopolist sets a single price, then to sell an additional unit she must reduce price on all units so that MR will be less than price. Monopolists maximize profit by producing where $MR = MC$. They then sell this output for the highest possible price according to the demand curve.

A monopoly will produce a smaller output and sell at a higher price than the equivalent competitive industry. Since monopolists are price setters, it does not make sense to ask what output they will produce at various prices. Hence, the concept of a supply curve is meaningless for the monopolist.

For a profitable monopoly to survive in the long run, barriers to entry are required. These barriers can be in the form of control over essential inputs, legal protection, patents, or internal scale economies. The monopolist can also create barriers through preemptive price cutting.

Price discrimination occurs when the monopolist sells different units of the same product at different prices with no cost justification. A requirement for successful discrimination is that resale of the product can be prevented. First-degree discrimination means that the monopolist charges the reservation price for each unit of output. The MR curve becomes the demand curve and output will be the same as under perfect competition. Second-degree discrimination means that the monopolist charges serveral different prices for different ranges of output. In this case, the MR curve becomes a step function. Output occurs where $MR = MC$. Third-degree discrimination means that the monopolist separates customers into several groups or classes and charges different prices to the members of the different groups. The group with the least elastic demand will be charged the highest price, and the group with the most elastic demand will be charged the lowest price.

The traditional measure of the net welfare cost of monopoly is the excess of social value over cost for the units of output which will not be produced because of the monopoly structure. This measure ignores the resources which are spent on securing and maintaining the monopoly position. It also ignores the possibility that X-inefficiency may occur as the result of the monopoly structure.

Multiplant monopolists produce each successive unit of output in whichever plant has the lowest marginal cost. They produce to the point where overall marginal cost equals marginal revenue.

With bilateral monopoly, market price and output are indeterminate. If the buyer has total bargaining power, then output will be expanded to the point where the marginal cost of buying another unit is equal to marginal value (as reflected in the demand curve). If the seller has total power then output will be expanded to the point where marginal cost of production equals marginal revenue.

With a positive discount rate, the monopolist will conserve more of a fixed resource for the future than a competitive industry would.

KEY TERMS

Barriers to Entry
Bilateral Monopoly
Cartel
Input Monopoly
Monopoly

Natural Monopoly
Perfect or First-Degree Price
   Discrimination
Preemptive Price Cutting
Price Setter

Rent Seeking
Second-Degree Price
   Discrimination
Third-Degree Price
   Discrimination

QUESTIONS

1. If the monopolist's demand curve is $P = 200 - 10Q$, and his marginal cost curve is $MC = 100 + 5Q$, what are the monopolist's profit maximizing price and output?

2. Graphically illustrate the impact of an increase in demand on price and quantity under a monopolistic market structure. Illustrate the impact of an increase in marginal cost.

3. In Figure 11.7, the MC curve crosses the MR curve at a corner point. If the MC curve crossed the MR curve in a horizontal segment, the monopolist might feel pressure to change her prices. Why?

4. "If the average total cost curve dips below the demand curve at any point, then monopoly is profitable." Is this statement true? Why?

5. Most small towns have only one bakery. Does such a bakery constitute a monopoly? Why or why not? What keeps more bakeries from opening in these towns?

6. What is consumers' surplus with a perfectly discriminating monopoly? What is the net welfare cost to society of such a monopoly?

7. Explain why MC cannot intersect MR in the inelastic region of the monopolist's demand curve.

8. A regional basketball monopolist can separate his customers into two groups—tall customers and short customers. The demand curve for the tall customers is $P = 40 - 0.5Q$, and the demand curve for the short customers is $P = 18 - 0.25Q$. The monopolist's marginal costs are roughly constant at \$10. Calculate the profit-maximizing outputs and prices for the two groups if the monopolist practices third-degree discrimination. Compare the prices and demand elasticities for the two groups. Are they what we would expect? Why? Is it likely that this monopolist can successfully price discriminate? Why?

9. The market demand curve for gizmos is $P = 100 - 5Q$. The gizmo industry is currently monopolized, and the monopolist's total cost function is $TC = 300 + 20Q$. If the monopolist can practice first-degree discrimination, what will her output be? How does this output compare to the output which would occur with no discrimination?

10. A monopolist operates plant 1 and and plant 2. The marginal costs of the two plants are $MC_1 = 120 - 15Q + 3Q^2$ and $MC_2 = 90 - 26Q + 9Q^2$. Calculate the overall marginal cost for the first 10 units of output and indicate where each successive unit will be produced.

11. A single buyer faces an upward-sloping supply curve given by $P = 40 + 10Q$. Graph the supply curve and the curve representing the marginal cost of buying an additional unit. How do the two curves compare? Why?

12. Can a perfectly discriminating monopolist maximize profit along the inelastic portion of the demand curve? Why or why not?

13. Price discrimination tends to be more common in the sale of services (for example, discrimination by income for medical services, by age for air travel) than in the sale of manufactured goods. Explain.

14. In making efficiency comparisons between a monopolist and a competitive firm, the marginal cost function of the monopolist is said to correspond to the supply function of the competitive industry. Explain.

15. A multinational firm operates two plants in different countries. The marginal costs per additional unit of output and the prices are shown below for each output level.

Output	Plant 1 (MC_1)	Plant 2 (MC_2)	Price ($)
1	1.2	0.2	5.5
2	1.8	0.3	4.5
3	2.4	0.4	4.0
4	2.5	0.7	3.6
5	2.9	1.5	3.3
6	3.0	2.4	3.0
7	3.1	2.8	2.7
8	3.2	3.0	2.4
9	3.4	3.2	2.1
10	3.8	3.3	1.8

a. Construct the marginal cost for the multinational as a whole.

b. Determine the profit-maximizing output in each plant.

c. Suppose the government in the country where plant 2 is located decides to levy a tax of $2 per unit. What are the new profit-maximizing outputs of the multinational?

d. Suppose the government in the country where plant 2 is located imposes a unitary tax on the worldwide profits of the firm (the tax is a fixed percentage of the profits). What will be the likely response of the firm? Justify your answer.

16. a. Explain briefly how the market for physicians' services conforms to the necessary conditions for third-degree price discrimination. Why doesn't a doctor who discrim-

inates in pricing lose richer patients to other doctors—say, young doctors just building up their practices?

b. What justification can there be for permitting price discrimination in medical services? Is it any different from permitting discrimination in electric utility rates?

c. How would you classify the structure of the market for medical services—competitive, monopolistic, oligopolistic? Explain.

d. Why don't doctors and hospitals advertise and compete for patients? Would this improve the quality of care and/or reduce its prices to the patient?

THE REGULATION OF MONOPOLY

12.1   INTRODUCTION

In the last chapter we studied the behavior of the monopolist. We saw that if the monopolist is left alone to determine price and output, then, in general, too little will be produced from a social point of view. In this chapter we will look at the regulation of monopoly in theory and practice. What measures can, and should, be taken to alter the monopolist's behavior in the desired direction?

Even before tackling the question, "How should we regulate?" we must answer the question, "Whom should we regulate?" For the most part, we have discussed the extreme case of pure monopoly. But, in reality, most monopolies are of a weaker form. Economists generally argue that any firm with any control over the price of its product has some monopoly power. Does this imply that all such firms should be regulated? Clearly the answer is no, for one must realize that regulation itself is costly.

In order to determine which firms warrant regulation, we must be able to measure and compare the amount of monopoly power. In Section 12.2, five different approaches to the measurement of monopoly power will be discussed. One of those is the Herfindahl index, which is most commonly used by the federal government today in deciding when action against monopoly is needed.

After examining the measures of monopoly power, we will focus our attention on policies designed to reduce the welfare loss of monopoly. These policies include price regulation, taxes, and the antitrust laws. Price regulation is intended to induce the monopolist to produce a larger output by setting a price beyond its control. Taxes can be used to alter the monopolist's output or to simply redistribute income and alleviate the equity problems associated with monopoly. Antitrust laws are designed to prevent the acquisition of substantial market power. In this sense, the antitrust laws are preventive measures. But they also regulate the practices of firms which do gain market control.

In Sections 12.5 and 12.6, we will discuss the regulation of a natural monopoly. We said that natural monopoly occurs as the result of economies of scale which result in an average cost function that is downward sloping over the entire range of market demand. Society benefits from monopoly in this case, because a single firm can serve the entire market at a lower cost than multiple firms could. But measures must be taken to prevent the natural monopolist from exploiting the monopoly position.

Finally, in Section 12.7, two applications will be presented. The first application examines the use of an import fee to counter OPEC's monopoly price. The second looks at the impact of tariffs and quotas when the domestic industry is monopolized.

12.2   MEASURES OF MONOPOLY POWER

In the last chapter we talked about the extreme case of pure monopoly. There are other degrees of monopoly. Economists generally consider any firm that can alter its price, through an adjustment in its output, to have some monopoly power.

However, a very small amount of monopoly power may not warrant regulation or any other market intervention. Clearly, before we can ascertain whether a problem exists and what, if anything, should be done, we must be able to measure· the amount of monopoly power.

The Lerner index

The ability to charge a price higher than MC is characteristic of monopoly. Using this information, Abba Lerner suggested an index to measure monopoly power.[1] This index, called the Lerner index, is defined as (price $- MC$)/price.

Since profit maximization implies $MC = MR$, and price $= AR$, we can also write the Lerner index as $(AR - MR)/AR = 1 - (MR/AR)$. But $MR/AR = (1 - 1/\eta)$ where η is the elasticity of demand. Thus, the Lerner index equals $1/\eta$, which makes intuitive sense. Note that for a firm in a perfectly competitive industry, η is infinity and, hence, $1/\eta$ is 0. The firm has no power to raise its price. If the demand elasticity is low, the firm will have a high degree of monopoly power.

Unfortunately, the Lerner index is not as simple to calculate as it might first appear. Note that the demand elasticity we are talking about is the elasticity of the demand *facing the particular firm*. This is the same as the elasticity of demand for a product if there is only one firm producing the product. But if there are several firms then we can only infer the elasticity of demand facing each firm from the number of firms and the elasticity of demand for the product.

We could also compute the Lerner index if we knew the firm's marginal cost, but even if the monopolist knew his marginal cost, he would probably be reluctant to reveal it. So we will more than likely have to infer it from the monopolist's behavior. To do so, there are two things we might look at:

1. We can sometimes examine other periods when there was no monopoly in the industry. This is possible if the industry has periodic episodes of competition. Economic historians such as Peter Temin and Donald McCloskey have used this method to measure monopoly power in the iron and steel industry in the nineteenth century in the United States and Great Britain, respectively.

2. An alternative is to examine other markets where the monopolist acts like a competitor. This method works in those cases where, for instance, the monopolist has a monopoly domestically and acts like a competitor in the international market. Since a price-discriminating monopolist equates marginal revenues in the two markets, and in the international market $MR = AR =$ price $= MC$, we get a measure of the marginal cost of the monopolist from the price charged in the international market. This is illustrated in Figure 12.1, which also illustrates that there are some problems with this approach to measuring monopoly power.

In Figure 12.1 we have shown the marginal cost curve rising slowly and foreign price quite high to illustrate the problems with this method of measuring monopoly power. First, we find the point of intersection of the MC curve with the foreign demand curve (which is horizontal at the foreign price since the monopolist is a

---

[1]Abba P. Lerner, "The Concept of Monopoly and the Measurement of Monopoly Power," *Review of Economic Studies*, June 1934, pp. 157–175.

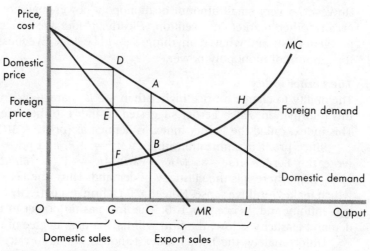

FIGURE 12.1   Measuring monopoly power of a monopolist who acts as a competitor in the international market.

price taker in the foreign market). This gives us the point H. Since the monopolist equates marginal revenue in both markets, the marginal revenue in the domestic market is EG, and, hence, the point on the domestic demand curve that gives domestic quantity and domestic price is the point D. We, thus, have the domestic sales and export sales shown in Figure 12.1.

What is the measure of monopoly power? One can use the Lerner index and say that since the marginal cost of the monopolist for the total output is $HL = EG$, and domestic price is DG, we have the Lerner index equal to $(DG - EG)/DG = DE/DG$. But if there were to be no exports, the equilibrium of the monopolist would be given by $MR = MC$, or the point B, and the quantity and price would be given by the point A on the demand curve. The Lerner index would be AB/AC since price equals AC and marginal cost equals BC. Note that DE/DG is much lower than AB/AC. (In our figure DE/DG is about half of AB/AC.) Thus, the domestic price is higher, the domestic quantity is lower, the monopolist's profits are higher, and yet the measure of monopoly power is lower, in the case where there is an international market!

The proper measure of domestic monopoly power is DF/DG, since FG is the marginal cost of domestic output. But there is no way of inferring FG from the price charged in the foreign market. What we are able to measure is the total monopoly power of the monopolist. We can take this approximately to be a weighted average of domestic monopoly power and foreign monopoly power (which is 0), weighted by the respective sales—domestic and export, respectively. Since the Lerner index,

$$\frac{\text{Domestic price} - \text{export price}}{\text{Domestic price}}$$

measures total monopoly power, we have the domestic monopoly power given by

Domestic monopoly power

$$= \frac{\text{domestic price} - \text{export price}}{\text{domestic price}} \times \frac{\text{domestic sales} + \text{export sales}}{\text{domestic sales}}$$

An alternative way of looking at this problem is to consider the relationship we derived in Section 11.7 between the prices that a discriminating monopolist charges in two markets. There we showed that

$$p_1(1 - 1/\eta_1) = p_2(1 - 1/\eta_2) \text{ or}$$

$$\frac{p_2}{p_1} = \left(1 - \frac{1}{\eta_1}\right) \Big/ \left(1 - \frac{1}{\eta_2}\right)$$

Let

$p_1 = \text{domestic price}$
$p_2 = \text{foreign price}$

Then, since η_2, the price elasticity of foreign demand, is ∞, we have

$$\frac{p_2}{p_1} = 1 - \frac{1}{\eta_1} \quad \text{or} \quad \frac{1}{\eta_1} = 1 - \frac{p_2}{p_1} = \frac{p_1 - p_2}{p_1}$$

And we saw earlier that the Lerner index is $1/\eta_1$. Thus, the Lerner index of monopoly power equals

$$\frac{\text{Domestic price} - \text{foreign price}}{\text{Domestic price}}.$$

Measures of monopoly power based on price discrimination

The existence of price discrimination is evidence of monopoly power because price discrimination shows clearly that the monopolist has control over prices. Furthermore, if we know the elasticities of demand we can calculate a measure of monopoly power, as the preceding discussion shows. In fact, if there are two markets, then since we know the market prices the monopolist is charging, we need to know only one of the two elasticities of demand. In the previous example, we had $\eta_2 = \infty$. This enabled us to get an estimate of the monopoly power.

Suppose that η_2 is not known exactly. We can still get some estimates of monopoly power by making some assumptions about η_2. If, for example, the monopolist is charging three times the price in one market as compared to the other one, we have $p_1/p_2 = 3$. Thus,

$$\frac{p_2}{p_1} = \frac{1}{3} = \left(1 - \frac{1}{\eta_1}\right) \Big/ \left(1 - \frac{1}{\eta_2}\right)$$

If $\eta_2 = 2, \dfrac{1}{\eta_1} = \dfrac{5}{6}$

If $\eta_2 = 4$, $\dfrac{1}{\eta_1} = \dfrac{3}{4}$

If $\eta_2 = \infty$, $\dfrac{1}{\eta_1} = \dfrac{2}{3}$

Thus, we can get some bounds on the amount of monopoly power by making some reasonable guesses about η_2.

Measures based on profit rates

Frequently, the monopolist earns above-normal profits. We can, therefore, think of measuring monopoly power by comparing the accounting profit rate in an industry or a firm with the normal profit rate. There is, however, the question of what is "normal." How do we treat the return to special entrepreneurial talents? Furthermore, even the competitive firm can earn an economic profit in the short-run until entry erodes it. These profits cannot be called monopoly profits.

Conversely, those who buy a right to a monopoly have to calculate the purchase price as a cost, and when this is done the profit rate appears normal. But this does not imply that there is no monopoly. For instance, a taxi driver in New York City paying $45,000 for a medallion (or license to operate a taxicab) would include this in her investment cost, and we might say that she is just earning a "normal" profit from her business. Suppose we can say this about every cab driver. Then we have the paradox that everyone in this industry (or profession) is earning a normal rate of return, and yet we say the industry is a monopoly.

This discussion demonstrates that there are serious problems with using profit rates to evaluate the extent of monopoly power. And one must use extreme care in interpreting the results of such an analysis.

Concentration ratios as measures of monopoly power

Concentration ratios measure the size of the largest firms' share in total industry sales (or profits or assets). For instance, considering sales as our measure, an n-firm concentration ratio, denoted by CR_n, is the proportion of total industry sales accounted for by the n largest firms. It is customary to consider four-firm and eight-firm concentration ratios denoted as CR_4 and CR_8, respectively, although we will see that this procedure has several drawbacks.

The idea behind concentration ratios is that in a competitive industry sales are more evenly distributed among firms, whereas in a monopolistic industry, sales are concentrated in a few large firms. (In the extreme case of a pure monopoly, sales are concentrated in a single firm.)

Suppose there are five firms in an industry, and the shares of the firms arranged by decreasing size are as follows:

Firm	Market Share
1	0.50
2	0.30
3	0.10

4	0.06
5	0.04

We can compute the cumulative shares for the *n* largest firms for $n = 1, 2, 3, 4, 5$. These cumulative shares are:

Cumulative Number of Firms	Cumulative Market Share
1	0.50
2	0.80
3	0.90
4	0.96
5	1.00

Thus, $CR_2 = 0.8$, $CR_3 = 0.9$, and so on. We can plot the cumulative percentage of sales against the cumulative number of firms from largest to smallest. The curve we get is called the *concentration curve*. This is shown in Figure 12.2 for three typical industries. Industry A is more concentrated than industries B and C. But whether B or C is more concentrated depends on whether we look at the four-firm concentration ratio (CR_4) or the eight-firm concentration ratio (CR_8). If we look at CR_4, B is more concentrated than C. If we look at CR_8, then C is more concentrated than B. This is the basic defect of concentration ratios.

There are also other problems with concentration ratios. Are we considering sales, profits or assets? Also, the concentration ratio does not take into account the number of firms. For instance, in our example of five firms, $CR_4 = 0.96$. In another

FIGURE 12.2   Concentration curves for three typical industries.

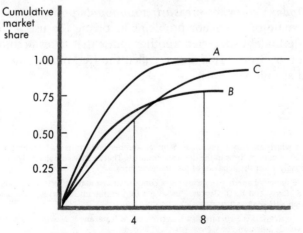

Cumulative number of firms from largest to smallest.

industry with 100 firms, suppose $CR_4 = 0.98$. These two numbers are really not comparable.[2]

In spite of all these defects, concentration ratios have played a major role in many antitrust cases initiated by the Justice Department. Many of these defects are, however, corrected in the Herfindahl index.[3]

Concentration ratios in U.S. manufacturing

The U.S. Census Bureau publishes quinquennial concentration statistics for some 450 manufacturing "industries" and 1300 manufacturing "product classes." The 1977 census shows the following distribution[4]:

Four-Seller Concentration Ratio (percent)	Number of Industries	Percentage of U.S. Mfg. Value Added
0–19	87	22.8
20–39	163	33.2
40–59	125	24.9
60–79	49	12.4
80–100	25	6.6
Total	449	

Thus, highly concentranted industries (those in which four sellers controlled more than 80 percent of total sales) are relatively rare. Indeed, no cases of pure monopoly, with a single seller controlling 100 percent of industry sales, are encountered. To find pure monopolies one has to look at regulated utilities (such as local residential telephone companies) or firms that have recently introduced new innovative products. At the nationwide manufacturing level, perfectly competitive industries are also rare. Most manufacturing activity occurs in industries of intermediate seller concentration, that is, in "loose oligopolies."

The Herfindahl index for measuring monopoly power

To avoid some of the major problems involving the use of concentration ratios, Orris C. Herfindahl suggested another index that takes account of the entire size distribution of firms.[5] This index, called the Herfindahl index and denoted by HI is defined as follows:

$$HI = \sum_{i=1}^{n} s_i^2$$

[2]It is not clear which industry is more competitive. Another problem is that concentration ratios are usually based only on the distribution of firms in the domestic industry. That is, they completely ignore foreign competition, which could dramatically affect the behavior of the domestic firms.

[3]An exhaustive survey of alternative measures of concentration and the effects of mergers on concentration ratios can be found in B. Curry and K. D. George, "Industrial Concentration: A Survey," *The Journal of Industrial Economics*, March 1983, pp. 203–255.

[4]See F. M. Scherer, "Market Structure," in J. Eatwell, M. Milgate, and P. Newman, eds., *The New Palgrave: A Dictionary of Economics*, vol. 3, Stockton Press, New York, 1987, p. 343.

[5]Orris C. Herfindahl, "A General Evaluation of Competition in the Copper Industry," in *Copper Costs and Prices 1870–1957*, Johns Hopkins Press, Baltimore, 1959, chap. 7.

where n is the number of firms in the industry and s_i is the market share of the ith firm ($i = 1, 2, \ldots, n$). This index reflects both the numbers of firms and their relative sizes.

In June 1982, the antitrust division of the Justice Department announced that in the division's future antitrust cases, it will use the Herfindahl index to measure concentration of market power, instead of the four-firm and eight-firm concentration ratios that had been used until then. In view of its widespread use, we will examine this index in some detail.

For the example we considered earlier, we compute the Herfindahl index as

$$HI = (0.50)^2 + (0.30)^2 + (0.10)^2 + (0.06)^2 + (0.04)^2$$
$$= 0.3552$$

If, instead, all firms had equal market shares then each share would be 0.2 and the Herfindahl index would be

$$HI = 5(0.2)^2 = \frac{1}{5}$$

If there are n firms in an industry and all have equal shares, the share of each firm will be $1/n$ and the Herfindahl index will be $n(1/n)^2 = 1/n$, which is the reciprocal of the number of firms. If there is only one firm, its share is 1 and the Herfindahl index is 1. Thus, the Herfindahl index lies between 1.0 and $1/n$ where n is the number of firms.

We know from elementary statistics that the variance (σ^2) of market shares[6] is

$$\frac{1}{n}\left[\sum_{i=1}^{n} s_i^2 - n\left(\frac{1}{n}\right)^2\right]$$

Hence, we get

$$HI = n\sigma^2 + \frac{1}{n}$$

Thus, the Herfindahl index depends solely on the number of firms n in the industry and the variance of the market shares. Instead of the variance of market shares we can also use other measures such as coefficient of variation of output (or sales) to compute the Herfindahl index.

A very small HI indicates that there are many firms of roughly equal size. A value closer to 1 indicates a small number of firms and/or very unequal shares. Thus, a larger HI is interpreted as indicating greater monopoly power.

---

[6]This is simply a restatement of $\frac{1}{n}\left[\sum_{i=1}^{n}\left(s_i - \frac{1}{n}\right)^2\right]$. The average share is, of course, $1/n$.

REGULATION OF MONOPOLY

In the previous chapter we discussed the problem of welfare loss due to monopoly. Several policies have been suggested to regulate monopolies, with the objective of reducing the welfare loss. These suggestions fall under four basic categories: (1) price regulation, (2) lump-sum taxes, (3) per-unit taxes, and (4) antitrust laws.

Price regulation

Suppose monopolists cannot charge a price higher than a ceiling price $\bar{p}$. How would monopolists choose their profit-maximizing output? To answer this question we have to determine the marginal revenue curve under a price ceiling and then the profit-maximizing output is found by the intersection of the marginal revenue curve and the marginal cost curve.

Figure 12.3 shows the marginal revenue curve when the government imposes a price ceiling $\bar{p}$. DD is the demand curve or the AR curve in the absence of the price ceiling. Over the range of output 0 to $\bar{Q}$, the price is constant, and, hence, MR = price = $\bar{p}$. After that, price is given by the relevant portion of the demand curve, and marginal revenue is given by the corresponding portion of the downward-sloping MR curve. Thus, the marginal revenue curve under a price ceiling $\bar{p}$ is the colored line in Figure 12.3. We can consider three situations depending on whether the price ceiling $\bar{p}$ is lower, equal to, or higher than the price given by the intersection of the demand curve and the marginal cost curve. The case where $\bar{p}$ is at the level where the marginal cost curve intersects the demand curve is the most straightforward. It is shown in Figure 12.3. In this case the monopoly solution and the competitive solution coincide, and there is no welfare loss due to monopoly.

In Figure 12.4 we show the case where price is regulated below the competitive level. In this case the price charged by the monopolist is lower than the competitive price, but the quantity produced is also lower than the competitive output. The competitive equilibrium is at the point A, and the monopolist's equilibrium is at the point B. The welfare loss is given by the triangle ABE. (Note that we are using

FIGURE 12.3 Price regulation of monopoly with price fixed at the competitive level.

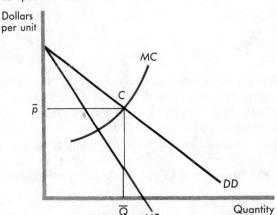

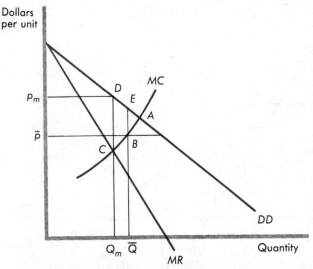

FIGURE 12.4 Price regulation of monopoly with the price fixed below the competitive level.

the traditional measure of welfare cost.) However, the welfare loss associated with an unregulated monopoly is equal to the triangle *ACD*. Thus, by imposing a price ceiling, the welfare cost of monopoly is reduced.

Note, however, that we obtained this result because $\bar{p}$ is above the level of the point *C*, which is the point of intersection between the *MC* curve and the *MR* curve. If $\bar{p}$ is set below this point, then the output under price regulation will be less than Q_m (the output under unregulated monopoly), and the welfare cost will be higher than with an unregulated monopoly. Thus, it does not make sense to regulate the price at a level below that given by the point *C* where *MR* = *MC*.

Finally, in Figure 12.5 we show the case where the regulated price is above the competitive level. With no price regulation the quantity produced by the monopolist is Q_m and the price charged is p_m. With the price regulation, quantity produced is $\bar{Q}$ and price charged is $\bar{p}$. Thus, quantity is higher and price lower. However, $\bar{p}$ is higher than the competitive price p_c, and $\bar{Q}$ is lower than the competitive quantity Q_c. The welfare cost of unregulated monopoly is *ACD*, and the welfare cost of the price regulated monopoly is *ABE*, which is lower. The result is similar to the one in Figure 12.4. What then is the difference? The difference is merely that in the case presented in Figure 12.4, price equals marginal cost. Whereas in the case presented in Figure 12.5, price is higher than marginal cost and, thus, the monopolist has higher profits (or lower losses in case of a short-term loss). Thus, the basic difference between the two cases is in the profits the monopolist makes.

Lump-sum taxes
The case of lump-sum taxes is easy to analyze. Since this type of tax is like a fixed cost, the *MC* curve for the monopolist does not change. Hence, the output and price remain unchanged. (However, a sufficiently high tax can induce exit in the long run.) The only change is that the monopolist's profits fall. Thus, there is no

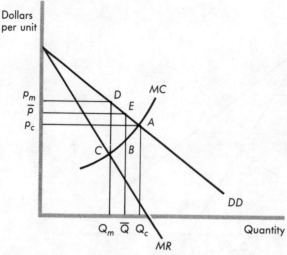

FIGURE 12.5   Price regulation of monopoly with the price fixed above the competitive level.

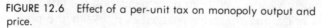

change in the welfare cost, the way we have been measuring it. There will only be some redistribution of income.

Per-unit tax

The case of a per-unit tax is different. This causes an upward shift in the MC curve by an amount equal to the tax. The effect is that the quantity produced declines and the price increases, although the increase in price is less than the amount of the per-unit tax. This is illustrated in Figure 12.6. For simplicity we have assumed that MC is constant, so that the MC curve is horizontal. MC_1 is the initial marginal cost curve, Q_1 is the initial output, and p_1 is the price. With the imposition of a

FIGURE 12.6   Effect of a per-unit tax on monopoly output and price.

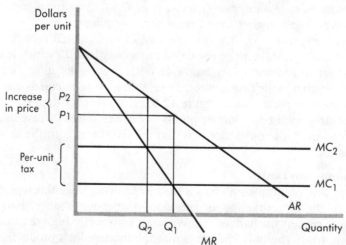

per-unit tax, the *MC* curve shifts up to MC_2. Q_2 is the new quantity and p_2 the new price. Note that the increase in price is less than the per-unit tax.

Antitrust laws and regulation of monopolies

In the preceding chapter we discussed the welfare loss due to monopoly. This took only the inefficiency aspects into account. There are many who also judge the income distribution consequences of monopoly and imperfect competition as being detrimental to the ideal of equity. Thus, both on the grounds of efficiency and equity there has been an impetus toward legislation against monopoly. During the last 100 years there have been a series of *antitrust laws* designed to restrain monopoly and foster competition. The term "antitrust" arises from the fact that the earliest monopolies were, as will be explained later, *trusts*. The terms "antitrust laws" and "trustbusters" are still used even though they no longer relate to trusts.

The purpose of antitrust laws is to promote competition and thereby ensure: (1) optimal allocation of society's resources across markets and the minimization of costs within each market, (2) maximization of dynamic efficiency by promoting a high rate of technological progress and by pressuring firms to innovate, and (3) promotion of equity by eliminating the income inequality generated by monopoly profits and restraints that limit economic opportunity. In addition, competition also helps in the attainment of other goals. Since economic power is not concentrated in a few hands, it cannot be used to manipulate the political process.

Three laws, with their numerous amendments, constitute the basis of antitrust policy in the United States. These are the Sherman Act (1890), the Clayton Act (1914), and the Federal Trade Commission Act (1914). The Federal Trade Commission Act also established the Federal Trade Commission (FTC). This agency, besides enforcing antitrust legislation, is active in the area of consumer protection. It administers legislation such as Trademark, Truth-in-Lending, and Fair Packaging and Labelling acts.

The Sherman Act

The Sherman Act was the first antitrust law. The post-Civil War expansion of the railroad system and the industrial revolution created large markets. The resultant large national firms led to the demise of small local firms. One common organization that developed was the *trust*, which was a combination of several corporations under the trusteeship of a single board of directors. These directors managed the affairs of all corporations jointly, and the individual corporations received trust certificates which entitled them to their share of profits. The holders of the trust certificates were interested only in their profits and not in running the business. Since the trust could control all the firms in a market, it eliminated competition. This was expected to raise profits, and the popularity of trusts grew rapidly. The trusts eliminated small competitors by means of localized price wars and preferential treatment from the railroads. The most famous of these trusts was the oil trust under John D. Rockefeller. But his oil trust was not alone. There were trusts in sugar, tobacco, whiskey, lead, and so on. The wealthy owners of the trusts were nicknamed "robber barons."[7]

The public protests against the trusts led to the passage of the Interstate Com-

---

[7]For some stories see Mathew Josephson, *The Robber Barons*, Harcourt, Brace and World, New York, 1962.

merce Act (1887) and the Sherman Act (1890). The Interstate Commerce Act established the Interstate Commerce Commission (ICC), which began regulating the railroads. The Sherman Act was the first antitrust law and probably one of the shortest pieces of legislation. Among other provisions, it makes it illegal to form trusts and to monopolize markets. The act, however, was very vague. It did not clearly define what the word "monopolize" meant. It did not make clear whether existing monopolies were illegal or just the formation of new monopolies or even attempts at formation of new monopolies.

Actually the Sherman Act was obsolete even before it was passed. In 1888 the state of New Jersey legalized intercorporate ownership, and this led to the formation of *holding companies*. A holding company is a corporation established for the sole purpose of acquiring a controlling stock interest in two or more corporations in an industry in order to run their affairs jointly. Companies usually have common stock (which has voting rights) and preferred stock (which has preference in distribution of dividends and not voting rights). Thus, by owning slightly over 50 percent of the common stock one can control the whole company. Actually, since many of the shareholders do not vote or are so widely dispersed that they cannot take active interest in the affairs, one can sometimes control the company with only 10 percent of the common stock. By more complicated "pyramiding" procedures, it is possible to control several corporations with very little investment. Since the holding company was a more efficient way of controlling corporations, many individuals used this method instead of trusts. Some of the well-known holding companies are American Can, American Tobacco, U.S. Rubber, and U.S. Steel.

The vague language of the Sherman Act gave a lot of latitude in interpretation by lawyers and the courts. In 1911 the Supreme Court argued that not every big corporation can be accused of monopolizing. Only the intention of exercising monopoly power and unreasonable actions that restrain trade were deemed illegal under the Sherman Act. Under this rule, known as "the rule of reason," Rockefeller's Standard Oil and Duke's American Tobacco Company (both controlling about 90 percent of their markets) were found guilty and were dissolved. This ruling narrowed the scope of the Sherman Act.

The Clayton Act (1914) and the Federal Trade Commission Act (1914)
These two pieces of legislation were enacted in 1914 because in the years following the Sherman Act, powerful new businesses came into being in many industries (steel, cans, and so on). It was believed that the Sherman Act could attack existing trusts but could not prevent the formation of new ones. The Clayton Act prohibited specific practices (some forms of price discrimination, exclusive contracts, tying contracts, requirement contracts, interlocking directorates, and so on), when the effect would be to "substantially lessen competition or tend to create a monopoly."

The Federal Trade Commission Act created the FTC and empowered it to outlaw "unfair methods of competition." Earlier, only the department of Justice could initiate antitrust suits. During the period 1910 to 1940, 346 cases were handled by the Justice Department, and 620 cases were handled by the FTC.[8]

---

[8]Richard A. Posner, "A Statistical Study of Anti-Trust Enforcement," *Journal of Law and Economics*, October 1970, pp. 370–390.

The three main laws—the Sherman Act, Clayton Act, and FTC Act—were repeatedly amended in response to real or perceived threats to competition. One famous amendment was the Robinson Patman Act (1936) which was designed to protect small independent retailers and wholesalers from mass distributors. The act forbade price discrimination. Another famous amendment was the Celler-Kefauver Act (1950) which was designed to discourage mergers.

How effective all this antitrust legislation has been is open to question. Critics say that most of the cases drag on for years (the *United States* v. *IBM* suit settled in 1982 was initiated in 1969), and the penalties imposed are incredibly small fines (usually no imprisonment). Still it is possible that these acts have a deterrent effect. They are violated in many cases, but perhaps the situation would have been much worse without them.

At the purely theoretical level, there is no reason to break up any single existing monopoly on grounds of overall economic efficiency. This argument is based on the theory of the second best. However, this theory, discussed in Chapter 18, is not of much practical value as its implementation involves knowledge that no government is likely to possess.

12.4   AVERAGE COST PRICING UNDER MONOPOLY

Suppose that the government wishes to eliminate all (economic) profits for the monopolist and so sets price where price equals the average cost of the unregulated monopolist's output. If monopolists are allowed to maximize their profit, the situation will be as shown in Figures 12.4 or 12.5, and the conclusions derived there apply.

However, this is not what is meant by average cost pricing. Average cost pricing means that price equals average (total) cost, and both price and output correspond to the point where the average cost curve intersects the demand curve as shown in Figure 12.7. The monopolist will not want to produce $\overline{Q}$ but will typically be

FIGURE 12.7   Effects of average cost pricing.

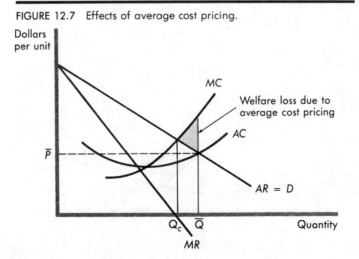

required to satisfy market demand at the regulated price $\bar{P}$. The output $\bar{Q}$ is higher than the competitive output Q_c. The price is also lower than the competitive price. There is a welfare loss shown by the shaded triangle in Figure 12.7. Note that this time the welfare loss is due to overproduction—the increase in consumer satisfaction is less than the increase in the cost of resources.

In the previous example, the demand curve intersects the average cost curve along its upward-sloping portion. We will now consider the case where the demand curve intersects the long-run AC curve ($LRAC$) to the left of its minimum point or in the region of economies of scale. Figure 12.8 depicts this scenario.

We generally argue that the output, corresponding to the intersection of $LRMC$ and the demand curve, is socially optimal, but in this case, since $LRAC$ is declining at A, $LRMC$ is less than $LRAC$. If the firm produces Q_c at a price of P_c, it will suffer losses and exit the industry. The lowest single price (and, hence, the largest output) at which this monopolist can cover costs is P_{ac}. Thus, in this sense, average cost pricing is optimal.

12.5   REGULATION OF NATURAL MONOPOLIES AND THE THEORY OF MARGINAL COST PRICING

In the last chapter, we mentioned that there are many cases where monopoly arises naturally because of economies of scale. These monopolies, called natural monopolies, occur in those cases where the average cost of production declines over the entire range of market demand (as in Figure 12.8). This implies that one firm can produce the entire output more cheaply than multiple firms could. Examples are gas pipelines, telephone companies, electric utilities, and some railroads. The monopolistic firm, if left alone, does not produce a socially optimal level of output. But regulation can bring about the optimal output if the regulators are able and willing to make the necessary calculations.

FIGURE 12.8   A case where average cost pricing for a monopoly is optimal.

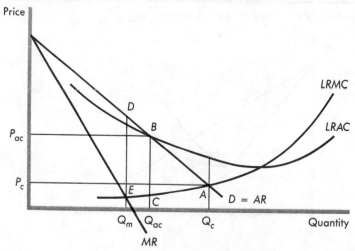

Our discussion of price regulation in Section 12.3 and average cost pricing in Section 12.4 gives some clues about the nature of price regulation in the case of natural monopolies. There are three types of regulation: (1) marginal cost pricing, (2) averaging cost pricing, and (3) price discrimination.

Marginal cost pricing

Consider first the case of marginal cost pricing. Price is set at the level corresponding to the intersection of the demand and MC curves, and the monopolist is required to provide the entire quantity demanded at that price. Thus, the socially optimal output is produced.

A problem occurs, however, since by definition the natural monopolist's $LRAC$ curve is downward sloping over the entire range of demand. Thus, marginal cost is less than average cost at the optimal output (as in Figure 12.8), and marginal cost pricing results in losses for the monopolist.

One solution to this problem is to subsidize the monopoly from general tax revenues for the losses it incurs. Another solution, adopted by Electricité de France (which is staffed by some great economists like M. Boiteux), is for the government to operate the electric utility and charge a price equal to marginal cost.[9]

It is easy to say that prices should be set equal to marginal cost, but it is very difficult to implement the rule in practice. This is particularly so with many of the natural monopolies we are talking about where investments have to be lumpy (building a new electric generating plant involves a large amount of fixed investment). There is an enormous amount of literature on marginal cost pricing in the case of electric utilities.[10] It is not possible to review here all this literature, but we will discuss a few aspects of the marginal cost pricing problem to clear some mistaken notions. The most important aspect pointed out by Boiteux is that "marginal cost pricing" does not always imply that price equals marginal cost! Of course, the discussion by Boiteux applies to publicly owned utilities, but the argument goes like this:

Suppose that there is an electric utility. It has a certain capacity and can supply a certain number of kilowatt hours of electricity. Once it is built, sunk costs are sunk, and the proper pricing rule is to set price equal to marginal cost. By marginal cost we mean marginal short-run operating costs. As demand increases, however, this electric utility cannot supply the total quantity demanded, and may have to raise the price to the point where quantity demanded is equal to the existing capacity. What Boiteux suggests is the following rule: Set price equal to short-run marginal operating cost if quantity demanded is less than or equal to capacity at that price. If quantity demanded exceeds capacity at this price, then set price above short-run marginal cost at a level that equates quantity demanded to the available capacity.

This rule is illustrated in Figure 12.9. Suppose marginal operating costs are constant. The available capacity is C. By capacity we mean here the maximum possible output. When the demand is given by D_1D_1, we set price $p_1 = MC$. When

[9]See M. Boiteux, "Marginal Cost Pricing," in J. R. Nelson, ed., *Marginal Cost Pricing in Practice*, Prentice-Hall, Englewood Cliffs, N.J., 1964. (This paper was originally published in French in 1956.)

[10]For some early discussion see the book edited by J. R. Nelson, ibid., and also A. E. Kahn, *The Economics of Regulation*, vol. 1, Wiley, New York, 1970.

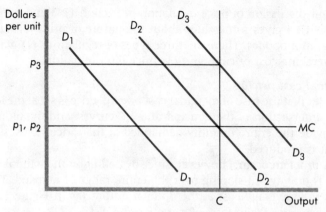

FIGURE 12.9   Marginal cost pricing with a fixed capacity and increasing demand.

the demand curve shifts to D_2D_2, price p_2 is still equal to MC. Thereafter price keeps on increasing. When the demand curve is D_3D_3, price is set at p_3. As the demand curve keeps shifting to the right, price keeps on rising. At some point, new capacity will be added. Boiteux suggests a rule for investment in new capacity, but since this involves intertemporal decisions (treated later in Chapter 20) we will not discuss it here. Anyhow, there are two rules: a short-term pricing rule and a long-term investment rule. Once new capacity is added, then price falls again to the new level of marginal costs. This is shown in Figure 12.10. Initially, capacity is C_1, and demand is given by D_1D_1. Price is $p_1 = MC_1$. When demand increases to D_2D_2 price rises to p_2, but when the new capacity comes into existence so that capacity is C_2, price falls to $p_3 = MC_2$, the new marginal cost. When demand increases to D_3D_3, price stays at p_3, but when demand increases to D_4D_4 price increases to p_4. The

FIGURE 12.10   Marginal cost pricing with shifting capacity and increasing demand.

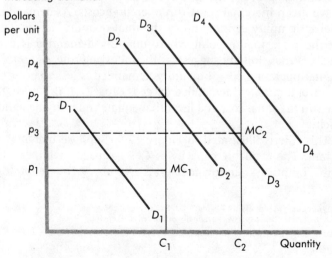

price will keep on increasing until additional capacity comes on line, at which point price falls to the point of the new marginal cost.

Vickrey makes a similar argument with reference to marginal cost pricing of water.[11]

> A more important consideration that is especially significant in the case of water supply is that new supplies come in very high lumps. What marginal cost pricing would require here is almost precisely the reverse of what very often happens. When a new supply is brought in, this increases costs, and this is very often used as a justification for an increase in the rates. The increase is even quite often postponed until the new supply becomes available, on the ground that only those who benefit from using the new supply should be called upon to pay for it. What ought to be done, however, if demand grows gradually is to increase the water rates for a period before the new supply is available sufficiently to curtail demand to the capacity of the old supply. . . . Then when the new supply becomes available the rate should be dropped sharply to the point where the new supply is fully utilized, . . . being subsequently raised as demand grows so as to keep the actual consumption within the capacity of the new supply.

Figure 12.11 shows what the marginal cost pricing rules suggested by Boiteux and Vickrey (and many others) imply for prices if investments are lumpy. In practice, it is politically not feasible to implement a price structure as shown in Figure 12.11. There are also many questions as to what is to be treated as fixed cost and what as variable cost in the computation of marginal cost. However, the idea of marginal cost pricing appealed to the regulatory authorities so much that an act was passed in 1978, called the Public Utility Regulatory Policies Act (PURPA). Following this Act, the Federal Energy Regulatory Commission (FERC) issued regulations in June 1979 requiring electric utilities to report "marginal cost calculations" as well as accounting cost calculations.

Under pressure to produce some number for marginal cost, many electric utilities hired consultants who generated some figures. However, the PURPA reg-

[11]W. S. Vickrey, "Responsive Pricing of Public Utility Services," *The Bell Journal of Economics and Management Science,* vol. 2, no. 1, 1971, pp. 337–346.

FIGURE 12.11   Pattern of prices over time under the marginal cost pricing rule with lumpy investments.

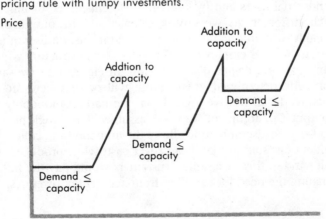

ulations do not make much sense *because there is no single number for marginal cost.* What we have is a marginal cost schedule (or *MC* curve) that gives marginal costs for various levels of output, and one cannot devise efficient prices without knowing where the demand curve is. The single number needed for marginal cost pricing is given by the intersection of the demand curve and the marginal cost curve.[12]

Average cost pricing

Compared with the marginal cost pricing rule, it would seem that the average cost pricing rule is easier to implement. All one has to do is check to see that the firm is earning a "fair" rate of return on capital. If it is earning a higher than fair rate of return, then price is too high. But what is "fair"? Ideally, the realized rate of return is the opportunity cost. But as we've seen, it is hard to account for such things as entrepreneurial talent, and, thus, it is difficult to calculate actual rates of return as well as fair rates of return. We will further discuss these problems in the next section.

We have also seen (in Figure 12.7) that average cost pricing *can* involve a welfare cost, and, in fact, we can (by drawing the curves in Figure 12.7 suitably) show that the welfare cost of average cost pricing can be higher than the welfare cost of monopoly pricing. But the case of natural monopoly, shown in Figure 12.8, is different. In this case even if there is a welfare loss (equal to the area of triangle *ABC*) it is definitely less than the welfare loss due to monopoly (which is given by the triangle *ADE*, in Figure 12.8). Thus, in this case we can say that average cost pricing is definitely better than monopoly pricing.

Both marginal cost pricing and average cost pricing are designed to induce the monopolist to expand output. As a monopoly's output approaches the optimal output (Q_c in Figure 12.8), the cost of the monopoly to society is reduced. A third tool used to induce the monopolist to increase output is a type of price discrimination.

Price discrimination

Many natural monopolies are allowed to price-discriminate. In fact, most electric utilities charge discriminatory prices. They employ a combination of second- and third-degree discrimination by charging different prices to residential, commercial, and industrial users and by charging different prices for different units of output to each customer. As we saw in Chapter 11, the output of the discriminating monopolist will, in general, be larger than for the nondiscriminating monopolist.[13]

Many utilities employ a declining block rate structure which was discussed as a form of second-degree discrimination. In Figure 11.7 we saw that if the blocks are properly determined, then output will occur where *MC* equals *D* or at the competitive level. But we argued that the natural monopoly will suffer a loss at that output. Our argument, however, assumed that a single price was being charged. Second-degree discrimination allows the monopolist to collect additional revenues on initial units sold so that it can cover costs while producing the socially optimal output. And in this case, utility customers would pay the full cost of production, eliminating the need for subsidies from general tax revenues.

---

[12]For further discussion see Section 12.7.3 on peak-load pricing.

[13]Under third-degree discrimination, total output can be less than in the absence of discrimination.

12.6 REGULATION OF NATURAL MONOPOLIES IN PRACTICE

In the previous sections we discussed the marginal cost pricing and average cost pricing approaches to the regulation of natural monopolies. To implement the marginal cost pricing approach one needs a complete knowledge of the cost conditions as well as the demand conditions. In practice, regulators do not have complete knowledge of cost and demand conditions, and hence they use the average cost pricing approach by focusing on the rate of return on invested capital. We will discuss this approach with reference to the case of electric utilities.

The state public utility commissions, which approve the prices that the utilities can charge, allow the utilities to cover their variable costs of production and earn a fair rate of return on invested capital, which is called the "rate base." If the realized rate of return is higher than this "fair" rate or "normal" rate, then the argument goes that price must be higher than average cost, and this is a signal for the regulators to reduce the price. Conversely, if the realized rate is below the normal rate, then this is a signal for the regulators to increase the price.

What is the fair or normal rate of return? This is supposed to be the cost of capital (the rate at which capital can be borrowed from various sources) which has been estimated in recent years to be between 10 and 14 percent. There is a considerable amount of controversy as to how to measure this cost of capital. There is an extensive literature in this area as well as a wide range of estimates.[14] Once the overall rate of return is determined, the electric utility is allowed to price-discriminate. It will typically charge different rates to residential, commercial, and industrial customers, as well as different rates for different units to the same customer. The unit price per kwh is likely to be higher for residential customers than for industrial customers because the industrial customers can more easily switch to alternative competing fuels.

There are several problems with this approach to utility regulation. The utilities have no incentive to hold down costs. If costs rise, the regulators permit a higher price to cover these costs. Since all variable costs are covered, the managers of utilities have an incentive to increase the variable costs by having expense accounts, payment of higher-than-necessary wages, and so on.

Since the rate structure is based on an allowed rate of return on invested capital or the so-called rate base, one way the utility can increase its profits is to increase the amount of its capital stock or the size of the rate base. This tendency will be more pronounced if the allowed rate of return exceeds the actual cost at which the utility can borrow additional funds. This tendency for utilities to "overcapitalize" is called the *Averch-Johnson effect*.[15] As a consequence of this type of rate regulation, electric utilities would be inclined to carry more reserve capacity than is needed and to invest in more capital intensive methods of production such as nuclear plants instead of fossil fuel plants.

---

[14]There is the problem of how to compute the cost of equity capital and debt capital and how to weigh the two. A survey of this literature can be found in F. D. Arditti. "A Survey of the Empirical Research on the Cost of Capital to Electric Utilities," in H. Levy, ed., *Research in Finance*, JAI Press, Greenwich, Conn., 1980.

[15]This was pointed out in H. Averch and L. L. Johnson. "Behavior of the Firm under Regulatory Constraint," *American Economic Review*, December 1962, pp. 1053–1069. Since then there has been an extensive literature on the existence or nonexistence of the Averch-Johnson effect and on measurement of its magnitude.

At the same time, there will be a tendency for the natural monopoly to suppress or slow down the introduction of technological innovations. This follows automatically from the results we observed that a natural monopoly regulated by the rate of return has few incentives to cut costs, and technological innovations do cut costs. A good example of this is the slowness with which AT&T introduced automated switching equipment. Although this equipment was introduced in the 1920s and several advances took place over time, it was not until the mid-1970s that AT&T completely shifted to the new system. Several other advances in digital technology have also been introduced only very slowly. The introduction of new products and new services will also be slow under the present system of regulation where the monopoly does not get the rewards from the introduction of these products and services.

Alternative solutions to these problems are to have unregulated monopolies or direct government ownership. In several foreign countries, many of the natural monopolies—utilities, railroads, and so on—are operated by governments. Some are run efficiently, some are not. Thus, the evidence is rather mixed. As for the difference between regulated and unregulated utilities, Stigler and Friedland compared electric rates in regulated and unregulated states between 1912 and 1937 and found that there was very little difference in the rates charged.[16]

12.7 APPLICATIONS

Regulation is a form of market intervention designed to adjust the monopoly outcome and improve social welfare. In this section we will look at the impact of two types of intervention in the international market and their effect on the behavior of a monopoly. In the first application, we discuss the use of an import fee to counter the behavior of a foreign monopoly, OPEC. As we will see, this measure primarily attacks the equity problem associated with monopoly, since output is only minimally affected. The second application examines the impact of trade restrictions on the behavior of a domestic monopoly. The third application we discuss is that of peak-load pricing, where discriminatory pricing leads to increased efficiency.

12.7.1 Import fee on oil

On January 1, 1973, the price of oil was about $2 a barrel. By the end of 1973, after the Arab oil embargo, the price rose to about $12 a barrel—a sixfold increase. By mid-1980, following the Iran-Iraq war, the price rose to about $40 a barrel (a twentyfold increase in 7 years). Since then the oil price has fallen, but the enormous increase in the price of oil has resulted in large income transfers from the oil consuming nations to OPEC (Organization of Petroleum Exporting Countries).

We will discuss the effect of import fees imposed by oil-consuming nations on these income transfers. Let us assume that OPEC behaves like a monopolist equating

[16]George Stigler and Clair Friedland, "What Can Regulators Regulate? The Case of Electricity," *Journal of Law and Economics*, October 1962, pp. 1–16.

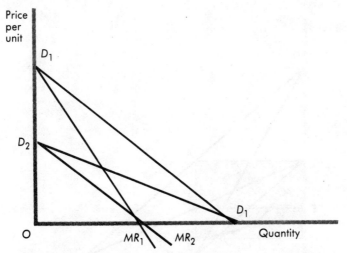

FIGURE 12.12   Effect of an import fee on the demand curve for imports.

MC to *MR*. Figure 12.12 shows the effect of a 50 percent import fee on the demand for imports. In Figure 12.12, D_1D_1 is the demand curve for imports by the oil-consuming nations, and MR_1 is the corresponding marginal revenue curve for OPEC. With an import fee of 50 percent, the demand curve swings to D_2D_1 where D_2 is the midpoint of OD_1 on the vertical scale. The points on the demand curve D_1D_1 show the prices that consumers are willing to pay for different quantities. The points on the demand curve D_2D_1 show the prices that OPEC receives for different quantities. If the import fee were 25 percent, OD_2 would be three-fourths of OD_1 on the vertical scale, and if the import fee were 75 percent, OD_2 would be one-fourth of OD_1 on the vertical scale.

Marginal costs for oil production are very low. So to analyze the effects of the import fee on OPEC's output, we will assume them to be 0. In this case, the *MR* curves with or without the import fee both intersect the *MC* curve at the same point. Thus, output does not change. The only thing that changes is the price OPEC receives and the profit it makes. This is shown in Figure 12.13. Without import fees the profit OPEC makes is given by the entire shaded area D_2ABC. With the import fee these profits are reduced to the cross-hatched area *EFBC*. The governments of the oil-importing nations collect D_2AFE as revenues. In fact, in the case of zero marginal costs, by increasing the import fee to a high enough percentage, one can actually eliminate OPEC's profits. As the import fee is raised, the demand curve D_2D_1 swings toward the horizontal axis, and the price OPEC receives falls. Finally, when the demand curve D_2D_1 passes through the point *B*, the price OPEC gets is exactly equal to its average cost of production, and OPEC's profits are completely eliminated.

This analysis, of course, depends on the assumption of zero marginal costs of production. This may be an unreasonable assumption since marginal costs, although negligible for Saudi Arabia and other Gulf states, are not negligible for

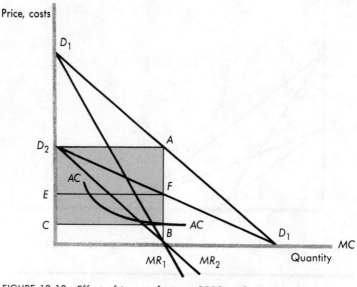

FIGURE 12.13   Effect of import fees on OPEC profits.

other OPEC members. In this case the effect of the import fee would be to curtail output. Consider, for instance, the case where marginal costs are constant but not negligible.

In Figure 12.14 the marginal revenue curve with no import fee is labelled 1 and the marginal revenue curves for higher and higher levels of import fees are labeled 2, 3, 4, respectively. The corresponding quantities are X_1, X_2, X_3, X_4. Thus, the quantity imported decreases when the import fee is raised.

FIGURE 12.14   Effect of higher import fees on OPEC output.

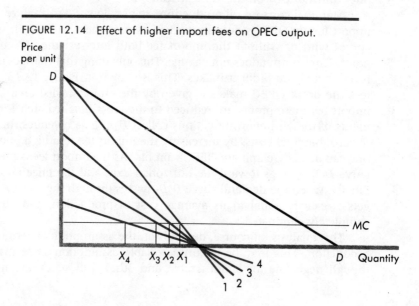

12.7.2 Effects of tariffs and import quotas under competition and monopoly

Under perfect competition, an import tariff or an import quota normally increases domestic production and thus employment. We will show that this need not be the case with monopoly and thus, workers in a monopolized industry may oppose tariffs and quotas.

First, let us again consider the case of perfect competition. In Figure 12.15, DD is the domestic demand curve and SS the domestic supply curve. P_f is the foreign or world price at which world supply is perfectly elastic. Without any import tariffs, the domestic price is also equal to P_f. Hence, domestic quantity supplied is Q_1, but domestic quantity demanded is Q_4. The difference $Q_4 - Q_1$ is made up by imports. If a tariff T is imposed, the domestic price level rises to $P_f + T$, domestic quantity supplied rises to Q_2, and domestic quantity demanded falls to Q_3. Thus, imports decline to $Q_3 - Q_2$. Since domestic production rises to Q_2, domestic employment will also rise, and workers benefit from the tariff.

The effect of import quotas is similar to that of tariffs under perfect competition. In Figure 12.15 the effect of an import quota of $Q_3 - Q_2$ on domestic production and domestic price is the same as that of an import tariff T. The imports will be $Q_3 - Q_2$, domestic production will be Q_2, and domestic price will be $P_f + T$. The government would have to issue import licenses in the amount $Q_3 - Q_2$. If these are issued at random, the lucky importers who obtain the import licenses will reap the benefit $(Q_3 - Q_2)T$. However, if the government auctions the import licenses then it will get revenues of $(Q_3 - Q_2)T$, the same amount as with the imposition of the tariff. The welfare cost of import quotas will then be the same as under tariffs. Also, as we increase the level of the tariff or decrease the size of the import quota, domestic production and employment increase.

Under monopoly the situation is different. The monopolist tries to equate marginal revenue with marginal cost. The situation is shown in Figure 12.16. DD is the domestic demand curve. MR is the corresponding marginal revenue curve. $LRMC$ is the marginal cost curve and $LRAC$ the long-run average cost curve. P_f is the foreign price. P_1 is the price corresponding to the minimum point of the average

FIGURE 12.15 Effects of tariffs under perfect competition.

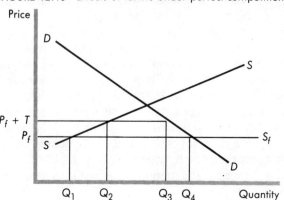

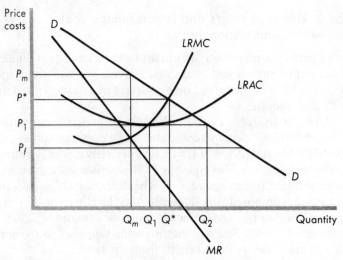

FIGURE 12.16   Effects of tariffs under monopoly.

cost curve. P^* is the price where the $LRMC$ curve intersects the demand curve DD. Finally, Q_m is the output where $MR = LRMC$ and P_m is the corresponding price. This is the price the monopolist charges in the absence of any pressure from imports.

If the market price is less than P_1 the monopolist produces nothing. Thus, the minimum tariff level needed for domestic production is $P_1 - P_f$. If the tariff level is less than this, there is no domestic production. All the domestic demand is met by imports. With the tariff at $P_1 - P_f$, domestic price is P_1, domestic production is Q_1, domestic quantity demanded is Q_2, and imports are $Q_2 - Q_1$. Now as the tariff level rises the monopolist moves up the marginal cost curve, domestic production increases, domestic quantity demanded decreases, and imports fall. Finally, at the tariff level $P^* - P_f$, domestic production and domestic quantity demanded are both Q^*, and there are no imports. If the tariff level is raised further, the monopolist takes advantage of this protection offered and cuts production. Eventually, if the tariff reaches $P_m - P_f$ or higher, the monopolist charges the monopoly price P_m and produces output Q_m. Thus, in the case of monopoly an increase in the tariff rate can actually result in a decline in output (and employment).

The effects of import quotas under monopoly are also similar to those of tariffs. In Figure 12.16, the maximum number of imports that can be permitted is $Q_2 - Q_1$. For import levels higher than that there will be no domestic production. For any other levels of the import quota, the domestic price will rise to the corresponding point between P_1 and P^*. To find the market price, all we have to do is measure a horizontal distance equal to the import quota between the $LRMC$ curve and the demand curve. This is shown in Figure 12.17. Let the import quota be q. We then measure a horizontal distance equal to q between the marginal cost curve and the demand curve. This gives us the market price as P_2. Q_2 is the domestic monopolist's output. $Q_3 - Q_2 = q$ gives imports. Q_3 is the total quantity demanded. In the figure we also show again the price P_1 where $LRMC = LRAC$ (the minimum point on the $LRAC$ curve). At that price the monopoly output is Q_1, domestic demand is Q_4, and

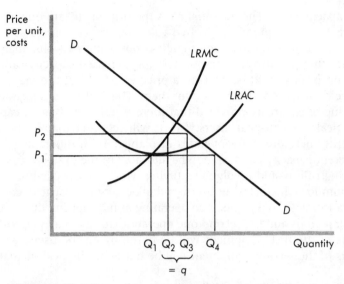

FIGURE 12.17 Effects of import quotas under monopoly.

imports are $Q_4 - Q_1$. This is the maximum level of quota one can set if any domestic production is to occur.[17]

12.7.3 Peak-load pricing

Peak-load pricing is a form of price discrimination in which the firm charges a higher price for peak use than for off-peak use. Telephone companies have followed this practice for a long time. The charge during the day is higher than during the night or on weekends. Peak-load pricing has also been extensively discussed in the case of pricing electricity.[18] Actually, the idea of peak-load pricing need not be confined to the case of large public enterprises such as public utilities and telephones. The principles of peak-load pricing are, in fact, equally applicable to such private enterprises as hotels, restaurants, health clubs, airlines, theaters, and to some degree most retail establishments.[19] In fact, we do observe theaters charging a lower rate for shows before 6 p.m., hotels charging low off-season rates, restaurants charging a lower price for basically the same meal at lunch than at dinner, airlines offering off-season low rates, and so on.

In all these cases the demand for the service fluctuates predictably during the peak and off-peak periods. The demands have different elasticities, and furthermore there are cost differences between the two periods. Any expansion in the output during the peak period can be done only if the firm builds sufficient capacity. A telephone company has to add more lines to accommodate higher peak demand. A hotel should have sufficient rooms to accommodate the rush at peak demand. During off-peak periods, however, the output can be expanded with no increase

[17]$Q_2 - Q_1$ in Figure 12.16 equals $Q_4 - Q_1$ in Figure 12.17.

[18]See the symposium on peak-load pricing in *Bell Journal of Economics*, Spring 1976, pp. 197–206.

[19]See Thomas Nagle, "Economic Foundations for Pricing," *Journal of Business*, 1984, pp. 5–20.

in capacity costs. The marginal costs the firm incurs are only operating costs. This leads to the frequently suggested rule that the customers at the peak should be charged a price equal to the marginal operating cost plus marginal capacity cost (since they are the ones responsible for increased capacity) and the customers at the off-peak should be charged a price equal to just the marginal operating cost, since capacity is a "free" good for them. This is the rule suggested by Kahn for the pricing of electricity provided that there is only one type of capacity serving both the peak and off-peak users.[20] (We will see later that in the case of electricity, usually there are different kinds of plants.) With different types of capacity, the different capacity costs have to be allocated to the different customers. The proper pricing rule would involve identifying which capacity is not a free good in equilibrium for which class of users, and allocating the capacity costs accordingly. For instance, with two plants, one operating at full capacity during both peak and off-peak periods and the second one operating during peak periods only, the capacity costs of the first equipment will be borne by all the users, whereas the capacity costs of the second equipment will be borne by the peak-demand users only.

EXAMPLE 12.1 Pricing of Electricity

An example of price discrimination in different forms is the pricing of electricity. Demand for electricity fluctuates seasonally, with heavy demand in midsummer if it is used for cooling (air-conditioning) and heavy demand in midwinter if it is used for heating. It also fluctuates between weekdays and weekends (many production facilities are closed on weekends) and even during different hours of the day (with a low around say 4 a.m. and peak during the day). Twice as many kilowatt hours may be required at the daytime peak as at the night-time trough. Such variation occurs in almost every country in the world.

Electricity is costly to store and therefore must be produced as it is used. To avoid blackouts, a power system must have enough capacity to satisfy the peak demand. However, different power plants have different cost structures. A large nuclear or coal-fired plant has low fuel costs but high capital costs. This plant is justified if it can operate most hours of the year. A small turbine plant has high fuel costs but low capital costs, and these are used only for a few hours at a time and for only a fraction of the year to satisfy peak demands. Some utilities also have pumped storage plants. Water is pumped up to a reservoir during off-peak hours using low-cost electricity. It is then used during peak-hours to run hydroelectric plants. Only about three-quarters of the electricity used in pumping the water up is recovered when the water flows down. However, this can be more economical than other methods of generating electricity during peak hours. Yet another way of satisfying peak demand is by purchasing electricity from another utility. This is expensive because it must be transmitted over long distances. Thus, supply of electric power comes from the following sources:

1. Primary generators: These are large coal-fired and nuclear-powered steam

---

[20]A. E. Kahn, *The Economics of Regulation*, vol. 1, Wiley, New York, 1970, pp. 89–103. Kahn also suggested that if, at a price equal to the short-run marginal cost, the capacity is fully utilized during the off-peak period, then the off-peak users should also bear some of the marginal capacity costs because the capacity is not a free good to them either.

generators. They spin constantly because they are too costly to stop and start. They can generate electricity at low marginal cost.

2. Secondary generators: These are smaller steam generators or jet turbines (and hydro plants) that can be started and stopped at short notice. Their marginal costs are higher than for primary generators.

3. Borrowed electricity: The marginal costs of borrowed electricity are generally higher than for secondary generators.

Thus, the marginal cost of producing electricity is much greater during peak periods than during off-peak periods. Unless demand for electricity is perfectly inelastic during both the periods, gains in economic efficiency are possible by charging different prices for electricity during the peak and off-peak periods.

Peak-load pricing for electricity is not used much in the United States, although peak-load pricing has been in use for a long time in the case of telephones and it is also used by airlines, restaurants, hotels, theaters, and even retailers. What is common is second- and third-degree price discrimination in the form of *declining block pricing* and charging different rates to residential, commercial, and industrial customers (see price discrimination in Section 12.5).

In France, however, Electricité de France adopted peak-load pricing in 1958 for nonresidential customers. The rates vary by season, day of week, and hour of day. There are three rates: base, shoulder, and peak. The shoulder rates are almost twice the base rates, and the peak rates are about 66 percent above the shoulder rates. In addition, the high voltage customers have to pay a maximum demand charge which is over 14 times the charge for the base period. Thus the rate differences are high, and this creates powerful incentives to vary the use by time of day. The French industry has responded by scheduling many production operations accordingly. Such vast differences in time-of-day rates require costly metering equipment but with the progress in computer technology this is not a big problem. One can schedule the whole operation by a computer. It is for households that the metering costs are still high, and, moreover, it is so difficult to vary household operations by time of day. Thus peak-load pricing is probably less feasible for households (peak-load pricing is currently used on an experimental basis for residential customers in North Carolina).

12.8   SUMMARY AND CONCLUSIONS

The Lerner index of monopoly power is equal to $(P - MC)/P$ or $1/\eta$. A higher Lerner index indicates greater monopoly power. The ability to price-discriminate indicates monopoly power. Furthermore, if we know one elasticity and the prices charged, we can determine the second elasticity.

Monopoly is frequently associated with above-normal profits. Thus, in theory, we can infer the amount of monopoly power by comparing a firm's actual profit rate with the average or normal profit rate. In practice, it is extremely difficult to determine the extent of monopoly from a comparison of accounting profit rates.

Concentration ratios measure the size of the largest firms' share in total industry sales, profits, or assets. The idea is that a large concentration ratio indicates the presence of firms which are large relative to the market and, hence, have some monopoly power. A concentration curve illustrates the entire size distribution of firms.

The Herfindahl index is equal to the sum of the squared market shares for all firms in the industry. If firms are equal in size then $HI = 1/n$ where n is the number of firms. Otherwise, $HI > 1/n$. This index reflects both the sizes and number of firms. A larger HI is interpreted as indicative of more monopoly power.

By imposing a price ceiling at the level where the MC curve intersects the demand curve, regulators can induce the monopolist to produce the competitive output.

Lump-sum taxes do not affect the position of the monopolist's MC curve and, hence, do not affect his output. They merely redistribute income from the monopolist to the government. A per-unit tax shifts the monopolist's marginal cost curve upward, thus reducing output and increasing price.

There are three basic pieces of antitrust legislation—the Sherman Act, the Clayton Act, and the FTC Act—designed to limit the acquisition of monopoly power and to restrict the behavior of firms with monopoly power. These laws have been repeatedly amended.

Average cost pricing means that both price and quantity correspond to the point where the AC curve intersects the demand curve. If $MC > AC$ at this point, then the welfare cost of unregulated monopoly can be larger or smaller than the welfare cost from average cost pricing. But with natural monopoly, average cost pricing reduces welfare loss in comparison to unregulated monopoly. Under natural monopoly, marginal cost pricing results in losses to the firm. It is also difficult to implement marginal cost pricing, especially when investment must be lumpy. Average cost pricing will induce the natural monopolist to expand output, thus, reducing the social cost of monopoly.

By allowing natural monopolies to price-discriminate, we can induce them to expand output and reduce the welfare cost of monopoly.

In practice, regulators use the average cost pricing approach for natural monopolies. Electric utilities generally have restrictions on the rate of return they are allowed to earn.

When marginal costs are negligible, an import fee can reduce the foreign monopolist's profit with little impact on output. The reduction in profit is transferred to the importing government. Increasing a per-unit tariff may induce the domestic monopolist to increase or decrease output and, hence, employment.

KEY TERMS

Antitrust Laws	Concentration Ratio	Lerner Index
Average Cost Pricing	Federal Trade Commission Act	Marginal Cost Pricing
Averch-Johnson Effect	Herfindahl Index	Sherman Act
Clayton Act	Import Fee	Trust
Concentration Curve		

QUESTIONS

1. Explain the advantages of the Herfindahl index over a four-firm or eight-firm concentration ratio.

2. As a new firm enters an industry, what happens to the Herfindahl index? Can we make a general statement?

3. We said that a lump-sum tax does not affect the output of the monopolist (unless it is high enough to induce exit), and, hence, the welfare cost of monopoly is unchanged. How would the analysis differ if the monopoly engages in rent-seeking activities?

4. Can a concentration curve ever be downward sloping? Can it ever be convex to the origin? Why?

5. Demonstrate graphically that the welfare cost of average cost pricing can exceed the welfare cost of monopoly pricing.

6. Over time a firm may lose its natural monopoly status. What factors could bring this about?

7. In Figure 12.16, choose a tariff between $P^* - P_f$ and $P_m - P_f$. Indicate the monopolist's marginal revenue curve and the profit-maximizing output under this tariff.

8. What is the impact of an import fee on domestic output and price? Does your answer depend on the market structure of the domestic industry?

9. For a natural monopolist:

   a. MC is less than MR

   b. MC is less than AC

   c. Price is constant

   d. $MC = AR$

   Explain your choice.

10. What is the "efficiency dilemma" when there is a natural monopoly?

CHAPTER 13

PRICING IN PRODUCT MARKETS: MONOPOLISTIC COMPETITION AND OLIGOPOLY

13.1   INTRODUCTION

We have now examined in detail the two extreme market structures: monopoly and perfect competition. In reality, most industries lie in the gray area between the two extremes. In this chapter we will look at two such intermediate industrial structures.

1. Monopolistic competition is characterized by a large number of firms, each of which has a little market power because it offers a differentiated product. Yet all the firms are in competition because their products are close substitutes. Examples are the retail clothing, hair styling, and restaurant industries.

2. Oligopoly consists of a few firms which dominate the industry and among whom there is frequently intense rivalry. Examples are automobile manufacturing and cigarette production.

In some sense it can be argued that monopolistic competition is closer to the extreme of perfect competition, whereas oligopoly is closer to monopoly.[1] As we will see, there are no barriers to entry under monopolistic competition and, hence, there are no economic profits in the long run. Also, monopolistically competitive firms behave independently with competition taking the impersonal form characteristic of perfect competition. Under oligopoly, however, there is intense personal rivalry. Also, barriers to entry are present which allow for long-run profit, as in the case of monopoly.

13.2   PRICING UNDER MONOPOLISTIC COMPETITION

Monopoly and perfect competition are really two extremes, and many industries fall in between. There are very few pure monopolies, since there are very few commodities for which close substitutes do not exist. Similarly, there are very few commodities that are entirely homogeneous to make the assumption of perfect competition realistic. There is, thus, a large grey area between these two extremes. Although the French economist Cournot pointed this out in 1838, it was in the early 1930s that economists began turning their attention to this middle ground between monopoly and perfect competition.

In 1933, Edwin H. Chamberlain of Harvard University published his book: *The Theory of Monopolistic Competition: A Re-Orientation of the Theory of Value*. It was received very enthusiastically, and many economists talked of the "Chamberlainian revolution." In the same year, but 6 months later, Joan Robinson of Cambridge University in England published a similar book: *The Economics of Imperfect Competition*. Chamberlain spent a lot of his time later differentiating his product from that of Joan Robinson.[2] Although there are similarities in the books, there are major

---

[1]An elaboration of the parallel between monopolistic and perfect competition can be found in Harold Demsetz, "Do Competition and Monopolistic Competition Differ?" *Journal of Political Economy*, February 1968, pp. 146–148.

[2]Joan Robinson is said to have remarked: "I'm sorry I ruined his life."

differences as well. For instance, Chamberlain treated at length product differentiation and advertising, which were neglected by Joan Robinson. Joan Robinson discussed problems such as price discrimination and monopolistic and monopsonistic exploitation not covered by Chamberlain.

We shall start our discussion by defining monopolistic competition. Monopolistic competition is said to exist when there are many firms, as in perfect competition, but each firm produces a product that is slightly differentiated from that of others. Examples of this are numerous: retail clothing stores, restaurants, barber shops, dry cleaners, and so on. There are several distinguishing characteristics of monopolistic competition:

1. *Product differentiation:* Products are heterogeneous rather than homogeneous. However, products are only slightly differentiated. The output of one firm is a close (but not perfect) substitute for the outputs of other firms. Differentiation grants each firm some monopoly power, whereas the presence of close substitutes provides competition.

There are many sources of differentiation. Some of these are: chemical composition, advertising, packaging, brand names, location, and design. The products do not have to be physically different. They must simply be perceived as somewhat different by consumers.

2. *Nonprice competition:* Since the products are only slightly differentiated the different firms try to play up the difference in their products in order to increase their demand. They do this in a variety of ways such as advertising the differences or adding some frills (free car wash with gas fill up).

3. *Large number of firms and freedom of entry and exit:* In monopolistic competition, as in perfect competition, there is a large number of firms and there is the same freedom of entry and exit. When firms in an industry are making a profit, new firms enter the industry with slightly differentiated products and drive profits down. Thus, in the long run, no firm is able to make an above-normal profit.

4. *Independent behavior:* The economic impact of one firm's decisions is spread sufficiently evenly across the entire group so that the effect on any single competitor goes unnoticed. This implies that conscious rivalry is missing or that competition is impersonal. Each firm behaves independently.

The term "monopolistic" refers to the small monopoly power that firms have by virtue of their differentiated product. The term "competition" implies that there is a large number of firms and there is freedom of entry and exit so that firms cannot make above-normal profits in the long run. Because of the monopolistic component the demand curve facing each firm is downward sloping. Each firm has some control over the price of its product.

The firm's demand curve

The concept of an industry is somewhat nebulous when differentiated products are concerned, and we will discuss this problem later. Chamberlain instead talked of a product group made up of all the products that are close substitutes. We can then talk of the total or product group demand curve. Such a demand curve is a typical downward-sloping curve. In Figure 13.1 the group demand curve is D_g.

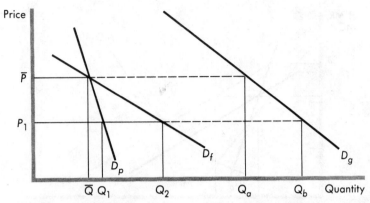

FIGURE 13.1 The group demand curve, proportionate demand curve, and perceived demand curve under monopolistic competition.

The group demand must somehow be divided up among the members of the group. Chamberlain assumed that all firms in the group are roughly identical so that they face similar cost and demand conditions. Thus, if all firms charge the same price, they will have identical market shares. In Figure 13.1, the curve D_p is the proportionate demand curve, or the demand curve facing a particular firm when all firms charge the same price. It is obtained by horizontally dividing the group demand curve by the number of firms. D_p is clearly a short-run curve, since we hold the number of firms constant when constructing it.

The firm, however, does not perceive D_p to be its demand curve. If the current price and quantity are $\overline{P}$ and $\overline{Q}$, then the firm perceives its demand curve to be D_f in Figure 13.1. D_f is more elastic than D_p. It is the demand curve facing the firm if all other firms continue to charge $\overline{P}$. The perceived demand curve is more elastic than the proportionate curve because if only one firm reduces price, then that firm can capture sales and market share from other firms. Similarly, if only one firm increases price, it will lose customers and market share to other firms. For example, in Figure 13.1, if one firm alone reduces price from $\overline{P}$ to P_1, then its sales will increase from $\overline{Q}$ to Q_2. But if all firms reduce price to P_1, then each firm's sales increase only to Q_1. Why do sales increase at all when every firm reduces price? Because the group demand curve is downward sloping. $Q_1 - \overline{Q}$ is simply $Q_b - Q_a$ divided by the number of firms. In other words, when all firms act together, market shares do not change.

Why does the individual firm perceive its demand curve to be D_f? Because under monopolistic competition there is a large enough number of firms that each firm believes its actions will go unnoticed. Each monopolistically competitive firm behaves independently, so each believes that it can adjust price without other firms following its lead.

Short-run equilibrium

Consider Figure 13.2, where D_p and D_f are as previously defined, MC is the firm's marginal cost curve, and MR_f is the marginal revenue curve corresponding to the firm's perceived demand curve. Suppose that momentarily all firms are charging

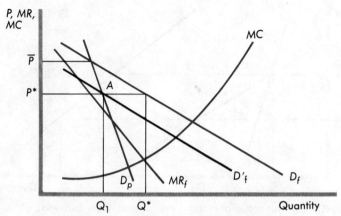

FIGURE 13.2   Short-run adjustment under monopolistic competition.

$\overline{P}$. The firm, believing its marginal revenue curve to be MR_f, has an incentive to expand output to Q^* and reduce price to P^*.

But since all firms are identical, each firm will attempt to increase output to Q^* and charge a price of P^*. Yet if all firms charge P^*, then each firm can only sell Q_1. With price equal to P^* and each firm producing Q^*, the market won't clear. There will be a surplus.

As each firm realizes that it can sell only Q_1 at a price of P^*, its perceptions of demand change. The perceived demand curve shifts to intersect D_p at the point A. The firm's new perceived demand curve is D'_f and indicates the quantities that the individual firm can sell at various prices if all other firms continue to charge P^*. Corresponding to D'_f is a new perceived marginal revenue curve. The firm will equate the new perceived marginal revenue with marginal cost and adjust output accordingly. But once again, all firms adjust output and price, each firm's perceptions change, and so on until an equilibrium point is reached.

Short-run equilibrium for the monopolistically competitive firm is illustrated in Figure 13.3. In equilibrium, each firm produces Q_e and charges a price of P_e. Each firm perceives that it is maximizing profit because $MR_f = MC$. And finally, the market clears because the point (Q_e, P_e) lies on the firm's proportionate demand curve.

Long-run equilibrium

Under monopolistic competition there are no barriers to entry or exit in the long run. In Figure 13.3, the firms are earning an economic profit in short-run equilibrium. The amount of the individual firm's profit is the shaded rectangle. (We could have instead illustrated a short-run equilibrium with losses incurred.) The profit will induce new firms to enter this product group. (Losses would, of course, induce exit.)

As new firms enter, each firm's proportionate demand curve shifts to the left and becomes more steep. This is because the overall product group demand must be divided among a larger number of firms. (Exit would cause D_p to shift rightward for the remaining firms.) Firms now find that they are unable to sell Q_e at a price

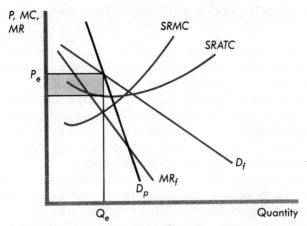

FIGURE 13.3   Short-run equilibrium under monopolistic competition.

of P_e. Firms will continue to enter, causing all firms to adjust output and price until an equilibrium with no economic profits or losses is reached.

A long-run equilibrium situation is illustrated in Figure 13.4. Each firm perceives that it is maximizing its profit so that there is no incentive to adjust output. But each firm is just covering its full economic cost so that there is no incentive to enter or exit. And finally, because (Q_e, P_e) lies on the proportionate demand curve, the market clears.

The long-run equilibrium position has aspects of both monopoly and perfect competition. There are no economic profits, which is characteristic of perfect competition. But $MR < P$, which is characteristic of monopoly. One should also note that the firms maximize only their perceived profit. Actual profits are not maximized as this would require that $MR_p = MC$.

FIGURE 13.4   Long-run equilibrium under monopolistic competition.

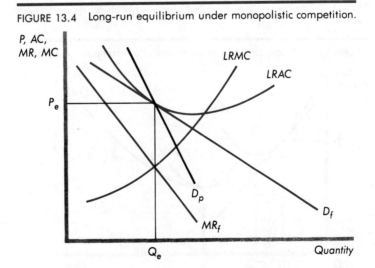

13.3 EXCESS CAPACITY UNDER MONOPOLISTIC COMPETITION

As shown in Figure 13.4, the long-run equilibrium for the firm under monopolistic competition is at the point where the perceived demand curve is tangent to the *LRAC* curve. Since the demand curve is downward sloping, the *LRAC* curve also has to be downward sloping at this point. Thus, unlike perfect competition, the firm's equilibrium will never be at the minimum point of the *LRAC* curve. Hence, it is argued that the firm's output under monopolistic competition is not the ideal output and that, because of excess capacity, there is a wasteful use of society's resources. Production costs are higher than necessary.

Ideal output is that output which is associated with the minimum point of the *LRAC* curve. *Excess capacity* is the difference between ideal output and the output actually attained by the firm in long-run equilibrium.

As argued by Cassels, the excess capacity under monopolistic competition can be divided into two parts.[3] This is shown in Figure 13.5; OQ_E is the long-run equilibrium output. OQ_I is the ideal output, the output corresponding to the minimum point of the *LRAC* curve. $SRAC_1$ is the short-run average cost curve corresponding to the optimal plant for output OQ_E, and $SRAC_2$ is the short-run average cost curve corresponding to the optimal plant for output OQ_I. OQ_M is the output corresponding to the minimum point of $SRAC_1$.

The excess capacity $Q_E Q_I$ can be decomposed into two parts:

1. $Q_M Q_I$ due to not building the technically optimal scale of plant (being on $SRAC_1$ instead of $SRAC_2$)

2. $Q_E Q_M$ due to not operating the plant built at the point of minimum average cost

Chamberlain, however, argues against treating the higher production cost due to excess capacity as a social loss, contending that product differentiation is not

[3]John M. Cassels, "Excess Capacity and Monopolistic Competition," *The Quarterly Journal of Economics*, May 1937, pp. 426–433.

FIGURE 13.5 Excess capacity under monopolistic competition.

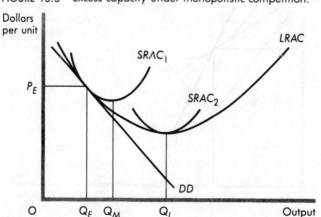

worthless. People may be willing to pay for this differentiation and variety in the form of excess capacity. Thus, the ideal output is not necessarily the one given by the minimum point of the *LRAC* curve. Of course, excessive proliferation of products of different quality is a waste of society's resources, but the cost of boredom produced by having uniform products has to be taken into account as well.

13.4   MONOPOLISTIC COMPETITION AND ADVERTISING

An essential characteristic of monopolistic competition is product differentiation. In order that consumers be informed about the differences in its product, a firm needs to advertise its product. However, there is informative advertising and persuasive advertising. Advertising, particularly in newspapers which also quote prices, has certain advantages. It saves consumers the costs of searching and shopping. However, much of television and radio advertising is geared to differentiating the product and developing brand loyalty.

The Federal Trade Commission (FTC) is empowered to prohibit unfair methods of competition and unfair acts or practices. Advertisers must be able to substantiate any claims made in their advertisements. For example, in 1977, the FTC ordered Warner-Lambert to stop making claims that its oral antiseptic Listerine could prevent or cure colds. In addition, Warner-Lambert was required to run corrective advertising stating that "contrary to prior advertising, Listerine will not help prevent colds or sore throats or lessen their severity." The FTC also requires firms to state in their advertising that sale items are actually available in their stores. Otherwise, firms can attract customers with advertisements for one product and then encourage them to buy another product. This kind of sales tactic is known as "bait and switch." The FTC encourages comparative advertising—advertising that compares the product of one firm with the products of competing firms.

In addition to curbing misleading advertising, the FTC is empowered to promote informational advertising. In 1978 it ruled that states and professional organizations could no longer ban advertisements for contact lenses, eye glasses, and eye examinations. It also ruled that it is illegal for the American Medical Association to restrict advertising by doctors. The aim of these regulations is to provide information for consumers about prices charged for different medical services.

Advertising expenditures in the United States are about 2 percent of GNP. Some economists believe that the benefit is much higher than this amount because of the increased information provided to consumers who save the cost of searching and shopping. Others, like Galbraith, argue that advertising promotes "contrived obsolescence" and a wasteful use of resources. Often the firms, by their advertising, mold the tastes of consumers so that the firms determine which products the consumers will buy. Thus, Galbraith attacks advertising as a violation of consumer sovereignty.[4]

Recent years have seen a growth in comparative advertising. In 1983, it accounted for over 35 percent of all television commercials. However, this sort of

---

[4]John Kenneth Galbraith, *The Affluent Society*, Houghton-Mifflin, Boston, 1958.

advertising has brought several lawsuits as well. The following are two of numerous examples of comparative advertisements being contested:

1. Carnation promoted its New Breed dog food as better than all brands. When a smaller competitor demonstrated that dogs find its product more savory than New Breed, Carnation was forced to modify its advertisements. Carnation changed its advertisement saying that New Breed is the best of all "leading brands."

2. Eastern Airlines' advertisement claiming to be "America's favorite way to fly" irritated American Airlines, which submitted evidence to show that Eastern is actually America's least favorite way to fly. But when Eastern came back with independent surveys and figures which showed that Eastern carried more passengers than other airlines, American Airlines' claim was denied.

What is the effect of advertising on prices charged to the consumer? Advertising increases costs, but it also shifts the demand curve. The net effect could be a fall or a rise in price, and since we are considering two different demand curves it could also mean a fall or rise in quantity. In Figure 13.6 we show a case of a decrease in price and an increase in quantity. In Figure 13.7 we show a case of an increase in price and an increase in quantity.[5] In both figures, the definition of variables is as follows:

	Without Advertising	With Advertising
Average total cost	ATC_1	ATC_2
Demand curve	DD_1	DD_2
Equilibrium point	A_1	A_2
Price	P_1	P_2
Quantity	Q_1	Q_2

[5]One can draw another diagram to show an increase in price and a decrease in quantity as well.

FIGURE 13.6 Effects of advertising on price and output (a decrease in price and an increase in quantity).

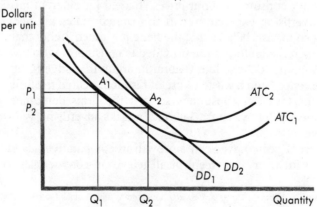

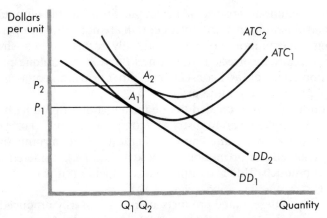

FIGURE 13.7 Effects of advertising on price and output (an increase in price and an increase in quantity).

The preceding analysis, however, is very simplistic and ignores one important aspect of advertising in real life, namely its role when consumers are uncertain about the quality of the product they purchase. Klein and Leffler argue that in practice advertising does increase the price, but consumers necessarily receive something when they pay a higher price for an advertised brand.[6] Firms making heavy expenditures on advertisement have to make sure that they maintain high-quality production. A sufficient investment in advertising implies that a firm will not engage in short-run quality deception, since the advertising expenditures produce a non-salvageable cost gap between price and production cost. Consumers are, therefore, assured of high quality even if they pay a higher price. This is the case with products whose quality is costly to determine before purchase. According to Klein and Leffler, it is not that it pays a firm with a "best buy" to advertise more, but rather that advertising implies the supply of "best buys" or more correctly the supply of promised high-quality products.[7]

13.5 CRITICISM OF THE THEORY OF MONOPOLISTIC COMPETITION

As mentioned earlier, the model of monopolistic competition was received very enthusiastically in the 1930s, and many economists talked of the "Chamberlainian revolution." Yet, despite its almost instant success, it later generated a lot of criticism and controversy. The attacks on this model were numerous; we will mention only a few of them.

Problems with the product differentiation assumption
The downward-sloping demand curves are derived from the assumption of product heterogeneity. This is inconsistent with the assumption that the cost curves or

[6]Benjamin Klein and Keith B. Leffler, "The Role of Market Forces in Assuring Contractual Performance," *Journal of Political Economy*, August 1981, pp. 615–641.

[7]Further discussion of the role of advertising in providing information can be found in Chapter 14.

demand conditions are the same for all firms. If the outputs of two firms are genuinely different, then the costs per unit are not really comparable. Furthermore, the long-run equilibrium of a firm with only normal profit as shown in Figure 13.4 is also logically incorrect. If the firm is providing a unique product and making super-normal profits as a consequence, other firms can compete away these profits only by providing the same product.

Another problem created by the introduction of product heterogeneity is that it is difficult to define an industry or "competing group." For example, tea, coffee, soft drinks, beer, wine, and liquor could form a chain of competing products. Under perfect competition or monopoly these would be considered as different homogeneous products. Under monopolistic competition it is not clear where we draw the line.

Finally, differentiated products are not necessarily produced by different firms. For instance, the fact that there are different brands of soaps and detergents—Biz, Bold, Camay, Cascade, Cheer, Comet, Dash, Ivory, Joy, Mr. Clean, Oxydol, Safeguard, Tide, and Zest—does not mean that this market is one of monopolistic competition. All these (and many more not mentioned here) are produced by a single firm, Proctor and Gamble, which has more than half of the market in soaps, cleansers, and detergents.[8] What we have here is an oligopoly of multiproduct firms (Lever Brothers is another big dominant firm in this area with many products of its own).

The predictive content of the theory

Another important criticism of the theory of monopolistic competition is that it is not useful for making any predictions. This criticism made by Stigler is based on the argument (which we discussed in Chapter 1) that the test of a theory is not whether it is descriptively accurate but whether it accurately predicts the effects of changes in the economic environment.[9] Unlike the theories of perfect competition and monopoly, the theory of monopolistic competition does not provide unambiguous predictions of the effect of changes in costs or demand on the price of the product, the size of the plant, or the number of firms in the industry.[10]

Consider, for instance, the question of the effect of an excise tax on output and price. We analyzed this problem earlier under both perfect competition and monopoly and derived predictions about the effects of excise taxes on output and prices under some assumptions about the slopes of the demand and supply curves. No such predictions emerge from the monopolistic competition model because we do not know whether few or many firms leave the industry when the share of the market for this taxed product falls. The existence of advertising further complicates

[8]This example is from Jesse W. Markham, "Comment," *American Economic Review*, May 1954, pp. 54–55.

[9]George Stigler, "Monopolistic Competition in Retrospect," *Five Lectures on Economic Problems*, Macmillan, New York, 1950, pp. 12–24.

[10]Although the controversy on Chamberlain's theory and its criticism by the Chicago school is beyond the scope of our discussion here, it is interesting to mention that Archibald argued that Stigler and Friedman attacked Chamberlain's theory of monopolistic competition not on the grounds of poor predictive record but on the grounds of consistency, simplicity, relevance, and so on—that is, on the basis of the theory's assumptions rather than predictions. See G. C. Archibald, "Chamberlain vs. Chicago," *Review of Economic Studies*, October 1961, pp. 2–28; "Reply to Chicago," *Review of Economic Studies*, February 1963, pp. 63–71; and M. Friedman, "More on Archibald vs. Chicago," *Review of Economic Studies*, February 1963, pp. 65–67.

the situation. We can obtain some predictions by introducing restrictions on the way some of the variables affect each other.[11]

One prediction of the monopolistic competition model, that of long-run excess capacity and unexploited economies of scale (discussed earlier in Section 13.3) does not appear to be corroborated by empirical evidence.

All this discussion of the monopolistic competition model does not mean that it has been useless. In fact, the enormous literature criticizing it implies that it did raise a lot of issues that were not considered in earlier models of perfect competition and monopoly. It has prompted economists to think of the problems of selling costs, advertising, nonprice competition, and so on.[12]

Some other things that this controversy has highlighted are:

1. We cannot judge theories on the basis of realism of assumptions. The theory has to be useful in deriving some observable predictions.

2. We have to be careful in defining costs, capacity, and so on in a manner consistent with the other assumptions of the model.

13.6 OLIGOPOLISTIC MARKETS

We have now examined the two extreme market structures—monopoly and perfect competition. And we have looked at a market structure which combines aspects of both monopoly and competition—monopolistic competition. In the following six sections we will study another market structure which lies between monopoly and perfect competition: *oligopoly.*

Oligopoly is a market structure in which a small number of rival firms dominate the industry. The leading firms are well aware that their actions are interdependent. An extreme case of oligopoly is *duopoly* where there are only two firms.

The term oligopoly means "few sellers." But the small number of sellers is important only in that it allows firms to recognize their interdependence. If there are two stores situated close together and selling similar goods to the same type of customers, and one of them cuts prices, it has to guess how the other store is going to react. Will it leave its prices unchanged, cut them by the same amount, or cut them more? In oligopoly, although competition is lacking in the sense that we discussed for perfect competition and monopolistic competition, there is sometimes intensive rivalry or competition in the popular sense of the word.

There are several important differences between oligopoly and monopolistic competition:

1. In oligopoly, entry of new firms is difficult, and relatively few sellers dominate the industry. In monopolistic competition, entry of new firms is easy, and a large number of sellers compete with each other.

---

[11]See J. Hadar, "On the Predictive Content of Models of Monopolist Competition," *Southern Economic Journal*, July 1969, pp. 67–73.

[12]See Robert L. Bishop, "The Theory of Monopolistic Competition after Thirty Years: The Impact on General Theory," *American Economic Review*, May 1964, pp. 33–43, for a positive view on Chamberlain's contribution.

2. In oligopoly, the product can be homogeneous (cement, steel) or differentiated (cars, soaps, cigarettes). In monopolistic competition, the sellers offer differentiated products.

3. In oligopoly, the actions of the firms are interdependent. In monopolistic competition, they are independent to a large extent.

4. In oligopoly, prices are relatively rigid, they do not change frequently except when there are price wars or when there is collusive price fixing. In monopolistic competition, prices can change frequently.

EXAMPLE 13.1   Texaco versus Pennzoil: A Dispute between Two Oligopolists

In 1983 Gordon Getty sought to increase the value of the 40 percent of the stock he controlled in Getty Oil, and so the company was considered to be for sale. The price of Getty shares rose from $50 in January 1983 to $80 in mid-December. Pennzoil tendered for 20 percent of Getty stock at $100 a share and then offered $112.50 for 32 million shares of Getty stock. Texaco then stepped in and offered $128 a share for the whole company.

Pennzoil sued Texaco for $7.53 billion in punitive damages and interest. It won the case in the courts, then Texaco declared bankruptcy, and finally in December 1987 the case was settled with Texaco agreeing to pay Pennzoil $3 billion.

How did Pennzoil arrive at $7.53 billion? It argued that since its cost of finding oil was $10.87 a barrel, the 1 billion barrels of Getty Oil's reserves it would have obtained were worth $10.9 billion. However, it would have paid $3.4 billion for these reserves. The difference of $7.5 billion is the damage it suffered because of Texaco's action.

However, this reasoning does not make sense. Pennzoil's cost of finding new reserves is irrelevant to the argument. If Pennzoil's cost of finding oil was $25 a barrel, it could have claimed a damage of $21.6 billion. Texaco should be thankful to Pennzoil that this was not the case. What is relevant is how Pennzoil would have added value to Getty's reserves.[13]

Texaco was a shrinking oil company with the shortest longevity of domestic oil reserves (7.8 years) among the major oil companies. It could be expected to pump out Getty's oil much more quickly than Pennzoil, giving those barrels a higher value for Texaco than for Pennzoil. Furthermore, since Texaco bought the whole company (which Pennzoil did not plan to do), it could integrate Getty oil with its own operations. However, Pennzoil did not have a large unused marketing network or better known name than Getty's. It did not have better production techniques. Thus, it is difficult to see how the acquisition of Getty Oil by Pennzoil would have added value to the reserves of Getty. Thus, the market valuation of $2.7 billion (based on the price of $80 for Getty stock before Pennzoil stepped in) was a fair value of these 1 billion reserves under Pennzoil's ownership. However, Pennzoil was to pay $3.4 billion, that is, $700 million more. Thus, Texaco actually saved Pennzoil $700 million, and hence it should have been Pennzoil that owed Texaco $700 million.

Suppose that Pennzoil did not intend to develop Getty's reserves but was going

---

[13]See Thomas Hopkins, "Pennzoil 'Owes' Texaco $700 Million," *The Wall Street Journal*, August 18, 1987, p. 32.

to sell its share. Assuming that it would have gotten $128 for each of the 32 million shares of Getty it owned and for which it paid $112.50 a share, the maximum damage it could claim is $496 million. But even this reasoning is not valid, because the fact that the reserves were worth $128 to Texaco does not mean they were worth that much to Pennzoil.

In summary, the $3 billion settlement of the Texaco-Pennzoil case does not make economic sense. Pennzoil came out of it a clear winner.

13.7   PRICE AND QUANTITY DETERMINATION IN DUOPOLY

Since interfirm rivalry is a basic feature of oligopoly we have to study the effect of this rivalry first. To do this we will initially concentrate on the case of duopoly—two sellers. We will discuss four models: (1) the classical models of Cournot and Edgeworth, (2) Hotelling's spatial equilibrium model, (3) Stackelberg's model, and (4) the modern game theory model. There have been other models, but these will illustrate the type of problems we encounter in the analysis of duopoly (or oligopoly).

The essential difference among duopoly and oligopoly models is in the formulation of firm expectation concerning rival reaction to a change in its price, output, location, and so on. Cournot's approach is based on the assumption that each duopolist believes that its opponent will not change the *quantity* supplied. Edgeworth's approach is based on the assumption that each of the duopolists believes that its opponent will maintain the current *price*. Stackelberg's approach is based on the assumption that one of the duopolists is a "leader" and the other the "follower." It is, therefore, a model of *asymmetric* duopoly. The game theory approach assumes that each duopolist believes that its opponent will adopt the most profitable countermove to any move the first makes. We will now explain these approaches in greater detail.

The models by Cournot and Edgeworth are based on naive conjectures about the reactions of the opponents. They can, therefore, be considered as simplistic versions of a class of models called *conjectural variations* models, in which firms are assumed to conjecture that changes in their own decisions will induce reactions from others. A special class of such models is the *consistent conjecture model* proposed by Bresnahan,[14] Perry,[15] and others (cited later). Perry explains the consistency condition for a duopoly, in which firms' decisions are output quantities, as follows:

> Each firm's first-order condition defines its profit maximizing output as a reaction function on (1) the output of the other firm and (2) the conjectural variation about the other firm's response. Thus, a conjectural variation by one firm about the other firm's response is consistent, if it is equivalent to the derivative of the other firm's reaction function with respect to the first firm's output at equilibrium. (Perry, p. 197.)

[14]Timothy F. Bresnahan, "Duopoly Models with Consistent Conjecturers," *American Economic Review*, December 1981, pp. 934–945.

[15]Martin K. Perry, "Oligopoly and Consistent Conjectural Variations," *Bell Journal of Economics*, Spring 1982, pp. 197–205.

Further elaboration of the consistent conjecture duopoly model is too complex to warrant inclusion here.[16] The simple models of Cournot and Edgeworth can be explained diagrammatically, and although naive, give an idea of what goes on in duopoly with more complicated conjectural variations. Furthermore, even the consistent conjecture model has been criticized as inconsistent, and more developments will be forthcoming.[17]

Cournot's solution

The French mathematical economist Cournot published his theory of duopoly in 1838.[18] Although most of his models were crude and involved very unrealistic assumptions, his method of analysis has been useful for subsequent theoretical development in the area of duopoly and oligopoly. Cournot assumes that:

1. There are two profit-maximizing duopolists, say A and B
2. Each duopolist produces an identical product
3. Both duopolists sell at identical prices
4. Each duopolist fully knows the linear market demand curve
5. Both duopolists act independently without collusion
6. Each duopolist acts under the assumption that its rival's output will remain exactly where it is now

The last assumption is very naive, because it implies that the duopolists do not learn from experience, but this assumption gives a determinate solution to the problem.

Cournot's example is that of mineral water from two adjacent springs produced at zero long-run marginal cost. The analysis is illustrated in Figure 13.8. DQ_c is the demand curve. Since $MC = 0$, the competitive output is OQ_c (the quantity demanded at price 0). Let MR_1 be the marginal revenue curve corresponding to the demand curve DQ_c. Equating MR_1 to MC, we get the monopoly output as OQ_1, monopoly price as OP_1, and monopoly profits as OP_1AQ_1. This would be the solution if the two duopolists colluded. Cournot's solution to the duopoly problem proceeds as follows.

Suppose initially that A is the only seller. A behaves like a monopolist, produces output $OQ_1 = 1/2\ OQ_c$, sells at a price OP_1, and makes a profit OP_1AQ_1.

Now B enters the market. Since Cournot assumes that each duopolist expects its rival *never* to change its output, B expects A to always market OQ_1. Thus, B cannot sell anything above a price of P_1. Below a price of P_1, B can sell the quantity demanded in excess of OQ_1. For example, at a price of P_3, B can sell Q_1Q_3. The demand curve for duopolist B can be viewed as the portion of the market demand AQ_c, where quantity is measured from the point Q_1 (Q_1 becomes B's origin). Du-

---

[16]The model is also called a "rational conjecture model." Some other papers are: G. Bramness, "The General Conjectural Model of Oligopoly," University of Warwick Discussion Paper no. 142, 1979; D. Ulph, "Rational Conjectures in the Theory of Oligopoly," *International Journal of Industrial Organization*, June 1983, pp. 131–154; and J. Laitner, "Rational Duopoly Equilibrium," *Quarterly Journal of Economics*, December 1980, pp. 641–662.

[17]L. Makowski, "Rational Conjectures Aren't Rational, Reasonable Conjectures Aren't Reasonable," Economic Theory Discussion Paper no. 66, University of Cambridge, 1983.

[18]Antoine-Augustin Cournot, *Researches into the Mathematical Principles of Wealth* (1838). The book was translated into English by N. T. Bacon, with a bibliography of mathematics of economics by Irving Fisher (New York, Macmillan Company, 1897). Cournot (1801 to 1877) was the first mathematical economist.

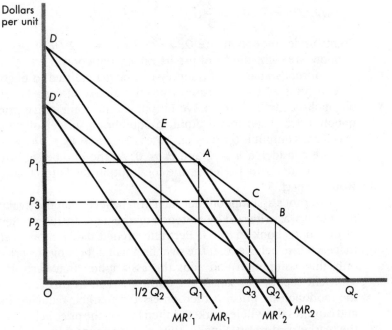

FIGURE 13.8 Cournot's solution to the duopoly problem.

opolist B's marginal revenue curve is now MR_2 where output again is measured from Q_1. The second duopolist's marginal revenue will equal marginal cost at an output of Q_1Q_2. So Q_1Q_2 will be duopolist B's initial profit-maximizing output. Total output has increased with B's entry, and, hence, product price falls.

Now A realizes that B has entered the market and reevaluates the situation. Duopolist A expects that B will always sell $Q_1Q_2 = Q_2Q_c$. Duopolist A's new demand curve is $D'Q_2$, which is obtained by horizontally subtracting B's output from the market demand curve. The new marginal revenue curve for A is MR_1' which intersects the horizontal axis at $1/2$ (OQ_2). Hence, A, in an attempt to maximize profit, reduces output to $1/2$ (OQ_2). The combined output now declines, and product price increases.

Now B reevaluates the situation. B's new expectation is that A will always continue to sell $1/2$ (OQ_2). B's new demand curve is constructed as before and becomes EQ_c with $1/2$ OQ_2 as the origin. B's new marginal revenue curve is MR_2' and crosses the horizontal axis at an output of $1/2$ $(OQ_c - 1/2$ $OQ_2)$. Duopolist B, thus, maximizes profit by increasing output to $1/2$ $(OQ_c - 1/2$ $OQ_2)$. Total output for the market has increased, and, thus, market price falls.

This process goes on, A decreasing output, B increasing output, until both A and B produce the same output of $1/3$ OQ_c. The total output produced by A and B together is $OQ_3 = 2/3$ OQ_c, and the price charged is $OP_3 = 2/3$ OP_1, shown in Figure 13.8. Thus, we have the following results: (1) The output under duopoly is less than the competitive output OQ_c but greater than the monopoly output OQ_1. (2) The price under duopoly is two-thirds of the price under monopoly. (3) Total profits to the two duopolists are:

$$OP_3CQ_3 = \frac{2}{3} OP_1 \times \frac{2}{3} OQ_c = \frac{4}{9} \cdot OP_1 \cdot OQ_c$$

Profits under monopoly are $OP_1 \times 1/2 \, OQ_c = 1/2 \, OP_1 \cdot OQ_c$. Thus, profits under duopoly are eight-ninths of profits under monopoly.

Cournot's analysis of duopoly can be generalized to oligopoly or the case of several firms and to the case of positive marginal cost. Let n be the number of oligopolists, Q_c the competitive output, P_c the competitive price, and P_m the monopoly price. Then total output in equilibrium under oligopoly is $nQ_c/(n + 1)$. Each firm's output is $Q_c/(n + 1)$. Price is $2P_m/(n + 1) + nP_c/(n + 1)$. In the duopoly case we considered $n = 2$ and $P_c = 0$. As the number of firms tends to infinity, $n/(n + 1)$ tends to 1. Hence, the total output tends to Q_c and price to P_c, as one would expect.

Cournot's assumption that each firm believes that the rival firm will not change its output was criticized by a French mathematician Joseph Bertrand in his review of Cournot's book in 1883. Bertrand argued that a more realistic assumption is that each firm believes that the rival firm will not change its price. Bertrand changes only this assumption and adds the assumption that each of the duopolists has sufficient capacity to satisfy the entire market. In this case A will first start with the monopolistic price, B then enters the market, reducing the price somewhat, and captures the whole market. A then lowers the price below B's price and captures the market and so on. Finally, the price war ends when price is $MC = 0$, and the total output produced is equal to the competitive output.

Chamberlain also changes Cournot's assumptions slightly. He replaces Cournot's assumption of a naive belief in fixed output with the assumption that firms recognize their interdependence. His argument runs as follows: A starts with output OQ_1 and price OP_1 in Figure 13.8, and B produces Q_1Q_2 as was the case with Cournot. A, however, then realizes that B will change its behavior if A changes its output and that the maximum (joint) profit occurs at output level OQ_1. A, therefore, cuts output to $1/2 \, OQ_1$ leaving B to produce $1/2 \, OQ_1 = Q_1Q_2$. A stable solution is reached which is the monopoly solution. There is no explicit collusion. There is only some understanding of mutual benefit.

Edgeworth's solution

The model proposed by the English economist Edgeworth in 1897 is similar to Bertrand's in that each duopolist assumes that its rival will not change its price. The only difference is that Edgeworth assumes that neither of the duopolists can produce an output as large as the competitive output. Figure 13.9 shows the situation. For the sake of simplicity we will assume that the two duopolists have identical marginal costs of 0 and that the maximum possible output is the same for both. The entire market is divided equally between A and B when both firms charge the same price. DE is the demand curve facing A, and DF is the demand curve facing B assuming prices are equal. The total competitive output is EF. The maximum output A can produce is OL, and the maximum output B can produce is OM ($OL = OM$). If the duopolists collude, the total output produced is $1/2 \, EF$ which is shown as GH. A produces OG, and B produces OH ($OG = OH = 1/2 \, GH$), and they charge the monopoly price OP_1.

Now suppose that there is no collusion. Then one of the duopolists, say A,

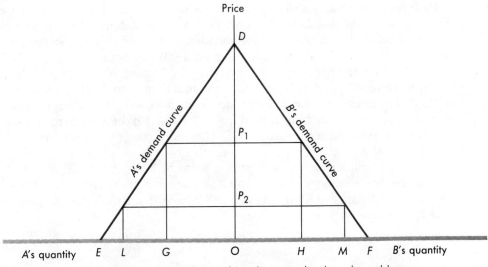

FIGURE 13.9   Edgeworth's solution to the duopoly problem.

reduces the price slightly below OP_1. Then all of B's customers go to A. But A can provide only an amount OL. Thus, B is left with sales equal to EL (or MF). Rather than accept the reduction in revenue, B reduces the price slightly below A's price and captures all of A's customers, but B can serve only OM. This process goes on until price falls to OP_2 and each of the duopolists produces the maximum possible output. A sells OL, and B sells OM.

However, the price OP_2 is not stable, because one firm can raise its price and increase its revenue (which increases profit in this case since $MC = 0$). Thus, for instance, A will try to raise the price, assuming that B will keep the price of OP_2, and there is no danger of losing customers to B since B is producing its maximum output. A raises its price all the way to OP_1. Now B realizes that any price increase up to OP_1 would lose it no sales and raises prices almost up to OP_1. Now A responds by cutting price below B's price, and the process goes on all over again. There is no determinate solution in this case (unlike Cournot's solution). The prices will now fluctuate in the range P_1P_2.

Hotelling's spatial equilibrium model

Hotelling proposed a solution to the duopoly problem in which the products of the duopolists are differentiated in the eyes of the buyers by virtue of the location of the duopolists. Buyers are uniformly distributed (one per unit of distance) along a line KL, and the duopolists A and B locate themselves at X_A and X_B, respectively, on the line, as follows:

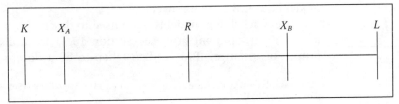

Each buyer purchases a single unit from A or B and transports the purchase home. It is assumed that $LRMC = 0$ for each seller and demand is completely inelastic. We also assume that the transportation costs, paid by the customer, are cx where x is the distance of the customer from a sales point (X_A or X_B).

A and B have some leeway in setting prices, but A never sets its price so high that buyers along KX_A find it cheaper to buy from B than from A. (Doing so would put A out of business.) Similarly, B does not set its price so high that buyers along $X_B L$ find it cheaper to buy from A than from B. Thus, A has the sheltered market KX_A, and B has the sheltered market $X_B L$. They both compete for the market in between X_A and X_B.

Hotelling's solution says that there is a point in between X_A and X_B, say R, such that the delivered price from X_A and X_B is the same. If the distance of R from X_A is x and the distance of R from X_B is y, and P_A and P_B are the prices charged by A and B, respectively, then at R

$$P_A + cx = P_B + cy$$

A gets all the customers along KR, and B gets all the customers along RL. A's profit is $P_A \cdot KR$, and B's profit is $P_B \cdot RL$.

A has an incentive to move toward X_B and expand its sheltered market. Similarly, B has an incentive to move toward X_A and expand its sheltered market. Hence, a stable solution is reached when both A and B locate themselves at the midpoint of KL.

Hotelling's solution is interesting because it shows how the sellers' location at the same point has increased the transportation costs. If the duopolists colluded and split the market, with A and B locating at one-quarter and three-quarters the distance from K to L, then the transportation costs would be minimized. (They would be half of what they are under the assumption of competition among the duopolists.) Hotelling's solution also explains the phenomenon that sellers tend to locate themselves in close proximity. Thus, it explains the concentration of business districts and firms in many cities. Since the firms are located close to each other, they have to compete with each other by advertising and by product differentiation, as well as by price.

Stackelberg's solution

Another solution to the duopoly problem that is often mentioned is the Stackelberg solution.[19] The difficulty of oligopoly theory is that oligopolists are in a game theory situation (described in the next section) and these situations cannot be put in the form of a pure maximization problem. Stackelberg's idea was that this can, nevertheless, be done in a duopoly if we assume that one of the firms is a *leader* and the other a *follower*. The model is thus one of *asymmetric duopoly*. In Cournot's model both firms are followers.

The Stackelberg model is often used to describe industries in which there is a leader, or a dominant firm (see Section 13.11 for a discussion of the dominant firm). For instance, IBM is often taken to be a dominant firm in the computer

---

[19]This was suggested by the German economist Heinrich von Stackelberg (1905 to 1946) in his thesis *Marketform und Gleichgewicht* (1934).

industry. Smaller firms in this industry wait for IBM's announcements for new products and prices and then adjust their own products and prices accordingly.

In the Stackelberg model, firm 1, the dominant firm, tries to maximize its profits, but it recognizes that its own choice of output will influence firm 2's (the follower's) choice of output via its reaction function. The details of the Stackelberg solution cannot be easily worked out without the use of calculus, and hence we will omit them. One thing is obvious: The dominant firm will produce more output than the follower. As for the total industry output, *with linear demand functions,* we said earlier that the output under Cournot duopoly is two-thirds of the competitive output, and under Bertrand's assumption it is equal to the competitive output. It can be shown that under the Stackelberg solution, total output is three-fourths of the competitive output, with the dominant firm producing twice as much as the follower. We can, therefore, summarize the industry outputs under the different models as follows:

- Competitive solution: Q_c
- Monopoly solution: $1/2\ Q_c$
- Cournot's duopoly solution: $2/3\ Q_c$
- Bertrand's duopoly solution: Q_c
- Stackelberg's duopoly solution: $3/4\ Q_c$

13.8 GAME THEORY APPROACHES

Almost all the economic problems we have discussed until now involved maximizing (profit, utility, and so on) or minimizing (cost, disutility, and so on) by the economic agents (firms, consumers). In the case of duopoly (and oligopoly), as is clear from the models of Cournot and Edgeworth that we have discussed, this problem gets complicated because each agent's actions depend on the other agents' actions as well. One firm's desire to maximize profits will be opposed by the other firm's desire to maximize its profits. To solve this type of problem, von Neumann and Morgenstern suggested what is known as *game theory.*[20] This theory looks at any decision-making problem where a person's return (or *payoff*) depends on not only his or her own choice but the other person's choices as well, as a *game*. If there are only two people (or firms) involved, it is called a two-person game. Otherwise, it is called a multiple-person game. In the case of a two-person game, if one individual's profit is the other individual's loss and vice versa, it is called a *zero-sum two-person game.* However, many problems in economics are non-zero-sum games.

There are two concepts that are necessary for analyzing any problem using the game theory approach: *strategy* and a *payoff matrix.* Strategies are alternative

[20]John von Neumann and Oskar Morgenstern, *Theory of Games and Economic Behavior*, Princeton University Press, Princeton, N.J. The book first appeared in 1944, but the revised edition of 1947 is the more standard reference. Von Neumann (1903 to 1957), a Hungarian-born mathematical genius, was one of the three coinventors of the hydrogen bomb. Morgenstern (1902 to 1977) was a professor of economics at Princeton University.

courses of action, and a payoff matrix is a table of numbers showing a person's returns (or payoffs) for various combinations of that person's and her or his rival's strategies. Consider the case of two duopolists A and B where each has two strategies: to cut prices by 5 percent or to make no change. The payoff matrices for A and B are shown in Table 13.1. The game is not a zero-sum game since the sum of the two payoffs is

$$\begin{bmatrix} -140 & -20 \\ -40 & 0 \end{bmatrix}$$

For a zero-sum game, all such sums must be 0. If A and B collude, clearly the best strategy is to make no changes in the price.

A common decision rule in game theory is the *maximin decision rule*. It says to choose the strategy which maximizes the minimum payoff. Though somewhat pessimistic, the rule is reasonable under oligopoly, where each firm might expect its rival to respond in a manner that ensures that the worst possible outcome will be realized.

Suppose A's strategy is to cut its price. Assuming that B responds to cause A to do its worst, A will end up with a loss of \$60,000. But what if A's strategy is not to cut price? Assuming again that B reacts, causing A to do its worst, A will lose \$80,000. Since A could be worse off with the second strategy, A chooses to cut its price.

Similarly, consider B's two strategies. If B cuts the price, and A responds to cause B to do its worst, B loses \$80,000. If B makes no change and A causes B to do its worst, B loses \$100,000. Thus, B is better off cutting the price by 5 percent.

TABLE 13.1   Payoff Matrices for Two Duopolists*

Payoff Matrix for A

		A's Strategy	
		Cut Price 5%	Make No Change
B's Strategy	Cut Price 5%	−60	−80
	Make No Change	+60	0
	Column Minimum	−60	−80

Payoff Matrix for B

		A's Strategy		Row Minimum
		Cut Price 5%	Make No Change	
B's Strategy	Cut Price 5%	−80	+60	−80
	Make No Change	−100	0	−100

*Profits are denoted by +, losses by −, both in thousands of dollars.

Thus, both *A* and *B* end up cutting prices by 5 percent, and they both lose—total losses are $140,000. The best joint strategy is not to change the prices. However, they individually choose strategies that harm both. This problem is known as the *prisoners' dilemma*. The situation described there is that of two prisoners locked up in two different rooms who are told that the following deal is being given to both of them:

1. If a prisoner confesses but the partner does not, the cooperating prisoner gets off with a 1-year sentence whereas the partner gets a sentence of 13 years. (The confession becomes state's evidence.)

2. If they both confess, each gets a sentence of 10 years. (The sentence for the crime is 13 years but it gets reduced to 10 because of the confession.)

3. If both prisoners keep quiet, since the district attorney's evidence is weak, they each get charged with a smaller crime and get a 2-year sentence.

The question is: What will each prisoner do? The payoff matrices for the two prisoners *A* and *B* are shown in Table 13.2. Clearly, the best course of action for both prisoners is to keep quiet. However, each prisoner, assuming the partner will cause her or him to realize the worst payoff, will confess. As with the duopoly example, *A* looks at the column minima of *A*'s payoff matrix and chooses to confess. *B* looks at the row minima of *B*'s payoff matrix and chooses to confess. Thus, both the prisoners are worse off.

The prisoner's dilemma arises from a lack of communication and from distrust among the prisoners. If the prisoners can communicate with each other and trust

TABLE 13.2   Payoff Matrices for Prisoners' Dilemma*

Payoff Matrix for Prisoner A

		Prisoner A's Strategy	
		Confess	Keep Quiet
Prisoner B's	Confess	− 10 years	− 13 years
Strategy	Keep Quiet	− 1 year	− 2 years
	Column Minimum	− 10 years	− 13 years

Payoff Matrix for Prisoner B

		Prisoner A's Strategy		Row
		Confess	Keep Quiet	Minimum
Prisoner B's	Confess	− 10 years	− 1 year	− 10 years
Strategy	Keep Quiet	− 13 years	− 2 years	− 13 years

*The minus sign indicates that a stay in prison has disutility.

each other, then they will arrive at a solution that is optimal for both. Similar conclusions apply to all economic problems where the "game" is comparable to the example in the prisoners' dilemma.

13.9   PRICING UNDER OLIGOPOLY

The previous analysis of duopoly illustrates the problems arising from rivalry among firms. In an oligopolistic situation, any firm's lowering of price can be interpreted by other firms as an attempt to eliminate them by capturing their markets. This kind of price reduction is called *predatory price cutting*. The other firms respond by cutting their prices, and the round of price cutting goes on. This chain of price cuts is called a *price war*. Such price wars have occurred in several industries: the railroads in the 1870s, oil production in the 1880s, cigarette manufacturing in the 1930s. These price wars reduce the profits for each firm, and those firms that reduce prices below their costs might even go out of business. If lowering prices is suicide in eliminating profits, so is raising prices. A firm that raises prices unilaterally in an oligopolistic industry will lose customers to the other firms.

The net conclusion of all this discussion is that there is an incentive for firms in an oligopolistic industry either to (1) not change prices or (2) collude with each other in changing prices. We shall discuss these two possibilities.

Kinked demand curve

In 1939 two papers, one by Hall and Hitch, and the other by Sweezy, argued that oligopolistic firms have "sticky" prices.[21] One reason for this is that the oligopolistic firm faces a *kinked demand curve*. This is shown in Figure 13.10. All firms currently charge a price P_0. D_1D_1 is the demand curve that a particular oligopolistic firm faces if the other firms *do not change* their prices. D_2D_2 is the demand curve this firm faces if all firms charge the same price.

[21]R. L. Hall and C. J. Hitch, "Price Theory and Business Behavior," *Oxford Economic Papers*, May 1939, pp. 12–45, and Paul M. Sweezy, "Demand under Conditions of Oligopoly," *Journal of Political Economy*, August 1939, pp. 563–573.

FIGURE 13.10   A kinked demand curve.

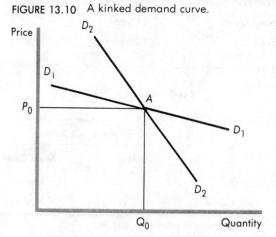

Suppose A is the current position of the firm, with price P_0 and quantity Q_0. The argument behind the kinked demand curve goes like this: If the firm raises price, the other firms do not, since they stand to gain by capturing the sales of this firm. However, if the firm reduces price, the other firms respond by matching the price reduction. Thus, the demand curve that this firm faces is given by the segment of D_1D_1 to the left of A and the segment of D_2D_2 to the right of A. This is shown in Figure 13.10. The demand curve has a kink at A.

The marginal revenue curve corresponding to the kinked demand curve is shown in Figure 13.11. MR_1 is the marginal revenue curve corresponding to D_1D_1, and MR_2 is the marginal revenue curve corresponding to D_2D_2. To the left of Q_0, the demand curve is given by the segment of D_1D_1 and, hence, the marginal revenue curve is given by the corresponding segment of MR_1. To the right of Q_0, the demand curve is given by the segment of D_2D_2, and hence the marginal revenue curve is given by the corresponding segment of MR_2. At the quantity Q_0, there is a sudden drop in marginal revenue—from point B to point C in Figure 13.11. The marginal revenue curve for the kinked demand curve in Figure 13.10 is, thus, given by the line $EBCF$ in Figure 13.11.

The consequence of this is that there is some range within which changes in the firm's marginal costs will not result in changes in price and quantity. This is shown in Figure 13.12. Note that for both MC_1 and MC_2 the price and quantity given by the equilibrium condition $MC = MR$ are the same.

The kinked demand curve is derived on the assumption that price increases by one of the oligopolistic firms are not followed by others but price decreases are promptly followed. Stigler examined price histories of seven industries to see if this was indeed the case.[22] The seven industries were cigarettes, automobiles, anthracite coal, steel, dynamite, gasoline, and potash. He found that the vast majority of the

[22]G. J. Stigler, "The Kinky Oligopoly Demand Curve and Rigid Prices," *Journal of Political Economy*, October 1947, pp. 432–449.

FIGURE 13.11   Marginal revenue curve corresponding to a kinked demand curve.

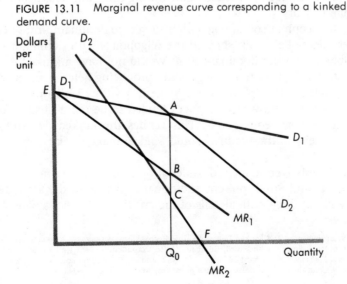

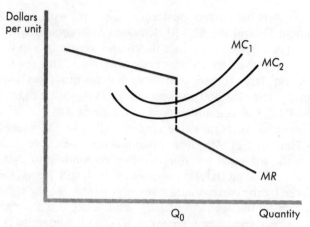

FIGURE 13.12   Price stickiness with a kinked demand curve.

recorded price episodes were not in keeping with the assumptions of the theory of the kinked demand curve. This was a test of the assumptions of the theory. Stigler also conducted other tests. These were tests of the implications of the theory, that prices are less flexible under oligopoly than under monopoly or oligopoly with collusion. He studied a number of oligopolistic and nonoligopolistic U.S. industries over a complete business cycle from June 1929 to May 1937 and found the following results:

   1. A comparison of 19 oligopolies with two monopolies showed that even though the monopolies experienced greater output variation, they tended to have less flexible prices. This refutes the kinked demand theory.

   2. A comparison of five oligopolies (rayon, copper, pineapple canning, typewriters, and midwestern oil) during, and outside of, periods of collusion showed that prices tended to be less flexible during collusion. This again refutes the kinked demand theory.

   3. A comparison of oligopolies subject to dominant firm price leadership with other oligopolies again showed the oligopolies with dominant firms to have less flexible prices, and dominant firms would not have a kinked demand curve.

   4. A comparison of 6 oligopolies producing heterogeneous goods (soap, tractors, grain binders, plows, tires, linoleum) with 13 oligopolies producing homogeneous goods showed that prices tended to be more flexible for industries producing homogeneous goods. This refutes the kinked demand curve as greater homogeneity of the product would tend to make the kink more pronounced.

Stigler's tests were criticized in detail by Efroymson. Primeaux and Bomball, and Primeaux and Smith present additional evidence on the kinked demand curve.[23] We will not discuss the details of the criticism of Stigler's work here, but Stigler's

[23]C. W. Efroymson, "The Kinked Demand Curve Reconsidered," *Quarterly Journal of Economics*, February 1955, pp. 119–136. W. J. Primeaux and M. R. Bomball, "A Re-Examination of the Kinky Oligopoly Demand Curve," *Journal of Political Economy*, July–August 1974, pp. 851–862; and W. J. Primeaux and M. C. Smith, "Pricing Patterns and the Kinky Demand Curve," *Journal of Law and Economics*, April 1976, pp. 189–199.

own assessment of the criticism of his study is in his 1978 paper, where he complains that the kinked demand curve is "a piece of scripture; it is to be taught and it is to be quoted in suitable contexts, but it is not to be tampered with."[24] Stigler complains that almost all textbooks on principles and price theory devote a few perfunctory pages to the kinked demand theory. According to Stigler, in 1940 about a quarter of the books mentioned it. In the mid-1970s about two-thirds of the books mentioned it, and the theory was repeated in subsequent editions. The book by Reid, however, reviews the theory and evidence on the kinked demand curve and tries to show that it need not be buried as Stigler suggests.[25]

The issue of price rigidity

The basic empirical observation that the kinked demand curve was supposed to explain is price rigidity. Stigler's argument is that this could as well be explained by transaction costs. If it is the kink that leads to inflexible prices, monopolists should have more flexible prices, since monopolists do not face a kinked demand curve. The empirical evidence is exactly the opposite: Monopolists change prices less frequently than do oligopolists. Thus, any theory in which prices are rigid only because individual oligopolists fear "upsetting the applecart" is suspect.

In a further, more detailed study, Stigler and Kindahl collected data for several industries from January 1, 1957 to December 31, 1966 from buyers on actual transaction prices paid for a number of products.[26] These data were further analyzed by Carlton, who studied the relationship between the average length of a spell of price rigidity and CR_4, the four-firm concentration ratio.[27] He found that the two were positively related, that is, the higher the concentration ratio, the greater is price rigidity, as measured by the average length of time over which prices did not change. A partial summary of a measure of price rigidity by product group is given in Table 13.3. A "pairing" means a transaction over time for a good of constant specification.

What all this evidence suggests is that oligopolists tend to change prices more often than duopolists and duopolists more often than monopolists. Why is the obvious question. One possible reason is that there may be some fixed costs associated with price changes.[28] If so, then firms have to consider how these costs compare with the benefits from price changes. If we can show that the benefits from price changes vary across market structures, then we can explain why price rigidity varies by market structure.

Rotemberg and Saloner compare duopoly and monopoly and show that duopolists have a greater incentive than monopolists to change prices in response to a change in costs.[29] However, the incentive to change prices in response to changes

[24]G. J. Stigler, "The Literature of Economics: The Case of the Kinked Oligopoly Demand Curve," *Economic Inquiry*, April 1978, pp. 185–204.

[25]Gavin C. Reid, *The Kinked Demand Curve: Analysis of Oligopoly*, Edinburgh University Press, Edinburgh, 1981.

[26]G. Stigler and J. Kindahl, *The Behavior of Industrial Prices*, NBER General Series no. 90, Columbia University Press, New York, 1970.

[27]D. W. Carlton, "The Rigidity of Prices," *American Economic Review*, September 1986, pp. 637–658.

[28]This idea was first suggested by Robert Barro, "A Theory of Monopolistic Price Adjustment," *Review of Economic Studies*, January 1972, pp. 17–26.

[29]J. Rotemberg and G. Saloner, "The Relative Rigidity of Monopoly Pricing," *American Economic Review*, December 1987, pp. 917–926.

TABLE 13.3   Price Rigidity by Product Group

Product Group	Number of Buyer-Seller Pairs	Average Duration of Spells of Price Rigidity (months)
Steel	348	13.0
Nonferrous metals	209	4.3
Petroleum	245	5.9
Rubber tires	123	8.1
Paper	128	8.7
Chemicals	658	12.8
Cement	40	13.2
Glass	22	10.2
Truck motors	59	5.4
Plywood	46	4.7
Household appliances	14	3.6

Source: D. W. Carlton, "The Rigidity of Prices," American Economic Review, September 1986, pp. 637–658.

in demand is higher for monopolists than for duopolists. In practice, the cost effect dominates the demand effect, and, hence, the monopolist may adjust prices more sluggishly than duopolists. A detailed presentation of their arguments would be quite lengthy for our purpose, but the main points to note from all our discussion on price rigidity are:

1. The kinked demand curve is not an adequate explanation of price rigidity under oligopoly.

2. In fact, the empirical evidence suggests that prices are more rigid under monopoly than under duopoly which, in turn, are more rigid than under oligopoly.

3. One explanation for this is a fixed cost of price adjustment.

4. Firms will compare the costs and benefits of price adjustment, and the latter depend on market structure.

5. Comparing duopoly and monopoly, whether the benefits are higher under duopoly than under monopoly depends on whether cost changes or demand changes prompt the price adjustment. In practice, the cost effect dominates the demand effect.[30]

13.10   CARTELS

The preceding discussion of pricing under oligopoly is based on the assumption that firms act independently even though they are interdependent in the market.

[30]The issue of price rigidity has been an active area of research in industrial organization. We have presented only a few of the findings.

Alternative methods of pricing are based on the assumption that firms, instead of competing with each other, enter into pricing agreements with each other. Interfirm agreements that restrain market competition, whether explicitly or implicitly, are referred to as *collusion*. Adam Smith, in his book *Wealth of Nations*, noted this tendency for firms to collude saying: "People of the same trade seldom meet together, even for merriment and diversion, but the conversation ends in a conspiracy against the public or in some contrivance to raise prices." We will now discuss the different forms of collusion. A cartel is one such form.

A *cartel* is a group of firms whose objective is to limit the scope of competitive forces in the market. One of the most famous cartels is OPEC, the Organization of Petroleum Exporting Countries. OPEC was formed in 1960 but was not really an effective cartel until it raised the price of oil from $2.12 a barrel on January 1, 1973 to $11.65 a barrel by the end of 1973, following the Arab-Israeli Yom Kippur War. This unprecedented price increase eventually led to the predictable result—an entry of new firms. It led to the discovery of new oil fields and development of existing high-cost oil fields in Alaska and the North Sea. This increased the supply and forced OPEC producers to further restrict production.

A cartel can be formed by producers within a country, in which case it is called a domestic cartel, or by producers (or governments) in different countries, in which case it is called an international cartel. OPEC is an example of the latter. As for domestic cartels, formal collusive agreements are generally outlawed in the United States. Hence, what we find is tacit collusion. This is found with some regularity in such industries as steel, paperboard, petroleum, and electrical equipment.

Paradoxically, the federal and state governments promote the formation of informal cartels in some cases by *legislating* higher-than-competitive prices, a cutback in supply, or even an increase in demand. The following are some examples (although many of the regulations are in the process of being abolished):

1. Federal laws set minimum prices above competitive levels for many agricultural commodities.

2. For a long time, the Civil Aeronautics Board (CAB) regulated interstate airline service, setting fares at high levels to accommodate even the higher-cost carriers.

3. The Federal Communication Commission (FCC) fixed rates for telephone and telegraph companies and radio and television broadcasting.

4. The Interstate Commerce Commission (ICC) promoted high prices for interstate barge and ship companies, buses, railroads, and trucks.

5. Many state governments set minimum prices for electric and telephone rates, insurance rates, rates on buses, subways, and taxis, and even for some consumer items like liquor.

As we have seen, raising price above the competitive level produces an excess supply. To tackle this problem the government has to restrict output. With agricultural commodities this is done by using *acreage allotments*. For other commodities and services this is done by *licensing* (airlines, taxi cabs, utilities, and so on).

The major functions of a cartel are price fixing and market division. Two problems must be faced before these two functions can be performed. First, the firms must be able to reach a collusive agreement. Second, once the agreement is reached, the firms must be able to enforce it over time.

Reaching agreement on a collusive price is not always easy. Different firms might have widely different cost conditions and different expectations about future demand. Thus, they have different perceptions of what price should be. The type of product is also important in reaching a collusive agreement. If the good is homogeneous, the firms have only to agree on a single price. When the good is not homogeneous, it is necessary to set a whole array of prices for different qualities. In the case of OPEC, for instance, the cartel sets different prices for heavy and light crude oil and there has been some haggling about what this price difference should be. There are also substantial differences in costs of production between Saudi Arabia and the North Sea producers. Expectations about future demand also vary among the different members of OPEC.

Once the collusive agreement is reached, there is the question of how long it can last. This depends on whether any member of the cartel cheats by reducing its price and, thus, increasing its market share. Once widespread cheating starts, a price war can break out, and this will result in a breakup of the cartel. However, if the members of the cartel realize that this is in nobody's interest, they can take steps to come together even after some temporary bursts of cheating. This is what has happened with OPEC repeatedly, although how long this can go on is an open question. Very few international cartels have managed to last more than 5 years. OPEC has had a much longer than expected life.

The life expectancy of a cartel depends on several factors:

1. The price elasticity of demand: If demand is fairly elastic, then a larger reduction in output is necessary to increase price. And, of course, a larger output reduction is more difficult to attain and maintain. One determinant of demand elasticity is the availability of substitutes. The copper cartel formed by Chile, Peru, Zaire, and Zambia was unsuccessful because of the availability of close substitutes which made the demand for copper quite elastic.

2. The stability of demand: A stable demand is conducive to cartel survival because constant adjustment of output, and the associated negotiation, are unnecessary.

3. The ability to control a substantial share of actual and potential output: It is especially important that the cartel control a substantial share when the elasticity of supply is large. For example, as OPEC raised the price of oil, the quantity supplied from new fields and from nonmembers increased dramatically. This increase undermined OPEC's power.

4. The political climate, in the case of international cartels: The rivalry between Iran and Iraq has contributed to the instability of OPEC. In fact, many possible international cartels actually do not come into existence because of political rivalries among the producing nations. The possibility of a cartel in chromium, gold, or manganese is remote because South Africa and the Soviet Union will not join together. A coffee cartel composed of Brazil and Columbia or a tea cartel composed of India and Sri Lanka is possible, but has not come into existence. (The latter is not possible under the current political climate.) In this case a coffee cartel could induce consumers to switch from coffee to tea, and a tea cartel could induce consumers to switch from tea to coffee.

As mentioned earlier, a cartel has to perform two functions: (1) fixing of price and (2) allocation of output among members. The way these functions are performed depends on how the cartel is organized. We shall discuss two types of cartels: (1) the perfect or centralized cartel and (2) the market-sharing cartel.

In the *perfect cartel*, the objective is to maximize the total profits of the member firms. This implies that each firm produces output where marginal costs are the same for all firms and equal to the marginal cost and marginal revenue for the cartel as a whole. If there are n firms with marginal costs given by MC_i ($i = 1,2, \ldots ,n$) and MC_T and MR_T are, respectively, the marginal cost and marginal revenue for the cartel as a whole, then we have

$$MC_1 = MC_2 = \ldots = MC_n = MC_T = MR_T$$

The situation is exactly the same as in the case of a multiplant monopolist discussed in Section 11.9. The MC curve for the cartel is constructed from the MC curves for the individual firms the same way the MC curve for the multiplant monopolist was constructed from the MC curves of the individual plants. The allocation of total output between the different firms in the cartel is done the same way a multiplant monopolist allocates total output between the different plants. Further, in a centralized cartel, the inputs are all purchased at the same price by all member firms, as in the case of a multiplant monopoly.

The centralized cartel makes all the decisions regarding prices, output, output allocation, profit distribution, and so on. Herein lie the problems with this type of cartel. In a multiplant monopoly, the monopolist may not produce any output from some of the plants. Similarly, in a centralized cartel some of the firms may get very little or may not get any output allocation. If this is the case, the firm that gets no output allocation will drop out of the cartel and go on its own. By not producing any output for a length of time the firm can lose its goodwill, experienced labor force, and established marketing channels, and, hence, might decide it is not worthwhile to stay in the cartel. The exit of some firms can undermine the cartel. This is what gives rise to a market-sharing cartel.

In a *market-sharing cartel* there is no centralized body making all the economic decisions regarding prices, output, and profits. The cartel merely allocates output among the different firms. There are two ways in which this is done: (1) nonprice competition and (2) quotas.

Nonprice competition is usually found in "loose" cartels. The cartel sets a minimum price, and each firm is allowed to sell all it can at that price. Examples of this are haircutting, theater tickets, medical services, and legal services. The only requirement in this is that firms do not reduce price below the cartel price. The sellers compete with each other but *not* by price competition. The competition is nonprice competition and takes the form of advertising, customer credit policies, and product variation.

Under the *quota system* each firm is allocated a certain quota. The quota any firm gets depends on: (1) the bargaining ability and importance of the firm, (2) relative sales of the firm in a precartel base period and the productive capacity of the firm, and (3) geographical location (for example, the agreement between Du Pont and ICI to divide the North American and European chemical markets).

The bargaining ability of a firm will also depend on the costs of production of the firm relative to those of other firms. The firm with the lowest costs of production has the best chance of surviving in a price war. For instance, in the case of OPEC, Saudi Arabia has the best bargaining ability by virtue of its enormous productive capacity as well as low costs of production.

In both of the market-sharing methods, one needs some penalizing and policing arrangements. In a quota system a penalty has to be imposed on those who exceed the quota by accident or design. Where minimum cartel prices are fixed, penalties must be imposed on price cutters. Policing price agreements is usually more difficult than policing quotas. In the case of price agreements one has to get data on "transaction" prices and these differ typically from "posted" or "list" prices. Since this information is usually difficult and costly to obtain, the method commonly followed is to observe buyer shifts—is a firm picking up business it would not otherwise be doing? If this is the case, then one can suspect that the firm is cheating. In those transactions where the bidding is done by sealed bids and the bids are later publicly opened, giving the name of the individual firm and the price at which the product is offered, one can easily identify who is doing the price cutting.

EXAMPLE 13.2 The Collapse of the Tin Cartel

In 1986 the world watched the simultaneous collapse of two commodity cartels: oil and tin.[31] Although the economic impact of oil is much wider than that of tin, both of them suggest that cartels do not work for too long. During the period of overpricing, new sources are developed, substitutes are invented, and economies of use are achieved by means of investment in research. For instance, in the case of the OPEC cartel, several new countries started producing oil, and several investments were made in energy conservation devices. Eventually, when the cartel collapses, many of these investments are entrenched and irreversible, either because of vested interests or because they embody the latest technological advances. Because of these factors, the producers in the cartel face an ever-declining demand and probably a lower price than one that would have prevailed had the cartel never existed.

In the case of tin, because of the high price maintained by the cartel, tin lost its place as a container material for beverages and gave place to aluminum and plastics. The aluminum beer can is a lasting monument of the cartel's price actions.

Unlike OPEC, which consisted of petroleum-producing countries, the tin cartel, which was called the International Tin Council (ITC) included 22 members, 16 of them consumer countries. The consumer countries had joined the ITC after the Korean War when tin was occasionally scarce. The United States was at one time a consuming member but dropped out in 1982. Like OPEC, the ITC imposed quotas

---

[31]William D. Sharpe, "Tin Cartel Joins OPEC on the Crash List," *The Wall Street Journal*, April 7, 1986, p. 23, and R. M. Bleiberg, "Tin in a Box: One of the World's Oldest Cartels Has Come to Grief," *Barron's*, November 18, 1985, p. 11.

on its producers, but unlike OPEC it tried to regulate supply and demand through the operation of a buffer stock. The buffer stock manager in London used the LME (London Metals Exchange) for purchasing and selling tin.

Malaysia, Indonesia, and Thailand are the three biggest producers of tin, and together they accounted for 45 percent of total world production of 192,000 metric tons in 1984. However, tin is not a major export earner for them (it is rubber). Only for Bolivia (which produced 10 perecent of total world output in 1984) was it of serious concern, but it was not even a member of ITC.

The actual collapse of the tin cartel during late 1985 and early 1986 came when the buffer stock manager, in an effort to keep the price above the ITC floor of $5.20 a pound, bought tin not only in the open market but through forward contracts. When he ran out of funds and the market price fell, he could not buy any more; he also was stuck with forward contracts which amounted to 60,000 metric tons (or about one-third of the world's yearly production). In a rescue operation the LME settled the contracts at a price of $3.90 a pound. The buffer stock operation was suspended, and the free market price soon fell below $3.00 a pound. The thing that kept prices ballooning was the purchase of huge amounts of tin by the buffer stock manager. The cartel members were well aware of these purchases and that the high price was attracting other supplies, but presumably they did nothing.

Buffer stock operations also exist in other commodities (cocoa, rubber). The rubber cartel known as the International Natural Rubber Organization (INRO), which includes Malaysia, Indonesia, and Thailand, also operates with a buffer stock operation. But the INRO has never indulged in forward purchases. If the INRO keeps rubber prices artificially high, it will also encourage research into and increased use of synthetic rubber and face the same fate as the other cartels.

13.11   INFORMAL, TACIT COLLUSION

A cartel is a formal collusive agreement. Oligopolists who cannot manage to form a cartel but recognize that their actions are interdependent sometimes operate on informal collusive agreements. These take two forms: gentlemen's agreements and price leadership.

Gentlemen's agreements are informal oral understandings among oligopolists that they will maintain a certain minimum price. These agreements are often ratified by nothing more than a handshake over lunch or dinner. An example of a long-standing gentlemen's agreement was the one in the iron and steel industry. Under the leadership of the U.S. Steel Corporation, iron and steel producing firms in the United States agreed to quote a uniform price according to a system called "Pittsburgh Plus." Under this system, every firm asked to give an offer price for steel would quote U.S. Steel's published price at its Pittsburgh mills (the basing point) plus railroad freight cost from Pittsburgh to the point of destination. This rule was to apply regardless of where the steel was actually produced and shipped. This single *basing point system* was later expanded to a multiple basing point system and to the cement industry.

The system, which operated very successfully throughout the first half of the twentieth century, was abandoned in 1948 after some legal attacks. Two dramatic examples of the effectiveness of gentlemen's agreements follow:[32]

• On May 26, 1936, the Navy department received bids from 31 steel companies for the delivery of a lot of rolled steel. Every company offered to deliver the steel at a price of $20,727.26.

• On April 23, 1936, officers of the U.S. Engineer Office at Tucumcari, New Mexico, opened sealed bids from 11 firms for the delivery of 6,000 barrels of cement. All 11 firms had submitted bids identical to the sixth demical point—$3.286854 per barrel.

Although gentlemen's agreements are now illegal in the United States (in the 1960s a grand jury indicted General Electric, Westinghouse, and 27 other manufacturers of heavy electrical equipment for price fixing), they are quite common. In fact, it is estimated that about one-third of all U.S. firms are involved in some form or other of tacit collusion.

Yet another form of informal tacit collusion is that of price leadership. *Price leadership* arises when one (or a few) firms typically initiate price changes and the rest of the firms in the industry follow. Note that the price changes can be either up or down. This removes the kink in the demand curve that we discussed earlier. In some cases the price leader can change over time, as happened in the cigarette industry. Although there are many varieties of price leadership, the most common one is the so-called umbrella price leadership, where the dominant firm, controlling a major portion of the industry's output, sets a price that maximizes its profit and then allows the smaller firms in the industry to sell all they want at this price. Examples of this form of price leadership are: aluminum (Alcoa), automobiles (General Motors), banking (Chase Manhattan), breakfast cereal (Kellogg), cigarettes (American and Reynolds), farm equipment (International Harvester), petroleum (Standard Oil), steel (U.S. Steel), and tin cans (American Can, Continental Can). The informal arrangement to follow the dominant firm avoids any legal problems faced by the firms under explicit collusion. The smaller firms tend to follow the dominant firm either out of fear or as a matter of convenience.

The problem facing the dominant firm is to determine the price that will maximize its profit while allowing the small firms to sell all they wish at that price. The situation is illustrated in Figure 13.13. The small firms are price takers, and the short-run supply curve is the horizontal sum of their marginal cost curves, above minimum average variable cost. This curve is labelled MC_s. The market demand curve is DD'. The dominant firm behaves like a monopolist and equates MR to its marginal cost, labelled MC_d. But before we can derive the dominant firm's MR curve, we need its demand curve.

We can first observe that at a price of Od, MC_s crosses DD'. This means that the small firms will supply the full quantity demanded in the market at this price, leaving nothing for the dominant firm. So the quantity demanded from the dom-

[32]These are cited from Max E. Fletcher, *Economics and Social Problems*, Houghton Mifflin, Boston, 1979, pp. 172–173. The second example cited by Fletcher is from F. Machlup, *The Basing Point System*, Blakiston, Philadelphia, 1949, p. 2.

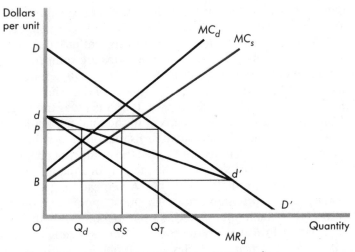

FIGURE 13.13   Price determination by a dominant firm.

inant firm at a price of Od or higher is 0. We can also note that below the price OB, the small firms are willing to produce nothing. Hence, for prices below OB, the demand curve facing the dominant firm is the portion $d'D'$ of the market demand curve. Finally, for prices between OB and Od, the quantity demanded from the dominant firm is the quantity demanded in the entire market minus the quantity supplied by the small firms. For example, the quantity demanded from the dominant firm at a price OP is Q_d, which equals $Q_T - Q_s$. The dominant firm's full demand curve is thus $dd'D'$.

MR_d is the marginal revenue curve corresponding to dd'. (Unless the dominant firm prices along the region dd', the model breaks down and we have monopoly.) The dominant firm equates MR_d with MC_d and sets price at OP. The dominant firm then produces Q_d while the small firms produce Q_s. And since, by construction $Q_d + Q_s$ is the total quantity demanded at price OP, the market clears.

In actual practice the analysis of price leadership is more complicated. There can be more than one dominant firm. There could be product differentiation, geographical differences among sellers, and so on. It is impossible to say anything concrete when all these complications are introduced. The analysis presented here captures the major important aspects of pricing in oligopoly under a dominant firm.

13.12   MERGERS

If firms in an oligopolistic industry cannot form a cartel or accept price leadership or form a gentlemen's agreement, they have another course open that will save them from any price wars. This is to eliminate rivalry through merger.

A *merger* is the consolidation of two or more independent firms into a single firm. A merger is termed "friendly" if it is supported by the management of the acquired firm and "hostile" if it is not. There are three kinds of mergers: (1) horizontal mergers, (2) vertical mergers, and (3) conglomerate mergers.

A *horizontal merger* combines two firms that produce the same product in the same geographic market. Since the two firms are competitors, the merger reduces the number of firms in the market. During the 1890s a series of horizontal mergers consolidated 200 steel firms into 20. Twelve of these firms were combined to form U.S. Steel in 1901. After this merger, U.S. Steel was the largest industrial firm in the United States and had 65 percent of the total market for steel.

A *vertical merger* combines two firms that previously had an actual or potential customer-supplier relationship. That is, the product of one firm is used as an input by the other firm. An example is the merging of a manufacturer of computers with a producer of electronic components. A vertical merger replaces a market transaction by an intrafirm transaction. The most important motive for vertical mergers is security—in the input markets, output markets, or both. The acquiring firm can merge with a firm that distributes its products through its outlets. This is called *downstream integration* and is designed to obtain security in the product markets. If the acquiring firm merges with a firm supplying inputs, it is called *upstream integration*. This is designed to obtain security in the input markets. In some cases vertical integration is dictated by the technology of production, as in the case of the iron and steel industry where the hot iron has to go directly into steel production. Otherwise, the delivered iron has to be reheated. Vertical integration eliminates the costs of transactions but also involves higher costs in coordinating two distinct operations.

A *conglomerate merger* is a merger that is neither horizontal nor vertical. These mergers have three motives: extending the market, expanding the product line, and pure investment. A merger between the *New York Times* and the *Los Angeles Times* would be a merger that is intended to expand the market. Both are newspapers but they serve distinct geographic area. A merger between General Motors and Winnebago Industries (a manufacturer of motor homes) would be a merger designed to expand the product line. General Motors needs to make only a few changes in its assembly lines. It can market the motor homes through the existing network. The acquisition of Montgomery Ward by Mobil Oil corporation is an example of a merger that has been justified on pure investment grounds only. It is a conglomerate merger that is not designed to expand markets or product line.

This classification of mergers is for convenience in analysis. There would, of course, be many mergers that fall in more than one of these categories.

Merger activity in the United States has proceeded in "waves"—some periods experiencing high merger activity and others none. Following the rapid industrialization of the U.S. economy, there were close to 3,000 mergers during the period 1896–1903. The mergers were "mergers for monopoly" and created such corporate giants as American Can, American Tobacco, and Standard Oil (each with a 90 percent share of its respective market) and U.S. Steel (with a 65 percent share of the steel market). Other big corporations formed during this period include Du Pont, Eastman Kodak, International Harvester, International Paper, United Fruit, and U.S. Rubber. In the following years, the pace of merger activity slowed down. However, in 1909 General Motors was formed through the consolidation of Buick, Cadillac, and Oldsmobile with Chevrolet being merged later. General Motors tried to acquire Ford as well but could not raise the necessary funds. In 1911, another famous corporation, IBM, was formed.

Another series of mergers (close to 7,000) took place from 1916 to 1929. These were "mergers for oligopoly." (These mergers created significant rivals to the monopolies created by the mergers from 1896 to 1903.) During this later period, Bethlehem Steel was formed to compete with U.S. Steel, Continental Can was formed to compete with American Can, and so on. There were also many vertical mergers involving firms in such industries as automobiles, chemicals, food, metals, and petroleum.

Between the Great Depression and the end of World War II, there was not much merger activity. However, there were more than 17,000 mergers from 1950 to 1970. In the 1960s there were many conglomerate mergers. These mergers were not designed to gain monopoly but were aimed at reducing risk through product diversification. However, this product diversification went too far in some instances. As an example, the International Telephone and Telegraph Company (ITT), which was originally in the communications business, diversified into car rentals (Avis), hotels and motels (Sheraton), home building (Levitt), insurance, consumer loans, publishing, and many other activities. Another example is the formation of Ling-Temco-Vought (L-T-V), which was ranked 335 on the *Fortune* list of 500 in 1961 but rose to rank 22 in 1968 by acquiring more than 30 companies including Braniff Airways and Jones and Laughlin Steel. All this merging created an enormous debt load for L-T-V, and it had to divest itself of many of the component companies in subsequent years. The late 1970s and early 1980s have seen a lot of merger activity again—mainly with big oil companies—Du Pont acquiring Conoco, U.S. Steel acquiring Marathon Oil, and Texaco acquiring Getty Oil. During recent years merger activity has again increased enormously starting in 1985.[33]

The effect of mergers on competition is a debatable issue. One has to study each case separately. Mergers, as in the period 1896 to 1903, that created "monopolies" are obviously anticompetitive. Mergers such as those in the period 1916 to 1929 that created firms contesting these monopolies probably increase competition. Of course, a merger of two oligopolistic firms would affect competition, whereas a merger of two firms in perfect competition might not. It is often argued that in a market with two dominant firms, the creation of a large "number three" firm increases competition.

13.13   SUMMARY AND CONCLUSIONS

Monopolistic competition is characterized by a large number of firms producing differentiated products. The firms behave independently, and nonprice competition is prevalent. There are no barriers to entry or exist.

Short-run equilibrium under monopolistic competition requires that each firm perceives that it is maximizing its profit and that the market clears. This requires

---

[33] According to *Mergers and Acquisitions* magazine, in 1987 there were 3,469 deals worth about $149 billion. The biggest deals were the acquisition of Standard Oil of Ohio by British Petroleum (worth $7.6 billion), Southland by Thompson ($4.0 billion), and Viacom by National Amusement ($3.1 billion).

that *MC* be equal to perceived *MR* at the output where the proportionate and perceived demand curves intersect.

Since there are no barriers to entry, economic profits induce new firms to enter the monopolistically competitive market. Entry will cease when a new equilibrium with zero profit is attained. This requires that the *LRAC* curve is tangent to the firm's perceived demand curve at the output where *MC* equals perceived *MR*. (The opposite changes will be prompted by short-run economic losses.)

Since in long-run equilibrium, the monopolistically competitive firm operates on the downward-sloping portion of the *LRAC* curve, per-unit production costs are not minimized, or scale economies are not fully exploited. But one can view the higher (than under perfect competition) per-unit production costs as the cost of variety or product differentiation.

The impact of advertising on output and price is unclear because, although the average total cost curve shifts upward, the demand curve shifts to the right.

The model of monopolistic competition has been criticized on the grounds that it contains conflicting assumptions, and has little predictive power.

Oligopoly is characterized by few sellers who are well aware of their interdependence. The product can be homogeneous or differentiated. Barriers to entry are present. Prices tend to be inflexible.

The Cournot model of duopoly is based on the assumption that each firm believes that its rival will maintain its current output. The resulting output is smaller than under perfect competition and the resulting price is higher. But both quantity and price approach the competitive levels as the number of firms increases.

The Bertrand model is based on the assumption that each firm believes that its rival will maintain its current price. Firms successively undercut each other's price until the competitive outcome is reached.

Edgeworth modifies Bertrand's model by assuming that neither firm can produce the full quantity demanded in the market at a price of 0. There is no determinate solution in this model.

In the Hotelling model, products are differentiated by location. Each firm moves toward the other in order to shelter a larger market share. Eventually, both firms wind up in the same location resulting in a waste of transportation resources.

Game theory can be used to analyze the behavior of oligopolists. The maximin decision rule says that the firm chooses the strategy with the best of the worst outcomes. This is a reasonable rule if the firm believes that its rival will react so that it realizes the minimum possible payoff. If rival firms match price cuts but not price increases, then the firm faces a kinked demand curve. The corresponding *MR* curve will have a gap. As long as *MC* stays within that gap, profit-maximizing output and price remain constant.

The purpose of a cartel is to limit the scope of competition. The major functions are price fixing and market division. A cartel will be most successful when demand is inelastic and stable, it can control a substantial share of actual and potential output, and the political climate is conducive to cooperation.

Tacit collusion can take the form of a gentlemen's agreement or price leadership. Dominant firm price leadership involves price setting by the dominant firm with smaller firms allowed to produce all they want at that price.

A merger is the consolidation of two or more independent firms into a single firm. A horizontal merger combines firms that produce the same product in the same market. A vertical merger involves the consolidation of two stages of production. And a conglomerate merger is neither horizontal nor vertical. The impact of the merger on the extent of competition must be judged on an individual basis.

KEY TERMS

Basing Point System
Bertrand Model
Cartel
Collusion
Comparative Advertising
Conglomerate Merger
Cournot Model
Downstream Integration
Edgeworth Model
Excess Capacity
Gentlemen's Agreement

Horizontal Merger
Hotelling Model
Ideal Output
Kinked Demand Curve
Market-sharing Cartel
Maximin Decision Rule
Merger
Monopolistic Competition
Nonprice Competition
Oligopoly
Payoff Matrix

Perfect Cartel
Predatory Price Cutting
Price Leadership
Price War
Product Differentiation
Product Group
Strategy
Upstream Integration
Vertical Merger
Zero-sum Game

QUESTIONS

1. Illustrate a monopolistically competitive firm in short-run equilibrium suffering a loss. Describe the adjustment process to long-run equilibrium.

2. Explain the relationship between the perceived demand curve and the proportionate demand curve under monopolistic competition. Which curve determines the firm's choice of output and price? Why must the two intersect at the equilibrium point?

3. Explain why we cannot determine whether a monopolistically competitive "industry" will have more or fewer firms than would be present under perfect competition.

4. Does the soft drink industry conform more closely to monopolistic competition or oligopoly? Support your answer.

5. In the Hotelling model, explain why a firm that sets price so high that it loses its sheltered market will have no customers.

6. In the Cournot model, explain why the two duopolists' marginal revenue curves are parallel. (Assume that the market demand is linear.)

7. In the kinked demand model of oligopoly, at what price does the kink occur? How useful is the model in explaining pricing under oligopoly?

8. In the Edgeworth model, will an increase in demand increase price? Why or why not?

9. Explain why the maximin decision rule is more appropriate under oligopoly than under perfect competition or monopolistic competition.

10. In a market-sharing cartel where price is set, will the agreement be easier to police when the product is homogeneous or differentiated? Why?

11. When price is determined by a dominant firm, explain the impact of a reduction in market demand. Explain the impact of an entry by a small firm.

12. Give an example of a horizontal, vertical, and conglomerate merger. What was the objective in each case?

13. "The higher the concentration in an industry, the higher will be the price rigidity." Evaluate this statement.

14. Two independent vendors are selling hot dogs on an isolated beach. Both hot dog stands are easily movable.

    a. Assume that people do not mind the walk to the hot dog stand. Where will the two vendors locate? Explain.

    b. As the sand heats up, customers become less willing to walk the distance and choose the nearest vendor. As the day becomes hotter, what happens to the relative locations of the two vendors? Why?

CHAPTER 14

PRICING IN PRODUCT MARKETS:
SOME EXTENSIONS

14.1   INTRODUCTION

In the preceding four chapters we discussed four different forms of market organization: competitive markets, monopolies, monopolistically competitive markets, and oligopolies. A study of these different forms of organization is a first step in the analysis of any industry. However, when we begin examining real world markets, we have to take account of several complications. In real world markets, buyers do not perceive all sellers' products as identical, and not all buyers are well informed, either about the price or the quality of the product they buy.[1] In such markets, sellers have to undertake product selection and advertising. Although we discussed product differentiation and advertising in the previous chapter, we did not consider consumers' response to them, nor did we consider the interaction between advertising, product differentiation, and market structure. There is now an enormous literature on this subject, and we will present some of these issues and findings in Sections 14.2 and 14.3.

We have also examined the sources and role of profits. An interesting debate centers on whether differences in the profit rates of firms are due primarily to differences in market structure or to differences in firm efficiency. We will look at this question and some of the empirical evidence in Section 14.4.

Finally, in Section 14.5, we will discuss a new controversial model of market organization. This is the theory of "contestable markets" that has been recently suggested by Baumol and his coauthors.

The topics in this chapter are given somewhat limited coverage. A complete presentation is beyond the scope of this book but would be included in a course on industrial organization. The purpose in presenting a limited coverage of issues is to give an idea of how the theories and the four basic models presented in the previous four chapters need to be extended when it comes to an analysis of real world markets.

14.2   PRODUCT DIFFERENTIATION AND MARKET STRUCTURE

Product differentiation is one of the most important characteristics of modern markets. Sellers differentiate their products in a number of ways: selection of location, selection of type of service, physical differences in the product supplied, brand labelling, and so on. Customers like to avoid driving long distances or going places where there is only one shop. Thus, location of sales outlets is very important. Customers also like fast and courteous service. They hate to stand in long lines. They also like attractive goods and buy some brand names because of assurance of quality. A large part of product differentiation is actually a consequence of consumers' demand for variety, because of differences in tastes. However, suppliers can, through aggressive advertising, create an image of differentiated products even when differences are minor.

One question that is often asked is whether product differentiation leads to

---

[1]Work on the consequences of imperfect buyer information about price started with a paper by G. J. Stigler, "The Economics of Information," *Journal of Political Economy*, vol. 69, June 1961, pp. 213–225.

monopoly power. Of course, product differentiation can confer some power over price. But to confer any monopoly power, product differentiation must somehow lead to a deterrence of entry. There are examples of markets with considerable product differentiation and negligible barriers to entry as in the case of restaurants. There are also examples of markets with product differentiation and substantial barriers to entry, as in the case of breakfast cereals.[2] So, the question is what produces entry deterrence? In his classic book, Bain argues that product differentiation might, in some cases, impose barriers to entry if consumers prefer established brands to new brands.[3] In a world where there is some uncertainty about product quality and consumers incur some costs in the acquistion of information, it is rational on the part of consumers to stick to known brands and shift to new brands only if there is considerable price advantage or expectation of higher quality. Marketing analysts have observed that if a product is virtually identical to established competitive products it has little chance of marketing success. If brand loyalty is important, then established firms' advantages might often depend heavily on buyers' uncertainty about the attributes of new brands, and, thus, a firm that is first in the market often has a considerable advantage.[4] Other firms entering the market with a "me too" strategy will not be successful. This aspect of consumer behavior gives monopoly power to a firm introducing a pioneering product. This conclusion is plausible given that consumers have a limited ability to receive, store, retrieve, and process information about different products. The marketing literature on consumer behavior emphasizes this point.[5]

Along with product differentiation, advertising is also an important characteristic of modern markets, and the two are intertwined. Does advertising create entry deterrence? Entry deterrence requires some asymmetries between established firms and new entrants because if firms entering an industry face the same demand and cost conditions as the established firms, the established firms cannot prevent entry. One argument presented by Joe Bain and others is that advertising provides established firms with advantages over potential entrants because it creates brand loyalty. New firms trying to enter the market have to overcome the preference consumers have for the established brands. This requires them to advertise more heavily and increases their cost.

However, brand loyalty created by advertising does not necessarily prevent entry. Brand loyalty deters entry only if it gives sufficient power to established firms to drive an entrant's profits to 0 while the established firms earn positive profits. If incumbent firms cannot prevent entry by advertising, then we cannot say that advertising creates entry barriers.

Apart from the brand loyalty argument, established firms may have a strategic advantage over potential entrants even if they face the same demand and cost conditions. The advantage arises from the leadership position of the established firms, which enables them to take actions prior to entry that places the entrants

---

[2]See R. Schmalensee, "Entry Deterrence in the Ready-to-Eat Breakfast Cereal Industry," *Bell Journal of Economics*, vol. 9, Autumn 1978, pp. 305–327.

[3]J. S. Bain, *Barriers to New Competition*, Harvard University Press, Cambridge, Mass., 1956, chap. 4.

[4]See R. Schmalensee, "Product Differentiation Advantages of Pioneering Brands," *American Economic Review*, vol. 72, June 1982, pp. 349–365.

[5]See J. R. Bettman, *An Information Processing Theory of Consumer Choice*, Addison-Wesley, Reading, Mass., 1979.

at a strategic disadvantage. Salop calls this *preentry asymmetry.*[6] Strategic actions might involve overinvestment in productive capacity or overinvestment in advertising capital, but the effects of the two actions can be different. If an established firm overinvests in productive capacity, it can deter potential entrants because the capacity commitment makes the threat of a price war credible.

In the case of advertising capital, however, an increased investment may be a handicap. When an established firm overinvests in advertising capital, it has a large group of loyal or captive customers who will not sample the new entrant's product. A large captive market reduces the established firm's incentive to respond aggressively to entry. It cannot reduce prices and raise advertising expenditures because it sacrifices profits that it can earn from its captive market (it has to charge the same price to all customers). This inability of the established firm to cut prices and respond aggressively to entry is known as the "fat-cat effect." In fact, an established firm may find it optimal to underinvest in advertising if it chooses to deter entry because by lowering its stock of goodwill it establishes a credible threat to cut prices in the event of entry. This is known as a choice to maintain a "lean and hungry look." Two other strategies, in relation to investment in advertising, are the "top dog strategy," which is overinvestment to be tough, and the "puppy-dog strategy," which is underinvestment in advertising that accommodates entry by turning the established firm into a small, friendly, nonaggressive puppy dog. Fudenberg and Tirole[7] discuss the conditions under which these different strategies are optimal. Their main conclusion is that overinvestment in advertising may not always deter entry, whereas underinvestment might sometimes deter entry.[8] Furthermore, established firms might choose to advertise to accommodate entry.

In summary, established firms have first-move advantages, and they can use advertising to deter entry, but the relationship between advertising expenditures and entry deterrence is very complex. In some specific cases we may be able to say that advertising deters entry and thus reduces competition, but we cannot make a general statement to that effect.

14.3   ADVERTISING AND MARKET STRUCTURE

> Advertising is a subject about which the ratio of poetic opinion to systematic analytics approaches infinity. Like romance, advertising is an activity to which people have been exposed and about which little is known.—*Harold Demsetz*[9]

The relationship between advertising and market structure is rather complex. Many questions are raised in this regard. Does advertising lead to monopoly? Is there more advertising under monopoly than under competition? To answer such questions we will consider (1) the effect of market structure on advertising, and (2) the effect of advertising on market structure.

---

[6]S. C. Salop, "Strategic Entry Deterrence," *American Economic Review,* May 1979, pp. 335–338.

[7]Drew Fudenberg and Jean Tirole, "The Fat Cat Effect, the Puppy-Dog Ploy and the Lean and Hungry Look," *American Economic Review,* May 1984, pp. 361–366.

[8]That firms might choose to underinvest in advertising to deter entry was suggested in R. Schmalensee, "Advertising and Entry Deterrence: An Exploratory Model," *Journal of Political Economy,* August 1983, pp. 636–653.

[9]*Journal of Industrial Economics,* December 1983, p. 229, in a paper by J. Arndt and J. L. Simon.

The effect of market structure on advertising.

A question that is often asked is whether monopoly (or oligopoly) can lead to too much advertising. Kaldor and Telser have suggested that monopoly can lead to a socially excessive level of advertising.[10] However, since monopolists appropriate only a part of the social gain from informative advertising, they may in some circumstances undersupply advertising.

Advertising can lead to two types of results: It can increase the overall demand for the product advertised, and it can increase the demand for the product of the advertising firm, at the expense of products supplied by other firms in the industry. In the former case, the benefits of advertising accrue to all the firms in the industry manufacturing the product. If the industry is monopolized, then advertising which increases the market demand for the product must also increase the monopolist's demand. Thus, the monopolist finds it profitable to undertake this type of advertising. For example, electric utilities frequently advertise that electric heat is somehow better than gas or oil heat.

With a large number of firms in the industry, no single firm has much of an incentive to engage in advertising that will increase overall market demand. In these cases, any such advertising is usually done by some association of producers. The citrus growers association advertises that orange juice is good for you. The dairy products association advertises the benefits of drinking milk or eating cheese. In a competitive industry, since an individual firm can sell as much as it pleases at the ruling market price, no individual firm has an incentive to advertise.

Where the benefits of advertising accrue to the firm, each individual firm has an incentive to advertise. But the perfectly competitive firm has nothing to advertise because its product is completely homogeneous.

In the case of oligopoly, the situation is different. The oligopolists advertise to capture a higher share of the total sales, which will be expanding with advertising. But even though advertising by oligopolists can increase the total demand for the products, a large proportion of the amount spent by each oligopolist can go to waste in cancelling the rivals' effort. This wasteful advertising can be avoided if the oligopolists coordinate their advertising policies with the purpose of joint profit maximization. In actual practice, however, this does not seem to happen. Scherer quotes an example showing that in the soap and detergent industry, enormous sums spent on advertising ($275 million in 1967 or roughly 11 percent of sales) do little more than cancel out rival messages because aggregate consumption of these products is almost unaffected by advertising.[11]

To summarize our discussion, in a competitive industry, no individual firm has an incentive to advertise because the benefits from advertising accrue to all firms in the industry while the advertising firm bears the costs. Under monopoly, the monopolist receives all the benefits, but in this case advertising is done only to increase the demand for the product, since there is no question of capturing rival firms' sales. Under oligopoly, advertising has two benefits—increasing the demand for the product, and capturing sales from rivals. However, in those cases when advertising does not increase total demand, all the advertising is somewhat

[10]N. Kaldor, "Economic Aspects of Advertising," *Review of Economic Studies*, vol. 18, 1950, pp. 1–27. L. G. Telser, "Advertising and Competition," *Journal of Political Economy*, vol. 72, December 1964, pp. 537–562.

[11]F. M. Scherer, *Industrial Market Structure and Economic Performance*, 2d ed., Houghton Mifflin, Boston, 1980, p. 389.

wasteful as it cancels the efforts of all firms trying to capture a bigger share of a pie that is not increasing in size. Thus, incentives to advertise are higher under oligopoly than under perfect competition or monopoly. But so are the possibilities of wasteful advertising and high social cost.

The effect of advertising on market structure

One question that has often been raised is whether advertising leads to monopoly power. It has been observed that the most important variable explaining differences in profitability between industries is the advertising-sales ratio. That is, the higher the advertising-sales ratio in an industry, the higher the profitability.[12] Based on this evidence, some economists have argued that advertising leads to brand loyalty, and this, in turn, leads to monopoly power. However, there is not much empirical support for this argument. Lambin examines 16 product classes in eight European countries and finds that the relationship between brand loyalty and advertising expenditure is on the average weak.[13] However, there are considerable differences between the different industries. Thus, we cannot depend on the connection between profitability and advertising expenditures via brand loyalty.

One other possible explanation for the observed correlation between advertising and profitability is that through pioneering new brands or making important improvements in quailty, some firms enjoy a favorable image in the minds of consumers and thus enjoy brand loyalty and earn above-normal profits. The firms do advertise, but this is for "image reinforcement." That is, advertising is designed to preserve the favorable image or brand loyalty. Thus, it is not the case that advertising expenditures are a causal factor in brand loyalty. Advertising is instead undertaken to preserve brand loyalty which itself is due to some other factors. Even some pioneering companies that stopped advertising their products later found that it was essential to advertise. For instance, the Hershey Company did not advertise its chocolates for a long time but then gave up this policy. IBM enjoyed a big market share and considerable price advantage over its competitors without much advertising.[14] Even so, when it introduced personal computers, it spent a lot of money on advertising, because it was not a pioneer in that field. There is, however, another difference between mainframe and personal computers. In the former case, the buyers are major corporations and educational institutions. In the latter case, the buyers are mostly individuals. For the sale of mainframe computers, IBM maintained a large and efficient sales force. Thus, there was less advertising through the usual channels.

In those cases where one firm enjoys considerable price advantage because of brand loyalty arising from a pioneering brand, in order for rival firms to enter and capture some share of the market, they must undertake intensive advertising. Thus, it is not advertising that leads to brand loyalty but it is the existence of brand loyalty that leads to high advertising expenditures. The established firms have to advertise

[12]A survey of this literature is in W. S. Comanor and T. A. Wilson, "The Effect of Advertising on Competition: A Survey," *Journal of Economic Literature*, vol. 17, June 1979, pp. 453–476.

[13]J. J. Lambin, *Advertising, Competition, and Market Conduct in Oligopoly Over Time*, North Holland, Amsterdam, 1976.

[14]Brian T. Ratchford and Gary T. Ford, "A Study of Prices and Market Shares in the Computer Mainframe Industry," *Journal of Business*, vol. 49, April 1976, pp. 194–218.

less but the rivals have to advertise a lot to get in. By virtue of their large market share, the established firms might also reap economies of scale in advertising.

In summary, the observed association between profitability rates and advertising-sales ratios does not imply any causal link between the two. Both are simultaneously affected by other factors.

Advertising as information

Some economists believe that advertising not only fails to create monopoly power but that it is a bulwark of competition. This view is summarized by Yale Brozen, who argues that advertising provides useful information about firms (their existence, size, location, and so on) and their products (their existence, prices, and qualities) and therefore reduces entry costs and makes demand curves more elastic than without advertising.[15]

An example that supports this view is the study of eyeglasses by Lee Benham.[16] In some states all advertising by prescription eyeglass dispensers is prohibited. In other states, there are no advertising restrictions. Benham argues that prohibition of advertising causes prices to rise by preventing firms from realizing significant economies arising from high sales volume. From a sample of 154 purchases, Benham found that prices were 25 to 30 percent higher in states with total advertising bans than in states without restrictions or with only weak restrictions. However, the eyeglass case is not typical. On the opposite side, Scherer gives a large number of examples where nationally branded products sell at a substantially higher price than private label products.[17]

There is, however, an element of truth in the argument that advertising provides useful information about firms and their products. At least advertisements inform consumers about the existence of some products and induce consumers to try them. Philip Nelson goes on to argue that firms will advertise more if they are confident that their product is sufficiently good that it will be repeatedly purchased after an advertising-induced trial.[18] He, therefore, concludes that heavily advertised goods are the best buys.

Nelson distinguishes between two types of goods: goods with "search qualities" and goods with "experience qualities." We might call these *search goods* and *experience goods*, respectively. Examples of search goods are clothing, footwear, furniture, and jewelry. We can assess their quality merely by looking and comparing among different stores and brands. Examples of experience goods are durables such as motor vehicles, instruments, electronic equipment, and appliances and nondurables such as beer, wine, foods, tobacco products, drugs, and perfumes. We can assess their quality only by trying them. In the case of search goods there can be

[15]Yale Brozen, "Entry Barriers, Advertising and Product Differentiation," in H. J. Goldschmid et al., eds., *Industrial Concentration: The New Learning*, Little Brown, Boston, 1974.

[16]Lee Benham, "The Effect of Advertising on the Price of Eye Glasses," *Journal of Law and Economics,"* vol. 15, October 1972, pp. 337–352.

[17]Scherer, *Industrial Market Structure*, pp. 381–384. Clorox, a leading nationally advertised brand, was found to be selling at a price 50 percent higher than the supermarkets' own house brands. Bayer aspirin was selling at a price twice that of the store brand aspirin.

[18]Philip Nelson, "Advertising as Information," *Journal of Political Economy*, vol. 82, July–August 1974, pp. 729–754, and "The Economic Consequences of Advertising," *Journal of Business*, vol. 48, April 1975, pp. 213–241.

very little scope for misleading advertising, since customers can be fooled only to a limited degree. In the case of experience goods, there is a larger scope for misleading advertising because at least first time experimenters can be fooled. However, the consumer will not be repeatedly fooled. Thus, the incentive for misleading advertising is less for lower-priced, frequently purchased items than for higher-priced, infrequently purchased ones. Nondurable experience goods are typically cheaper and bought more frequently than durable experience goods; hence, there is less incentive for misleading advertising of nondurable experience goods.

In addition to search goods whose qualities can be determined by inspection and experience goods whose qualities can only be determined after purchase, there is another category, "credence goods" defined by Darby and Karni.[19] These are goods whose characteristics cannot be determined reliably even after use. An example would be a preventative drug. Now if consumers think that heavily advertised goods are the best buys, then firms producing low-quality goods will have an incentive to undertake intensive advertising, particularly in the case of credence goods.

Another classification system for goods is that of "convenience goods" and "shopping goods" by Porter.[20] Convenience goods are goods that are usually purchased without consulting a retailer. Shopping goods are goods for which retailers serve as an important source of consumer information. Porter finds no association between advertising and profitability across markets in the case of shopping goods. He finds a strong positive association in a sample of convenience goods.

What all this discussion suggests is that the response of consumers to advertising varies a lot with the nature of the goods under consideration. Questions like "Does advertising cause profits?" or "Does advertising give monopoly power?" are too simplistic and cannot be given any general answer. What we need is an analysis that takes into account the nature of the good under consideration, how consumers process information and react to advertising, how producers perceive the consumers' response, and so on.[21]

If advertising conveys information then consumers will demand it. Telser suggests a theory in which advertising supplies information to consumers in response to their demands.[22] He argues that the equilibrium between the supply and demand for advertising will determine the total quantity provided. Most studies on advertising concentrate on the *effects* of advertising. By contrast Ehrlich and Fisher study the *determinants* of advertising.[23]

An alternative view on advertising as information to that in the papers by Nelson cited earlier is the view that advertising may indirectly signal quality. That is, the heavily advertised goods are the "best buys." This is the view expressed in

[19]M. Darby and E. Karni, "Free Competition and the Optimal Amount of Fraud," *Journal of Law and Economics*, vol. 16, April 1973, pp. 67–88.

[20]M. Porter, "Consumer Behavior, Retailer Power, and Performance in Consumer Goods Industries," *Review of Economics and Statistics*, vol. 56, November 1974, pp. 419–436.

[21]See G. R. Butters, "A Survey of Advertising and Market Structure," *American Economic Review*, vol. 66, May 1976, pp. 392–397.

[22]Lester G. Telser, "Towards a Theory of the Economics of Advertising," in *Issues in Advertising*, ed. D. G. Tuerck, American Enterprise Institute, Washington, D.C., 1978.

[23]I. Ehrlich and L. Fisher, "The Derived Demand for Advertising: A Theoretical and Empirical Investigation," *American Economic Review*, June 1982, pp. 366–388.

the papers by Klein and Leffler (see Section 13.4 of the preceding chapter for a discussion of their arguments) and Kihlstrom and Riordan.[24]

In summary, there is not much evidence to show that advertising, in general, promotes brand loyalty, deters entry of new firms into an industry, increases monopoly power, or increases profitability. In particular cases we might find some evidence for these claims, but as a general proposition there is no simple direct relationship between advertising and brand loyalty, entry deterrence, monopoly power, or increased profits. Perhaps the most important use of advertising is as a provider of information and as a signal of quality in markets where information about products or product quality is scarce.

EXAMPLE 14.1   The Ban on Broadcast Advertising of Cigarettes

Since the 1964 surgeon general's report on the harmful effects of cigarette smoking, the federal government has pursued policies to discourage cigarette smoking. The first move, in 1965, required health warnings on cigarette packages. Then in 1967, the Federal Communication Commission applied the Fairness Doctrine to cigarette advertising. This meant that broadcast stations that carried cigarette advertisements had to offer free time for antismoking messages. Finally in 1971 the federal government banned all broadcast advertising of cigarettes.

Did the ban on broadcast advertising of cigarettes have the desired effect of reducing cigarette consumption? Many empirical studies investigating this question came to the conclusion that the advertising ban had no effect on cigarette consumption.[25] In a study done soon after the ban, Hamilton argued that the 1964 surgeon general's report and the antismoking advertisements aired during the period of the Fairness Doctrine created health-scare effects that were successful in reducing cigarette consumption.[26] However, with the 1971 ban, the antismoking advertisements also disappeared and the consumption of cigarettes actually increased. Hamilton argued that his analysis showed that the cigarette advertisements had no effect and the antismoking advertisements had a negative effect on cigarette smoking.

Schneider, Klein, and Murphy also argued that the advertising ban was not effective in reducing cigarette consumption.[27] They contend that the 1953 health report and the 1964 surgeon general's report significantly reduced cigarette consumption. However, as the public became aware of the dangers of cigarette smoking, cigarette companies introduced filter-tip and low-tar cigarettes. This change in cigarette technology reduced the amount of tobacco per cigarette and reduced the health risks of smoking. Schneider, Klein, and Murphy argue that in estimating the demand for cigarettes and investigating the effect of the advertising ban, one should take account of these changes in cigarette technology and improvements in cigarette quality.

[24]R. Kihlstrom and M. H. Riordan, "Advertising as a Signal," *Journal of Political Economy*, June 1984, pp. 427–450.

[25]For a review of these studies and his own investigation see Robert E. MacAuliffe, *Advertising, Competition and Public Policy: Theories and New Evidence*, Lexington Books, Lexington, Mass., 1987, pp. 83–90.

[26]J. L. Hamilton, "The Demand for Cigarettes: Advertising, the Health Scare and the Cigarette Advertising Ban," *Review of Economics and Statistics*, November 1972, pp. 401–411.

[27]L. Schneider, B. Klein, and K. M. Murphy, "Governmental Regulation of Cigarette Health Information," *Journal of Law and Economics*, December 1981, pp. 575–612.

Thus, as far as the empirical evidence goes, the advertising ban has had no effect on cigarette consumption. Opponents of cigarette advertising object to the harmful effects cigarettes have on health. They, therefore, support the ban on cigarette advertising hoping that this will reduce cigarette consumption and improve health. Given the habitual nature of cigarette consumption, we might expect that the ban may not reduce cigarette consumption and the evidence shows that this is so. Thus, the advertising ban does not lead to improved health. But can it lead to a worsening of health? The answer is "perhaps yes."

If cigarette manufacturers are prevented from broadcast advertising, they have to resort to other costlier means of advertising. Further, with the restrictions on advertising, cigarette manufacturers find it less profitable to engage in research and development. They have reduced incentives to develop healthier cigarettes if they cannot easily inform consumers about the relative virtues of the new product. This means that consumers are exposed to greater health risks than would otherwise be the case if cigarette manufacturers competed with each other to develop safer products and communicated them to the customers through broadcast advertising. The advertising ban thus imposes some costs to society, although the magnitude of the cost cannot be measured because it depends on what new products might have been introduced without the ban.

14.4　MARKET STRUCTURE AND PROFITABILITY DIFFERENCES AMONG FIRMS

In the previous section we talked of differences in advertising-sales ratios as being one of the potential explanations for profitability differences among firms. One of the major questions often raised concerns the effect of market structure on profitability. There are essentially three competing theories on this: the classical theory, the anticlassical revisionist theory, and the managerial theory.

1. The classical theory: This theory follows Joe Bain's work, from the 1950s, and argues that profitability differences among firms are mainly due to differences among industries. It is, thus, the market structure of the industry that is important. Profitability of firms in an industry is primarily determined by the ability of the firms in that industry to limit rivalry among themselves and to impose barriers to entry. One of the important variables explaining differences in profitability is the concentration ratio of the industry. Empirical evidence shows a positive association between profitability and the concentration ratio.[28]

2. The anticlassical revisionist theory: This theory, advanced in the 1970s, holds that all markets are (at least approximately) competitive and scale economies are negligible.[29] However, within at least some industries there are persistent efficiency differences among firms. More efficient firms tend to grow at the expense of their

---

[28]This evidence is summarized in Leonard Weiss, "The Concentration-Profits Relationship and Anti-Trust," in H. J. Goldschmid et al., eds., *Industrial Concentration: The New Learning,* Little-Brown, Boston, 1974 and Scherer, *Industrial Market Structure,* chap. 9 (on "The Price and Profit Consequences of Market Structure").

[29]See H. Demsetz, "Industry Structure, Market Rivalry and Public Policy," *Journal of Law and Economics,* vol. 16, April 1973, pp. 1–10 and S. Peltzman, "The Gains and Losses From Industrial Concentration," *Journal of Law and Economics,* vol. 20, October 1977, pp. 229–263.

rivals and are more profitable. The greater the efficiency differences in an industry, the less equal are the market shares, and, thus, the higher is the concentration ratio. Also, the higher profits of the larger firms lead to higher average industry profitability. One can observe a positive association between concentration ratios and profitability but, according to the theory, this is due to the impact of efficiency differences on both the concentration ratio and average industry profitability and not because concentration facilitates collusion.[30] Note that the argument is similar to the one that we discussed earlier regarding the relationship between profitability and the advertising-sales ratio. Namely, there are some other variables that affect both. In fact, when efficiency measures are used (in addition to concentration ratio) to explain the differences between firms in their profitability rates, the concentration ratio actually has a negative effect on profitability. Thus, the positive correlation between the concentration ratio and profitability may be a spurious one.

3. *The managerial theory:* This theory is somewhat like the anticlassical theory. It stresses the importance of firm-level efficiency differences based largely on differences in organizational and managerial skills. Evidence for this hypothesis is presented in Mueller.[31] Again, when measures of efficiency are used (in addition to the concentration ratio) to explain profitability, it is found that the concentration ratio has a negative effect on profitability.

In summary, the classical theory says that interfirm differences in profitability are not due to differences among firms but rather are due to differences in market structure among the different industries in which they operate. Thus, industry effects are important; firm effects are not. The opposite view holds that it is differences in the efficiency level among firms that are important, not the differences among industries, which are spurious and arise from interfirm differences in efficiency. Schmalensee tested this simple hypothesis by using 1,775 business units operated by 456 firms in 242 manufacturing industries.[32] He decomposed the differences in profitability rates into different sources: differences between firms, between industries, and so forth. His findings are actually opposite from the findings of those who tested the anticlassical theory. He finds that (1) there are no firm effects, (2) industry effects are important and explain 75 percent of the differences in profitability between firms, and (3) market share effects are negligible. He states, however, that these findings do not necessarily mean that the classical theory is correct, because the analysis is descriptive and the year (1975) chosen for the analysis may have been atypical due to the severe recession and energy price shocks.

14.5 CONTESTABLE MARKETS

In the preceding section we talked of the classical and anticlassical theories of market structure. We said that the anticlassical theory held that all markets are (at

---

[30]Evidence in favor of this view is in Stephen Martin, *Market, Firm and Economic Performance,* N.Y.U. Graduate School of Business, New York, 1983, and D. J. Ravenscraft, "Structure-Profit Relationships at the Line of Business and Industry Level," *Review of Economics and Statistics,* vol. 65, February 1983, pp. 22–31.

[31]Dennis C. Mueller, *The Determinants of Persistent Profits,* Federal Trade Commission, Washington, D.C., June 1983.

[32]R. Schmalensee, "Do Markets Differ Much?" *American Economic Review,* vol. 75, June 1985, pp. 341–351.

least approximately) competitive. A new theory of market structure has recently been advanced by Baumol and his coworkers.[33] This is the theory of *contestable* markets. As we shall see, a contestable market has many of the characteristics of a competitive market.

A contestable market is one into which entry is absolutely free and exit is absolutely costless. The entrant suffers no disadvantage in terms of production techniques or perceived product quality relative to the incumbent. The crucial feature of a contestable market is its vulnerability to "hit-and-run entry." The presence of shadow entrants will force competitive behavior by the incumbents. The crucial assumption in perfect competition is price-taking behavior. In the theory of contestable markets this assumption is replaced with that of rapid entry and exit. The potential competitors have the same cost functions and can enter and leave *without loss of capital* before the incumbents change their prices. Sunk costs are thus assumed to be 0.

The use of the word "contestable" has been criticized by Shepherd.[34] By dictionary definition, a *contest* is a struggle whose uncertain outcome depends on a series of actions and reactions. Thus, every market is at least partly contestable. However, the hit-and-run entry does not permit a contest. Also, according to Baumol, actual entry need not occur. The existing firm (or firms) in the industry can prevent entry by anticipatory price restraint. If actual entry does not occur, there can be no contest. Shepherd suggests the use of the term "ultra-free entry" instead of "contestable." He also criticizes the assumption of ultra-free entry as inconsistent. If there are fixed costs, then entry cannot be at a small scale. The entering firm has to produce the same output as the incumbent firm, or the entering firm will have higher average total cost. Thus, the entry will be on a large scale, and it is implausible to assume that there will be no response by the incumbent.[35]

Many of the assumptions underlying the theory of contestable markets are open to question. The theory assumes that all producers have access to the same technology, there are no sunk costs and exit is entirely costless, incumbents cannot change prices instantly, and consumers respond instantly to price differences. Under such circumstances, the entrant undercuts prices, serves all of the market, and exits costlessly if price retaliation occurs. The entrant makes a profit if the incumbent is not minimizing costs or is making above-normal profits.

In practice, however, entry and exit are not costless. Production involves some sunk costs. Entry and exit take some time, and it takes time to liquidate commitments. It is questionable whether consumers respond instantly to differences between the prices of the entrant and the incumbent. As we discussed earlier, in Sections 14.2 and 14.3, consumers take some time to assimilate new information. However, the incumbent can change prices much faster. The contestable market theory assumes long lags in the price behavior of the incumbent firm and short lags in the behavior of consumers and the entry and exit of the entering firm. Traditional theory of industrial organization assumes the opposite—that prices can

---

[33]See W. J. Baumol, "Contestable Markets: An Uprising in the Theory of Industry Structure," *American Economic Review*, vol. 72, March 1982, pp. 1–15, and W. J. Baumol, J. C. Panzar, and R. D. Willig, *Contestable Markets and the Theory of Industry Structure*, Harcourt, Brace, Jovanovich, San Diego, 1982.

[34]W. G. Shepherd, "Contestability vs. Competition," *American Economic Review*, vol. 74, September 1984, pp. 572–587.

[35]For other criticisms of the ultrafree assumption, see the paper by Shepherd, ibid.

be adjusted faster than sunk capacity and that consumer response has significant delays. The empirical evidence supports the traditional view.

There is not much empirical evidence for the contestable markets theory. One industry, the airlines industry, is presented as an example of a contestable market. But Shepherd disputes this as well.[36] Under deregulation during 1975 to 1984, the airline industry has shown increased competition and more flexible pricing. It is easier for airlines to enter and compete on each others' routes. But there is the question of what the relevant market is, in the case of the airline industry. If we define the relevant market as the national market, then entry into the industry involves founding a new airline, and entry and exit are not costless (in fact, they involve substantial costs). Baumol and his coauthors define each *city-pair-route* as the relevant market. Under this definition, established airlines all act as potential entrants to each others' routes. Entry and exit can be almost costless. There is no new capital equipment involved. However, even with the addition of routes, entry is not ultrafree. Existing carriers have not been easily displaced, and they have often responded effectively. It takes time to build ground facilities and lure customers from the previous airline. The success of the entrant also depends on the connections provided, but if we consider this, we will be expanding the scope of the relevant market. Shepherd argues that airline competition can be explained well by established concepts of market structure and entry rather than by the contestable markets theory.

In a survey paper, Bailey and Baumol offer four possible cases where the contestable markets theory could be applicable: railroads, airlines, trucking, and telephone service.[37] Shepherd discusses these examples and argues that they are not satisfactory.[38] The arguments are similar to those in the case of airlines: that the relevant market is not properly defined and entry is not costless. There are, however, more empirical studies emerging on this issue and the debate of how relevant these studies are will go on for a while. For instance, in a study of the international liner shipping industry, Davies argues that sunk costs are low, and entrants and incumbents are symmetrically placed.[39] The Canadian data show frequent entry and exit, hit and run entry, and large-scale entry. Davies claims that ''far from being a theory without facts, the contestability principle is shown to be extremely relevant in the economic analysis of the shipping industry.'' Yet another paper that is sympathetic to the contestable markets theory is by Morrison and Winston, who study the empirical implications of the contestability hypothesis.[40]

In summary, questions have been raised about the usefulness of the contestable markets theory in modelling the behavior of modern markets. Some have argued that the traditional theories can adequately explain the observed behavior and that the new theory does not lead to any additional insights. In connection with their

[36]Shepherd, ibid.

[37]Elizabeth E. Bailey and William J. Baumol, ''Deregulation and the Theory of Contestable Markets,'' *Yale Journal of Regulation*, 1984, pp. 111–113.

[38]W. G. Shepherd, ''Illogic and Unreality: The Odd Case of Ultra-Free Entry and Inert Markets,'' in R. E. Grieson (ed.), *Antitrust and Regulation*, Lexington Books, 1986, pp. 231–252.

[39]J. E. Davies, ''Competition, Contestability, and the Liner Shipping Industry,'' *Journal of Transportation Economic Policy*, September 1986, pp. 299–312.

[40]S. A. Morrison and C. Winston, ''Empirical Implications and Tests of the Contestability Hypothesis,'' *Journal of Law and Economics*, April 1987, pp. 53–66.

theory, Baumol and his coauthors develop a useful analysis of multiproduct costs and prices and even critics of the contestable markets theory agree that this is useful.

14.6   SUMMARY AND CONCLUSIONS

To confer any monopoly profit, product differentiation must somehow lead to deterrence of entry. If consumers prefer established brands, then firms introducing pioneering products might acquire some monopoly power.

Incentives to advertise are higher under oligopoly than under monopoly or perfect competition. Under oligopoly, advertising serves to increase overall market demand and also to reallocate market shares.

Higher advertising-sales ratios are associated with greater profitability, but there is little support for the argument that advertising leads to brand loyalty, which, in turn, increases profitability. In fact, it appears that the existence of brand loyalty leads to heavier advertising (by late entrants). Advertising may enhance competition by reducing entry costs and increasing the elasticity of the product demand curves. Advertising may also reduce price by allowing firms to realize scale economies, but there is limited empirical support for this argument.

There are three competing theories concerning the source of profitability differences among firms. The classical theory argues that profitability differences among firms are due to differences in market structure. The anticlassical revisionist theory argues that differences in profitability among firms are due to differences in efficiency. The managerial theory again argues that differences in profitability are due to differences in efficiency but stresses organizational and managerial aspects of efficiency.

In a contestable market, entry is absolutely free and exit is absolutely costless. This assumption replaces the one of price-taking behavior in the model of perfect competition. Although it constitutes an important contribution, the theory of contestable markets has received extensive criticism.

KEY TERMS

Anticlassical Revisionist Theory	Convenience Goods	Search Goods
Classical Theory	Credence Goods	Shopping Goods
Contestable Market	Experience Goods	
	Managerial Theory	

QUESTIONS

1. Television advertising is considerably more expensive than other forms. What kinds of products are primarily advertised on television? Does this support our observation that oligopolists have the greatest incentive to advertise?

2. The managerial theory argues that differences in profitability among firms are due primarily to differences in managerial efficiency. If this is so, do the observed differences in profitability constitute differences in economic profit or merely differences in accounting profit? Why?

3. Brozen argues that advertising serves to provide important information. Does information content vary with the form of advertising? If so, which forms appear to be most informative?

4. Is the division of goods into convenience goods and shopping goods independent of the division into search goods and experience goods, or does there appear to be a strong correlation between the groups?

PART FOUR
PRICING IN
INPUT MARKETS

Part Four (Chapters 15 to 17) presents the theory of pricing in input markets. In Chapter 15 we consider the pricing of inputs under perfect competition in both the input and output markets. In Chapter 16 we consider the pricing of inputs under imperfect competition in the input and/or output markets. Although the theory is worked out for many inputs, in Chapters 15 and 16 we consider the labor input in greater detail. Chapter 17 is, therefore, devoted to special problems with other inputs: land and capital.

CHAPTER 15

EMPLOYMENT AND PRICING OF INPUTS IN COMPETITIVE MARKETS

15.1   INTRODUCTION

We began this book with an overview of supply and demand and the determination of price and output in the product market. We then started looking behind the demand and supply curves in more depth, that is, we examined the theory of consumer behavior to understand from where the demand curve comes. We studied production theory and cost theory, as well as the structure of the product market, to understand from where the supply curve comes. We are now ready to look at one more piece of the puzzle, namely, input markets. The following correspondence, with respect to the labor input, gives us an idea of just where input markets fit in:

	Output	Labor Input
Demand	Derived from preferences of consumers	Derived from production conditions
Supply	Derived from production conditions	Derived from preferences of workers

In this and the next two chapters we will discuss the pricing of inputs or factors of production in the input markets or what are commonly called the *factor markets*. As with pricing in the output markets, pricing in factor markets will depend on the way suppliers and demanders are organized. In this chapter we will discuss pricing of inputs in competitive markets. In the next chapter we will discuss pricing of inputs under imperfect competition.

In this chapter, many of our discussions and applications focus on a particular input—labor. (The student will find it useful to review what we have already said about labor supply in Chapter 5.) Labor is a particularly important and interesting input, but the other factors will be given more coverage in the subsequent chapters. It might be useful to point out that labor is not really a single input. There are all types of labor with different skills (or no skills), and these types are certainly not interchangeable. Yet in this chapter we talk about *the* wage rate and *the* quantity of labor employed. What we are really examining is the input market for a particular type of labor. We will discuss wage differences for different types of labor in Chapter 17.

15.2   PROFIT MAXIMIZATION IN RELATION TO FACTOR (INPUT) USAGE

In Chapter 10 we argued that if $MR > MC$, then another unit of output adds more to revenues than to costs, and, thus, expanding output increases profit. But, if $MR < MC$, then reducing output will subtract more from costs than from revenues, so that reducing output increases profit. Combining these observations, the firm clearly maximizes profit by expanding output to the point where $MR = MC$ but no further.

We can similarly argue that the firm will maximize profit by increasing its usage of input X just until

$$(MRP)_X = (MFC)_X$$

$(MRP)_X$ is the marginal revenue product of input X, which equals $\Delta TR/\Delta X$, where X is the quantity of input X employed. That is, $(MRP)_X$ tells us by how much total revenues will increase if one more unit of X is hired and other inputs remain constant. $(MRP)_X$ can also be expressed as

$$(MRP)_X = \frac{\Delta TR}{\Delta X} = \frac{\Delta Q}{\Delta X} \cdot \frac{\Delta TR}{\Delta Q} = (MP)_X \cdot MR$$

where $(MP)_X$ is the marginal product of X and MR is marginal revenue. $(MFC)_X$ is the marginal factor cost of X, which equals $\Delta TC/\Delta X$. $(MFC)_X$ tells us by how much total cost will increase if one more unit of X is hired and other inputs remain unchanged. Clearly, the firm should expand usage of X as long as $(MRP)_X > (MFC)_X$, because additional units add more to revenues than to costs. But the firm should expand usage of X only to the point where $(MRP)_X = (MFC)_X$. Once MFC exceeds MRP, additional input usage reduces profit.

The values of MRP and MFC will depend on the structures of the output market and input markets. In this chapter, we will assume perfect competition in both the output market and the input markets.

Under perfect competition in the output market, the firm is a price taker and $P = MR$. Hence,

$$MRP = P_0 \cdot MP = VMP$$

where VMP is the value of the marginal product and P_0 is the output price.

Also, if there is perfect competition in the input market, the firm can purchase all of the input that it wants at the market price. The input supply curve facing the firm is horizontal, and MFC equals input price.

Thus, with competition in both the output and input markets, profit maximization requires that

$$\text{Output price} \times \text{marginal product} = \text{input price}$$

And if we have several inputs, since output price is the same, we get

$$\frac{\text{Price of input 1}}{MP \text{ of input 1}} = \frac{\text{price of input 2}}{MP \text{ of input 2}} = \frac{\text{price of input 3}}{MP \text{ of input 3}} =$$

$$\dots \text{etc.} = \text{price of output}$$

We will illustrate this principle in the next section with a numerical example.

15.3 DEMAND CURVE FOR A SINGLE VARIABLE INPUT

We will first examine the case of a single variable input—labor. Consider a firm producing wheat. The farm, machinery, fertilizer, seed, and so on are all fixed. The only input that is varied is the number of workers, who are assumed to be homogeneous in ability.

Table 15.1 gives the changes in output, or marginal product of labor, as we increase the labor input. Assuming that each unit of output sells for $10, we compute the value of the marginal product (VMP). The wage rate per worker, or the price of labor, is $2,000. The firm employs labor to the point where the VMP = wage rate. Increasing the labor input beyond this point will result in a reduction in profit.

The number of workers hired from Table 15.1 is eight. If the wage rate is reduced to $1,000 the number of workers hired will be nine. If the wage rate is raised to $3,000 the number of workers hired will be seven.

The VMP curve will be rising at first and then falling, as shown in Figure 15.1. The VMP curve rises as long as MP of labor is increasing. Once we reach the point of diminishing marginal return, the VMP curve declines. Some part of the declining portion of the VMP curve gives the demand for labor curve. This is shown in Figure 15.2.

Note that if the wage rate is $5,000 from Table 15.1, we might conclude that the firm will employ five workers because this is where VMP = wage rate. However, this firm could not even cover its variable costs. The labor cost is $25,000 and

TABLE 15.1 Changes in Output as Labor Input Increases

Number of Workers	Maximum Output	Marginal Product	Value of Marginal Product (Marginal Product × $10)	Wage Rate	Increase in Profit (Value of Marginal Product − Wage Rate)
0				$2,000	
1	300	300	$3,000	2,000	$1,000
2	700	400	4,000	2,000	2,000
3	1,200	500	5,000	2,000	3,000
4	1,800	600	6,000	2,000	4,000
5	2,300	500	5,000	2,000	3,000
6	2,700	400	4,000	2,000	2,000
7	3,000	300	3,000	2,000	1,000
8	3,200	200	2,000	2,000	0
9	3,300	100	1,000	2,000	−1,000
10	3,300	0	0	2,000	−2,000

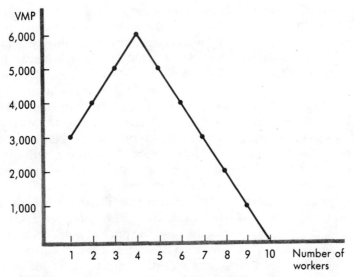

FIGURE 15.1   Value of marginal product (VMP) curve.

value of output is $23,000. Hence, the firm will not hire any workers and will shut down if the wage rate is $5,000. The condition that input price equals marginal product × output price holds only as long as the firm opts to hire any of the input. And the firm will employ the input in the short run as long as the revenue per unit of the input equals or exceeds the input price, which implies that variable costs are being covered.

Note that Figure 15.2 has been drawn on the assumption of a given output price $P_0 = \$10$. What will happen if the output price falls to, say, $8 per unit? The value of marginal product will fall (the fourth column in Table 15.1), and the VMP curve will shift to the left. We can easily see that at a wage rate of $2,000

FIGURE 15.2   Demand for labor by an individual firm.

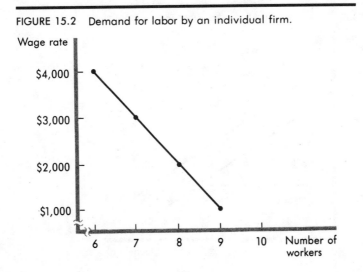

the firm will now hire seven workers and not eight. Also, at a wage rate of $4,000, we have VMP = wage rate when the number of workers hired is three, but the firm will not employ any workers because the value of total output (or total revenue) for three workers is $8 × 1,200 = $9,600 whereas the wage bill is 3 × $4,000 = $12,000. Thus, the firm cannot cover its variable costs.

In any case, it is easy to see that with a decline in output price, and the leftward shift in the VMP curve, the demand curve for labor in Figure 15.2 shifts to the left. With an increase in output price, it shifts to the right. This is an intuitive result. As product price rises, the firm expands output and, hence, needs more labor. The demand for the input is a *derived demand*. It is called a derived demand because it is derived from the demand for output. How much of the input a firm demands depends on the quantity of output the firm produces.

Figure 15.2 shows that as the wage rate falls, the firm demands a larger number of workers. However, when each firm hires more workers, and produces more output, the industry output rises and the price of output falls. With this fall in the price of output, as we have seen, the input demand curve of each firm shifts to the left. Thus, in deriving the industry demand curve for an input, we have to account for the effect of a price decline on the individual firms' input demand curves.

Figure 15.3 illustrates this point. We can aggregate the individual firms' demand curves for labor by horizontal summation, as we did with individual consumer demand functions in Chapter 2. We will call this demand curve, obtained by simple summation, the *aggregate demand curve*. It gives the quantity of labor demanded at each wage rate for the industry as a whole, *holding output price constant*. We can get such aggregate demand curves for each output price. In Figure 15.3, D_1D_1 is an aggregate demand curve, and D_2D_2 is another aggregate demand curve for a lower output price (with a lower output price we saw that each individual firm's demand curve shifts to the left).

Now when the wage rate falls from W_1 to W_2, more labor will be hired, but this will increase industry output with a consequent decline in the output price.

FIGURE 15.3   Demand curve for labor in a competitive industry.

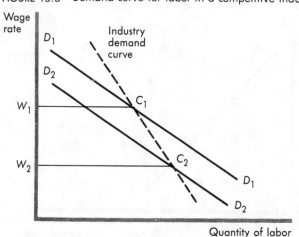

Thus, the aggregate demand curve for labor shifts to the left, and the amount of labor hired will be given by the point C_2 on D_2D_2 (not by the corresponding point on D_1D_1). The industry input demand curve is given by the dotted line C_1C_2 in Figure 15.3. This demand curve takes account of the decline in output price due to an increase in the industry output.[1]

Note that the industry demand curve C_1C_2 is steeper than the aggregate demand curves D_1D_1 and D_2D_2. How much steeper it is depends on how much the aggregate demand curve shifts with the decline in output price. If the elasticity of demand for output is high, then the decline in price for a given increase in output will be small. Thus, the shift in aggregate demand curve will be very small. So, the difference in the elasticities between the industry demand curve and the sum of the individual firms' demand curves depends directly on the elasticity of demand for the output. In all cases the industry demand curve will be less elastic than the sum of the individual firms' demand curves.

15.4 THE CASE OF SEVERAL INPUTS

Consider the case of two variable inputs: labor and capital. The firm will employ labor and capital to the point where the value of the marginal product of each factor is equal to the price of the factor. Thus

$$(VMP)_L = (MP)_L \cdot P_0 = P_L$$

and

$$(VMP)_K = (MP)_K \cdot P_0 = P_K$$

But these relationships themselves do not enable us to derive the demand curves for the inputs. We shall now show how these curves are derived.

The demand curve in Figure 15.2 was derived on the assumption that the quantity of capital is fixed. What if we vary the quantity of capital? The impact on the demand for labor depends on the nature of the relationship between the inputs.

If the inputs are *independent inputs*, a change in the quantity of one input has no effect on the marginal product of the other, so that the marginal product of labor will be independent of the amount of capital and vice versa. In this case, the demand curves for each factor can be derived separately as in the previous section.

Normally, however, inputs are *complementary inputs*, so that the marginal product of one input increases with higher usage of the other input. For example, if more tools and machinery are provided, each worker's marginal product should rise. Thus, the marginal product of labor, for each unit of labor, increases with a larger quantity employed of the complementary input (capital in this case). This means that the VMP_L curve and the demand for labor curve will shift to the right as the amount of capital is increased. This is shown in Figure 15.4.

[1]Note that we are assuming that the demand curve D_1D_1 is the aggregate demand curve for the industry output level corresponding to the wage rate W_1. Thus, C_1 is a point on the industry demand curve.

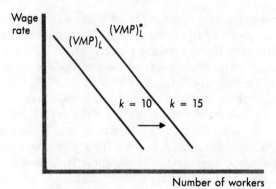

FIGURE 15.4   A shift in the demand curve for labor with increased usage of capital input.

Now consider the impact of a decline in the wage rate. The lower price of labor will make the firm hire more labor. But the lower wage rate also causes the marginal cost of output to fall so that the firm expands output. As the firm expands output, it will probably hire more capital. But as capital usage increases, the *VMP* curve and the demand-for-labor curve shift to the right, inducing a further increase in the quantity of labor employed.

The resulting demand curve for labor is shown in Figure 15.5 by the dotted line. It is flatter than the $(VMP)_L$ lines, which give the demand curves for labor for *given* values of the capital input. The increase in the quantity of labor demanded can be broken up into two parts in much the same way as was done in the theory of the consumer in Chapter 5. There the effect of a decline in the price of good X was broken up into a *substitution effect* and an *income effect*. Here we can do the same except that the income effect is called the *scale effect* or *output effect*. This is

FIGURE 15.5   Demand for labor allowing for changes in the capital input.

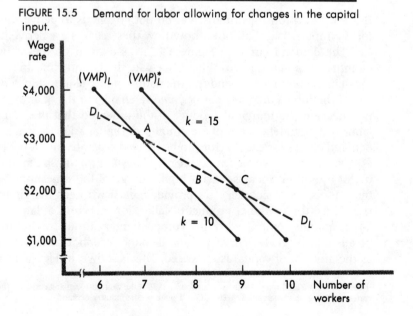

shown in Figure 15.6. Q_1 is the initial output level. The absolute slope of AB_1 is the ratio of the initial wage rate to the price of the capital input. Thus, bundle C represents the least cost input bundle for producing Q_1 with the initial wage rate. Now suppose that when the wage rate falls, the input price ratio is equal to the absolute slope of AB_2. If the firm expands output to Q_2, the optimal input bundle becomes D.

Now, as we did in Chapter 5 when we considered substitution effect and income effect in consumption, draw a line $A'B_2'$ parallel to AB_2 but tangent to the isoquant Q_1. The input bundle E represents the least-cost input bundle for the firm if it produces the initial output after the decline in the wage rate. Bundle E contains more labor and less capital than bundle C.

The movement from C to D can, thus, be decomposed into two components: a movement from C to E along the old isoquant—which is a pure substitution effect—and a movement from E to D—which is a scale effect or output effect. Also, the total increase in labor input from L_1 to L_2 can be decomposed into two parts: (1) an increase from L_1 to L_2' (the substitution effect) and (2) an increase from L_2' to L_2 (the scale effect or output effect).

Note that we cannot show the substitution and output effects on the diagram in Figure 15.5 because the curves are *for given values of the capital input,* whereas what we want to consider is movement along an isoquant (substitution effect) and movement to a higher isoquant (output effect). The substitution effect involves a reduction in capital usage. The output effect, in this example, involves an increase in capital usage. So the quantity of capital is not remaining constant.

We can decompose the movement from 7 units of labor to 9 units (A to C) in Figure 15.5 into the following: 7 to 8 (A to B) is movement along a demand curve

FIGURE 15.6   Substitution and scale effects of a decline in the price of labor.

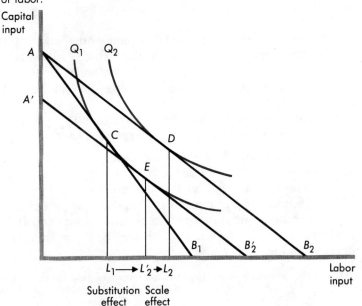

and 8 to 9 (B to C) is movement due to a shift in the demand curve. But these *do not* represent substitution and output effects.

In the theory of the consumer, we mentioned that sometimes the income effect can be negative. In this case the good under consideration is called an "inferior good." Similarly, in the case of the theory of production, the scale effect or output effect for an input can be negative. In this case the input is called an *inferior input* or *regressive input*.

The derivation of the industry demand curve now proceeds along the lines we discussed in Section 15.3 (Figure 15.3). With two variable inputs, a decline in the price of labor has two effects: (1) the substitution and output effects we described here and (2) the effect of output price when the industry output expands.

We have to take account of the first effect in deriving the individual firm's demand for labor. We have to take account of the second effect in deriving the industry demand curve for labor from the demand curves of the individual firms. Since we have explained this latter point earlier in Section 15.3, we will not go through it again.

15.5 ELASTICITY OF THE INPUT DEMAND CURVE

In the previous two sections we discussed the demand curve for labor by the individual firm and by the industry. For policy purposes, it is important to know what the elasticity of the input demand curve is. In the case of the labor input, we would like to know the wage elasticity of demand for labor. The factors influencing the elasticity of industry demand for an input can be summarized in four laws often called the Hicks-Marshall laws of derived demand, named after the two British economists, Hicks and Marshall.[2] These laws say that, other things equal, the own price elasticity of demand for an input is higher

1. When the price elasticity of demand for the product being produced is high
2. When other factors of production can be easily substituted for the input
3. When the supply curves of other factors of production are highly elastic
4. When the cost of the input is a large share of the total costs of production

The first three laws can be shown to always hold. There are conditions under which the last law may not hold, as will be explained later.

Elasticity of demand for the final product
An increase in input price leads to an increase in output price, and the greater the price elasticity of demand for the final product, the larger will be the decline in industry output for a given increase in price. The greater the decrease in output, the greater the decrease in input usage (other things equal). Thus, the greater the elasticity of demand for the final product is, the greater will be the elasticity of demand for the input.

[2]John R. Hicks, *The Theory of Wages*, St. Martin's Press, New York, 1966, pp. 241–247 and Alfred Marshall, *Principles of Economics*, 8th ed., Macmillan, London, 1923, pp. 518–538. Hicks's *Theory of Wages* was first published in 1932.

As we noted earlier in Section 15.3, the individual firm's demand for an input will be more elastic than the industry demand, although, as we noted, the difference between these two elasticities is not large if the elasticity of demand for the output is high.

Finally, we should also note that since the long-run elasticity of demand for output is higher than the short-run elasticity, we will have a corresponding result that the long-run price elasticity of demand for an input will be higher than the corresponding short-run elasticity.

Elasticity of substitution

The ability to substitute one input for another is reflected in the *elasticity of substitution* between the two inputs. A large elasticity indicates that the two inputs are close substitutes in production. Now if there is a close substitute available, then when the price of an input rises (other things constant), the firm can simply substitute the other input. So, if labor and capital are close substitutes, then when the wage rate rises, firms will substitute capital for labor, and the decline in employment will be greater. Hence, the demand for an input will be more elastic when close substitutes are available.

The elasticity of substitution is usually denoted by the letter σ. The elasticity of substitution between labor and capital is defined as

$$\sigma = - \left[\frac{\Delta(K/L)}{K/L} \Big/ \frac{\Delta(P_K/P_L)}{P_K/P_L} \right]$$

with Q constant. It shows the percentage change in the capital to labor ratio for a given percentage change in the input price ratio, holding the output level constant. If $\sigma = 1$, a 10 percent fall in the P_K/P_L ratio results in a 10 percent increase in the K/L ratio. Several studies have been conducted to empirically estimate σ. There is usually a great divergence in these estimates, depending on the type of data used, time period considered, and so on. In fact, many economists are skeptical of these estimates because of this diversity. Table 15.2 presents a typical set of estimates. Many of the estimates are close to 1.

Elasticity of supply of other inputs

The demand for an input will be more elastic if the supply curves of the other inputs are more elastic. Suppose there is an increase in the price of labor. The individual firm would like to substitute capital for labor. However, if the supply of capital (machines) is inelastic, then the firm would be limited in its ability to make a profitable substitution. This is because a small increase in demand for capital will cause a large increase in its price. Thus, the decline in labor usage will be smaller, and demand for labor will be less elastic.

Again, note that the substitution possibilities are higher in the long run than in the short run. In the long run, the producers of capital equipment can expand their capacity and new producers can enter the market. Thus, the long-run elasticity of supply of the other input would be higher than the short-run elasticity. Consequently, the long-run elasticity of demand for an input would be higher than the corresponding short-run elasticity.

TABLE 15.2 Estimates of Elasticity of Substitution between Labor and Capital, United States, 1949–1961

Industry	Elasticity
Food and kindred products	0.24
Tobacco manufacturers	1.18
Textile mill products	1.10
Furniture and fixtures	1.12
Paper and allied products	1.02
Chemicals	1.25
Petroleum and coal	1.30
Leather and leather products	0.86
Stone, clay, and glass	0.67
Machinery, not electrical	1.04
Electrical machinery	0.64
Transportation equipment	0.24

Source: C. E. Ferguson, "Time Series Production Function and Technological Progress in the American Manufacturing Industry," Journal of Political Economy, June 1965, pp. 135–147.

The share of the input in total costs

Finally, the share of the input in total costs is also an important factor in determining the elasticity of demand for an input. If the share of labor costs is only 10 percent, then a 10 percent increase in the wage rate, other things equal, would raise total costs by only 1 percent. However, if the initial share is 90 percent, a 10 percent increase in the wage rate would increase total costs by 9 percent. Since *MC* will increase more in the latter case than in the former, price will increase more in the latter case, and output and, hence, employment, will fall more in the latter case. Thus, the greater the share of labor in total costs, the higher the wage elasticity of demand for labor tends to be.

Although intuitively plausible, the law does not always hold. This argument suggests that the quantity of the input used per unit of output is independent of the price of the factor. In other words, the "law" is necessarily true only in the case where inputs must be combined in fixed proportions.

Empirical evidence

What is the magnitude of the wage elasticities of demand for labor in U.S. manufacturing? Hamermesh surveyed over 20 empirical studies and concludes that the absolute value of the wage elasticity of demand for labor in U.S. manufacturing is around 0.15 to 0.50, holding output constant (and 0.40 to 2.60 if we allow output to vary).[3] Although the range from 0.15 to 0.50 is wide, it does at least put some

[3]D. S. Hamermesh, "The Demand for Labor in the Long-Run," in O. Ashenfelter and R. Layard, eds., *Handbook of Labor Economics*, vol. 1, North Holland Publishing, Amsterdam, 1986, pp. 429–471.

limits on the claims one can make for the ability of wage subsidies to increase employment by changing the relative labor intensity of production at a fixed rate of output. In an earlier paper Hamermesh uses these estimates of wage elasticities to estimate the percentage changes in employment resulting from four policy changes suggested in 1975 to stimulate employment in a recession.[4] One of the policies was an employment tax credit of $4 per worker-day on each worker-day worked at a firm in excess of the previous year's employment. The estimated change in employment was 0.49 to 3.46 percent.

A word of caution

In the previous discussion we referred constantly to the industry demand for labor. In actual practice labor is mobile between industries, and the demand curve for labor summarizes the responses of a large number of industries. Thus, wage rates are not determined just by the demand of a particular industry. An engineer or an electrician can move between different industries. There are some specialized kinds of labor that are not mobile between industries (air pilots, air traffic controllers, and so on). But these are more of an exception than a rule, and even in these cases (although the skills are industry-specific), the workers themselves can move to other industries at their own cost. Their demonstrated ability in these professions can be taken as an indication of their ability to acquire other skills.

15.6 SOME COMMENTS ON THE DERIVED DEMAND FOR LABOR

In all our discussion we have talked of labor as homogeneous. This is indeed not so, and we can consider at least two categories of labor: skilled and unskilled labor. We would now have two wage rates—one for skilled and another for unskilled labor. When we talk of elasticity of demand, we mean the own wage elasticity. Furthermore, we have to consider not only capital-labor substitution but also labor-labor substitution, or the substitution possibilities between skilled and unskilled labor. Also, like capital, skilled labor will be in limited supply in the short run. It takes time to train skilled labor.

Empirical evidence on own wage elasticities suggests that the own wage elasticity is higher for production workers than nonproduction workers. This result appears to be a consequence of the fact that there is greater substitutability between capital and production workers than between capital and nonproduction workers.[5]

Labor unions also limit the scope of substitution of labor for other inputs. Since the power of a union depends on the elasticity of demand for labor (the higher this elasticity, the lower the union power), unions try to take measures that will lower the elasticity of demand for labor. The elasticity of demand for the final product depends on the availability of substitutes. Frequently, this substitute prod-

[4]D. S. Hamermesh, "Econometric Studies of Labor Demand and Their Application to Policy Analysis," *The Journal of Human Resources,* Fall 1979, pp. 507–525.

[5]D. S. Hamermesh and J. Grant, "Econometric Studies of Labor-Labor Substitution and Their Implications for Policy," *Journal of Human Resources,* Fall 1979, pp. 518–542. More recent evidence is summarized in D. S. Hamermesh, "The Demand for Labor in the Long-Run," in O. Ashenfelter and R. Layard, eds., *Handbook in Labor Economics,* vol. 1, North Holland Publishing, Amsterdam, 1986, pp. 429–471.

uct is an imported good. Unions try to seek quotas or tariffs on imports so that the competition from foreign goods is reduced.

One example is the demand for domestic farm labor. The elasticity of demand depends on (1) the supply of immigrant workers (legal and illegal) who are willing to work at wages below the wages of domestic workers and (2) the supply of imported farm products that compete heavily with domestically produced farm products. Farm labor unions seek to obtain government regulations that prevent illegal immigrants from accepting employment as farm workers and push for the imposition of tariffs and quotas on the imports of farm products. The first measure is an attempt to reduce the elasticity of supply of a substitute input, and the second measure is an attempt to reduce the elasticity of demand for output. According to the laws of derived demand in the previous section, both of these measures should decrease the elasticity of demand for domestic farm labor.

15.7   INPUT SUPPLY

In discussing input supply, we will differentiate among produced inputs (such as machinery or materials), labor, and natural inputs (such as land or ore). We must also be careful to distinguish between the total or market supply of an input and the supply curve of the input facing an industry or a firm. Also, in this chapter we will consider only input supply under competitive input market conditions.

We will first discuss the market or total supply of produced inputs, such as materials, because this topic requires little additional attention. The market supply for materials is determined in the same manner as the market supply for any output. That is, the fact that a product is an intermediate product rather than a final or consumer product is irrelevant for purposes of supply. And we have already discussed the derivation of a market supply curve from the firms' cost curves, for a competitive industry, in Chapter 10.

We have also already considered several aspects of labor supply in Chapter 5. There, we examined (1) the backward-bending supply curve of labor, (2) the effects of welfare programs and negative income tax on work effort, and (3) effects of progressive income tax on labor supply. However, in Chapter 5 we focused our attention on the individual's decision of how much labor to supply at various wage rates. That is, we were concerned with the individual worker's supply curve of labor. The market supply curve of labor is derived by horizontally summing all of the individuals' labor supply curves.

There is a common objection to the derivation of a labor supply curve in this manner, and now is a good time to discuss it. In Chapter 5, we treated the number of hours of labor supplied as the choice of the individual. But casual observation tells us that it is the employer rather than the employees that determine the number of hours worked in most cases. Except for self-employed workers, the worker can only marginally adjust work hours through overtime or perhaps extra sick time. But if workers' preferences are similar, then a marginal adjustment is all that would be needed when the standard workweek is determined by the typical worker's preferences. So is the standard workweek sensitive to worker preferences? Well, if most workers began looking for part-time work with only 30 hours per week, then in the long run the standard workweek would undoubtedly respond. So at least in the long run the typical worker's preferences determine the number of hours worked.

We have one last input supply to discuss, and that is the supply of natural inputs such as land. The market supply curve for these inputs is vertical because the quantities available are fixed. And the market supply curve tells us the quantities of the input available to all employers, at various input prices.

But does a vertical market supply curve imply that the supply curve of the input to one industry or one firm is also perfectly inelastic? Let's first consider the supply curve to the industry. If an input is employed in only one industry then the supply curve facing the industry coincides with the market supply curve. This is the case only for very specialized inputs. More commonly, inputs are mobile among several industries. For example, unskilled labor is mobile among so many industries that the supply curve of unskilled labor facing an industry will be close to horizontal at the market wage rate. Thus, in the case of unskilled labor, a single industry can generally employ all that it wants to, without affecting the wage rate. If an input is employed in only a few industries, then each industry faces an upward-sloping supply curve for the input. But in this case, the supply curve facing each industry will be more elastic than the market supply curve. This is because if input price in one industry increases, not only might new units of the input be drawn into the market, but existing units will relocate to take advantage of the higher input price. So in general, we can only say that the input supply curve to an industry is at least as elastic as the market supply curve.

The input supply curves facing the individual firms are, in this chapter, taken to be perfectly elastic at the current market price. This is because we have assumed that markets are perfectly competitive. Even if the input is employed in only one industry, there are enough firms in the industry so that none of them has any control over input prices.

15.8 DETERMINATION OF EQUILIBRIUM INPUT PRICE AND EMPLOYMENT

In the previous sections we have frequently referred to the industry demand for an input. And the industry we have talked of is an output industry. For some specialized inputs that are not mobile between industries, the industry demand is the total or market demand. (Examples of specialized types of labor skills that are immobile between industries are air traffic controllers and astronauts.) In actual practice, most inputs are mobile between industries. (Examples of mobile labor are secretaries and unskilled workers.) In this case the market demand for the input is the horizontal sum of the industry demands for the input. (The market supply of an input was discussed in the previous section.)

The intersection of the market demand and supply curves determines the equilibrium input price and the total quantity of the input employed. This is shown in Figure 15.7 for the case of labor. W^* is the equilibrium wage rate, and L^* is the equilibrium employment. W^* and L^* are determined by the intersection of the market demand for labor D and the market supply of labor S. If the wage is above W^*, then there will be an excess supply of labor, and if the wage rate is below W^*, then there will be an excess demand for labor.

Note that in equilibrium the wage rate W^* must be equal across all the industries among which the input is mobile. If one industry pays a higher wage rate, then workers from other industries will transfer until any wage discrepancy is eliminated.

As in the case of output markets, an increase in market demand for an input will cause an increase in equilibrium price and employment for the input. An increase in market demand can be brought about by an increase in input demand by any of the employing industries. Of course, if the industry employs a large fraction of the total, then a change in that industry's demand will have a larger impact on market demand and a larger impact on input price and total employment. A decrease in the market demand for an input clearly reduces equilibrium price and input employment.

An increase in market supply of an input will cause a decrease in input price and finally a decrease in market supply of an input will lead to an increase in input price.

15.9   APPLICATIONS

In the previous sections we have discussed the determinants of (1) market demand for labor, (2) market supply of labor, and (3) the equilibrium wage and employment. There are many government policies affecting the demand for labor, supply of labor, and the equilibrium in the labor market. We have mentioned one such policy in a previous section—the minimum wage law. We will discuss several policies and show how the theoretical tools we have developed in the previous sections can be applied to assess the impacts of these different policies.

FIGURE 15.7   Equilibrium wage rate and employment.

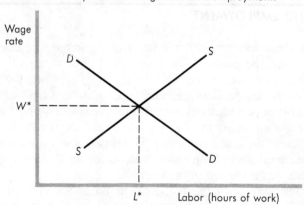

15.9.1 Effects of minimum wage laws

If a minimum wage law is to be effective, then the minimum wage $\overline{W}$ must be set above the market equilibrium wage W^*. An effective minimum wage law will produce unemployment. This is shown in Figure 15.8. Without the minimum wage law, employment is Ob. If the minimum wage rate is $\overline{W}$, then the wage rate will be $\overline{W}$ and the employment is Oa. However, at the higher wage rate $\overline{W}$, the quantity of labor supplied will be larger. More people will enter the work force, and those already working will want to work more hours. Thus,

ab = decline in employment hours
bc = increase in quantity of labor supplied

and

$ac = ab + bc$ = unemployment in hours

The observed unemployment ac is, thus, higher than the reduction in employment ab induced by the minimum wage law.

The enactment of minimum wage laws is often justified on grounds of equity. Whether such laws accomplish this purpose is open to question. It depends, in part, on the shapes of the demand and supply curves. This is shown in Figure 15.9.

In case (a) the decrease in employment ab is very small, although the unemployment ac is high. Most of this unemployment comes from bc, the increase in quantity supplied. In case (b) the decrease in employment ab is very large and accounts for most of the unemployment ac. Which of these cases applies in practice is an empirical question, but clearly the social cost of minimum wage legislation is greater in the second case.

The minimum wage laws in the United States started with the Fair Labor Standards Act of 1938, which provided for a minimum wage rate below which hourly wages could not be reduced, an overtime pay for workers who worked long hours, and restrictions on the use of child labor. In 1938 the minimum wage was

FIGURE 15.8   Effect of a minimum wage law.

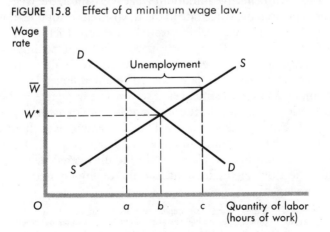

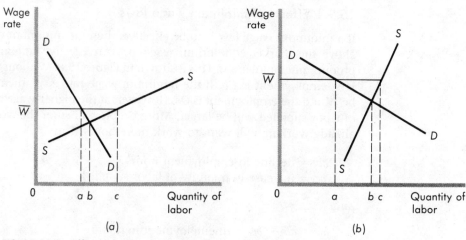

FIGURE 15.9   Effects of minimum wage laws on employment.

set at $0.25 per hour. The coverage was not uniform. It covered about 43 percent of all nonsupervisory wage and salary workers. Subsequent legislation increased this coverage. On January 1, 1987, the coverage was 83.3 percent, and the minimum wage was $3.35 per hour. In Table 15.3 we present the minimum wage and average wage in manufacturing for the period 1938 to 1987.

Since the minimum wage is specified in nominal terms, the real wage falls over time with inflation. Hence, there is pressure on Congress to legislate increases from time to time. In real terms, the minimum wage, thus, fluctuates over time, with jumps every time there is new legislation and a steady erosion until the next legislation. This is shown in Figure 15.10.

The effect of a minimum wage law on employment is shown in Figure 15.8, but this model applies only if *all* workers are covered by minimum wage laws. If there is only partial coverage, there may be no increase in unemployment. The unemployed workers in the covered sector will switch over to the uncovered sector and seek employment there. This will depress the wage rate in the uncovered sector. Thus, with effective minimum wage legislation, the wage rate in the covered sector goes up, and the wage rate in the uncovered sector goes down. The argument is easy to follow, but we will illustrate it in Figure 15.11.

Initially, the wage level is W_0 in both the sectors. Employment is L_c in the covered sector and L_u in the uncovered sector. With a minimum wage W_m in the covered sector, employment falls to L_c'. The unemployed labor $(L_c - L_c')$ attempts to find employment in the uncovered sector. The wage rate in the uncovered sector falls to the level W_1 so that the increase in employment $(L_u' - L_u)$ is less than $(L_c - L_c')$, because some workers will leave the market as the wage rate falls. Also, it is not true that the entire unemployed labor $(L_c - L_c')$ can switch from the covered sector and find employment in the uncovered sector. Thus, there will be a certain effect on unemployment. But the unemployment will be less than with total coverage.[6]

[6]Unemployed workers in the covered sector might decide to wait in the covered sector until an opening comes up. They could calculate the probabilities of a higher wage in the covered sector taking account of periods of unemployment and compare it with the lower wage and certain employment in the uncovered sector.

TABLE 15.3 The Minimum Wage and Manfacturing Wages

Year	Minimum Wage	Average Manufacturing Wage	Minimum Wage as Percentage of Average Manufacturing Wage
1938	$0.25	$0.62	40.3
1939	0.30	0.63	47.6
1945	0.40	1.02	39.2
1950	0.75	1.44	52.1
1956	1.00	1.95	51.3
1961	1.15	2.32	49.6
1963	1.25	2.46	50.8
1967	1.40	2.82	49.6
1968	1.60	3.01	53.2
1974	2.00	4.42	45.2
1975	2.10	4.83	43.5
1976	2.30	5.22	44.1
1978	2.65	6.17	43.0
1979	2.90	6.70	43.3
1980	3.10	7.27	42.6
1981	3.35	7.99	41.9
1987	3.35	9.81	34.2

FIGURE 15.10 Pattern over time of minimum wage rates in real terms.

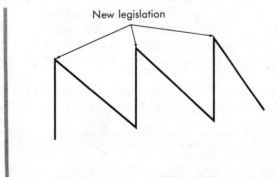

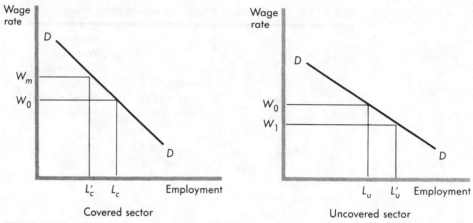

FIGURE 15.11   Effect of minimum wage law on wage rates in the covered and uncovered sectors.

EXAMPLE 15.1   What Went Right with Minimum Wages in the 1970s and 1980s?

Between 1973 and 1977 real minimum wage rose steadily but so did the difference between teenage white and nonwhite employment rates (for teens aged 16 to 19). Between 1977 and 1986 real minimum wage fell steadily but so did the difference between teenage white and nonwhite employment rates. The figures are roughly as follows:

Year	Real minimum wage (1986 dollars)	Difference between teenage white and nonwhite employment rates (%)
1973	3.60	20
1977	4.60	27
1986	3.30	22

The figures demonstrate that the minimum wage law works against the less privileged.[7] President Carter's Minimum Wage Study Commission found that "an explicit purpose of minimum wage was, and is, to protect adult workers from low-wage competition from youth." In fact, minimum wage laws also protect white workers from competition from less educated lower-skilled minorities.

There has been a large number of studies on the effects of minimum wage laws on unemployment.[8] The empirical evidence is mixed, but one predominant

---

[7]Michael S. Bernstam, in "Minimum Wage: Bulwark of the Privileged," *The Wall Street Journal,* June 15, 1987, p. 26, argues that demographic changes cannot explain these figures. So, the changes have to be attributed to the economic effects of minimum wage laws.

[8]See Finis Welch, *Minimum Wages: Issues and Evidence,* American Enterprise Institute, Washington, D.C., 1978, and Jacob Mincer, "Unemployment Effects of Minimum Wage Changes," *Journal of Political Economy,* August 1976 pp. S 87–S 104.

conclusion that emerges is that the employment opportunities for teenagers have been reduced because of minimum wage. Some found evidence of this reduction in the number employed, others found reduction in the hours worked (a switch from full-time employment to part-time employment). For adults, minimum wage laws seem to have negligible effect, since most of them earn a wage rate higher than the minimum.

Part of the reason that the effects of minimum wage laws on unemployment have been found to be small, is that there is a large degree of noncompliance. The enforcement is not strict, and penalties for noncompliance are small. Ashenfelter and Smith present some evidence that suggests that only 50 to 70 percent of covered workers who would have earned less than the minimum without the law are actually paid the minimum.[9] The rest are paid a wage below the minimum.

One other possibility is that employers might comply with the minimum wage law but reduce some fringe benefits. Thus, labor costs to employers would not go up as much as expected and employment would not decrease as much as expected.

One of the major objectives of minimum wage laws is to promote a more equitable income distribution by raising the wages of low-wage earners. However, as we showed earlier in Figure 15.11, the wage rate in the covered sector rises and the wage rate in the uncovered sector falls, thus, promoting a greater wage disparity. The low-wage earners in the uncovered sector are likely to get still lower wages because of increased pressure in this market coming from the unemployed in the covered sector. Thus, the income distribution consequences are likely to be the opposite of what were intended. Some lucky workers will get employment in the covered sector at a higher wage, but others will be either unemployed or employed in the uncovered sector at a lower wage. Gramlich studied the impact of minimum wage laws on income distribution but found very little effect.[10] Part of the reason could be the noncompliance mentioned earlier. Another reason is that he examined the distribution of family income. And as mentioned earlier, it is frequently the teenagers that suffer the effects of unemployment or reduced hours of work, and this would not have much of an impact on family income. Some of the teenagers might even come from middle- or high-income families.

15.9.2 Overtime pay

In Chapter 5 we derived the hours of work supplied by a worker and showed that the supply curve of labor can be backward bending, so that as the wage rate increases, the hours of work supplied by a worker could actually decrease. Suppose that the wage rate is a fixed amount per hour for the standard hours of work (say, 40 hours per week) and it is higher (say one-and-one-half times) for any overtime hours. It is common practice among employers to let existing workers work overtime at a higher wage rate rather than hire additional workers when their demand for labor is temporarily higher than normal. The employers, thus, save any costs of hiring and training new workers. Also, government-mandated insurance pre-

[9]Orley Ashenfelter and Robert S. Smith, "Compliance With the Minium Wage Law," *Journal of Political Economy*, April 1979, pp. 335–350. Work done by the National Council on Employment Policy (1984) shows about 8 million workers working below minimum wage.

[10]Edward Gramlich, "Impact of Minimum Wages on Other Wages, Employment and Family Incomes," *Brookings Papers on Economic Activity*, 1976, part II, pp. 409–462.

miums and other compensations are employee-related not hours-related. Thus, employers have further incentive to let existing workers work overtime. We will show that unlike the case of paying a higher wage rate, such overtime pay will, in general, increase hours of work supplied. This is shown in Figure 15.12.

We consider the workers' indifference curves between income and leisure, and we measure hours of leisure on the horizontal axis. The maximum hours of leisure (measured on a per-diem basis) is 24. Hours of work are, thus, measured right to left in Figure 15.12.

At the initial wage rate, AB_1 is the "budget line." The worker is on indifference curve I_1 and supplies H_1 hours of work. At a higher uniform wage rate, AB_2 is the budget line. The worker is on a higher indifference curve, but the hours of work supplied decline from H_1 to H_2 (note that hours of work are measured from right to left). With overtime pay the budget line has a kink and tilts upward after the standard hours of work (which we have assumed to be H_1 in Figure 15.12). The kinked budget line is shown as ACD. The worker is on a higher indifference curve I_3, and hours of work supplied increase to H_3.

Note that hours supplied of work need not always increase with overtime pay. Suppose the standard number of hours of work is greater than H_1. In this case the kink is at a point to the left of the point C in Figure 15.12. Then it can be verified (we are not showing it because it will clutter up the diagram) that hours of work may not increase. In some cases it will depend on how far left of C the kink occurs and how steep the new segment of the budget line is (how high the overtime pay rate is). And if the standard number of hours is less than H_1, so that the worker puts in overtime even without overtime pay, then the amount of overtime hours supplied might fall with the introduction of the overtime pay rate. But for any

FIGURE 15.12   Effect of overtime pay on labor supply.

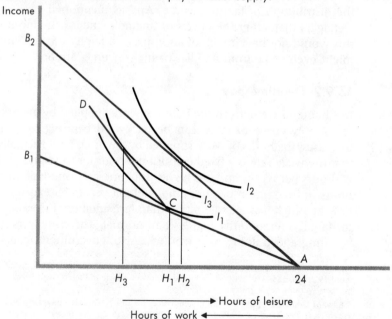

worker working just the standard number of hours, overtime pay will always increase the hours of work supplied.

It is important to realize that what we have discussed is only the supply side of the picture. To discuss the effect of overtime pay on actual hours worked we have to consider the demand side as well. We will, however, not pursue this in detail. Instead, we will make some casual observations.

As mentioned earlier, much of government-mandated insurance legislation, which is employee-related rather than hours-related, increases the fixed costs of hiring new employees and provides an incentive for employers to use overtime hours. The average weekly overtime hours of work in manufacturing in the United States was roughly 2.56 hours per employee between 1956 and 1963. It rose to 3.34 hours per employee in the period 1964 to 1977. This use of overtime hours reduces aggregate employment (in number of employees), and the U.S. Congress has introduced proposals periodically to increase overtime pay to twice the pay rate for standard hours. The argument is that this would increase the marginal cost of using overtime hours, and employers would hire new employees. There have been several estimates of the employment effects of this proposal—estimates showing that employment would increase by 0.3 to 0.4 percent. Ehrenberg and Schumann, however, argue that these estimates are overly optimistic.[11]

15.9.3 Piece wages versus time wages

Throughout our analysis we have assumed that workers are paid by the hour. This payment method is called time wages. This is the predominant method of wage payment in almost all countries. About 86 percent of U.S. employees are on time wages. An alternative method of wage payment is that of piece wages, where workers are paid by the work performed. Workers on piece rates usually earn more than those in comparable time-rate jobs. This is for two reasons. First, there will be a compensating wage differential. Second, the workers who opt for piece-rate jobs frequently work harder. We will consider each of these reasons.

Workers on piece rates find their earnings fluctuate based on their day-to-day productivity (headaches, stomach upsets, and so on can affect their productivity). Such pay fluctuations would not be there for workers on time rates. If the average total wage income is the same under both payment methods, then workers will prefer the time rate because of the stability in earnings and, if possible, switch into time-rate jobs. Thus, if the employer wants to use the piece rate, the employer will have to pay a higher average total wage for workers on the piece rate. There will have to be some wage differential to compensate for the higher fluctuations in income. Under the time-rate scheme, the employers bear the costs of fluctuations in worker productivity. Under the piece rate, employees bear the costs of fluctuations in productivity. The employer may find it desirable to shift the costs of fluctuations even if it requires an increase in average total wages. In some cases, the costs of fluctuations are shared by the employer and the employee, and time-rates and piece-rates are used in combination. This is the case of salespersons who receive a fixed salary (usually a low one) and, in addition, commissions based on sales.

[11]Ronald G. Ehrenberg and Paul L. Schumann, *Longer Hours or More Jobs? An Investigation of Amending Hours Legislation to Create Employment*, New York State School of Industrial and Labor Relations, Ithaca, N.Y., 1982.

It is also argued that workers will work harder on a piece rate than on a time rate because they have an incentive to put in the last ounce of their effort. This argument is not necessarily valid, because even with the time rate the employer can fire an employee who is lethargic and kills time, but marginal reductions in effort are frequently difficult to detect. Furthermore, the less motivated worker will do better on time-rate wages and, hence, will opt not to take a job paying piece rate.

Piece rates can be used only where the output of the worker is easily measurable. The garment industry is one which primarily uses piece rates. Other examples of workers on piece rates are auto repair mechanics and salespersons. Assembly line workers, however, have to work in coordination with others and, hence, cannot be paid on piece rates. Nor is it generally feasible to use piece rates with managers. Only about one-seventh of all employees in the United States are on piece rates.

Technological change, however, creates some problems even when the output can be clearly measured. For instance, if a new machine is invented and the same auto repair job can be done in less time than before, then the employer has to renegotiate the piece rate with the workers. Such renegotiation can be difficult and expensive. Thus, piece rates are less likely to exist in an industry undergoing rapid technological progress.

15.9.4 Occupational safety and health regulations

In 1970, Congress passed the Occupational Safety and Health Act, which directed the U.S. Department of Labor to issue and enforce safety and health standards for all private employees. The act requires every employer to furnish each employee a job which is "free from recognized hazards that are causing or likely to cause death or serious physical harm." The act, however, does not spell out how much health and safety is to be provided by the employer. Under the auspices of the act, an agency was created: the Occupational Safety and Health Administration (OSHA). The function of this agency is to determine standards which can be classified as specification standards and performance standards. Under specification standards, the agency specifies allowable technologies. Under performance standards, the agency specifies allowable outcomes (allowable rate of pollution, allowable noise, and so on). The firms must then choose a technology that conforms to these performance standards.

The purpose of all these standards is to reduce the exposure of workers to risks of loss of life or serious injury. If workers do understand the risks involved in the different jobs and there are compensating wage differentials for more risky jobs, then the OSHA regulations make some workers worse off. This is shown in Figure 15.13.

In Figure 15.13, *AB* is the job offer curve. It gives the different jobs that the employers can offer with different wage and risk combinations. It assumes that the wage rate increases with the riskiness of the job but does so at a decreasing rate.

The workers' indifference curves will be upward sloping with the slope increasing with increasing risk as shown in Figure 15.13. (Recall the indifference

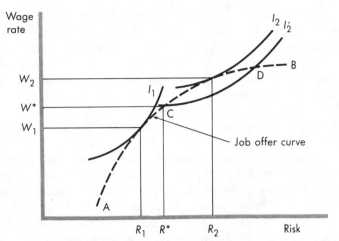

FIGURE 15.13 Effect of government regulation of risk on workers' utility.

curves for a "good" and a "bad" discussed in Chapter 4.) Here wage is a good and risk is a bad. We are assuming that workers dislike risk, that is, they are *risk averse*.

Worker 1 with indifference curve given by I_1 would choose a job with risk R_1 and wage W_1. Worker 2 who is less risk-averse and whose indifference curve is given by I_2 would choose a job with risk R_2 and wage W_2. Now suppose that the government mandates that no jobs with risk levels greater than R^* can be offered to workers. The job offer curve is now the truncated curve AC. Worker 2 will now get a job with risk level R^* and wage rate W^*. However, this worker is now on a lower indifference curve I_2' and is, thus, worse off. Worker 1 is unaffected by the mandate.

All this analysis assumes that (1) the worker has correct knowledge of the job risks involved, and (2) there are no external effects, that is, all potential hazards accrue to the worker making the decision. We will now consider the implications of these assumptions.

If the first assumption is violated, then the solution is to inform workers of the job risks involved. Thus, the government, instead of mandating the maximum permissible level of risk, can mandate the distribution of information on the risks involved in the different types of jobs and let the workers choose. In the absence of such information, the legislation of maximum level of risk can, in some cases, make workers better off. For instance, in Figure 15.13 worker 2 might choose the point D on the job offer curve, underestimating the risks involved and think that he or she is on the higher indifference curve I_2. However, the worker is actually on indifference curve I_2' and the government-mandated maximum risk R^* brings the worker to the point C on the same indifference curve. Thus, the worker is actually not worse off, although she or he might mistakenly think so. This is, of course, a somewhat artificial example, but it illustrates the point that when workers underestimate the risks involved in certain jobs, government-mandated maximum levels of risk can make workers better off, or at least no worse off.

The second problem of external effects (which we discuss in greater detail in Chapter 19 on externalities) points to the fact that workers undertaking risky jobs may take into account only their own private costs. There are also psychic costs for members of the family, close friends, and relatives. Also, the costs of medical treatment are borne by taxpayers, and some of the diseases can even be contagious. All of these external costs are not taken into account in the analysis in Figure 15.13, where only the indifference curves of the workers are considered. Thus, mandating maximum risk might make worker 2 worse off but make other affected individuals better off.

The violation of our assumptions does not allow us to conclude that the OSHA regulations are socially desirable. This discussion merely suggests that the simple analysis in Figure 15.13 needs to be modified to take account of these problems. In practice, one needs to evaluate the availability of information on risks involved in the different jobs and the magnitude of external effects in determining whether OSHA contributes positively to overall social welfare.

15.9.5 Are workers paid their marginal products?

Throughout our discussion we have assumed that the wage rate for a worker is equal to the value of the worker's marginal product. If this is so, the relationship between the wage rates and the values of marginal product should be given by the 45° line shown in Figure 15.14. In actual practice, however, the wage rates of workers within a firm vary much less than the workers' marginal productivities. The actual relationship between wages and marginal products is more like the flatter line *AB* in Figure 15.14.

Economists have advanced several explanations for this behavior. One argument is that it is not possible to measure workers' marginal productivity accurately, and many firms follow strict pay formulas based on education, experience, length of tenure in the job, and other considerations, which are all supposed to influence

FIGURE 15.14   Theoretical and actual relationships between workers' wages and marginal products.

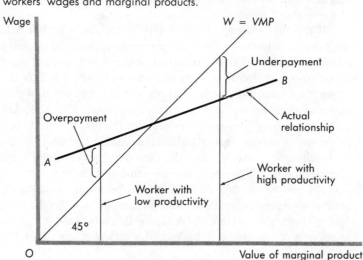

the worker's marginal product. In this case, the relationship between the wage rate and the value of the marginal product would be a line with a slope less than 1, such as the line *AB* in Figure 15.14. In statistical terminology, this is called a "regression effect" (a regression toward the mean).

Another argument is that workers prefer employment contracts with more gently sloping earnings as a means of smoothing out their earnings over a lifetime. Such smoothing would necessitate paying them more than the value of their marginal product in early years and less than the value of their marginal product in later years. But this payment pattern is feasible only when labor contracts are binding over the long term. Otherwise, employees can change jobs when their pay falls below the value of the marginal product.

Yet another argument suggested by Robert Frank is that workers care a great deal not only about the income they receive but also about what position they occupy in the income hierarchies of the groups to which they belong.[12] The less productive workers would not normally want to associate themselves with the more productive workers and, thus, have to be paid a compensating wage differential to induce them to stay in the same pool as the more productive workers. This accounts for the wage being higher than the value of the marginal product for workers with low productivity and lower than the value of the marginal product for workers with high productivity (as shown in Figure 15.14).

15.9.6 Labor as a quasi-fixed factor

In the theory of production discussed in Chapter 6 we considered capital as a fixed factor of production and labor as a variable factor of production. Although this was correct as a first approximation, in actual practice many of the costs associated with labor are also fixed costs.

With fluctuations in the demand for its products, a firm will adjust its variable factors of production to the point where the price paid for a factor is equal to the value of the marginal product of the factor. If there is a decrease in the demand for the firm's product, the firm will lay off some of its unskilled labor, which it will rehire when demand increases. However, the managers and the technical personnel cannot be as easily dispensed with. They are usually on longer-term contracts and, furthermore, will be more difficult to replace if fired. There are search, hiring, and training costs associated with this kind of labor. Thus, in the short run, the firm will treat these costs as sunk costs. This is why labor is often called a *quasi-fixed* factor.

In Figure 15.15, we consider the impact of search, hiring, and training costs on the firm's hiring and firing decisions when demand fluctuates. Let us define

VMP_1 = initial value of the marginal product of labor

VMP_2 = value of marginal product of labor following a decrease
   in product demand

W = wage rate

S = per-unit search, hiring, and training costs.

[12]See Robert H. Frank, "Are Workers Paid Their Marginal Products?" *American Economic Review,* September 1984, pp. 549–571. Also Robert H. Frank, *Choosing the Right Pond: The Economics and Politics of the Quest for Status,* Oxford University Press, New York, 1985.

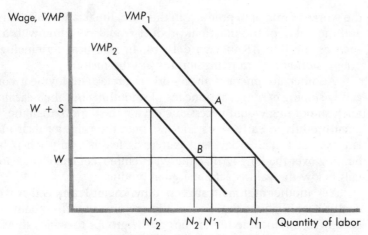

FIGURE 15.15 Response of firms treating labor as a quasi-fixed factor.

In the absence of any search, hiring, or training costs, the firm will initially employ N_1 units of labor. Following the decline in output demand, the firm will reduce employment to N_2. In both cases, the firm equates VMP to the wage rate.

Now in the presence of search, hiring, or training costs, the cost of hiring an additional unit of labor is $W + S$. Thus, the firm will initially hire labor until $W + S = VMP_1$, or it will hire N_1' units of labor. But once hired, the search, hiring, and training costs are sunk. The marginal cost of keeping an employee is only W. So when the output demand falls, the firm reduces labor usage only to N_2 (not N_2').

The way Figure 15.15 is drawn, N_2 is less than N_1'. But with sufficiently high hiring, training, and search costs, N_2 could be greater than N_1'. This would mean that none of the employees would be laid off as the result of the decline in demand. (But new employees would not be hired because the cost of a new unit of labor is $W + S$.)

If the decline in demand is permanent, then the number of units of labor will eventually be reduced to N_2'. As existing employees retire or leave, they will not be replaced unless VMP exceeds $W + S$ or unless the quantity of labor falls below N_2'.

15.10   SUMMARY AND CONCLUSIONS

The firm will maximize profit by increasing its usage of an input to the point where marginal revenue product is equal to marginal factor cost. Under perfect competition in the output market, marginal revenue product is equal to marginal product times output price or the value of the marginal product. And with competition in the input market, marginal factor cost equals input price.

The demand curve for a single variable input is a portion of the value of marginal product curve. The industry input demand curve is less elastic than the sum of the individual firms' input demand curves because it takes into account the change in output price which results from an expansion or contraction of industry output. With two variable inputs, the firm's input demand curve is no longer a portion of the *VMP* curve. This is because when the price of one input changes, output and the quantity of the other input also change. As the quantity of the other input changes, the *VMP* curve shifts. With two variable inputs, the impact of a change in input price on the quantity demanded by the firm can be broken down into a substitution effect and a scale effect.

The elasticity of demand for an input is higher when: (1) the elasticity of demand for the output is high, (2) other factors can be easily substituted for the input, (3) the supply curves of other inputs are highly elastic, and (4) the cost of the input is a large share of total cost. There are exceptions to rule (4).

The market supply for produced inputs is determined in the same manner as the market supply for a final product. The market supply of labor is the horizontal sum of the individual workers' supply curves. Each worker's supply curve is derived from his or her preferences for leisure and income. The market supply of natural inputs is fixed. The input supply curve facing an industry is at least as elastic as the market supply curve. Under competition, the input supply curve facing the firm is perfectly elastic. Equilibrium input price and employment are determined by the intersection of the market demand for the input and the market supply of the input.

An effective minimum wage law will result in unemployment. Part of the unemployment results from a reduction in quantity demanded while the rest results from an increase in quantity supplied. When minimum wage laws cover only some employees, the result is a decline in the wage of workers who are not covered.

Higher overtime pay rates will generally induce workers to supply additional hours. For workers currently working just the standard number of hours, overtime pay will always increase the number of hours supplied.

Workers paid piece rate generally earn more on average than workers in comparable time-rate jobs. Part of the pay differential compensates the employee for bearing the cost of fluctuations in productivity. Also, workers paid piece rate may work harder.

Laws limiting risk exposure in employment may make less risk-averse workers worse off. This is because the extra pay may more than compensate them for the added risk. This argument does not hold, however, if the worker is poorly informed concerning the amount of risk or if there are external effects.

In reality workers are not generally paid the precise value of their marginal product. This is because marginal product is frequently difficult to measure. Also workers may prefer smoother earnings over time.

In the presence of search, hiring, and training costs, the firm will hire workers only if *VMP* exceeds the wage rate plus the search, hiring, and training costs. But the firm will retain existing workers as long as *VMP* exceeds (or equals) the wage rate.

KEY TERMS

Aggregate Demand Curve
Complementary Inputs
Derived Demand
Elasticity of Input
   Demand
Elasticity of
   Substitution
Factor Markets
Fair Labor Standards
   Act
Independent Inputs
Industry Demand Curve

Inferior or Regressive
   Input
Marginal Factor Cost
Marginal Revenue
   Product
Market Demand for an
   Input
Market Supply of an
   Input
Occupational Safety and
   Health Act
Piece Wages

Quasi-Fixed Factor
Scale or Output
   Effect
Substitution Effect
Supply of an Input to
   a Firm
Supply of an Input to
   an Industry
Time Wages
Value of Marginal
   Product

QUESTIONS

1. Explain why the upward-sloping portion of the *VMP* curve cannot be part of the firm's input demand curve.

2. An increase in the demand for widgets will not increase the productivity of workers producing widgets. So why does the demand for labor increase?

3. Using Figure 15.3, explain why the industry demand for a single variable input will be more elastic when elasticity of demand for the output is high.

4. If a charitable organization donates shovels and other simple tools to landowners in underdeveloped countries, what will be the impact on the demand for labor? On the wage rate? Explain.

5. Discuss some of the factors that determine the wage elasticity of demand for drywall finishers.

6. Explain why unions are stronger when the demand for labor is less elastic.

7. Will the imposition of a minimum wage in the presence of search, hiring, and training costs cause more or less unemployment than in the absence of these costs? Why?

8. If a firm in equilibrium hires two variable inputs X and Y, and the marginal product of Y is twice that of X, what do we know about the relative input prices? Why?

9. Suppose a competitive firm's average and marginal product curves for labor are

$$AP = 100 - L$$
$$MP = 100 - 2L$$

If the market price of the product is $5, determine the firm's demand curve for labor in the short run when other inputs are fixed.

10. Will the supply curve of engineers to the computer industry be more or less elastic than the supply curve to IBM? Why?

11. Is the firm demand curve for labor more elastic when capital is variable or when capital is fixed? What does this tell us about the elasticity of demand for an input in the short run versus the long run?

12. Describe the effects on the market for skilled and unskilled labor if the current minimum wage is abolished.

13. It has been often suggested that the impact of unionization on wage levels of organized workers is most noticeable during periods of recessions. Evaluate this statement.

14. Why are labor unions less powerful today than they were, say, 10 years ago?

15. Examination of the 14 percent of the U.S. population in 1985 classified as receiving incomes below the officially defined poverty level (about $11,000 for a family of four) revealed that a substantial portion were *employed*, that is, these were the "working poor." Consider the following two policies:

   1. Pay a wage subsidy to employers who hire such workers at the minimum wage of $3.35 per hour (the subsidy equals the difference between the minimum wage and the current wage paid).

   2. Pay a cash grant to the worker which would give the worker the same utility as policy *1*.

   With income on the vertical axis and leisure on the horizontal axis, draw the indifference curves and the budget line. What is the economic interpretation of the slope of the budget line? Using this diagram answer the following questions:

   a. Which of the two policies gives the greater incentive to work?

   b. Which of the two policies has the lesser cost to the government?

16. "Minimum wages benefit most those who would otherwise earn wages close to the minimum, and least those whose wages are the lowest." Critically appraise this statement.

CHAPTER 16

EMPLOYMENT AND PRICING OF INPUTS UNDER IMPERFECT COMPETITION

16.1 INTRODUCTION

In the preceding chapter we discussed the problem of pricing of inputs under the assumption of perfect competition in *both* the product market and the input markets. The individual firm had no control over the price of its output or the prices of its inputs.

In this chapter we will relax these assumptions of perfect competition in the product and factor markets. In the product market we will relax the assumption of perfect competition by considering monopoly. In the factor market we will relax the assumption of perfect competition by considering *monopsony* (a single buyer of an input). These are the other extremes from perfect competition, and as we discussed earlier in Chapter 13, there is a large gray area in between. However, considering these extremes helps us understand the major differences in the pricing of inputs and the determination of input employment.

We will see later that the effects of minimum wage laws, of trade union on wages, and so on all depend crucially on whether we assume perfect competition in the product and factor markets. Thus, it should be noted that the discussion of the effects of different government and other policies from the previous chapter needs to be modified if the market organization in the product and/or factor markets is different. This will be made clear later in Section 16.5.

16.2 INPUT DEMAND UNDER MONOPOLY

In Chapter 15 we saw that the firm will maximize profit by increasing its use of input X to the point where

$$(MRP)_X = (MFC)_X$$

We also said that $(MRP)_X = \Delta TR/\Delta X = (MP)_X \cdot MR$, and $(MFC)_X = \Delta TC/\Delta X$, holding other inputs constant.

But in the last chapter we assumed that the output market was perfectly competitive, which means that $MR = P_0$, where P_0 is output price. $(MRP)_X$ for the competitive firm was thus equal to $(MP)_X \cdot P_0$, or the value of the marginal product of X, which we denote by VMP_X.

In this section we consider the demand for a single variable input by a firm which has a monopoly in the output market. As we know, the monopolist faces a downward-sloping demand curve for its product so MR is not equal to output price. This, in turn, means that under monopoly, $(MRP)_X$ is not equal to $(VMP)_X$. We will assume that the input markets are competitive so that MFC = input price.

Table 16.1 presents the calculations of MRP for a single variable input, labor. The first two columns summarize the short-run production function, and the second and third columns summarize the firm's demand curve for its output. $(MRP)_L = \Delta TR/\Delta L$ where L is the number of workers and TR is total revenue.

Figure 16.1 compares the MRP curve, or the monopolist's input demand curve, with the corresponding VMP curve. The MRP curve lies below the VMP curve. This

TABLE 16.1   Computation of Marginal Revenue Product for a Monopolist

Number of Workers	Maximum Output	Price per Unit of Output ($)	Total Revenue from Product ($)	Marginal Revenue Product ($)
0	0		0	
1	300	44.0	13,200	13,200
2	700	42.0	29,400	16,200
3	1,200	40.0	48,000	18,600
4	1,800	37.5	67,500	19,500
5	2,300	35.0	80,500	13,000
6	2,700	33.5	90,450	9,950
7	3,000	32.0	96,000	5,550
8	3,200	31.0	99,200	3,200
9	3,300	30.5	100,650	1,450
10	3,300	30.5	100,650	0

is because $VMP = MP \cdot P_0$ while $MRP = MP \cdot MR$, and the monopolist's marginal revenue is less than product price. From Figure 16.1 we see that for a given wage rate, the monopolist will hire less labor than if he behaved as a competitor. This is an intuitive result because the monopolist produces less output than would be produced under competition. So fewer units of the input are used.

From Table 16.1, we see that at a wage rate of $13,000 or below, the monopolist will hire five workers; at a wage rate greater than $5,550 but less than or equal to $9,950 the monopolist will hire six workers; and so on. How many workers will be hired at a wage rate of $16,200? The answer is none. Although $MRP = $16,200 with two workers, total revenue would not be sufficient to pay them. That is, at this wage rate the firm cannot cover its variable costs and will shut down in the short run. So in summary, if the monopolistic firm uses any labor, it will hire

FIGURE 16.1   Demand for labor under monopoly and the corresponding VMP curve.

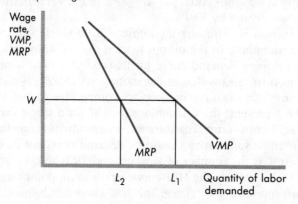

to the point where $(MRP)_L$ equals the wage rate. And the firm will employ labor as long as revenue per worker equals or exceeds the wage rate. Thus, a portion of the MRP curve is the input demand curve.

16.3 THE MONOPOLIST'S DEMAND CURVE FOR AN INPUT WHEN SEVERAL INPUTS ARE VARIABLE

In the preceding section we derived the demand curve for a single input, labor, holding the levels of other inputs constant. As we did in Section 15.4 of the last chapter, we will now consider the case of several variable inputs: labor and capital.

The monopolistic firm will employ labor and capital to the point where the marginal revenue product (MRP) of each factor is equal to the price of the factor. Thus, in equilibrium we will have

$$(MRP)_L = (MP)_L \times MR = P_L$$

and

$$(MRP)_K = (MP)_K \times MR = P_K$$

Thus, we get

$$\frac{P_L}{MP_L} = \frac{P_K}{MP_K} = MR$$

or

$$\frac{\text{Price of labor}}{\text{Marginal product of labor}} = \frac{\text{price of capital}}{\text{marginal product of capital}} = \text{marginal revenue}$$

Note that the first equality is the same as in perfect competition. However, the difference is that this ratio is equal to output price under perfect competition but equal to marginal revenue under monopoly.

$$\frac{P_L}{MP_L} = \frac{P_K}{MP_K} = \begin{array}{l} \text{Price of output under} \\ \text{perfect competition and} \\ MR \text{ under monopoly} \end{array}$$

These relationships do not, however, give us the demand function for labor when the capital input is variable. To get this we have to follow the procedure we used in Figure 15.4 and 15.5 of the last chapter. Since the procedure is *exactly* the same, we will not repeat the diagrams here. The only adjustment required is that the VMP curves be replaced with the MRP curves.

One other point worth mentioning concerns the derivation of the industry demand curve. In the case of perfect competition, we argued in Section 15.3 of the last chapter that we cannot get the industry demand curve by simply adding up the individual firms' demand curves. This is because with a decline in the input price, each firm expands employment, the industry employment rises, the industry output rises, and, hence, the product price falls and *VMP* changes. We have, therefore, to take account of this change in output price in deriving the industry demand curve. No such problem arises in the case of monopoly because the monopolist's demand curve for an input is the industry demand curve for that input.

16.4   INPUT SUPPLY UNDER MONOPSONY

In the previous sections we relaxed the assumption of perfect competition in the product market and allowed for the case that the firm faces a downward-sloping product demand curve. We will now relax the assumption of perfect competition in the input market and consider the case where the firm faces an upward-sloping input supply curve. Just as we considered the extreme case of pure monopoly (single supplier) on the output side, we can consider the extreme case of pure monopsony (single buyer) on the input side. The monopsonist faces the entire upward-sloping market supply curve and, thus, has to pay a higher price to attract more units of the input.

In our earlier analysis, the *VMP* (in the case of perfect competition) or the *MRP* (in the case of monopoly) was compared with the input price to arrive at the quantity of the input demanded by the firm. But now that the input price is not constant, the marginal factor cost is not equal to the input price. With an upward-sloping input supply curve, *MFC* exceeds input price. And the firm maximizes profit by hiring to the point where *MFC* = *MRP*. (And, of course, *MRP* = *VMP* with a competitive output market.)

Table 16.2 presents the calculation of *MFC*. The first two columns give the input supply curve. Note that average factor cost *AFC* is the same as input price. The *MFC* and *AFC* from Table 16.2 are graphically illustrated in Figure 16.2.

TABLE 16.2   Average, Total, and Marginal Factor Costs

Number of Units of Factor	Input Price or AFC	Total Factor Cost TFC	Marginal Factor Cost MFC
0		0	
1	10	10	10
2	11	22	12
3	12	36	14
4	13	52	16
5	14	70	18
6	15	90	20

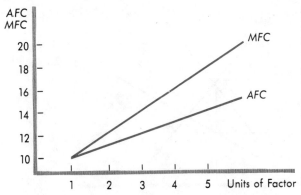

FIGURE 16.2 Average and marginal factor costs.

The relationship between *AFC* and *MFC* for an input is given by

$$\frac{MFC}{AFC} = 1 + \frac{1}{e_F} \quad \text{or} \quad MFC = P_F\left(1 + \frac{1}{e_F}\right)$$

where P_F is input price and e_F is the elasticity of input supply.[1] With a competitive input market, the individual firm's e_F is infinite, and, hence, $MFC = AFC = $ input price. With imperfect factor markets, $0 < e_F < \infty$ and $MFC > AFC$ in most cases. The exception is the backward-bending supply curve of labor, and, in this case, $MFC < AFC$ because $e_F < 0$.

Earlier, we defined the input demand curve for a firm under perfect competition in the output market as part of the *VMP* curve and, under monopoly, as part of the *MRP* curve. When we have monopsony in the input market there is no demand curve for the input. In fact, the concept of an input demand curve is meaningless because the firm is not a price taker. The firm determines the input price by the quantity that it employs. For a given input supply curve, the *MFC* curve is determined. The intersection of the *MFC* curve with the *VMP* curve (in the case of competition in the output market) or the *MRP* curve (in the case of monopoly) uniquely determines the quantity of the input employed. The price of the input is then determined from the input supply curve.

This is illustrated for the case of labor in Figure 16.3: *SS* is the input supply curve, *MFC* is the marginal factor cost curve, and *VMP* is the value of the marginal product of labor. In Figure 16.3 the employment *Q* is determined by the intersection of the *VMP* and *MFC* curves (the output market is assumed to be competitive). Once *Q* is determined, the wage rate *W* is obtained from the *SS* curve as the wage

[1]Consider, for example, labor.

$$TFC = W \cdot L$$
$$\Delta TFC = W \cdot \Delta L + L \cdot \Delta W$$
$$MFC = \Delta TFC/\Delta L = W + L \cdot \Delta W/\Delta L$$
$$\qquad = W(1 + L/W \cdot \Delta W/\Delta L) = W(1 + 1/e_L)$$

Since $W = AFC$, we have $MFC/AFC = 1 + 1/e_L$.

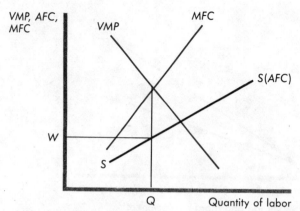

FIGURE 16.3 Employment under monopsony (for monopoly, change VMP to MRP).

rate corresponding to the employment Q. Note that under perfect competition, the wage rate is equal to VMP (the value of the marginal product of labor). Under monopsony the wage rate is below the VMP. Joan Robinson (1903 to 1983) called this difference the *monopsonistic exploitation of labor*.[2] We will see in the next section how labor, by forming a trade union, can counter this monopsonistic exploitation.

We will summarize the results on the demand for an input, such as labor, that we have derived up to now. This is presented in Table 16.3.

The results for monopsony in Table 16.3 are for the nondiscriminating monopsonist. We will now consider the case of wage discrimination by a monopsonist. Wage discrimination under monopsony is similar to the practice of price discrimination under monopoly (which we discussed in Chapter 11).

[2]See Joan Robinson, *The Economics of Imperfect Competition*, Macmillan, London, 1933.

TABLE 16.3 Summary of Results on Demand for Labor

Labor Market	Product Market	
	Perfect Competition	Monopoly
Perfect Competition	The VMP curve is the demand curve for labor. $W = VMP$ gives the level of employment.	The MRP curve is the demand curve for labor. $W = MRP$ gives the level of employment. Since $MRP < VMP$, we have $W < VMP$.
Monopsony	$MFC = VMP$ gives the level of employment, and the corresponding point on the supply curve gives the wage rate. The demand curve consists of a single point. $W < MFC$.	$MFC = MRP$ gives the level of employment, and the corresponding point on the supply curve gives the wage rate. The demand curve consists of a single point. $W < MFC$, $MFC = MRP$, $MRP < VMP$.

Suppose there are two labor markets with different supply elasticities e_1 and e_2. The monopsonist equates marginal factor costs in both markets. This equality is clearly necessary for profit maximization. For, if MFC were lower in market 1 than in market 2, the monopsonist could reduce cost by increasing employment in market 1 and reducing employment in market 2. And, of course, if MFC were lower in market 2, then the opposite adjustment would reduce cost. Hence, we have

$$MFC_1 = MFC_2$$

or

$$W_1 \left(1 + \frac{1}{e_1}\right) = W_2 \left(1 + \frac{1}{e_2}\right)$$

If $e_1 > e_2$, we have

$$1 + \frac{1}{e_1} < 1 + \frac{1}{e_2}$$

Hence, $W_1 > W_2$. That is, the monopsonist will pay a higher wage rate in the market with the higher elasticity of supply.

In our discussion in Chapter 11 on monopoly, we also mentioned the case of perfect discrimination where monopolists charge a different price to every customer. The monopolist charges customers their *reservation price*. Similarly, we can talk of perfect discrimination by a monopsonist. In this case the monopsonist pays workers their *reservation wage*.

The reservation wage for a worker is the minimum wage at which the worker is willing to work. Thus, the reservation wage for the first worker in Table 16.2 is $10, for the second worker it is $11, and so on. The monopsonist who is practicing perfect discrimination will pay the first worker $10, the second worker $11, and so on. In this case, the MFC curve is the supply curve of labor. And total employment will be higher since it is now given by the intersection of the VMP curve and the SS curve. This is shown in Figure 16.4. (In the case of monopoly, employment is determined by the intersection of the SS curve with the MRP curve). Thus, employment increases from Q_1 to Q_2 if the monopsonist practices perfect discrimination.

16.5   MONOPSONY, MINIMUM WAGE LAWS, AND TRADE UNIONS

Earlier, in Chapter 15, we argued that the effect of a minimum wage law is to produce unemployment. This is the case when the labor market is perfectly competitive. However, under monopsony the minimum wage law can increase the wages of workers without any reduction in employment and can sometimes even increase employment. We will soon see how this can happen.

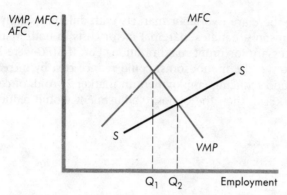

FIGURE 16.4 Increase in employment due to perfect discrimination by the monopsonist.

To analyze the effects of minimum wages under monopsony we have to study first the effect on the *MFC* curve, because it is the intersection of this curve with the *VMP* (or *MRP*) curve that determines employment. This effect is shown in Figure 16.5. Initially, the input supply curve is *SS'*, and the *MFC* curve is *DE*. We now impose a minimum wage $\overline{W}$. Since no labor is supplied below $\overline{W}$, the supply curve of labor becomes *ABS'*. Since the wage rate is constant over the range *AB*, we have *MFC* equals the wage rate over this range. After point *B*, the *MFC* is as it was before. Hence, the *MFC* curve becomes *ABCE* with the imposition of a minimum wage.

The important thing to note is that with a minimum wage, the *MFC* curve is flat until it hits the supply curve. Then the *MFC* curve turns vertically up and joins the original *MFC* curve. Since employment is determined by the intersection of the *MFC* curve with the *VMP* curve, and wages from the supply curve, all wage and employment combinations possible are bounded by the *VMP* and supply curves. This is shown in Figure 16.6. The wage and employment combinations possible are shown in thick lines. To demonstrate that minimum wages can increase employment, we will consider setting the minimum wage $\overline{W}$ at a level higher than W_1, where W_1 is the wage prevailing under monopsony. This is shown in Figure

FIGURE 16.5 Effect of minimum wage law on the *MFC* curve.

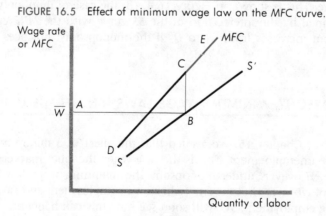

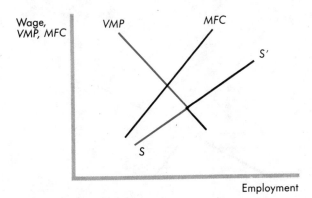

FIGURE 16.6 Wage and employment combinations produced by minimum wage laws (shown as colored lines).

16.7. Initially, employment is Q_1 and the wage rate W_1. With the minimum wage fixed at $\overline{W}$, the MFC curve is ABCD. Taking the point of intersection of the MFC curve with the VMP curve, we see that employment rises to Q_2. The wage rate is $\overline{W}$ as given from the supply curve ABS'.

We will now analyze the effects of different levels of the minimum wage $\overline{W}$. To do this we start with the initial position of wage and employment under monopsony and consider the extent of monopsonistic exploitation. This is shown in Figure 16.8 with the thick colored lines from Figure 16.6. Without minimum wage laws, Q_1 is employment and W_1 is the wage rate. The value of marginal product of labor at this level of employment is W_m. The degree of monopsonistic exploitation is $W_m - W_1$. If we fix the minimum wage at W_m, then employment will remain unchanged and the wage rate will be W_m. Thus, with minimum wage at W_m, all monopsonistic exploitation is removed.

FIGURE 16.7 Effect of minimum wage law on employment.

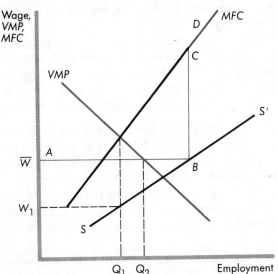

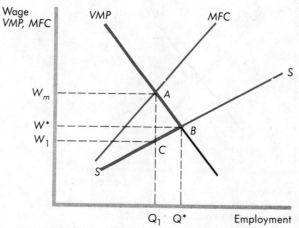

FIGURE 16.8   Increases in wages and employment with minimum wage laws.

The maximum employment that one can achieve by minimum wages is Q^*, the intersection of the *VMP* curve with the supply curve. This employment can be achieved by setting the minimum wage at W^*. However, setting minimum wages anywhere between W_1 and W_m will increase employment and wages above what would otherwise have prevailed under monopsony. Setting minimum wage above W_m will increase wages but will reduce employment below Q_1. And, of course, setting minimum wage below W_1 will have no effect.

The elimination of monopsonistic exploitation of labor can be achieved without minimum wage laws. It can be achieved by trade union organization of labor. The wage that the trade union wants to negotiate will depend on its objectives:

1. If the trade union wants maximum wages, with the current level of employment unchanged, it will negotiate the wage rate at W_m in Figure 16.8.

2. If the trade union wants maximum employment, it will negotiate the wage rate at W^* in Figure 16.8.

3. Intermediate levels between W^* and W_m correspond to various combinations of objectives of raising wages and employment. Note that although negotiating wages in the range W_1 to W^* raises employment and wages, the same increases in employment can be achieved at higher wage in the range W^* to W_m. Thus, the union is better off on the segment *AB* rather than *BC* in Figure 16.8.

In summary, the effect of minimum wage laws in labor markets that are competitive is to reduce employment or increase unemployment. If labor markets are characterized by monopsony, the effect may be to increase employment. However, empirical studies have shown that minimum wage laws have not increased employment. If anything, minimum wage laws seem to have increased unemployment at least in the market for teenagers. Thus, the empirical evidence supports the competitive model.[3] But what this may indicate is simply that the segment of

[3]See Finis Welch, *Minimum Wages: Issues and Evidence,* American Enterprise Institute, Washington, D.C., 1978. A readable nontechnical survey of economic research in this area is: Sar Levitan and Richard Belous, *More than Substance: Minimum Wages for the Working Poor,* Johns Hopkins Press, Baltimore, 1979.

the labor market covered by minimum wage laws is competitive. Monopsony elements are likely to exist in the labor market but at the higher end of the skill levels of the labor force. Workers at these levels are not affected by minimum wage laws. They are more affected by trade union activity. In Section 16.7 we will discuss examples where trade union activity increases both wages and employment in a monopsonistic situation.

16.6 LABOR EXPLOITATION UNDER MONOPOLY AND MONOPSONY

In the previous section we discussed how minimum wage laws or trade union bargaining can eliminate the "exploitation" of labor by a monopsonist and how the wage rate can be brought into equality with the *VMP* (value of marginal product).

If the product market is characterized by monopoly, then instead of *VMP* we have to consider *MRP*, and we saw earlier that *MRP* < *VMP*. Thus, there is an additional exploitation of labor that cannot be eliminated by minimum wage laws.

Employment under monopoly and monopsony is illustrated in Figure 16.9. The intersection of the *MRP* curve with the *MFC* curve gives *Q* as employment, and from the supply curve we get W_1 as the wage rate. The value of *MRP* for this level of employment is W_2, and the value of *VMP* for this level of employment is W_3. We can, thus, break down labor exploitation as follows:

$$W_2 - W_1 = \text{monopsonistic exploitation}$$
$$W_3 - W_2 = \text{monopolistic exploitation}$$
$$W_3 - W_1 = \text{total exploitation}$$

We saw earlier that $W_2 - W_1$ can be eliminated by minimum wage laws or trade union bargaining. But $W_3 - W_2$ cannot be eliminated by minimum wage laws. Raising the minimum wage to any point between W_2 and W_3 would merely reduce employment because the monopolist would equate *MRP* to the wage rate

FIGURE 16.9   Exploitation produced by monopoly and monopsony.

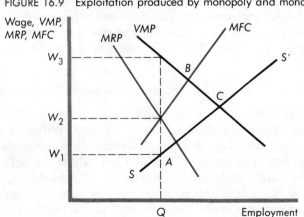

to determine how many workers to hire. How much of $W_3 - W_2$ can be eliminated depends on the bargaining strengths of the monopolist-monopsonist and the labor union. This is a case of *bilateral monopoly,* and as we said in Chapter 11, there is no determinate solution to this problem.

Without any labor union or minimum wage laws, the monopolist would equate *MRP* to *MFC* in Figure 16.9. She would hire a number of workers equal to Q and pay a wage rate W_1. With a minimum wage set at W_2, employment remains at the same level Q. If the labor union is strong, it can force the monopolist to forgo monopoly profits and move the equilibrium to the point B where both employment and the wage rate rise as compared to the point A. At point B there is no monopoly exploitation and $VMP = MFC$. The ideal competitive solution is, of course, given by the point C, but this point can be reached only in the following two cases:

1. If the labor union only negotiates increases in employment and lets the wage rate be given by the points on the supply curve SS', point C can be attained.

2. If the labor union negotiates increases in employment and also insists on the wage rate being determined by the points on the *MFC* curve, point C can be attained through perfect price discrimination by the monopsonist as illustrated earlier in Figure 16.4.

Thus, what happens to wages and employment depends on the respective powers of the monopolist and trade union and whether the labor union negotiates increases in employment only or both increases in employment *and* increases in wages.

16.7   APPLICATIONS

In the previous sections we discussed the demand for an input under monopoly in the product market and the supply of an input under monopsony in the input market. Although much of the discussion of the determination of input price and employment is often conducted under the assumption of perfect competition in both the product and factor markets (which we discussed in the last chapter), there are some interesting applications of the theories presented in this chapter. In the previous two sections, we discussed the effects of minimum wage laws and trade unions under monopsony. There are some special cases of this that deserve further discussion.

16.7.1 Monopsony in labor markets: The market for nurses

The essential feature of pure monopsony is that there is only one firm that is the buyer of an input in a particular market. A typical example of pure monopsony is a coal mining town where the mine is literally the sole employer. But this is very rare. A less extreme example is that of a firm which is a large employer, relative to the input market, and, hence, has to face an upward-sloping input supply curve.

A good example of this is the market for registered nurses (RNs). We will discuss developments in the 1960s to illustrate the problem of monopsony in the labor market, and then we will outline the recent developments. According to the data in Yett, 10 percent of all hospitals are the only hospital in an area, 30 percent of all hospitals are located in areas where there are only one or two hospitals, and more than 60 percent of hospitals are in areas where there are fewer than six hospitals.[4] Hospitals do act like cartels or monopsonists with respect to setting nurses' wages. Donald Yett conducted a survey of the largest hospital associations to determine whether they had wage stabilization programs—14 of the 15 hospital associations that responded said that they did have a wage stabilization program.

The effect of this monopsonistic wage setting is to create an artificial shortage of nurses. This is illustrated in Figure 16.10. *VMP* is the value of marginal product curve, *SS* the supply curve, and *MFC* the marginal factor cost curve. The monopsonistic firm (hospital) will equate *VMP* (or *MRP*) to *MFC*. This is given by the point A in Figure 16.10. The employment and wage rate of the firm would be at the point B, with the wage rate equal to W_1 and the quantity of RNs employed equal to Q_1. However, at the wage rate W_1 the monopsonistic firm would like to employ Q_2 nurses. Thus, there is a shortage of $Q_2 - Q_1$ nurses. This shortage is merely a consequence of the hospital trying to maximize its profits (equating *VMP* or *MRP* to *MFC*). And the nurses get paid less than the value of their marginal product, as we noted earlier.

In the early 1960s, hospitals found it difficult to hire more nurses, and they tried to solve the shortage problem by recruiting foreign-trained nurses and by lobbying for legislation to provide subsidies to increase the supply of nurses.

In the middle 1960s, two important events alleviated the shortage of nurses: (1) the passing of the Medicare and Medicaid bill and (2) collective bargaining among hospital nurses. Passage of the Medicare and Medicaid bill increased the demand for medical care. At the same time hospitals were reimbursed on a "cost-plus" basis. Since the costs of increased wages to nurses could be passed on to the government, the hospitals did not have much incentive for cost minimization. This factor contributed to the rapid rise in nurses' wages during the 1966–1969 period.

[4]Donald E. Yett, *An Economic Analysis of the Nursing Shortage*, D. C. Heath, Lexington, Mass., 1975, p. 221.

FIGURE 16.10   A monopsonistic market for registered nurses.

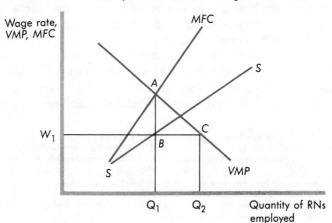

The other development was the unionization of nurses. In Section 16.5 we discussed the effects of unions on wages and employment. Under monopsony the unions can raise both wages and employment. In the case of nurses, the extent of unionization was not very large. The proportion of hospitals with at least one formal collective bargaining agreement rose from 15.7 percent to 27.4 percent in the 1970s. This is not a phenomenal increase. However, the effect of unions can often go beyond the workers covered by collective bargaining. Employers sometimes raise wages to prevent unionization and to avoid potential costs of bargaining.

Another factor relevant to our discussion was the passage of the Nurse Training Act by the federal government in 1964. This act subsidized nurses' training by providing scholarships and loans to students and grants for the construction of nursing schools. However, between 1966 and 1972 it is estimated that the federal subsidy program resulted in only about 1,500 additional nursing graduates per year. This amounts to a cost of $50,000 per active RN produced under the nurse training legislation. Many economists argue that an alternative policy of wage subsidy, which would increase the labor force participation of trained RNs, would have been 6 to 10 times cheaper than the nurse training program.[5] Assume that the wage elasticity with respect to the nurse participation rate is 1.0 (most estimates are around this figure). In 1969 the annual wage of an RN was around $8,000. A 1 percent increase in wage (or wage subsidy) is equal to $80 and since there were 630,000 RNs, the total cost would be $80 × 630,000 or approximately $50 million. But this would result in an increase of 1 percent in the number of RNs, or 6,300 nurses. Thus, the cost per additional RN is around $8,000, which is about one-sixth of the $50,000 which was the estimated cost under the nurses' training program. Although we have skipped some details in our calculations, we have given a rough idea of the costs involved under the two policy options and the impact on the number of RNs.

In any event, the shortage of nurses of the early 1960s diminished. The vacancy rate for RNs dropped from 23.2 percent in 1961 to 9.3 percent in 1971. Many economists believe that this decline was due primarily to the passage of the Medicare and Medicaid bill and the increase in unionization. It is suspected that the Nurse Training Act of 1964 did not contribute much.[6]

The nursing shortage of the early 1970s produced spectacular wage increases. The average maximum wage soared 39 percent. Enrollment in nursing programs shot up by more than 50 percent. However, training programs take at least 2 years to complete, with specialized programs taking longer. Thus, the time lags involved increased the number of nurses in the market in the late 1970s and made nursing a less attractive profession. This produced a decline in enrollment in nursing schools during the 1975–1980 period. Another round of wage increases between 1980 and 1982 reversed this downward trend, but enrollment did not grow as rapidly.

---

[5]Some studies that estimated the wage elasticity of RN's participation rate are: Lee Benham, "The Labor Market for Registered Nurses," *Review of Economics and Statistics,* August 1971, pp. 246–252; and Frank Sloan and S. Richupan, "Short-Run Supply Responses of Professional Nurses: A Microeconomic Analysis," *Journal of Human Resources,* Spring 1975, pp. 241–257.

[6]Some other papers that discuss the shortage problem and monopsony and union power are: C. R. Link and J. H. Landon, "Monopsony and Union Power in the Market for Nurses," *Southern Economic Journal,* April 1975, pp. 649–659, and Richard Hurd, "Equilibrium Vacancies in a Market Dominated by Non-Profit Firms: The 'Shortage' of Nurses," *Review of Economics and Statistics,* May 1973, pp. 234–240.

Between 1983 and 1986 again enrollment in nursing schools fell drastically from over 250,000 in 1983 to less than 200,000 in 1986. A survey by the American Hospital Association in 1986 found the percentage of unfilled nursing positions to be 14 percent. Hospitals that gave a bonus of $2,000, however, found it easy to fill the positions. Thus, as usual, the shortage was due to too low wages for nurses.

There are several factors that contributed to the increased demand and decreased supply of nurses in the 1980s.[7] On the demand side, the federal government introduced in 1983 the "prospective payment system" for Medicare patients, to reduce health care costs. It requires hospitals to assign patients to one or more of 486 "diagnostically related groups" (DRGs). Medicare then pays only a fixed amount for a particular DRG. Faced with a fixed payment, hospitals tried to limit patient days. The result was a shift from hospitals to home care and community clinics, which make intensive use of nurses. Other factors contributing to increased demand for nurses were the increased demand for health care (due to rising incomes and availability of health insurance) by the population as a whole as well as the increase in the elderly population (which needs more nursing care).

Several factors contributed to a decreased supply. The foremost was the availability of alternative options for women. Many women were going into financial services and self-employed small businesses, professions that are considered more prestigious than nursing. Even those who were trained as nurses found it attractive to go into "private practice," and this reduced the supply of nurses to hospitals (which frequently provide parking for doctors and even visitors but not to nurses, thus treating them as second-class citizens).

The increase in demand and decrease in supply create a shortage of nurses for the hospitals, but this shortage can be cured by raising the wages of nurses and making nursing a respectable profession. Nurses provide basic health care and even with increased wages, a top earning nurse will earn substantially less than an average physician.

The major factor characterizing the shortage of nurses in the 1980s is, therefore, not monopsony as it was in the 1960s and early 1970s discussed earlier.

16.7.2 Discrimination in employment

In the *Current Population Reports: Consumer Issue,* published by the U.S. Bureau of the Census, tables give median wage and salary income of blacks and whites, of males and females, and so on. From these tables one can easily see that there are income disparities between sex, age, and racial groups. For example, consider the following:

Black-White Ratio of Median
Wage and Salary Income for Full-
Time Workers

Year	Males	Females
1965	0.64	0.71
1975	0.77	0.99

[7]Timothy Tiergarthen, "This Nursing Shortage Is Different," *The Wall Street Journal,* November 11, 1987, p. 26.

These entries indicate that in 1965, the median salary income for full-time black male workers was 64 percent of the median salary for full-time white male workers. Note that the income disparity is less for females than for males and that the disparity declined over the period 1965 to 1975.

Examining these figures, many people want to conclude that racial discrimination is present. However, one must be careful not to simply attribute the entire salary disparity to discrimination, without more information. An operational definition of discrimination is "the valuation in the labor market of personal characteristics of the worker that are unrelated to productivity."[8] To isolate the impact of discrimination, we must first take account of many intervening factors like education, job stability, job experience, and so on which might affect productivity and, hence, explain part of the salary disparities.

A number of studies have tried to adjust the raw figures for two intervening factors: (1) blacks tend to be younger and less educated than whites (on the average) and (2) the average quality of schooling received by blacks is lower than that for whites. Adjusting for the observed differences in age, years of schooling, years of job experience, and so on produced estimates that suggest that about half the differences in the earnings can be explained by these observed measurable characteristics.[9] This leaves at most half of the disparity to be attributed to discrimination.

However, there is circular reasoning involved here. The factors mentioned here are true, but a question arises as to why blacks tend to invest less in schooling. There could be many explanations—lower expectation about the effects of education on earnings (which itself can be traced to social treatment), socioeconomic status of parents, cultural background, and so forth. Thus, the disparity in education might itself be attributed to discrimination.

Several theories concerning the sources of discrimination are based on (1) personal prejudice, (2) signalling, (3) monopsony. The personal prejudice theory says that some employers are prejudiced against some particular groups and, hence, underestimate their marginal product.[10] However, if a firm underestimates the marginal product of a certain class of labor, it will hire less of this labor and, thus, make less profit, compared with a nondiscriminating firm. Thus, the discriminating firm will be at a competitive disadvantage, and we should find firms that practice discrimination going out of business. We should also find discrimination declining over time. However, we do not find much evidence of either of these things happening. This leads us to suspect that there must be substantial monopolistic and oligopolistic sectors in the economy, since it is firms in these sectors that can afford to discriminate. In fact, it is common experience that blacks are more likely to be employed in competitive industries than in oligopolistic industries.

It should be noted that discrimination due to prejudice need not be confined to employers alone. It can be on the employees' side (some groups wanting to work only in segregated environments) or the consumers' side (some groups wanting to be served only by members of a certain group). Again, catering to these

---

[8]K. J. Arrow, "The Theory of Discrimination," in O. Ashenfelter and Albert Rees, eds., *Discrimination in Labor Markets*, Princeton University Press, Princeton, N.J., 1973.

[9]There is an enormous literature on this subject. A summary of many results can be found in Ray Marshall, "The Economics of Racial Discrimination: A Survey," *Journal of Economic Literature*, September 1974, pp. 849–871.

[10]See Gary S. Becker, *The Economics of Discrimination*, 2d ed., University of Chicago Press, Chicago, 1971.

prejudices would be inconsistent with profit maximization and can be done only under imperfectly competitive environments (monopoly, oligopoly, monopsony).

The signalling theory says that race and sex can be used as "signals" about the productivity of workers.[11] The employer cannot estimate correctly the marginal produce of each potential employee. So the employer uses some screening method for selecting employees with higher productivity. The theory says that race and sex are used as screening devices if previous experience indicates that productivity is correlated with these characteristics. The use of race or sex as a screening device may look like prejudice but really it is not. In essence, what the employer does is assign some average group characteristics to each member of the group. If the employer finds that workers living on the north side of a railroad are more productive than those living on the south side, then he or she may use the side of residence as a screening device. This would not be considered prejudice.

This method of screening on the basis of group differences becomes very costly to firms if members in a group are very dissimilar. The signals are not very reliable. Also, the firm must reduce its use of a signal over time if there are structural changes in the characteristics of the groups. For example, if more women want steady employment, an employer discriminating against women because they have traditionally not kept a job would be making a costly mistake. After a while, the employer, noting the structural change, would stop using sex as a screening device.

Finally, monopsony elements can be responsible for wage discrimination. Earlier, in Section 16.4, we discussed how under monopsony, there can be different wages paid to different groups based on their supply elasticities. Here is a case of discrimination that arises from the profit motive, not prejudice—It is profitable for the discriminators. The monopsonist might be able to segment the market into noncompeting groups based on sex or race. Then it would be profitable to practice discrimination.

However, as we noted earlier when we discussed the market for nurses, there are not many cases of monopsony that one can think of and even fewer cases of monopsonists discriminating on the basis of race and sex.

EXAMPLE 16.1   Who Is Sick, the Patients or the Doctor?

Through the Equal Employment Opportunity Commission (EEOC), the federal government is in charge of enforcing antidiscriminatory laws in civilian employment. However, many studies have found that the earnings of minorities and women employed by the federal government are substantially lower than the earnings of "similar" white males.[12] Thus, we can conlude that the "doctor" who is in charge of curing patients is himself sick.

Although discrimination is present in several government agencies, there is considerable variation in the relative (relative to white males) wages of blacks and

[11]The signalling theory has been developed in A. Michael Spence, "Job Market Signalling," *Quarterly Journal of Economics*, August 1973, pp. 355–374.

[12]The most exhaustive study is Sharon P. Smith, *Equal Pay in the Public Sector: Fact or Fantasy*, Princeton University, Industrial Relations Section, Princeton, N.J., 1977. Other studies are: G. J. Borjas, "Discrimination in HEW: Is the Doctor Sick or Are the Patients Healthy?" *Journal of Law and Economics*, 1978; J. E. Long, "Employment Discrimination in the Federal Sector," *Journal of Human Resources*, 1976; and D. A. Smith, "Government Employment and Black/White Relative Wages," *Journal of Human Resources*, 1980.

women employed by the different agencies. Borjas tries to explain these differences through a political approach to government behavior (that is, by assuming that the government's objective is to maximize its political support).[13] He finds that the relative wage of black males is higher in agencies with heavy black constituencies and in agencies which make expenditures in enforcing affirmative action programs in the private sector. Similarly, the relative wage of women in federal agencies also depends on the sexual composition of the constituency and on the aegncy's output. He argues that these findings suggest that the characteristics of a firm and the markets it serves might offer clues to the sources of employment discrimination in the private sector as well.

16.7.3 Economics of sports

The most prominent example of monopsony in the U.S. economy is major league sports such as baseball, football, basketball, and hockey. The players are much less valuable in any employment other than in one particular sport. Each of the leagues has a virtual monopoly for that sport, and the individual teams operate like a cartel.

The team owners restrict competition among themselves for the players by using the "draft" system and "reserve clauses." The draft system works the following way. At the end of the official season all teams are ranked on the basis of won-lost record. The worst team in each league is given the first choice of players entering the profession. The next poorest team has the second choice, the third poorest has the third choice, and so on. No team can bargain with a player who has been drafted by another team. However, the reserve clause permits a team to acquire the services of another team's player by purchasing the player's contract from the current owner. This switch does not increase the pay of the player, but the team that originally signed up the player may sell the contract at a profit. In essence, when players have signed up with a team, they have sold the rights to their playing skills. For instance, if a player has signed up for $40,000 with the L.A. Raiders and the Seattle Seahawks want to buy the player for $45,000, the player gets the same amount as before but the L.A. Raiders get $5,000. However, if the value of the marginal product of this player is more than $45,000 for the L.A. Raiders, then the team owners would not want to sell the contract to the Seattle Seahawks even at a profit of $5,000. Note that (as shown in Figure 16.3) under monopsony, the wage rate paid to the players is below the value of the marginal product of each player and, thus, there is considerable leeway for the bargaining of contracts. One can thus talk of the "exploitation" of players by the team owners.[14]

As we explained earlier in Section 16.5, the gap between the player's wage and the value of the player's marginal product can be closed or reduced if the players form a union and use collective bargaining. However, in this case the correct analysis is the one in Section 16.6, because the teams have a monopoly over the

---

[13]G. J. Borjas, "The Politics of Employment Discrimination in the Federal Bureaucracy," *Journal of Law and Economics,* October 1982, pp. 271–298.

[14]See G. W. Scully, "Pay and Performance in Major League Baseball," *American Economic Review,* December 1974, pp. 915–930. Scully estimates that in some cases the players were paid less than one-fifth of the value of their marginal product.

sale of tickets and other rights for the sport. Thus, the situation is one of monopoly *and* monopsony. There we explained the nature of solutions that are feasible, depending on the power of the labor union and whether the labor union is interested in higher wages or higher employment.

In the case of professional sports, if the existing players were organized into a union, they would be interested in getting a higher wage. Thus, the optimum point from the union's point of view is point B in Figure 16.11 with employment at Q_1 and wage rate W_2. Without any bargaining the equilibrium employment is at Q_1, and the wage rate is at W_1.

An important point to note is that there are actually markets for individual positions on teams and each will have its own wage and quantity. However, considering this will unduly complicate our analysis.

Now let us consider the effect of the formation of a new league. In this case, the new league competes with the original league for players. This is what happened with the formation of the American Football League, the World Football League, and most recently the USFL (which went out of existence quickly), in football; the American Basketball Association, in basketball; and the World Hockey League, in hockey. With the new league, the supply curve facing each league is more elastic, and the original league is no longer a pure monopsonist. The effect would be a rise in employment and wages and not as much monopsonistic exploitation (which is given by the distance between the supply curve and the *MFC* curve). This is shown in Figure 16.12. With the formation of the new league the existing league will face the flatter supply curve S_2 with the corresponding marginal factor cost given by MFC_2. The original supply curve is S_1, and the marginal factor cost curve is MFC_1. The initial equilibrium gives quantity Q_1 with a wage rate W_1. With the formation of the new league, the quantity increases to Q_2 and price to W_2. There is also less monopsonistic exploitation. However, the monopolistic exploitation still persists (given by the difference between *MRP* and *VMP*). This can be reduced by collective bargaining (or strikes).[15]

---

[15]During recent years, there were strikes by the members of the Baseball Players Association in 1981 and the Football Players Association in 1982 and 1987.

FIGURE 16.11   Collective bargaining in professional sports.

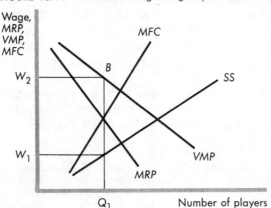

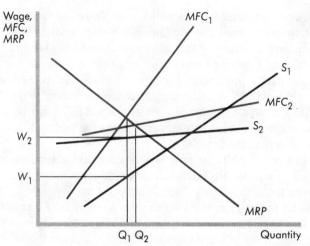

FIGURE 16.12   Effect of the formation of a new league on the wages of players.

16.7.4 College sports: The NCAA as a cartel

Until now we have discussed professional sports. The case of college sports is less obvious, but it is still a case of monopsony. The National Collegiate Athletic Association (NCAA) establishes athletic standards and official playing rules for college sports. It regulates the number of student athletes that universities can hire, it controls the televising of college football games, it fixes the prices for sporting events, and it sets the wages of student athletes.[16] The NCAA strictly enforces its regulations by imposing penalties and sanctions for all violations of its rules.

The NCAA was founded in 1906. Its membership has grown from 13 schools to over 700 colleges and universities. The NCAA regulates the earnings of college athletes so that the richest universities cannot buy up the most promising athletes. The wages paid to some of the college athletes are way below the value of their marginal product, and it is not unusual for some universities to cheat on the NCAA rules by paying some players under-the-table emoluments such as giving them $50 for a car wash or employing their close relatives. However, if these violations of the NCAA rules are detected, the NCAA imposes stiff penalties in the form of reducing a college's number of athletic scholarships, preventing the college or university from appearing in bowl games, preventing television broadcasting of the college's games (as happened with the University of Florida football program in 1984), and so on.

Colleges and Universities, however, do not protest against the penalties imposed by the NCAA and do not quit the cartel. Presumably, the cost of maintaining their athletic programs would really skyrocket if free competition were to be substituted.[17]

[16]The wages are tuition, room, board, books, and some "laundry money." However, since tuition, room, and board are not the same at all universities, there is a permissible range of price competition in the market.

[17]If competition were to be substituted, universities might have to sign up student athletes on long-term contracts, and then professional leagues would have to purchase the contract of the student athlete from the university.

As for the college athletes, they are willing to put up with lower wages while going to college because the colleges provide them with the necessary on-the-job training. Many of them are interested in maximizing their lifetime earnings rather than their proximate earnings while in school, although some athletes do turn professional before completing their college education. The universities bear the cost of training prospective professional athletes and receive revenues in the form of financial support from fans and alumni.

Although the NCAA operates like a cartel, there are some essential elements of its structure that are sources of trouble, and, in fact, many of the characteristics of market structure that are most often associated with successful cartels are absent in the case of the NCAA.[18] Some of these characteristics are

1. The number of firms: A successful cartel does not have a large number of firms. The NCAA has more than 600 members, and it is impossible to monitor all the actions of its members.

2. Restrictions on entry: Successful cartels have restrictions on entry that the NCAA does not have. Any college or university that states that it will abide by the rules of the NCAA can join.

3. Publications of violations: A cartel would like to be informed of all the violations by the members but would not like them to be known to the public. A cartel cannot function if its defects are laundered in the public. The NCAA violations are publicized in the press and on television when they are known. But before they are known, they are really a secret from all members.

4. Differences in costs and profits: A cartel's member firms cannot have wide discrepancies in costs because they all have the same pricing structure. The members of the NCAA, however, differ widely on the costs of their athletic programs and their size. Some big universities have multimillion-dollar programs; others have very small programs. This problem is partly solved by having separate divisions for the NCAA.

In spite of all these differences, the NCAA does function like a cartel in collegiate sports. The colleges and universities are willing to stay within the NCAA, in spite of stiff regulations, for the reasons mentioned earlier.

16.8 SUMMARY AND CONCLUSIONS

For a monopolist, $MRP < MVP$, and the monopolist's input demand curve is a portion of the MRP curve. The monopolist's demand curve for an input, thus, lies below the corresponding VMP curve. When several inputs are variable, the monopolist maximizes profit where the input price to marginal product ratio is the same for all inputs and is equal to marginal revenue.

A pure monopsonist faces an upward-sloping market supply curve of an input. This means that marginal factor cost exceeds input price. The monopsonist who is

[18]See James V. Koch, "A Troubled Cartel: The NCAA," *Law and Contemporary Problems*, Winter–Spring 1973, pp. 135–150.

a competitor in the output market hires where $VMP = MFC$. The monopsonist who is a monopolist in the output market hires where $MRP = MFC$. In both cases, input price is determined by the corresponding point on the input supply curve. For the perfectly discriminating monopsonist, the MFC curve is the input supply curve, and employment is the same as for a competitive input market. For a monopsonist discriminating between several markets, the highest wage rate will be paid in the market with the highest elasticity of input supply.

Under monopsony, a minimum wage law can increase the wage rate without reducing employment. In fact, employment may actually rise. This is because the minimum wage law flattens a portion of the MFC curve, so that MFC equals the wage rate over some region of employment.

When monopoly in the output market and monopsony in the input market are both present, employment occurs where $MRP = MFC$, and the wage rate is determined by the corresponding point on the labor supply curve. The difference between MFC and the wage rate is the monopsonistic exploitation of labor. The difference between MVP and MRP is the monopolistic exploitation. The monopolistic exploitation cannot be eliminated by minimum wage laws.

Monopsony in the market for nurses produced a "shortage" in the early 1960s. This shortage was alleviated by the passage of the Medicare and Medicaid bill and the unionization of nurses.

Discrimination in employment can be the result of prejudice, signalling, or monopsony power. We would expect competitive forces to reduce discrimination so that it is more likely to occur in monopolistic or oligopolistic sectors.

A prominent example of monopsony is major league sports. If players were organized into a union, wages could be increased. Also, the entrance of new leagues tends to increase both athletes' wages and employment and to decrease monopsonistic exploitation of athletes. A less obvious example of monopsony is the NCAA. The member colleges and universities function as a cartel.

KEY TERMS

Discrimination	Monopolistic Exploitation	Monopsony
Marginal Factor Cost	of Labor	Reservation Wage
Marginal Revenue	Monopsonistic Exploitation	Signalling
Product	of Labor	

QUESTIONS

1. How can a firm be a monopolist in the output market and face a perfectly elastic input supply curve? What is an example of this?

2. Using the data in Table 16.1, demonstrate that $(MRP)_L$ is also equal to $MR \cdot (MP)_L$. Explain the logic of this relationship.

3. If there are two employers of an input, how does the elasticity of each one's input supply curve compare to that of the market input supply curve? Why?

4. Graphically demonstrate that the wage bill for a perfectly discriminating monopsonist is lower than for a nondiscriminating monopsonist using the same quantity of labor.

5. Explain why the labor unions support the "Buy American" campaign. What is the impact on the wage rate and employment? Does it matter whether the labor market is competitive?

6. If labor is the only variable input, explain why the monopolist producing where $MR = MC$ must employ labor to the point where $W/(MP)_L$ equals marginal revenue.

7. Graphically illustrate the case where a minimum wage law reduces employment under monopsony.

8. Explain how the regulation of output price in a monopolistic industry can reduce the exploitation of labor. How are the relevant curves affected?

9. Do you believe that the male-female wage disparities of 20 years ago can be explained by monopsonistic profit maximization? Under this theory, which group would you expect to have been paid more? Why?

10. In Section 16.7.3 we analyzed the impact of a new league on athletes' wages and employment. Explain how the analysis changes if the presence of a new league reduces demand for tickets, television rights, and so on for the original league.

CHAPTER 17

WAGES, RENT, INTEREST, AND PROFIT

17.1   INTRODUCTION

In the previous two chapters we primarily discussed one factor of production: labor. Occasionally, when we discussed substitution effects we mentioned capital as the other factor of production. We will now discuss the other factors in greater detail.

Factors of production have traditionally been classified under the headings of *labor, land,* and *capital.* To these were supposed to correspond three categories of factor returns: *wages* to labor, *rent* to land and *interest* to capital. The distribution of total revenues into wages, rent, and interest is called the *functional distribution of income.* In the eighteenth and nineteenth centuries this functional distribution of income had major social significance. Land was owned by the aristocracy, capital (material assets other than land) by the bourgeoisie, and labor was confined to the working class. This classification lost its significance over time when it was discovered that it is not possible to indeed classify the returns to the different factors into the "functionally" distinct categories of wages, rent, and interest.

As for the term "profit," we explained earlier in Chapter 11 that we must distinguish between *accounting profit* and *economic profit.* When we use the term profit in a day-to-day usage what we mean is accounting profit. This also includes the returns to specialized factors of production (entrepreneurial skills and so forth). These are actually opportunity costs to the firm, and it is only the residual after taking account of these returns to specialized factors that we call economic profit. In this sense a major portion of accounting profit goes into the traditional returns to labor, land, and capital. For example, we might consider entrepreneurial skills as a specialized kind of labor. We will discuss profits in greater detail later in Section 17.5. For the present, we will confine our attention to a discussion of returns to the traditional factors: labor, land, and capital. But even here, as we will presently see, the distinction is not really very clear.

17.2   THE DISTINCTIONS BETWEEN LABOR, LAND, AND CAPITAL

The distinctions between labor, land, and capital are rather blurred. Land is traditionally defined as "natural and inexhaustible powers of the soil" and capital as "produced means of production." In other words, land is made by nature, capital by people. But this distinction loses its meaning when one takes into account all the human effort that goes into "land development" for agriculture or for other purposes. Thus, even in "land" there is a lot of human effort involved.

In modern society workers have a decision to make. Are they going to spend time working at unskilled jobs (which involve raw labor) or spend time in training for jobs with higher skills? This training is part of what is now called "human capital."[1] The studies on human capital were motivated by the observation that the growth of physical capital, at least as conventionally measured, explains a relatively small part of the growth in income in many countries. The idea of human

---

[1] See Gary S. Becker, *Human Capital,* Columbia University Press, New York, 1964.

capital is, however, very old. Alfred Marshall (1842 to 1924) in his *Principles of Economics* said: "The most valuable of all capital is that invested in human beings."

There is, thus, a labor element in land and a capital element in labor, and we shall see that there is also a land element in labor and capital. Thus, all returns to these factors cannot be really classified into strict categories such as wages, rent, and interest.

A more important distinction is that between *capital* and *income* or between *a source of productive services* and the productive *services* themselves. The distinction is also between a *stock* and a *flow*. In this classification, under capital we have (1) land, (2) machines and buildings, and (3) human training and skills. The first two can be sold as a stock or their services can be "hired" or "rented." For instance, an acre of land can be sold, or it can be rented for a year. A typewriter can be sold or rented for a year. It is only human training and skills that can be only hired or rented. They cannot be sold as a stock.

17.3   ECONOMIC RENT AND QUASI RENT

In our daily usage "*rent*" is the price paid *per unit of time* (month, year, etc.) for the services of a durable good. We can rent buildings, dryers, washing machines, typewriters, computers, cars, and so on, instead of buying them.

In economics, however, the term has a specific meaning. *Economic rent* is the excess of total payments to a factor of production (land, labor, or capital) over and above what is required to bring the particular factor into production. Suppose worker A is willing to work at \$3 an hour but B is willing to work at \$4 an hour. An employer needing two workers employs them both at \$4 an hour. Then A has received an *economic rent* or surplus payment of \$1 an hour. The classical economists applied the idea of rent to agricultural land only. In his book, *The Principles of Political Economy and Taxation* (1817), David Ricardo (1772 to 1823) argued that lands were cultivated in descending order of fertility. Initially, the most fertile land was cultivated, and, as the demand for corn grew, less fertile lands were brought under cultivation. He assumed that labor costs and return on capital were constant. The price of corn was equal to the cost of production (labor costs and return on capital) on the marginal land. However, a surplus was earned on the superior land over the marginal land mainly due to differential fertility. This surplus was called rent.

Figure 17.1 illustrates this point. There are three farms A, B, and C ordered by decreasing fertility or increasing marginal costs (which equal average costs). The marginal cost curve is shown as a thick line. When price is p_1, only farm A is cultivated. Since price equals average cost, there is no surplus or rent. When price rises to p_2, farm B also is brought under cultivation. For farm A, since price is greater than average cost, there is a surplus given by the shaded rectangle 1. As for farm B, price equals average cost and there is no surplus. When price rises to p_3, farm C is also brought under cultivation. There is no surplus on this land, but there is a surplus on farm B given by the shaded rectangle 3. As for farm A, the surplus increases and is now given by the two rectangles 1 and 2.

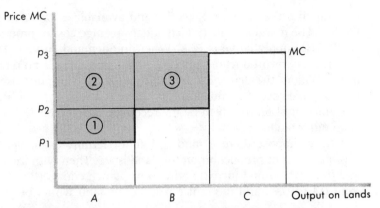

FIGURE 17.1 Increases in rent on fertile lands with increases in price of corn.

At the time Ricardo was writing, England's supply of corn was very low because of the Napoleonic wars. The high price of corn was blamed on "greedy" landlords who charged tenant farmers high rents. Ricardo's argument was that the rent was high because the price of corn was high and not the other way around. He argued that, since the price of the corn was equal to the cost of production on the marginal land ("no-rent" land), rent did not enter the price, nor would taxing the landlords have an effect on the price. The solution to the problem, according to Ricardo, was to allow free trade. With the importing of corn and the resulting fall in price, rents would fall (and so would domestic production), because the lands with inferior fertility would not be brought under cultivation.

Note that the emergence of rent does not depend on the existence of inferior lands. It arises from scarcity of fertile land. In fact, the availability of inferior lands acts as a dampening factor on the rents of lands of superior fertility. This is illustrated in Figure 17.2. On the horizontal axis we measure output, and assuming constant output per acre, we can also denote acres of land on the same axis.

FIGURE 17.2 Changes in economic rent with the availability of inferior lands.

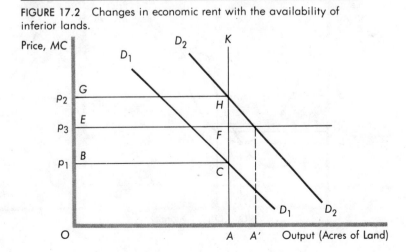

Suppose the amount of fertile land available is *OA*, and this is all of equal fertility. The marginal cost (which equals average cost of production) on this land is *OB*. The supply curve is *BCK*. When the demand curve is D_1D_1, all this fertile land is used for production, price $p_1 = MC$, and there is no rent. With the growth in population, the demand curve shifts to D_2D_2. The price rises to p_2, and, since the marginal cost of production is p_1, there is a rent or surplus going to landlords. The amount of rent is given by the rectangle *BCHG*. This is what happens if there is no other land available.

Now suppose there is land of inferior fertility available. The marginal cost (average cost) of production on this land is *OE*. Then with the increase in demand to D_2D_2, price would increase only to p_3 (which equals *OE*). Output would go up from *OA* to *OA'*, and the rent on the fertile land would be given by the area of rectangle *BCFE*.

Thus, rent arises because of scarcity of fertile land. It will be there whether or not there are inferior lands. Note also, in the above example, that when the demand curve is to the left of D_1D_1, price will still be p_1 (marginal cost *OB*), but not all the fertile land will be used.

Ricardo also argued that with the increase in the price of corn, production was pushed up both *intensively* (by producing more on the existing land) and *extensively* (by bringing less-fertile land under cultivation). We will illustrate this point with the use of typically shaped marginal cost *MC* and average cost *AC* curves shown in Figure 17.3. We have two farms, farm *A* and farm *B*. Farm *B* is less fertile than farm *A* and, hence, has a higher average cost curve. Initially, when price is p_1, only farm *A* is cultivated with production at Q_1. There is no rent since price = *MC* = *AC*. When price rises to p_2, the production on farm *A* rises to Q'_1. This is the result of intensive cultivation of farm *A*. Also, farm *B* is brought into production with output Q_2. Farm *B*'s output is called "extensive" cultivation. Also, for farm *B* there is no rent since price = *MC* = *AC*. But for farm *A* there is rent given by the shaded area, which is price minus *AC* times the quantity produced.

FIGURE 17.3   Intensive and extensive cultivation.

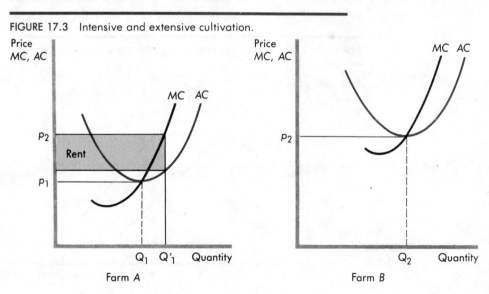

Farm A

Farm B

The above analysis enables us to predict the effects of *acreage controls*. If the acreage under production is controlled, existing landowners get higher and higher rents as the price of the produced grain rises. Usually, such policies are used to increase farm incomes. The result is only an increase in the income of landlords—not farm workers, or tenant farmers.

Until now we have considered economic rent on land only. Alfred Marshall argued that the concept of economic rent need not apply just to land. It can apply to any factor of production that is in fixed supply for a short or longer period. He said "in a sense all rents are *scarcity rents,* and all rents are *differential rents.*" What is true of land or natural resources is true of certain types of machines, human-made capital resources, and special human skills. Thus, the incomes received by all factors may contain an element of rent above the price necessary to keep the factor in its current employment, and the division of the price between necessary price and surplus depends on the time horizon we are considering. The term "quasi rent" ("sort-of" rent) is commonly used to depict the surplus accruing to factors of production other than land.

We can illustrate the concept of quasi rent with reference to labor. But before we do this, we will define a few terms. Suppose an individual is offered a job at $4 an hour. If this individual has an opportunity to take a similar job elsewhere at $5 an hour, she or he would reject the first offer because the *opportunity cost* (cost of alternative opportunities) is higher than the wage rate offered. Suppose the second job is a hazardous job and the individual is indifferent between the two jobs. Then the wage difference $5 − $4 = $1 is called a *compensating wage differential* (a wage differential that compensates for the job hazards). The difference is not economic rent. For instance, fire fighters, coal miners, and workers in other hazardous jobs have to be paid higher wages to compensate the workers for higher chances of loss of life. Richard Thaler and Sherwin Rosen compared average differences in wages with average differences in mortality by occupation groups.[2] A typical comparison that they present is as follows:

Occupation	Incremental Annual Deaths per 100,000 Workers	Estimated Annual Addition to Salary ($)
Fire fighters	44	77
Mine operators	176	310
Police and detectives	78	137

Note that the number of deaths for mine operators is 4 times higher than for fire fighters (and so also is estimated annual addition to salary). The data indicate that for an increase of 44/100,000 in the probability of death in a year, the worker demands $77 in annual increase in salary. From this the authors calculate the value of life as

$$\frac{\$77 \times 100,000}{44} = \$175,000$$

[2]Richard Thaler and Sherwin Rosen, "The Value of Saving a Life: Evidence from the Labor Market," in N. Terleckyj, ed., *Household Production and Consumption,* National Bureau of Economic Research, New York, 1975.

Not all wage differentials are compensating wage differentials. Some of the differences are pure rents created by scarcity—either natural or artificial. The high wages of beautiful models are due to the fact that God does not make too many of them. The high wages of doctors arise from the fact that the American Medical Association restricts the supply. As we have seen earlier, restricting the suppy will increase the rents for the present owners of that particular resource.

In any labor market with an upward-sloping supply curve, as long as there is no discrimination so that everyone gets the same wage, there will always be some rents accruing to some workers. This is illustrated in Figure 17.4. Different workers have different opportunity costs and, hence, different reservation wage rates (minimum wage rates at which they are willing to work).

In Figure 17.4, the first worker is willing to work at wage *OA*, the fiftieth worker at wage *OB*, and the hundredth worker at wage *OC*, and so on. If 50 workers are hired, everyone gets a wage = *OB*. The area under the supply curve is the summation of the opportunity costs of all the 50 workers. This is given by *OAFG*. The total wage bill is *OBFG*, and the area *ABF* represents the total rent accruing to the workers. Workers whose opportunity costs are low get higher rents.

If the number of workers employed goes up to 100, since the wage rate is *OC* and everyone gets paid the same, the earlier 50 workers get additonal rent given by the rectangle *BCDF*. The total opportunity cost is *OAEH*, and the total rent accruing to labor is given by *ACE*.

The above type of analysis was used by Walter Oi to analyze the cost of a military draft versus an all-volunteer army.[3] We will illustrate this with Figure 17.4. Suppose we need 100 soldiers. If we recruit them on a voluntary basis we have to pay a wage rate *OC*. However, we can fix the wage at *OB* and "draft" 100 soldiers. The impact of the draft policy is as follows:

1. The cost of the army goes down. The taxpayers save *BCEJ*.

2. The rent to the first 50 soldiers declines by *BCDF*.

3. As for the remaining 50 soldiers, their opportunity costs are *GFEH*. But they get only *FJHG* as wages. Hence, they lose *FEJ* in forgone opportunities. They also lose *DEF* in rent that they would have received under a volunteer army.

[3]Walter Y. Oi, "The Economic Cost of the Draft," *The American Economic Review*, May 1967, pp. 39–62.

FIGURE 17.4   Opportunity costs and rents for labor.

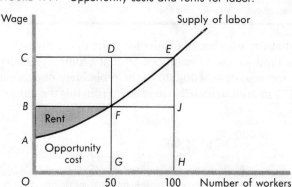

In summary, there is a redistribution of income between the soldiers and taxpayers. The loss of the first 50 soldiers is a loss in the economic rent they were receiving. The loss of the other 50 is not only a loss of economic rent but a loss of forgone opportunities as well.

In our example we assumed that the number of volunteers forthcoming at the fixed wage rate for the draft was 50 (half the number desired). But this can be any other number (< 100). In Walter Oi's example, the total number of soldiers desired was 472,000. He estimated that the wage rate for an all-volunteer army would have been $5,900. The draft army wage was $2,500, and the estimated number of volunteers at this wage was 263,000. Thus, 209,000 were real "draftees." This gives the following figures: (1) Saving for taxpayers

$$= (\$5,900 - \$2,500) \times 472,000$$
$$= \$1.6 \text{ billion}$$

(Area *BCEJ* in Figure 17.4). (2) Loss in rent to the soldiers who would have voluntarily joined the army at the draft wage (similar to area *BCDF* in Figure 17.4) is

$$(\$5,900 - \$2,500) \times 263,000 = \$894 \text{ million}$$

(3) Opportunity loss to draftees is roughly the loss of rental income which approximates

$$\tfrac{1}{2} (\$5,900 - \$2,500) \times 209,000 = \$355 \text{ million}$$

(We have assumed that area *DEF* = area *EFJ* in Figure 17.4.)

Although there are other factors not taken into account in the above analysis, such as the costs of administering the draft and the costs of draft evasion (going into a draft-exempt occupation, staying in school longer than planned, illegal activities), the above analysis gives some idea of the magnitude of income transfers involved. The above example also illustrates how economic rent can arise for labor and how methods to reduce this by force can result in opportunity loss for others.

EXAMPLE 17.1 How Much Is Life Worth?

Blomquist surveyed a number of studies that calculate estimates of the value of life.[4] To make the numbers comparable, he converts all values to June 1980 U.S. dollars using the consumer price index. (The number obtained by Thaler and Rosen will, therefore, be different from the one given earlier.) In the case of labor market studies, the estimates are based on compensating wage differentials (wage differentials that compensate for the job hazards). In the case of consumption activities (for example, installing smoke alarms in houses, use of seat belts in automobiles, and choosing to live in neighborhoods with less air pollution) the value of life is estimated from the extra costs the consumers are willing to incur for lesser risk of

---

[4]Glenn Blomquist, "Estimating the Value of Life and Safety: Recent Developments," in M. W. Jones Lee, ed., *The Value of Life and Safety*, North Holland Publishing, Amsterdam, 1982, pp. 27–40.

death. Some of the estimates are as follows (many others with detailed analysis of the limitations can be found in the paper by Blomquist):

Source	Authors	Value of Life (Thousands of 1980 dollars)
Implicit values from labor market activity		
Workers in risky occupations	Thaler-Rosen	494
Blue collar workers in manufacturing and construction	Dillingham	378
Males in manufacturing industries	Smith	2,785
Blue-collar workers	Viscusi	2,820
Implicit values from consumption activity		
Residential smoke alarms	Dardis	351
Auto seat belt use	Blomquist	466
Residential neighborhood air pollution	Portney	180

Source: The reference to the study by Thaler and Rosen has been given earlier. The other references are: G. Blomquist, ''Value of Life Savings: Implications of Consumption Activity,'' Journal of Political Economy, June 1979, pp. 540–558; R. Dardis, ''The Value of Life: New Evidence from the Marketplace,'' American Economic Review, December 1980, pp. 1077–1082; A. E. Dillingham, ''The Injury Risk Structure of Occupations and Wages,'' Ph.D diss., Cornell University, 1979; P. R. Portney, ''Housing Prices, Health Effects and Valuing Reductions in Risk of Death,'' Journal of Environmental Economics and Management, March 1981, pp. 72–78; R. S. Smith, ''Compensating Wage Differentials and Public Policy: A Review,'' Industrial and Labor Relations Review, April 1979, pp. 339–352; W. K. Viscusi, ''Labor Market Valuations of Life and Limb: Empirical Evidence and Policy Implications,'' Public Policy, Summer 1978, pp. 359–386.

An alternative method of obtaining the value of life is to calculate the present value of forgone earnings. This is the method used in compensation for accidents. This method is illustrated in Section 20.7.

17.4 CAPITAL, INTEREST, AND USER COST OF CAPITAL

We have discussed at length labor and land. We now turn to the third factor: capital. The term *capital* is defined in the Oxford American dictionary as "wealth or property that is used or invested to produce more wealth, the money with which business is started." In the finance literature, the term "capital" is used in the latter sense (money invested). However, in economics "capital" generally refers to the mass of long-lived and reproducible implements of production such as roads, bridges, factories, machines, and houses. These are also called "physical capital." They provide service over a period of time. Earlier, we talked of "human capital" in the sense that a worker also provides service over a period of time. However, the difference between physical capital and human capital is that the former can be bought and sold, but the latter cannot.

Since the production of physical capital takes up some of the current resources but returns flow only in the future, the choice of how much physical capital to produce involves decisions about current and future consumption. These decisions are called *intertemporal* decisions, and since a detailed discussion of this problem will lead us too far away from our main discussion here, we will treat them later in a separate chapter (Chapter 20). For the present we will make some convenient assumptions about these intertemporal decisions, to derive the supply function of capital. The demand function will be derived in the same way that we derived the demand for labor or any other input. The supply of labor was derived in Chapter 5 from the work-leisure choice of workers. The supply of capital depends similarly on choices between present and future consumption of individuals.

To illustrate these ideas let us assume that Robinson Crusoe, alone on an island, catches 10 fish per day. If he devotes one-tenth of his time for 10 days, he can build a net, and with the net he can catch 12 fish a day (or take some time off for leisure). Thus, Crusoe faces two choices: (1) catch 10 fish per day every day or (2) catch 9 fish per day for 10 days and catch 12 fish per day thereafter. The marginal product of the net is 2 fish per day. Now, assume that if Crusoe were to build another net, then he would be able to catch 13 fish per day. The marginal product of the second net is 1 fish per day. Next, suppose that one day a group of individuals land on this island. One of them has nets and rents them out in exchange for fish. The others just fish and are as productive as Crusoe. Now, if the rental price of a net is 2 fish per day, Crusoe will rent one net. If the rental price of a net is 1 fish per day, Crusoe will rent two nets. The number of nets rented is determined by equating the rental price to the marginal product (both expressed in terms of fish).

The building of machines, factories, roads, bridges, and so on all involve the same type of decisions that Crusoe faced in building a net. The decision is to use some labor and materials for the construction of capital equipment instead of producing goods for current consumption. Furthermore, the rental price of machines per hour (or day) would be equal to the value of marginal product of the machines per hour (or day). The demand curve for machines would be similar to the demand curve for labor shown in Figure 15.2 in Chapter 15. This demand curve for machines is shown in Figure 17.5. This is the demand curve for a competitive firm. For a monopolistic firm, we have to change *VMP* (value of marginal product) to *MRP* (marginal revenue product).

We now have to derive the supply curve. We will assume that as the rental price goes up, more machines will be supplied. We will not formally derive this result here because, as we said earlier, this involves an analysis of intertemporal decisions by consumers (treated later in Chapter 20). So, we will assume that the supply curve is upward sloping.

As we did with labor (in Chapter 15) we can also derive the market demand curve for machines and the market supply curve for machines; the intersection of the demand and supply curves gives us the equilibrium number of machines and the rental price. However, there are really many different kinds of machines. Also, physical capital includes buildings, roads, and bridges, in addition to equipment. Thus we have a real problem in constructing an aggregate measure of capital. The problem is not that simple with labor either. We cannot just count heads to get a

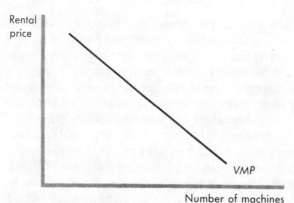

FIGURE 17.5   Demand curve for machines by a competitive firm.

measure of labor input. We have to take account of differences in skills and experience. However, the problems of getting an aggregate measure of capital are
more serious and there have been bitter controversies on this subject.[5]

Since we live in a monetary economy, it might seem best to convert the diverse
types of capital equipment into monetary terms or market values. In this case, one
might then think of taking the rental price of capital as the *rate of interest*, which
is nothing but the rental price of money. If you have $10,000 and you lend it to
someone at a 10 percent rate of interest for one year, you are, in essence, renting
your money for $1,000, and you get back the rent and the principal at the end of
the year (assuming that there is no default risk). A firm thinking of renting a
machine or other capital equipment at a price of $10,000 would compare the value
of the marginal product of the capital equipment with the return earned from, say,
a risk-free government bond.

However, it is not appropriate to take the rate of interest as a measure of the
rental price of capital for one main reason: When you lend (or rent) your money,
at the end of the time period you get your money back. The money you get back
may be worth less if there is inflation, but let us assume for the present that there
is no inflation. The same is not the case with machines. The machine would be
worth less because of depreciation and obsolescence. However, there may be some
tax deduction the firm can get if capital loss due to depreciation and obsolescence
is tax deductible. Also, if during the time period capital goods' prices have gone
up, then the capital equipment you have will be worth more at the end of the
period. Thus, the rental price of capital is not just the market rate of interest. You
have to add (and subtract) the factors mentioned. Assuming no taxes and no
inflation, the rental price of capital (also often called the *user cost of capital*) is given
by

$$c = q(i + \delta - g) \qquad\qquad [17.1]$$

[5]See G. C. Harcourt, *Some Cambridge Controversies in the Theory of Capital,* Cambridge University Press, Cambridge,
1972. This book has been translated into Italian, Polish, Spanish, and Japanese.

where

c = user cost of capital
q = price of a unit of capital
i = interest rate
δ = rate of depreciation (and obsolescence)
g = growth rate of prices of capital goods

The firm will compare c to the value of marginal product of a unit of capital.[6] Note that

qi = interest cost of borrowed funds
$q\delta$ = cost of depreciation and obsolescence. This is a capital loss, and
qg = capital gain due to a rise in the price of capital goods

The finance literature replaces i with r, the cost of financing the capital expenditure. We can consider two sources of finance: (1) debt (or borrowing), with interest rate i, and (2) equity (or the selling of stock), with cost of equity ρ. Then if β is the marginal proportion of funds obtained from debt and $(1 - \beta)$ from equity, we have

$$r = \beta i + (1 - \beta)\rho \qquad [17.2]$$

We now substitute r from Equation 17.2 for i in Equation 17.1.

The important thing to note is that money and physical capital (although we consider both in dollar terms) are not the same. Physical capital can depreciate, become obsolescent, and increase in value (take the phenomenal rise in the 1970s of housing prices). Money cannot depreciate, go out of fashion, or rise in value. (We are assuming no general inflation or deflation.)

17.5 PROFIT

We now come to the last of the components of the functional distribution of income: profit. We have previously emphasized the difference between economic profit and accounting profit and said that in long-run equilibrium, economic profits are 0 in a competitive industry.

For firms to operate as production units they need labor, land, and capital, but they also need an organizer. This organizer of a firm is called an *entrepreneur*. Entrepreneurs devote their time to bringing potential investors together, choosing plant location, hiring labor or executives, and financing the operation of the firm.

[6] In Chapter 15, Section 15.4, we wrote P_K/MP_K = price of output. What we mean by P_K is the rental price of capital or the user cost of capital.

There is, thus, labor and financial capital involved on the part of the entrepreneur. The entrepreneur incurs costs today for returns in the future. The amount of money attributable to the entrepreneur's efforts is sometimes called *normal profit*. This includes wages for labor (wages would be the amount the entrepreneur would have earned elsewhere in the competitive industry) and interest for investment expenditure (this is the return on investment that would have been earned elsewhere). But these are really opportunity costs. The term "profit" should, thus, refer to any excess over this normal profit. This excess is called "economic profit" or excess profit. It is the existence of this excess profit that lures new firms to enter an industry.

In a competitive industry, the excess profits disappear in the long run with the entry of new firms. This is not, however, the case with monopoly. Since entry is restricted, the excess profits may not disappear even in the long run. However, future excess profit can be capitalized and included in measuring the value of the firm. In this case the excess profit is a return to this capitalized value. When the monopoly is sold, this will be a cost to the new firm. Sometimes the excess profits earned by the monopolist are called "monopoly rent." The problem of monopoly profit is discussed in greater detail in Section 17.7.5 when we discuss the question of how much a monopoly is worth.

In the short run, even in a competitive industry, there can be some excess profits. But these excess profits cannot be capitalized because they are transitory.[7] They serve the useful purpose of signalling other firms to enter this market. With the entry of new firms these excess profits are likely to disappear. The excess profits for a monopoly are capitalized (and reflected in the value of the firm) because they are permanent.

Sometimes excess profits are not capitalized in the case of uncertainty.[8] Since the excess profits are not certain, the value of the firm does not increase by the capitalized value of the future profits. There will be some residual returns in each period (these residual returns can be positive or negative). If revenues and costs in the future are known with certainty, all net returns will be capitalized, and then there will be no such thing as residual return or excess profit.

Residual returns or excess profits can occur in

1. A competitive industry in the short run, particularly to those who first entered the industry—these are the "innovators"

2. A monopoly, although in this case the returns may be capitalized and then there is no such thing as residual returns

3. Conditions of uncertainty

The famous economist Joseph Schumpeter argued that profits result from the successful application of innovations (which are commercial applications of inventions).[9] Such successful innovations are made by the firms first entering a

---

[7] In practice this is not true. One has just to see how some stocks really jump up in price even with transitory excess profits.

[8] Actually, there is an uncertainty as to whether the short-run excess profits of a competitive firm will continue in the future, because of the uncertainty of the speed of entry of other firms.

[9] Joseph A. Schumpeter, *The Theory of Economic Development: An Enquiry into Profits, Capital, Credit, Interest, and Business Cycles*, Harvard University Press, Cambridge, Mass., 1934.

competitive industry, and these are the firms that make excess profits in the short run before others enter the industry. Some of the innovative firms obtain a patent for the innovation and, thus, form a monopoly. Thus, Schumpeter's innovative firms making profits (economic profits) fall under cases 1 and 2.

Another famous economist, Frank Knight, regarded profit as a return to taking risk.[10] This theory falls under category 3. Entrepreneurs who start a firm not only have to be rewarded for their labor input and investment but also for the risk they are taking. There is always the chance that the business might fail and that the entrepreneur might lose all the investment and effort. Profit is a reward for this risk. It is the existence of this reward that prompts many individuals to innovate and produce new products or produce old products by better production methods. It is the driving force behind all development. Thus these rewards serve a socially useful and productive purpose.

The profits earned by monopoly, however, do not serve a social purpose and are indeed found to involve some social costs.[11] The existence of monopoly profits results in a number of socially unproductive activities. The activities have been variously called "rent-seeking activities" or DUP (directly unproductive profit-seeking) activities.[12] There is a variety of estimates of the directly unproductive profit-seeking activities because there is no end to their scope. From lobbying efforts in Washington to simple lunches and dinners done to curry favors, there is a host of unproductive profit-seeking activities that one can think of. In fact, Mishan has estimated the losses from "nonproductive" activities at 50 percent of our total GNP.[13]

17.6   PERSONAL DISTRIBUTION OF INCOME

In the previous sections we discussed the determination of wages, rent, interest, and profit. This distribution of income into wages, rent, interest, and profit is called the *functional distribution of income*, and, as we said earlier, it had sociological significance for the classical economists. This is not so in modern societies. What is important is the *personal distribution of income*. This is the distribution of income to individuals or to families. It is this distribution that forms the basis of all discussions about inequality. There are, of course, policies that try to change the personal distribution of income by manipulating wages, prices, and profits. But these have often been found to have negligible effect on the personal distribution of income.

Table 17.1 shows the distribution of U.S. families' money income in 1980. A common measure of income inequality is the *Gini coefficient*, which is derived from the *Lorenz curve*. To construct a Lorenz curve, we plot the cumulative percentages of income against the cumulative percentages of families (arranged from the lowest

---

[10]Frank A. Knight, *Risk, Uncertainty, and Profit*, Houghton Mifflin, Boston, 1921.

[11]We discussed the problem of welfare cost of monopoly in Section 12.9 of Chapter 12.

[12]See J. N. Bhagwati, "Directly Unproductive Profit-Seeking (DUP) Activities," *Journal of Political Economy*, October 1982, pp. 988–1002.

[13]Ezra Mishan, *Economic Efficiency and Social Welfare*, Allen and Unwin, London, 1981.

TABLE 17.1   Distribution of U.S. Families' Money Income, 1980

Families Ranked by Income	Income Range ($)	Percentage of Total Income
Lowest 20%	0–10,286	5.1
Second 20%	10,287–17,390	11.6
Middle 20%	17,391–24,630	17.5
Fourth 20%	24,631–34,534	24.3
Highest 20%	34,534+	41.5
		100.0
Top 5%	54,060+	15.3

Source: U.S. Bureau of Census, Current Population Reports, Series P-60, August 1981.

to the highest income). The required numbers are given in Table 17.2, which are derived from the first and last columns of Table 17.1 (adding numbers successively). These number are plotted in Figure 17.6. The diagonal line is the *line of perfect equality* (20 percent of families receive 20 percent of income, 40 percent of families receive 40 percent of income, and so on). The closer the Lorenz curve is to the diagonal line the more equal the income distribution. Hence, a measure of equality should measure how close the Lorenz curve is to the diagonal. Such a measure is the Gini coefficient, which is defined as

$$\text{Gini coefficient} = \frac{\text{area between the Lorenz curve and line of equality}}{\text{area of the triangle under the line of equality}}$$

In Figure 17.6 it is

$$\frac{\text{Shaded area}}{\text{Area of triangle } ABC}$$

The Gini coefficient lies between 0 (perfect equality) and 1 (perfect inequality). For the United States the Gini coefficient has been around 0.4.

TABLE 17.2   Cumulative Percentages of Families and Income (Arranged from Low to High Income)

Cumulative Percentage of Families	Cumulative Percentage of Income
20	5.1
40	16.7
60	34.2
80	58.5
100	100.0

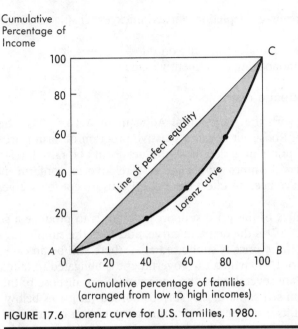

FIGURE 17.6   Lorenz curve for U.S. families, 1980.

There are many government policies that are designed to reduce income in-equality. In fact, the "Great Society" programs and the "War on Poverty" of the Johnson administration were meant to promote income equality. The results, how-ever, seem to show that not much has been accomplished. The Gini coefficients for the United States were 0.384 in 1950, 0.378 in 1961, and 0.375 in 1970. The Gini coefficient for 1980 was closer to 0.4 than to the figure in 1970. We have discussed the shortcomings of government programs in several parts of the book. The important thing to note, for the present, is that to study income distribution we have to look at the personal distribution of income and not the functional distribution of income. The functional distribution of income is more a resource allocation issue than an income distribution issue. It is more a question of efficiency than equity. No useful purpose is served in meddling with the functional distribution of income (manipulating wage rates, for instance) to achieve a more equitable personal distribution of income.

17.7   APPLICATIONS

In the previous sections we outlined the theory of economic rent and quasi rent and the theory of the user cost of capital. We will now illustrate the use of these theories in some practical applications.

First, with the theory of rent and quasi rent we will consider five problems:

1. Acreage restrictions in agriculture
2. Leasing of publicly owned lands for oil and gas exploration

3. Percentage depletion versus quick expensing as incentives for oil exploration

4. The windfall profits tax on oil

5. Monopolizing a competitive industry

17.7.1 Acreage restrictions

Beginning with the Agricultural Adjustment Act of 1933, the administration of Franklin D. Roosevelt began a massive program of farm price supports. The idea was that if prices of agricultural products could be raised, relative to other prices, then farmers' incomes would increase relative to nonfarm incomes. Farm price supports have been in effect since the 1930s except for a 2-year lapse from 1974 to 1976.

The effect of the price support program is to produce a surplus as shown in Figure 17.7. *DD* is the demand curve, and *SS* is the supply curve. The equilibrium price is P_e. If the price is supported at P_s, there will be an excess supply shown as *AB* in Figure 17.7, which the government is obligated to take care of.

There are several ways the government can dispose of this surplus. The government can sell some of this surplus abroad (at prices below the support price), as a part of its economic aid program or as part of commercial sales. Some of the surplus is used for school lunches and supplementing the food stamp program. Some of the surplus gets wasted in storage. The costs of all of this surplus disposal are, however, paid by the taxpayers.

An alternative method of reducing the surplus is to restrict production. One form of restriction on production is acreage restriction. To qualify for price supports, individual farmers are required to restrict the acreage which they cultivate. This program will result in a shift of the supply curve to the left. Since land is to be treated as a fixed factor, the resulting supply curve is something like a short-run supply curve, steeper than the long-run supply curve. In Figure 17.7 we show this as *S'S'*. The acreage restriction by itself may not remove the surplus completely, but it reduces the surplus from *AB* to *AC* as shown in Figure 17.7. Acreage restric-

FIGURE 17.7 Effect of price supports and of acreage restrictions.

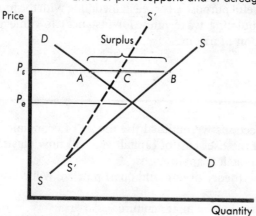

tions can be pushed to the point where the surplus can be eliminated completely, but in practice there is a danger of "overshooting the target" (producing a situation of excess demand) if this is attempted.

The result of acreage restriction is to increase the rents to the land under cultivation. For instance, in Figure 17.1 earlier, if lands B and C are removed from cultivation and the price of ouput increases above P_3, the rent to land A rises. Scarce resources always command some rents. The acreage restriction artificially makes land a scarce resource.

A restriction on the amount of farm labor to be employed or fertilizer to be used would have the same effect. However, such policies are hard to implement. Acreage restriction is the easiest to monitor.

17.7.2 Leasing of publicly owned lands for oil and gas exploration

When leasing publicly owned lands for oil and gas exploration, the government should attempt to collect the maximum possible rents from the oil companies while seeing that the most efficient level of production is achieved. There are three methods of collecting money from the oil companies.

1. Collect a percentage share of the value of output as royalties.
2. Collect a rent (called a lease bonus) at the time of the lease, through an auction. The oil company then keeps all the revenues from production.
3. Combine a royalty with a lease bonus scheme.

In practice, the third method is followed. The U.S. government first decides which lands should be commercially used for oil and gas exploration. The more promising lands are auctioned off to the highest bidder of the lease bonus. There is, in addition, a fixed percentage royalty that the government collects out of the revenues from well-head production (usually 12.5 percent). The less promising lands are awarded in a lottery, with the government again collecting a fixed percentage of the revenues from the well-head production (usually 16.6 percent).

Under the combined royalty-lease bonus scheme, the government gets less revenue, and the output is lower than under the pure lease bonus scheme. This is shown in Figure 17.8.

In Figure 17.8 MC is the marginal cost curve and P_0 is the market price for oil. The output that we would like the firm to produce is Q_0. The rent is P_0AC, and this is the rent that the government would be able to capture in a pure lease bonus scheme. (Of course, one has to subtract the total fixed costs and take into account the present values of all such rents in the future years.)

Suppose that there is a percentage royalty that the government receives. In this case, the price that the firm receives falls to P_1, the difference $(P_0 - P_1)$ being the royalty payment. Output will now fall to Q_1. The rent that the government can capture will be P_1BC. The royalty income that the government gets is P_0DBP_1. The sum of these two incomes is less than P_0AC. The difference is shaded triangle ABD. This represents the loss to the government under the joint royalty-lease bonus scheme as compared to the pure lease bonus scheme. Thus, output is lower, and

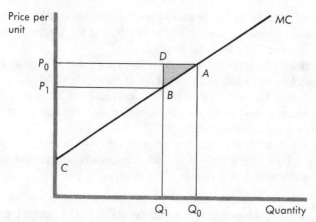

FIGURE 17.8   Rents and royalty payments on federally owned lands.

there is also a loss in revenue to the government. The argument here is similar to the analysis of the efficiency of lump sum taxes versus per-unit taxes.

Although the above analysis shows that the combined royalty-lease bonus scheme is inefficient, this practice is followed because of the existence of uncertainty in oil and gas exploration (which the previous analysis does not consider). Prior to any drilling, it is impossible to assess the exact magnitudes of the oil and gas reserves underlying any land. Lands which arc highly promising might not turn out to be giant oil fields. Under the pure royalty scheme the government assumes all the risks. Under the pure lease bonus scheme the oil company assumes all the risks. In the combined royalty-lease bonus scheme, the government and the oil company share the risks.

There is, however, an alternative method of sharing the risks besides the use of royalties. This is to share the lease bonus itself. This avoids the problem of restricting output below the socially optimal level as happens with the royalty scheme. The lease bonus is shared in a two-part bonus scheme (or multipart lease bonus if there are more installments of payments). In the two-part lease bonus scheme there are no royalty payments. The government leases the land to the highest bidder, but the lease bonus is paid in two installments. The first installment is due immediately, and the second installment is due prior to the commencement of commercial production. The oil company would have the option of not paying the second installment and cancelling the lease. The government can take the land and lease it again to the highest bidder.

It is not within the scope of this book to examine in detail the different policies regarding the leasing of public lands without considering in detail the different policies of risk sharing.[14] The foregoing analysis is based on some elementary principles that we have presented in the previous chapters of the book and abstracts from the problems of uncertainty.

[14]For an analysis of the different approaches to risk sharing, see Hayne E. Leland, "Optimal Risk Sharing and the Leasing of Natural Resources with Application to Oil and Gas Leasing on the OCS," *The Quarterly Journal of Economics*, August 1978, pp. 413–437.

17.7.3 Tax incentives for oil exploration: Percentage depletion versus quick expensing

The oil industry received for many years two major subsidies: (1) percentage depletion, and (2) quick expensing of the so-called intangible development costs. Of the two, percentage depletion is the much bigger subsidy in dollar terms but is also the one with little economic justification.

One of the basic principles of economics is that the most important decisions are those made at the margin. The market price is determined by the costs of the marginal producers. If the price has to be reduced or the output increased, the subsidies the government provides should be those affecting the behavior of the marginal high-cost producers. The percentage depletion allowance, however, does not conform to this basic principle. It rewards the lowest-cost, highest-profit producers and not the marginal high-cost producers. Thus, it represents pure income transfers to the oil industry and does not provide any incentive for increased exploration and production. To show this we must first discuss what the percentage depletion and the quick-expensing subsidies involve.

Suppose the total expenses for drilling an oil well are $500,000. The intangible expenses are the expenses for wages, fuel, repairs, hauling, supplies, and so on, as well as all expenses connected with dry holes. Suppose these are $400,000. The remaining $100,000 are expenses for tangible items (drilling equipment, pipes, and so forth).

The quick expensing of intangible costs means that the oil company can write off the $400,000 of expenses against income from other operations this year. Without the quick-expensing provision, these expenses would be written off over the life of the successful wells. The total tax liability, thus, does not change, but the quick expensing saves taxes this year as compared to saving some this year and the rest in future years. Thus, *it is like an interest free loan.* For instance, with a 50 percent tax rate, the tax refunds are $200,000 this year with quick expensing and $10,000 each year for the next 20 years without the provision. The oil company can use the $200,000 for other purposes or earn interest on it.

In the above example, the tangible expenses of $100,000, however, can be deducted against income only over time (say 20 years). Thus, this deduction would be $5,000 per year for 20 years.

Under an alternative scheme, the tangible expenses, instead of being deducted at a uniform rate, can be deducted at the rate at which the oil well is being depleted. For example, if the production rates in 3 years are at 15 percent, 20 percent, and 10 percent of the total reserves (which, of course, have to be estimated), then the tangible expenses deducted from income will be $15,000, $20,000, and $10,000 for the 3 years. By the time the oil well is completely depleted, all expenses would be written off. This method is called the *cost depletion method.*

The percentage depletion is entirely different. The oil company gets to deduct a certain percentage (usually 22 percent) of the gross revenues at the well-head. However, there is a maximum that the oil company can deduct. This maximum is 50 percent of the income using the cost depletion method. This provision works against high-cost producers, and in practice only the low-cost producers can get the benefit of percentage depletion.

For instance, consider two producers A and B. Suppose the price of oil is $25 per barrel. Producer A produces 8,000 barrels per year and producer B produces 16,000 barrels per year. Suppose the royalties, operating costs, and such are identical and that each producer can deduct $10,000 for tangible drilling costs for the cost depletion method. The results are shown in Table 17.3. Thus, producer A can get a deduction of $10,000 under the cost depletion method but only $5,000 under the percentage depletion method. As for producer B, she can get an extra $78,000 deduction if she uses the percentage depletion method rather than the cost depletion method. With a 50 percent tax rate she saves $39,000, which when calculated for 16,000 barrels, works out to be a subsidy of $2.44 per barrel. Of course, we have made an extreme assumption that royalties and operating costs are the same for the two producers. But the example illustrates the point that it is the low-cost producers that get the benefit of percentage depletion. Thus, the marginal costs of the low-cost producers go down, but those of the high-cost producers do not change. Thus, there will be no effect on output. There will only be an increase in the rents received by the low-cost producers. This is shown in Figure 17.9.

In Figure 17.9, MC_1 is the marginal cost curve under the cost depletion method. MC_2 is the marginal cost curve with the percentage depletion method. The low-cost producers get the higher benefit, and the producers at the margin get no benefit. Given the market price P_0, production is at Q_0. The output Q_0 does not change. However, there is an increase in the rents to the inframarginal producers. This is shown by the shaded area in Figure 17.9.

Percentage depletion is beneficial to the low-cost producers who have discovered their own oil wells. If the oil well is sold, most of the increased rent will be capitalized and included in the purchase price. Thus, for purchased wells the difference between percentage depletion and cost depletion is perhaps not great.

TABLE 17.3 Effects of Percentage Depletion on Low-Cost and High-Cost Producers

	Producer A	Producer B
1. Gross income	$200,000	$400,000
2. Royalties, taxes, and operating expenses	180,000	180,000
3. Net income (gross income minus royalties, etc.)	20,000	220,000
4. Deduction under cost depletion	10,000	10,000
5. Taxable income under cost depletion (net income minus deduction for cost depletion)	10,000	210,000
6. Deduction under percentage depletion (22% of gross income)	44,000	88,000
7. 50% of taxable income under cost depletion	5,000	105,000
8. Minimum of (6) and (7)	5,000	88,000
9. Percentage depletion allowance allowed	5,000	88,000
10. Extra deduction under percentage depletion	0	78,000
11. Extra tax benefit under percentage depletion (50% tax rate)	0	39,000

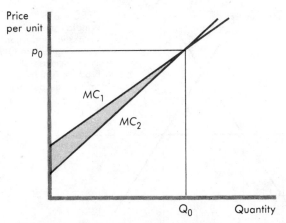

FIGURE 17.9   Effects of percentage depletion on marginal costs.

By contrast, the quick-expensing subsidy is like an interest-free loan available to all producers. It reduces the costs for marginal producers as well. Thus, it has a stimulative effect on exploration and development.

17.7.4 Taxation of rents and quasi rents: The windfall profits tax on oil

Throughout the 1970s, the OPEC cartel raised the price of oil continuously. In the absence of any price controls, the domestic price of oil would rise to the foreign price, and the domestic oil producers would receive high economic rents (also called "windfall profits"). However, imposing price controls on the domestic price of oil would discourage domestic production, encourage domestic demand, and, thus, increase imports. The average price paid by the consumers is a weighted average of domestic and import prices. Let

P_0 = controlled domestic price

P_1 = import price

Q_0 = domestic production

Q_1 = imports

Then the average price consumers pay is

$$P_c = \frac{P_0 Q_0 + P_1 Q_1}{Q_0 + Q_1}$$

Without any price controls, the average price consumers pay will be just P_1. Since with controls $P_1 > P_0$, we will have $P_c < P_1$. In other words, price controls will stimulate domestic demand and result in an increase in imports.

The effects of the OPEC price increase on OPEC's profits and the profits of domestic oil producers without price controls and with price controls is shown in Figure 17.10(a) and (b), respectively.

In Figure 17.10(a) P_0 is the initial (pre-OPEC) price of oil. P_1 is the OPEC price. DD is the domestic demand curve, and SS is the domestic supply curve. At the pre-OPEC price P_0, Q_1 is the domestic quantity supplied, Q_4 the domestic

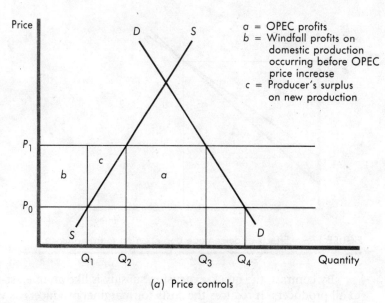

a = OPEC profits
b = Windfall profits on
    domestic production
    occurring before OPEC
    price increase
c = Producer's surplus
    on new production

(a) Price controls

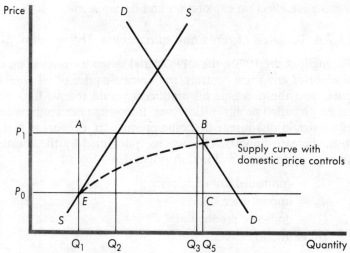

Supply curve with
domestic price controls

(b) Domestic price controlled at the original price

FIGURE 17.10   Effects of price increases by OPEC.

quantity demanded, and $Q_4 - Q_1$ the imports. When OPEC raises the prices to P_1, domestic quantity supplied rises to Q_2, domestic quantity demanded falls to Q_3, and imports fall to $Q_3 - Q_2$. Assuming that the price P_0 measures the marginal cost of OPEC output, the rectangle a gives the profit of OPEC producers, the rectangle b gives the increase in producers' surplus (or economic rent or windfall profits) to the pre-OPEC producers. Area c shows the producers' surplus arising from the new domestic production $(Q_2 - Q_1)$.

Figure 17.10(b) shows the consequences of a price control on domestic oil. Domestic price is controlled at price P_0. Domestic production will stay at the level

Q_1. The prices consumers pay will be a weighted average of P_0 and P_1. The controlled supply curve is, therefore, the dotted line shown in Figure 17.10(b). The domestic quantity demanded is now Q_5, and imports rise from ($Q_3 - Q_2$) to ($Q_5 - Q_1$). Note that Q_5 will be greater than Q_3 but less than Q_4 (the pre-OPEC quantity demanded). The OPEC profit now rises to the area $ABCE$. Thus, the domestic price conrol, which is designed to protect domestic consumers from "exploitation" by the oil companies, results in an increase in income transfers to OPEC producers.

Under the administration of President Jimmy Carter a proposal was made that would solve the problems of the wealth transfer to OPEC that price controls would involve, and the wealth transfer to the domestic oil companies if price controls were not imposed. The proposal was the windfall profits tax which would operate as follows: For all the wells in production before the OPEC price increase, a tax of $P_1 - P_0$ would be imposed. There would be no tax on new wells or alternative energy sources. This program would not affect total domestic supply because it would only tax the rents accruing to oil producers that were producing oil before the price increases by OPEC. To ensure that consumers were the beneficiaries of the tax, the plan also called for using the tax revenue to reduce income taxes and to support energy research. Thus, consumers would be satisfied that the oil companies were not ripping them off and, thus, would not oppose decontrol of domestic prices. The policy would also promote domestic production and reduce the dependence on imports.

There are, of course, some problems with the implementation of a plan like this. It is not true that output from the existing wells would be unaffected by the windfall profits tax. After the well becomes partly depleted, one has to use tertiary methods of production, and the cost of production would be higher than P_0. Actually, the windfall profits tax was designed to take care of these complications.

It was also estimated that the decontrol of domestic oil prices would itself make OPEC cut its price. In this case the decontrol (with windfall profits tax) would be all the more desirable. However, it has been argued that the windfall profits tax makes it more difficult for oil companies to raise funds for investment.[15]

The example is a good illustration of the effects of taxation of rents. The idea that economic rents can be taxed without affecting the supply of goods and services prompted the economist Henry George (1839 to 1897) to suggest, in his book *Progress and Poverty* (1879), a single tax, a tax on land rents. Henry George almost got elected as Mayor of New York City in 1886 on a platform that consisted of the "single-tax movement." However, the proposal lost its support over the years. From a practical point of view, it is hard to determine what rents are, and land is not the only factor of production to which rents accrue. Earlier in Section 17.3, we discussed the concept of quasi rent, which makes the point that rents can accrue to other factors as well. Anyway, the windfall profits tax was a case where rents could be identified and, therefore, taxed.

17.7.5 How much is a monopoly worth?

In Chapter 11 we discussed the theory of pricing under monopoly. There we assumed the monopoly to exist and then asked what the profit-maximizing output

---

[15]One of the problems with the windfall profits tax was deciding what was new versus old oil. Lots of illegal or questionable schemes were developed aimed at circumventing the law.

was. Here we will ask the question: How much is a monopoly worth? In other words, suppose we start with a competitive industry. How much is the monopolist willing to pay for the right to purchase and monopolize the industry?

To answer this question we have to consider not monopoly profits but the excess of rent under monopoly over rent under competition.[16] As explained earlier, in Figure 17.4 the area under the supply curve gives the opportunity cost of the resources used; subtracting this from the total revenue we get the rent to these resources. We will use this result in the following analysis.

We will assume that the monopolist's marginal cost curve represents the supply curve of the industry if it were to be operating competitively. There are, thus, no cost advantages or disadvantages with either of these market organizations. This assumption will enable us to compare the rents to resources under competition and monopoly. The situation is described in Figure 17.11. P_c and P_m are prices under competition, and monopoly and Q_c and Q_m are outputs under competition and monopoly, respectively. Under monopoly we have:

$$\text{Revenues} = OP_mAQ_m$$
$$\text{Cost of resources} = OCQ_m$$
$$\text{Rent} = OP_mAC$$

Under competition we have:

$$\text{Revenues} = OP_cDQ_c$$
$$\text{Cost of resources} = ODQ_c$$
$$\text{Competitive rent to resources} = OP_cD$$

[16]The following discussion is based on Harold Demsetz, "Purchasing Monopoly," chap. 7 in David C. Colander, ed., *Neo-Classical Political Economy*, Ballinger Publishing, Cambridge, Mass., 1984. For a detailed discussion of this and other related issues such as welfare cost of monopoly, see this paper.

FIGURE 17.11   Profit from monopolizing a competitive industry.

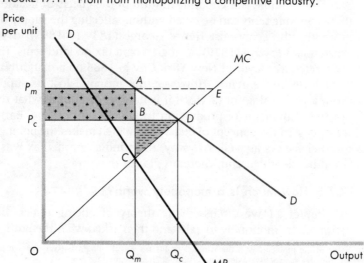

If the monopolist were to purchase the competitive industry, he would have to fully compensate all the productive resources. The factors producing $Q_c - Q_m$ would no longer be employed in the monopolized industry. The monopolist could purchase them for Q_mBDQ_c and resell them for Q_mCDQ_c (their opportunity cost) or merely pay them CBD to leave the industry. Either way, the net cost to the monopolist would be CBD. The resources producing Q_m would continue to be employed in the monopolized industry and would need to be paid OP_cBQ_m.

The profit from purchasing the monopoly would, thus, be monopoly revenues OP_mAQ_m minus the sum of CBD and OP_cBQ_m. But this is equal to the difference between monopoly rent OP_mAC and competitive rent OP_cD. Taking away the common area OP_cBD we are left with the difference $P_mABP_c - BCD$, or the area filled with pluses minus the area filled with minuses in Figure 17.11.[17]

What can we say about these two areas? This will depend on the elasticities of the demand and supply curves. The more elastic the demand curve, the greater will be the monopoly rent; the more elastic the supply curve, the smaller will be the competitive rent.

The important conclusion from this analysis is that the monopoly rent OP_mAC does not measure the *profit from monopolization*. This latter profit is much smaller in value.

17.8   SUMMARY AND CONCLUSIONS

The distribution of revenues into wages, rent, and interest is called the functional distribution of income. The return to labor is wages, the return to capital is interest, and the return to land is rent. However, it is not possible to classify the returns into functionally distinct categories.

Economic rent is the excess of total payments to a factor of production over and above what is required to bring the particular factor into production. The classical economists applied the idea of rent to land only. Hence, economic rent accruing to other factors is sometimes called quasi rent. In any input market with an upward-sloping supply curve, as long as there is no discrimination, there will always be some rent accruing to some units of the factor.

The rental price of capital is *not* the rate of interest. The interest rate must be adjusted for the rate of depreciation and the growth rate in the prices of capital goods.

Accounting profit includes the return to many specialized factors of production. Normal profit includes the opportunity cost of the entrepreneur's labor and financial capital. Economic profit is the excess profit—that is, profit over and above normal levels. Excess profit can occur in a competitive industry in the short run, in a monopoly, or under conditions of uncertainty.

The Lorenz curve graphically illustrates the cumulative personal distribution of income. The Gini coefficient measures inequality in the distribution—the coef-

[17]Actually, at the higher price P_m more resources would be forthcoming, and if these resources must also be compensated, the area to be subtracted can be as large as the triangle ACE shown in Figure 17.11.

ficient is the area between the Lorenz curve and the line of perfect equality divided by the area under the line of perfect equality.

Acreage restrictions reduce supply, increase price, and increase the rents to land under cultivation. Publicly owned lands are leased for oil and gas exploration under a combined royalty-lease bonus scheme. Under this arrangement, government revenues are smaller and output is lower than under a pure lease bonus scheme.

Quick expensing of intangible development costs reduces costs for all oil producers and, thus, stimulates exploration and production. However, percentage depletion benefits only the low-cost producers. Since marginal producers are not affected, there will be little impact on output. A tax on existing rents, such as the windfall profit tax, does not affect supply but rather merely transfers rents from the producers to the government. The profit from purchasing and monopolizing a previously competitive industry is much less than monopoly rent.

KEY TERMS

Accounting Profit	Gini Coefficient	Profit from Monopolization
Acreage Restrictions	Human Capital	Quasi rent
Compensating Wage	Interest	Quick Expensing of
Differential	Lease Bonus	Intangible Costs
Debt-Equity Ratio	Leverage	Real Rate of Interest
Economic Profit	Lorenz Curve	Rent
Economic Rent	Nominal Rate of Interest	Royalty
Financial Capital	Normal Profit	User Cost of Capital
Functional Distribution	Percentage Depletion	Wages
of Income	Physical Capital	Windfall Profits Tax

QUESTIONS

1. With the rapid increase in the demand for computers, the quasi rents of computer engineers increased substantially. Explain what has happened to the supply curve of computer engineers over time and, consequently, what has happened to these rents.

2. Does the full difference between the wages of doctors and the average wage rate constitute a quasi rent? Why or why not?

3. Walter Oi implicitly assumes that those with the lowest opportunity cost (and not already enlisted) will be drafted. If draftees are really randomly chosen, does Oi's analysis overstate or understate the full cost of the draft?

4. Based on Oi's analysis and your answer to question 3, can you make an economic case for allowing draftees to pay someone to replace them in the army?

5. We previously discussed the licensing of taxis in New York City through the issuance of medallions, which can be resold. Explain why medallions command such a high price when taxi drivers argue that their profits are negligible.

6. Can the Lorenz curve intersect the line of perfect equality? Why or why not?

7. How does the Lorenz curve for the distribution of aftertax income compare with the curve for pretax income? How do the Gini coefficients compare?

8. How will acreage restrictions affect per-acre usage of labor, fertilizer, capital, and so on? Can you determine the impact on total usage of these inputs? How are intensive and extensive cultivation affected?

9. If a monopolist can reduce the costs of production, what will the profit from purchasing and monopolizing a competitive industry be?

10. We argued that the windfall profit tax would not affect the supply of domestic oil. Is this still true if producers fear that the tax will one day apply to fields currently being developed? Why? How does this expectation affect the ability to capitalize future rents?

PART FIVE
OTHER TOPICS

Part Five (Chapters 18 to 21) presents a discussion of some important topics that students in microeconomics should be familiar with. Chapter 18, on welfare economics and general equilibrium analysis, discusses a few aspects of welfare economics not covered in Chapter 9 and provides an introduction to general equilibrium analysis. Chapter 19 discusses conditions under which a case for government intervention in markets is often made (externalities and public goods). Chapter 20 discusses aspects of consumer and producer choices over time (intertemporal choice). Finally, Chapter 21 provides an introduction to imperfect information and uncertainty in microeconomic problems, two important aspects that we have ignored in all the previous chapters.

CHAPTER 18

WELFARE ECONOMICS AND GENERAL EQUILIBRIUM ANALYSIS

18.1   INTRODUCTION

The purpose of welfare economics is to explain how a socially efficient allocation of resources can be identified and achieved. In Chapter 9 we discussed some conditions laid down by the Italian economist Vilfredo Pareto for economic efficiency. Welfare economics based on Pareto's conditions is known as *Paretian welfare economics*. We also pointed out (in Section 9.8 of Chapter 9) that since interpersonal comparisons of utility are ruled out, Pareto's criterion for improvement in welfare (that at least one person should be made better off and no one worse off) is not useful for the evaluation of many economic policies. Since most policies benefit some and hurt others, the criterion just maintains the *status quo* in many suboptimal situations. In this chapter we will consider some modifications that have been suggested to Pareto's conditions. We will discuss the compensation criterion and the social welfare function. Furthermore, since most of the book has been devoted to partial equilibrium analysis, we will give an introduction to general equilibrium analysis.

In the literature on welfare economics, a distinction is drawn between what is called the "old" and the "new" welfare economics, although what is called "new" is not new by recent standards. (It was new in 1940.) The essence of the old welfare economics is contained in the famous book by the British economist A. C. Pigou (1877 to 1959), (Alfred Marshall's successor at Cambridge University), *The Economics of Welfare* (it first appeared in 1912 as *Wealth and Welfare*). The old welfare economists assumed measurable and interpersonal comparison of utility. For instance, Pigou regarded as "evident" that "any transference of income from a relatively rich man to a relatively poor man of similar temperament, since it enables more intense wants to be satisfied at the expense of less intense wants, must increase the aggregate sum of satisfaction" (1932 edition of *The Economics of Welfare*, p. 89). By contrast, the new welfare economics is based on Pareto's principle of excluding interpersonal comparison of utility. Actually, Pareto's writings appeared earlier than Pigou's book, but they were popularized in English in the 1930s. The new welfare economics (also called Paretian welfare economics) started around 1938 with

1. A paper published in 1938 by Lionel Robbins criticizing interpersonal comparisons of utility

2. The Kaldor-Hicks criterion of compensation published in 1939

3. Bergson's paper on social welfare functions published in 1938

18.2   THE COMPENSATION CRITERIA

Around 1938 there was a discussion among some famous British economists (Harrod and Robbins) regarding the repeal of the corn laws in 1846, and whether the gain to the community as a whole might be regarded as exceeding the loss to the landlords. If we rule out interpersonal comparisons of utility, obviously we cannot say anything. It was in this connection that Kaldor and Hicks suggested that if the losers of any policy change (here the landlords) could be compensated for their loss and after that the gainers of the policy change could be still better off than before, then the policy change can be regarded as having increased the community's welfare. This is called the *Kaldor-Hicks criterion*. The Kaldor-Hicks criterion says: Allocation *A* is socially preferable to *B* if those who gain from a change to *A* could compensate those who lose from a change to *A* and still be better off than at *B*.

However, 2 years later, another economist, Tibor Scitovsky, argued that the reverse can also happen, that is, those who will lose from the change to *A* can bribe those who will gain and still be better off in *B* than in *A*. (In the above example the landlords could bribe the consumers.) Hence, he suggested a double criterion which is known as the *Scitovsky double criterion*, and it runs as follows: Allocation *A* is socially preferable to *B* if the gainers could bribe the losers into accepting the change and simultaneously the losers could not bribe the gainers into not making the change.

However, the Scitovksy criterion did not solve the problem of comparing two situations on the basis of potential compensation. In 1955 another economist, W. M. Gorman, showed that the Scitovsky criterion can lead us in circles. For example, if we have four possible allocations *A, B, C,* and *D*, then the Scitovsky criterion applied pairwise can show that *A* is better than *B*, *B* is better than *C*, and *C* is better than *D*. This should imply that *A* is better than *D*, but it is possible that the Scitovsky criterion shows that *D* is better than *A*. Thus, we go in a circle.[1]

All this discussion may lead us to conclude that the compensation criteria are not useful in practice. This is not so since the theoretically possible problems need not arise in practice. In fact, James Buchanan argues that the productivity of economists should be directed toward finding social rearrangements, contracts, and compensations that can achieve higher social welfare.[2]

18.3 THE SOCIAL WELFARE FUNCTION

The compensation criteria discussed earlier consider the "efficiency" aspects only and not that of distribution. The compensation principle asks only whether losers *could* be compensated; it does not require that they *actually* be compensated. It is argued that whether, and in what manner, compensation should take place, if it should take place at all, is a moral issue. Another problem with the compensation criteria is that they allow comparison between a few alternatives but do not tell us the state that achieves the maximum possible welfare. It was thought that these

[1]The papers referred to here are: N. Kaldor, "Welfare Propositions in Economics," *Economic Journal*, 1939; J. R. Hicks, "The Foundations of Welfare Economics," *Economic Journal*, 1939; T. Scitovsky, "A Note on Welfare Propositions in Economics," *Review of Economic Studies*, 1941; W. M. Gorman, "The Intransitivity of Certain Criteria Used in Welfare Economics," *Oxford Economic Papers*, 1955.

[2]J. M. Buchanan, "Positive Economics, Welfare Economics, and Political Economy," *Journal of Law and Economics*, 1959, pp. 124–138. In another paper (*American Economic Review*, May 1975, p. 227) Buchanan refers to a small book by W. H. Hutt, *A Plan for Reconstruction* (London, 1943) in which Hutt proposed that the postwar British economy be swept clear of all restrictions through the device of compensating all persons and groups who would lose by the change.

problems could be solved by considering a *social welfare function* which was first suggested by the economist Abram Bergson in 1938.[3]

The social welfare function is a sort of social indifference curve and gives the various combination of the utilities of the different individuals that result in the same level of social welfare. To show this diagrammatically we will consider only two individuals A and B in the society, whose utilities we will represent by U_A and U_B. The social welfare function is

$$W = f(U_A, U_B)$$

In Figure 18.1 we show the social indifference curves. They show the different combinations of U_A and U_B that give the same level of social welfare. Social indifference curves are negatively sloped because as A is made better off, B must be made worse off, and vice versa. Making A and B both better off, or one better off and the other equally well-off, would result in a movement to a higher indifference curve. In Figure 18.1, W_2 represents a higher level of social welfare than W_1. Note that social indifference curves need not be convex to the origin.

Samuelson saw great promise for social indifference curves and remarked that "the foundation is laid for the economics of the good society."[4] Once we formulate the social welfare function and the social indifference curves, we are well equipped to compare different policies and investigate policies that maximize social welfare subject to the available economic resources.

In a dictatorship, the social welfare function and social indifference curves reflect the value judgments of the dictator. In a democracy, the value judgments of individuals can be expressed by voting. However, Arrow pointed out that there is no way of evaluating social welfare by a democratic vote.[5] This result is commonly known as *Arrow's impossibility theorem*.

[3] Abram Bergson, "A Reformulation of Certain Aspects of Welfare Economics," *Quarterly Journal of Economics*, February 1938, pp. 310–334.

[4] P. A. Samuelson, "Social Indifference Curves," *Quarterly Journal of Economics*, 1956.

[5] K. J. Arrow, *Social Choice and Individual Values*, Wiley, New York, 1951.

FIGURE 18.1 Social indifference curves.

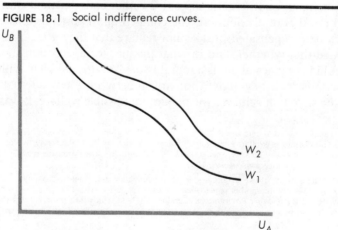

Arrow laid down some commonsense basic requirements for the derivation of social welfare functions. One of these requirements is that social welfare choices should be *transitive*. In other words, if A is preferred to B, and B is preferred to C, then A is preferred to C. Consider, however, the following rankings of three policies A, B, and C by three individuals Bob, Carol, and Ted (1 is the highest rank).

		Policies	
	A	B	C
Bob	1	2	3
Carol	2	3	1
Ted	3	1	2

Consider policies A and B. Bob and Carol both prefer A to B. Thus, a majority vote between A and B will lead to a choice of A. Consider policies B and C. Bob and Ted prefer B to C. Thus, a majority vote between B and C will lead to a choice of B. Thus, A is preferred to B, and B is preferred to C. This should imply that A is preferred to C. However, when we consider A and C, we find that both Carol and Ted prefer C to A. Thus, a majority vote between A and C will lead to a choice of C. This is also sometimes known as the *voting paradox*.

The above method of voting by ranks does not take into account the intensity of the preferences of the different individuals. This is indeed the idea behind the compensation principle. If my preference to have a dog is very intense, so that it is worth, say, $700 to me, and five of my neighbors are mildly annoyed by it (and the annoyance is worth, say, $100 to each) then clearly, if a compensation scheme can be worked out, I will have the dog. But a majority vote would turn down the dog.

The criterion of the social welfare function, and even the Kaldor-Hicks criterion based on potential, not actual, compensation, requires an assumption of omniscience on the part of the individual evaluating the different policies. Such an assumption is totally unrealistic because individuals' utilities are highly subjective, and it is very difficult for others to evaluate them. Only actual compensation will help an evaluation. However, in many instances it is not clear to whom compensation is to be made. For instance, in a critique of the Kaldor-Hicks criterion, Stigler asks: "Could not the real income of the society be increased by bribing potential thieves instead of hiring policemen?"[6] But who are the potential thieves? In any case, they need to be punished, not provided compensation.

Buchanan criticizes the concept of a social welfare function arguing that it arose from a fixation of economists with the idea of maximizing something.[7] "Economists crossed the bridge from individual to social maximization because they wanted to be able to say something about policy alternatives. . . . This is the bridge which economists should never have crossed, and which has created major intel-

[6]G. J. Stigler, "The New Welfare Economics," *American Economic Review*, 1943, pp. 355–356.

[7]J. M. Buchanan, "A Contractarian Paradigm for Applying Economic Theory," *American Economic Review*, May 1975, pp. 225–230.

lectual confusion."[8] Instead, he suggests that economists should work on deriving compensation schemes. If an observed position is inefficient, there must be ways of securing agreement on change, agreement that produces mutual benefits. Economics, he argues, is a "science of contract."

18.4   THEORY OF THE SECOND BEST

The *theory of the second best*, introduced by Lipsey and Lancaster, argues that if all the conditions required to achieve a Pareto optimum cannot be satisfied, then trying to achieve as many of the conditions as possible is not necessarily the second-best alternative.[9] In general, if one of the Paretian optimum conditions cannot be fulfilled, a second best optimum is achieved only by departing from all other optimum conditions. The reason for this is that if one marginal condition is violated, we have to maximize the relevant objective function subject to this constraint, and the new marginal conditions are not the same as the old ones.

The theory of second best has negative implications for several policy choices. For instance, suppose that some markets in the economy are monopolistic. A Pareto optimum cannot be achieved. However, breaking up some of them is not necessarily a better alternative. (Breaking up all of them will be a better solution but not some of them.) The theory of second best rarely gives us a positive prescription. The problem is that when some of the Paretian conditions are violated, we have to derive new conditions for optimality and see that they are satisfied. But the knowledge required to determine these new conditions is rarely available. Thus, in many practical applications, when discussing an industry it is customary to assume that the marginal conditions are satisfied in the other industries. Thus, the existence of second-best theory is acknowledged and then conveniently ignored.[10] Another alternative is to use the *third-best solution*, which says that governments should just pursue policies that promote free entry into and exit from markets instead of trying to regulate or forcibly break up existing monopolies.

The problem of actual implementation of second-best solutions has been emphasized in the following comment by Harry G. Johnson:

> The fundamental problem is that, as with all second-best arguments, determination of the conditions under which a second-best policy actually leads to an improvement of social welfare requires detailed theoretical and empirical investigation by a first-best economist. Unfortunately policy is generally formulated by fourth-best economists and administered by third-best economists; it is therefore very unlikely that a second-best welfare optimum will result from policies based on second-best arguments.[11]

[8]Ibid., p. 226.

[9]R. G. Lipsey and Kelvin Lancaster, "The General Theory of the Second Best," *Review of Economic Studies*, 1956–1957, pp. 11–32.

[10]See, for instance, C. K. Rowley, *Steel and Public Policy*, McGraw-Hill, London, 1971. The author states: "Despite this important caveat, policy discussion in this book ignores the problems presented by second best theory and proceeds as if the marginal conditions were already satisfied in non-steel sectors of the economy."

[11]Harry G. Johnson, "The Efficiency and Welfare Implications of the International Corporation" in I. A. McDougall and R. H. Snape, eds., *Studies in International Economics*, North Holland Publishing, Amsterdam, 1970, p. 101.

18.5   INTERDEPENDENT UTILITIES

In all the preceding analysis we assumed that the utility for each individual depended only on what the individual consumed. In actual practice there is the problem of "keeping up with the Joneses" or "exceeding the Joneses." The utility an individual gets depends not only on the individual's consumption but also on the consumption of others (this effect could be positive in the case of altruism and negative in the case of egotism or envy). In this case the marginal conditions considered in Chapter 9 get very complicated. They involve additional terms regarding the *MRS* and *MRT* for others. No specific rules can be laid down without specific knowledge of this interdependence. As regards welfare, again we cannot say that the availability of more goods will increase welfare. In some cases, one can argue that an increase of output makes the community worse off, since, no matter how the additional goods are distributed, the additional envy generated cannot be adequately compensated for out of these goods.

Although the idea of interdependent utilities is intuitively plausible, the first major application was in Duesenberry[12] who used it to derive the *relative income hypothesis of consumption*, which, simply stated, says that

1. Consumers are not so much concerned with their absolute level of consumption as they are with their consumption *relative* to the rest of the population.

2. Present consumption is not influenced merely by present levels of absolute and relative income but also by levels of consumption attained in previous periods.

18.6   APPLIED WELFARE ECONOMICS

The discussion in the preceding sections suggests that application of the theories in welfare economics to practical situations is rather difficult. In 1971, Harberger presented an open letter to the economics profession pleading that three basic postulates should be accepted as providing a conventional framework for all applied welfare economics.[13] These postulates were:

1. The competitive demand price for a given unit measures the value of that unit to the demander.

2. The competitive supply price for a given unit measures the value of that unit to the supplier.

3. When evaluating the net benefits or costs of a given action (project, program, or policy), the costs and benefits accruing to each member of the relevant group should normally be added without regard to the individuals to whom they accrue.

[12]J. S. Duesenberry, *Income, Saving, and the Theory of Consumer Behavior,* Harvard University Press, Cambridge, Mass., 1949.

[13]A. C. Harberger, "Three Basic Postulates for Applied Welfare Economics: An Interpretive Essay," *Journal of Economic Literature,* September 1971, pp. 785–797.

The basic approach to be used is the evaluation of consumers' and producers' surpluses. This is the method we employed in Chapter 11, and in other applications in subsequent chapters. The limitations of this approach were mentioned in Chapter 9.

18.7 PARTIAL AND GENERAL EQUILIBRIUM ANALYSIS

Partial equilibrium analysis is a technique that uses the ceteris paribus (holding all other things constant) assumption to simplify the economic analysis. It is used for two types of problems:

1. To analyze economic changes in any particular industry or sector of the economy that involve that individual industry or sector alone. For instance, a strike at a small cement plant might affect only the output of that plant and the workers there.

2. To assess first order or initial effects of policies or events. For instance, a general strike of all workers at General Motors will initially affect only the output of General Motors and the incomes of the workers there. Partial equilibrium analysis studies these initial effects. Later there will be ripple effects on the entire economy, but this is the area of general equilibrium analysis.

General equilibrium analysis, by contrast, is concerned with the interdependence of all economic units and all sectors in the economy. If the equilibrium in one sector is disturbed by a policy or an event, then when this sector tries to achieve a new equilibrium, it disturbs the equilibrium in all the remaining sectors, and these sectors in turn approach a new equilibrium. General equilibrium is achieved only when all economic units are in equilibrium *simultaneously.* Macroeconomic theories tend to be of a general equilibrium character, whereas microeconomic theories tend to be of a partial equilibrium character, although it is difficult to offer any such generalization.

General equilibrium analysis has two purposes: (1) to provide a means of analyzing the economic system as a whole and (2) to study the second-, third-, and higher-order effects of an economic change. Returning to the example of a strike of all workers at General Motors, the initial effect is on the output of General Motors and the incomes of the workers. The secondary effects are reduced demand for steel, reduction of domestic disposable income, consequent decrease in demand for all consumer goods, and so on.

The French economist Leon Walras (1834 to 1910) was one of the first to produce a comprehensive mathematical analysis of general economic equilibrium.[14] He tied together the theories of production, exchange, money, and capital. Discussion of general equilibrium theory requires a mathematical treatment which is beyond the scope of this book.[15]

[14]Leon Walras, *Elements of Pure Economics*, William Jaffe, trans., Irwin, Homewood, Ill., 1954.

[15]It is interesting to note that Walras, who is considered a mathematical economist, failed twice the entrance examination to the Ecole Polytechnique in Paris for lack of preparation in mathematics. He entered Ecole des Mines in 1854. Leaving school after a year he tried literature unsuccessfully. Schumpeter called Walras the greatest of all economists.

Until recently, general equilibrium analysis has been mainly discussed in theory and has had very few applications. The only general equilibrium model that was applied was the input-output model. This model, discussed in the next section, makes grossly simplifying assumptions. It assumes constant returns to scale, no substitution among inputs in production, and so on. Recently, however, models have been developed that allow for substitution on the production and consumption side, and are computable.[16] Since these models are difficult to explain without the use of mathematics we will discuss the input-output model in the next section. This will at least show what general equilibrium analysis involves.

18.8 INPUT-OUTPUT ANALYSIS

Input-output analysis is a technique for studying the general interdependence among the different sectors of the economy. It was developed by W. Leontief as an application of general equilibrium analysis.[17] However, it makes several important simplifications to reduce general equilibrium analysis to manageable proportions:

1. Input-output analysis deals with the total quantity of each commodity demanded by all consumers and produced by all producers.

2. In its simplest version, the analysis assumes quantities demanded to be given rather than being determined by prices.

3. Input-output analysis assumes constant returns to scale and fixed production coefficients. To produce 100 cars the inputs required are 100 times the inputs required for the production of 1 car. Furthermore, production of each car requires a fixed amount of steel, other materials, labor, and so on. There is no substitution among inputs. This assumption is not valid in the long run but may be all right in the short run. This is one of the major limitations of the technique, because by the time the data on input coefficients for a large number of industries are gathered, the numbers could be out of date.

The technique of input-output analysis was popular in the 1950s, but interest in the method has waned since. The data requirements are enormous, particularly if tables with 500 or more sectors are constructed. It has thus become customary to construct more manageable smaller input-output models for specific sectors.

Suppose we want to study the effect of an increase in the demand for automobiles. Then input-output analysis will enable us to trace the impact of this change on the steel industry, the rubber industry; in fact, through the entire economy. We cannot consider such a complex model. However, we will consider a simple illustrative example with three sectors.

Consider three sectors: manufacturing M, nonmanufacturing NM, and households H. The flows (in dollar terms) between the sectors are shown in Table 18.1.

[16]John B. Shoven and John Whalley, "Applied General Equilibrium Models of Taxation and International Trade," *Journal of Economic Literature*, September 1984, pp. 1007–1081.

[17]W. Leontief, *The Structure of the American Economy*, Oxford University Press, New York, 1951.

TABLE 18.1 An Input-Output Table Giving Intersector Flows (billions of dollars)

Sector Producing	Sector Purchasing			Total Sales
	M	NM	H	
M	900	1,200	900	3,000
NM	900	1,200	900	3,000
H	1,200	600	0	1,800
Total production	3,000	3,000	1,800	7,800

Table 18.1 shows the following:

1. The total output of the manufacturing sector M is 3,000. Of this, 900 is sold to the manufacturing sector M, 1,200 to the nonmanufacturing sector NM, and 900 to the household sector H. The 900 sold from M to M comes from the fact that the steel industry sells to the auto industry, and there are some other similar sales between components of the aggregate.

2. The total output of NM is 3,000. Of this, 900 is sold to M, 1,200 to NM, and 900 to H.

3. The total output of H is 1,800. Of this, 1,200 is sold to M and 600 to NM. Note that there are no sales from H to H. Households produce the labor input which is sold to the manufacturing and nonmanufacturing sectors. There are no internal sales.

In Table 18.2 we present the input-output coefficients. These are obtained by dividing the entries in Table 18.1 by the column totals. What the numbers show is that it takes 0.3 units of M, 0.3 units of NM, and 0.4 units of H to produce 1 unit of M. Similarly, it takes 0.4 units of M, 0.4 units of NM, and 0.2 units of H to produce 1 unit of NM.

The input-output coefficients in Table 18.2 can be used as follows: Suppose the household demand for manufactured goods increases to 1,200 (with demand for nonmanufactured goods remaining at 900). By how much will the output of manufactured and nonmanufactured goods have to increase to meet this increased

TABLE 18.2 Input-Output Coefficients

Sector Producing	Sector Purchasing	
	M	NM
M	0.3	0.4
NM	0.3	0.4
H	0.4	0.2
Total production	1.0	1.0

demand by the households? To answer this question, we have to solve the equations:

$$M = 0.3M + 0.4NM + 1,200$$
$$NM = 0.3M + 0.4NM + 900$$

The first equation says that of the total output M of manufactured goods, 0.3 M goes as internal input, 0.4 NM goes into the production of nonmanufactured goods, and 1,200 is left for consumption by households. Similarly, of the total output NM of nonmanufactured goods, 0.3 M goes into the manufacture of manufactured goods, 0.4 NM goes as internal input, and 900 is left for consumption by households.

Solving the two equations, we get $M = 3,600$, and $NM = 3,300$. Thus, a 300-unit increase in final demand for manufactured goods by households results in an increase of 600 in the output of manufactured goods and an increase of 300 in the output of nonmanufactured goods. Note that the reason for this is that not all the increase in M is available for final consumption. Part of it becomes an internal input, and part goes into NM. Also, an increase in the output M necessitates an increase in NM.

Note also that the wages of households increase by 300. This increase is given by the input coefficients of H in Table 18.2. The increase is

$$0.4(600) + 0.2(300) = 240 + 60 = 300$$

We have measured everything in billions of dollar terms—final demands as well as inputs. The implied assumption is that prices do not change. Thus, households increase their demand for output by \$300 billion and, hence, provide more labor input worth \$300 billion. Of this, \$240 billion worth of labor input goes into the output of M, and \$60 billion worth goes into the output of NM.

If price changes are allowed, the analysis gets very complicated. We have to consider the input-output table in terms of physical inputs and outputs rather than in dollar terms as we have done here. Our purpose here is to illustrate the general equilibrium effects of changes in economic conditions on final outputs of different categories of goods.

18.9   SUMMARY AND CONCLUSIONS

A change constitutes a Pareto improvement only if it renders someone better off and nobody worse off. The Kaldor-Hicks compensation criterion defines a change to be an improvement in social welfare if those who gain can compensate the losers and still be better off. This criterion does not require that compensation actually take place. If it does take place, then Pareto's condition can be used. The Scitovsky criterion considers a change to be an improvement in social welfare if it passes the Kaldor-Hicks test and does not pass the Kaldor-Hicks test in reverse.

A social welfare function aggregates the utility of all the individuals in a society.

A change is then considered an improvement if it puts society on a higher social indifference curve.

The theory of second best argues that if all of the conditions required to achieve a Pareto optimum cannot be satisfied, then trying to achieve as many of the conditions as possible is not necessarily the second best alternative.

In applied welfare economics, many economists believe that the best approach is the evaluation of consumer and producer surpluses.

Partial equilibrium analysis uses the ceteris paribus condition. It is appropriate for analyzing changes that affect only one industry or sector. It can also be used to evaluate first-order or initial effects of a change. General equilibrium analysis is concerned with the interdependence of all economic units. Input-output analysis is a technique for studying the general interdependence among the different sectors of the economy.

KEY TERMS

Arrow's Impossibility
   Theorem
General Equilibrium
   Analysis
Input-Output Analysis

Kaldor-Hicks Compensation
   Criterion
Partial Equilibrium
   Analysis
Pareto Criterion

Scitovsky Criterion
Social Welfare Function
Theory of the Second
   Best
Voting Paradox

QUESTIONS

1. Can a collective action which harms a majority satisfy the Kaldor-Hicks criterion? Why? Will such an action be approved by majority vote? Could it be approved if the buying and selling of votes were permitted?

2. Suppose that all programs providing aid to farmers were eliminated. What would be the immediate effect on employment in that sector? What other sectors would be likely to be affected?

3. In a purely competitive economy, only trade which constitutes a Pareto improvement will occur. Do you agree with this statement?

4. Is a change which satisfies the Kaldor-Hicks criterion more likely to take place when many or few people are involved? Why?

5. If all the members of society have identical preferences, will choices made by majority vote be transitive?

CHAPTER 19

EXTERNALITIES, PUBLIC GOODS, AND GOVERNMENT INTERVENTION

19.1   INTRODUCTION

In Chapter 1 we defined the economic problem as the determination of the efficient use of scarce resources to produce a maximum output, taking into account the production possibilities and consumers' preferences and tastes. In this chapter, we shall discuss the circumstances under which the market mechanism can fail to achieve an efficient allocation of resources. This is often called *market failure*. The major sources of market failure are:

1. *Certain forms of market organization:* Examples include monopoly and oligopoly.
2. *Externalities:* The behavior of some individuals or firms affects the welfare of others. For example, a chemical firm dumping wastes in a river can increase production costs for fishermen.
3. *Existence of public goods:* These are goods for which one individual's consumption need not exclude another individual's consumption. For example, if there is one apple and *A* eats it, then *B* cannot have an apple. However, if there is a public park and *A* uses it, it does not exclude *B*'s using it. The park is, thus, a public good, and an apple is not.

We discussed monopoly and oligopoly in Chapters 11, 12, and 13. In this chapter we will discuss the problems of externalities and public goods.

Many economists argue that the mere existance of externalities and public goods does not by itself justify government intervention in markets. They argue that private markets exist for "internalizing" externalities (we will explain this term in Section 19.3) and for private provision of public goods ("privatization" of public goods). We will outline these arguments as we proceed, and we will discuss the case for government intervention in markets (see Section 19.10). We will also discuss the problems of consumer protection and occupational licensing—two areas in which the government has acted as a "big brother" in trying to protect consumers.

Finally, we will discuss some controversies that have arisen in practice because of government intervention in the presence of externalities and public goods.

19.2   EXTERNALITIES IN CONSUMPTION AND PRODUCTION

In Chapter 9 we discussed the conditions for efficiency in consumption and production and overall economic efficiency. These conditions involved marginal rates of substitution (*MRS*) and marginal rates of transformation (*MRT*). The conditions were derived on the assumption that production costs are borne only by the producer of the product and that the utility derived from consumption is enjoyed by only the purchasers. This is not always so. Some products have *external effects* or *externalities* (which are also called *spillover effects* or *neighborhood effects*). The externalities could be *positive externalities* (these involve external benefits) or *negative externalities* (these involve external costs). We will first give examples of positive and negative externalities in consumption and production and then discuss how they change the conditions of efficiency discussed in Chapter 9.

1. Positive externality in consumption: An example of this is vaccinations. They help not only the person vaccinated but also the entire neighborhood that the person lives in by preventing the spread of contagious diseases.

2. Negative externality in consumption: Suppose a person rides a noisy motorcycle. The rider gets an enjoyment from it (usually the greater the noise, the greater the enjoyment). But for other people living in the neighborhood, the noise is a nuisance.

3. Negative externality in production: An oft-quoted example is that of a paper mill that produces paper and waste that is dumped into a river. The riverside residents and the fishers are hurt by the waste.

4. Positive externality in production: An oft-quoted example is that of the production of honey. Beekeepers try to put their beehives on farms because the nectar from the plants increases the production of honey. The farmers also receive advantages from the beehives because the bees aid pollination of the plants. We will now analyze the consequences of these externalities.

The famous book by the British economist A. C. Pigou, titled *Wealth and Welfare* (1912), was the first to deal with externalities in a systematic way. Pigou argued that in the presence of externalities, even if we have perfect competition we do not achieve a Pareto optimum. The social benefit or cost is a combination of private and external benefits or costs. We will use the following notation to denote these costs and benefits:

MPC = marginal private cost
MEC = marginal external cost
MSC = marginal social cost

and

$$MSC = MPC + MEC$$

Also,

MPB = marginal private benefit
MEB = marginal external benefit
MSB = marginal social benefit

and

$$MSB = MPB + MEB$$

Overall economic efficiency requires that $MSC = MSB$ for each product. The reason is obvious. As long as $MSB > MSC$, production should be expanded because additional benefit exceeds additional cost. Similarly, if $MSB < MSC$, then production should be decreased.[1] Consequently, we should have for each pair of products equality between the marginal social rate of transformation $MSRT$ and the marginal social rate of substitution $MSRS$. Thus, in the conditions derived in Chapter 9, we have to substitute the word "social" in all the marginal rates MRT and MRS. If only the marginal private costs are considered, the economy will not reach economic efficiency. For economic efficiency consumers and producer must weigh the full social benefits of consumption or production.

One way to get producers and consumers to weigh social benefits and costs is to impose taxes and subsidies which bring private benefits or costs into line with social benefits or costs. We will now illustrate how these taxes and subsidies would work.

Negative externality in production

Figure 19.1 illustrates the case of a negative externality in production. Since we are assuming that there are no externalities in consumption, the demand curve DD shows the marginal private and social benefits ($MPB = MSB$). The competitive supply curve, however, reflects only the marginal private costs. The MSC curve lies above the competitive supply curve. The optimal output is Q_0 with a price P_0. But the competitive market, if left alone, will product Q_1 with a price of P_1. Thus, there is a tendency to overproduce. At the optimal quantity of output Q_0, the price would be P_0, but marginal private cost would be C_0. Thus, the government could levy a per unit tax of $(P_0 - C_0)$ on the firm, increase marginal private cost by $(P_0 - C_0)$, and reduce output from Q_1 to Q_0. Consumers would pay P_0, the full marginal social cost of production. The revenue from the tax could be used to pay for the external damages from the production of this product (for example, in the case of the paper mill, the tax revenues could pay for the cleaning up of the river or for alternative ways of paying for the damages to those hurt by the waste dumped in the river). Note, however, that the tax revenue could be more or less than the external damage. The revenue would equal $(P_0 - C_0) \times Q_0$ whereas the total external cost would equal the area between MSC and MPC up to Q_0.

[1]For simplicity, we are assuming that there is only one level of output for which $MSB = MSC$.

FIGURE 19.1   Negative externality in production.

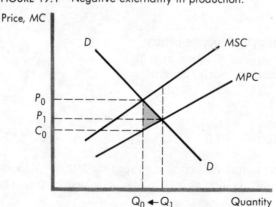

Finally, the net gain to society from the tax is given by the shaded area in Figure 19.1. This is the excess of costs over benefits for the units which are eliminated by the tax. It is the summation of $(MSC - MSB)$ over the output range Q_0 to Q_1.

Positive externality in production

This case is illustrated in Figure 19.2. In this case, since there are external benefits, the MSC curve is below the MPC curve ($MSC < MPC$). Since the demand curve gives the marginal social (private) benefit, the optimal level of output Q_0 is given by the intersection of the demand curve with the MSC curve. However, if left alone the competitive market will produce Q_1 where the demand curve intersects the MPC curve. Thus, too little will be produced from the social point of view. At the output level Q_0, producers receive a price of P_0, but their marginal cost is C_0. Thus, output can be increased by providing the producers a subsidy equal to $(C_0 - P_0)$. The consumer pays the marginal costs of production C_0 minus the external benefit $(C_0 - P_0)$ or a price P_0. In the previous case, we had a tax equal to the marginal external cost. In the present case, we have a subsidy equal to the external benefit. Where does the government get the money to pay the subsidy? It could collect it from the people reaping the external benefit. But again, the expenditures on the subsidy may not equal the total external benefit.

The net benefit to society from the subsidy is given by the shaded area in Figure 19.2. This is the excess of social benefit over social cost for the extra units produced as the result of the subsidy.

Negative externality in consumption

This is illustrated in Figure 19.3. Since there are no externalities in production, marginal social cost and marginal private cost are equal, and the competitive supply curve reflects the common marginal cost. However, on the demand side, the demand curve reflects only the marginal private benefit MPB. And since the marginal social benefit is less than the marginal private benefit, the MSB curve is below the MPB curve.

The optimal quantity is again Q_0 (the point where $MSB = MSC$). In the absence

FIGURE 19.2   Positive externality in production.

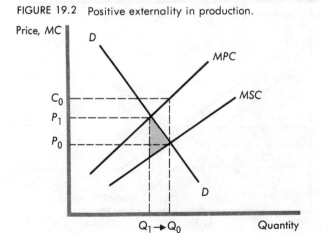

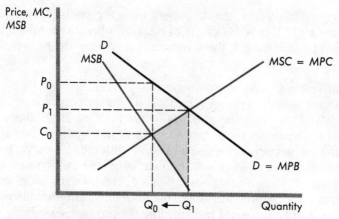

FIGURE 19.3   Negative externality in consumption.

of any intervention, the quantity supplied and consumed is Q_1, and the price is P_1. Thus, there is an overproduction of the commodity as compared to the socially optimal level.

To restrict the output to Q_0, the price has to be raised to P_0. But the supply price for Q_0 is C_0. Hence, a tax equal to $(P_0 - C_0)$ needs to be levied. The price the consumer pays is, thus, P_0, which equals the marginal private cost of production C_0 plus the cost of externality in consumption $(P_0 - C_0)$. Again, the revenue generated from the tax could be used to compensate those who are hurt by the external cost arising from the consumption of this product. Again, the area of the shaded triangle measures the net benefit of the tax to society.

Positive externality in consumption

This is illustrated in Figure 19.4. Again, the MSC (which equals MPC) curve is the supply curve. The demand curve DD is the MPB curve. Since there are external benefits, $MSB > MPB$, and the MSB curve lies above the demand curve.

The socially optimal quantity is given by Q_0 where $MSB = MSC$. Without any intervention, the quantity produced is Q_1, and the price is P_1. Thus, there is un-

FIGURE 19.4   Positive externality in consumption.

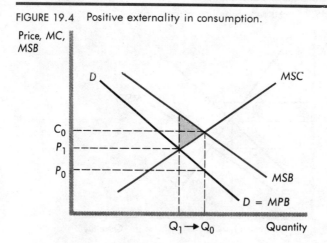

derproduction as compared to the socially optimal level. If Q_0 is produced, the market price will be P_0 but the marginal cost of production will be C_0. Thus, the consumers need to be given a subsidy equal to $C_0 - P_0$. The producers will get C_0 but the consumers pay P_0. At least part of the cost of the subsidy $(C_0 - P_0) \times Q_0$ could possibly be collected from those reaping the external benefits arising from the consumption of this good.

Again, the net benefit to society from the subsidy is measured by the area of the shaded triangle in Figure 19.4. It is the excess of social benefit over social cost for the output range Q_1 to Q_0.

Summary

We might summarize our results as follows: (1) In the presence of externalities, the socially optimal level of output Q_0 is given by the condition $MSB = MSC$. (2) The private production of output Q_1 is given by the condition $MPB = MPC$. (3) To bring about an output of Q_0 we can use the tax and subsidy programs shown in Table 19.1. These correspond to the four cases we considered.

We did not consider combinations of taxes and subsidies, but these combinations are possible if there are externalities in both consumption and production. For example, there might be positive externalities in consumption and negative externalities in production (suppose for the sake of argument that this is the case with a vaccine). We will illustrate this case of externalities in consumption and production in Figure 19.5. The socially optimal output is Q_0. We can bring about this output if we subsidize consumers by AB and tax producers by AE. Alternatively, we can just tax producers by BE. The tax of BE on producers would solve all the efficiency problems. Equity considerations might, however, require that both a subsidy and a tax be imposed.

Note that we could have the socially optimal output produced in the absence of intervention when there is an external benefit in consumption and an external cost in production. In Figure 19.5, this would require that the demand and supply curves intersect at Q_0. In this case, taxes and subsidies would only be warranted on the grounds of fairness. Furthermore, the subsidy would have to equal the tax or the optimal output would no longer be produced.

19.3   THE COASE THEOREM

The preceding analysis was based on the argument that in the presence of externalities the government should intervene by levying taxes on those imposing ex-

TABLE 19.1   Taxes and Subsidies in the Presence of Externalities

Condition	Tax or Subsidy	Amount of Tax or Subsidy*
$MSC > MPC$	Tax producers	$MSC - MPC$
$MSC < MPC$	Subsidize producers	$MPC - MSC$
$MSB < MPB$	Tax consumers	$MPB - MSB$
$MSB > MPB$	Subsidize consumers	$MSB - MPB$

*These amounts are measured at the socially optimal output.

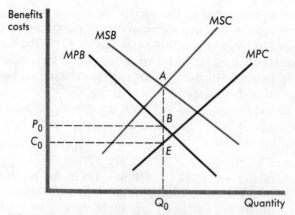

FIGURE 19.5   Externalities in consumption and production.

ternal costs and subsidizing those who contribute external benefits. This argument, which originated from Pigou's book in 1912, was challenged by Ronald Coase (about 50 years later), who argued (what might appear obvious in retrospect) that the presence of externalities does not necessarily mean that government should intervene.[2] After all, the government intervention, or the administering of the subsidies and taxes, will cost something. And if these costs are higher than the social benefits from intervention (given by the areas of the triangles in Figures 19.1 to 19.4) then government intervention will not increase social welfare.

Coase argued, in addition, that there is a possibility of private deals that would achieve the same result as government taxes and subsidies. Consider the case of the paper mill dumping waste in a river and, thus, hurting the fishing. In Figure 19.6, Q_0 is the socially optimal output but the competitive market produces Q_1. If the paper mill reduces the output from Q_1 to Q_0, the net loss in the producer's and consumer's surplus is ACE but the gain to the fishers is $ABCE$ (the excess of MSC over MPC for the output range Q_0 to Q_1). Since $ABCE$ is larger than ACE so that the gain to the fishers is larger than the loss to the consumers and producers, it

[2]Ronald H. Coase, "The Problem of Social Cost," *Journal of Law and Economics,* October 1960, pp. 1–44.

FIGURE 19.6   Possibility of private deals under externalities.

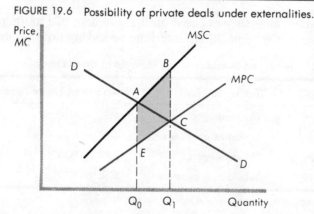

should be possible for the fishers to bribe the producers and consumers to cut production to Q_0. Thus, the socially optimal level of output could be achieved without government taxing or subsidizing. Of course, if the number of people involved is large, the bargaining costs could be very high.

Coase also argued that it would make no difference to the allocation of resources, how the property rights to a contestable resource (here, the river) were assigned. If the property rights to the river were assigned to the fishers, then the paper mill would have to pay the fishers compensation for dumping the waste in the river. This compensation would have to be equal to $MSC - MPC$ per each unit in Figure 19.6, because that is the measure of harm done to the fishers. The paper mill would have to take the costs of compensation into account when calculating its costs. Thus, its private marginal cost curve would no longer be MPC but would now be MSC in Figure 19.6. Thus, the *externality has been internalized*. The output of the paper mill would now be the socially optimal level Q_0.

The same would be the case if the paper mill were to be assigned the property rights to the river and, thus, had the right to dump wastes in it. Fishers could then bribe the paper mill not to dump waste. The amount of the bribe would be the difference $MSC - MPC$. When the paper mill calculated its costs, it would have to add to MPC the amount of this bribe (it is the cost of the forgone bribe by increasing output). Thus, again the cost curve the firm would be looking at would be the MSC curve. The externality has again been internalized. Of course, to whom the property rights to the river are assigned (the paper mill or the fishers) will make a difference in income distribution, but Coase is assuming the absence of income effects.

The Coase theorem can be summarized as follows: Under perfect competition, if income effects and transactions costs are ignored, voluntary agreements among the different parties concerned will lead to a socially optimal output even in the presence of externalities, and the result will be the same regardless of which party is assigned the property rights to the contestable resource.

The assumptions of the Coase theorem are that the income effects are small and that transactions costs are negligible, and both assumptions are unlikely to be valid in practice. Suppose there is a large river into which several industrial plants are dumping waste; millions of people are using the river water for drinking purposes and recreational facilities. Obviously, it is impossible to assign property rights to anyone, and it is impossible for private parties to get together and reach an agreement. An example of this situation is the Ruhr basin in West Germany with a lot of industries polluting the rivers in the area. What are the possible solutions?

First of all, it does not make any sense to say that the industries should not pollute the water at all. There is a *socially optimal level of pollution*, and this is not in general zero pollution. Figure 19.7 shows the marginal costs MSC and marginal social benefits MSB for improvements in water quality. We denote water quality as ranging from 0 (uselessly dirty water) to 100 (pure water). The marginal cost of cleaning goes up as we reach higher and higher levels of purity. The marginal benefits also decline as we go to higher and higher levels of purity. For example, going from 95 percent pure to 100 percent pure may not make as much difference as going from 45 percent pure to 50 percent pure (for almost all uses except drinking, perfect purity is not necessary).

The optimal quantity of pollution is Q^*. If water quality is at Q_1 ($< Q^*$), then

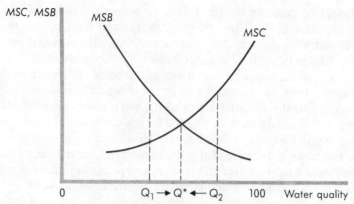

FIGURE 19.7   Determination of optimal level of pollution.

it pays to increase it since the extra benefit is greater than the extra cost. If the water quality is at Q_2 ($> Q^*$), then it pays to decrease it because benefits forgone are less than costs saved.

The diagram is, of course, of little practical value because there are, in practice, many insurmountable problems in measuring *MSB* and *MSC*. It does, however, illustrate the point that there is such a thing as the optimal level of pollution and that it need not be zero pollution (100 percent purity).

EXAMPLE 19.1   The Optimal Speed Limit

The optimal speed for a driver and the optimal speed limit imposed by the government are two distinct concepts. A driver's optimal speed is determined by equating the private marginal benefit of increased speed (value of reduced travel time) to the private marginal cost (increased fuel usage and increased probability of an accident). For the society, however, the driver driving at high speeds imposes external costs by increasing the probability of accidents for others. The generally accepted rationale for imposing speed limits on highways is that there are external costs in driving that increase as speed increases. For instance, the 55 mph speed limit was introduced to reduce total gasoline consumption in the United States and to reduce the rate of accidents.

Jondrow, Bowes, and Levy try to estimate the private and socially optimal speed limits.[3] They use estimates obtained by others for the change in accident probability per mile with respect to speed, change in gasoline used per mile with respect to speed, and the amount of crude oil imported by the United States. These are necessary to calculate the accident externality and the gasoline consumption externality components in the socially optimal speed limit. To estimate the private optimum they use the revealed preference of the drivers, that is, how fast they actually drive if unencumbered by a speed limit.[4] They also assume that all drivers

[3]J. Jondrow, M. Bowes, and R. Levy, "The Optimal Speed Limit," *Economic Inquiry*, July 1983, pp. 325–336. The paper gives several references to earlier studies on the evaluation of the 55 mph speed limit.

[4]The average speed limit of drivers on the German Autobahn is estimated to be 85 mph. This can be an overestimate for U.S. drivers due to differences between the driving habits of U.S. and German drivers and the technical capabilities of the cars. However, the calculations of Jondrow et al. are just illustrative.

are rational and informed, and, other things equal (value of time and life), they would drive at the same speed.

Based on these calculations, Jondrow et al. obtain the following optimal speed limits (we are presenting only some of the results):

Value of Time ($ per hour)	Value of Life ($ thousands)	Private Optimum (mph)	Social Optimum (mph)
5	100	60.8	56.9
5	1,000	53.4	48.2
5	10,000	29.4	24.7
10	100	86.0	80.5
10	1,000	75.7	68.2
10	10,000	41.5	34.9
15	1,000	92.4	83.6
15	1,715	85.0	75.5
15	10,000	50.9	42.8

Jondrow et al. also estimate the costs of a suboptimal speed limit. They use value of time as $15 per hr and value of life as $1.715 mill. Thus, the socially optimal speed limit is 75.5 mph. Total miles travelled (on main rural and urban interstate roads) in 1976 was 676 billion miles. The reduction in the probability of being killed by reducing the speed limit from 75.5 to 55 mph is equal to 1.38×10^{-8} per mile. This implies a saving of about 9,330 lives at a cost of $29.6 billion per year. The cost per life saved is thus $3.2 million or about $1.5 million above the value that individuals place on their own lives. How does this compare with the cost of other federal safety efforts? A comparison of this cost with the costs of saving life by 57 federal safety efforts estimated by Graham and Vaupel reveals that only 12 are more expensive.[5]

19.4 POLICIES TO REGULATE POLLUTION

Given that there is a nonzero optimal level of pollution, what are the appropriate policies to achieve it? There are three types of policies: (1) pollution standards, (2) pollution taxes, and (3) pollution licenses. The "standards" policy is a method of direct control, whereas the other two are indirect methods. For the implementation of the "standards" policy and the "licensing" policy we need to know the optimal pollution quantity whereas for the implementation of the tax policy we need to know $(MSC - MSB)$ at the optimal level of pollution.

[5]J. Graham and J. Vaupel, "The Value of a Life: What Difference Does it Make?" *Risk Analysis*, March 1981, pp. 89–95.

19.4.1 Pollution standards

The standards policy is the one that is most frequently used in practice though, from the economic point of view, it is the least efficient. The Environmental Protection Agency (EPA) was set up in 1970 with the specific task of monitoring air pollution, water pollution, and toxic and hazardous wastes. It is in charge of setting standards for environmental quality, imposing taxes on polluters, monitoring waste disposal firms and waste disposal technologies, and so on.

Not much economic analysis goes into the formulation of environmental policies. The way the standards method of pollution control works is as follows: The EPA estimates the volume of discharge from each source that is justified on a rough benefit-cost comparison. Then it gives each source a quota or permit that specifies the allowed discharge of the residual. Of course, a new permit would be required after each change in output, product mix, technology, or any other variable affecting the source's discharge. Problems arise as to how to allocate the permissible discharges among the different producers. We cannot use discharge per unit of output because outputs of oil refiners, steel mills, and food processors differ. Even for firms producing the same output, the pollution problems result in a lot of litigation, since the courts argue that disparities in costs should be taken into account in assigning discharge permits. Because of these complexities, the rule often followed in practice is to set standards at approximately a uniform percentage abatement from previous discharges for existing sources, and a uniform percentage abatement from an estimated discharge level for new sources. However, since costs of pollution abatement vary greatly among sources, a requirement of a uniform percentage abatement is an inefficient policy (the efficient policy would equate the marginal cost of pollution abatement for all sources). Finally, direct control of pollution is wasteful because firms spend a lot of time negotiating with government and circumventing the complex rules. They pay high salaries to individuals skilled in dealing with officials in Washington rather than those skilled in increasing productivity. Direct controls also lead to government interference with the production technique of firms. Firms have to get approval on every new technology they use. They sometimes have some forms of technology, that they would not normally use, thrust on them. A good analogy that points out the limitations of the standards approach to pollution control is that of labor markets where government would decide how much of each kind of labor is needed by each employer and then issue permits for the employment of labor.

A good example that shows the defects of pollution standards is that referring to automobile emissions.[6] In 1970 Congress decided to get tough with the automobile companies, and that year's Clean Air Act amendments instructed EPA to reduce by about 90 percent (in 5 to 6 years), new car emissions for the three air pollutants: hydrocarbons HC, carbon monoxide CO, and nitrogen oxides NO_x. The standards set were as follows (the figures are grams per mile):

Year	HC	CO	NO_x
1967 (uncontrolled)	8.70	87.0	4.0

[6]See Edwin S. Mills, *The Economics of Environmental Quality*, Norton, New York, 1978, pp. 209–214.

1973–1974	3.00	28.0	3.1
1975	0.41	3.4	2.0
1976 and beyond	0.41	3.4	0.4

In 1970 it was uncertain whether it would be possible to make cars that would meet the 1975–1976 standards, what it would cost, or what the benefits of improved air quality would be. The NO_x standard raised problems of technology. *HC* and *CO* are products of incomplete combustion, whereas NO_x is a normal product of combustion. Thus, modifications that reduced *HC* and *CO* emissions would increase NO_x emissions.

The automobile industry lobbied and obtained delays in meeting those standards. The EPA granted a delay in 1973 and Congress changed the law in 1974 and 1975, in response to the energy crisis. In the 1977 Clean Air Act Amendments, Congress modified the emission standards. The original hydrocarbon and carbon monoxide standards were put off until the 1980 model year, and the NO_x standard was raised to 2.0 grams per mile through 1980, and 1.0 gram per mile for 1981 and beyond.[7]

The automobile industry had two choices—either to clean up the internal combustion engine or to develop alternative engine types. Since the latter course of action would have taken a lot of time, the automobile industry decided to add a catalyst to the exhaust system of the internal combustion engine. The catalyst, however, requires low-lead gasoline and considerable care in automobile operation to avoid burning it out. Furthermore, the owners lack an incentive to replace the catalyst because the car's drivability and fuel consumption are likely to improve if it burns out. If many owners failed to maintain the catalyst, the level of air pollution would be the same as before. The net result of the arbitrary and stringent standards and deadlines has been an enormous cost to automobile drivers. These costs are shown in Table 19.2.

19.4.2 Pollution taxes

Under the taxation scheme there is a tax per unit of waste dumped. The tax should correspond to the marginal cost of cleaning up the waste at the optimal level of pollution. Suppose the government imposes a tax of $10 per unit of waste. Then the firms will dump as much waste as they want at this price. The firms will take the costs of cleanup into consideration when undertaking production.

Pollution taxes have been widely used in France, Germany, and Great Britain; they have not been as common in the United States and Japan, which have relied more on the direct control method. There are a few states (for example, Vermont, Maryland, and Michigan) that charge fees for waste disposal in waterways (the fees are supposed to reflect the cost of environmental damage). At the national level there are taxes on leaded gasoline and taxes on sulphur content of coal, oil, and natural gas. There are also rebates if a firm makes an effort to prevent sulphur

---

[7]Lawrence J. White, *The Regulation of Air Pollution Emissions from Motor Vehicles,* American Enterprise Institute, Washington, D.C., 1982, discusses details of the standards and the costs of these pollution emission standards.

TABLE 19.2 The Costs per Automobile of Emissions Regulation (1968–1981 current dollars)

Year	Equipment Only	All Other Costs	Total
1968	14	0	14
1969	15	0	15
1970	24	0	24
1971	25	0	25
1972	25	170	195
1973	44	488	532
1974	49	541	590
1975	119	187	306
1976	126	197	323
1977	123	343	466
1978	133	369	502
1979	148	411	559
1980	222	684	906
1981	600	951	1,551

Note: Other costs are present lifetime value of fuel penalty, maintenance, and unleaded gasoline premium.
Source: R. W. Candall, H. K. Guenspecht, T. E. Keeler, and L. B. Lave, Regulating the Automobile, Brookings Institution, Washington, D.C., 1986, table 3.1, p. 30. Their calculations are based on data in Lawrence J. White, The Regulation of Air Pollution Emissions from Motor Vehicles, American Enterprise Institute, Washington, D.C., 1982.

from escaping into the atmosphere. Furthermore, there are taxes on pesticides and other hazardous chemicals.

19.4.3 Pollution licensing

Of the three methods of pollution control we have been discussing, this is the most efficient, although it is also the least utilized. The way it works is as follows: On the basis of benefit-cost analysis, the government determines the optimal level of pollution (this can be done for each category of pollution, but we can assume for simplicity, that there is only one kind). Suppose that the government determines that in a specified area, about 10 million units of waste per year can be dumped. It then auctions off *pollution licenses* of this amount. The holder of the license for X units has the right to dump X units of waste during the year in the specified area. The strictly limited supply of licenses ensures that the pollution level does not exceed the limit set. The producers of goods take the costs of reducing wastes versus the costs of obtaining the licenses into account. The price of the license is bid up by the firms with the highest pollution abatement costs. The purchasers of the licenses are the polluters. If the conservationists want to reduce the level of pollution below the level set by the government, they can buy the licenses and not use them. Furthermore, a firm that buys a license can later sell it to some other firm if the original purchaser finds ways of reducing wastes. In this method, firms are able to make rational choices and calculations without government intervention, unlike the case of direct controls.

In the early 1980s the U.S. government started an emissions trading program. Hailed by Senator Pete Dominici as "the one bright idea that has emerged during the 1980's," the emissions trading program represents the first large-scale attempt to use economic incentives in environmental policy in the United States. However, Tietenberg argues that though the program is a definite improvement over the policies of the clean air acts of the 1970s, the cost savings actually achieved from the program have been considerably less than expected.[8]

EXAMPLE 19.2 Gasoline Mileage Standards

In the 1975 Energy Policy and Conservation Act Amendment, the U.S. Congress included gasoline mileage standards for cars. These are called CAFE (corporate average fuel economy) standards. They required sales-weighted fleet-average fuel economy to rise from 18 to 27.5 miles per gallon (mpg) by the 1985 model year with subsequent standards to be set later. In addition to CAFE standards, there were two other regulations to reduce gasoline consumption: the 55 mph speed limit on highways (which was relaxed only in late 1987) and a "gas guzzler" tax on cars that consume too much gasoline. At the same time that these policies were enacted, the government was encouraging gasoline consumption by imposing price ceilings on crude oil and refined products.

Between 1973 and 1980 crude oil prices increased from $3 to $40 a barrel, and with the increase in gasoline prices, U.S. car manufacturers would have manufactured gas-saving cars even without the CAFE standards. It was only after the oil price decline since 1981 that the CAFE standards became a constraint on automobile manufacturers. However, for different reasons, the United Auto Workers (UAW) and the car manufacturers found themselves supporting the CAFE standards and lobbying for their extensions even after 1985.[9]

The UAW supported the CAFE standards even though they raised the costs for automobile manufacturers and that meant fewer cars sold, because the law applied separate CAFE standards for domestic and imported cars. Given General Motors' and Ford's success in the manufacture of large cars, they had to manufacture enough small cars to meet the CAFE standards. Since the U.S. companies were not competitive with Japan and Korea in the manufacture of small cars, without CAFE they would have imported small cars from abroad. In short, CAFE served as a *nontariff trade barrier* for small car imports.

Chrysler also supported the CAFE standards for the same reason. Even though it had a worse fuel economy record than GM and Ford for a given weight of the car and engine power, it met the CAFE standards because it was forced to end its production of large cars during its brush with bankruptcy in the late 1970s. Thus

---

[8]T. H. Tietenberg, *Emissions Trading: An Exercise in Reforming Pollution Policy*, Brookings, Washington, D.C., 1985.

[9]Robert W. Crandall, "Single-Digit Oil and Auto Mileage Standards Don't Mix," *The Wall Street Journal*, April 3, 1986. Also see the editorial in *Barron's*, August 4, 1986, "Unwise at Any Speed: Those Absurd Gasoline Mileage Standards Should Be Scrapped."

continuation of CAFE standards would put pressure on GM and Ford but not on Chrysler.

Even GM and Ford argued for a continuation of CAFE in 1987 and 1988 model years, possibly to constrain major large-car competitors in the world like Mercedes, Volvo, BMW, Peugeot, and Saab from exporting freely to the United States. Thus, again the CAFE program serves as a nontariff trade barrier.

The CAFE program was an anomaly and even an absurdity in an era of declining oil prices. However, there were many vested interests in favor of its continuation, and curiously enough these were the UAW and the big three automobile manufacturers, each for a different reason.

Another law to reduce gasoline consumption was the 55 mph speed limit. Again, whatever economy in gasoline consumption was desired could have been achieved by a gasoline tax. Blair, Kaserman, and Tepel estimate that the 55 mph speed limit should have reduced gasoline consumption by 1.4 percent.[10] Using a price elasticity of demand for gasoline of -0.4, they estimate that the same results could have been achieved by a price increase of 3.4 percent.

19.5   PUBLIC GOODS

About half of the U.S. federal budget is used for more or less public goods such as the military, science, energy, environment, transportation, and law and order. In a number of papers written in the 1950s Paul Samuelson laid out the theory of *pure public goods*. A pure public good is one that provides nonexcludable and nonrival benefits to all people in a given society. *Nonexcludability* means it is technically impossible or extremely costly to exclude any individual from the benefits of a good. *Nonrivalry* means that there is no rivalry among the consumers because the enjoyment of the good by any one person does not reduce its availability for others. A classic example is that of a lighthouse. When the light is on, it is difficult to prevent any nearby ship from seeing it and taking advantage of it (nonexcludability), and one ship's use does not affect other ships' ability to use it (nonrivalry). In reality, there are no pure public goods. Even a lighthouse might send out coded electronic transmission that can be unscrambled only by rented equipment. In this case, nonexcludability does not apply. Also, if there is a dense concentration of ships, the ships with the high masts can blot out the light so that other ships cannot see it. In this case, consumption is no longer nonrival.[11]

The private market economy does not do well at providing public goods. If no one can be excluded from consumption there is no way to charge a price for

[10]R. D. Blair, D. Kaserman, and R. Tepel, "The Impact of Improved Mileage on Gasoline Consumption," *Economic Inquiry*, April 1984, pp. 209–217.

[11]Note, however, the criticism of the lighthouse example in R. H. Coase, "The Lighthouse in Economics," *The Journal of Law and Economics*, October 1974, pp. 357–376. Coase argues that the lighthouse example often cited as a public good is not a good illustration. He gives a sketch of the history and evolution of the British lighthouse system, which raises its revenues from the consumers of the service (ships calling on British ports). The service is operated by the Lights Advisory Committee representing Shipowners, Underwriters and Shippers, which is consulted on the budget. Thus, there is no need for government intervention in this case. Coase says: "Despite the extensive use of the lighthouse example in the literature, no economist, to my knowledge, has ever made a comprehensive study of lighthouse finance and administration. The lighthouse is simply plucked out of the air to serve as an illustration—economists should not use the lighthouse as an example of a service that could only be provided by the government."

the good and, therefore, no incentive for private entrepreneurs to produce and sell it. Even if people could be selectively excluded from consuming it, the nonrivalry in consumption means that it is inefficient to exclude anyone. Since it costs nothing to provide the good to each additional customer after the first, social welfare is maximized by giving away the good free. The fact that, once a good is produced, the marginal cost of provision of the good to any individual is 0, leads to the *free-rider problem*. In other words, every individual wants to get a free ride and does not want to pay for the provision of the good because it is possible to get it free once someone else pays for its provision.

The failure of the market to deal efficiently with the provision of public goods leads many economists to suggest that the government should step in and produce them. There are, of course, some economists who argue that the costs of government bureaucracy and interference with liberty are so great that except in the case of pure public goods, like national defense, it is best to leave the production of many so-called public goods to the private sector. The argument is that private individuals will get together and organize clubs to produce these goods efficiently. This is called the *club theory*.[12] We shall discuss this after outlining the main issues concerning the provision of public goods.

In our discussion we have to distinguish between two types of public goods: (1) pure public goods such as national defense, law and order, and basic research (and space programs) and (2) goods that fall in between the pure public goods and private goods. These include goods where partial exclusion is possible. Examples are education, environmental quality, transportation, and community and regional development. Also, there are three issues to be discussed: (1) determination of how much to produce, (2) determination of how to cover costs, and (3) determination of how to distribute the benefits.

19.6 OPTIMALITY CONDITIONS FOR THE PROVISION OF PUBLIC GOODS

We have consistently argued that the competitive market will provide the optimal quantity of a private good because output will be expanded just to the point where $D = S$. And the demand curve represents the full social benefit of additional units MSB, and the supply curve reflects the marginal social cost of production MSC.

Again, with public goods, output should be expanded to the point where $MSB = MSC$. But a market demand curve, which we derived by horizontally summing individuals' demand curves, no longer reflects MSB. This is because all individuals simultaneously benefit from each unit of the public good.

Figure 19.8 illustrates the derivation of a marginal social benefit curve for a public good from individuals' demand curves. For simplicity, we will consider two individuals A and B. MV_A represents the marginal value (or benefit) of the public good to A. This is individual A's demand curve for the good. MV_B is B's marginal value curve or demand curve for the good. In other words, the Xth unit of the good provides XD benefit to A and XE benefit to B. But both A and B receive this

[12]See J. M. Buchanan, "An Economic Theory of Clubs," *Economica*, February 1965, pp. 1–14.

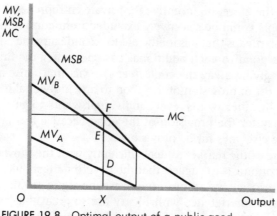

FIGURE 19.8 Optimal output of a public good.

benefit. So the *MSB* for the *X*th unit is $XD + XE$ which equals XF. Because of the nonrivalry in consumption with the public good, the *MSB* curve is derived by vertically summing the individuals' marginal value (or demand) curves. In Figure 19.8 the *MSB* curve is shown by the thick colored line. The optimal output is now given by the intersection of the *MSB* curve with the marginal cost (both private and social) curve. The optimal output is, thus, OX units of the public good.

In actual practice there is the problem of how to obtain the marginal benefits or valuations of individuals. With goods whose benefits accrue to a very large number of individuals, it is usually the bureaucrats who estimate the social benefits and social costs. An underestimation of social costs and/or an overestimation of social benefits results in an overproduction of the public good. As a consequence there can be a net social loss. This is illustrated in Figure 19.9.

The output corresponding to the intersection of the marginal social benefit *MSB* and the marginal social cost *MSC* curves is given by X_0. This is the optimal

FIGURE 19.9 Net welfare loss due to overproduction of a public good.

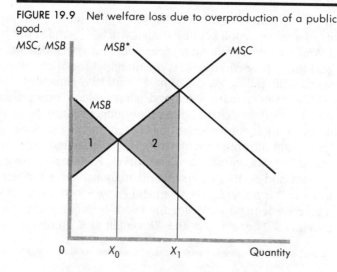

level of output. However, suppose the bureaucrats overestimate the *MSB* (in the interests of their own department). (The underestimation of costs can be similarly analyzed.) The curve *MSB** shows the overestimated benefits. The actual production is X_1. The net social benefit when the output is X_0 is given by the shaded area 1. However, if output is X_1, there is also a social loss given by the shaded area 2. If area 2 is larger than area 1, then society would be better off without any of the good.

With the production of goods in government hands, it is often alleged that the costs invariably go up. The conservative economist Gordon Tullock suggests a "bureaucratic rule of two" which says that the transferring of any production activity from the private to the public sector results in a doubling of the unit costs of production. It is also customary to quote the famous Parkinson's law[13] which says that employment in government agencies grows at a constant rate whether the work to be done rises, stays constant, or declines. Thus many economists suggest that except for pure public goods such as defense and law and order, the government should not enter into the area of direct production or provision of public goods. We shall now discuss the methods suggested for the private provision of public goods.

19.7 PRIVATE PRODUCTION OF PUBLIC GOODS

Examples of private production of public goods are hard to come by, but one can imagine market provision of broadcasting, police, fire protection, and outdoor recreation facilities such as parks. There is also an increasing pressure on state and local governments to consider user finance of many of these activities. In view of this, it is interesting to see whether the production of some public goods can be left to private enterprise.

There have been some papers that have attacked the classical proposition that free markets will underproduce public goods.[14] These papers have argued that for an *excludable* public good, undersupply will not be a problem since the competitive market can provide the good efficiently. Thompson, in fact, argues that an over-supply will result. His analysis, however, is based on the unrealistic assumption that producers have full knowledge of the demand curves of all consumers and can extract all their consumers' surplus. He also assumes free entry. Hence, competition for the consumers' surplus forces down the price and leads to oversupply.

Demsetz analyzes the production of public goods the same way one analyzes production with joint supply. As an example he says: "Just as the slaughtering of a steer provides goods to both leather users and meat consumers, so the production of a public good yields benefits that can be enjoyed by more than one individual." Thus, Demsetz treats the same public good consumed by different individuals as different goods being supplied jointly. Since competitive markets can efficiently produce goods in joint supply, it follows that they can do so with public goods as

[13]C. Northcote Parkinson, *Parkinson's Law*, Houghton Mifflin, Boston, 1957.

[14]Two papers that illustrate the arguments are: Earl A. Thompson, "The Perfectly Competitive Production of Public Goods," *Review of Economics and Statistics*, February 1968, pp. 1–12, and Harold Demsetz, "The Private Production of Public Goods," *Journal of Law and Economics*, October 1970, pp. 292–306.

well. However, the analogy with joint supply is not appropriate. In the case of joint supply (of beef and leather), a large number of consumers are competing for the goods jointly supplied. In the case of a public good, treated as different goods for different consumers, there is only one consumer for each good.

One of the key assumptions made by both Thompson and Demsetz is that preferences of individual consumers are completely known to sellers of the public good. William Oakland shows that once this key assumption is relaxed, the classical conclusion that, if left to the private sector, there will be an underproduction of public goods, still holds true, even for excludable public goods.[15]

19.8   PROBLEMS WITH UNIFORM PRICING OF PUBLIC GOODS

Suppose that there is a nonrival but excludable public good, and the government follows a socially optimal provision policy. In other words, it provides an amount for which $MSB = MSC$. If all users have to be charged the same price, and that price is set so that they are all willing to buy the full amount provided, then most users will wish to buy more units than they can, and none wishes to buy fewer units. This is shown in Figure 19.10. Suppose, for illustration, that there are only two individuals X and Y. Curves X and Y show the marginal values of each unit for the two individuals. Since each unit of the public good can be consumed by both X and Y, the total social value of a unit of the good is given by the curve $X + Y$, which is the vertical summation of the two curves X and Y. Suppose the good can be provided at a constant marginal cost OA. Then the marginal social benefit of the output is equal to the marginal social cost at the output level Q_0. To induce X to consume Q_0 units of the output, price must be P_X. But at price P_X

[15]William H. Oakland, "Public Goods, Perfect Competition, and Underproduction," *Journal of Political Economy*, September–October 1974, pp. 927–939.

FIGURE 19.10   Problem with uniform pricing of public goods.

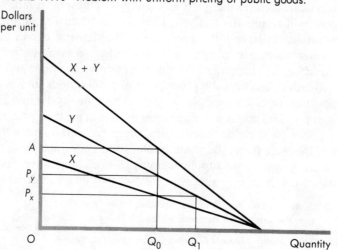

individual Y would want to consume Q_1 units of output, which is greater than Q_0. Thus, with uniform pricing for the public good there will be some individuals who will want to consume more than is provided. If we can somehow charge price P_x for X and price P_y for Y, then both individuals will freely choose to consume Q_0 units of the output and, furthermore, the production costs are completely covered because $P_x + P_y = OA$. Such a situation, where (1) the socially optimal amount of the public good is provided (where $MSB = MSC$), (2) each individual is charged a price equal to the marginal value for the individual, and (3) production costs are covered, is called a *Lindahl equilibrium*.

This system of charging different prices to the different consumers is similar to the pricing of joint products considered by Alfred Marshall. The joint products are priced according to the demand for each product. In Figure 19.10, suppose that X and Y are two products jointly produced. The curves X and Y are the demand curves for these products. OA is the marginal cost of production. Then P_x and P_y are the prices charged for the two products.

How can one find the Lindahl equilibrium? Suppose sets of prices are proposed which just cover costs. Individuals are asked to record how much of the good they wish to consume at the various prices. When we find a set of prices for each individual at which all individuals want to consume the same amount of the good, we have found the Lindahl equilibrium. This mechanism, of course, assumes that individuals reveal their preferences truthfully. This, however, may not be the case because of the free-rider problem we discussed earlier.

19.9   REVELATION OF PREFERENCES FOR PUBLIC GOODS

As we have discussed earlier, the problem of preference revelation is an important issue in the provision of public goods. All individuals try to underreport their own valuation, because once the good is produced they can get a free ride. The free-rider problem has long been regarded as insolvable in a world of imperfect information and self-interest. However, during the last few years some economists have devised what is known as an *incentive-compatible mechanism*. This is the mechanism by which even self-interested individuals are induced to reveal their true preferences. The mechanism was first developed by Clarke and Groves around 1971 and since then has been extended in several directions. It is beyond our scope to discuss these later developments, but we will outline the essentials of the original suggestions even though there are some drawbacks which have been fixed in the subsequent literature. We shall follow the development in Tideman and Tullock.[16]

Consider the case of three voters and three options to choose from. All three voters are asked to state which option they prefer and the amount of money they are willing to pay to secure their preferred option. We shall presently see why each voter has an incentive to respond truthfully. After the voters' responses are obtained,

[16]T. Nicholas Tideman and Gordon Tullock, "A New and Superior Process for Making Social Decisions," *Journal of Political Economy*, December 1976, pp. 1145–1159. The paper by T. Groves and J. Ledyard, "Optimal Allocation of Public Goods: A Solution to the Free Rider Problem," *Econometrica*, May 1977, corrects some problems with earlier work.

each voter is levied a Clarke-Groves tax, which is actually a bizarre tax. The voters' responses and their taxes are shown in Table 19.3.

Voter A values options 1, 2, and 3 at $50, $20, and $10, respectively. Voter B values them at $10, $60, and $20, and voter C values them at $40, $10, and $55. On the basis of total value, option 1 will be chosen.

Now consider voter A. Without A's vote, the total values are $50, $70, and $75 for options 1, 2, and 3, respectively. This is shown in the bottom part of Table 19.3. Thus, option 3 will be chosen. Since A's vote changes the outcome from option 3 to option 1, the Clarke-Groves tax on voter A will be $75 − 50 = $25. If option 3 is chosen, voter A gets a benefit of $10. By revealing her or his preferences, A sees that option 1 is chosen. A's increase in benefit is $40. The net benefit after tax is $40 − 25 = $15. This is shown in the last two columns of the top part of Table 19.3.

Voter B's vote does not change the outcome, and B pays no tax.

Without C's vote, the total values are $60, $80, and $30 for options 1, 2, and 3, respectively. Thus, option 2 will be chosen. Since C's vote changes the outcome from option 2 to option 1, C's tax is $80 − 60 = $20. The benefit to C from voting is $40 − 10 = $30. The net benefit after tax is $30 − 20 = $10.

Note that if voter A understated preferences to avoid the tax (for example, if A stated that option 1 benefited him or her only $30), then with A's vote option 2 is chosen and without it option 3 is chosen. Thus, A's tax is reduced to $75 − 70 = $5. But the benefit for A from voting is $20 − 10 = $10 and the after tax benefit is $10 − 5 = $5. Thus, A is made worse off. The tax we have obtained is very high, but this is because we have considered only three individuals. With a large number of individuals, the tax will be minuscule.

The above example illustrates how, through a peculiar tax scheme, individuals can be made to reveal their preferences. There are, however, many practical difficulties in implementing the tax scheme. First, for the case of a large number of consumers, each has very little incentive to go to the trouble of giving a detailed value report, since each report has very little effect on the amount of the public

TABLE 19.3   Clarke-Groves Tax for Public Goods

| Voter | Differential Values of Options (dollars) | | | | Net Benefit of Voting after Tax |
	1	2	3	Tax	
A	50	20	10	25	15
B	10	60	20	0	0
C	40	10	55	20	10
Total	100	90	85		

Total without the Individual's Vote			
A: B + C	50	70	75
B: A + C	90	30	65
C: A + B	60	80	30

good supplied. Also, the costs of administering the scheme for a large number of individuals can be prohibitive. These costs can be reduced by requiring only a sample of the total population to report their marginal valuations. Only these individuals will pay the Clarke-Groves tax, whereas all individuals pay a cost-share or a general tax.

The Tideman and Tullock process has been criticized in detail by Riker, but we will not pursue this criticism here because it will be too lengthy for our purpose.[17] What the criticism suggests is that there are many problems with preference-revealing mechanisms. Furthermore, there is not necessarily a large class of practical applications that correspond to the simple ones discussed here that can be solved as simply. Nevertheless, what this literature suggests is that the free-rider problem can, in principle, be solved.

EXAMPLE 19.3 Captain MacWhirr's Problem

The following example is similar to the demand-revealing process for determining preferences for public goods.[18] The similarity is that both are solutions to an information problem. The solution in each case is obtained by separating the information revealed by the individual from what the individual is entitled to.

In the novel *Typhoon*, Joseph Conrad poses a classic problem of information revelation. Two hundred Chinese workers are being transported home on a ship commanded by Captain MacWhirr, after working for seven years in various tropical colonies. Each worker's accumulated savings of silver dollars are stored in his own wooden chest. However, the ship runs into a violent storm, all the wooden chests get smashed, and the silver dollars are all scattered between decks. A riot ensues among the Chinese workers as they try to recover their silver dollars. To stop the conflict, the captain sends the first mate and some men to pick up all the money with a plan to return it to the rightful owners. However, the captain has a big problem. How is he going to determine how much money each worker had? If he asks the workers, of course, each worker will overstate the amount. In the story, the captain imposes an arbitrary solution which he thinks is fair. This is to assume that all men had the same amount of money, and he gives an equal share of the total to each worker.

This solution is not fair. Let us assume that only the captain knows the total amount of money and that each worker knows the amount he had but not the total amount or the amount that anybody else had. The captain's mistake is to assume that each worker is entitled to get the amount he states. Under this scheme, of course, each worker has an incentive to overstate his share. The way to solve this problem is to cut the link between the claim each worker makes and the amount he is entitled to.

A straightforward method of doing this is as follows: Let the maximum amount to which an individual worker is entitled be the difference between the total amount of money and the total amount claimed by everyone else. If the individual claims

[17]William H. Riker, "Is a 'New and Superior Process' Really Superior?" *Journal of Political Economy*, August 1979, pp. 875–890.

[18]This interesting example is from Gene E. Mumy, "A Superior Solution to Captain MacWhirr's Problem: An Illustration of Information Problems and Entitlement Structures," *Journal of Political Economy*, October 1981, pp. 1039–1043.

less than this maximum entitlement, he gets what he claims. But if he claims more, he gets penalized and actually gets less than this maximum amount he is entitled to. The result of this rule is that no worker has an incentive to overstate (or understate) his share and reveals the correct amount he actually had. This means that each worker is entitled to the exact amount he had. (A formal mathematical proof is given in the paper by Mumy.)

19.10 GOVERNMENT INTERVENTION IN MARKETS

Governments directly control a lot of economic activities in socialist and communist countries. However, even in the United States, the government intervenes in a larger number of markets. The major role of the government is in the conduct of fiscal and monetary policies which are discussed in books on macroeconomics. In adddition, the United States government intervenes in the functioning of product and factor markets through a series of regulations. Some examples are:

1. Antitrust laws aimed at preserving competition in the economy
2. Minimum wage laws, which we discussed in Chapter 16
3. Agricultural price support programs
4. Motor vehicle pollution control acts (which we discussed earlier in this chapter)
5. A host of regulations on consumer protection, which are listed in the next section
6. Regulations regarding licensing of occupations (discussed in Section 19.12)

The list can be expanded to several pages. In view of the large role of the government, we have to examine the purpose of government interventions and the way they come about.

There are two main goals of government intervention: income redistribution and better allocation of resources. Regarding the first goal, there is a detailed study by Benjamin Page which examines a wide range of issues: taxes, social welfare programs, spending on public goods, economic regulation, and the legal system.[19] Page finds that government policies are making income inequality worse.

Regarding the resource allocation objective, we discussed in the preceding sections two reasons for market failure: externalities and public goods. These two factors along with monopoly and oligopoly (discussed in Chapters 11, 12, and 13) have formed the basis for government intervention in markets. There are, broadly speaking, two theories of government intervention for the purpose of improving resource allocation—the public interest theory and the economic theory.

The public interest theory
The public interest theory has a long tradition in economics. According to this theory, the market mechanism plays a major role in the optimal allocation of goods and services, but the public will act through the government to correct any failures

---

[19]Benjamin I. Page, *Who Gets What From Government*, University of California Press, Berkeley, 1983.

in this allocation that might arise due to monopoly, externalities, or the existence of public goods. The theory rests on the assumptions that the government responds to a public demand for the correction of inefficient allocations and that the government can remove these inefficiencies at a lower cost than private organizations.

If this theory is correct, we should be observing that government regulates monopolies, controls the output of public goods, and taxes or subsidizes externalities. In practice, however, we observe government not tackling these problems and instead intervening in other situations where there is no evidence of any market failure. Government restrictions on foreign trade in the form of tariffs and quotas and government protection of inefficient industries and certain monopolies are examples of such actual behavior.

A common explanation for these inefficient government activities is that there are certain special interest groups that lobby strongly for government intervention because they benefit from it. This idea is more adequately developed in the economic theory of regulation propounded by Stigler and others who regard government intervention as another commodity whose equilibrium price and output are determined by demand and supply conditions.[20]

The economic theory

In the economic theory of regulation, introduced by Stigler and developed by Peltzman, regulation is treated like any other good. The equilibrium price and output are determined by the demand for and supply of regulation. Stigler argues that the behavior of governments can be modelled as part of the market mechanism.

Regulation confers benefits on some producers and groups by providing direct subsidies or controlling entry of rivals. Examples of direct subsidies are subsidies to farmers and airmail subsidies to domestic airlines (which until 1968 received airmail subsidies of $1.5 billion annually whether they carried mail or not). Prime examples of control of entry are the Civil Aeronautics Board (CAB), which controlled entry of airlines over different routes and the Federal Deposit Insurance Corporation (FDIC) which controlled entry of commercial banks. The regulations result in a transfer of wealth from one group to another. Thus, the commodity that is being transacted is transfer of wealth by government intervention. The price of this commodity takes the form of open bribes, campaign contributions, or more subtle forms of payment such as lucrative jobs for relatives of politicians and free time as volunteers at elections.

Let us first consider the demand side. The demanders are the firms or groups that benefit from the government subsidies or government controls over entry. There is, however, one problem on the demand side. Once a regulation comes into being, it benefits *all* the firms in the regulated industry, including those that did not contribute their time or money to politicians. This is the free-rider problem. Thus, regulation is more likely to occur in those cases where the beneficiaries form a small group. In this case it is easier to police the activities of individual members, and it is also easier to solicit lobby funds.

On the supply side, the political regulator wishes to maximize votes and, thus,

[20]G. J. Stigler, *The Citizen and the State*, University of Chicago Press, Chicago, 1975, and Sam Peltzman, "Toward a More General Theory of Regulation," *Journal of Law and Economics*, 1976, pp. 211–240. A criticism of these theories can be found in R. Posner, "Theories of Economic Regulation," *Bell Journal of Economics and Management Science*, Autumn 1974, pp. 335–358, and J. Hirschleifer, "Comment," *Journal of Law and Economics*, August 1976, pp. 241–244.

ensure security of tenure. (The price of wealth transfers is taken to be votes.) The number of votes the political regulator gets depends on such factors as the total transfers to the beneficiary group, costs of forming the beneficiary group, mitigation of opposition, lobbying, and the probability of opposition by the taxed group.

The economic theory of regulation gives some insights into the government regulatory process. It provides an explanation for why "inefficient" regulations may come about. The politician process will introduce a regulation whenever the regulators and the beneficiary group can agree on a price. The economic theory has its critics as well. Posner argues that though the economic theory is an important advance over competing theories, it does not enable us to predict specific industries in which regulation will be found.[21] The theory does not tell us what number of members in the beneficiary group will maximize the likelihood of regulation. For instance, agriculture (with farm subsidies) is not a very concentrated industry, whereas telephone and electric utilities are, and all of these are regulated. Posner argues that the economic theory is "still so spongy that virtually any observation can be reconciled with the theory." However, as Stigler argues, the main contribution of the economic theory is that it tells us to look, as precisely and carefully as we can, at who gains and who loses, and how much, when we seek to explain a regulatory policy.[22]

19.11 CONSUMER PROTECTION

Governments formulate several regulations to "protect" consumers from exploitation by producers or special interest groups. Sometimes this exploitation occurs because consumers are not well informed, and in this case the government regulations serve a useful function. In other cases the government policies, although intended to "protect" the consumer, might actually do more harm than good. This is particularly so where governments start tinkering with prices as in the case of agricultural price support programs, minimum wage laws, and maximum interest rates.

The following is a partial list of different forms of consumer protection regulations, each with a different motive and consequence.

1. Requirements that the composition or possible effects of commodities be disclosed to consumers through labels or in advertising. For instance, in the case of tobacco products, each advertisement has a footnote: "SURGEON GENERAL'S WARNING: Smoking By Pregnant Women May Result in Fetal Injury, Premature Birth, And Low Birth Weight." The effectiveness of this warning is open to question. There was once a cartoon in the *New Yorker* where one of the employees of a company manufacturing hot dogs asks: "Of course, the consumers have a right to know what is in a hot dog. But do they *really* want to know it?"

[21] Posner, "Theories of Economic Regulation," pp. 347–348.

[22] A critical appraisal of various theories of regulation can be found in Paul L. Joskow and Roger G. Noll, "Regulation in Theory and Practice: An Overview," in Gary Fromm, ed., *Studies in Public Regulation*, Cambridge, Mass., MIT, 1983.

2. Requirements that commodities meet minimum standards prescribed by the government as in the case of milk, meats, drugs, and cars. We discussed earlier the case of pollution standards in Section 19.4.1. The analysis of standards for different commodities is similar.

3. Prohibition of the sale of various goods such as drugs and guns. In the United States from 1920 to 1933 there was prohibition of the manufacture, sale, or transportation of alcoholic beverages. This period, called the Prohibition Era, became famous for extreme violence and a wild way of life. The widespread lawlessness gave the 1920s its nickname "Roaring Twenties." In Section 2.7.4 of Chapter 2, we presented an analysis of illegal activities.

4. Setting of maximum prices. An example of this is setting maximum interest rates with the idea of protecting individuals from "overcharging" by banks. Another example is that of "rent control" to protect renters from "exploitation" by landlords. We have discussed price controls in general in Section 2.7.3 of Chapter 2. We have also discussed rent control in Section 10.9.2 of Chapter 10. There we argued that it is not necessarily true that renters are "exploited" by landlords and analyzed the consequences of rent control. In the case of interest rate ceilings, there would be many consumers who would not be able to obtain loans at any price. During recent years there have been many suggestions made to put a ceiling on the interest rates charged on credit cards. Many of the big banks have been charging enormously high rates (18 to 20 percent) on Mastercard and Visa accounts. The banks argue that they have to maintain such high rates because of high delinquency rates on loans. However, the banks at the same time send credit cards to a large number of consumers with questionable credit and lure them into the "credit card trap." The argument against interest rate ceilings is the usual one—that it prevents some customers from obtaining credit at any price, even if they are willing to pay. However, it is also true that banks indulge in a credit card campaign. The proper action for the government is to make consumers aware of the banks that charge lower rates and to make banks disclose the true costs of credit. Dissemination of information rather than interest rate ceilings would be the proper form of consumer protection.

5. Restrictions on persons permitted to supply certain commodities or services. Examples are qualifications and registration requirements for lawyers, medical practitioners, and teachers. The problems associated with these restrictions are discussed in the next section on occupational licensing. Another regulation is that of allowing only doctors to prescribe drugs. Some of the drugs have such minor side effects that pharmacists can safely prescribe them. Thus, the restriction that all prescription drugs have to be recommended by doctors alone is not really consumer protection. In many cases consumers are hurt because they have to bear the unnecessary costs of going to a doctor.

6. Compulsory education for children. This restriction is imposed because of the externalities arising from the consumption of education.

There is no end to the list of consumer protection policies. The above discussion gives an idea of the different types of policies and their consequences to the consumer. Some of the policies, however, have curious legal implications. There is an amusing example of this provided by Stigler.[23] A professor of finance at the Harvard Business School taught his class how to predict short-term interest rates based on a regression model. The model worked well for the period 1960 to 1968. A 1969 graduate of the school used the model he had learned while working for a respected company. The model, however, did not predict well for 1969 and 1970, and the graduate lost his job. He then sued the Harvard Business School and the professor, charging that the professor had taught him something that was demonstrably false. The lower court ruled in favor of the school and the professor, but, on appeal, this decision was overturned. The judge argued that: "It seems paradoxical beyond endurance to rule that a manufacturer of shampoos may not endanger a student's scalp but a premier educational institution is free to stuff his skull with nonsense." On further appeal the case was decided in favor of the school and the teacher. What this suggests is that just as banks and financial institutions have to disclose details of interest rates on credit according to the Truth in Lending Act of 1968, universities should conform to a "Truth in Teaching Act." However, since there is no such thing as "the truth" that professors can teach, all that such an act can do is make universities provide a disclaimer: "Whatever you have learned at this citadel of learning cannot be mechanically applied in practice."

19.12   OCCUPATIONAL LICENSING

Licensing requires that a person cannot engage in an activity without a license from a duly recognized authority.[24] Thus, doctors and lawyers are licensed by state authorities with the permission of the professional bodies, the American Medical Association (AMA) and the American Bar Association (ABA), respectively. Practicing without a license in these areas is an offense punishable by civil and/or criminal sanctions. Licensing is a stricter requirement than *certification*. Certification implies that the person with a certificate from a recognized authority has the required competence in that area. A degree in education certifies that the teacher is qualified to teach. However, some individuals, without a degree in education, are also hired as teachers. Universities often expect professors to have a Ph.D. degree. But some professors continue to teach even if they do not have a Ph.D. degree, and it is not a civil or criminal offense.

Occupational licensure is widespread: lawyers, doctors, pharmacists, accountants, dentists, sanitarians, psychologists, veterinarians, barbers, and so on. "Hypertrichologists are licensed in Connecticut, where they remove unsightly hair with the solemnity appropriate to their high sounding title."[25]

The main arguments in favor of licensing are:

1. It is difficult for consumers to obtain and appraise information (as to who is a good doctor, a good lawyer, or a good barber).

[23]George J. Stigler, *The Citizen and the State: Essay on Regulation,* University of Chicago Press, Chicago, 1975, pp. 189–191.

[24]The discussion here is based on Chapter IX titled "Occupational Licensure," in Milton Friedman, *Capitalism and Freedom,* University of Chicago Press, Chicago, 1962.

[25]Quoted in ibid., p. 140, from a book by Walter Gelhorn: *Individual Freedom and Governmental Restraints,* Louisiana State University Press, Baton Rouge, La., 1956.

2. Potential risks of mistakes are great (an incompetent doctor can produce a lasting disability in a patient, an incompetent lawyer can ruin a case, an incompetent plumber can ruin the pipes, and so on).

3. Spillover and neighborhood effects can occur.

The first argument can be adequately solved by certification. It does not justify licensing. The second argument also does not justify licensing. If a plumber ruins the pipes, it is up to the customer and the plumber to settle the score. If a physician harms a patient (and only the patient), then the physician and the patient can settle the damages between themselves. It is actually the last argument, neighborhood effects, that is a relevant justification for licensing. The simplest and most obvious example is that of physicians, who by treating their patients poorly, unleash an epidemic. In this case both the physicians and the rest of society would be interested in having a licensing scheme whereby only "competent" physicians can practice medicine and, thus, prevent epidemics.

However, the main justification often offered for licensure is not this neighborhood effect but that individuals are incapable of judging the abilities of a doctor, lawyer, plumber, or barber. They must be protected against their own ignorance. If the occupation of plumbing is to be restricted to those who have the competence to do a good plumbing job, clearly only plumbers are capable of judging who is a competent plumber. If the occupation of medicine is to be restricted to only competent doctors, clearly only doctors are capable of judging who is competent. Although this argument appears plausible, in practice the professional bodies granting licenses in their respective professions have used the licensing power as an entry-controlling device to ensure a high level of income for the practitioners of that profession. The result has invariably been the establishment of monopoly power by the restriction of entry, and nowhere has this been more evident than in the case of medicine, where the AMA has exercised strong power in restricting entry.

The AMA is perhaps the strongest trade union in the United States.[26] It limits the number of people who can enter the medical profession. The reason it has such great power is that in almost every state in the United States a person must be licensed to practice medicine, and to get a license doctors must graduate from an approved school. In almost every state the list of approved schools is identical to the list of schools approved by the Council on Medical Education and Hospitals of the AMA. The licensure provision is, thus, the key to the effective control the AMA has. The argument usually given for controlling entry is that the members of the medical profession want to raise what they regard as the standards of quality of the profession. This argument, however, may be only a rationalization that is given to restrict entry and ensure a high income for those in the medical profession. It is not true that every minor ailment requires a high-quality physician to treat it. Hence, although the average quality of service for those who get medical care could be higher with restriction of entry than without, if we take into account the large number of cases that do not get medical care, the average quality might be sub-

---

[26]See Reuben A. Kessel, "The AMA and the Supply of Physicians," in R. H. Coase and M. H. Miller, eds., *Essays in Applied Price Theory by Reuben A. Kessel*, University of Chicago Press, Chicago, 1980, pp. 37–53 for a discussion of the role of the AMA in the restriction of medical care in the U.S.

stantially lower than if there were free entry. The reasoning is similar to the argument that if we restrict automobile output to only a fixed number of Cadillacs, then the quality of automobile service will be higher than it is now.

Even the argument that the average quality of medical care (for those who obtain it) is higher with restriction of entry might not be correct. As Friedman argues, "Under the interpretation of the statutes forbidding unauthorized practice of medicine, many things are restricted to licensed physicians that could perfectly well be done by technicians and other skilled people who do not have a Cadillac medical training."[27] The talents of many well-trained physicians who could devote full-time energies to research and advancement of medical knowledge are perhaps wasted in the performance of tasks that could be left to technicians. Under free entry there would be a hierarchy of physicians qualified to serve different tasks: treating minor ailments, treating major ailments, and doing research. Under these conditions, the quality of medical care would improve over time because of increased research.

Nor is it true that every physician or surgeon currently practicing is competent. Currently, it is not easy to get physicians to testify against a fellow physician facing the sanction of being denied the right to practice. Thus, it is very difficult for private individuals to collect from physicians and surgeons for malpractice. Nor are medical practitioners supposed to say anything bad about another member of the profession. Thus, knowledge about the competence of different physicians and surgeons is rarely available. Once a medical practitioner gets certified by the AMA, nothing more needs to be said. High income is also ensured by the restriction of entry even if the quality of care provided by the medical practitioner deteriorates.

One other consequence of restricting the amount of conventional medical care is the rise in the number of chiropractors and other substitutes. There is also a tremendous growth in the "health industry"—health clubs, health foods, and so on. Some of these developments are not bad, but they have been receiving excessive attention because of the high cost of conventional medical care.

All this discussion on the quality of medical care in the United States and the effect of the policies of the AMA suggests that entry requirements are not an obvious method for improving the quality of the members of the profession. Friedman cites an amusing example of entry requirements for barbers in the state of Maryland (the entry requirement law was subsequently declared invalid by the courts).[28] This law required that "neophyte barbers must receive formal instruction in the scientific fundamentals for barbering, hygiene, bacteriology, histology of the hair, skin, nails, muscles and nerves, structure of the face and neck, elementary chemistry relating to sterilization and antiseptics, diseases of the skin, hair, glands and nails, haircutting, shaving and arranging, dressing, coloring, bleaching, and tinting of the hair." Whoever wrote this law has shown some technical skill.

Since the preceding discussion of the AMA by Friedman and Kessel, some changes have taken place in the medical profession. In the early 1960s economists were blaming the AMA for creating a shortage of doctors by keeping a tight reign on medical school enrollments, a policy that was claimed to be responsible for

[27]Friedman, *Capitalism and Freedom,* p. 156.
[28]Ibid., p. 142.

pushing up physicians' fees. Since then barriers to entry have been substantially lowered and the number of doctors has expanded rapidly. This expansion has taken place through a rise in medical school enrollment from some 32,000 per year in the early 1960s to over 80,000 in the late 1980s, as well as a substantial influx of doctors from foreign medical schools. The number of doctors consequently expanded from about 259,000 in 1960 to about 553,000 in 1985. This increase has been higher than the rate of population growth and, hence, the number of doctors per 100,000 population has increased from around 146 in 1960 to 231 in 1985. With all this increase, however, the costs of medical care have risen more than twice as fast as the consumer price index. Why is this so?

There are several reasons for this paradox.[29]

1. Though physicians account directly for less than 20 percent of total health care costs, they virtually control the total process of health care: prescription of drugs, office visits, admission to hospitals, and the course of treatment. An important feature of the medical market is that consumers are uncertain about the quantity, quality, and price of the medical care they require. The specialized nature of medical practice, the anxiety of patients about their health, and the emergency of some medical problems, all contribute to the fact that decisions are left to the doctors. They "call the tune."

2. The widespread use of health insurance and the Medicaid and Medicare programs where payment is made by a third party contributes to the ineffectiveness of price constraints on consumption of health care services.

3. Many have even suggested that doctors will either raise their fees or induce demand for added treatment when more physicians enter their service area (see Example 2.7 in Chapter 2). There is no economic reasoning for this "inducement hypothesis," though there is substantial empirical evidence in its favor. One possible argument is that since advertising and overt competition are suppressed, the increased number of physicians reduces the amount of information consumers obtain about their skill levels and the prices charged.

In summary, the high price of health care can no longer be blamed on the restriction of entry into the medical profession by the AMA as in the early 1960s. The growth in Medicare and Medicaid programs and other types of third party insurance, the physicians' control over the total health care costs, and the "inducement hypothesis" explain why the price of health care has risen so dramatically in spite of a substantial increase in the number of doctors per capita.[30]

19.13 SOME APPLICATIONS TO TRANSPORTATION

The principles of private and social costs that were discussed in the beginning sections of this chapter can be illustrated with applications in transportation economics, for example, highway congestion and optimal tolls and mass transit.

---

[29]See Example 2.7: "Supplier Induced Demand: The Case of Physicians" in Chapter 2, and Example 7.3: "Why Are Medical Costs Out of Control" in Chapter 7. Also, see the discussion on medical insurance in Section 9.10.2 of Chapter 9 and the discussion on moral hazard in Chapter 21 (Section 21.7).

[30]See "Why More Doctors Won't Mean Lower Bills," *Business Week,* May 11, 1981, pp. 130 and 135.

19.13.1 Highway congestion and optimal tolls

The costs of automobile travel consist of: (1) costs of vehicle operation, and (2) time costs of travel. There are other unforeseeable costs of being involved in an accident. The greater the highway congestion, the slower the traffic moves, and all these costs increase.

With average costs rising, marginal costs exceed average costs. Thus, an additional vehicle on the road, by increasing the overall cost of traffic, will impose a positive (though small) cost on *all* the vehicles on the road. By setting the price at marginal cost, we get the socially optimal level of highway congestion. However, the highway toll will not be equal to the marginal cost. The drivers pay their average costs and pay the difference between marginal cost and average cost as the toll. This is shown in Figure 19.11. *DD* is the demand curve, *MC* and *AC* are, respectively, the marginal cost and average cost curves. The optimal level of road congestion is *OC*, and the optimum toll is *AB*. *OF* would be the level of congestion without any tolls.

Note that in Figure 19.11 *OG* is the constant vehicle operating cost (assumed for simplicity to be the same for each vehicle), and *GH* is the minimum average cost per mile for the trip. (This includes fuel costs and time costs.) For simplicity we have drawn *AC* and *MC* as straight lines. Since *OH* represents the minimum average cost, at this point *MC* = *AC*. For the demand curve, the vertical axis is the price (cost per mile) and the horizontal axis is the number of miles driven which, in our example, is directly proportional to the level of congestion on the road.

19.13.2 Mass transit

Suppose that a subway (or bus system) is used for transportation. The subway riders get some benefits, and by equating the marginal benefits and marginal costs, we get the price that users of the subway system pay. This is shown in Figure 19.12. MB_s is the marginal benefit curve of subway users. *MC* is the marginal cost

FIGURE 19.11 Optimal tolls on highways.

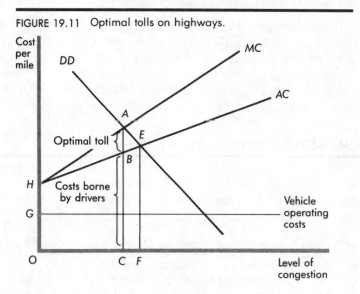

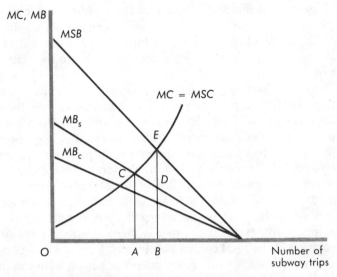

FIGURE 19.12 Optimal pricing of mass transit.

curve for subway use. The equilibrium quantity is *OA*, and the eqilibrium price is *AC*.

However, the subway system confers benefits on car drivers through reduced congestion and traffic time. In the calculation of total benefits to society this ought to be taken into account. This benefit curve for car owners is shown as MB_c In Figure 19.12. However, the *MC* curve represents the full marginal social cost. Summing the two benefits MB_c and MB_s, we get the marginal social benefits as *MSB*.

The intersection of *MSB* and *MC* curves gives *OB* as the optimal level of output. However, since the demand curve for subway users is MB_s, to induce subway users to increase the trips to *OB* the price has to be reduced to *BD*. Thus, the optimal price is *BD*, and the optimal output *OB*. However, if the price is *BD*, the marginal costs are not fully covered (the shortfall is *DE*). But a shortfall in revenues can be covered by taxes on car users. Also, if the subway system increases property values, then we have to include another marginal benefit of property owners. Now the total *MB* curve is obtained as a summation of the *MB* curves for car drivers, subway users, and property owners.

19.14 SUMMARY AND CONCLUSIONS

If production or consumption involves a positive externality, then the competitive output will be less than the socially optimal output. If production or consumption involves a negative externality, then the competitive output will be greater than the socially optimal output. The socially optimal output can be brought about by taxing the party imposing the external cost or subsidizing the party contributing the external benefit. The socially optimal output occurs where marginal social benefit equals marginal social cost.

Coase argued that the presence of externalities does not necessarily warrant government intervention because intervention is itself costly, and private deals could achieve the same result. Coase further argued that it makes no difference to the allocation of resources how the property rights to the contestable resource are assigned.

There are three types of policies designed to achieve the optimal level of pollution. Under the popular pollution standards scheme, the EPA estimates the justifiable volume of discharge from each source and sets a quota at that amount. The permissable discharge must then be allocated among the various producers. The policy is inefficient because differences in pollution abatement costs are frequently ignored. Under the pollution taxation method there is a tax charged per unit of waste dumped. Under pollution licensing, pollution permits are auctioned off and can then be resold. There are strict limits on the number of permits.

A pure public good is characterized by nonexcludability and nonrivalry in consumption. Nonexcludability means that individuals who do not contribute to the provision of the good cannot be excluded from the benefit once it is produced. Nonrivalry in consumption means that one person's consumption of the public good's benefits does not reduce the availability of benefits to others. It is economically inefficient to exclude anyone from the consumption of a public good, once it is produced. The provision of a public good should be expanded to the point where MSB equals MSC. The MSB curve is derived by vertically summing the individuals' marginal value or demand curves.

A Lindahl equilibrium occurs where $MSB = MSC$ for the public good, each individual pays a price equal to marginal value, and production costs are covered. The Clarke-Groves tax is a method for providing individuals with the incentive to correctly reveal their preferences for a public good.

There are two theories of government intervention for the purpose of improving the allocation of resources. According to the public interest theory, government intervention is needed to correct market failures that arise because of monopoly, externalities, or the existence of public goods. According to the economic theory, regulation is an economic good. The amount of regulation is determined by demand for and supply of intervention.

Governments formulate many regulations to protect consumers from exploitation by producers or other groups. In many instances, consumer information programs would be a better approach.

The most common argument in favor of licensing is that consumers are unable to evaluate the competence of members of certain professions and mistakes in assessing competence can be very costly. Certification rather than licensing would solve this problem. Furthermore, since current members of the profession grant licenses, licensing power has been used to restrict entry and establish monopoly power.

When highways are congested, each additional car imposes an external cost on all other drivers. A toll can be used to bring about the optimal amount of highway congestion. The marginal social benefit curve for mass transit is the vertical sum of the marginal benefit to subway riders and the marginal benefit to car drivers. To bring about the optimal quantity of ridership, the subway ticket price must be less than MC.

KEY TERMS

Coase Theorem
Economic Theory of
  Government Intervention
  (or Regulation)
Free Rider Problem
Incentive-Compatible
  Mechanism
Lindahl Equilibrium
Marginal External Benefit
Marginal External Cost
Marginal Private Benefit

Marginal Private Cost
Marginal Social Benefit
Marginal Social Cost
Market Failure
Negative Externality in
  Consumption
Negative Externality in
  Production
Nonexcludability
Nonrivalry in Consumption
Pollution Licenses

Pollution Standards
Pollution Taxes
Positive Externality in
  Consumption
Positive Externality in
  Production
Public Interest Theory
  of Government
  Intervention
Pure Public Good
Socially Optimal Output

QUESTIONS

1. Give an example of a good or service whose production involves an external benefit or an external cost. Give an example of a good or service whose consumption involves an external cost or benefit.

2. What is the economic justification for government subsidization of education?

3. When the consumption of a good involves external benefits, can subsidizing the producers bring about the socially optimal output? Why or why not?

4. Explain why it is Pareto inefficient to exclude anyone from consuming a pure public good once it is produced.

5. Is a radio broadcast a pure public good? How does the private sector manage to provide radio broadcasts? Do you think that the socially optimal quantity is provided? Why or why not?

6. Suppose that there are empty seats in your classroom. Is your economics lecture then characterized by nonrivalry in consumption? Can an individual who doesn't pay tuition be excluded? Is it efficient to exclude those who don't pay? Does the situation change if the classroom is crowded?

7. Give an example of a good which is characterized by nonexcludability but *not* by nonrivalry in consumption. Give an example of a good which is characterized by nonrivalry in consumption but *not* by nonexcludability. Which type of good do you think the private sector is more likely to provide? Why?

8. Why is the free-rider problem more likely to occur when a large number of people are involved?

9. Under Lindahl pricing, is it possible for an individual who benefits from a public good to be assigned a price of 0? Why?

10. With an external cost in production, is society clearly better off under perfect competition than with a monopoly in that industry? Why?

INTERTEMPORAL CHOICE

20.1 INTRODUCTION

In the previous chapters we ignored the time dimension, except to consider the distinction between the short run and the long run and the choice of present vs. future consumption. We will now examine problems that explicitly involve time.

Almost all problems in economics involve making choices that have consequences over a period of time. Consumers have to choose how much of their income to spend now and how much to save for the future. Producers have to decide how much to invest in new equipment now that will generate output over a number of years. Students have to decide how many more years of schooling they are going to "invest" in before entering the job market. All these choices involving time are called *intertemporal choices*.

In real life, decisions involving the future are even more complex because few aspects of the future are certain. Thus, intertemporal decision analysis must take into account uncertainty. We will, however, omit this problem and assume that future costs and returns are known. This is just a matter of simplifying our analysis and proceeding step by step.

Before we analyze the problem of intertemporal choice we have to define two concepts that enable us to evaluate some future costs and returns at the present time: *discounting* and *present values*.

20.2 DISCOUNTING AND PRESENT VALUES

We all know that $100 in hand today is not the same as $100 to be paid in one year. We would prefer the $100 today. But would we prefer the $100 today to $105 to be paid in 1 year? The answer depends on the rate we use to discount future payments. Suppose that we can deposit the $100 today at 10 percent interest. In one year we will have $110 or (1 + interest rate)($100). In this case, $100 today is equivalent to $110 in one year. We would clearly not prefer the promise of $105 to be paid in 1 year to $100 today. We can, however, work backward and calculate the present worth of $105 payable in one year. $105/(1.10) equals approximately $95.45. That is, $95.45 could be invested today to yield $105 in one year's time. The $95.45 is called the "present value" of the future $105. Thus, the *present value* (often abbreviated *PV*) of a future payment is the amount received today that would be equivalent in value to the future payment. The *discount rate* is the rate of interest we use in converting a future payment to its present value.

The above example considered a single payment, but sometimes payments are received over a period of time. Suppose the annual rate of interest is r, and it is constant over the entire period we are considering. We will, henceforth, express r in decimal form so that a 10 percent rate of interest means $r = 0.10$. Then $100 today is worth $100(1 + r)$ a year from now. This amount can be invested again at a rate of interest r to get $100(1 + r)(1 + r) = 100(1 + r)^2$ at the end of 2 years. At the end of 3 years we get $100(1 + r)^3$, and so on.

Conversely, if we are promised $100 now and $100 at the end of each of the next 3 years, the present values are calculated as follows:

$100 for the amount received now

$\dfrac{\$100}{(1 + r)}$ for the amount received a year from now

$\dfrac{\$100}{(1 + r)^2}$ for the amount received 2 years from now

$\dfrac{\$100}{(1 + r)^3}$ for the amount received 3 years from now

The total present value for this payment stream is, therefore,

$$\$100 \left[1 + \frac{1}{1 + r} + \frac{1}{(1 + r)^2} + \frac{1}{(1 + r)^3} \right]$$

For different values of r we can calculate the present value. For example, when $r = 0.05$ or at a 5 percent rate of interest, the present value is:

$$PV = (\$100 + \$95.24 + \$90.70 + \$86.38) = \$372.32$$

For $r = 0.10, 0.15,$ and 0.20 the present values are as follows (one can easily check these on a hand calculator):

r	PV
0.10	$348.68
0.15	328.32
0.20	310.64

As the interest rate rises, the present value of the income stream falls.

Although many income streams are finite in time, sometimes it is convenient to talk of perpetual income streams. Suppose we buy a bond from which we receive interest of $100 at the end of this year and $100 at the end of every year thereafter, forever. This is called a *perpetual bond* or *perpetuity*. The present value of this income stream is

$$PV = \frac{\$100}{1 + r} + \frac{\$100}{(1 + r)^2} + \frac{\$100}{(1 + r)^3} + \cdots$$

$$PV = \$100 \left[\frac{1}{1 + r} + \frac{1}{(1 + r)^2} + \frac{1}{(1 + r)^3} + \cdots \right]$$

Now, we know that the sum of the infinite series $x + x^2 + x^3 + \ldots$ is $x/(1 - x)$ provided that x is less than 1 in absolute value. Since $1/(1 + r) < 1$, we can define $x = 1/(1 + r)$ and substitute to get

$$\frac{1}{1+r} + \frac{1}{(1+r)^2} + \frac{1}{(1+r)^3} + \ldots = \frac{\dfrac{1}{1+r}}{\left(1 - \dfrac{1}{1+r}\right)} = \frac{1}{r}$$

Hence, the present value of our perpetuity is $100(1/r) = \$100/r$. Suppose the rate of interest is $r = 0.05$. Then the present value (and, hence, the price) of the bond is \$2,000. If $r = 0.10$, the price of the bond falls to \$1,000. Thus, the higher the rate of interest, the lower the price of the bond. So, in this case of a perpetual bond, the bond price varies inversely with the rate of interest.

In actual practice, bonds are not perpetuities. They have a fixed maturity. Most bonds pay interest every year and are redeemable at face value at the end of the maturity period. But the examples we have given show that bond prices fall when interest rates rise and bond prices rise when interest rates fall.

20.3   CHOICE OF INVESTMENT PROJECTS

The net present value rule

One of the many important applications of the use of present values is the choice of investment projects. Many investment projects such as the building of factories, dams, and power plants involve costs at the beginning of the project and return revenues from the project only after a certain time. In these cases there are two questions to consider: (1) Should an investment project be undertaken? (2) Given a number of investment projects that are worth undertaking, which is the best or how should we rank them?

The present value method provides an answer to both of these questions. In answering these questions we compute net present value, denoted by *NPV*. It is defined as

$$NPV = PV \text{ of benefits (or revenues)} - PV \text{ of costs}$$

The answer to the first question is: Invest if $NPV > 0$. The answer to the second question is: Rank the projects according to *NPV*. Choose the project with the highest *NPV* first.

Where do these answers come from? When we begin talking about multiperiod decisions, profits in various periods are no longer independent. Thus, the goal of profit maximization in each period is no longer reasonable for the firm. Instead, we treat the goal of the firm as the maximization of the present value of the entire stream of profits. Now, if *NPV* for a project is positive, then that project increases the present value of profits and, hence, should be undertaken. Similarly, projects with the highest *NPVs* add the most to the present value of profits and, thus, should be undertaken first. A few examples will illustrate this reasoning.

In Table 20.1 we present the stream of costs and returns for a hypothetical investment project over a number of years. Costs are assumed to be \$200 for each

TABLE 20.1   Stream of Costs and Returns for a Hypothetical Investment Project

Year	Costs	Returns
1	$200	0
2	200	0
3	200	0
4	0	$100
5	0	100
6	0	100
7	0	100
8	0	100
9	0	100

of the first 3 years. The returns from the project begin only after the third year but then continue forever at $100 per year. Let us assume that all the numbers in Table 20.1 are beginning-of-period numbers. That is, costs are due and returns are received at the beginning of the year. We can now compute present values of costs and returns.

$$PV \text{ of costs} = \$200 + \frac{\$200}{1 + r} + \frac{\$200}{(1 + r)^2}$$

and

$$PV \text{ of returns} = \$100 \left[\frac{1}{(1 + r)^3} + \frac{1}{(1 + r)^4} + \cdots \right]$$

The stream of returns is the same as a perpetuity of $100 with the first two payments missing. Thus, the PV of returns is equal to $\$100(1/r) - [\$100/(1 + r)] - [\$100/(1 + r)^2]$. This is also equal to $\$100/[r(1 + r)^2]$. We can now calculate the PV of costs and returns for different values of r. These are shown in Table 20.2. Thus, if the rate of interest is 5 percent or 10 percent, the NPV is positive and the project

TABLE 20.2   Present Values of Costs and Returns at Different Interest Rates

Interest Rates r	PV of Costs	PV of Returns	NPV
0.05	571.88	1,814.06	1,242.18
0.10	547.11	826.45	279.34
0.15	525.14	504.10	−21.04
0.20	505.55	347.22	−158.33

is worth undertaking. But it is not worthwhile if the rate of interest is 15 or 20 percent or higher.

The *NPV* criterion assumes that there is no uncertainty about the stream of costs and revenues and that there are no limits on the amount of funds the investor can borrow. Some alternative criteria for choice among investment projects are discussed at length in textbooks on corporate finance. The criteria suggested are payback period, average return on book, internal rate of return, and profitability index (benefit-cost ratio). However, all these rules have shortcomings, and, with suitable modifications, the *NPV* criterion can be shown to be the best of all criteria. We will not discuss these alternative criteria in detail, but we will mention some of them briefly, and indicate their relationship to the *NPV* criterion.

The profitability rate criterion

The *profitability rate* that is often referred to in books on finance is simply the ratio of *PV* of returns to *PV* of costs. If this ratio is > 1, then the investment project is worth undertaking. Otherwise, it is not. But if this ratio > 1, then $NPV > 0$. Thus, the *NPV* rule and the profitability rate rule always give the same answer to the questions of whether an investment is worthwhile.

The internal rate of return rule

The *internal rate of return IRR* is the rate of interest at which *PV* of returns $=$ *PV* of costs. In other words, it is the rate of interest at which the *NPV* is 0. In the example in Table 20.2 this rate falls somewhere between 0.10 and 0.15. For $r = 0.14$ we have *PV* of costs $= 529.33$ and *PV* of returns $= 549.62$. Hence, $NPV = +20.29$. Since $NPV = -21.04$ at $r = 0.15$, the internal rate of return will be roughly 0.145 or 14.5 percent.

The internal rate of return rule for investment says to invest if $r < IRR$. Otherwise, do not invest. It might appear that this rule gives the same answer to our question about investment as the *NPV* rule. This is true, however, only if the *NPV* is a smoothly declining function of the rate of interest r, as it is in Table 20.2. If, instead, there are multiple solutions to the internal rate of return, then the *IRR* rule gives an implausible answer. For instance, in Figure 20.1, $NPV = 0$ for two values of r. Both r_1 and r_2 are internal rates of return. If the market rate of interest is less than r_1, then according to the *IRR* rule we should invest. However, for values

FIGURE 20.1   Multiple solutions to internal rate of return.

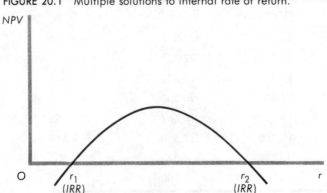

of $r < r_1$, net present value is negative, and so we lose money. Thus, we should not use the *IRR* rule in these cases.

This example is not artificial. There are many real world cases where investment projects have *terminal costs*. These are cases where there are large clean up costs after a few years of operation. For example, in strip mining of coal, or phosphate mining, there are returns during the mining process but there are large costs of land reclamation after the mining is done. Many chemical plants have large cleanup costs after a few years of dumping of wastes. It is in cases such as these that problems with the use of the *IRR* arise.

Let us consider an example of a coal mine with 3 years of operation. The costs and returns are as follows:

Year	Costs	Returns	Explanation
1	4,000	0	Costs of opening the mine
2	0	25,000	Returns from the output
3	25,000	0	Costs of land reclamation and closing the mine

All costs and returns accrue at the beginning of the year.

The *NPV* for this mining project for different rates of interest is shown in Table 20.3. Note that $NPV = 0$ for $r = 0.25$ and $r = 4.00$. Thus, the internal rate of return has the values: 25 percent and 400 percent! However, at market rates of interest less than 25 percent, *NPV* is negative. The *PV* of costs is higher than the *PV* of returns, and, hence, the investment is not worth undertaking. The graph of *NPV* against r for this example will be like the one shown in Figure 20.1.

The above example shows that investments with large terminal costs at a future date are not worth undertaking unless interest rates are high. Projects with returns in the near future and costs in the distant future become less and less attractive as the rate of interest *falls* (over some range). This is just the converse of the other

TABLE 20.3   Net Present Values from the Operation of a Coal Mine

r	PV of Costs	PV of Returns	NPV
0.05	26,676	23,810	−2,866
0.10	24,661	22,727	−1,934
0.20	21,361	20,833	−528
0.25	20,000	20,000	0
0.50	15,111	16,667	1,556
1.00	10,250	12,500	2,250
2.00	6,778	8,333	1,555
4.00	5,000	5,000	0

result we found earlier that projects with costs in the near future and returns in the distant future become less and less attractive as the interest rate *rises*.

Choice between investment projects

We will now answer the second question: How do we rank different projects? The *NPV* rule says to rank the projects according to their *NPV* and choose the project with the highest *NPV* first. The *IRR* rule says to rank the projects by their *IRR* and choose the project with the highest *IRR* first. The profitability rate rule says: Rank projects by the ratio of *PV* of returns to *PV* of costs and choose the project with the highest ratio. This is also known as the *benefit-cost ratio rule*. We will illustrate these with some examples.

Consider the case of the project with costs and returns as in Table 20.1. We will call this project *A*. Suppose a second project, project *B*, gives the same returns as project *A* ($100 each year after 3 years) but involves a cost of $550 in the first year and no costs in the second and third years. Thus, *PV* of costs for project *B* = $550 at all rates of interest.

Consider, first, the *NPV* rule. If the market rate of interest is 5 percent, so $r = 0.05$, then project *A* has a higher *PV* of costs than project *B*. Since both have the same *PV* of returns, *NPV* for project *A* < *NPV* for project *B*. Thus, project *B* is ranked higher than project *A*. The reverse is the case for $r = 0.10$. At this rate of interest project *A* is ranked higher than project *B*.

Consider the *IRR* rule next. Let us assume that the multiple solution problem we discussed earlier does not exist and the *NPV* is steadily declining as the rate of interest rises. This means that we can use the *IRR* rule to decide whether an investment is worth undertaking or not. We saw earlier that the *IRR* for project *A* is 0.145. For project *B* we find the *IRR* by equating *PV* of returns to *PV* of costs, which is 550 at all rates of interest. Since we saw earlier that *PV* of returns is 549.62 for $r = 0.14$, the *IRR* for project *B* is close to 0.140. Thus, project *A* will be ranked higher than project *B*, *at all rates of interest*.

Finally, the ranking by benefit-cost ratio or the ratio of *PV* of returns to *PV* of costs gives the same answer in this case as the ranking by *NPV*, because the *PV* of returns is the same for the two projects. However, one can easily construct examples where the two criteria will give opposite answers. Consider the following two projects.

	Project 1	Project 2
PV of returns	400	200
PV of costs	100	25
NPV	300	175
Ratio of PV of returns to PV of costs	4	8

Using the *NPV* criterion, project 1 is ranked higher than project 2. Using the profitability ratio criterion, we have the opposite ranking: project 2 is ranked higher than project 1.

The *NPV* criterion is preferred to the other criteria because *NPV* is the net discounted total profit, and we would like to maximize total profit, not profitability rate. The same argument goes for the *IRR* criterion. Implicitly, this criterion assumes that funds can be reinvested at any time, at the *IRR*, which is not the case. The *NPV* criterion, by concentrating on the total net discounted profit, gives the correct answer because this is the quantity we would like to maximize.

In Section 20.7 we will give some examples that use *NPV* in different contexts. But before that we will discuss the problems of intertemporal choices in consumption and production.

20.4 INTERTEMPORAL CONSUMPTION DECISIONS

In Chapter 5 (Section 5.8.1) we considered a consumer's choice between current and future consumption. This is what is known as a two-period model. In other words, we consider only two periods: present and future. In reality there are more time periods over which decisions are made, but the two-period model gives us enough insights into the basic problems.

We will first review the analysis of Chapter 5 (Section 5.8.1) and then extend it to cover different interest rates for borrowing and lending. Let us define the following:

y_0 = current income
y_1 = future income
c_0 = current consumption
c_1 = future consumption
r = rate of interest (for saving and borrowing)

We have to determine c_0 and c_1 given y_0, y_1, and r. We will assume that the consumer's preferences can be represented by indifference curves that are convex, downward sloping, and nonintersecting, as shown in Figure 20.2. What we need now is the budget line. Since the present discounted value of future income y_1 is $y_1/(1 + r)$, maximum current consumption is $w_0 = y_0 + y_1/(1 + r)$. Alternatively, consumers can save their entire present income which will be worth $y_0(1 + r)$ in the future. Thus, maximum future consumption is $w_1 = y_1 + y_0(1 + r) = w_0(1 + r)$. The slope of the budget line is, therefore, equal to $-(1 + r)$.

In Figure 20.2 the consumer's equilibrium is at point A with current consumption c_0 and future consumption c_1. At this point the slope of the indifference curve is equal to the slope of the budget line. We saw in Chapter 4 (Section 4.5) that the slope of the indifference curve (in absolute value) is equal to the ratio of the marginal utilities of c_0 and c_1. Thus, we have the relationship

$$\frac{\text{Marginal utility of } c_0}{\text{Marginal utility of } c_1} = 1 + r$$

at the equilibrium point.

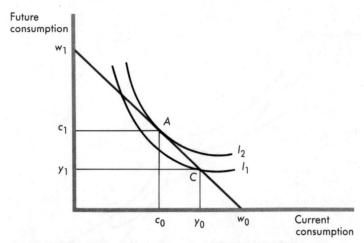

FIGURE 20.2   Choice between current and future consumption.

We discussed in Chapter 5 how the consumer could borrow (or save) to increase (or decrease) current consumption c_0 over current income y_0. In Figure 20.2 the consumer would be at the point C and on indifference curve I_1 if the consumer were unable to borrow or save. But by saving some of the current income for the future, the consumer can reach the point A on the higher indifference curve I_2. One can also show the reverse case—that of the consumer borrowing against future income. Since we discussed this earlier in Chapter 5 we will not go through it again.

We will next consider the impact of a change in the rate of interest. Suppose there is a rise in the rate of interest r. What will happen to current and future consumption? In particular, is the individual better off or worse off? We can show that things can go either way. Figure 20.3 illustrates this point.

In Figure 20.3 BB is the initial budget line. With a rise in the interest rate the budget line rotates to $B'B'$ through the point C, which involves no saving or borrowing.

Now consider two individuals with indifference curves given by I_1, I_1', and I_2, I_2', respectively.[1] Individual 1 is on indifference curve I_1 and moves to a higher indifference curve I_1' when the interest rate rises. However, individual 2, who is on indifference curve I_2, moves to the lower indifference curve I_2'. Note that individual 1 is a saver, with current consumption less than current income, and individual 2 is a borrower, with current consumption higher than current income. Thus, the result makes intuitive sense. A rise in the interest makes savers better off and borrowers worse off.

We can now extend the analysis to consider the case where the consumer faces different interest rates for borrowing and saving. Suppose that the consumer gets an interest rate r_1 for saving and has to pay an interest rate r_2 for borrowing. We will assume that $r_2 > r_1$. This is usually the case. We all know that if we get a 6 percent rate of interest on our savings accounts, we usually pay around 12

---

[1] These are, of course, only portions of the indifference curves.

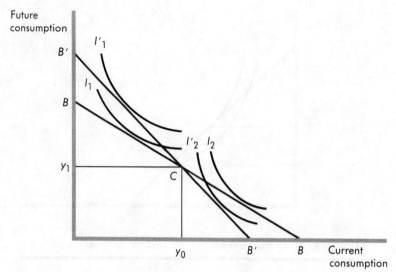

FIGURE 20.3   Effect of an increase in the interest rate on consumer behavior.

percent for our consumer loans. What will the budget line look like under these circumstances? The budget line in this case is shown in Figure 20.4. The consumer can increase current consumption over current income y_0 by converting some or all of future income into current income at the rate of interest r_2. Similarly, the consumer can increase future consumption over y_1 by saving some or all of y_0 at a rate of interest r_1. Since $r_2 > r_1$, the budget line has a kink at the point C, with CB_0 being steeper than CB_1. We can analyze the behavior of the consumer by superimposing the indifference curves on the budget line. Since this analysis is

FIGURE 20.4   Budget line for a consumer who faces different interest rates for borrowing and lending.

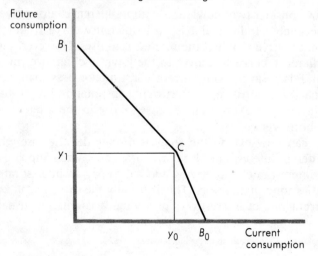

straightforward, we will not pursue it further. We can also study the effect of changes in borrowing and/or saving rates by the same procedure as that used in Figure 20.3.

In the above analysis we implicitly assumed that prices were constant. The consumer is indifferent between various bundles of present and future goods and services. Thus, indifference curves must be expressed in real terms, and consumption must be expressed in real terms. If prices are not constant, then we must adjust for changes in the price level. Let's suppose that

$$P_1 = P_0(1 + g)$$

so that g is the growth rate of prices or the inflation rate. The relationship between maximum real current consumption w_0 and maximum real future consumption w_1 is now

$$w_1 = \frac{w_0(1 + r)}{1 + g}$$

since w_0 invested now will become $w_0(1 + r)$ in the future period but will be worth only $[w_0(1 + r)]/(1 + g)$ in real terms. Thus, the slope of the budget line (in absolute terms) becomes $w_1/w_0 = (1 + r)/(1 + g)$. For example, if the rate of interest is 5 percent and the inflation rate is also 5 percent, the absolute slope of the budget line is $(1 + 0.05)/(1 + 0.05) = 1$. That is, current goods can be substituted for future goods at the rate of 1 to 1.

The impact of a change in the rate of inflation can be easily analyzed by adjusting the slope of the budget line. It should also be noted that the coordinates of the point C in the previous diagrams would be real income in each period.

20.5 INTERTEMPORAL PRODUCTION DECISIONS

In the preceding discussion we considered the equilibrium of a consumer with *given* current income y_0 and future income y_1. We can relax this assumption by considering the production side and the production possibilities. The resources an individual has at hand can be used to produce current goods (or current income y_0) or future goods (or future income y_1). For instance, the resources can be used to produce all consumption goods now or some resources can be used for building better machines that will increase the production of consumption goods in the future. Similarly, the individual can attend school now and increase future productivity or can work more now.

We can depict the production possibilities between current output and future output by a production possibilities curve. This curve is similar to the one we discussed in Section 6.9 of Chapter 6 except that instead of two goods X and Y we have current output y_0 and future output y_1. This is shown in Figure 20.5. By superimposing the indifference curves on the production possibility curve, we can get the optimum for a producer-consumer who has no scope for exchanging current

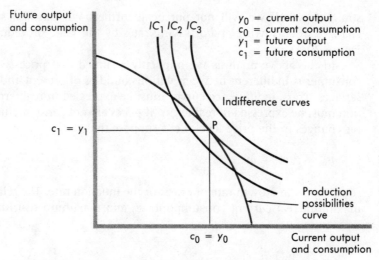

y_0 = current output
c_0 = current consumption
y_1 = future output
c_1 = future consumption

FIGURE 20.5 Equilibrium for the producer-consumer with no exchange.

for future goods or vice versa. In other words, the individual's consumption must equal production in each period. The optimal point is at P in Figure 20.5. The level of utility or satisfaction corresponds to IC_2.

Now if there is a market for present and future goods our producer-consumer can convert present goods into future goods and vice versa. This means that consumption no longer has to equal production in each period. The consumption possibilities are no longer directly constrained by the production possibilities curve.

Let us assume an interest rate of r. An individual producing at point R in Figure 20.6 produces y_0 in the current period and y_1 in the future. Maximum current consumption is w_0 where

$$w_0 = y_0 + \frac{y_1}{(1 + r)}$$

and the individual's maximum future consumption is w_1 where

$$w_1 = y_1 + y_0(1 + r)$$

In fact, the individual producing at R can consume anywhere along the line B_2, which is that person's "budget constraint" or "wealth line." We have seen earlier that the slope of B_2 is $-(1 + r)$.

We can construct a budget line corresponding to each point on the production possibilities curve. Since the interest rate is given to be r, all the budget lines will be parallel. For the individual producing at point T, the budget line is B_3. For the individual producing at S or V, the budget line is B_1.

The individual must now choose the production bundle (which determines the budget line) and the consumption bundle (given the budget line) to maximize satisfaction. Figure 20.7 illustrates the production and consumption equilibrium

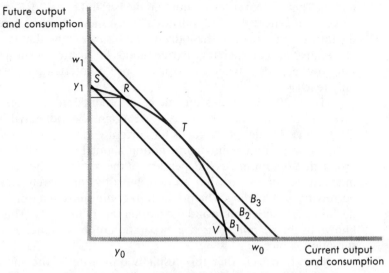

FIGURE 20.6 Budget lines when future goods can be exchanged for current goods and vice versa.

for a saver. Clearly, with a higher budget line, higher indifference curves can be reached. Thus, the individual will choose the production bundle corresponding to the highest possible budget line. In Figure 20.7, this production bundle is T, where a budget line is tangent to the production possibilities curve. The individual, thus, produces y_0 in the current period and y_1 in the future. Next, the consumer must choose the consumption bundle which maximizes satisfaction subject to budget

FIGURE 20.7 Production and consumption equilibrium for the saver.

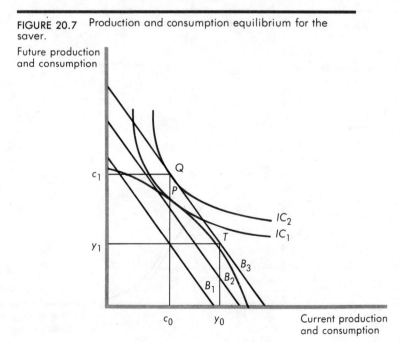

line B_3. The optimal consumption bundle is Q in Figure 20.7, where an indifference curve is tangent to B_3. The individual consumes c_0 in the current period and c_1 in the future. Since $c_0 < y_0$, the individual is a saver. Note that the individual is better off because she can exchange current goods for future consumption. The individual can now reach IC_2, whereas in the absence of intertemporal exchanges she could only reach IC_1.

Figure 20.8 illustrates the choice of production and consumption for a borrower. In this case, $c_0 > y_0$ and $c_1 < y_1$. Again, the individual is better off with the ability to exchange future goods for current goods.

One important point worth noting about Figures 20.7 and 20.8 is that the production optimum T is independent of the nature of the indifference curves. The indifference curves can shift around, but this will merely change the amount of borrowing and lending. The production optimum is determined solely by the production possibilities curve and the market rate of interest r. This result is commonly known as the *separation theorem* (separation of the production optimum from consumption choices).

Note, however, that this result is only true at the individual level. If the preferences of all individuals change, then this will change the aggregate level of borrowing and lending, which, in turn, will change the rate of interest r. This will have an effect on the production optimum. This brings up the question of how the market interest rates are determined, which we will discuss in the next section.

EXAMPLE 20.1 Effects of Price Controls on the Supply of Natural Gas

In Chapter 2 (Section 2.7.3) we discussed the effects of price controls and argued that they result in a decrease in the quantity supplied and an increase in the quantity

FIGURE 20.8 Production and consumption equilibrium for a borrower.

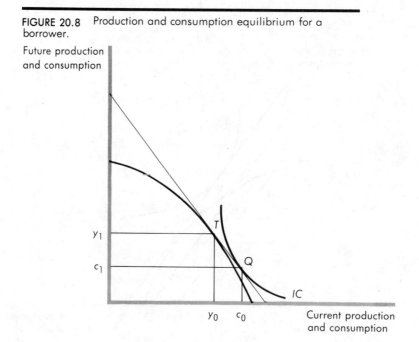

demanded. This result is true for non-storable commodities but not for commodities whose supply can be changed over time. To illustrate the problem we will consider the supply of natural gas.

There are two effects we have to consider: (1) the effect on exploration and, hence, future supply and; (2) the effect on current supply from existing wells.

As far as future exploration is concerned, price controls, if they are effective, will curtail exploration activity because the net present value (*NPV*) of the future stream of earnings will decline and some exploration activity that was marginally profitable before price controls would no longer be undertaken. This would affect future supply of natural gas.

As far as existing wells are concerned, the choice of the producers is how much to supply now as opposed to supplying in future periods. Assuming for simplicity a two-period case, the producers would adjust their current quantity supplied to the point where $P_1 = P_2/(1 + i)$ where P_1 is the current price, P_2 is next period's price, and i is the interest rate.

With prices controlled at $\bar{P}$, since a price $\bar{P}$ received next period is worth only $\bar{P}/(1 + i)$ this time period, it pays the producers to increase the quantity supplied this time period. They will do this to the point where the current market price is equal to $\bar{P}/(1 + i)$. Of course, there is an important geological constraint, namely, that rapid pumping out of existing wells depletes the total supply. In any case, the immediate effect of price controls would be to increase the current quantity supplied, and to create shortages in future time periods.

This seemingly perverse but natural reaction of producers, and the increase in the quantity supplied following price control, might delude politicians and customers into believing that the natural gas producers were overcharging the customers. This would be detrimental to any rational policy making.

20.6   HOW ARE INTEREST RATES DETERMINED?

In the previous section we saw that given the production possibilities curve, the rate of interest determines the production optimum y_0, y_1 and the indifference curves determine the consumption optimum c_0, c_1. Based on this we have some individuals who will be savers and, hence, lenders, and some individuals who will be borrowers. We can aggregate the total amount of lending and borrowing for each rate of interest. This will give us the current demand for borrowed consumption goods and the current supply of loanable consumption goods at the different rates of interest.[2] The resulting demand and supply curves are shown in Figure 20.9. The intersection of these two curves determines the rate of interest.

The individual preferences might change, but as long as the aggregate demand and supply curves do not change, there will be no change in the rate of interest. However, if there is a general shift of preferences for current over future consumption, the demand curve for borrowing will shift to the right and the supply curve will shift to the left. These shifts will occur because of increased borrowing

---

[2]We can, as well, consider the future period and draw the demand and supply curves for future goods. It does not make any difference.

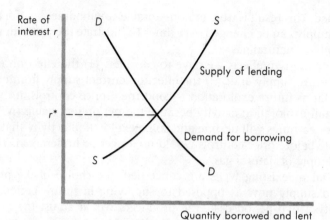

FIGURE 20.9   Determination of the market rate of interest.

by the previous borrowers, and an increase in the number of borrowers because some individuals who were lenders might turn into borrowers. This will result in a rise in the rate of interest, and, as noted earlier, this will result in an optimum production level where y_0 is higher and y_1 is lower. The final equilibrium will be reached where the quantity supplied by lenders is equal to the quantity demanded by the borrowers at an increased level of current production y_0.

20.7   APPLICATIONS

We will now examine several issues that illustrate the importance of the time dimension. First, we will consider the impact of a change in property tax rates on the present value of a home. In particular, we will look at the effects of California's Proposition 13. Next, we will try to answer the question "Are you worth your weight in gold?" by presenting some present value calculations for lifetime earnings. The third application focuses on the "publish or perish" edict facing college faculty and presents some estimates of the value of publications. Finally, in the last section, we will demonstrate that the consumer's decision to purchase a durable good is in many ways similar to the firm's decision to invest. We will consider several aspects of durable goods markets.

20.7.1   Housing prices and Proposition 13

On June 7, 1978, California voters approved a statewide property tax limitation known as Proposition 13. One of the most persuasive arguments in favor of the proposition was that property taxes had increased to such an extent that families could no longer afford to purchase housing. Furthermore, those who lived in rental housing supported the proposition believing that the high taxes contributed to their high rents. This reasoning turned out to be flawed.

The reduced property taxes were instantly capitalized, and housing prices rose. An empirical study done by Kenneth Rosen found that a $1 reduction in property taxes resulted in roughly a $7 increase in property values.[3] Since, as shown in Section 20.2, the present value of an income stream of $1 per year is $1/r$ where r is the rate of interest, this implies that the savings in property taxes were capitalized at the rate of about 14 percent (which was roughly the rate of interest at that time).

As the price of houses increased, all those who had bought houses earlier felt wealthier. However, this wealth could be converted into purchasing power only by selling the house. For those who remained in California, selling the house they owned implied buying another house which also had appreciated in price. Thus, only those who moved out of the state could capture the increase in wealth.

As for rents, they remained unchanged. This is to be expected because the rental price is determined by the demand for and supply of rental housing, and the reduction in property taxes had no effect on either demand or supply in the short run. In the long run, if demand does not change and the supply of rental housing increases, then the rental price will fall. However, property taxes are usually too small a portion of total costs to have any substantial effect on the supply of housing. In large metropolitan areas it is the land values that comprise a major portion of the cost. Thus, the effect of changes in property taxes on the supply of housing in such areas is likely to be small. There is a considerable debate among economists on whether the property tax on rental housing is a tax on profits, and, hence, not shifted to the consumer, or whether it is an excise tax and, thus, largely shifted to the consumer.[4] The evidence in California supports the view that it is more like a profits tax than an excise tax.

20.7.2 Present value of lifetime earnings: Are you worth your weight in gold?

Suppose that you start your career at the age of 25 and you earn an annual income of $30,000 for the next 40 years.[5] At an annual rate of interest of 10 percent, the present value of this income stream is:

$$\frac{\$30,000}{1.1} + \frac{\$30,000}{(1.1)^2} + \ldots + \frac{\$30,000}{(1.1)^{40}} = \$293,371$$

Actually, as a rough approximation (since 40 years is a long enough period to be considered a perpetuity), we can take the present value as $30,000/r$ where r is the rate of interest. At a 10 percent rate of interest, this present value is $300,000.

We can now try to answer the question of whether you are worth your weight in gold. This depends on the price of gold. The price of gold is quoted in dollars per troy ounce, and since there are approximately 14.6 troy ounces per pound, we will take the price of gold as $6,000 per pound (which implies a price of $411 per troy ounce). Thus, you are worth your weight in gold only if your weight is <50 pounds.

[3]Kenneth T. Rosen, "The Impact of Proposition 13 on House Prices in Northern California: A Test of the Interjurisdictional Capitalization Hypothesis," *Journal of Political Economy*, February 1982, pp. 191–200.

[4]For a theoretical discussion of this issue see Peter Mieszkowski, "The Property Tax»An Excise Tax or a Profits Tax?" *Journal of Public Economics*, vol. 1, 1972, pp. 73–96.

[5]See Harry G. Johnson, "Are You Worth Your Weight in Gold?" in Harry G. Johnson and Burton Weisbrod, eds., *The Daily Economist*, Prentice-Hall, Englewood Cliffs, N.J., 1973, pp. 30–33.

However, your income is not going to stay at $30,000 for the next 40 years. Suppose your income grows at the rate of 5 percent per year. Then the present value becomes

$$\frac{30,000}{1.1} + \frac{30,000(1.05)}{(1.1)^2} + \frac{30,000(1.05)^2}{(1.1)^3} \cdots$$

Since $1.05/1.1 \cong 1/1.05$, this implies that the effective rate of interest is 5 percent. In general, the rate of capitalization of the income stream will be equal to the rate of interest minus the rate of growth of income.

At the 5 percent rate of interest, the present value of your lifetime earnings will be approximately $600,000. Now you are worth your weight in gold if your weight is <100 pounds. One can make the calculations with different values for the price of gold, starting income, growth rate of income, and the rate of interest. If the price of gold rose to $600 per troy ounce, there would be many individuals who would not be worth their weight in gold. Of course, with a higher inflation rate income will grow at a higher rate but the interest rate will also rise. We will assume that these two effects cancel out.[6]

Razin and Campbell calculated present values of lifetime earnings for holders of bachelor's degrees in various fields using National Science Foundation data for 1968 on yearly earnings of scientific manpower.[7] They used an interest rate $r = 0.03$. Some of the results they obtained were (rounded to the nearest thousand):

Bachelor's Degree	Present Value of Lifetime Earnings
Mathematics	342,000
Economics	340,000
Computer Science	307,000
Physics	283,000
Biological Science	216,000

Since then, however, the relative importance of computer science versus other fields has changed. Thus, one cannot place too much emphasis on comparisons of present values based on a single year's data. More importantly, these numbers do not give us an idea of what college degrees in the respective fields are worth since the abilities of individuals in the different fields tend to differ. As for the returns to college education in general, we have to subtract from these numbers the present values of costs of college education (which include the actual costs incurred as well as the cost of foregone earnings). After doing all these calculations (and allowing for differences in ability) we may end up with much smaller numbers than those

[6]As an anecdote, it is worth noting that the Ismaili community used to weigh the late Aga Khan III (1877 to 1957) every year on his birthday and present him with gold equal to his weight. Surely, this gave him no incentive to do any dieting. But he lived long anyway.

[7]Assaf Razin and James D. Campbell, "Internal Allocation of University Resources," *Western Economic Journal*, September 1972, pp. 308–320.

presented. However, there is no easy way of calculating the present value of psychic satisfaction from a college education.

20.7.3 Present value of publications

In the case of college professors, some economists have also calculated the present values of articles published. An example of this is the paper by Tuckman and Leahey who calculated the present value of the *first* article by an assistant professor to be $12,340 (at an interest rate of 5 percent).[8] The present value declines to $4,310 for the fifth article and to $1,544 for the thirtieth article. One can argue that it is very unlikely that an individual publishing thirty articles will be at the assistant professor level. However, the present value of the thirtieth article at the associate professor level is $826 and it is still lower ($686) at the full professor level. The present values are much lower if a discount rate of 10 percent is used, instead of 5 percent.

The data used by Tuckman and Leahey were from a survey conducted by the American Council of Education (ACE) in the academic year 1972–1973. The data consisted of 973 full-time male faculty employed at universities in the field of economics. Of these 515 were full professors, 245 associate professors, 185 assistant professors, and 28 were instructors.

One other interesting feature of the study by Tuckman and Leahey is that the present values are lower for books published than for articles published. However, their results take into account only the present value of incremental salaries due to publicaton. In the case of books, there is the present value of the stream of royalties that needs to be taken into account.

It should be noted that all these numbers are some sort of averages. Articles vary considerably in length as well as quality, and the present values differ considerably. Perhaps this is an example where the computation of present values has been really stretched quite far.

20.7.4 The market for durable goods

When purchasing a durable good like a car or a washing machine, the consumer is, in effect, purchasing a stream of services. The consumer will purchase the good if the present value of the stream of services plus the discounted salvage value exceeds the purchase price. Or we can state that the maximum price a consumer is willing to pay is the present value of services plus the discounted salvage value. The present value of this stream of services will, of course, vary across consumers. The salvage value is either the scrap value at the end of the product's useful life or the price of the good on the used-good market, depending on how long the consumer keeps the good.

In this section we will examine two aspects of the durable goods market. We will consider optimal durability, the impact of an increase in the discount rate on durability, and the impact of a change in durability on product price. The second aspect we will consider is obsolescence. In particular, we will examine obsolescence due to style changes.

[8]See Howard P. Tuckman and Jack Leahey, "How Much Is an Article Worth?" *Journal of Political Economy*, October 1975, pp. 951–967.

Let us first analyze durability.[9] We will assume, for simplicity, that the good provides a constant flow of services for a certain number of years (years of durability) and then breaks down. It is reasonable to assume that the marginal cost to the manufacturer of increasing durability of the good will be increasing. However, in the computation of present values, the services in the distant future receive less and less weight. Hence, the increment to present value will be decreasing with increasing durability. The shape of the total cost curve and the present value curve will, therefore, be as shown in Figure 20.10. The corresponding increment to PV curve and MC curve are shown in Figure 20.11. Since the increment to PV is the present value of the additional year's services, the increment to PV curve can be viewed as the demand curve for durability. If all consumers are identical, then the socially optimal durability is given by the point Q with y years of durability.

We will now consider the impact of a change in the discount rate on durability and the demand for durable goods. An increase in the rate of interest, that is the rate at which future service flows are discounted, will shift the present value curve downward from PV_1 to PV_2 as shown in Figure 20.12. The increment to PV for each unit of durability also falls so that the increment to PV curve shifts downward as well. This is shown in Figure 20.13. Optimal durability declines from y_1 and y_2.

The increase in the discount rate, thus, causes the present value of a stream of services from a durable good to decline for two reasons. First of all, the PV of a fixed stream of services declines as the discount rate increases. Second, product durability declines, which reduces the length of the service stream. Since the price the consumer is willing to pay for a durable good is the present value of the service stream (which may vary among consumers) plus discounted salvage value, an increase in the discount rate reduces the demand for the durable good and, hence, reduces price.

But what happens to salvage value? Let's suppose that the consumer plans to

[9]The full analysis of optimal durability is more complicated than this simple analysis we have presented here. A more thorough analysis and an argument that durability of consumption goods is the same under competition or monopoly can be found in P. L. Swan, "Durability of Consumption Goods," *American Economic Review*, December 1970, pp. 884–894. Further discussion of this problem is in E. Sieper and P. L. Swan, "Monopoly and Competition in the Market for Durable Goods," *Review of Economic Studies*, July 1973, pp. 333–351.

FIGURE 20.10   Impact of durability on present value and total cost.

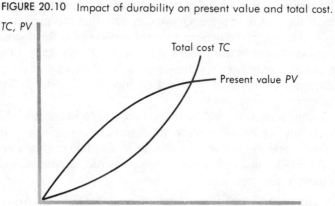

Years of durability

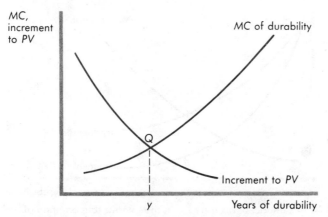

FIGURE 20.11   Determination of optimal durability for a consumption good.

sell the good on the used good market. At any point in time, the price that someone is willing to pay for the used good is the present value (at that time) of the stream of services over the remaining life of the good. So a reduction in durability reduces the price of used goods as well, reinforcing the reduction in the demand for new goods.

We can similarly examine the impact of style changes which produce obsolescence. Let's suppose first that style changes are anticipated as in the case of cars. The services provided in later years have to be discounted more heavily because they do not provide as much satisfaction as before if new goods with newer styles are being introduced. This is equivalent to a rise in the interest rate. Hence, both durability and price will fall. If style changes are unanticipated, then they will not affect the price of the product when it is new. However, once the style change is announced, the present value of the remaining service stream declines, and the price of the used good falls.

We will now discuss whether it is profitable to restrict resale. If the new goods and used goods compete with each other, some manufacturers who have a mo-

FIGURE 20.12   Impact of an increase in the discount rate on the PV curve.

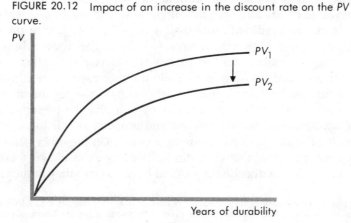

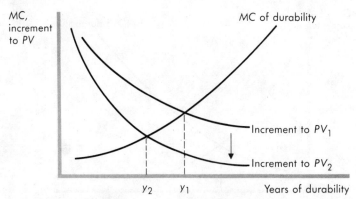

FIGURE 20.13 Impact of an increase in the interest rate on optimal durability.

nopoly in the manufacture of the durable good can try to reduce this competition by various means such as introduction of new models (or new editions of a text-book) or outright prohibition of resale. Consumers who typically purchase new goods will take into account the reduced resale value, and this will reduce their demand for the product. But the reduction in the availability of used goods will induce some of the customers from the used-good market to enter the new-good market, thus, increasing demand. What happens to the quantity sold and to the profits of the manufacturer depends on the degree of substitutability of the used good for the new good, the elasticity of demand, and the cost curves of the manufacturer.[10]

There are many problems associated with an analysis of durable goods. The purpose of our discussion here is to illustrate how present value considerations enter in the determination of durability and the prices of new and used consumption goods.

EXAMPLE 20.2   Effect of the Tax Reform Act of 1986 on Land Values

The tax reform act of 1986 eliminated some of the tax breaks for ownership of houses, condominiums, and commercial real estate. It was expected that the new law would have a large negative impact on land values and real estate prices. Real estate experts predicted more than a 20 percent decline in the price of more expensive houses. However, when one looks at the details of the tax law, there is no reason to believe that the tax law would have such effects. The tax breaks for owner-occupied housing, principally the mortgage interest and property tax deductions, were retained. Interestingly enough, the argument was that the lower tax rates would lower house prices by reducing the present discounted value of the tax breaks (mortgage interest and property tax deductions) and thereby increasing the aftertax cost of buying a house. On the other hand, those supporting the new tax argued that since prospective buyers would get a tax cut overall, even after mortgage deduction they would have more money in their pockets and so be

[10]A more detailed analysis of this problem can be found in D. K. Benjamin and R. C. Kormendi, "The Interrelationship between Markets for New and Used Durable Goods," *The Journal of Law and Economics,* October 1974, pp. 381–401.

likely to increase their spending on housing. This would have a positive impact on land values and real estate prices. Which of these two effects will be the predominant one? It is easy to see that the effect of a general tax cut is to increase all spending, not just on housing, whereas the effect of the reduced income subsidy from tax deductions for mortgage interest and property taxes affects the expenditures on housing only at the margin. Thus, unless tax reform leads to lower interest rates, it can be expected to lead to an increase in the cost of home ownership.

Supposing that the tax reform act leads to lower housing prices, who actually would be hurt by lower housing prices? Young people who don't own their first home would obviously benefit. People in their middle years who already own a house but may buy a bigger one will benefit. Their current property may be worth less, but the one they intend to buy will also be cheaper. The only group that would be hurt would be older people selling their last house, but these people would have a large appreciation in the value of their house during the past decades anyway. In fact, the generational consequences of the rise in housing prices can be seen from the fact that in 1973 a 30-year-old male needed 21 percent of his income to pay the mortgage on a medium-priced home, whereas in 1984 the figure was 44 percent.

In his famous book, *Progress and Poverty* (1879), Henry George pointed out long ago that wealth accruing in land operates like a tax on productive factors like labor and capital, in the economy.[11] His proposal was to lower the value of land as close to 0 as possible by taxing away all the rent and to use the money to reduce (or eliminate) taxes on the productive factors.

The tax policy in the United States for the past few decades, and particularly after 1981, was exactly the opposite. The several tax breaks, from home mortgage interest deduction to rapid depreciation of buildings, resulted in the return to real estate being taxed at a much lower rate than returns to labor and other forms of investment. The generous tax breaks for rental and owner-occupied housing were supposed to increase the quantity of housing and make it affordable. Instead, the value of the tax breaks was capitalized into higher prices for land and existing structures.[12]

Another argument made (this one by the National Apartment Association) was that as a consequence of the tax reform act, apartment rents would rise 40 percent and property values decline by 28 percent. Since the value of rental property is the capitalization of future income, if rents go up, the property values have to go up unless the rate of interest goes up substantially (so that the present value declines dramatically). Another set of circumstances under which this can happen is where tax breaks rather than rents are a major portion of the income from rental property so that even if rents go up, the total income declines. The argument that rents would go up was based on the following reasoning: The end of the tax subsidy for new rental housing would make rental housing unattractive as an investment, and this would reduce the supply of new rental housing. However, even this

[11]Henry George (1839 to 1897) was by turns a sailor, prospector, printer, reporter, editor and publisher of a newspaper, orator, political activist, and finally a writer on political economy. His book *Progress and Poverty* (1879) was a bestseller on economic theory and policy and began a worldwide movement for land reform and taxation. He was a precursor to supply-side economics, a pioneer on tax limitation, and insisted that land rent set an upper limit on government expenditure.

[12]Michael Kinsley, "Let's Hear It for a Drop in Home Values," *The Wall Street Journal*, June 5, 1986, p. 27.

argument is not completely valid because there is the demand side as well. The tax reform act could make housing more affordable to the middle-income groups so those living in rental apartments could move to owner-occupied housing. This would reduce the demand for rental housing. The net effect on apartment rents is not clear.

20.8   SUMMARY AND CONCLUSIONS

The present value of a stream of future payments is the amount received today that would be equivalent in value to the future payments. An increase in the discount rate reduces *NPV*. The present value of a perpetuity is the dollar amount of the annual payment divided by r, where r is the discount rate. The net present value rule says that only projects with an $NPV > 0$ should be undertaken and that projects should be ranked from highest to lowest according to their *NPV*s. The *NPV* rule leads to the maximization of present value of the firm's profits.

Utility maximization requires that

$$\frac{\text{Marginal utility of current consumption}}{\text{Marginal utility of future consumption}} = 1 + r$$

An increase in the interest rate makes savers better off and borrowers worse off. If borrowers and savers face different rates of interest, then the budget constraint will be kinked.

In analyzing intertemporal consumption decisions, consumption and income must be expressed in real terms. A consumer-producer with no possibility of intertemporal exchange (consumption must equal production in each period) will produce where the production possibilities curve is tangent to an indifference curve. When intertemporal exchange is possible, the individual will produce where the slope of the production possibilities curve is $-(1 + r)$ and consume where the slope of an indifference curve is $-(1 + r)$. All consumers are at least as well off with intertemporal exchange.

The intersection of the current demand for borrowed goods and the current supply of loanable goods gives the equilibrium interest rate in a simple two-period model.

The reduction in California's property taxes led to an increase in housing prices because the property tax savings were immediately capitalized.

As the discount rate increases, optimal product durability declines, the demand for the durable good declines, and the price of the durable good falls, other things equal.

KEY TERMS

Benefit-Cost Ratio Rule	Internal Rate of Return	Intertemporal Choice
Discounting	Rule	Intertemporal Exchange

Net Present Value Rule   Present Value   Separation Theorem
Perpetual Bond or Perpetuity   Profitability Rate Criterion

QUESTIONS

1. Calculate the *NPV* for the investment project in Table 20.1 assuming that costs are due at the beginning of the period but returns are received at the end. Use a discount rate of 10 percent.

2. In Figure 20.3, we examined the impact of a change in the interest rate on savers' and borrowers' well-being. Can you determine the impact of the increase in the interest rate on each group's current and future consumption? Assume that both current and future consumption are normal goods.

3. Use a diagram such as Figure 20.7 to examine the impact of an increase in the interest rate on production and consumption when intertemporal exchange is possible.

4. "If all members of society are equally productive and have the same preferences, there can be no intertemporal exchange." Examine the validity of this statement in the context of our simple two-period model.

5. Joe Delinquent is a consumer with a fixed income each period but a credit rating so bad that he is unable to borrow. What does his intertemporal budget constraint look like?

6. Assuming that the interest rate for borrowing exceeds the interest rate for lending, draw an intertemporal budget constraint for an individual with fixed income in both periods. What happens to this budget constraint if interest received on savings is taxed? What happens if interest paid on borrowing is tax deductible?

7. Calculate the present value of $100 received at the end of 1 year, 2 years, and 3 years, when the interest rate is 5 percent for the first year, 8 percent for the second year, and 10 percent for the third year.

8. In the analysis of durable goods, we argued that an increase in the discount rate will reduce the demand for durable goods, ceteris paribus. One of the things we held constant was prices. If the increase in the discount rate is due to a rise in the general level of prices, does our result hold?

9. There has been much debate concerning the life expectancy of the tax limitations contained in Propostion 13. In other words, will the law be repealed in the future under pressure for increased spending and the associated need for additional revenue? How do Californians apparently assess the permanence of the limitations?

CHAPTER 21

UNCERTAINTY AND IMPERFECT INFORMATION

21.1 INTRODUCTION

The previous chapters in the book ignored two major problems that are likely to be encountered in practice: uncertainty and imperfect information. We have assumed throughout that prices, costs, revenues, profits, and so on are all known with certainty. For instance, we have assumed that a firm making production decisions is absolutely certain about the prices it will be paying for the inputs and the price it will get selling the output. Clearly, this is rarely the case. Both the demand and supply of inputs as well as outputs fluctuate over time. This raises the question of how production and consumption decisions are made under uncertainty. The area of uncertainty in microeconomics is so vast that it is not possible to even give a summary of the main results in a single chapter. We will, therefore, consider only a few of the important and basic problems and those, too, in a single-period context. The problem of multiperiod decision making under uncertainty is way beyond the scope of intermediate books in microeconomics.

The second problem which we will discuss in this chapter is that of *imperfect information*. This concept is related to uncertainty but deserves separate treatment. Throughout the book we have assumed that consumers, producers, workers, and so on have complete information about the choices available to them. In practice, this is not so. Consumers have to search for the lowest price. Workers have to search for information concerning alternative jobs. All these problems form an area called the "economics of information." Information is itself a commodity which economic agents can acquire only at some cost. There is a point at which each consumer stops searching for a lower price or each worker stops searching for an alternative job. This explains why the same product can sell at different prices or workers with the same qualifications get different wages.

Before we discuss these issues, we need to discuss a few basic results in probability theory. First, we will explain the concepts of probability, expected values, and risk.

21.2 UNCERTAINTY, PROBABILITIES, AND EXPECTED VALUES

The term "probability" is used to give a quantitative measure to the uncertainty associated with uncertain events. There are two concepts of probability: *objective probability* and *subjective probability*. Objective probability is a concept based on long-run relative frequencies. Consider the case of a box containing three white balls and six red balls, all of equal size, weight, and so on (identical except for color). We shake the box and draw a ball (without looking at it). Will the ball drawn be white or red? Of course, we are uncertain about the outcome, but we can express our uncertainty by saying that the probability that the ball drawn is white is $\frac{1}{3}$ and the probability that it is red is $\frac{2}{3}$. What we mean by this is that if we conduct the experiment of mixing the box well, drawing a ball without looking at it (and replacing it before the next draw), a large number of times, then in approximately one-third of the cases, the ball drawn will be white, and in the remaining two-thirds of the cases it will be red. Many practical problems involving uncertainty are not as simple as drawing balls from a box, nor do they refer to any repetitive phenomena. Hence, what we use is the concept of subjective probability.

Some early discussions of uncertainty in economics were couched in terms of objective probability. For instance, Frank Knight drew a distinction between risk and uncertainty.[1] Knight described a situation as a risky one if we can assign definite objective probabilities to the outcomes. A situation is described as uncertain if no such objective probabilities can be assigned. Knight concluded that entrepreneurial decisions and profits belong in the theory of uncertainty, not in that of risk. The problem with Knight's analysis is that he does not develop a theory of uncertainty. Since the time that Knight wrote his book, there has developed a theory of probability that depends on subjective beliefs.[2] Thus beliefs of consumers and producers can be given a probability interpretation. We will therefore use the word "uncertainty" to describe any situation where the probability of an outcome is not 0 or 1. The distinction made by Knight is no longer followed by writers in the area of uncertainty in economics.

Subjective beliefs can be translated into probabilities by using betting odds. For instance, suppose we consider a game between the Miami Dolphins and the Seattle Seahawks. If we say that

Probability that the Dolphins win = $\frac{1}{2}$

Probability that the Seahawks win = $\frac{1}{4}$

Probability that the game is a draw = $\frac{1}{4}$

then we are willing to bet 2 to 1 for the Dolphins against the Seahawks and we are willing to bet 1 to 1 for the Seahawks against a draw. Of course, consistency requires that we are also willing to bet 2 to 1 for the Dolphins against a draw. There have been examples given of some betting odds that do not result in a set of probabilities that are mutually consistent, but we need not bother about such examples here.

A *random variable* is a variable whose value is uncertain but whose probability distribution is known. In the above example, the outcome of the football game is a random variable. Suppose a firm cannot predict its profits but can describe its profits in probabilistic terms. Then the firm's profits are a random variable.

If a random variable X takes on values $x_1, x_2, \ldots x_n$ with probabilities $p_1, p_2, \ldots p_n$ (note $p_1 + p_2 + \ldots + p_n = 1$) then the *expected value* of the random variable is denoted by $E(X)$ and is defined as

$$E(X) = p_1 \cdot x_1 + p_2 \cdot x_2 + \ldots + p_n \cdot x_n$$

For instance, suppose a firm is not certain what its profits are going to be next year but it believes that there is an even chance (probability) that they will stay the same as this year, and that if they change, there is an equal chance (probability) that they will go up $100 million or go down $100 million. If this year's profits

[1] See Frank H. Knight, *Risk, Uncertainty and Profit*, Houghton Mifflin, New York, 1922.

[2] The pioneering essay is Frank Ramsey, "Truth and Probability," written in 1926. Ramsey was an English mathematician at Cambridge who died in 1930 at the age of 26.

are $400 million, then we have the following probability distribution for next year's profits:

Probability that profits are $400 million = $\frac{1}{2}$

Probability that profits are $300 million = $\frac{1}{4}$

Probability that profits are $500 million = $\frac{1}{4}$

Expected profits are

$$E(\text{profits}) = \tfrac{1}{2}(400) + \tfrac{1}{4}(300) + \tfrac{1}{4}(500) = \$400 \text{ million}$$

Suppose the firm has an alternative investment in mind for which the probability distribution of profits is as follows:

Probability that profits are $400 million = $\frac{1}{2}$

Probability that profits are $0 = $\frac{1}{4}$

Probability that profits are $800 million = $\frac{1}{4}$

That is, if profits change, there is an even chance that they go up by $400 million or go down by $400 million. Again,

$$E(\text{profits}) = \tfrac{1}{2}(400) + \tfrac{1}{4}(0) + \tfrac{1}{4}(800) = \$400 \text{ million}$$

Thus in both the cases expected profits are $400 million, but one can describe the latter case as riskier than the former. There is a chance of making much higher profits, but there is also a chance that all profits will be wiped out. Thus, we need some measure of the risks involved. This is given by the variance of profits around the mean. If we denote the mean or expected profit by $\bar{x}$, then the variance $V(X)$ of the random variable X is given by

$$V(X) = p_1(x_1 - \bar{x})^2 + p_2(x_2 - \bar{x})^2 + \ldots + p_n(x_n - \bar{x})^2$$

It is customary to denote expected values with the symbols M or m (they are mean values) and variance with σ^2. In the above example, in the first situation the variance of profits is:

$$V(\text{profits}) = \tfrac{1}{2}(0)^2 + \tfrac{1}{4}(-100)^2 + \tfrac{1}{4}(100)^2 = \frac{(100)^2}{2}$$

Usually, it is the square root of the variance, called the *standard deviation*, that is used to measure the risk. In this case this is $100/\sqrt{2}$. Let us denote this by σ_1.

In the second situation, the variance of profits is

$$\tfrac{1}{2}(0)^2 + \tfrac{1}{4}(-400)^2 + \tfrac{1}{4}(400)^2 = \frac{(400)^2}{2}$$

The standard deviation, which is the square root of this, is $400/\sqrt{2}$. Let us denote this by σ_2.

In our analysis of uncertainty we will use the expected values and variances of profits, prices, costs, and so on. Usually the firm can increase its expected profits only by making more risky investments, and this will increase the variance of the profits. However, after a while even undertaking more risky investments does not help the firm to increase expected profits that much. This can be depicted in the profit opportunities curve of the firm, which is shown in Figure 21.1.

However, if the firm believes that higher risk is bad, since higher expected profits are good, the indifference curves (indifference curves between a bad and a good) are as shown in Figure 21.2.

In Figure 21.3 we show the equilibrium of the firm with respect to the optimal level of expected profits and variance of profits. AB is the profit opportunities curve. The highest indifference curve the firm can reach is I_1, with C as the point of tangency.

21.3 ATTITUDES TOWARD RISK

In the preceding section we argued that a higher variance of profit is bad. This need not always be the case. There are some individuals who love taking huge risks. For them risk is not a "bad," it is a "good." There are others who are indifferent. Finally there are those who do not like risks. These individuals are said to be *risk averse*. We will give a more formal definition of these terms.

Suppose that you toss a coin and you win $100 if it shows a head and you lose $100 if it shows a tail. That is, you expect to win $100 with probability $\frac{1}{2}$ and you expect to lose $100 with probability $\frac{1}{2}$. Your expected return is:

$$\tfrac{1}{2}(100) + \tfrac{1}{2}(-100) = 0$$

FIGURE 21.1   Profit opportunities for a firm.

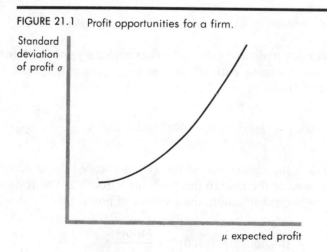

Standard deviation of profit σ

μ expected profit

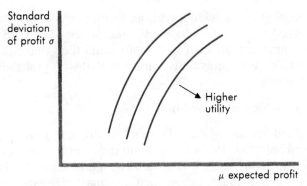

FIGURE 21.2   Indifference curves for a firm.

This is called a *fair gamble*. A fair gamble is a gamble whose expected return is 0. Suppose you ask an individual how much he or she is willing to pay to play this game (or gamble). A risk lover will pay some positive price to play this game. A risk-neutral individual will pay a zero price, that is, play if it is free. An individual afraid of taking any risks will demand some money to play this game. We now have these definitions:

• Individuals are said to be *risk averse* if they are not willing to undertake a fair gamble.

• Individuals are said to be *risk neutral* if they are indifferent between accepting or rejecting a fair gamble.

• Individuals are said to be *risk loving* if they are eager to undertake a fair gamble.

The utility function of income will be different for these three groups of individuals. We will explain these differences after explaining a theory called the *expected utility theory*.

FIGURE 21.3   Optimum level of risk for the firm.

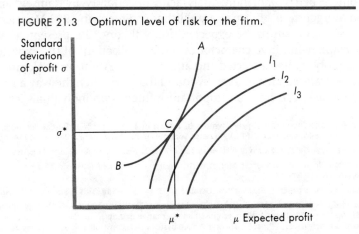

Suppose that an individual with an income of $800 is offered a fair gamble that gives $100 with probability $\frac{1}{2}$ and takes away $100 with probability $\frac{1}{2}$. The initial utility for this individual is $U(\$800)$. After the gamble the individual gets a utility of $U(\$700)$ with probability $\frac{1}{2}$ and $U(\$900)$ with probability $\frac{1}{2}$. The expected utility is therefore

$$U^* = \tfrac{1}{2}U(\$700) + \tfrac{1}{2}U(\$900)$$

It is a weighted average of the utilities of the different prospects, weighted by the respective probabilities. However, without the gamble, the expected utility for the individual is $U(\$800)$, since it is certain (with probability 1). The expected utility theory says that individuals behave as if they maximize expected utility. Hence, in this case if $U(\$800)$ is greater than U^*, the individual will not take the gamble. This will be the case for a risk-averse individual. If $U(\$800)$ and U^* are equal, the individual will be indifferent. This is the case of a risk-neutral individual. If $U(\$800)$ is less than U^*, the individual will be anxious to undertake the gamble. This is the case of a risk lover. These three situations are shown in Figure 21.4. In each case point A corresponds to $U(\$700)$. Point B corresponds to $U(\$900)$. Point C, which is the midpoint of AB, is half the sum of these and hence corresponds to the expected utility U^*. Point D corresponds to $U(\$800)$. For the risk-averse individual, point D is higher than point C. For the risk-neutral individual they are both the same. For the risk lover, point C is higher than point D.

The expected utility theory was first formulated by Daniel Bernoulli about 250 years ago.[3] He observed that different individuals responded differently to the same gambles. Thus, it is not the expected money value of the prizes but the expected utilities of the money values that mattered. Bernoulli suggested that individuals behaved as if they maximized expected utility. The maximization-of-expected-utility hypothesis is interesting because it can explain certain real world phenomena. For instance, insurance is typically an unfair gamble, that is, the expected money returned to the insured is less than the cost of the insurance. However, many individuals buy it because they are risk averse.

Bernoulli's hypothesis was later derived from more fundamental assumptions about the behavior of individuals facing uncertainty, by Ramsey[4] and von Neumann and Morgenstern.[5] In a paper published in French in 1953 Maurice Allais presented a severe criticism of the expected utility theory.[6] He presented examples to show the counter-intuitive character of some implications of the expected utility theory. This problem has attracted the attention of several psychologists as well. For instance, Kahneman and Tversky found that very often the way a gamble is described or "framed" can have an important influence on individuals' choices.[7] According

[3]A translation of the original paper written in French in 1738 appears as Daniel Bernoulli, "Exposition of a New Theory on the Measurement of Risk," Louise Sommer, trans., *Econometrica*, January 1954, pp. 23–26.

[4]F. P. Ramsey, *The Foundations of Mathematics and Other Logical Essays*, Routledge, London, 1931, chap. 7.

[5]John von Neumann and Oscar Morgenstern, *Theory of Games and Economic Behavior*, Princeton University Press, Princeton, N.J., 1944.

[6]Maurice Allais's paper in *Econometrica*, October 1953, pp. 503–546. This is known as the *Allais paradox*.

[7]Daniel Kahneman and Amos Tversky, "The Framing of Decisions and the Psychology of Choice," *Science*, January 1981, pp. 453–458. These authors proposed an alternative descriptive model of economic behavior called "prospect theory" in their paper: "Prospect Theory: An Analysis of Decision Under Risk," *Econometrica*, March 1979, pp. 263–297.

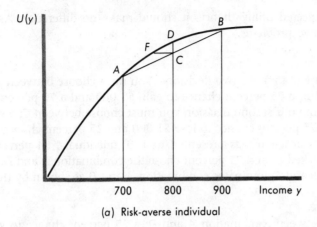

(a) Risk-averse individual

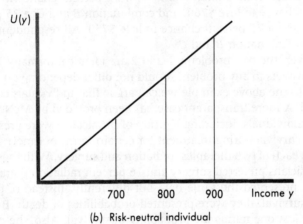

(b) Risk-neutral individual

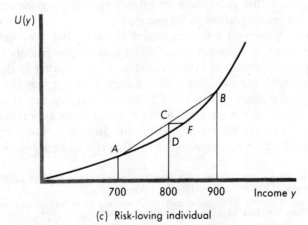

(c) Risk-loving individual

FIGURE 21.4   Utility functions for different attitudes toward risk.

to the expected utility theory, it should make no difference. As an illustration, consider two problems.

Problem 1

You are asked to make two decisions. You must choose between *A*: a sure gain of $240 and *B*: a 25 percent chance to gain $1,000 and a 75 percent chance to gain nothing. In your second decision you must choose between *C*: a sure loss of $750 and *D*: a 75 percent chance to lose $1,000 and 25 percent chance to lose nothing. When this problem was presented to 150 individuals, 84 percent picked *A*, 87 percent picked *D*, and 75 percent chose the combination *A* and *D*. However, combination *B* and *C* dominates combination *A* and *D* as shown by the next problem.

Problem 2

Choose between combination *A* and *D*: a 25 percent chance to win $240, and a 75 percent chance to lose $760, and combination *B* and *C*: a 25 percent chance to win $250, and a 75 percent chance to lose $750. All respondents to this problem picked the combination *B* and *C*.

However, the two problems 1 and 2 are identical formally.

The answers to any problem should not differ depending on how the question is framed. In the above example we can argue that individuals could not calculate things well. A more transparent case has been provided by McNeil et al.[8] Different groups of individuals, including a group of physicians, were presented with probabilities of survival during treatment for certain forms of cancer for 1 year and for 5 years, for each of two therapies: radiation and surgery. With these data 84 percent of the physicians preferred surgery and 16 percent radiation therapy. Then another group was presented the same data but differently. Instead of presenting probabilities of survival, they were presented probabilities of death. But the probability of dying is just one minus the probability of survival. Also, the calculation is very trivial. However, the proportion of physicians choosing surgery over radiation therapy fell from 84 percent to 50 percent!

We have presented a few examples to show that how individuals actually respond to uncertain situations depends on how the uncertainty is presented.[9] This is contrary to the theory of expected utility. In our further analysis, however, we will proceed with the expected utility theory. It is not that these results are not important in the study of economic behavior. It is just that this will take us too far off the main track we are following.[10] Yet another alternative to the expected utility theory has been offered by Loomes and Sugden.[11] However, we have already deviated quite a bit from expected utility theory and hence we will not discuss it.

---

[8]B. J. McNeil, S. G. Pauker, H. C. Sox, Jr., and A. Tversky, "On the Elicitation of Preferences for Alternative Therapies," *New England Journal of Medicine*, vol. 306, 1982, pp. 1259–1262.

[9]See the collection of papers in Daniel Kahneman, Paul Slovic, and Amos Tversky, eds., *Judgment under Uncertainty: Heuristics and Biases*, New York, Cambridge University Press, 1982.

[10]For an application of the ideas of Kahneman and Tversky to the theory of consumer behavior, see Richard Thaler, "Toward a Positive Theory of Consumer Choice" in *Journal of Economic Behavior and Organization*, vol. 1, 1980, pp. 39–60.

[11]G. Loomes and R. Sugden, "Regret Theory: An Alternative Theory of Rational Choice under Uncertainty," *Economic Journal*, December 1982, pp. 805–824.

21.4   INSURANCE AND GAMBLING

People who are risk averse will be willing to pay to avoid risk. This is the basis of all insurance. Suppose I have an income of $900 a week but if I am sick, I might lose $200 a week. I think there is a 50-50 chance of this happening. If I do not insure, my expected utility is given by the point C in Figure 21.4(a). Going back to that figure and drawing a horizontal line CF, we note that the point F corresponds to the same level of utility. Thus, if someone gave me a guaranteed income of $800 − CF my utility would be given by the point F, and I should be equally happy. So, I am willing to pay the insurance company a weekly premium equal to

$$\$900 - (\$800 - CF) = \$100 + CF$$

provided they guarantee that I get $900 a week even if I am sick. *On the average,* the insurance company pays me $100 per week, and so its expected profits are equal to CF per week.

The income $800 − CF is called the *certainty equivalent* income for the risky situation. It is that level of income offered with certainty that yields the same utility as the expected utility from the risky incomes. The difference between the expected income (here it is $800) and the certainty equivalent income is called the *cost of risk*. In our example the cost of risk is CF. The fraction of expected income an individual is willing to sacrifice for the sake of certainty is called the *risk premium*. In our example the risk premium is $CF/\$800$. Note that the more curved the utility function in Figure 21.4(a) is, the greater the cost of risk (and the risk premium) will be.

The cost of gambling is the opposite of the case of insurance. Again, refer to Figure 21.4(c). Suppose the gambler has a certain income of $800 with utility given by the point D. Consider the uncertain prospect given by $900 with probability $\frac{1}{2}$ and $700 with probability $\frac{1}{2}$. The expected utility is given by the point C, which gives a higher utility than the point D, and the gambler is eager to take the uncertain income. How much is the gambler willing to pay for this uncertain income? Draw a horizontal line CF. The certainty equivalent income is given by the point F in Figure 21.4(c). This income is $800 + CF. The expected income is $800. Thus, the gambler would be willing to pay a price up to DF to take the gamble. Note again that the more curved the utility function is, the higher the price the gambler is willing to pay.

In actual practice, we observe that the same person who buys insurance also gambles. How can we explain this? In a famous article, Friedman and Savage suggested that the utility function of a tyical individual would have both concave and convex segments (concave at low and high incomes and convex in between) as shown in Figure 21.5.[12] Suppose the individual has income y_0 and is at the point B on the utility function $U(y)$. For a loss equal to L, the points that yield expected utility will lie on the line segment AB (depending on the probability of

[12]M. Friedman and L. J. Savage, "The Utility Analysis of Choices Involving Risk," *Journal of Political Economy,* August 1948, pp. 279–304.

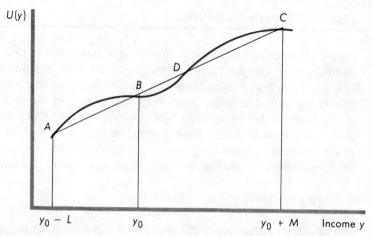

FIGURE 21.5 Utility function of an individual who buys insurance and also gambles.

loss). Since the utility function is above the line *AB*, the individual would be better off buying insurance [as in Figure 21.4(*a*)].

Now consider gambles (lotteries) that pay a large sum *M* (with a small probability). Since the probability of receiving *M* is small, the expected utility will lie close to *B* (along the line segment *BD*). Since the points along this line segment are above the utility function $U(y)$, the individual would pay for the gamble (lottery ticket) as in Figure 21.4(*c*). Note that a large payoff with a high enough probability (say 50 percent) and a high price would give an expected utility less than $U(y)$, and the individual would not buy the lottery. The hypothesis is that there is only a small convex segment in the utility function and this explains why individuals buy lottery tickets with a small price that promise to yield big payoffs (although with a very small probability).

21.5   ASYMMETRIC INFORMATION: THE MARKET FOR LEMONS

In the preceding section we saw that a risk-averse individual would be better off by buying insurance against unforeseen calamities (illness, fire, and so on). We also saw that the insurance company can profit by providing the insurance. However, there is one major informational problem with the provision of insurance contracts. The problem arises from the fact that one party (the insurance company) has less information than the other party (the customer) about the risks involved. The customer would have better knowledge than the insurance company about the probability of her getting ill. This is a case of *asymmetric information*.

An illustration of the problems created by asymmetric information is the market for lemons discussed by Akerlof.[13] The word "lemon" is used to denote a defective

[13]George A. Akerlof, "The Market for 'Lemons': Qualitative Uncertainty and the Market Mechanism," *Quarterly Journal of Economics*, August 1970, pp. 488–500.

product. Consider the market for used cars. We will, without any loss of generality, consider used cars which are identical except for quality differences (that is, of the same vintage, size, and observable accessories). Some of these cars are of good quality and others are just lemons, they break down constantly and require an abnormal number of repairs. The owners of used cars know whether the car they own is a lemon. But they all claim that their car is a good car. The buyers, of course, cannot tell whether a car is good or a lemon. As a result the market price of used cars will depend on the average quality of the used cars available for sale. In this case sellers of lemons will get more than what their cars are worth, and sellers of good-quality cars will get less than what their cars are worth. Since buyers will not pay a price above what the average car is worth, the owners of high-quality cars will withdraw their cars from the market. This changes the distribution of used cars on the market, the average quality goes down and so does the average price buyers are willing to pay. Again, cars with better-than-average quality go off the market, and the process goes on until no transactions take place. In effect the "lemons" drive out the good cars from the market. This phenomenon is also known as *adverse selection*, where only bad-quality products are left in the market and good-quality products are not offered.

The problem here is that buyers and sellers are not able to communicate accurate information. However, in practice, numerous institutions arise that counteract the adverse effects of quality uncertainty suggested by the lemons model. In the case of used cars one obvious institution is that of used car dealers that provide guarantees with the cars they sell. The more reputable dealers have their reputation at stake and this gives a certain assurance of quality. There are also automotive service centers that can check the quality of used cars and customers can get some information on quality at a cost.

Some other institutions that counteract the effects of quality uncertainty are brand names, chain stores, named restaurant and motel chains (Sheraton, Hilton, Holiday Inn, Howard Johnsons, and so on) and licensing practices (doctors, lawyers). In all these cases, there is a certain assurance of quality. The consumer usually pays a higher price (a higher price for a Whopper at Burger King and a higher price for a pizza at Pizza Hut than a hamburger or pizza at local restaurants), but there is an assurance of some standards of quality. In fact, one might even argue that often customers would interpret the higher price as an indicator of higher quality (particularly in the case where sellers depend on repeat purchases). Scitovsky first wrote a note on this problem of inferring quality on the basis of price.[14] Stiglitz provides an exhaustive survey of the literature on the dependence of quality on price.[15]

In the following sections we will discuss alternative methods of dealing with the problem of asymmetric information and adverse selection suggested by the lemons model.

[14]T. Scitovsky, "Some Consequences of the Habit of Judging Quality by Price," *Review of Economic Studies*, 1945, pp. 100–105.

[15]J. E. Stiglitz, "The Causes and Consequences of the Dependence of Quality on Price," *Journal of Economic Literature*, March 1987, pp. 1–48.

21.6   THE INSURANCE MARKET AND ADVERSE SELECTION

As we said earlier, the insurance markets are characterized by asymmetric information. The insurance company has less information about the risks (illness, accident proneness, and such) of the insured than the insured individuals themselves. We will now illustrate the problem of adverse selection.

Suppose that there are two groups of individuals, the high-risk group (H of them) and the low-risk group (L of them). The probabilities of an illness (or accident) are P_H and P_L for the high and low groups respectively ($P_H > P_L$). Both groups participate in the insurance program, and the company cannot distinguish them. The weighted average probability of illness (or accident) for the whole group is

$$\bar{P} = P_H \cdot \frac{H}{H + L} + P_L \cdot \frac{L}{H + L}$$

Note that $P_H > \bar{P} > P_L$. If the cost of illness (or accident) is C, the insurance premium I for a full coverage will be given by

$$I \geq C\bar{P}$$

If individuals know their own risks, since $\bar{P} > P_L$, the individuals with low risk may not be willing to buy the insurance policy whereas the high risk individuals would be anxious to accept it. If the low-risk individuals drop out, the insurance company has to raise the premium, and only the high-risk individuals will buy the insurance. The low-risk individuals will have no insurance at all.

The insurance company can get the low-risk people to reveal themselves by offering coinsurance or some deductibility scheme. This process is known as "self-selection." The insurance company can confront individuals with a structured set of choices with different rates of coinsurance, amounts of deductibility, length of contract, and so on. From the choices made, the insurance company can infer the risk characteristics of individuals. However, the information problem is not completely solved. The information conveyed by the individual's choice of a particular contract depends on the set of contracts available to the individual.

With two groups of individuals with different probabilities of disaster (illness, accidents, and so on) there cannot, theoretically speaking, be a single insurance policy. If at all, there have to be two insurance policies, and it can be shown that the high-risk individual obtains complete insurance and the low-risk individual obtains insurance with a large deductible. The low-risk individual obtains only partial insurance. Indeed with a continuum of individuals with differing probabilities, it has been shown that there can be no equilibrium in the insurance market.[16]

How important are all these problems of adverse selection in practice? Pauly maintains that "despite the outpouring of theoretical models of markets with adverse selection, there has as yet been no conclusive application of those models to

---

[16]M. Rothschild and J. Stiglitz, "Equilibrium in Competitive Insurance Markets: An Essay on the Economics of Imperfect Information," *Quarterly Journal of Economics*, November 1976, pp. 630–649.

the health insurance industry."[17] Pauly gives several reasons that adverse selection and the problems suggested in the theoretical literature have not been of great consequence in practice.[18]

21.7   THE PROBLEM OF MORAL HAZARD

Another problem often mentioned in connection with insurance (although it occurs in almost every activity) is that of *moral hazard*. Moral hazard in the case of insurance arises whenever an individual's behavior that affects the expected loss is altered by the quantity of insurance obtained. For instance, let P be the probability that an individual will get into an accident. The problem of moral hazard is that the probability P is higher with insurance than without insurance. That is, individuals who buy the insurance will drive more carelessly because they are insured, and, thus, the probability of their getting into an accident is greater. Similarly, if an individual buys insurance against sickness, there are two forms of moral hazard. First, the individual will spend less on preventive health care, and, thus, the probability of getting sick rises. Second, the purchase of insurance induces an individual to spend more resources on the treatment of the illness than would otherwise be the case. In fact, the probability of disaster (sickness, accident, fire) can be so much higher with insurance than without that a mutually beneficial insurance policy may fail to exist, or complete insurance may fail to exist. The individual has to bear part of the risk through coinsurance and/or deductibles.

The problem of moral hazard is pervasive and not special to insurance markets. Adam Smith, in his book *Wealth of Nations* (1776, p. 700) describes it in the following words: "The directors of such companies, however, being the managers of other peoples' money than of their own, it cannot well be expected, that they should watch over it with the same anxious vigilance with which the partners in a copartnery frequently watch over their own."

Moral hazard occurs in all economic activities where economic agents do not bear the full consequences of their actions. In such instances the economic agents maximize their own utility to the detriment of others. The problem of moral hazard in the case of medical insurance was discussed by Arrow in 1963 and since then has attracted wide interest.[19]

21.8   SIGNALLING AND SCREENING

In the previous sections we discussed the consequences of asymmetric information. The lemons model showed the problem that sellers of high-quality products have

[17]Mark V. Pauly, "Taxation, Health Insurance, and Market Failure in the Medical Economy," *Journal of Economic Literature*, June 1986, pp. 629–675. The quotation is from p. 650.

[18]See also Mark V. Pauly, "What Is Adverse about Adverse Selection?" in R. S. Scheffler and L. F. Rossiter, *Advances in Health Economics and Health Services Research*, Jai Press, Greenwich, Conn., 1986, pp. 281–286.

[19]K. J. Arrow, "Uncertainty and the Welfare Economics of Medical Care," *American Economic Review*, December 1963, pp. 941–973.

when products of both high and low quality are marketed side by side and buyers have no way of learning about the quality. Spence suggested a solution to this problem.[20] He argued that if sellers of a high-quality product could find some activity that was less costly for them than for sellers of a lower-quality product, then it might pay them to undertake this activity as a *signal* of higher quality. The buyers, too, would learn that the signal was associated with higher quality.

One application of signalling, that we discussed earlier, is in insurance. An individual with low risk is more willing to coinsure than an individual with a high risk. Thus, the level of coinsurance is a potential signal of risk level. Another application that Spence himself considered is in education. Education increases productivity but more importantly it can act as a signal of high productivity if workers with high productivity can acquire it at a lower cost than workers with low productivity.

Consider two kinds of workers: workers with high productivity P_H (there are H of them) and workers with low productivity P_L (there are L of them). Of course, $P_H > P_L$. The average productivity is

$$\overline{P} = P_H \cdot \frac{H}{H + L} + P_L \cdot \frac{L}{H + L}$$

where we are measuring productivity in terms of the value of goods produced. If employers cannot distinguish between workers, they may pay each worker a wage $W = \overline{P}$. However, one way in which workers with higher productivity can distinguish themselves is by acquiring a *signal* such as education. If all high-productivity workers are educated and none of the low-productivity workers are, the employers will find who the high-productivity workers are and pay them a wage $W_H = P_H$ and pay a wage $W_L = P_L$ for the low-productivity workers. There will thus be an equilibrium, and it will be sustainable. The question is: Under what conditions will this take place?

Suppose that the costs of education are C_H for the high-productivity workers and C_L for the low-productivity workers. We have to have $C_H < C_L$. Furthermore, we should have

$$C_L > P_H - P_L$$

so that it is not worthwhile for the low-productivity worker to invest in education. We also should have

$$C_H < P_H - P_L$$

so that it is worthwhile for the high productivity worker to invest in education. Note that if education is used as a signal, those with education get a wage $W_H = P_H$ and those with no education get a wage $W_L = P_L$. Thus, we should have the condition

$$C_H < (P_H - P_L) < C_L$$

[20]M. Spence, "Job Market Signalling," *Quarterly Journal of Economics*, August 1973, pp. 355–379, and *Market Signalling*, Harvard University Press, Cambridge, Mass., 1974.

The above equilibrium is called a *separating equilibrium* wherein the two groups of workers separate themselves by getting or not getting education.

However, other equilibria are also possible. Suppose that $C_L > P_H - P_L$ so that low-productivity workers do not find it worthwhile to invest in education. Since every worker gets a wage $\bar{P}$ if no one gets educated and there is no separation, if $C_H > P_H - \bar{P}$ then it would not be worthwhile for the high-productivity workers to get educated either, and there will be an equilibrium with no one getting educated. Thus, in the presence of differential information multiple equilibria are possible.[21] Also note that, in the above model, since education does not increase productivity, it is a waste from the social point of view. Where education is used merely as a signal, there is a social cost; high-ability individuals would attend school longer than they would in the absence of low-ability individuals.

This view of education as a signal has serious implications for educational policy. In its extreme form (as in the model that we considered, where education has no effect on productivity) the theory suggests that earnings differences associated with education do not merely reflect improvement in individuals' productive capacity caused by education but rather employers' use of education as a signal to identify preexisting differences in productivity. The value of education is merely to place the right person in the right job.[22]

Before 1973 the prevalent view of education was that it increased individuals' productivity and hence could be regarded as an investment in human capital.[23] However, these models of human capital do not explain how information about an individual's productivity gets transmitted to potential buyers of the individual's services. The signalling model suggests that the level of education conveys such information. In its extreme form, the signalling hypothesis suggests that education has nothing to do with productivity, that its use is only as a signal. Furthermore, if some individuals have education, others who are more talented have to acquire even more education just to signal their superior talents. This leads to an overinvestment in education and a "rat race," which is a waste from the social point of view because it does not lead to any increased productivity.[24]

There have been many studies to test the signalling theory. Riley reviews the tests done before 1979 and argues that the studies were not well designed to test the signalling theory and hence do not constitute adequate tests.[25] He suggests an alternative method of testing the signalling model, based on the fact that some occupations need screening and others do not. The jobs where screening is used are those where employers cannot infer the individual's productivity by direct observation. In Riley's model individuals either accumulate minimum education

[21]See J. E. Stiglitz, "The Theory of 'Screening,' Education and the Distribution of Income," *American Economic Review*, June 1975, pp. 283–300. Also, J. E. Stiglitz and A. Weiss, "Alternative Approaches to Analyzing Markets with Asymmetric Information: Reply," *American Economic Review*, March 1983, pp. 246–249.

[22]K. J. Arrow, "Higher Education as a Filter," *Journal of Public Economics*, July 1973, pp. 193–216, presents a model where individual productive ability is completely unaffected by education and education is solely used as a signal and discusses the implications of the model.

[23]See Gary S. Becker, *Human Capital*, N.B.E.R., New York, 1964, and Jacob Mincer, *Schooling, Experience and Earnings*, N.B.E.R., New York, 1974.

[24]G. A. Akerlof, "The Economics of Caste, and of the Rat Race and Other Woeful Tales," *Quarterly Journal of Economics*, November 1976, pp. 599–617.

[25]John G. Riley, "Testing the Educational Screening Hypothesis," *Journal of Political Economy*, October 1979, pp. S-227–S-252.

for an unscreened job or continue in school and later accept a screened job. It follows that the discounted lifetime earnings of those individuals choosing screened jobs will, for any given educational level, be less than the lifetime earnings of those in unscreened jobs. Riley claims that his results confirm this, and thus there is evidence in favor of the signalling hypothesis. The screenist interpretation of schooling as a provider of skills and information (signal) offers a more complete explanation than traditional human capital theory.

Liu and Wong also confirm the signalling hypothesis of education.[26] They find that firms offer higher initial wages to individuals with educational certificates in the absence of better information on productivity of new employees. They also find that after the new employee has been with the firm for some time, employers no longer continue to pay individuals on the basis of educational certificates. They also find evidence in favor of two conjectures: (1) The role of educational screening is more important for high-skilled jobs than for low-skilled jobs, and (2) educational screening is performed by firms each time a new employee is hired regardless of whether the employee has previously worked in the labor market.

Another study of the screening hypothesis by Miller and Volcker also claims support for it and concludes that "for the most part screening was alive and well in Australia."[27] Using the data from the April 1981 census of 1980 graduates in Australia, Miller and Volcker compare the salaries of graduates employed in areas where they might be expected to utilize skills acquired at the university, with salaries of graduates of equivalent background not so employed. If employers place little premium on skills acquired and use the awarding of degrees only as a filter, there will be no differences in the salaries of the two groups. Miller and Volcker find that this was indeed the case.

In summary, there is some evidence to show that education is indeed used as a signal by which employers screen prospective job applicants. Its role is not merely to improve the skills of individuals but also to provide information on individuals' abilities.

21.9   SUMMARY AND CONCLUSIONS

Economic agents have to constantly face uncertainty. They are uncertain about prices, costs, market conditions, and so on. By uncertainty we mean those situations where the several possible outcomes can be described by a probability distribution. In economics the probabilities we use are often subjective probabilities. Given a probability distribution for the several possible outcomes, a firm can calculate the mean and variance for revenues, costs, and profits. Similarly, a consumer can calculate mean and variance of utility.

Individuals can be classified as risk averse, risk neutral, and risk loving depending, respectively, on whether they are not willing to, indifferent to, or eager to undertake a fair gamble, that is, a gamble whose expected return is 0.

---

[26]P. W. Liu and Y. C. Wong, "Educational Screening by Certificates: An Empirical Test," *Economic Inquiry*, January 1982, pp. 72–83.

[27]Paul W. Miller and Paul A. Volcker, "The Screening Hypothesis: An Application of the Wiles Test," *Economic Inquiry*, January 1984, pp. 121–127.

The expected utility theory says that individuals behave as if they maximize expected utility. Although this theory has been criticized and shown to be at times contradictory to observed behavior, we employ it in our discussion because it is the simplest and most widely accepted theory. Based on the expected utility theory we explain why risk-averse individuals will buy insurance and risk-loving individuals will pay to gamble. We also explain why the same individual will buy insurance and gamble as well.

The provision of gambling is not very costly, but the provision of insurance has several problems. These are problems of adverse selection and moral hazard. The problem of adverse selection arises from the fact that the insurance company has less information than the insured about the risk involved.

Akerlof's model of the market for lemons (bad used cars) highlights the problems created by asymmetric information. Where buyers are uncertain about the quality of used cars and offer to pay only a price for average quality, the better quality cars disappear from the market because the sellers of these cars do not get a fair price. Similarly, if an insurance company which is uncertain about the risk quality of the applicants offers an insurance premium appropriate for average risk, individuals with lower risk drop out (they will consider the premium very high). Thus only the individuals with high risk will get an insurance. This is the problem of adverse selection. However, economic institutions do arise to solve this problem. There are agencies providing information at a cost.

The problem of moral hazard arises because those who get insurance have an incentive to take greater risks or spend more money on cures than they normally would do because the insurance company pays for it. Moral hazard is supposed to arise in all situations where individuals do not fully bear the consequences of their actions.

One way individuals can convey information about their productivity, degree of risk, or other attributes to the other party (employer, insurance company, and so on) is by acquiring a signal. There has been much controversy as to whether higher education serves to increase individuals' productivity or just acts as a signal. There has been some evidence in favor of the signalling theory, that higher education does act as a signal and that wage differences due to education are not solely due to increased productivity.

We have omitted from our discussion models of search where consumers acquire information about prices by searching for the lowest price, or workers search for the highest wage. Searching by consumers and workers and advertising by sellers and employers are ways of conveying information. We have also omitted discussions of the stock market and futures markets.

KEY TERMS

Adverse Selection	Expected Value	Risk Neutral
Asymmetric Information	Moral Hazard	Risk Premium
Certainty Equivalent	Objective Probability	Screening
Cost of Risk	Risk Averse	Signalling
Expected Utility Theory	Risk Loving	Subjective Probability

QUESTIONS

1. Calculate the expected monetary value to you of the following games:

   a. I toss a coin. If it shows heads you pay me $20. If it shows tails I pay you $40.

   b. I toss a coin. If it shows heads you pay me $2,000. If it shows tails, I pay you $4,000.

2. In the previous question suppose I charge you $9 to play game *a*. Will you play it? If I charge you $999 to play game *b* will you play it? Give reasons for your answers.

3. Will a risk-averse individual gamble? Will a risk lover purchase insurance? Give reasons and explain your answers with a graph.

4. A new hamburger place has opened right across from Burger King. Local residents mostly eat at this new place. Tourists all eat at Burger King. Explain why this is so.

5. Suppose stock *A* has an equal chance of going up 20 percent and going down 10 percent. Stock *B* has an equal chance of going up 30 percent and going down 20 percent during the same period. What is the expected return for the two stocks? Which one will a risk-loving individual prefer?

6. The probability of your house catching fire is 1/10,000. If you estimate that the damage in case of a fire is $1 million, what is the expected loss due to the fire? If the insurance company asks for a premium of $150 would you pay it? Explain your answer with a figure.

7. Pizza Hut charges $12 for a pizza. A new pizza place charges $10 for the same kind of pizza. My friend says that the pizza from the Pizza Hut has to be better because it charges a higher price and that we should go there, not to the new place. Explain the logic in this statement.

8. A monopolist faces the following demand function:

$$Q = 150 - CP$$

The constant *C* is not known, but the monopolist believes that there is an equal chance that it is 10 or 15. What price should the monopolist charge so as to maximize the expected revenue?

9. Suppose that your utility function is

$$U(Y) = 1000Y - 10Y^2$$

You are asked to choose between two prospects:

   a. $Y = 30$ and $Y = 50$ each with probability $\frac{1}{2}$

   b. $Y = 40$ with probability 1 (certainty)

Which one will you choose? What is the certainty equivalent income for choice *a*? Define the cost of risk and risk premium for prospect *a*.

10. Explain the meaning of the following terms and their implications for economic policy:

   a. Adverse selection

   b. Moral hazard

   c. Signalling

11. Suppose that there are 100 workers in a factory, half of them with productivity of $12,000 and the other half with productivity of $6,000. The owner pays everyone a wage rate of $9,000. Suppose that the workers with high productivity observe that in a similar neighboring factory the owner pays $12,000 for the educated workers and $6,000 for the uneducated workers and decide that they should get an education. If the costs of an education are $5,000 for the workers with high productivity and $7,000 for workers with low productivity, will the workers with high productivity get an education?

12. What is the moral hazard problem in health insurance? Suppose that once a person pays for health insurance, all health care is free. How do the long waiting lines at doctors' offices mitigate the problem of moral hazard?

GLOSSARY

Accounting Cost the cost concept used by accountants. Accounting cost can differ dramatically from economic cost (or opportunity cost).

Accounting Profit the excess of total revenue over total accounting cost. Accounting cost does not take into account all opportunity costs so that accounting profit generally exceeds economic profit.

Acreage Restrictions a policy designed to reduce agricultural output by restricting the amount of land cultivated.

Additive Utility the case where total utility for a bundle of commodities is equal to the sum of the utilities for the individual commodities.

Adverse Selection the case where only products of a lower quality remain in a market, or only individuals with greater risk purchase insurance.

Anticlassical Revisionist Theory (of profit) holds that all markets are competitive and scale economies are negligible. Profitability differences are due to differences in firm efficiency.

Arc Elasticity an elasticity measured between two distinct points.

Arrow's Impossibility Theorem any social decision rule must violate at least one of the requirements of rational choice.

Asymmetric Information the case where one party has better information about the probability of an outcome.

Average Cost cost per unit of output.

Average Cost Pricing the setting of a monopolist's price equal to average total cost where both price and output correspond to the intersection of the average total cost curve and the demand curve.

Average Fixed Cost fixed cost per unit of output. Average fixed cost is equal to total fixed cost divided by quantity produced.

Average Product output per unit of factor employed. Average product can be computed for each factor. Average product equals total product divided by factor quantity.

Average Revenue revenue per unit of output sold. Average revenue is equal to total revenue divided by quantity sold. When a single price is charged, average revenue equals output price.

Average Total Cost total cost per unit of output. Average total cost is equal to total cost divided by quantity produced. Average total cost is also the sum of average fixed cost and average variable cost.

Average Variable Cost variable cost per unit of output. Average variable cost is equal to total variable cost divided by quantity produced.

Averch-Johnson Effect the over-utilization of capital by an electric utility as a result of rate of return regulation.

Barriers to Entry impediments to the entry of new firms into an economically profitable industry.

Basing Point System a pricing system under which freight charges are calculated from a base point, regardless of the actual point of origin.

Benefit-Cost Ratio Rule the same as the profitability rate criterion.

Bilateral Monopoly a situation where there is only a single buyer of a monopolist's output.

Black Market a market which develops as the result of attempts to control price below the equilibrium level.

Budget Line a locus of points representing the various combinations of two goods which a consumer can just afford with a given income and for given prices of the two goods.

Capital-Saving Technological Change an improvement in technology which shifts the production isoquants in such a way that the optimal capital-to-labor ratio declines at the original factor price ratio. This is the same as labor-using technological change.

Cardinal Theory of Utility treats utility as measurable with cardinal numbers. The units of measurement are called utils.

Cartel a group of firms acting together to control output and price.

Centralized Cartel a cartel for which a central group makes all decisions concerning price, outputs, profits, etc.

Certainty Equivalent the amount of income received with certainty that yields the same utility as the expected utility associated with a given distribution of uncertain incomes.

Ceteris Paribus the condition that all other things remain constant.

Change in Demand a shift of the demand curve resulting from a change in one of the factors which was held constant in the construction of that curve.

Change in Quantity Demanded a change in the quantity of a good which consumers are willing and able to purchase that results from a change in the price of the same good, ceteris paribus. Graphically, a change in quantity demanded is represented by a movement along a demand curve.

Change in Quantity Supplied a change in the quantity of a good which sellers are willing and able to provide that results from a change in the price of the same good, ceteris paribus. A change in quantity supplied is graphically represented by a movement along a supply curve.

Change in Supply a shift of the supply curve resulting from a change in one of the factors which was held constant in the construction of that curve.

Change in Technique a change in an input ratio resulting from a change in a factor price ratio.

Classical Theory (of profit) holds that profitability differences among firms are mainly due to differences among industries.

Coase Theorem holds that under perfect competition, if income effects and transaction costs are ignored, voluntary agreements among the parties concerned can lead to a socially optimal allocation of resources even in the presence of externalities. Furthermore, the resulting allocation will be the same, regardless of which party is assigned the property rights to the contestable resource.

Cobb-Douglas Production Function a production function of the form $Q = aL^bK^c$ where a, b, and c are constants, Q is output, and L and K are the quantities of inputs employed.

Cobweb Model a simple dynamic model of output and price where quantity supplied in any period depends on the price in the previous period. Quantity demanded depends on the price in the same period.

Collusion explicit or tacit agreement among firms concerning price, output, or other matters.

Compensating Wage Differential the portion of the wage rate which is necessary to induce workers to accept hazardous or unpleasant jobs.

Compensation Criterion defines a change to constitute an improvement in social welfare if those who benefit would still benefit after fully compensating those who are harmed.

Complementary Inputs a pair of inputs such that an increase in the usage of one causes the marginal product of the other to rise.

Complements A is said to be a complement to good B if an increase in the price of A causes a decrease in the demand for good B. A decrease in the price of the complement would cause an increase in the demand for good B. Cross-price elasticity is negative for complementary goods.

Completeness of Preferences the assumption that the consumer is capable of ranking all possible commodity bundles. For any two commodity bundles A and B, the consumer either prefers A to B, prefers B to A, or is indifferent between A and B.

Concentration Curve a curve showing cumulative market share for each number of firms where firms are ranked from largest to smallest.

Concentration Ratio the proportion of the total market controlled by the largest four or eight firms.

Conglomerate Merger a merger which is neither horizontal nor vertical.

Conspicuous Consumption the consumption of items which are valued because of their high price or snob appeal.

Constant Cost Industry an industry where firms can enter or exit and all firms can expand or contract output without affecting the cost structure of the individual firms.

Constant Returns to Scale the case where a proportionate change in all inputs changes output by that same proportion.

Consumer's Surplus the maximum amount which a consumer would be willing to pay for a specified quantity of a good minus what the consumer must actually pay to obtain that quantity of the good.

Consumption Efficiency requires that the marginal rate of substitution (in consumption) be the same for all individuals consuming each pair of goods.

Contestable Market a market into which entry is absolutely free and from which exit is absolutely free.

Contract Curve the locus of points in an Edgeworth box diagram which represents efficient allocations of goods (in the case of consumption) or inputs (in the case of production).

Convenience Goods commodities that are usually purchased without consulting a retailer.

Cost of Risk the difference between the expected income and the certainty equivalent income.

Credence Goods commodities whose attributes cannot be reliably evaluated by the consumer even after use.

Cross-Price Elasticity of Demand a measure of the responsiveness of the demand for one good to a change in the price of another good, ceteris paribus. Cross-price elasticity equals the ratio of the percentage change in demand for one good to the percentage of change in the price of another good, which is the same as $\Delta Qx/\Delta Py \cdot Py/Qx$. Cross-price elasticity will be positive for substitutes and negative for complements.

Deadweight Loss the reduction in the sum of consumers' surplus, producers' surplus, and government surplus. This is also known as the welfare cost of a policy change.

Debt-Equity Ratio the amount of money owed by a corporation divided by the amount of stockholder equity.

Declining Industry an industry characterized only by exit and no entry because the demand for the industry's product is continuously declining.

Decreasing-Cost Industry an industry where the general expansion of output by existing firms or the entry of new firms causes each firm's LRAC curve to shift downward. The long-run supply curve for a competitive decreasing-cost industry will be downward sloping.

Decreasing Returns to Scale the case where a proportionate increase in all inputs causes output to increase by a smaller proportion.

Demand Curve a curve showing the quantity of a commodity which the consumer(s) would be willing and financially able to purchase at each price, ceteris paribus. A demand curve can be constructed for an individual consumer of the entire market.

Derived Demand the demand for an input by a producer which is derived from the demand for the output by the consumers.

Discounting the act of converting a stream of future returns into a present value.

Discrimination the valuation in the labor market of personal characteristics which are not related to productivity.

Diseconomies of Scale (internal) factors which cause long-run average cost to increase as the firm's output increases. The firm's long-run average cost curve will be positively sloped in the presence of scale diseconomies.

Disequilibrium a situation characterized by pressure to change. Market disequilibrium occurs when price is such that quantity demanded is not equal to quantity supplied.

Downstream Integration a merger in which the acquiring firm merges with a firm which utilizes or sells its output.

Dual Problem the alternative linear programming problem which can be solved in order to obtain shadow prices.

Duopoly an extreme case of oligopoly where there are only two firms.

Economic Profit the amount by which total revenue exceeds full opportunity cost. Economic profit is sometimes also called pure profit.

Economic Region of Production the downward-sloping portions of all isoquants.

Economic Rent the excess of total payment to a factor of production over and above what is required to bring that particular factor into production.

Economic Theory of Intervention (or regulation) holds that regulation is like any other commodity, with its price and quantity determined by the forces of demand and supply.

Economies of Scale (internal) factors which cause long-run average cost to decrease as the firm's output increases. The firm's long-run average cost curve is negatively sloped in the presence of scale economies.

Edgeworth Box Diagram a diagram used to describe efficiency conditions and to demonstrate how the allocation of some goods and resources can be improved through exchange.

Elasticity of Input Demand a measure of the responsiveness of the quantity demanded of an input to a change in the price of that input. Mathematically, elasticity of input demand equals percentage change in quantity of input demanded divided by percentage change in input price.

Elasticity of Substitution a measure of the responsiveness of the input ratio to a change in the input-price ratio. The elasticity of substitution is equal to the absolute value of the ratio of the percentage change in the input ratio to the percentage change in the input-price ratio.

Engel Curve a curve illustrating the various amounts of a commodity which a consumer (or consumers) would be willing to purchase at various income levels, ceteris paribus.

Equilibrium a state of rest. Market equilibrium occurs where quantity demanded equals quantity supplied so that there is no pressure on price to change.

Equilibrium Price the price corresponding to the intersection of the demand and supply curves. The equilibrium price is also called the market clearing price.

Equilibrium Quantity the quantity corresponding to the intersection of the demand and supply curves. It is both the quantity demanded as well as the quantity supplied at the equilibrium price.

Excess Capacity the amount by which plant capacity exceeds actual output.

Excess Demand the amount by which quantity demanded exceeds quantity supplied at a price below the equilibrium price. Another term for excess demand is shortage.

Excess Supply the amount by which quantity supplied exceeds quantity demanded at a price above the equilibrium price. Another term for excess supply is surplus.

Expected Utility Theory argues that individuals behave as if their objective were to maximize expected utility.

Expected Value the average or mean value of a random variable.

Experience Goods commodities whose attributes can be evaluated only after using them.

Export Subsidy monetary assistance granted by the government to exporters of a specified commodity.

External Benefit the portion of the benefit associated with an economic decision that accrues to someone other than the party making the decision.

External Cost the portion of the cost associated with an economic decision that accrues to someone other than the party making the decision.

External Diseconomies of Scale factors beyond the control of the individual firm that cause each firm's average cost curve to shift upward as industry output is expanded or as new firms enter the industry.

External Economies of Scale factors beyond the control of the individual firm that cause each firm's average cost curve to shift downward as industry output is expanded or as new firms enter the industry.

Factor Markets the markets for the inputs into the production process.

Fair Gamble a gamble with an expected return equal to zero.

Financial Capital the total amount of money subscribed by the owners (stockholders) and creditors (bondholders) of a firm (corporation).

First-Degree Price Discrimination the charging of a different price for each unit of output. The prices charged are the reservation prices or maximum prices.

Fixed Costs costs which do not vary with the level of output. Fixed costs are the costs of the inputs which do not vary with changes in output. Since all inputs are variable in the long run there are no fixed costs in the long run.

Fixed Proportions Production Process a production process characterized by an elasticity of substitution equal to zero. The isoquants in this case are right angles.

Free Mobility of Resources a requirement for perfect competition that all inputs be mobile both geographically and between jobs.

Free Rider Problem the problem of public good provision resulting from the incentive for an individual to understate his preference for a public good in hope of obtaining the good at a lower cost.

Freedom of Entry and Exit a characteristic of perfect competition requiring that there be no barriers to new firms entering the market or existing firms exiting the market in the long run.

Functional Distribution of Income the classification of total revenue into wages, rent, and interest.

General Equilibrium Analysis an analysis which examines the impact of a change in one market on all of the various markets in the economy.

Gentlemen's Agreement an informal oral understanding among oligopolists that they will maintain a certain minimum price.

Giffen Good *see* Giffen Paradox.

Giffen Paradox the case where an increase in price leads to an increase in quantity demanded. This occurs in theory for an inferior good with an income effect that is stronger than the substitution effect. The uncompensated demand curve for such a good will be positively sloped and thus violate the law of demand.

Gini Coefficient an index of inequality in a distribution. A higher value indicates greater inequality. The Gini coefficient is equal to the area between the Lorenz curve and the 45 degree line multiplied by two.

Growth Maximization Model a model of firm behavior based on the assumption that managers satisfy instincts of power, dominance, and prestige by pursuing growth as an objective.

Herfindahl Index a measure of monopoly power in an industry. The Herfindahl index is equal to the sum of the squared market shares for all firms in the industry.

Hicksian Method a method of decomposing a change in quantity demanded into the substitution effect and the income effect. Under this method the substitution effect involves a movement along a single indifference curve whereas the income effect involves a movement between indifference curves. This is the theoretically correct method of decomposition.

Homogeneous Product a commodity such that the product of one seller is viewed by consumers as identical to the product of another seller.

Homogeneous Production Function a special case of homothetic production function where a proportionate change in inputs causes output to change by a proportion which does not vary with changes in the input bundle.

Homothetic Production Function a production function such that the ratio of marginal products is unaffected by a proportionate change in the inputs.

Horizontal Merger the combination of two firms that sell a similar product in the same geographic market.

Human Capital skills or knowledge which render the worker more productive.

Ideal Output the output associated with the minimum point on the firm's LRAC curve.

Identification Problem the problem of identifying a demand curve or a supply curve from simple observations on price and quantity when both curves are shifting.

Import Tariff a tax charged on the importation of a commodity. The tax can be levied on a per-unit basis or it can vary with the value of the commodity.

Incentive-Compatible Mechanism a mechanism by which self-interested individuals are induced to reveal their true preferences for a public good.

Income Consumption Curve a curve showing the combinations of two commodities that the consumer would purchase at various levels of income, holding prices constant. The curve consists of a series of tangency points between indifference curves and parallel budget lines.

Income Effect the portion of a change in quantity demanded which is attributable to the change in real income that results from the change in price.

Income Elasticity of Demand a measure of the responsiveness of demand to a change in income, ceteris paribus. Income elasticity equals the ratio of percentage change in demand to percentage change in income, which is the same as $\Delta Q/\Delta Y \cdot Y/Q$. Income elasticity is positive for a normal good and negative for an inferior good.

Increasing-Cost Industry an industry where the general expansion of output by existing firms or the entry of new firms causes each firm's LRAC curve to shift upward. The long-run supply curve for a competitive increasing-cost industry will slope upward.

Increasing Returns to Scale the case where a proportionate increase in all inputs causes output to increase by a larger proportion.

Independent Inputs a pair of inputs such that a change in the usage of one has no effect on the marginal product of the other.

Independent Products products such that the cost of producing one product is unaffected by a change in the output of another product.

Indifference Curve the locus of points representing the various combinations of two commodities that yield a given total utility. An indifference curve can be constructed for any level of utility.

Industry a group of firms that sells a well-defined product or closely related set of products.

Inferior Good a commodity such that an increase in consumers' incomes causes a decrease in demand and a decrease in consumers' incomes causes an increase in demand. Income elasticity for an inferior good is negative.

Inferior Input see Regressive Input.

Inflection Point a point of change in a function's curvature. Mathematically, the inflection point corresponds to a value of zero for the second derivative.

Initial Endowment the original quantities of goods allocated to an individual before any trade takes place.

In-Kind Subsidy full or partial provision of a particular commodity by the government. Examples include food stamps and housing assistance.

Input Monopoly an input market characterized by a single seller of a factor of production with no close substitutes.

Input-Output Analysis a technique for studying the general interdependence among the different sectors of the economy.

Interest the payment received for lending money or the cost of borrowing funds.

Intermediate-Run Elasticity an elasticity computed over a time period between the short run and the long run in length.

Internal Rate of Return Rule an investment criterion which ranks projects according to their internal rates of return and approves only projects with an internal rate of return greater than the interest rate. The internal rate of return for a project is the discount rate which yields a net present value of zero.

Interpersonal Utility Comparison the problem of weighing changes in utility for two or more individuals. Pareto viewed this problem as impossible to solve.

Intertemporal Choice a choice involving time.

Intertemporal Exchange the exchange of commodities across time.

Isocost Line the locus of points representing all of the combinations of two inputs which the firm can purchase for a given total cost, at specified input prices.

Isorevenue Line the locus of points representing the various combinations of two products that yield a specified total revenue at given product prices.

Joint Products products which must be produced in fixed proportions so that a change in the output of one product automatically results in a proportionate change in the output of the other product(s).

Kaldor-Hicks Compensation Criterion see Compensation Criterion.

Kinked Demand Curve the oligopolist's demand curve when rivals match price reductions but not price increases.

Labor-Saving Technological Change an improvement in technology which shifts the production isoquants in such a way that the optimal capital-to-labor ratio increases at the original factor price ratio. This is the same as capital-using technological change.

Laspayre Index a cost-of-living index which uses base-period expenditure shares to weight the various price changes.

Law of Demand the requirement that the quantity demanded of a commodity varies inversely with its price, ceteris paribus. The law of demand requires that demand curves be negatively sloped.

Law of Diminishing Marginal Productivity the requirement that as equal increments of the variable input are added, holding technology and the quantities of all other inputs constant, eventually the increment to output (or marginal product) will decline. This is also known as the Law of Diminishing Returns.

Law of Diminishing Marginal Rate of Substitution in Production the requirement that as one input is substituted for another, eventually the marginal rate of substitution will decline. This law insures that isoquants will be convex to the origin.

Law of Diminishing Marginal Utility the requirement that as the consumption of a particular commodity increases, ceteris paribus, the marginal utility of that commodity will eventually decline.

Law of Diminishing Returns *see* Law of Diminishing Marginal Productivity.

Law of Supply the requirement that the quantity supplied of a commodity varies directly with its price, ceteris paribus. The law of supply implies that supply curves will be positively sloped.

Lerner Index a measure of monopoly power which is equal to (price − *MC*)/price.

Lindahl Equilibrium a situation where the socially optimal output of a public good is provided, each individual's price is equal to marginal value, and production costs are fully covered.

Linear Programming a mathematical technique which can be used to locate a constrained maximum or minimum value when the objective function and all constraints are linear.

Long Run a period of time sufficient for all economic agents to fully adjust to a change. In the case of production, the long run is the period of time sufficient to alter the quantities of all inputs into the production process.

Long-Run Elasticity a measure of the full responsiveness of quantity after consumers (in the case of demand) or sellers (in the case of supply) have had sufficient time to completely adjust. Long-run elasticities can be computed for price changes, income changes, or changes in some other variable.

Long-Run Expansion Path a curve showing the optimal combinations of two inputs for various levels of output when the input price ratio is held constant and both inputs can be adjusted. The curve consists of a series of tangency points between the isoquants and parallel isocost lines.

Lorenz Curve a curve illustrating the cumulative distribution of income or wealth.

Luxury Good a commodity with an income elasticity greater than one. As income increases, the demand for a luxury increases more than proportionately.

Managerial Efficiency *see* Production Efficiency.

Managerial Theories of the Firm theories of firm behavior which emphasize the separation of ownership from control in the modern corporation.

Managerial Theory (of profit) argues that differences in profitability among firms are primarily due to firm-level efficiency differences based largely on differences in managerial skills.

Marginal Cost the cost of an additional unit of output. Graphically, marginal cost is the slope of the total cost curve. Mathematically, marginal cost equals $\Delta TC/\Delta Q$.

Marginal Cost Pricing the setting of price at the level corresponding to the intersection of the marginal cost curve and the demand curve.

Marginal Factor Cost the increase in total cost resulting from a one-unit increase in input usage, ceteris paribus.

Marginal Product the increment to total product attributable to a one-unit increase in an input, holding other inputs constant. Marginal product can be calculated for any input in the production process.

Marginal Rate of Substitution the rate at which one commodity can be substituted for another without changing total utility. The marginal rate of substitution of X for Y is equal to the absolute value of the slope of the indifference curve.

Marginal Rate of Technical Substitution the rate at which one input can be substituted for another input in the production process without affecting total output. Graphically, the marginal rate of technical substitution is equal to the absolute value of the slope of the isoquant. Mathematically, it is equal to the ratio of marginal products for the two inputs.

Marginal Rate of Transformation the marginal rate of transformation of product A for product B is equal to the reduction in the output of B that is necessary to increase the output of A by one unit, holding inputs constant.

Marginal Revenue Product the change in total revenue resulting from a one-unit increase in input usage, ceteris paribus.

Marginal Utility the increase in total utility resulting from a one-unit increase in the consumption of a particular commodity, holding the quantities of other commodities constant.

Market a group of firms or individuals transacting a particular commodity.

Market Competition a market structure with somewhat less stringent requirements than perfect competition. Market competition requires a homogeneous product, perfect knowledge, and enough firms that they behave as price takers.

Market Demand Curve a curve showing the quantity of a commodity which would be demanded by all consumers in the market at each price, ceteris paribus.

A market demand curve can be obtained by horizontally summing individual consumer's demand curves.

Market Failure the provision by a competitive market of an output quantity which is not socially optimal.

Market-Sharing Cartel a cartel in which the member firms mutually determine market shares.

Market Structure the type of organization characterizing an input or output market. The four standard market structures are perfect competition, monopoly, oligopoly, and monopolistic competition.

Market Supply Curve a curve showing the quantity of a commodity which would be provided by all suppliers in the market at each price, ceteris paribus.

Maximum Decision Rule a decision criterion which says to choose the strategy which maximizes the minimum possible payoff.

Merger the consolidation of two or more independent firms into a single firm.

Monopolistic Competition a market structure characterized by many small independent sellers of a differentiated product and no barriers to entry.

Monopolistic Exploitation of Labor the amount by which the value of marginal product for labor exceeds the marginal revenue product of labor.

Monopoly (pure) a market structure characterized by a single seller of a product with no close substitutes.

Monopsonistic Exploitation of Labor the amount by which the marginal factor cost of labor exceeds the wage rate.

Monopsony (pure) the case of a single buyer of a commodity (generally an input).

Moral Hazard the case where an individual's behavior which might affect expected loss is altered by the quantity of insurance purchased.

Natural Monopoly the case where the average cost of production declines over the entire range of market demand. This implies that one firm can produce the entire output more cheaply than multiple firms could.

Necessity a commodity with a positive income elasticity less than one. As income increases, the demand for a necessity increases less than proportionately.

Negative Externality in Consumption the case where consumption imposes costs on parties other than the consumer.

Negative Externality in Production the case where production imposes costs on parties other than the producer.

Net Present Value Rule an investment criterion that ranks projects according to their net present values and approves only projects with positive net present values. The net present value is simply the present value of returns minus the present value of costs.

Neutral Technological Change an improvement in technology which shifts the production isoquants in such a way that the optimal capital-to-labor ratio is unaffected at the original factor price ratio.

Nominal Rate of Interest the amount of money paid for the use of borrowed funds for a period of time (usually one year), divided by the amount of money borrowed.

Nonexcludability the infeasibility of excluding any individual from enjoying the benefits of a commodity once that commodity is provided.

Nonprice Competition rivalry among firms which takes the form of advertising or variation in the product's design or quality.

Nonrivalry in Consumption a property of public goods that allows an additional consumer to enjoy the benefits of a commodity without reducing the availability of benefits to others.

Normal Good a commodity such that an increase in consumers' incomes leads to an increase in demand and a decrease in consumers' incomes leads to a decrease in demand. Income elasticity for a normal good is positive.

Normal Profit the opportunity cost of owner-supplied resources. This is a profit only in the accounting sense.

Oligopoly a market structure characterized by only a few interdependent sellers of a homogeneous or differentiated product and substantial barriers to entry. The interdependence commonly leads to intense rivalry.

Opportunity Cost the value of a resource in its next best use. This is the cost concept most relevant to economic decisions and is thus sometimes called economic cost.

Ordinal Theory of Utility treats utility as measurable only on an ordinal basis. In other words, the consumer can rank commodity bundles in order of preference but cannot state by how much bundle A is preferred to bundle B.

Output Effect *see* Scale Effect.

Paasche Index a cost-of-living index which uses current-period expenditure shares to weight the various price changes.

Pareto Criterion defines a change to be an improvement in social welfare only if it constitutes a Pareto improvement.

Pareto Improvement a change in the allocation of resources that renders at least one person better off and nobody worse off.

Pareto Optimum a resource allocation for which there are no Pareto improvements.

Partial Equilibrium Analysis an analysis which focuses on the impact of a change in one market on the outcome in that market without considering the interrelationships with other markets.

Payoff Matrix a table showing an individual's returns for various combinations of the individual's and the rival's strategies.

Perfect Cartel a group of firms where each member's output is set at a level which maximizes the group's total profit.

Perfect Competition a market structure characterized by perfect knowledge, free mobility of resources, a homogeneous product, freedom of entry and exit, and enough sellers and buyers that each behaves as a price taker.

Perfect Knowledge a characteristic of perfect competition requiring that all economic agents have perfect information on prices, costs, wage rates, and so on, for both the present and the future.

Perfect Price Discrimination *see* First-Degree Price Discrimination.

Perpetual Bond or Perpetuity a bond which pays a specified amount of interest each period without termination.

Physical Capital the durable manufactured inputs into the production process such as buildings, machinery, tools, etc.

Piece Wages a payment method under which workers are paid according to the amount of work accomplished.

Plant Capacity the output corresponding to the minimum point on the average total cost curve for that plant.

Point Elasticity an elasticity measured at a single point or for arbitrarily small changes.

Positive Externality in Consumption the case where consumption bestows benefits on parties other than the consumer.

Positive Externality in Production the case where production bestows benefits on parties other than the producer.

Predatory Price Cut a reduction in price for the purpose of eliminating rivals by capturing their market shares.

Preemptive Price Cutting the reducing of price for the purpose of deterring entry into a market by potential rivals.

Present Value the amount received today that would be equivalent in value to a specified future payment or stream of payments.

Price Ceiling a maximum price above which the market price is not allowed to rise.

Price-Consumption Curve a curve showing the various combinations of goods X and Y that the consumer would purchase for various prices of commodity X, holding the price of Y and income constant. The curve consists of a series of tangency points between indifference curves and budget lines where all of the budget lines have the same vertical intercept.

Price Control a government imposed limit on the price of a commodity. An upper limit is called a price ceiling and a lower limit is called a price floor.

Price Discrimination the charging of different prices for the same product when those differences are not cost justified.

Price Effect the total change in quantity demanded resulting from a change in price. The price effect is equal to the sum of the income effect and the substitution effect.

Price (own) Elasticity of Demand a measure of the responsiveness of quantity demanded to a change in the price of the same good, ceteris paribus. Price elasticity is equal to the absolute value of the ratio of percentage change in quantity demanded to percentage change in price which is the same as $|\Delta Q/\Delta P \cdot P/Q|$. Demand is said to be elastic if price elasticity exceeds one and inelastic if price elasticity is less than one.

Price Elasticity of Supply a measure of the responsiveness of quantity supplied to a change in price, ceteris paribus. Price elasticity of supply is equal to the ratio of percentage change in quantity supplied to percentage change in price.

Price Floor *see* Support Price.

Price Leadership a situation such that one or a few firms typically initiate price changes and the other firms in the industry follow.

Price Rationing the manipulation of price by the government in an attempt to control the quantity of a good consumed. The most common form of price rationing is the imposition of an excise tax in order to reduce consumption.

Price Setter an economic agent (buyer or seller) with perceptible control over the prevailing market price of a product.

Price Taker an economic agent (consumer or seller) who is so small relative to the market that she cannot exert any perceptible influence on price.

Price War a situation in which rivals successively undercut one another's prices.

Private Benefit the portion of the benefit associated with an economic decision that accrues to the party making that decision.

Private Cost the portion of the cost of an economic decision which accrues to the party making that decision.

Producers' Surplus the amount producers receive for a given quantity of a commodity in excess of the minimum amount they would have been willing to accept for that quantity.

Product Differention the case where consumers perceive similar products to have distinguishing characteristics but to be close substitutes.

Product Group a group of all the products that are close substitutes.

Production Efficiency requires that the marginal rate of technical substitution be the same for (a) all products that a single firm produces using any given pair of inputs and (b) all producers producing the same output.

Production Function a statement of the functional relationship between inputs and outputs.

Production Isoquant the locus of points representing the various combinations of two inputs which will yield a specified total output. An isoquant can be constructed for any level of output.

Production Possibility Curve a curve showing the various combinations of two outputs that result from efficient allocations of given inputs.

Production Transformation Curve the curve showing the various combinations of two products that the firm can produce with a given set of inputs.

Profitability Rate Criterion an investment criterion which ranks alternative investments according to their profitability rates and approves only investments with a profitability rate greater than one. The profitability rate is simply the ratio of present value of returns to present value of costs.

Public Interest Theory of Government Intervention holds that the government responds to a public demand for the correction of inefficient allocations and that the government can correct these inefficiencies at a lower cost than private organizations.

Pure Competition a market structure with slightly less stringent requirements than perfect competition. Pure competition requires only a large number of traders and a homogeneous commodity.

Pure Public Good a commodity characterized by nonexcludability and nonrivalry in consumption.

Quantity Allotment a limitation imposed by the government on the quantity of a commodity that may be consumed. Quantity allotments were imposed for many commodities during World War II.

Quasi Rent the surplus accruing to factors of production other than land.

Real Income the purchasing power associated with a specified nominal income.

Real Rate of Interest the rate of interest adjusted for inflation.

Regressive Input an input such that an increase in output results in a decrease in usage at constant input prices. Regressive inputs are also called inferior inputs.

Rent the return paid to an input that is fixed in quantity.

Rent Seeking activity and expenditure for the purpose of maintaining or securing monopoly power.

Reservation Wage the minimum wage at which an individual is willing to work.

Ridge Line a line separating the downward-sloping portions of a series of isoquants from the upward-sloping portions. Ridge lines bound the economic region of production

Risk Averse characteristic of an individual who is unwilling to undertake a fair gamble.

Risk Loving characteristic of an individual who is eager to undertake a fair gamble.

Risk Neutral characteristic of an individual who is indifferent between accepting or rejecting a fair gamble.

Risk Premium the fraction of expected income that an individual would be willing to give up in exchange for certainty.

Royalty a share of the value of output, usually expressed as a percentage.

Sales Maximization Model a managerial theory of firm behavior based on the assumption that managers attempt to maximize sales revenue subject to a minimum profit constraint.

Scale Effect the portion of the change in input usage resulting from the change in output caused by a change in input price.

Scitovsky Criterion defines a change in the allocation of resources to constitute a social improvement if those who benefit from the change could bribe the losers into accepting it *and* the losers could not bribe the gainers into foregoing it.

Screening the evaluation of individual characteristics by direct observation.

Search Goods commodities whose attributes can be evaluated by inspection and comparison.

Second-Degree Price Discrimination the charging of several different prices for different ranges or groups of output.

Selective Excise Tax a tax levied on each unit of a particular commodity.

Separation Theorem states that when intertemporal exchange is possible, the production optimum is independent of consumption preferences.

Shadow Price the change in the value of the objective function which would result from a one-unit relaxation of a constraint, without relaxing the other constraints.

Shopping Goods commodities for which retailers serve as an important source of information.

Shortage *see* Excess Demand.

Short Run a period of time which is too short for all economic agents to fully respond to a change. In the case of production, the quantities of some inputs cannot be altered in the short run.

Short-Run Elasticity a measure of the initial responsiveness of quantity when consumers (in the case of demand) or sellers (in the case of supply) have not had time to fully adjust. Short-run elasticities can be computed for price changes, income changes, or changes in some other variable.

Signalling the use of a readily observable characteristic to infer unobservable qualities.

Slutsky Method a method of decomposing a change in quantity demanded into the substitution effect and the income effect. Under this method, both the income and substitution effects involve movements between indifference curves. Though theoretically incorrect, the Slutsky method is operational whereas the Hicksian method is not.

Social Benefit the sum of private benefit and external benefit.

Social Cost the sum of private cost and external cost.

Socially Optimal Output the quantity of output for which marginal social benefit equals marginal social cost.

Social Welfare Function a function specifying the relationship between social welfare and individuals' welfare or utility.

Specialization in Consumption the consumption of only one commodity. Specialization in consumption generally results from concave indifference curves but can also occur with convex indifference curves.

Stages of Production based on the behavior of average product and marginal product, economists have divided a production process with a single variable input into three stages. The economically meaningful range is given by stage II with marginal product greater than zero and average product falling.

Strategy one of several alternative courses of action.

Substitutes good A is said to be a substitute for good B if an increase in the price of A causes an increase in the demand for B. A decrease in the price of the substitute would cause a decrease in the demand for good B. Cross-price elasticity is positive for substitute goods.

Substitution Effect the portion of a change in quantity demanded which is attributable solely to the change in relative prices.

Sunk Cost a cost which cannot be recovered by selling or renting a resource. This is a cost only in the accounting sense.

Supply Curve a curve showing the quantity of a good which would be offered for sale at each price, ceteris paribus. A supply curve can be constructed for an individual supplier or for the entire market.

Support Price a minimum price below which the market price is not allowed to fall. This is also known as a price floor.

Surplus

Survivor Principle firms operating at or moving toward the minimum point on the long-run average cost curve should be the ones which "survive" over time in a competitive market.

Tatonnement Process a process by which an auctioneer calls out a price, compares the quantity demanded with the quantity supplied, adjusts price in the indicated direction and repeats the process until the market clearing price is found. Trade takes place only at the market clearing or equilibrium price.

Technological Change a change in the state of the arts available for combining and transforming resources into goods and services.

Theory of the Second Best argues that if all of the conditions required to achieve a Pareto optimum cannot be satisfied, then trying to fulfill as many conditions as possible may not be the second best alternative.

Third-Degree Price Discrimination the charging of different prices to different groups of consumers. The individuals within a particular group all pay the same price.

Time Wages a payment method under which workers are paid by the hour.

Total Product the total quantity of output that can be produced with a specified input bundle.

Total Revenue the total amount of money the seller receives for a specified quantity of a commodity sold. When a single price is charged, total revenue is equal to price times quantity sold.

Transaction Costs the costs of negotiating a contract or agreement.

Transitivity of Preferences the condition that if bundle A is preferred to bundle B and bundle B is preferred to bundle C, then bundle A must be preferred to bundle C. Transitivity of preferences precludes the intersection of indifference curves.

Trust a fiduciary arrangement under which a trustee administers property for a group of beneficiaries. Combinations of firms often use this legal device to jointly manage their interests.

Upstream Integration a merger where the acquiring firm merges with the supplier of an input.

User Cost of Capital the rental cost of physical capital expressed as a percentage of its value.

Utility the satisfaction that a consumer derives from the consumption of goods and services.

Utility Maximization Model a general managerial theory of firm behavior based on the assumption that managers attempt to maximize their utility subject to a minimum profit constraint.

Valuation Ratio the ratio of the stock market value of a firm to its accounting or book value.

Value of Marginal Product the marginal product of an input multiplied by the price of the output.

Variable Costs the costs of the inputs which vary with the level of output.

Vertical Merger the combination of firms that previously had an actual or potential customer-supplier relationship.

Voting Paradox the possibility that the choices made by majority vote will not be transitive.

Wages the return to labor for its contribution to production.

Welfare Cost *see* Deadweight Loss.

Windfall Profits Tax a tax on the profits of oil companies attributable to OPEC price increases.

X-Inefficiency the failure of the firm to maximize the output produced from its given inputs due to poor managerial motivation and an inefficient market for knowledge.

Zero-Sum Game a game where one party's gain equals the sum of the other parties' losses.

INDEX